Glass, alcohol and power in Roman Iron Age Scotland

Dominic Ingemark

With drawings of the glass by Marion O'Neil

National Museums Scotland

Published in 2014 by
NMS Enterprises Limited – Publishing
a division of NMS Enterprises Limited
National Museums Scotland
Chambers Street
Edinburgh EH1 1JF

www.nms.ac.uk

British Library Cataloguing in Publication Data

A catalogue record of this book is available
from the British Library.

ISBN: 978 1 905267 81 1

Publication layout and design by
    NMS Enterprises Limited – Publishing.
Cover design by Mark Blackadder.
Cover images: Fragments of glass from Torwoodlee, Selkirkshire
    (front) and Traprain Law, East Lothian (back) © National
    Museums Scotland.
Printed and bound in Great Britain by
    Henry Ling Ltd, Dorchester, Dorset

Published by National Museums Scotland as one of a series of
titles based on the collections and scholarship of the Museum.

For a full listing of NMS Enterprises Limited – Publishing titles
and related merchandise visit:

www.nms.ac.uk/books

Contents

Introduction and methodology

The Roman glass vessels and window glass from non-Roman/native contexts

List of figures

List of plates

Acknowledgements

FIRST and foremost I would like to thank Dr Fraser Hunter, Principal Curator of Iron Age and Roman collections at National Museums Scotland. Dr Hunter put a great deal of effort into editing text, arranging production of the illustrations and maps, and ensured that this book came into being. His in-depth and detailed knowledge of the Iron Age cultures of Scotland has been extremely valuable, and I am most grateful for his contribution to this book.

While preparing the manuscript, I enjoyed the privilege of working with two of the leading experts on Roman glass in the world – Dr Hilary Cool, Barbican Research Associates and Professor emerita Jennifer Price, University of Durham. Dr Cool functioned as a reviewer of the manuscript for the National Museum of Scotland, and offered extensive and valuable comments that significantly improved the text. Professor Price acted as my assistant PhD supervisor during a research period at the University of Durham, and in this capacity she generously shared her extensive knowledge of Roman glass, commenting on an earlier draft of the catalogue. It should also be stressed that it is thanks to Professor Price that some fragments which otherwise would have remained unidentified could be classified.

I also extend my thanks to Professor Helle Vandkilde, Aarhus University, Denmark. The seminars – and the course on elites in prehistory in particular – that Professor Vandkilde conducted when she worked in Lund were extremely inspiring, and they certainly contributed to the analysis. Professor emeritus Örjan Wikander, Lund University, Sweden – my former PhD supervisor – was of assistance at an earlier stage of this work, when he kindly imparted his in-depth knowledge of Roman culture. Towards the end of my PhD studies, I spent six months in Edinburgh and during this time Professor Ian Ralston acted as my assistant supervisor. I remember with pleasure his kind and generous manner in sharing his knowledge on Scottish archaeology.

I also want to thank the following persons affiliated with National Museums Scotland. Dr David Clarke, former Keeper of Archaeology, always believed in this project, and his support contributed to this publication. Working with Marion O'Neil – a most skilful archaeological illustrator – has been a special privilege. Her eye for detail and her great thoroughness have been invaluable. Jim Wilson and Ian Scott patiently brought out finds from the hoards of the Museum, and their kind and humorous stance has made my work less arduous. The computer skills of Craig Angus have been of great assistance, particularly in finalising the illustrations. Lynne Reilly has functioned as editor, and she has created a beautiful book. Dave Cowley at the Royal Commission on the Ancient and Historical Monuments of Scotland produced the excellent maps.

Thanks to Dr Jacek Andrzejwoski and Professor P. J. Cherian for photographs of objects in their collections and to Neil McLean for the new photographs of Scottish material.

It has been both a pleasure and a great privilege to work in Scotland. During the years I have met with much kindness, received help and not least encouragement from people in museums, university departments and archaeological organisations across the country. I extend my thanks to all of them.

I have received generous financial support from the following: Axel Emanuel Holmbergs stipendiefond, Berit Wallenbergs stiftelse, Craafordska stiftelsen, the Dorothy Marshall Bequest, Helge Ax:son-Johnsons stiftelse, Hildur Gabrielsons donation, the Gunning Gift, Kungliga Humanistiska Vetenskapssamfundet Lund, Stiftelsen Elisabeth Rausings minnesfond, Sven Kristenssons donation, Vetenskapssocieten i Lund.

Dominic Ingemark
January 2014

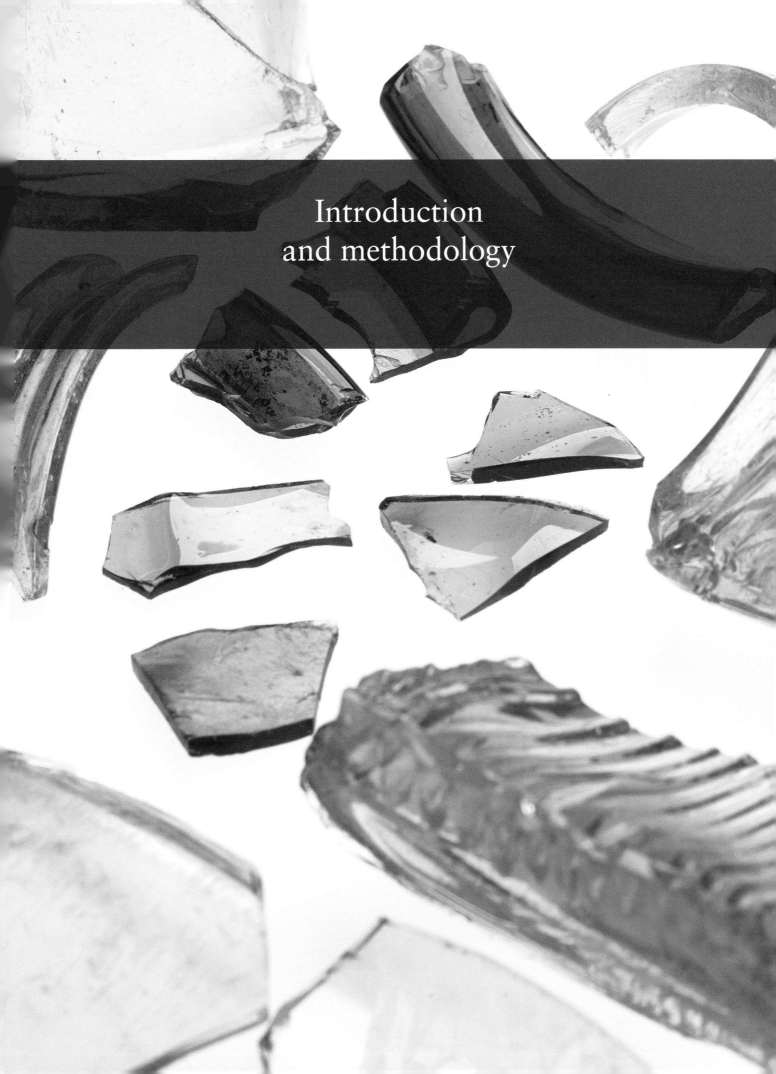

Introduction
and methodology

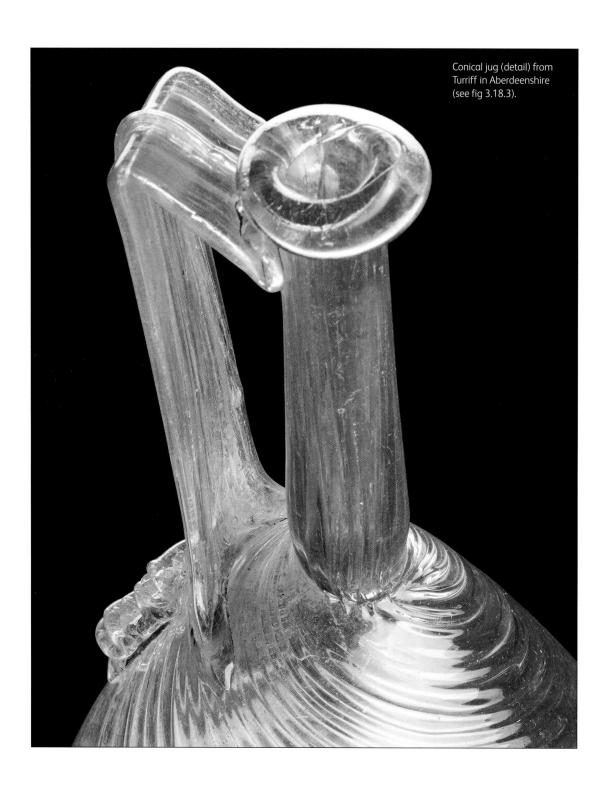

Conical jug (detail) from Turriff in Aberdeenshire (see fig 3.18.3).

1
Introduction

1.1 Primary aims and goals

ROMAN glass from indigenous sites is a key source material for studying the impact of Rome on Iron Age Scotland, but it has never been properly studied. This work fills that gap. Detailed analysis of often tiny fragments reveals the impressive objects they once were – desirable objects, laden with power and symbolism for the recipient groups. This study is based on the Roman glass vessels found on non-Roman/native sites north of Hadrian's Wall, dated mainly to the Roman Iron Age (AD 1–400). Geographically this area primarily lay beyond the frontiers of the Roman Empire, despite various attempts by the Roman army to conquer Britain in its entirety and brief interludes when north Northumberland and Lowland Scotland were incorporated within the boundaries of Rome.

The key reasons behind the choice of material for this case study were: the importance of Roman glass as export articles; the manageable size of the material, which allows comprehensive study; and the high standards of glass research in Britain. It is important to stress, however, that all that can be offered on the basis of the study of a single material is a partial picture of the whole.

Taking the glass as a starting point, I hope to shed some light on aspects of Roman-native relations, most importantly the exchange of goods and ideas. The material is far too fragmented and much too scattered to make a contribution to glass studies as such; instead, it constitutes a case study for a discussion of wider topics in the Roman Iron Age/Roman period.

One of the primary problems considered in this work is whether the finds of glass on native sites represent loot or plunder, as is sometimes argued in earlier scholarly works, or whether they were the outcome of some peaceful enterprise such as trade, exchange or gift giving. And is it possible to arrive at some understanding as to the scale of this exchange, whatever its nature? Was it a mere trickle of trinkets of Roman manufacture, as advocated in academic works of relatively recent date? Or was it a flow of predominantly quality goods of a greater scale than we hitherto have been led to believe?

Other key issues I wish to address are:

(a) Whether the imported Roman goods – in particular the Roman vessel glass – might not just have denoted status, but also functioned as an instrument for obtaining influence and power.

(b) How the cup, or its alcoholic contents, served as a symbol of the leader's 'generosity', and more importantly, how it functioned as an instrument of lordly power.

(c) Whether the glass found on some sites may once have formed parts of Roman drinking sets, as was the case in Free Germany, possibly reflecting some understanding of Roman drinking customs, and how knowledge from and of distant

Figure 1.1

Finds of Roman glass on native/non-Roman sites; uncertain sites are marked with question mark.

D. Cowley/ F. Hunter

0   100 km

realms could have functioned as a means for the elite to gain or maintain influence and power through its ability to create social barriers.

In order to interpret the archaeological material, theories and models derived from archaeological, anthropological and sociological research will be applied. The focus is on the broader meaning of this material, so discussion of individual sites is limited, although key details are summarised in Appendix A. In my study I have utilised various strands of evidence derived from a vast geographical area which fall within numerous scholarly specialities, fields and disciplines, most importantly glass studies; British and Continental prehistoric archaeology; Roman and Classical archaeology, ancient history and more specifically Roman social history; Medieval history and literature; anthropology and sociology. It goes without saying that it lies well beyond the capability of any scholar to procure expert knowledge within all these fields, but I hope that this work will provoke the interests of other specialists.

1.2 Secondary aims and goals

Despite a long interest in Roman-native trade and relations, there are surprisingly few in-depth studies of Roman imports in Iron Age contexts in the area north of Hadrian's Wall. One can only speculate on why this is the case, but it is in my view clear that the study of northern Britain has long suffered from an unfortunate dichotomy between Roman military archaeology and prehistoric or 'native' archaeology. With this work I hope to make a contribution, not only to our understanding of Roman-native trade and contacts, but the understanding of the individual sites. Roman material has long been essential for the dating of native sites, and hopefully the results from this study may also be of some use in dating different phases at these individual sites.

Throughout the catalogue – chapter 3 – I discuss finds of Roman glass from other areas beyond the borders of Rome, with a particular emphasis on the finds from Free Germany. In the case of these finds, especially the Scandinavian material, I have attempted to give a detailed description of the contexts of the finds. The reasons for this are two-fold: these finds from funerary contexts constitute a significant analogy to the Scottish material, and may be of assistance in interpreting the latter. Simultaneously, particulars of the context of these discoveries have been available in the Scandinavian

languages and German only, and it seems desirable to make this information accessible to an English-speaking audience.

1.3 Limits of the study

There are, of course, many limitations in an investigation of this kind. Originally it was my ambition to produce a complete study of all finds of Roman vessel glass found on non-Roman/native sites,[1] but for various reasons this has proven unfeasible. The material from a limited number of sites, four in total, was still with the excavators. At the time of writing, however, I had some information concerning the identification of these finds, which therefore were included in the study. Similarly the material from 13 sites is reported as missing, but nevertheless it is possible to include this material based on published accounts. In two cases I have neither been able to access the material, nor have I had enough information on it, and thus it was not included in the present study.[2]

In total, the study includes material from 64 sites – the majority of which belong to the Roman Iron Age – but the reader will also find references to finds from 13 sites excavated after the closing date for the catalogue in 2007, which means that 77 Iron Age sites have yielded Roman glass. In addition, I have studied the material from nine sites that are not included in the study. This material was either demonstrated not to be Roman glass or, in some cases, the material was of Roman date but does not come from native sites.[3]

Notes

1 The first version of this work was presented as a PhD thesis at Lund University (Ingemark 2003) and updated by further research trips in 2007, 2010 and 2013; the catalogue was, however, closed in 2007. A number of the finds discovered after 2007 have been studied but are not included in the catalogue – a summary is included in ch. 3.26.
2 See ch. 3.26.
3 See ch. 3.26; Appendix A.

2

Methodology and representativity

2.1 Identification and classification of the glass vessels

THE overwhelming majority of finds of Roman glass from non-Roman/native contexts north of Hadrian's Wall come from various types of settlements; hence, it is highly fragmented (fig. 2.1). Consequently the methods used, and the difficulties discussed below, primarily concern the study of a fragmented material. Most, if not all, of these methods are conventional and well established; however, for the benefit of the reader I have given a brief outline of the methods and classificatory schemes utilised.

Two different methods were used in the identification of the material. On the one hand, I studied the shape of the fragments, the techniques employed in the manufacture of the vessels, and how they were decorated; in other words the common method applied to most fragmented archaeological materials, which needs no further explanation.

On the other hand, I utilised a method of identification developed by Frans Herschend in 1973. This is based on the fact that all glass produced before the twentieth century AD is more or less bubbly. The laws of physics govern the shape and direction of these bubbles. For example a long, narrow neck has long, elongated bubbles which run more or less vertically, whereas a vessel of a spherical shape has spherical bubbles. Even a minute fragment, which cannot be identified otherwise, gives an indication of the shape of the vessel.[1] Although Herschend's method has certain drawbacks in that one can only establish the shape of the part where the fragment came from, in its simplicity it is a practical method to aid in the identification of the material.

Equally important as determining the shape of the vessel is establishing its colour. Ascertaining the colour of a glass vessel may at first seem to be a straightforward and unproblematic task; yet, to the best of the author's knowledge, no practical solution to this problem exists today, despite various attempts to find an objective way of determining the colour of glass.[2] Instead, there are a number of different factors that affect how we perceive and classify a colour: physical, chemical, physiological and not least psychological factors.[3] Particularly important are factors such as the thickness of the glass and the light in the room where the fragments are studied.

Traditionally the colour of the glass has been classified by giving a verbal description, for example 'amber', which in more recent research has been replaced by a more neutral description – in this case 'yellow-brown'. This way of classifying colour in glass cannot be said to be entirely objective, and therefore several archaeologists and glass scholars have advocated the use of colour atlases.[4] Ulf Näsman has argued that the employment of these may be considered subjective to some extent, but to a lesser degree than the traditional verbal description.[5] Originally it was my intention to use the Munsell Colour Chart, but this turned out to be unfeasible, for several reasons:

(a)   The Munsell Colour Chart is not intended for determining transparent and glossy colours: indeed, it is inappropriate for colours of this kind;

Figure 2.1

The nature of the material: fragmentary glass from Traprain Law.

(b) Roman glass is found in a wide array of different colours – both transparent and opaque – and a number of these are missing altogether from the colour atlas.

(c) The division between different shades of colour is not fine enough to be of practical use.

(d) In many cases the colour of the fragments is not homogeneous.

Lacking alternatives, I have therefore chosen to use the traditional verbal description of colour, despite its drawbacks.

The taphonomy of the glass is also an important factor in identification. A glass – or pottery – vessel is made to withstand extended use and for this reason certain parts are strengthened. In an important study by Ewan Campbell he pointed to the effects of this, namely that rims, bases and handles form larger fragments, whereas body sherds tend to be of smaller size.[6] Of the unidentified material – discussed in chapter 3.25 – a significant proportion consists of small body fragments.

The degree of breakage in native/non-Roman contexts appears to be higher than in Roman contexts. Perhaps this was a result of the extended use of many of the native sites, where small sherds which had not been swept up were trampled on for generations. Or possibly the value of the glass – which was occasionally reused or remelted – was higher in a native than in a Roman context. In other words, the sherds of a broken vessel were more meticulously collected in native contexts. Whatever the cause, the result is that the classification and quantification of the material is rendered more difficult.

Despite these difficulties, it has been possible to identify a substantial part of the total assemblage. In the present study several different typologies have been used. Those studying the glass found in Free Germany have traditionally employed the typology of Hans-Jürgen Eggers (1951). This study, in spite of its scholarly qualities, is impaired by a very strong bias towards funerary material. Occasionally other older studies/typologies, such as Anton Kisa's (1908) or Morin-Jean's (1913) are also referred to, but these have rarely been used extensively in the classification of the material.

The most commonly employed typology is that of Clasina Isings (1957), which is based on a genuine understanding of the material; moreover it is very flexible, and it has thus won general acceptance among scholars. However, for various reasons, it is not entirely unproblematic to use. Isings' study was written not long after the Second World War,[7] at a time when many museums' collections had been lost, or were in a state of complete

disarray. It also focuses on the intact funerary material, but we cannot presuppose that all types or varieties that once existed have survived as intact objects. Despite its drawbacks, I make use of this typology, as it is so widely accepted and understood.

In 1998 Jennifer Price and Sally Cottam published a handbook on Romano-British glass vessels. This typology allows for more variation than Isings'. Moreover, this work was based on extensive studies of fragmented settlement material as well as intact grave-material. There is no numerical ordering of the forms; rather each form is described according to its perceived function/ form, the manufacturing method used, and characteristic features, for instance: *Conical beaker with ground exterior surfaces and facet-cut/relief decoration*, or *convex wheel-cut cup*. I have found Price and Cottam's handbook most useful, and I refer to it as well as Isings in the catalogue. In the descriptions of the glass, and the methods employed in the manufacture, I have made use of the same terminology as two of the leading scholars within the field of glass studies, namely Hilary Cool and Price.[8]

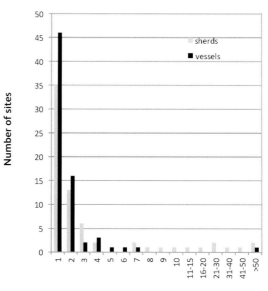

Figure 2.2

Number of sherds/vessels found on different sites; small numbers of both sherds and vessels dominate. The sites with over 50 sherds are Torwoodlee (73) and Traprain Law (366); Traprain Law has over 50 vessels (n=101).

The closest parallels for the assemblage of Roman glass on non-Roman/native sites north of Hadrian's Wall come from Roman Britain. The quality of the research on Roman glass from this area is very high indeed and it has been extensively published through the meticulous work of leading glass historians such as Donald B. Harden, Dorothy Charlesworth, Cool, Price and Denise Allen. Rather than giving endless lists of Romano-British parallels, I have chosen to give a brief summary of what is known about the distribution of different types and forms: two excellent works which can be used as overviews, and which I refer to throughout this work, are Cool and Price's *Roman vessel glass from excavations in Colchester, 1971–85* (1995); and Price and Cottam's *Romano-British Glass Vessels: A Handbook* (1998). I have chosen to follow the former in the way the catalogue is structured.

In the case of the material from the parts of Continental Europe which once belonged to the Roman Empire, as well as material from areas occupied by the Roman Empire in North Africa and the Middle East, I have chosen to give a list of parallels in the footnotes as there are no overviews of the same quality as in Britain. These lists of parallels are by no means complete, for in recent years there has been a great deal of research done for example in France, Germany and Spain, but they should give some idea of a type's distribution. With regard to Roman glass from areas beyond the borders of Rome, I have chosen to present this material in greater depth, in particular the Scandinavian parallels.

2.2 Quantifying the glass assemblages

When studying fragmentary material, one has to be aware that the number of fragments to a large extent reflects the conditions of deposition. Merely comparing the number of fragments can therefore be strongly misleading, giving an utterly distorted picture of what was once there. For this reason, archaeologists studying material from different deposits within a site, or from different sites, need to have an accurate analytical tool or method which allows for and enables a comparison between the assemblages. It is important to stress that the native assemblages of Roman glass are very small. Moreover, they are fragmented to a much greater degree than is normally found on Roman sites,[9] rendering comparison difficult.

There are four basic methods of quantification which have been applied to pottery as well as glass:

(a) Fragment count.
(b) Weight.
(c) Estimated vessel equivalents (EVE).
(d) Estimated minimum or maximum numbers of vessels (EMN).

The two first methods are self-explanatory. The calculation of EVEs can be based on either weight, surface area or the proportion of a measurable part of the vessel.[10] In the case of estimated minimum number of vessels (EMN), fragments of the same colour, type and size – for example a rim fragment and a base fragment – are counted as one vessel. The estimated maximum number of vessels method is the opposite, as all non-joining fragments are assumed to have belonged to different vessels.[11]

There are drawbacks and disadvantages with all these methods. Many assemblages of Roman glass consist of a variety of different vessels, ranging from large and heavy storage vessels to small and light drinking vessels. As a consequence, the fragment count and weight methods give a biased picture of the size of the original assemblage. The estimated vessel equivalents method (EVE) is considerably more time-consuming than the other methods of quantification. More importantly, however, in cases with a low level of retrieval – such as the native sites – the calculated figures are very low indeed, thus under-emphasising the size of the assemblage.

One of the drawbacks with the minimum numbers of vessels method (EMN) is that the assemblage size strongly influences the result. With an increasing size of the assemblage, the estimated number of vessels does not increase at the same rate.[12] This makes it difficult to compare assemblages of different sizes. The advantage of the EMN, however, is its simplicity, and the fact that it is far less time-consuming than calculating EVEs. More importantly, EVE is a method more suited to the study of large Roman assemblages with a relatively low degree of fragmentation, and not for the small native assemblages. I have therefore chosen to use estimated minimum numbers (EMN).

2.3 The representativity of the glass

A crucial problem in the study of Roman–native interaction is whether we should regard the exchange as minor and insignificant, or whether it took place on a larger scale than hitherto believed. Although an estimation of the minimum number of vessels can provide an idea of how many vessels reached the site, it might – for example, in the case of extensive recycling – belie the true size of the original assemblage.

Unlike the glass of other periods, Roman glass is a stable and durable soda–lime–silica glass, which normally survives the passage of time extremely well.[13] There are a number of factors, some of which have been touched upon already, that determine how much of the original glass assemblage can be retrieved through archaeological excavation, hence forming the basis for the calculation of estimated minimum numbers (EMN):

(a) With the exception of a limited number of finds from funerary contexts, and a single find from a ritual deposit, the overwhelming majority of finds of glass come from settlement sites. Consequently, very few intact objects have survived the passage of time, and most material is in a highly fragmented state. Once deposited as grave gifts or hoards, the objects were in effect taken out of circulation, and the chances of survival and archaeological retrieval are likely to be greater than in the case of the settlement material.

(b) A significant number of the finds are represented by a single fragment, which indicates that in most cases when a vessel was broken, the sherds were meticulously swept up. These may have been discarded and removed from the dwelling, in which case the likelihood of retrieval is small. In some instances, discussed below, the broken vessels were reused or possibly recycled.

(c) A small category of finds show clear signs of deliberate reuse (fig. 2.3).[14] Fragments of vessel glass such as a base of a cylindrical cup, blue-green bottles, the rim of an oil flask as well as a piece of window glass were turned into gaming pieces or polishers by knapping; similarly, the handle of an oil flask, a rim of a tubular-rimmed vessel and a tubular pushed-in base were used for beads.[15] Of the sites yielding such finds, seven are of certain Roman Iron Age date, one of possible Roman Iron Age date, whereas two are, or may be, of early Medieval date. Most evidence (discussed later) seems to imply that the glass reached the native sites in the Roman Iron Age as intact vessels, rather than having been imported as cullet, whereas this need not be the case of the material from the early Medieval sites.[16] It is noteworthy that the limited reworking of glass fragments in a cold state stands in contrast to the more extensive reuse of fragmented Roman pottery. In-depth study of the Roman pottery from native/non-Roman sites by Louisa Campbell has identified more than a hundred sites on which gaming counters, spindle whorls, weights, polishers and suchlike objects made of samian (and to a much lesser extent also coarse-ware) were discovered.[17] The contrast between the materials is marked. No less than 107 sites have yielded reworked Roman pottery, in comparison to a mere seven sites with reused Roman glass. However, this

Figure 2.3

Reused glass fragments from Traprain Law. a) Handle reused as bead, and two sherds reused as gaming counters (GV 211, 538, 1273; bead height, 17mm). b) Base reused as gaming counter (GV 1231; diameter 45mm).

Figure 2.4

Glass bangles from Knowes, East Lothian.

has to be seen in the light of potential recycling of Roman glass in a native context.

(d) It is still a matter of discussion whether recycling of Roman glass took place on native sites, although recent evidence seems to suggest this. It is very likely that the core of glass bangles was often manufactured from recycled Roman glass (fig. 2.4),[18] but views concerning the sites of production differ, leaving the problem unresolved.

As the question of recycling is of fundamental importance for the interpretation of native assemblages of Roman glass, it seems appropriate to expand upon this matter. H. E. Kilbride-Jones, Robert Stevenson, Roy Newton and J. Henderson and M. M. B. Kemp have all argued[19], based on the finds distributions, that the manufacture of these bangles occurred on native sites. In contrast, Price[20] has put forward the notion that these were of Roman manufacture, made in the *vici* of the Roman forts in northern Britain – again based on the distribution patterns of these objects. The recent dis-

covery of glass-working debris from the manufacture of glass bangles at a Roman – possibly to be seen as rural – site at Thearne, near Hull, demonstrates that some glass bangles were indeed manufactured within the province, but, while valuable, the finds from a single site do not lay the matter to rest.[21]

There can be little doubt that the core of most objects was made of remelted Roman glass, as determined both by scientific methods and ocular examination. Many finds have a blue-green core, and blue-green bottle glass was readily available on the native sites.[22] There are also rare examples of highly-coloured pillar-moulded bowls being remelted to form bangles, such as the finds from Traprain Law and Dod Law (fig. 2.5; plate 1).[23] Using anthropological analogy as a point of departure, Thea Haevernick has demonstrated that manufacture of this kind was easy to set up and move, and that it leaves little trace.[24]

Julian Henderson has shown that there was Iron Age production of glass beads in Culbin Sands, Morayshire.[25] Similarly it has been argued by Michael Erdrich, Kristina Giannotta and by William Hanson that glass-working employing Roman glass took place at Traprain Law.[26] Excavations at Mine Howe, Tankerness, Mainland Orkney have yielded a minimum of five different objects manufactured from remelted blue-green bottle glass. There are also remains of what may have been debris from glass-working. In addition, a small number of glass fragments were either partly melted or otherwise affected by heat. It thus appears that some small-scale glass-working may have taken place on the site, and this may be linked to the other high-temperature crafts that we know took place at Mine Howe.[27] Recent excavations of what appears to be a high-status settlement and industrial site at Culduthel Mains Farm, Inverness, included debris from bead manufacture and enamelling of metal objects, in the form of molten glass waste and off-cuts from glass rods. Also there are finds of what may be fragmented Roman glass,[28] but these are difficult to link to the production. The raw material in this production, which took place from 150 BC to AD 60, was imported glass ingots.[29] Thus we know that there was a knowledge of glass-working in the native societies.

In the light of this evidence, would it not be possible to suggest that a manufacture of bangles took place on both Roman and native sites, both sides of Hadrian's Wall? While this is an area where further scientific work would be very desirable, it seems fair to conclude that much Roman glass which arrived on native sites would have been recycled after breakage.

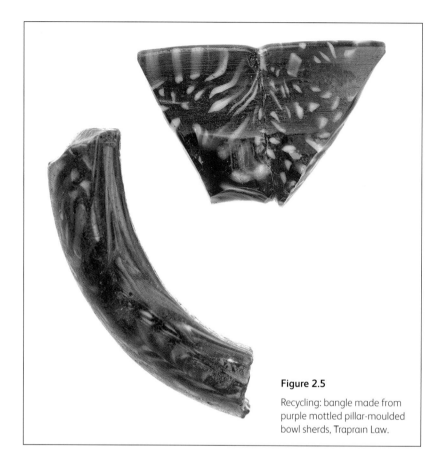

Figure 2.5

Recycling: bangle made from purple mottled pillar-moulded bowl sherds, Traprain Law.

Notes

1 Herschend 1972–73.
2 There are ways of determining the colour of glass in an objective way in a laboratory. For economic and practical reasons these methods have been used very little in archae-ological research. See Sanderson & Hutchings 1987.
3 Itten 1971, 12–13; Osborne 1980, 14–15; Agoston 1987, 5.
4 See for example Gerharz et al. 1986; Newton & Davidson 1996 (1989), 188; Rütti 1991b, 109.
5 Näsman 1984, 16.
6 Campbell 2007, 84–85.
7 Isings 1957, v.
8 Cool & Price 1995.
9 This is based on my personal observations, having worked with assemblages from native, Romano-British and Roman sites.
10 Cool & Baxter 1999.
11 Orton 1990, 94.
12 Cool & Price 1995, 9.
13 Newton & Davidson 1996 (1989), ch. 4.
14 Besides glass, other types of Roman imports were also reused, such as samian and copper-alloy objects (Erdrich et al. 2000, 449; Hunter 2007a, 37).
15 Waulkmill, Tarland, Aberdeenshire (ch. 3.5, Appendix A, G:2); Leckie broch, Stirlingshire (ch. 3.23, Appendix A, K:4); Dalmeny Park, Midlothian (ch. 3.25, Appendix A, M:2);

Covesea, Morayshire (ch. 3.25, Appendix A, F:2); Traprain Law, East Lothian (chs 3.8, 3.22, 3.23, Appendix A, N:2); ?Ardeer / ?Luce Sands (ch. 3.23, Appendix A, P:1); Lochspouts, Ayrshire (ch. 3.23, Appendix A, P:5); Dunadd, Argyll (ch. 3.22, Appendix A, J:1); Whithorn, Wigtownshire (ch. 3.23, Appendix A, Q:2); Keiss Harbour, Caithness (ch. 3.23, Appendix A, D:3).
16 See discussion in ch. 4.6.
17 Campbell 2012, 4–5.
18 Newton 1971, 13–15; Henderson & Kemp 1992, 43–45.
19 Kilbride-Jones 1938a; Stevenson 1954–56, 1976; Newton 1971; Henderson & Kemp 1992.
20 Price 1988.
21 www.historyofglass.org.uk/pdfs/study-days/Study_Day_ Mar_09.pdf [accessed 4 March 2014]; Campbell 2008. At the time of writing the author had little information on this discovery. I would like to thank Dr Fraser Hunter for bringing this find to my attention.
22 See chs. 3.23; 4.3.
23 Newton 1971, 13.
24 Haevernick 1981a, 8–11.
25 Henderson 1989, 67.
26 Erdrich et al. 2000, 447.
27 See ch. 3.26; Appendix A, B:2
28 Murray 2007, 25; Canmore ID 163581: 'Old Town of Leys' (= Culduthel) www.rcahms.gov.uk [accessed 5 March 2014].
29 Dr Fraser Hunter pers. comm.

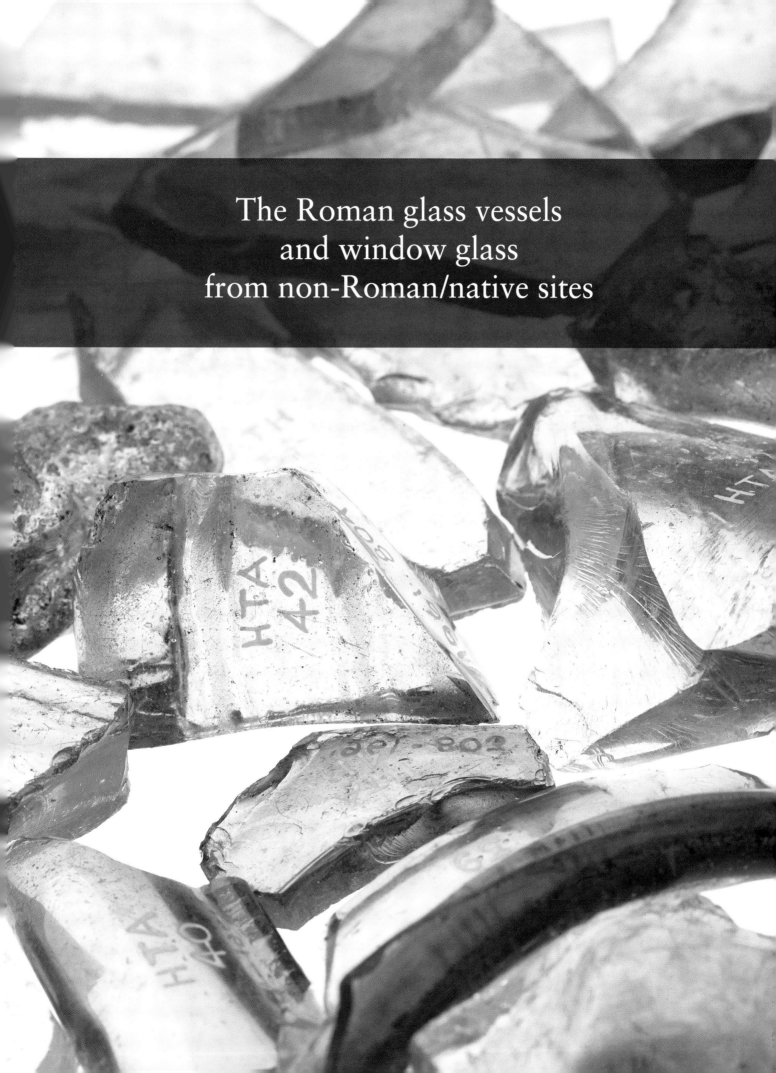

The Roman glass vessels
and window glass
from non-Roman/native sites

A snake-thread glass sherd
from Covesea (see fig. 3.4.5).

3
Catalogue

Introduction

EACH positively identified form, group of forms or category of glass is discussed in a separate chapter. Given the fact that the majority of glass assemblages come from non-Roman/native settlement sites – hence were strongly fragmented – parts of the material remain unidentified or cannot be classified with certainty. This is dealt with in chapter 3.25 'Miscellaneous fragments (including post-Roman finds)'.

At the end of the catalogue there is also a chapter that deals with lost, missing and dismissed material, as well as with recent finds (3.26). The closing date of the catalogue is 2007, but some later discoveries (and rediscoveries for that matter) have been included. The observant reader will also find that single finds made prior to this date were still with the excavators and could not be studied for practical reasons. My ambition has been that the distribution maps should comprise all finds known to me, including those which have been made after 2007, and not only those in the catalogue.

One of many difficulties in working with fragmentary material is that some material can be classified to type – or even to subtype – whereas other material can only be identified as belonging to a larger group of vessels made with a specific method of manufacture (e.g. snake-thread glass). This is obviously of great importance for how the catalogue is best arranged from a logical perspective. In working with the fragmented material from Colchester, Hilary Cool and Jennifer Price faced the same problems.[1]

To my mind, Cool and Price's catalogue works very well, and I have chosen to follow this. This division of the material is roughly chronological – 'cast' glass is therefore placed before blown glass, because blown glass represents a later invention. It has to be noted though, that this invention happened well before the Claudian invasion of Britain. An exception to the chronological arrangement is that all polychrome blown vessels are placed early in the catalogue; in this case the categories include both early and late material.

After the cast material and the polychrome blown glass, the glass is divided into functional categories: cups and beakers of different types, bowls of various categories, jars, jugs, unguent bottles and oil-flasks, followed by large bottles. These are also arranged in a rough chronological order. At the end I have placed the window glass.

In the practical organisation of the catalogue, I have chosen to focus on those features most crucial for my overall argument. The following aspects are discussed:

- A general description of the form or type.
- The dates of manufacture and use within the Roman world.
- The function of the objects within the Roman world.
- Parallel finds from Roman contexts.
- A detailed description of the finds from non-Roman native contexts in Scotland and north Northumberland and a discussion of these
- Parallel finds from other areas beyond the borders of the Roman Empire.

In the discussion on the finds from non-Roman native sites, these are roughly arranged from north to south, following the old (i.e. pre-1975) county divisions for consistency with previous works, although the Inner and Outer Hebrides are grouped together in a single category (fig. 8.1).

Many of the finds come from Traprain Law in East Lothian. In these cases, the entry gives the museum registration number (in the form GV xxx), any older numbers, and the excavation area and level (if not specified, these are unknown). For more recent excavations the site code and find number are given. A brief summary of each site can be found in Appendix A.

Abbreviations used in the description of the glass

Dims = dimensions
W = width
WT = wall thickness
RD = rim diameter
BD = base diameter
PH = present height

All measurements are in millimetres.

Chronological references

In British scholarly works there are different means of referring to the date of a specific form or category of find, and I sometimes follow the tradition of stating which emperor was in power. For the sake of convenience I will give a short list of emperors referred to:

- Augustus 27 BC–AD 14
- Tiberius AD 14–37
- Gaius (Caligula) AD 37–41
- Claudius AD 41–54
- Nero AD 54–68
- The Flavian dynasty AD 69–96
  (Vespasian AD 69–79;
  Titus AD 79–81;
  Domitian AD 81–96)
- Trajan AD 98–117
- Hadrian AD 117–138
- Antoninus Pius AD 138–161
- Marcus Aurelius AD 161–180

Finds in the catalogue with accompanying photographs or illustrations are denoted with an asterisk*, e.g. GV 110*.

Notes

1   See Cool & Price 1995.

3.1 Pillar-moulded bowls

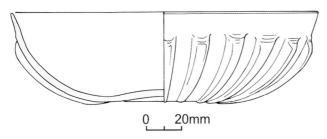

Figure 3.1.1

Pillar-moulded bowl, Radnage, Buckinghamshire [scale 1:2].
After Harden et al. 1988, 51

0   20mm

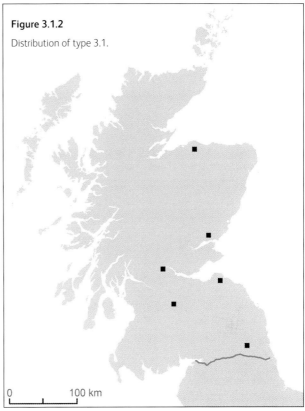

Figure 3.1.2

Distribution of type 3.1.

0   100 km

A general description of the type

The pillar-moulded bowl is thick-walled, with a shallow or deep convex body and prominent ribs on the outside.[1] The inside surface and the outer rim are ground and polished and display a dull surface, while the remainder of the outside is glossy. Wheel-cut horizontal grooves are often found in the interior. While they usually occur on the lower body, there are examples with wheel-cut grooves below the rim. The bowls vary in size; the rim diameters are $c.100$ to $c.220$mm, the heights $c.50$ to $c.85$ mm.[2]

The denomination 'pillar-moulded' used among English-speaking glass historians derives from Apsley Pellatt of the Falcon Glass Works, London.[3] The antiquarian Charles Roach Smith, a friend of Pellatt's, came to use the same term in 1859,[4] a term which has been employed ever since. Pillar-moulding – a new technique, invented at the beginning of the nineteenth century by James Green – had little to do with the ancient manufacturing methods; however, among scholars today it is generally agreed that the term is technically meaningless.[5]

There has been much debate on the actual manufacturing method, a debate which is still very much on-going. Many glass historians support the ideas that are put forward by Keith Cummings, who prefers the term mould-pressing. Cummings suggested that molten glass was poured on a flat surface to form a thick flat disc. A mould with a rib pattern was pressed into the disc. The still-soft disc was then sagged, or slumped, on a mould to give it a bowl shape. After annealing the bowl was polished on the inside, and on the rim.[6]

A theory related to that of Cummings' which has won some support in the scholarly world has been put forward by Rosemarie Lierke. She suggests that the pillar-moulded bowls were made on a device resembling a potter's wheel; the blank was sagged/slumped over a convex mould which was mounted on a slowly rotating turntable.[7] Nevertheless, there are several other suggested manufacturing methods, a number of which have been carried out more or less successfully in modern experiments. W. A. Thorpe advocated the idea of mould-pressing.[8] Frederick Schuler advanced the idea that they were cast, using the *cire-perdue* or lost wax method.[9]

In Isings' typology, pillar-moulded bowls are divided depending on the general shape of the vessel and how the ribs are executed;[10] however Jennifer Price and Sally Cottam do not make such a distinction.[11] Since the Scottish material is so fragmented, I have chosen to use the colour rather than the shape as a typological criterion. In this particular case, this is of much greater value, as the colour of the vessels can be used as a dating instrument. Pillar-moulded bowls are either polychrome or monochrome. The latter are in strong colours, such as deep blue, dark green, yellow-brown and yellow-green, or in common blue-green glass.[12] Monochrome vessels in opaque white or pale blue are known, but extremely rare.[13]

The polychrome ones are made in marbled or mille-fiore glass, with two or more colours (see pl. 2).[14] There are a number of colours, some of which imitate semi-precious stones.[15] One frequent variant is purple with opaque white dots. This is the same colour as that of *vasa murrina* mentioned by Pliny the Elder[16] and other classi-cal authors.[17] Anton Kisa identified *vasa murrina* with glass,[18] but A. I. Loewenthal and Donald Harden have made a convincing case for it to be fluor-spar,[19] the glass being an imitation.[20] This is shown in the following passage from Pliny the Elder's *Natural History*:

> There is, furthermore, opaque white glass and others that reproduce the appearance of fluor-spar, blue sapphires or lapis lazuli, and indeed, glass exists in any colour.
>
> Pliny the Elder, *Historia Naturalis*, 36.75.198

A passage found in *Periplus maris Erythraei* also sup-ports Loewenthal's and Harden's suggestions:

> Several sorts of glassware. Imitation murrhine ware made in Diospolis. *Periplus maris Erythraei* 6

Dating the type

The earliest examples of pillar-moulded bowls date to the early Augustan times.[21] They represent the continu-ation of the Hellenistic glass production methods, which were later replaced by the blowing technique. Early finds have been made in the House of Livia, Palatine Hill, Rome,[22] Livia's villa at Prima Porta outside Rome,[23] and in Magdalensberg, Austria.[24]

Both polychrome and monochrome vessels were produced during this period. However, the production of strongly coloured monochrome bowls ceased around the mid-first century, and marbled polychrome some-what earlier.[25] In other words, these variations of pillar-moulded bowls went out of production only a few years after Britain became part of the Roman Empire. During the second half of the first century there was a clear de-cline in quality and craftsmanship, common blue-green being the only colour still in production. This produc-tion came to an end in the Flavian period.[26]

The earliest British finds date to the period immedi-ately after the Claudian invasion, as shown by finds from some of the earliest Roman sites, such as Colchester, Essex.[27] Finds have also been made on numerous Neronian and Flavian sites, after which there is a sharp decline.

The function of the vessels

Pillar-moulded bowls are considered to be tableware, intended for drinking as well as serving. Price has sug-gested that the function varied depending on size and shape.[28] It may well be that smaller, thinner, deep bowls were used as drinking utensils' whereas larger, shal-lower, much heavier bowls were used for serving food.

The finds from Roman contexts

Pillar-moulded bowls constitute one of the most recur-rent and geographically most widely distributed types of Roman glass, both within the Empire and beyond its most distant outposts. However, there is a possibility that this type is over-represented in the archaeological record for the following reasons:

- Fragments of pillar-moulded bowls are easily identified in the glass assemblages, due to the methods of manufacture and distinct decora-tion.[29] In a period when an increasing number of types were manufactured in blown rather than cast glass, the dull inside surface and the glossy outside surface make even minute fragments immediately recognisable. Furthermore, the dis-tinct design with raised ribs distinguishes it from other types of cast vessels, while the colours are readily identifiable.
- In contrast to many other types of Roman glass vessels, pillar-moulded bowls do not break easily, and there are many cases in which vessels appear to have remained intact and in use for extended periods of time, often surviving for several decades. This is probably due to the simple form, its execution in thick glass, and most importantly the methods of manufacture and the quality of craftsmanship: the vessels appear to have been annealed correctly, render-ing them more resistant to blows.

Yet even taking this into account, it seems that pillar-moulded bowls actually were one of the most common types of glass in their day. Given that the type was pro-duced for a long period of time (a century) from the early Augustan period and into the Flavian period, in all prob-ability on numerous sites across the Roman Empire,[30] this is hardly surprising.

At the time of the Roman attempts to expand into northern Britain, several subtypes of pillar-moulded bowls – the polychrome vessels and strongly coloured monochrome vessels – were no longer in production. This is reflected in the sharp decline of finds of these sub-types on Flavian sites in southern Britain. Nevertheless, a number of finds in these colours, as well as some in blue-green glass, have been discovered in Roman forts and civilian settlements of Flavian date in northern Britain.[31] This requires an explanation, and the most plausible one seems to be that these durable bowls were the personal property of officers and soldiers serving in the Roman army who brought them with them to their new camps in the north, rather than being commodities offered for sale by traders following the army, although the latter cannot be entirely excluded.

In other parts of Roman Britain, pillar-moulded bowls constitute an extremely common type of glass in assemblages dating to the first century AD.[32] Sites belonging to the first phase of Roman occupation, i.e. those founded after the Claudian invasion and the following Neronian period, have the highest percentage of bowls in polychrome or strongly coloured glass. As for sites in the Flavian period or later, they exhibit relatively few, if any, vessels in those colours. Still, it is important to bear in mind that the majority of finds – even on very early Roman sites – are in blue-green glass. This is the case with Colchester, for example, which was founded during the reign of the emperor Claudius.[33]

The pattern of distribution of pillar-moulded bowls in the other parts of the Roman Empire largely resembles that in Britain, though many finds have been made in earlier contexts, dating from the Augustan period onward. Vessels have been discovered on a great number of sites in the vast area that once constituted the Empire. Large numbers of finds have been unearthed in the very core of the Empire – Italy itself;[34] they are nearly as numerous in the north-western, western and northern provinces,[35] in the eastern provinces,[36] and in North Africa.[37]

In the areas lying beyond the borders of Rome, pillar-moulded bowls are indubitably the most common type of Roman glass; we will return to this topic below.

The finds from non-Roman contexts in Scotland and north Northumberland

A minimum of seven pillar-moulded bowls have been found on six native sites north of Hadrian's Wall. One fragment of a blue-green bowl was unearthed during the excavations of the Iron Age settlement at Birnie, in Morayshire (fig. 3.1.4.2).[38] One fragment of a small polychrome bowl in deep blue, opaque yellow and opaque white was discovered during the excavations of a souterrain in Tealing, Angus (figs 3.1.4.4, 3.1.5; pl. 3).[39] Excavations of a dun at Castlehill Wood, Stirlingshire yielded a fragment of a large polychrome bowl in purple glass with opaque white spots (figs 3.1.4.3, 3.1.5; pl. 3).[40] From Traprain Law, East Lothian there are two joining fragments of a small, deep polychrome bowl in purple with opaque white spots (figs 3.1.4.5, 3.1.5; pl. 3).[41] In addition, there are two small fragments of a monochrome bowl in blue-green glass. During the excavations of Hyndford crannog, Lanarkshire, two fragments of a large blue-green bowl were unearthed (fig. 3.1.4.1).[42] From an Iron Age roundhouse at West Whelpington, Northumberland there is a possible find of a monochrome blue bowl.[43] Unfortunately, this find has been lost since the excavations took place and thus no positive identification could be made.

In addition to these finds, there are two glass bangles which were made of remelted polychrome pillar-moulded bowls: one bangle in purple glass with opaque white spots from Traprain Law (fig. 2.5; pl. 1),[44] and one in the same colours from Dod Law, Northumberland. Chemical analysis demonstrated that the same type of glass was used for these.[45] There has been a debate concerning the origin of the glass bangles; most have argued that the production took place on the native sites, whereas one scholar has contended that these were of Roman manufacture. As yet this question remains unresolved (see chapter 2.3).

The native assemblage of pillar-moulded bowls differs from those typically found in Roman contexts in that there is evident preference for polychrome or strongly

Figure 3.1.3

Polychrome bowl from Espe, Fyn, Denmark.
National Museum, Copenhagen: NM C 1309

coloured vessels. On Roman sites, in particular those which post-date the Neronian period, the bulk of the pillar-moulded bowls are in common blue-green glass; only a minor part are polychrome or in strong colours. However, a number of the Roman sites of Flavian date in northern Britain have yielded small numbers of polychrome vessels, thereby demonstrating that these sturdy vessels were in use well after production had ceased.

With the exception of the blue-green bowls from Birnie, Hyndford and Traprain Law – which may be of Flavian date – the manufacture of all other finds predates the Roman invasion in AD 78/79–83. Trying to establish when these vessels reached native hands thus becomes problematic, as they either represent acquisitions made before the Roman arrival in northern Britain, or exchange during or after the Agricolan invasion. There are very few other Roman imports which can be positively demonstrated to pre-date the Flavian period,[46] and considering that vessels of this type were in use on Roman sites in northern Britain, the later date seems more plausible.

Save the Tealing find, which was a small vessel, all others appear to have been large. The former was in all probability a drinking vessel, whereas the function of the remainder could either have been vessels for serving and

presenting food, or drinking vessels. Finds of the same type have been made in funerary contexts and settlements in Free Germany. In the case of the former, the pillar-moulded bowls formed parts of drinking sets which included objects of both Roman and indigenous make. This might imply that the vessels functioned as drinking vessels in Iron Age societies, although it cannot be excluded that they were employed as vessels for serving food.

Polychrome bowls

Castlehill Wood, Stirlingshire.[47] K:2

HH 582*, NMS. Rim fragment. Purple with opaque white spots. Ground on inside, and on rim. PH 54; W 34; WT 4.5–10.

Tealing, Angus.[48] I:4

FR 547*, NMS. Body fragment. Deep blue with opaque white spirals and marbled in opaque yellow. Remains of one narrow rib. Ground on inside, shiny on outside. Curved. Dims 13 x 14; WT 1.8–4.8.

Traprain Law, East Lothian. N:2

GV 682* (V 21 177), Area K, Level 2, NMS. Two joining rim fragments. Purple with opaque white spots. Remains of rib. Ground on inside and rim. PH 23; W 36; WT 3.2–4.8.

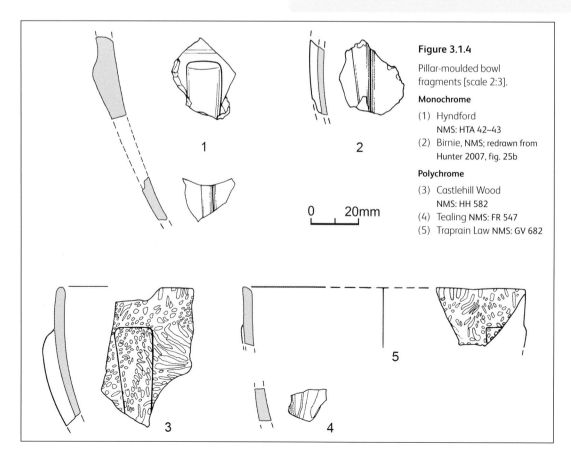

Figure 3.1.4

Pillar-moulded bowl fragments [scale 2:3].

Monochrome

(1) Hyndford
NMS: HTA 42–43

(2) Birnie, NMS; redrawn from Hunter 2007, fig. 25b

Polychrome

(3) Castlehill Wood
NMS: HH 582

(4) Tealing NMS: FR 547

(5) Traprain Law NMS: GV 682

0   20mm

Monochrome bowls in strong colours

West Whelpington, Northumberland. U:7

One possible find. Lost? Fragment of a blue pillar-moulded bowl.[49]

Monochrome bowls in blue-green glass

Birnie, Morayshire. F:3

DS 98 sf.312*, with the excavator; ultimately NMS. Body fragment. Blue-green. Remains of one raised rib. Outside surface dull showing traces of heavy wear; inside surface pitted, ground/ abraded band on the lowest part. Dims 37 x 25; WT 2.3–5.7.

Hyndford, Lanarkshire. O:1

HTA 42*, NMS. Body fragment. Blue-green. Part of one rib, with tooling mark on upper edge. Ground on inside. Occasional small bubbles. Worn on rib. Dims 32 x 26; WT 10.

HTA 43*, NMS. Body fragment. Blue-green. Remains of one rib. Ground on inside. Worn on rib. Dims 20 x 14; WT 2.5.

Traprain Law, East Lothian. N:2

TLF 04 find 344, NMS. Body fragment from immediately below the rim. Blue-green. Ground on both sides. Dims 7 x 6; WT 2.5. Probably same vessel as TLF 05 600. F/W zone 20.

TLF 05 find 600, NMS. Body fragment. Blue-green. Ground on inside. Worn after breakage. Dims 8 x 5; WT 3.2.

The finds from other areas beyond the borders of the Roman Empire

Pillar-moulded bowls are one of the most widely distributed types of Roman vessel glass outside the Roman Empire. A number have been discovered in Free Germany, and in funerary contexts they are sometimes found in pairs. During the excavation of a burial mound with the remains of an inhumation burial – no skeletal material was preserved – at Store-Dal, Østfold, Norway, two shallow monochrome pillar-moulded bowls were found together with a bronze patera in a large bronze cauldron. Several other objects were unearthed in the same grave: an iron knife, two silver brooches, a gold ring, glass beads, a bone comb, etc.[50]

In Espe, Funen, in Denmark, two polychrome vessels in deep blue and opaque white (fig. 3.1.3; pl. 2) were found in a grave excavated in 1871 together with a number of other finds: a repaired large bronze kettle, fragments of a bronze skillet or ladle, bronze mountings from drinking horns, a fossil amulet, a silver fibula, a necklace with beads in glass and amber, etc.[51]

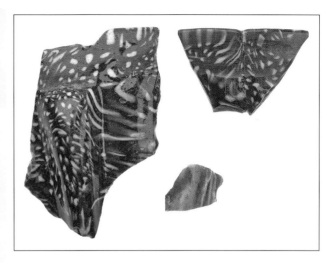

Figure 3.1.5

Polychrome bowl fragments from Castlehill Wood (left), Traprain Law (right) and Tealing (bottom).

In 1964 a grave-field in Sörby-Störlinge, Öland in Sweden, threatened and partly destroyed by ploughing, was excavated. In one of the graves, a stone cist in what had originally been a mound, the remains of an inhumation burial were found. The grave had been looted, probably in ancient times. However, the excavation yielded fragments of two blue-green pillar-moulded bowls, the remains of one or two drinking horns, spurs, fragments of a shield and a sword-sheath and pottery. It was suggested by the excavator that the grave had originally also contained a bronze kettle.[52]

In the 1920s a number of stray finds were made in what was first believed to be a Roman camp at Westick bei Kamen, Kreis Unna, Nordrhein-Westfalen, Germany. Later excavations, in the 1930s and 1963, proved this to be a native settlement. Among the finds is a fragment of a blue-green pillar-moulded bowl.[53] Another settlement find was made at Castrop-Rauxel, Kreis Reckling-hausen, Nordrhein-Westfalen: a fragmented pillar-moulded bowl in natural coloured green.[54]

Excavations of the settlement site of Feddersen Wierde, Mulsum, Landkreis Cuxhaven, Niedersachsen in Germany from 1955 to 1963 yielded two fragments of a blue-green bowl.[55] In 1883 a grave-mound near Beitkow, Brandenburg, Germany was excavated by the inhabitants of the nearby village. Not much is known about the context, except that the grave contained skeletal remains, a blue-green pillar-moulded bowl, a bronze cauldron, and a wine-strainer in bronze.[56] A monochrome bowl in brown glass was found at a burial ground at Weißenfels-Buedefeld, Landkreis Weißenfels, Sachsen-Anhalt, Germany.[57]

In 1908, a farmer in Lübsow (formerly Kreis Greifenberg, Pommern, Germany, now Lubieszewo, Poland) discovered a burial mound with the remains of a cremation. This site, one of several burial mounds, was extremely rich and contained a large number of finds. Particularly notable is a drinking set consisting of two pillar-moulded bowls, two silver goblets, the remains of two drinking horns, a bronze ladle, a bronze jug, a bronze cauldron and several other objects. In the grave there was also a mirror, a gold and silver brooch, etc.[58]

Other Polish finds are: one bowl from a cremation burial at Łęg Piekarski (monochrome);[59] two blue-green bowls from what probably was a cremation burial at Kossin (formerly Kreis Pyritz, Pommern, now Kosin Pyrzyce); two blue-green bowls were discovered with a sieve and ladle set, a drinking horn, etc. in a burial at Wichulla, Posen, now Goslawice (Opola);[60] there are also finds from Szczecin[61] and Debe (polychrome).[62] The prestige and value of this type of bowl was clearly very high, and in Poland a number of pottery copies of pillar-moulded bowls have been discovered (fig. 3.1.6).[63]

Polychrome bowls have also been found in the Black Sea region.[64]

A few finds have been made in Africa: for example, Fezzan, Sahara (south-western Libya),[65] Kush, Sudan[66] and Heïs, Somalia (monochrome).[67] In Roman times – in particular from the era of Augustus onwards – the Arabic peninsula formed an important node along the trade route to the east, and finds of Roman glass of different types have been made on a number of sites. Pillar-moulded bowls have been unearthed at Timna[68] and Qana, Yemen. During the excavations of a tumulus containing an inhumation burial in Bahrain a pillar-moulded bowl in deep purple with white marbling was found. In this bowl lay a string of beads in agate, crystal and amethyst, an ivory comb and an ivory pin; across it was a copper spatula. Several other glass and pottery vessels were also found.[69]

A number of sites in the United Arab Emirates (UAE) have also yielded finds of pillar-moulded bowls. The excavations at Ed-Dur, the Emirate of Umm al-Qaiwain, UAE yielded a great number of fragments of pillar-

Figure 3.1.6 Ceramic copies of pillar-moulded bowls from Polish Przeworsk culture cemeteries; late 1st to 2nd century AD.

(a–b): Łęgonice Małe site II (Odrzywół commune, Przysucha district, Mazowieckie province) (inv. no. PMA/IV/5222:17).

(c–d): Sierzchów (Bolimów commune, Skierniewice district, Łódzkie province) (inv. no. PMA/IV/264:9).

Photos taken by Roman Sofuł for State Archaeological Museum in Warsaw

moulded bowls, polychrome as well as monochrome.[70] At Dibba al Hisn, Sharjah, UAE a tomb containing no less than 15 skeletons was rich in finds of pottery, metal, and glass. Two intact pillar-moulded bowls and a number of fragmentary examples were discovered at this site.[71] Two pillar-moulded bowls were found in tombs of a cemetery at Mleiha, Sharjah, UAE.[72] In addition to these, pillar-moulded bowls have been found at Kush, Ras al-Khaima, UAE,[73] and at Bidya, Fujairah, UAE.[74]

A pillar-moulded bowl was found at Ashur, Iraq,[75] and at least two, possibly four, pillar-moulded bowls have been found in Iran. One was discovered on a site on the coast of the Caspian Sea at Amlash, Guilan.[76] Excavations of a number of cairn burials at Tepe Yahya in the Soghun Valley in south-eastern Iran revealed a small pillar-moulded bowl.[77] In 1979 Customs on the Iran–Turkey border seized a large number of glass vessels which were to be smuggled out of the country. Nothing is known of their provenance; however, they may well have come from looted graves in Iran. This collection – now in the Bazargan collection in the National Museum of Iran – includes two monochrome bowls in pale green and pale blue-green glass.[78]

Several finds have been made on the south-eastern coast of India (fig. 3.1.7). For example, six to eight bowls, several in strong colours, were found in Arikamedu, Pondicherry[79] A pillar-moulded bowl was also discov-

ered in Dharanikota, Andhra Pradesh.[80] Excavations in Taxila, Punjab, Pakistan,[81] and in Begram, Afghanistan,[82] have also yielded bowls of this type (polychrome and monochrome). Most exotically, three fragments of polychrome bowls were found in a grave – where Liu Xing, the son of king Guang Wu, was buried in AD 67 – in Ganquan, Hanjiang County, Jiangsu Province, China.[83]

Notes

1 There is also an extremely rare sub-type with an attached conical foot; however, less than a dozen of these are extant. See: Berger 1960, Taf 2.22; Grose 1989, 247–49; Lazar 2000, 63, fig. 1.
2 Price & Cottam 1998a, 44.
3 Pellatt 1849, 104–6.
4 Roach-Smith 1859, 121–22.
5 Harden et al. 1988, 20.
6 Cummings 1980, 26–29; See also Gudenrath 1991, 222.
7 Lierke 1993; Lierke 1996, 56–57; Weinberg & Stern 2009, 35.
8 Thorpe 1938, 11.
9 Schuler 1959. For a picture of the results of Frederic Schuler's experiments, see: Whitehouse 2003, 81.
10 Isings 1957, 17–21.
11 Price & Cottam 1998a, 44–46.
12 Cool & Price 1995, 15.
13 Price 1995a, 145.
14 Grose 1989, 245.
15 Kisa 1908, 512.
16 Pliny the Elder, *Historia Naturalis*, 33.2.5; 37.78.204.
17 See Trowbridge 1930 [1922], 83–94.
18 Kisa 1908, 532–69.
19 Loewenthal & Harden 1949; see also Bromehead 1952.
20 Loewenthal & Harden 1949, 33.
21 Cool & Price 1995, 16.
22 Grose 1977, 21–22, fig. 5.2.
23 To be published by the present author.
24 Czurda-Ruth 1979, 26–34.
25 Berger 1960, 10–11, 19.
26 Cool & Price 1995, 16.
27 Harden 1947, 294; Charlesworth 1985a, MF 3:F 2; Cool & Price 1995, 15–26.
28 Price 1995a, 147.
29 Harden 1947, 288.
30 Price 1995a, 147.
31 Not surprisingly pillar-moulded bowls form a very small portion of the glass assemblages in the militarised north. At Castleford, Yorkshire, for example, pillar-moulded bowls make up 3 % of the total glass assemblage (Cool & Price 1998, 141, 144).
32 Cool & Price 1995, 15–19; Price & Cottam 1998a, 44–46 with references.
33 Harden 1947, 294; Charlesworth 1985a, MF 3:F 2; Cool & Price 1995, 15–26.
34 Italy: Aquileia (Calvi 1969, tav. 9); Bologna (Meconcelli

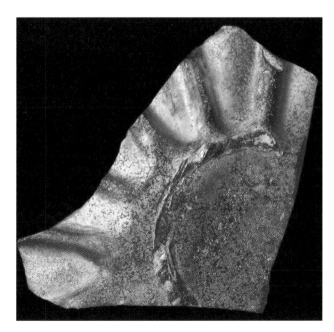

Figure 3.1.7

Pillar-moulded bowl fragment from Pattanam, Kerala, India.

Courtesy of Prof. P. J. Cherian; see Cherian 2013

Notarianni 1979, 42–43); Claterna (Maggio, Ozzano dell'E-milia) (Meconcelli Notarianni 1987); Cosa (Grose 1974, 37, fig. 1: 6–7); Luni (Roffia 1973, 465–66); Settefinestre (De Tommaso 1985, 177); Livia's villa at Prima Porta outside Rome (to be published by the present author); The Palatine, Rome (Sternini 2001, 24, 33, fig. 4); Herculaneum (Scatozza Höricht 1986, 25–31); Morgantina, Sicily (Grose 1982, fig. 4).

35 **The Netherlands**: Nijmegen (Isings 1980, fig. 1); Velsen (van Lith 1977, 16–22); Valkenburg (van Lith 1978–79, 11–37. **Luxembourg**: Hellingen (Thill 1975, Taf. 20:3). **Germany**: Weisenau (Behrens 1925, Abb. 1:10–11; Kessler 1927, Abb. 4); Cologne (Kisa 1908, Abb. 43); Mainz (Behrens 1925–26, 62); Xanten (Charlesworth 1984, 284–85, 287–88); Asberg (van Lith 1984, 223–30); Nida-Heddernheim (Welker 1974, 18–24; Welker 1985, 13–14); Hofheim (Ritterling 1913, 371–72); Oberstimm (Garbsch 1978, 279). **France**: Normandy (Sennequier 1994, fig. 2). **Portugal**: Conimbriga (Alarcão & Alarcão 1965, est. 1). **Spain**: Pasaje Cobos (Price 1987c, fig. 2:6). This, and the following lists, represent but a few of the many sites on which finds have been made.

36 **Slovenia**: Poetovia (Ptuj) (Subic 1974, fig. 7); Polhov gradec (Petru 1974, Tab. XI:8 & Tab. XI:9 (footed bowl). **Croatia**: Stenjevac (and other sites) (Damevski 1974, 69, Tab. 7:3). **Romania**: Tomis (Bucovală 1984, fig. 4). **Greece**: Acanthus, Ierissos, Chalkidike (Trakosopoulou 2002, 84); the Agora, Athens (Weinberg & Stern 2009, 35); Monasteraki Kephala, Knossos, Crete (Carington-Smith 1982, 270); the Unexplored Mansion, Knossos, Crete (Price 1992b, 420–21); Tarrha, Crete (Buechner 1960, 110). **Cyprus** (Vessberg & Westholm 1956, 128; Åström 1964, 122–25, fig. 2:1). **Lebanon**: Beirut (Jennings 2000, 47–50, fig. 4; Jennings 2002, 128, fig. 3). **Israel**: Ashdod (Barag 1967, 36, fig. 16:10). **Jordan**: Araq el-Amir (Lapp 1983, 44, fig. 19:5).

37 **Tunisia**: Carthage (Foy 2003, 62–63, fig. 7). **Libya**: Forte della Vite, Tripolitana (Price 1985c, 69); Sidi Khrebish, Benghazi (Price 1985d, 291). **Egypt**: Quseir al-Qadim on the Red Sea coast (Meyer 1992, 17–19).

38 Appendix A, F:3.
39 Appendix A, I:4.
40 Appendix A, K:2.
41 Appendix A, N:2.
42 Appendix A, O:1.
43 Appendix A, U:7.
44 Stevenson 1954–56, 215–17; Newton 1971, 13.
45 Newton 1971, 13.
46 Hunter 2007a, 22.
47 Feachem 1956–57, 35; identified by Dr Donald B. Harden.
48 Thorpe 1940, 134.
49 The find is described in the first report, when the excavators were not aware of an earlier Iron Age phase. Although the passage is rather lengthy, it is worth quoting *in extenso*:

The only other piece of glass was from site 19. It was a small fragment of a blue glass vessel with a ridge on the outer surface. Mr R. J. Charleston of the Victoria and Albert Museum has been kind enough to examine the piece, and comments: 'These alternatives seem possible, in descending order of probability: (a) A Roman survival,

from a 'pillar-moulded' bowl. This is by no means unlikely, bearing in mind the Roman pieces which have turned up in Anglo-Saxon finds, the fragment of cameo glass found in a (?) Viking context in Norway etc. A piece of blue glass, even fragmentary, might have been an attractive object in the Middle Ages. (b) Seventeenth century. This was a period of experimentation in glass, but I do not know of anything with which this fragment might be at all plausibly associated. (c) Islamic medieval importation. This glass does not strike me as Islamic in its general quality.' If the piece is a survival of the Roman period it may possibly have been reused in a brooch or similar ornament (Jarrett 1962, 219).

However, in later excavations a pre-Roman Iron Age or Roman Iron Age phase was discovered (Jarrett & Evans 1989, 134). I find it plausible that the fragment derived from one of the roundhouses of the Roman Iron Age.

50 Petersen 1916, 38, 41; Ekholm 1937a, 16–18, fig. 4.
51 Engelhardt 1871, 448; Ekholm 1937a, 16, fig. 3.
52 *Statens Historiska Muséer och Kungl. Myntkabinettet – Samlingarnas tillväxt* 1965, 34–35; Hagberg 1965, 44–45; Lund Hansen 1987, 91, 471.
53 *CRFB* D7, IX-12-5/5.1; Fremersdorf 1970b, 52.
54 *CRFB* D7, XI-06-1/6.8; Fremersdorf 1970c, 88.
55 *CRFB* D4 XXI-02-14/3.2.
56 Weigel 1890, 39-41; *CRFB* D1, V-08-1/1.3.
57 *CRFB* D6, VIII-18-8/1.4, Taf. 89:3 & 124:2; Schmidt & Bemman 2008, 120, 126.
58 Pernice 1912, 141–42, Abb. 10; Eggers 1940, 14; Eggers 1949–50, 61, 93; Eggers & Stary 2001, 100–1, Taf. 284: 12 & 13, Taf. 296.
59 Leciejewicz 1960, pl. 26.
60 Eggers 1951, 110, Karte 178.
61 Eggers & Stary 2001, 94, Taf. 269: 2 & 3.
62 Eggers 1951, 178, Karte 49.
63 *CRFB* P3, 169–75.
64 Sorokina 1967, 77, Abb. 3.16.
65 Caputo 1951, fig. 70; Wheeler 1956, 194.
66 Stern 1981, 40, fig. 2:21.
67 Stern 1993, 52–53, no. 29.
68 Comfort 1958, 207.
69 During-Caspers 1980, 13–17, pls XXV & XXVI.
70 Whitehouse 1998, 13–25, fig. 4 to fig.6; Whitehouse 2000, 93–98, fig. 5 to fig.11.
71 Jasim 2006, 221–22, figs. 31–34, figs 35.2–35.5.
72 Jasim 1999, 79–80, fig. 20.
73 Price & Worrell 2003, 153.
74 Jasim 1999, 80 with references.
75 Jasim 2006, 221 with references.
76 Kunisch 1967, 182, Abb. 4.
77 Lamberg-Karlovsky & Fitz 1987, 755, fig. 8.
78 Kordmahini 1994, 40–41.
79 Wheeler 1946, 102; Stern 1992, 117.
80 Stern 1991, 143, pl. XXXVI.
81 Stern 1992, 117.
82 Hackin 1939, 34, 62–63, pl. IX, fig. 22 & pl. XXVI, fig. 61; Hackin 1954, 95.
83 Tanichii 1983, 83–84, fig. 5

3.2 Cast and lathe-turned vessels

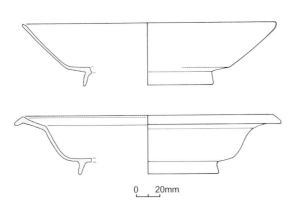

Figure 3.2.1

Cast and lathe-turned vessels [scale 1:3].

Top: bowl, Watercrook, Cumberland.
After Charlesworth 1979d, fig. 93:165

Bottom: bowl with wide rim, Colchester, Essex.
After Price & Cottam 1998a, fig. 13b

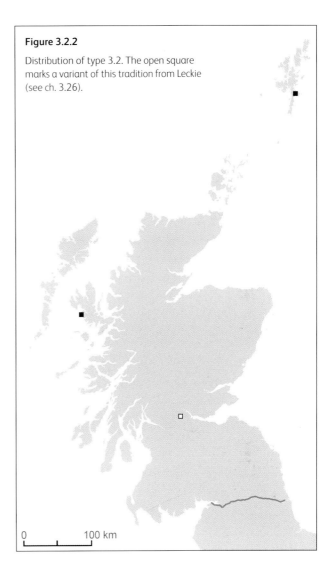

Figure 3.2.2

Distribution of type 3.2. The open square marks a variant of this tradition from Leckie (see ch. 3.26).

A general description of the type

A find from Clickhimin, Shetland, belongs to a 'family'[1] of high-quality cast and lathe-turned vessels characterised by angular carinated shapes manufactured in the first and second century AD. (See also a recent find from Fiskavaig, chapter 3.26.) This family includes two closely related classes: one in coloured glass, one in colourless glass. Until relatively recently, the commonly held view among glass historians was that the strongly coloured type went out of production around the mid-first century AD, whereas colourless vessels were manufactured – or at least in use – until the mid-second century AD.[2]

Price has recently put forward convincing evidence for a more complex picture concerning the period of production for strongly coloured glass, which suggests that polychrome mosaic glass was still in manufacture in the Flavian period, and probably into the second century AD. These finds differ only in detail from those of earlier date, and Price suggests that many of the Romano-British finds are in fact of later manufacture.[3]

The earliest finds of this 'family' date to the Augustan and Julio-Claudian periods, and were manufactured in polychrome opaque glass, monochrome opaque glass or monochrome glass in strong translucent colours. The shapes resemble contemporary styles in fine-ware pottery, i.e. samian/*terra sigillata*,[4] for example bowls of Dragendorff type 27. Some of the vessels even have colours – opaque red and orange – similar to that of pottery.[5] (A glass vessel from Leckie broch, Stirlingshire – originally believed to be samian – turned out to be a glass vessel of this type; chapter 3.26.) The samian in turn derived its forms from Roman bronze and silver vessels,[6] and it has been suggested by David Grose that the later class of colourless lathe-turned glass may have been directly influenced by the shapes and forms used for silver vessels.[7]

Price and Cottam differentiate between two related classes of cast and lathe-turned vessels: bowls and plates with simple vertical or sloping rims, convex or almost straight sides and base rings (class I), and bowls and plates on base rings with wide horizontal rims, sometimes with overhanging rims (class II).[8] Both classes are characterised by a dull surface on both the inside and outside of the vessel as a result of the lathe cutting and polishing.[9] As no part of the rim or body of the Clickhimin find survived, it is not possible to establish with certainty to which of these classes it belonged.

The bodies are straight, of conical or convex shape. The base rings are vertical or diagonal. Bowls and small plates often have small, high base rings, whereas large plates have wide, often low base rings. There is a considerable variety in size, with rim diameters ranging from 60 mm to 300 mm.[10] The majority of vessels are plain. However, wheel-cut decoration occurs, albeit rarely, on vessels of both classes. The finest examples of this, decorated with a 'bead and bar' pattern, are the well-known finds from the Cave of Letters in the Judean desert, which were carefully wrapped in palm leaves and hidden away during the Bar Kokhba revolt in AD 132–135.[11] Other variations have been found, such as a large bowl from the province of Palencia, Spain, which is covered by oval facets.[12]

Donald Harden was the first to recognise this class of vessels in his 1936 study of the glass from Karanis, Egypt, in which he put forward the idea that they were manufactured in Alexandria, Egypt.[13] At the time few parallels were known outside Egypt, but today numerous finds have been made, not least in Italy and southern France. And although there is little to prove or disprove Harden's claim, another view is that much of this class of vessels may well originate from Italy or southern France rather than from Egypt.[14] David Grose has proposed that peripatetic craftsmen may have produced the vessels at many different places.[15]

Dating the type

The earliest finds of colourless cast glass of this class from Britain date to the early Flavian period. The type was relatively common throughout the Flavian, Trajanic and Hadrianic periods. Grose has suggested a shorter time span for this type, and put forward the idea that the Cave of Letters finds deposited in AD 132–135[16] might be heirlooms.[17] However, Cool and Price suggest that they continued in use until the mid-second century[18] on the basis of finds made in Antonine contexts in Scotland at Inveresk, East Lothian,[19] and at Cramond, Midlothian.[20]

The function of the vessels

Nothing is known with certainty about the function of these vessels. However, it seems likely that they were used for serving and presenting food.

The finds from Roman contexts

Most finds of cast and lathe-turned vessels on Roman sites in northern Britain are in colourless glass. However, the relatively high number of finds in coloured glass suggests that production of coloured glass continued into the Flavian and later periods.[21] In both coloured and colourless glass, vessels with wide rims (class II) seem to dominate.[22] Cast and lathe-turned vessels have been found on numerous sites in the rest of Britain. For example, a unique find of a class I bowl with wheel-cut relief decoration of papyrus-sprays was made in the Roman villa of Park Street outside St Albans (Verulamium), Hertfordshire.[23]

Vessels belonging to the colourless class of most relevance here come from all over the area which once constituted the Roman Empire. Finds of colourless cast and lathe-turned vessels have been found in the northwestern, northern, western,[24] eastern[25] and North African[26] provinces, as well as Italy itself.[27]

The finds from non-Roman contexts in Scotland and north Northumberland

The Clickhimin find is a fragment of a small bowl or a plate with a high base ring, in colourless glass with slight yellow tinge (fig. 3.2.3). This was unearthed during the excavations of a broch and wheelhouse on a small islet in a loch on Shetland.[28] Although such vessels are relatively frequent on Roman sites in northern Britain, finds of this type are rare in native contexts north of Hadrian's Wall. There is the find from Clickhimin and a find not included in the catalogue from Fishavaig, Skye. (And also a vessel of a related type resembling samian from Leckie broch, Stirlingshire.) Similarly, finds of this type are exceedingly rare beyond the borders of the Roman Empire, with only a handful of finds from north-east Africa and Arabia. The Clickhimin find was probably manufactured somewhere in the central parts of the Empire between the Flavian and the Antonine period.

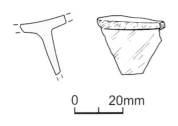

Figure 3.2.3

Cast vessel fragment from Clickhimin, Shetland [scale 2:3].

Shetland Museum: CLN 79173, redrawn from Hamilton 1968, 138, fig. 62:2

0   20mm

Clickhimin, Shetland.[29] A:1

CLN 79173*, Shetland Museum. Base fragment of a cast and lathe-turned vessel, bowl/plate? Part of a high base ring. Colourless with a yellow tinge. Dims 22 x 28; WT 4.0.

The finds from other areas beyond the borders of the Roman Empire

To my knowledge there are only two other finds of colourless cast and lathe-turned vessels beyond the borders of the Roman Empire. One comes from Aksum in Ethiopia and is a class II plate or bowl;[30] the other of the same class comes from Sedeinga in the kingdom of Meroë (northern Sudan).[31] However, vessels in polychrome and strong monochrome colours have been found on at least one site in Free Germany: outside Wroclaw, Lower Silesia, Poland (formerly Sacrau, Breslau, Niederschlesien).[32] There are also a number of finds of this category from Africa and Arabia: Candace, Ethiopia;[33] Kush, Sudan;[34] Heïs, Somalia,[35] and Timna, Yemen.[36]

Notes

1 In classifying the wide range of cast vessels, David Grose has suggested the word 'family', an overarching description of several closely related 'classes' manufactured in the same technique and general style. The classes in turn include different shapes and variations (Grose 1989, 241).
2 Cool & Price 1995, 38.
3 Price 2002.
4 Berger 1960, 24–30; Grose 1989, 241 ff; Grose 1991, 8–9.
5 Allen 1998b, 22.
6 Mutz 1972, 172–76.
7 Grose 1991.
8 Price & Cottam 1998a, 53–59.
9 Cool & Price 1995, 38.
10 Price 1987c, 72.
11 Barag 1963, fig. 40.
12 Price 1987c, fig. 4.1.
13 Harden 1936b, 50; Grose 1991, 12.
14 Cool & Price 1995, 41.
15 Grose 1991, 16.
16 Barag 1963, fig. 40.
17 Grose 1991, 15.
18 Cool & Price 1995, 38.
19 Thomas 1988.
20 Maxwell 1974, 199.
21 Price 2002.
22 Price & Cottam 1998a, 55–59 with references.
23 Harden 1945, 68–69, fig. II.
24 **The Netherlands:** Maastricht (class II) (Isings 1971, 22). **Germany:** Asberg (class II, resembling Dragendorff 27)

(van Lith 1984, 223); Trier (class II, facet-cut decoration) (Goethert-Polaschek 1977, 25, Abb. 5); Oberstimm (class II, coloured glass) (Garbsch 1978, 279, Taf. 107: E 14). **France:** Saintes (class II) (Hochuli-Gysel 1993, 81, Abb. 2). **Austria:** Magdalensberg (class II) (Czurda-Ruth 1979, 67–72, 76–79). **Portugal:** Conimbriga (class II, facet-cut decoration) (Alarcão & Alarcão 1965, 59–61, 168, est. III & IV). Numerous finds of both plain and facet-cut vessels have been made in **Spain.** Facet-cut vessels of class II have for example been made at: Barcelona, Cádiz, León, Palencia, Tarragona and Seville (Price 1987c, 72–80).
25 **Syria:** Dura Europos (Clairmont 1963).
26 **Egypt:** Karanis (Harden 1936b, 50); Quseir al-Qadim (Morrison 1989, 194, 196, fig. on p. 197).
27 In **Italy** finds of class II in both coloured and colourless glass have been made at Cosa (Grose 1973–76, 178–79); Luni (Roffia 1973, 467); Settefinestre (De Tommaso 1985, 176, tav. 47); Livia's villa at Prima Porta, outside Rome (to be published by the present author); San Lorenzo in Lucina, Rome (Ingemark 2012, 322); Ostia and Paestum (Grose 1991, 17).
28 Appendix A, A:1.
29 Hamilton 1968, 133.
30 Morrison 1989, 194, 196, fig. on p. 197.
31 Cool 1996, 205, fig. 3.1.
32 Fremersdorf 1939b.
33 Stern 1977.
34 Stern 1981, 38.
35 Stern 1987, 26–29.
36 Comfort 1958, 207.

3.3 Vessels with marvered blobs

Figure 3.3.1

Vessels with marvered blobs [scale 1:3].

Left: amphorisk, ?Lebanon.

After Harden et al. 1988, 112

Right: jug, Locarno, Switzerland.

After Biaggio Simona 1990, fig. 6

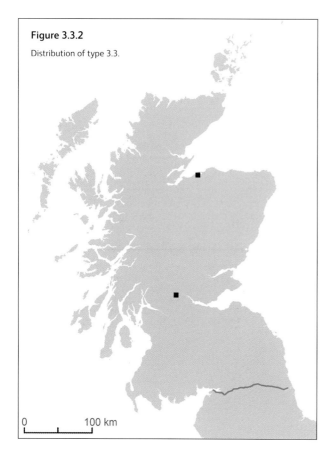

0   20mm

Figure 3.3.2

Distribution of type 3.3.

0   100 km

A general description of the type

The first detailed study of vessels with marvered blobs was written in 1938 by Fritz Fremersdorf, who named this style of decoration *Buntgefleckter Oberfläche*, a term used since in German scholarly work.[1] Strong colours such as deep blue, yellow-brown, dark green and purple are often used as ground colour. However, vessels are also known in natural green, blue-green and colourless glass. The applied blobs are in opaque colours such as white, red, yellow and blue.[2] This decoration was achieved by rolling the gather in small chips of glass and marvering them flush with the surface before inflating the vessel.[3]

In most scholarly work glass with more than one colour is termed 'polychrome'. However, I have chosen to distinguish between glass vessels with blobs in one colour – bichrome, and vessels with blobs in two or more colours – polychrome (pl. 4). In the north-western provinces most finds are bichrome, usually in coloured glass with opaque white. Vessels with applied blobs in two or more colours are rare in this area, and most finds of this variety are concentrated in southern Switzerland, in northern Italy, and the Adriatic region.

A wide range of different vessel types were decorated with marvered blobs, such as cups of Isings Form 12 (Hofheim cups),[4] jugs of Isings Forms 13,[5] 14,[6] 52[7] and 55,[8] amphorisks of Isings Form 15 (pl. 4),[9] beakers of Isings Form 37,[10] bowls of Isings Form 44,[11] bath flasks of Isings Form 61,[12] jars of Isings Form 67a–c,[13] *askoi*,[14] and *skyphoi*.

In 1938 Fremersdorf also put forward the hypothesis that vessels with a decoration of marvered blobs were manufactured in the area of northern Italy or in the northern Adriatic area.[15] Most scholars agree with Fremersdorf.[16] His hypothesis that a Syrian workshop from Sidon (modern Saida on the Lebanon coast) which later moved to Italy was one of the first to introduce this kind of decoration is, however, less convincing. This hypothesis was based on finds of *skyphoi*-handles with traces of this type of decoration, and bearing a maker's mark in Latin and Greek respectively, many of which have been found in Italy. Fremersdorf suggested that the Italian finds and the use of Latin indicates that the manufacture moved from the Syrian coast to Italy.[17] However, the use of Latin and the Italian finds could equally be explained by an export from Syria to Italy.

Dating the type

The earliest dated finds come from graves in the Canton of Ticino (Tessin) in southern Switzerland dating to between the early Tiberian and the Claudian period,[18] while finds from Vindonissa in Switzerland date between AD 20/30 and AD 70.[19] In Britain most finds are made on sites of Claudian and Neronian date, such as Kingsholm, Gloucestershire,[20] and Colchester, Essex.[21]

Finds have also been made on a small number of Flavian sites, for example in the annexe ditch of the Flavian fort at Carlisle, Cumbria.[22] The latest British find known to me is a globular or discoid jug (Isings Form 52) in dark brown with opaque white spots found in an early to mid-second-century context at Eastgate in Gloucester, Gloucestershire. Fragments of an amphorisk (Isings Form 15) have been unearthed in a second-century deposit at Exeter, Devon.[23] These late finds are survivals of an earlier manufacture.

The function of the vessels

Marvered blobs were used as a decoration for a wide range of objects, several of which are discussed elsewhere in this work.[24] These objects were vessels for drinking and serving wine, as well as for serving and presenting food.

The finds from Roman contexts

Very few finds of vessels with marvered blobs have been made in Roman contexts in northern Britain and all of these are bichrome. The northernmost find comes from Camelon, Stirlingshire.[25] In addition, finds have (for example) been made in Carlisle, Cumbria.[26] South of the militarised zone, glass vessels with marvered blobs have been found on a number of sites of Claudian, Neronian and early Flavian date; most of these vessels were also bichrome. However, polychrome vessels have been found at a few sites: Colchester, Essex,[27] Carmarthen, Carmarthenshire,[28] and Caersws *vicus*, Powys.[29]

Whereas polychrome vessels are relatively rare in other parts of the Empire (most finds being of the bichrome variant),[30] there is a concentration of finds in southern Switzerland, northern Italy and the Adriatic region.[31] Relatively few finds from the central parts of Italy have been published,[32] but a number of hitherto unpublished finds from Pompeii could suggest that we have to alter our view on how widely this type was distributed.

The finds from non-Roman contexts in Scotland and north Northumberland

Two fragments of glass with marvered decoration have been found in non-Roman/native contexts in Scotland, from the Culbin Sands, Morayshire,[33] and Leckie broch, Stirlingshire (figs 3.3.4–5).[34] The Culbin find is from a sand dune and could, in theory, be from any period. This find also has some odd features: a polished or worn surface and a rare ground colour – natural green with applied blobs in deep blue, opaque white and opaque yellow (pl. 5, left). Despite these oddities, the find is in all likelihood of Roman date, but whether it belongs to the same class as the Leckie find is unclear.

The find from Leckie is in deep blue glass with applied blobs in opaque yellow and opaque white (pl. 5, right). The finds from Culbin Sands and Leckie are convex-curved vessels, but could not be identified to type. However, judging by the shape it is likely that these fragments originate either from amphorisks or flagons. It is noteworthy that both fragments are of the rare polychrome variant mainly found in southern Switzerland, northern Italy and the Adriatic area.

Figure 3.3.3

Amphorisk with marvered blobs, ?Lebanon.
Height: 117 mm; diameter: 32 mm.

Collection of The Corning Museum of Glass, Corning,
New York: 59.1.88

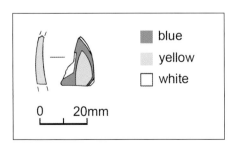

blue
yellow
white

0   20mm

Figure 3.3.4

Sherd with marvered blobs, Leckie [scale 2:3].
Hunterian Museum: A.1980.240

To my knowledge there is not a single find of a polychrome vessel from Roman sites in northern Britain, and a mere three finds from southern Britain. Although single finds of vessels decorated with marvered blobs have been made in Romano-British contexts of Flavian or later date, the majority are of Claudian-Neronian date. The polychrome vessels found on the Continent date from the Tiberian/Claudian to the Flavian period.

Leckie broch has yielded a relatively wide range of Roman imports. It is notable that this assemblage includes a substantial proportion of glass of early date, but whether this indicates that these finds reached native hands before the Agricolan invasion is difficult to ascertain as vessels of this type are found on early Flavian sites in Roman Britain.

Culbin Sands, Morayshire. F:2

BIB 78*, NMS. Base fragment of convex-bodied vessel. Green bubbly glass with marvered dots in deep blue, red, opaque white and opaque yellow. Inner surface ground or polished. Dims 26 x 21; WT 3.1.

Leckie, Stirlingshire. K:4

A 1980 240*, Hunterian Museum. Body fragment of a convex-bodied vessel in deep blue glass, with marvered dots in opaque yellow and opaque white. Dims 19 x 15; WT 3.

Finds from other areas beyond the borders of the Roman Empire

On the whole, finds from outside the borders of the Roman Empire are rare. However, several finds have been made in the Black Sea region. A Hofheim cup (Isings Form 12) is in the Odessa Museum, Ukraine. A handled beaker of Isings Form 37 was found in Kertsch, Crimea, Ukraine, and a ewer of unknown provenance is reported to have come from southern Russia.[35]

At ed-Dur, Umm al-Qaiwain, United Arab Emirates, a ewer was found. This was in light yellow-brown glass with spots in blue, yellow and white. A flask shaped in the form of a bunch of grapes and three bronze vessels (a bowl, a strainer and a ladle) were found in the same grave.[36]

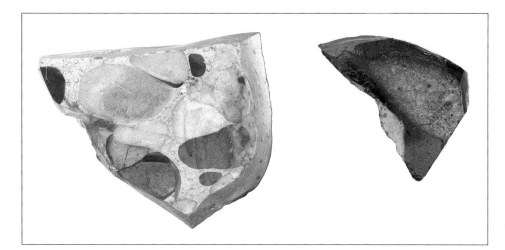

Figure 3.3.5

Sherds with marvered blobs.

Left: Culbin Sands

NMS: BIB 78

Right: Leckie broch

Hunterian Museum: A.1980.240

Notes

1 Fremersdorf 1938.
2 Fremersdorf 1938, 116; Biaggio Simona 1990.
3 Price & Cottam 1998a, 30.
4 Sorokina 1967, Abb. 3.
5 Biaggio Simona 1990, Fig. 4.
6 Biaggio Simona 1990, Fig. 3.
7 Biaggio Simona 1991, tav. 41.
8 Biaggio Simona 1991, tav. 40.
9 Fremersdorf 1938, Taf. 14; von Saldern 1980b, 44; Harden et al. 1988, 112; Biaggio Simona 1990, Fig. 7.
10 Sorokina 1967, Abb. 3.
11 Faider-Feytmans 1940, 218, pl. 3.
12 See Harden et al. 1968, 58.
13 See Fremersdorf 1938, Taf. 14; Harden et al. 1988, 111.
14 Anonymous *sine anno*, cover.
15 Fremersdorf 1938, 116–21.
16 Cool & Price 1995, 56.
17 For a discussion on Fremersdorf's ideas, see Berger 1960, 34.
18 Biaggio Simona 1990, 102.
19 Berger 1960, 34.
20 Price & Cool 1985, 43, 46, fig. 17.
21 Harden 1947, 295–96; Cool & Price 1995, 107–9.
22 Cool 1992, 65.
23 Charlesworth 1979b, 228.
24 See 'Jugs or flagons with globular or conical bodies', ch. 3.18; 'Small globular flasks with looped handles – *aryballoi*', ch. 3.22; 'Tubular-rimmed bowls', ch. 3.14; 'Jars with globular bodies and collared rims', ch. 3.16.
25 Unpublished, referred to by Price 1995a, 156.
26 Price 1990a, 166; Cool 1992, 65, 67, fig. 10.
27 Harden 1947, 295–96, pl. 87–88.
28 Unpublished, referred to by Cool & Price 1995, 157.
29 Cool & Price 1989, 33, 38, fig. 20 no. 20.
30 **The Netherlands:** Nijmegen (Isings 1968, 10); Velsen (van Lith 1977, 43–45; van Lith & Isings 1981, 100). **Belgium:** Houdeng-Goegnies (Faider-Feytmans 1940, 218, pl. 3). **Luxembourg:** Hellingen. **Germany:** Weisenau bei Mainz

(Behrens 1925, Abb. 1; Behrens 1925–26, Abb. 1.4–1.6); Mainz (van Lith 1977, 44, footnote 232). From Xanten comes a rare find of a *rhyton* in blue-green glass with blobs in blue and opaque white. Several indeterminate fragments in blue with opaque white, and a blue fragment with blobs in red and opaque white were also part of the assemblage (Charlesworth 1984, 285). Finds have also been made in Breslau, Kempten, and Mayen (Fremersdorf 1938, 116). **France:** Arles (Harden et al. 1988, 111).

31 **Switzerland:** A wide range of objects decorated with marvered blobs have been found in the Vanton of Ticino (Tessin): Muralto (Fremersdorf 1938, 116; Simonett 1941, Abb. 90 & 95; Biaggio Simona 1990, fig. 2, fig. 3 & fig. 7; Biaggio Simona 1991, tav. 30, 40–41, fig. 30 & fig. 35) and Locarno (Biaggio Simona 1990, fig. 4 & fig. 5; Biaggio Simona 1991, tav. 40–41, fig. 28). Finds have also been made at Baden/Aquae Helveticae, and Vindonissa (Berger 1960, 33–34, Taf. 4.60–4.71). **Slovenia:** Lubljana (Fremersdorf 1938, Taf. 14). From northern **Italy** a number of sites have yielded finds: Aquileia (Fremersdorf 1938, 116; Calvi 1969, tav. 15); Adria (Anonymous *sine anno*, cover); Bagnolo nel Bresciano (Fremersdorf 1938, 116); Bologna (Meconcelli Notarianni 1979, 54, fig. 39); Claterna (Meconcelli Notarianni 1987, fig. 13 no. 10), and Cosa (Grose 1974, 42, fig. 4 no. 22).

32 The fact that so few finds of this type are to be found in the literature may not give the full picture of the distribution. One find comes from Livia's villa outside of Rome (to be published by the author), there is only a single published find from Pompeii (Scatozza Höricht 1990, 44), and no published finds at all from Herculaneum. Dr Hilary Cool has kindly informed me of this and pointed to the fact that there are a number of finds from Pompeii – as yet unpublished – which could suggest a wider distribution for vessels with marvered blobs than hitherto known.

33 Appendix A, F:2.
34 Appendix A, K:4.
35 Fremersdorf 1938, 116; Sorokina 1967, 71, 77, Abb. 3.4–3.6.
36 Whitehouse 1998, 42–43, fig. 10 no. 101, pls 2c & 12.

3.4 Snake-thread glass

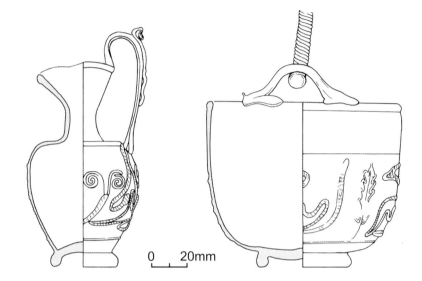

Figure 3.4.1

Snake-thread vessels [scale 1:2].

Left: oinochoë, Köln (Cologne), Germany.

After Harden et al. 1988, 128

Right: cylindrical cup/miniature bucket, Köln (Cologne), Germany.

After Harden et al. 1988, 127

0   20mm

A general description of the type

The use of threads applied to the surface of a vessel was a common way of decorating glass vessels during the Roman period. The snake-thread is a specific and distinct type of this form of decoration.[1] The name snake-thread glass derives from the German *Schlangen-fadengläser*, first conceived by the scholar Anton Kisa.[2] The threads look like snakes, hence the name. Roughly, one can talk of two groups of snake-thread glass:

(a) One with threads in contrasting colours such as opaque yellow, blue, red and white on colourless or greenish colourless glass. Gilded threads also occur, but are very rare. In this group patterns in general are abstract, although leaves and ivy leaves are recurring features.[3] The threads have diagonal slashing.

(b) The other group consists of colourless glass with self-coloured threads. Figurative motifs are not uncommon, a group called 'Flower and Bird' being the best known.[4] The threads on the latter group have waffle-iron or honeycomb patterns, rather than the more common diagonal slashing.

Snake-thread decoration was used on a wide variety of vessel types: flasks (fig. 3.4.3), cups and beakers (fig. 3.4.7; pl. 6),[5] many of which have undecorated variants, as well as variants with other kinds of decoration. In

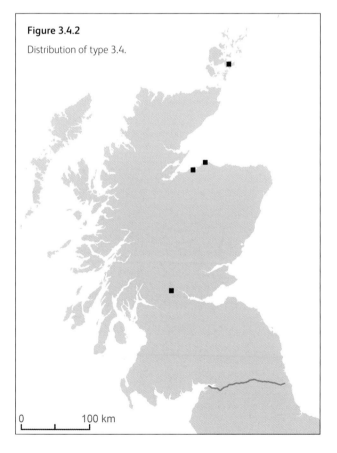

Figure 3.4.2

Distribution of type 3.4.

0   100 km

addition to these there are rare and rather peculiar types, such as dropper flasks in the shape of helmeted heads or sandals.[6] In some cases snake-thread decoration was combined with other types of decoration, for example indentations.[7]

Where the snake-thread process was invented and where it was produced have been matters for scholarly debate since the 1920s, and this debate is still ongoing. I have therefore chosen to discuss this type of glass in more detail. Kisa was the first to discuss snake-thread glass in depth. He wrote one of the most important pieces of scholarly research on glass – *Das Glas im Altertume* – by the turn of the twentieth century; it was post-humously published in 1908. At that time the majority of finds had been made in and around Köln (Cologne) in Germany, and very few outside the north-western provinces, which led him to draw the conclusion that snake-thread glass was an invention and product of this area. He suggested that there were two areas of produc-tion: one of high-quality, i.e. colourless, glass in Köln; and one of lower quality, i.e. greenish glass, in Namur, Belgium.[8]

However, a number of finds in the east discovered after this time made several scholars, most importantly, Fritz Fremersdorf and Donald Harden, suggest produc-tion in the east, the latter arguing for Alexandria, Egypt and Syria as likely areas of production. Harden pro-posed a simple model in 1934 of the different possibili-ties regarding the origin of the snake-thread glass:

(a) The ware was made only in the east, where it enjoyed little popularity, but nevertheless was exported widely westwards.

(b) The ware was made only in the west, and occasional examples were exported eastwards.

(c) The ware was first made in the west and was introduced almost at once to eastern workshops by migrant artisans.

(d) The ware was first made in the east and was introduced almost at once to western workshops by migrant artisans.[9]

The idea that snake-thread glass could have been inven-ted in the Rhineland and subsequently spread to the east was primarily advocated by Fremersdorf, who had changed his view on the matter in 1939.[10] This is con-trary to the traditional belief that movements of ideas as well as people within the glass industry always went from the east to the west.

Dan Barag proposed in an important paper from 1969 that the group called 'Flower and Bird', which has only been found in the east, was the origin of the snake-thread glass. This might have been a substitute for more expensive relief-cut vessels first produced in the late second century, possibly in Alexandria. In the early third century it spread into the east and also the west, where a new style evolved.[11] It has also been suggested that the eastern tradition of snake-thread glass was brought to Spain, where a group of vessels with self-coloured threads have been found.[12]

To summarise, although no direct proof for the production of snake-thread glass has been discovered on glass-working sites, the distribution patterns of certain variants of the type have been interpreted as indicators of a minimum of three different areas of production:

(a) The north-western provinces.

(b) Egypt and the Syrian coast.

(c) Southern Spain.

Dating the type

The main reason why the problem concerning the origin of snake-thread vessels has been so hard to solve stems from difficulties in dating the objects. Kisa dated the finds from Köln between Domitian (AD 81–96) and Septimius Severus (AD 193–211), assuming that they were contemporary with the coins found in the graves. This was already in question at the beginning of the twentieth century, when several scholars suggested a date of *c.* AD 200 for the earliest vessels of this type.[13]

Figure 3.4.3

Snake-thread flasks, Koblenz, Germany.
British Museum: 1868,0501.257

Fremersdorf put forward a hypothesis, also based on associated coins in graves, that the technique was invented in Köln around AD 160–170 by immigrant glass blowers, and that it continued till the early fourth century, culminating in the so-called 'Masterpiece' in AD 300. The date given by Fremersdorf for the latter is based on several late coins, including one of Galerius Maximianus (AD 292–305), and on the argument that the skills necessary in producing an object of this kind would require decades of practice.[14] The early dates based on numismatic evidence have been criticised by Barag, who points out that the coins were worn and can only provide us with a *terminus post quem* date.[15]

Dela von Boeselager has presented a plausible alternative to Fremersdorf's late dating of the 'Masterpiece' and other related types of snake-thread glass, on the basis of many different types of evidence. She shows that vessels with similar decoration and quality are of a considerably earlier date, for example a jug from Cortil-Noirmont, Brussels, Belgium, which dates to the early third century.[16] Her argument is that these vessels were antiques or heirlooms when they were put in graves.[17]

With few exceptions the British finds have not been found in closely dated contexts.[18] Most dated finds from the Continent show clearly that snake-thread glass was produced from the late second to the third century, and it can safely be assumed that the British finds are of roughly the same date. In some cases identification of a fragmented material has made clear what type of vessel these originated from – for example, cylindrical cups with fire-rounded rims and base rings – which are types with known dating.

The function of the vessels

The fragments of snake-thread glass from Mine Howe, Covesea, and Culbin Sands are minute, and it could not be established what kind of vessel they originated from. The most common types, however, are beakers and flasks. As for the Leckie broch find, which is discussed elsewhere, this was clearly a wine cup.[19]

The finds from Roman contexts

Until some 30 years ago very few finds of snake-thread glass had been made in Britain.[20] New excavations have brought many examples to light; however, those sites on which glass of this type has been discovered have seldom yielded more than one or two fragments.[21] Snake-thread glass has been found on a number of sites in northern Britain, military as well as civilian.

The overwhelming majority are of the polychrome type, although on rare occasions vessels with self-coloured threads have come to light. Most of the fragments are undiagnostic, but most of the identified material came from stemmed beakers or stemmed flasks. There is also a rare find of a cylindrical cup with snake-thread decoration from Castle Street, Carlisle, Cumbria.[22] One of the largest collections of snake-thread glass in Roman Britain lies in the north: Piercebridge, County Durham. From this site there are no less than seven finds (one of which came from the eastern part of the Empire).[23]

If we turn to the Midlands and southern Britain, the lion's share of these finds are from settlements,[24] and it was only recently that an intact find from a funerary context was made; a footed amphorisk found in Gloucester.[25] Due to the high degree of fragmentation, most of the finds are undiagnostic. The forms of vessels which have been identified consist primarily of cylindrical cups, stemmed beakers and stemmed flasks.[26]

In other parts of the north-western provinces, numerous finds of snake-thread glass have been made, many of which come from funerary contexts. Many finds have been discovered on sites near or on the *Limes* in Germany, which may explain their frequency in Free Germany.[27] Snake-thread glass has also been found on a number of sites in the Netherlands, Belgium, Luxemburg and in France.[28] Finds of vessels in colourless glass with self-coloured threads predominantly come from Egypt and Syria-Palestine.[29] Outside this area snake-thread glass of this type is scarce, with rare finds in Switzerland, Hungary, Italy, Cyprus, Portugal and Spain.[30]

The finds from non-Roman contexts in Scotland and north Northumberland

Four fragments from a minimum of four vessels with snake-thread decoration have been found in native contexts north of Hadrian's Wall; in addition, there is one fragment of a stemmed vessel, a beaker or flask possibly decorated in the snake-thread technique from Waulkmill, Tarland in Aberdeenshire. Two of these finds, a cylindrical cup with a fire-rounded rim from Leckie broch, Stirlingshire[31] and the find from Tarland, are discussed elsewhere.[32]

One fragment of a vessel in clear, colourless glass with snake-thread decoration in opaque blue was found at Mine Howe (fig. 3.4.5).[33] The fragment is of minute size and slightly distorted as a result of being exposed to heat; hence nothing can be said of the vessel's original type or even general shape. The function of this site remained unclear at the time of writing, but the archaeological evidence suggests that different crafts – possibly including simple glass working – took place there.[34]

The remaining two finds were found in Covesea and Culbin Sands (figs 3.4.4–5; pl. 8). Both sites are situated in Morayshire, the distance between the two being a mere 30 km. The Sculptor's Cave, Covesea, is situated on the coast. The excavations of this site yielded a varied and atypical assemblage of Roman imports, including Roman glass and pottery. It was a ritual rather than a settlement site.[35] Culbin Sands is a relatively large area – 18 km² – of sand dunes along the coast. Most archaeological material from this area is the result of casual finds; thus, little can be said about the context. It has been argued that there was manufacture of glass beads in this area.[36]

Both fragments are minute, undiagnostic body sherds in clear colourless glass with applications in opaque blue, i.e. of the polychrome type probably manufactured in the north-western provinces. Although these fragments could not be identified to type or even shape, it is clear that they were produced in the second or third centuries AD. Sherds of snake-thread glass vessels are relatively frequently found on Romano-British sites, but despite extensive excavations few of these have yielded more than the odd sherd. This suggests that the material from native/non-Roman sites from beyond the borders of Rome represents an exclusive category of Roman imports.

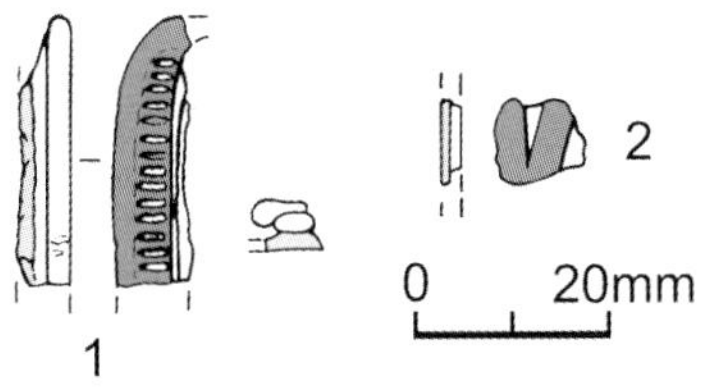

Figure 3.4.4

Snake-thread glass fragments [scale 2:3].

(1) Covesea
NMS: HM 217

(2) Culbin Sands
NMS: BIB 79

Covesea, Morayshire. F:1

HM 217*, NMS. Body fragment. Clear, colourless, trail in opaque blue. Slightly curved body. Applied trail, with horizontal (?) slashes. Dims 7 x 26; WT (with trail) 5.3.

Culbin Sands, Morayshire. F:2

BIB 79*, NMS. Body fragment. Clear, colourless glass, with trail in opaque blue. Applied trail in the shape of a 'V'. Dims 8 x 7; WT (with trail) 2.3, (without) 0.8.

Mine Howe, Tankerness, Orkney. B:2

MH00* find 1854. Body fragment. Clear, colourless glass, with a trail in opaque blue. Applied trail in the shape of a 'U'. Distorted by heat. Dims 9 x 7; WT (with trail) 3.0, (without trail) 2.0.

Figure 3.4.5

Snake-thread glass sherds.

Left upper: Mine Howe.

Left lower: Culbin Sands. NMS: BIB 79

Right: Covesea. NMS: HM 217

Finds from other areas beyond the borders of the Roman Empire

Finds of glass vessels decorated in snake-thread technique are by no means infrequent in Free Germany. While we cannot know for certain why this was the case, it is possible to point to two different factors which may explain this fact. First, many of the finds from within the Roman Empire are from sites on or in the vicinity of the *Limes*, and cities such as Köln have been pointed out as possible production sites. Second, there seems to have been a certain preference for glass vessels with different types of decoration.

Around 50 glass vessels decorated in snake-thread technique are known from Free Germany. As several of these were uncovered in cremation graves, the exact number of vessels could not be established on the basis

Figure 3.4.6

Himlingøje 1949, (grave 2), Zealand.

National Museum, Copenhagen

of the fragmented and melted remains. At least 20 – perhaps as many as 25 – vessels are known from the Nordic countries. Of these, no less than 18 come from Denmark. Fragments of a minimum of two vessels have been found in Sweden, and there are four or five likely further examples. Finally, from Finland there is an almost intact drinking horn. In addition to these, 17 come from an area around the mouth of the river Wisla, Poland. Most finds are concentrated in three areas: south-east Zealand with eight finds; Møllegårds-marken, northern Funen with seven or eight finds; and the Wisla area. These finds consist of three types of vessels: tall beakers of Eggers type 189, stemmed beakers of Isings Form 86/Eggers type 197 and drinking horns of Eggers type 246.

The very rich site of Himlingøje, Præstø Amt, Zealand was discovered by gravel diggers as early as 1829. Although it is clear that the finds came from one or several inhumation graves, not much is known about the context of these finds. One of the most notable finds is a stemmed snake-thread beaker of Isings Form 86/Eggers type 197. An undecorated cylindrical cup of Isings Form 85b, as well as a drinking horn in glass of Eggers type 247 were also found. In addition, the excavation yielded a number of bronze vessels and objects, including a Hemmoor vessel and a ladle and sieve. Also noteworthy are two silver beakers and a serpent-head finger-ring in gold. Another grave, excavated in 1949 and discussed elsewhere, contained a beaker of Eggers type 189 among an impressive number of other grave gifts (figs 3.4.6–7; pls 6 & 7).[37]

A snake-thread beaker of Eggers type 189 was found in a grave at Rislev (Kirkebakken), Præstø Amt. This site was investigated in 1896 and unfortunately little is known about the context. In addition to the glass beaker, a ladle and sieve in bronze, as well as some pottery sherds, were found.[38]

During a gravel dig in 1929 at Lærbrogård, Vråby, Præstø Amt, two graves were accidentally discovered; these were two inhumation burials. Two beakers of Eggers type 189 were uncovered in grave 1, both with applied threads in opaque white and blue. Two sets of bronze ladle and sieve, two finger-rings in gold, fragments of a silver fibula, some fragments of silver sheet, and at least 30 black and white gaming pieces in glass, were also found.[39]

In 1869 or 1870, what later turned out to be an exceptionally rich grave was partly uncovered at Valløby (Møllehøj), Præstø Amt. This was later examined, first by the local school teacher in 1871, and in 1872 by the archaeologist C. Engelhardt. Fragments of two glass beakers were discovered, one of which was a beaker of

Figure 3.4.7

Snake-thread beaker and other grave-goods: Himlingøje 1949, (grave 2), Zealand.

National Museum, Copenhagen: NM I C 24137 & 6-9/49

Eggers type 189 in clear, colourless glass, with applied threads in opaque white and blue. In addition to these, a large number of objects were unearthed. In a small chamber behind the deceased's head was a samian bowl, two silver goblets, four bronze vessels, a ladle and sieve in bronze, and the bronze mountings for a drinking horn. In the actual grave over 100 gaming pieces in glass, four bronze vessels, a pottery vessel, three finger-rings in gold, a serpent-head arm-ring in gold, and two fibulae, were found.[40]

In 1873 a farmer in Nordrup by, Sorø Amt, Zealand, found a grave while digging for gravel. The objects were brought to the National Museum in Copenhagen, which sent two archaeologists to the site. The grave contained the skeletal remains of an adult woman, and a number of finds were made: two snake-thread beakers of Eggers type 189 in clear, colourless glass with applied threads in opaque white and blue, a fragment of a bronze vessel, a ladle and sieve set in bronze, and a silver and gold fibula. On the chest of the deceased were several objects, probably wrapped in a bundle of cloth or birch bark: a silver fibula, an amber bead, 25 glass beads, an amulet in the shape of a miniature bucket made in bronze, a bone comb, and a small round bronze box containing what may have been an ointment.[41]

A large burial ground in Møllegårdsmarken, Gudme, Odense Amt, Funen, Denmark, was excavated in the years 1959 to 1966. This lies near the important Iron Age settlement Gudme. Glass was found in a number of graves; however, the custom of cremating the dead dominated and consequently most finds are melted and thus beyond recognition. The excavator Erling Albrechtsen reports that glass lumps with opaque white and blue threads were found in no less than seven or eight graves.[42]

A beaker of Eggers type 189 has also been discovered at Hjortsvang, Skanderborg Amt, Jutland. Almost nothing is known about the context of this find; only that it is reported to have come from a grave-mound. A bronze ladle, one or two fibulae, and some beads, may have originated from the same grave.[43]

At least two finds of melted fragments of snake-thread glass vessels were found during excavations in 1870 at the large Iron Age grave-field Kannikegård, Bodilsker Amt, Bornholm. In grave 265 – a cremation burial – fragments of what is believed to have been a beaker of Eggers 189 were discovered; while in grave 317, also a cremation burial, melted lumps in greyish colourless glass with threads in opaque white, red and green were found.[44]

Two certain finds of snake-thread glass vessels have

been made at two sites in Sweden. In addition, there is fragmentary and melted material from two cremation burials – with the remains of up to five vessels – which has been interpreted as finds of snake-thread glass.

During construction work at a building site for a small house at Tuna Farm, Badelunda (Västerås), Västmanland, in 1952, a hitherto unknown grave-field was discovered on a hillock. The oldest grave on the site (grave X), a rich grave of Iron Age date, is of primary interest here. Unfortunately much had been disturbed, but it was clear that a wooden coffin was placed in the centre of a stone setting. The grave gifts were exceptionally rich, and include a tall beaker of Eggers type 189 with applied opaque white and blue threads, the remains of a wooden cask, a serpent-head finger-ring, a serpent-head arm-ring, two gold hairpins, and several other finds in gold. Two silver spoons, three bronze vessels (including two of Hemmoor type), and several glass beads, were also found.[45]

At Gödåker, Tensta, Uppland, archaeological excavations in a small grave-field consisting of some 18 cairns and standing stones took place in 1915, in the early 1920s and the 1950s. In grave number 1 a bronze vessel placed in a basket of birch bark contained the remains of a cremation; within the bronze vessel were around 70 fragments from a minimum of three vessels.[46] Two of these finds have opaque coloured threads, but it remains unclear if these originally came from vessels with snake-thread decoration or not: one was in blue-green glass with applied opaque white and self-coloured threads; the other in colourless with a yellowish tinge with applied threads in opaque white.

The burial-mound Gullhögen, Husby Långhundra, Uppland, was excavated during the years 1988 to 1993. During these excavations three graves were found: one of pre-Roman Iron Age, one of Roman Iron Age, and one of Viking Age date. Grave B – that of Roman Iron Age date – appears to have been the burial of a high-status person, and on the basis of the finds the excavator Birgit Arrhenius suggested that this was a woman.[47] Two or possibly three fragmentary glass vessels were found: the melted remains of one or two snake-thread vessels, and a painted cylindrical cup.[48] Other finds include the melted remains of what might have been a silver fibula, beads in glass and amber, remains of a comb,[49] and a snake-head ring.[50]

At Östra Varv, Varv, Östergötland, a grave was discovered while levelling and building the foundations for a cottage. When this happened is not entirely clear; however, the archaeologist Hjalmar Stolpe wrote a brief report on the find in 1895. The grave was clearly an inhumation, as not just one, but two, mandibles were found. The finds consisted of a drinking horn in glass with applied threads in opaque white and blue in a simple pattern on the body and stylised ivy leaves below the rim, the bronze mountings for another drinking horn, the remains of two shields, two iron spear heads, two iron knives, a bone comb, and a fibula in bronze.[51]

On the whole very few Roman objects found their way to Finland. A rich grave of an extremely rare type was found at Soukainen, Laitila, in south-western Finland. Building activity during the making of a sports ground for the local school revealed a cairn with two stone cists in the centre. A drinking horn in colourless glass with applied threads in opaque white and blue, similar, though not identical, to that of Östra Varv, Östergötland, Sweden, was unearthed. The excavations also yielded a sword, two iron spear heads and the remains of a shield, a dice, a pair of tweezers, and a bronze vessel of Hemmoor type.[52]

Excavations of an inhumation burial in 1910 at Daspig, Kreis Merseburg, Sachsen-Anhalt, Germany,

yielded fragments of a colourless drinking horn of Eggers type 246 with applied white threads.[53] At Leuna, Kreis Merseburg, Sachsen-Anhalt, Germany, a number of inhumation burials were discovered. Among the rich finds was a fragmented snake-thread beaker of Eggers type 189, decorated with an ivy-leaf pattern.[54]

In 1927 and 1928 a grave-field in what was then Pollwitten, Kreis Mohrungen, Ostpreußen (now Polowite, Morag, Poland), was excavated by Dr Gaerte from Köningsberg. Unfortunately the original report as well as the finds were destroyed in the final stages of the Second World War. In six of the excavated graves no less than twelve beakers of Eggers type 189 were found.[55] Finds of Eggers type 189 have also been made in Krossen, Ostpreußen (now Krosno, Poland); Horodnika, Poland; Rostolty, Poland; Elblag, Poland; Willenberg, Westpreußen (now Wielbark, Szczytno, Poland);[56] Beszowa, Lubnice,[57] and other sites. In total some 30 finds of snake-thread beakers have been made – primarily in funerary contexts – in present-day Poland.[58]

Notes

1   Cool & Price 1995, 61.
2   Kisa 1908, 444.
3   See Harden et al. 1988, 123–29.
4   Barag 1969, 61.
5   See Doppelfeld 1966, Abb. e; Fremersdorf 1959, Taf. 9–33, 35–65.
6   See Harden et al. 1988, 134–37.
7   Fremersdorf 1959, Taf. 17 & 43; Price & Cool 1993, 151.
8   Kisa 1908, 470.
9   Harden 1934, 54.
10 Fremersdorf 1939a, 13.
11 Barag 1969, 55.
12 Raddatz 1973, 30–31.
13 Barag 1969, 56.
14 Fremersdorf 1959, 7–11.
15 Barag 1969, 58.
16 von Boeselager 1989, 29–30.
17 von Boeselager 1989, 34–35.
18 Cool & Price 1995, 62.
19 See ch. 3.8.
20 Price 1978a, 75.
21 Cool & Price 1995, 62.
22 Cool & Price 1991, 168.
23 Cool & Price 2008, 238, fig. 10.2.
24 Price & Cottam 1998a, 32.
25 I would like to thank Dr Hilary Cool for making me aware of this hitherto unpublished find.
26 Cool & Price 1995, 61–62.
27 **Germany:** Köln (see, for example: Behrens 1925, Abb. 7;

Fremersdorf 1955a, Taf. 24:2; Fremersdorf 1959; Doppelfeld 1966, 52–59; Fremersdorf & Polónyi-Fremersdorf 1984, 68–70, 86; Päffgen 1989, Abb. 4:6–7, Abb. 6). Finds have been unearthed at Zugmantel, Saalburg, Arnsburg, Rückingen (Fremersdorf 1939a, 13–14, Abb 2.3); Nida-Heddernheim (Welker 1974, 126–28; Welker 1985, 47–48); Laurentzberg (Follmann & Piepers 1963, 539–45, Abb. 28:7); Bonn (Follmann-Schulz 1990, 120, Abb. 3); Worms (von Pfeffer 1976), and Regensburg (von Schnurbein 1977, 73–74).
28 **The Netherlands:** Stein (Isings 1971, 14, fig. 2:24); Gulpen (Isings 1971, 21, fig. 11:58); Esch is a particularly prolific site, with finds of flasks, beakers and cups (van den Hurk 1977, 100–1, fig. 12, fig. 14, fig. 16 & fig. 17, pl. I). **Belgium:** Cortil-Noirmont, Tongeren, etc. (Mariën 1984). **France:** Normandy (Sennequier 1994, fig. 2 & fig. 3); Jonchery-sur-Suipppes, Marne (Lantier 1929, 14, fig. 25); Besançon (Koltes 1982, 52–53, pls 32 & 33).
29 Barag 1969.
30 **Switzerland:** Cham-Hagenhorn (Rütti 1983); **Hungary:** Intercisa/Dunaújváros (Barkóczi 1988, 107; Barag 1969, 63; Rütti 1983, Abb. 11); **Italy:** Rome (Barag 1969, fig. 2); **Cyprus:** Idalium (Harden et al. 1968, 63); **Portugal:** Conimbriga (Alarcão & Alarcão 1965, 168, est. III nos 91 & 94). **Spain:** see Raddatz 1973, 30–31.
31 See 'Cylindrical cups with fire-rounded rims and base rings', ch. 3.8.
32 See 'Beaker or flask with a beaded stem', ch. 3.5.
33 Appendix A, B:2.
34 To be published by the present author.
35 Appendix A, F:1.

36   Appendix A, F:2.
37   Norling-Christensen 1951; Schou Jørgensen et al. 1978; Lund Hansen 1987, 412–13.
38   Lund Hansen 1987, 416; Ekholm 1958b, Abb. 1b.
39   Broholm 1954; Lund Hansen 1987, 413.
40   Engelhardt 1873; Lund Hansen 1987, 413.
41   Engelhardt 1875, 21 ff; Petersen 1890–1903, pl. II fig. 2, pl. III fig. 9; Lund Hansen 1987, 411.
42   Albrechtsen 1971, 243; Albrechtsen 1968, 295; Lund Hansen 1987, 420–25.
43   Lund Hansen 1987, 429.
44   Vedel 1872, 139, 143; Ekholm 1937b, 339; Lund Hansen 1987, 417–18.
45   Stenberger 1956, Lund Hansen 1987, 451; Nylén & Schönbäck 1994, 32, fig. 27.

46   Almgren 1916; Lund Hansen 1987, 443; Andersson 2002, 241–42, fig. 1.
47   Arrhenius 2006, 10–11; see also the discussion in Andersson 2001, 226–27.
48   Henricson 2006, 81.
49   Arrhenius 2006, 10–11
50   Andersson 2001, 222.
51   Stolpe 1896; Lund Hansen 1987, 444.
52   Kivikoski 1954; Kivikoski 1973, 39–40, Abb. 191.
53   *CRFB* D6, VII-10-4/1.1.
54   *CRFB* D6, VII-10-12/1.14, Taf. 88: 1a & 1b.
55   Eggers 1966.
56   Eggers 1951, 178–79.
57   Garbacz 2001, 230.
58   Stawiarska 2005, with references.

3.5 Beaker or flask with a beaded stem

Figure 3.5.1

Left: flask with beaded stem, Koblenz, Germany.

After Harden et al. 1988, 132

[scale 1:2]

Right: beaker with a beaded stem, Köln (Cologne) Germany.

After Stern 2001, 165

Figure 3.5.2

Distribution of type 3.5.

0   100 km

A general description of the type

Only the stem of this find from Waulkmill, Tarland in Aberdeenshire, was preserved. Stems are found on a wide variety of cups, beakers and flasks from the first to the fourth centuries AD. These categories of vessel glass can roughly be divided into three main groups:

(a) Beakers of first-century date, mainly manufactured in strong colours such as emerald green, dark purple and deep blue, but also in blue-green glass. This group includes cups and beakers of Isings Forms 36a, 38a and 40.[1]

(b) Flasks or amphorisks of second- to third-century date in the shape of a bunch of grapes or a large shell – Isings Form 91b–c.[2] These, however, seem to be rare.

(c) Beakers and flasks of different shapes and types dating from the mid-second to the early fourth century, including Isings Forms 36c, 86 and 93.[3] These were in most cases manufactured in clear, colourless glass, but also in greenish colourless, blue-green or dark green glass with snake-thread or other trailed-on decoration. Some vessels in this group were furnished with a highly elaborate decoration such as applied doves in open-work flasks,[4] or applied scallop shells on beakers or flasks,[5] which sometimes were combined with snake-thread decoration.

The colour of the Tarland Waulkmill find, greenish colourless, suggests that it belongs to the last group. The

Figure 3.5.3

Snake-thread beaker: Himlingøje 1828/Baunehøj, Zealand.
National Museum, Copenhagen: NM MCMXXXII-XL

majority of vessels in this group, regardless of shape, were decorated with so-called snake-threads in either strong, contrasting colours or with self-coloured snake-threads.[6]

There is considerable variation in the shape of these vessels.[7] Beakers have tall, cylindrical bodies (Doppelfeld Form l),[8] cylindrical bodies with applied handles (cantharoi),[9] pear-shaped or ovoid bodies, sometimes with indents (Isings Form 86), bell-shaped bodies (Isings Form 36c),[10] or conical bodies (Doppelfeld Form m).[11] The flasks have ovoid bodies,[12] sometimes with indents (Isings Form 93),[13] globular bodies combined with two handles,[14] or a round, flat body (Doppelfeld Form c).[15] Vessels decorated with plain self-coloured trails, are also known.[16] Both stemmed vessels with snake-thread decoration of the specific types discussed above,[17] and other related forms of vessels with decorations such as doves and scallop shells, were in all likelihood manufactured in the north-western provinces.

Dating the type

On the whole, finds of stems in Roman Britain are rare. Nevertheless, as argued above, a majority of the vessels which are decorated in the snake-thread technique are more or less contemporary with finds of this kind made on the Continent,[18] from the second half of the second century to the third or early fourth century AD. At Colchester, Essex, a stem was found in a context post-dating AD 225.[19] At Rapsley, Ewhurst, Surrey, fragments of another type of stemmed vessel, a goblet with pincered scallop shell decoration, was found in a layer post-dating AD 225.[20]

The function of the vessels

As only the stem is preserved on the Tarland Waulkmill find, it is unclear whether it originated from a beaker or a flask. Little is known about these types, but it may be suggested that they were used for drinking and serving wine.

The finds from Roman contexts

Finds of actual stems and feet are relatively rare on Romano-British sites in northern Britain. The excavations at Cramond, Midlothian, yielded two fragments in colourless glass of a stemmed vessel.[21] In York, Church Street produced a foot in colourless glass;[22] from Blake Street there is a stem and two feet in colourless glass;[23] and from Fishergate there is also a find.[24] From Aldborough, Yorkshire, there is a fragment of the lower body, stem and foot of a beaker or flask.[25] In addition to these, fragments of snake-thread glass have been found on a number of sites in the area,[26] and it is likely that some of these come from stemmed vessels.

A similar picture can be presented for the rest of Roman Britain: a limited number of fragmented stems, and a greater number of body fragments of snake-thread vessels which may have come from stemmed beakers or flasks. Numerous finds of stemmed and footed vessels have been made in other parts of the north-western provinces, the majority of which have snake-threads in contrasting colours or self-coloured snake-threads. The majority of these come from graves; however, there are also settlement finds.[27]

The finds from non-Roman contexts in Scotland and north Northumberland

A gamekeeper digging a sandpit discovered a stone cist burial, and the remains of teeth and small parts of bone suggest that it was an inhumation burial. Unlike most finds of vessel glass from funerary contexts, which are more or less intact, the find from Waulkmill, Tarland, Aberdeenshire, consists of a single fragment – a beaded stem in greenish colourless glass (figs 3.5.4–5).

There are two possible ways of interpreting this find: either it was a *pars-pro-toto* gift, that is a fragment representing the intact object, or it was intended as a crude gaming piece. Notwithstanding the fact that this grave contained a set of gaming pieces in quartzite and glass, the interpretation as a *pars-pro-toto* gift seems more plausible, as it would differ quite significantly from all the other pieces in its crudeness and awkward shape.

A miniature cauldron was discovered in the same grave, and possibly there is some connection between the two finds, as both cauldrons and cups or beakers – assuming that it was a beaker rather than a flask – were symbols of power in the Iron Age, and both were linked to the serving of mead or other alcoholic beverages.[28] The cauldron was also a symbol of death.[29]

In the discussion of the identification above, it was argued that the stem from Waulkmill, Tarland, once constituted a vessel decorated in snake-thread technique. The colour and shape of this find implies a mid-second to early fourth-century AD date. This find is unique, as not a single other find of a stemmed vessel has been discovered in a native context north of Hadrian's Wall. It is possible however, that three related finds of snake-thread glass from Mine Howe, Tankerness, Orkney,[30] the Sculptor's Cave, Covesea, Morayshire,[31] and Culbin Sands, Morayshire,[32] may have been stemmed vessels. although these were in clear, colourless glass and not greenish colourless glass.[33] Stemmed vessels are also sparse finds on Roman sites in northern Britain, as in the rest of Britain. This scarcity may be more apparent than real, as finds of this type are difficult to identify.

Waulkmill, Tarland, Aberdeenshire. G:2

EQ 290*, NMS.[34] Fragment of beaded stem. Greenish colourless. H: 28; W: 24; diameter of the 'bead': 21.

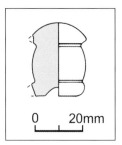

Figure 3.5.4

Beaded stem, Waulkmill, Tarland [scale 2:3]..

NMS: EQ 290

Figure 3.5.5

Beaded stem, Waulkmill, Tarland.

NMS: EQ 290

Finds from other areas beyond the borders of the Roman Empire

Stemmed beakers of Isings Form 86/Eggers Type 197 have been found in Free Germany.[35]

Notes

1 Isings 1957, 50–54, 56.
2 Isings 1957, 109–10; see Fremersdorf 1959, Taf. 50–51, 148–53.
3 Isings 1957, 50–52, 103, 110–11.
4 See Fremersdorf 1959, Taf. 80–81.
5 See Fremersdorf 1959, Taf. 82–83; Doppelfeld 1970, Abb. 1; Friedhoff 1989, Abb. 2 no. 26. However, it is important to note that applied scallop-shells are also found on other types of vessels; see Harden 1968a, 67.
6 For a discussion concerning this technique, see 'Snake-thread glass', ch. 3.4.
7 See Doppelfeld 1966, Abb. e.
8 See Fremersdorf 1959, Taf. 14–15; von Pfeffer 1976, Taf. 27; Harden et al. 1988, 138–39.
9 See van der Hurk 1977, fig. 16, pl. I:2.
10 See Harden et al. 1988, 123.
11 Fremersdorf 1959, Taf. 17–18.
12 Fremersdorf & Fremersdorf-Polónyi 1984, 68; Harden et al. 1988, 132.
13 Fremersdorf 1959, Taf. 43.
14 van der Hurk 1977, fig. 17, pl. I:3.
15 See Fremersdorf & Fremersdorf-Polónyi 1984, 69–70; Harden et al. 1988, 124–26.
16 Price & Cottam 1998a, 104–5; see van der Hurk 1977, fig. 15.
17 For a more extensive discussion concerning the area/s of manufacture for snake-thread glass, see ch. 3.4.
18 For a more extensive discussion on the dating of snake-thread glass, see ch. 3.4.
19 Cool & Price 1995, 85.

20 Harden 1968a, 64; Harden 1968d, 308.
21 Maxwell 1974, 197–98. Fragments not illustrated.
22 Charlesworth 1976b, 17, fig. 13 no. 52.
23 Cool 1995a, 1575, fig. 742.
24 Hunter & Jackson 1993, 1336.
25 Charlesworth 1959a, 54, pl. III, 4. Colour not described.
26 For a discussion on these, see ch. 3.4.
27 **The Netherlands**: Esch (van der Hurk 1977, 100–2, fig. 10–fig. 17); Nijmegen (Fremersdorf & Fremersdorf-Polónyi 1984, 69); Stein (Isings 1971, 18–19). **Belgium**: Overhespen and Tongeren (Mariën 1984, fig. 10 to fig. 13). **Germany**: excavations in Köln (Cologne) have yielded a significant number of finds (Fremersdorf 1926, Abb. 1; Fremersdorf 1959, Taf. 11–12, 14–15, 17–18, 22–23, 30–41, 43–45, 47, 62–63, 67–69, 80–83; Fremersdorf 1961, Taf. 136–37; Doppelfeld 1965–66, Abb. e, Taf. 50–51, 91–92, 129; Harden et al. 1968, 65; Doppelfeld 1970, Abb. 1; Fremersdorf & Fremersdorf-Polónyi 1984, 68; Harden et al. 1988,

123; Friedhoff 1989, Abb. 2:26; Päffgen 1989, Abb. 3:17, 4:6; von Boeselager 1989); Koblenz (Harden et al. 1988, 132); Worms (von Pfeffer 1976, Taf. 27); Zugmantel (Fremersdorf 1939a, 13–14, Abb. 2), and Trier (Goethert-Polaschek 1977, 183–84, Taf. 15:170). **France**: Strasbourg (Fremersdorf & Fremersdorf-Polónyi 1984, 70); Normandy (Sennequier 1994, fig. 3), and Viotte, Besançon (Koltes 1982, 53).
28 See ch. 5.
29 Green 1998.
30 Appendix A, B:2
31 Appendix A, F:1.
32 Appendix A, F:2.
33 For a discussion concerning the types of vessels decorated in snake-thread glass, see ch. 3.4.
34 Whimster 1981, 411.
35 See ch. 3.4.

3.6 Arcaded beaker

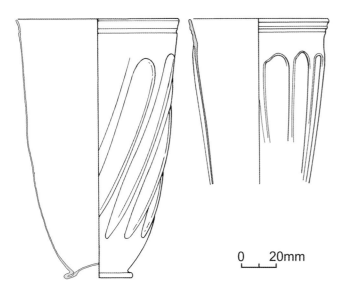

Figure 3.6.1

Arcaded beakers, Wroxeter, Shropshire [scale 1:2].
Left: with diagonal arcading. Right: with vertical arcading.

After Price & Cottam 1998a, fig. 27a–b

0 ___ 20mm

Figure 3.6.2

Distribution of type 3.6.

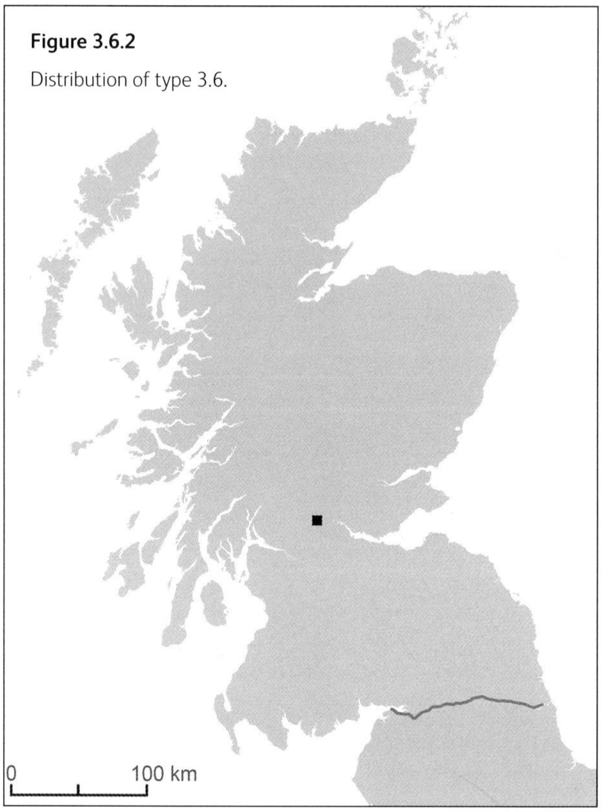

0 ___ 100 km

A general description of the type

Beakers of Isings Form 33 have vertical rims, cracked off and ground smooth. Below the rim are one or more horizontal wheel-cut grooves. The upper body has a straight side tapering in, i.e. is slightly conical in shape. The lower body curves in to a small tubular pushed-in base ring, with a domed base. The vessels were made in clear, colourless, greenish colourless or pale green glass. Rim diameters are *c.*75–100mm, heights 140mm or more.[1]

All beakers are decorated with a pattern in low relief, and there are two variations. One has separate elongated ovals, the other has the ovals set next to each other forming an arcaded pattern. At Vindonissa in Switzerland, both variations were found.[2] The arcaded beakers either have vertical or diagonal arcades; the excavations at Wroxeter, Shropshire, have yielded examples of both sub-types.[3] A very rare variation has an arcaded pattern combined with indents, where the relief pattern encircles the indents as on one found at Red House, Corbridge, Northumberland.[4]

There has been some discussion concerning the making of the decoration. Ludwig Berger suggests they were tooled with the help of fine tools.[5] However, Edith

Welker has put forward more convincing arguments for the low relief being achieved by applying threads and then marvering them, with the vessel then reheated in the glory-hole to give it its typical appearance.[6] Some vessels however, *e.g.* one from Kretz, Mayern, Germany,[7] appear to have been reheated but not marvered.

In 1957 Clasina Isings suggested that beakers of this type were manufactured in northern Italy or southern Switzerland on the basis that there is a clear concentration of finds in that area.[8] Despite a lack of other evidence, I am inclined to support Isings' views on since the picture has not changed in any major respects despite half a century of excavations.

Dating the type

The earliest British finds are pre-Flavian or early Flavian, and it appears they were contemporary with the Continental finds.[9] From Colchester, Essex, there is a find from a context dated to AD 49–75,[10] and at Usk, Gwent, excavations yielded a fragment from a Neronian context.[11] Most British finds date to the last third of the first century.[12]

The function of the vessels

In all likelihood these beakers were used for drinking wine.

The finds from Roman contexts

On the whole, finds of beakers of Isings Form 33 are infrequent in Britain,[13] and this is also the case in northern Britain. Fragments of a colourless beaker were found at the mid-Flavian fort at Elginhaugh, Midlothian.[14] Excavations at South Shields, Tyne & Wear have also yielded a find of an arcaded beaker,[15] and from the Agricolan supply base at Red House, Corbridge, Northumberland, there are fragments of a colourless vessel.[16] Finds have been made on a limited number of sites in the Midlands and southern Britain.[17] Comparatively few finds of beakers of Isings Form 33 have been made in the north-western and western provinces,[18] whereas a number of finds have been made in Switzerland and northern Italy.[19]

The finds from non-Roman contexts in Scotland and north Northumberland

Only one find of an arcaded beaker has been made in a native context north of Hadrian's Wall: two joining fragments from Leckie broch, Stirlingshire (fig. 3.6.3). This beaker is of Neronian or Flavian date, and belongs to a type that is relatively rare in Roman Britain. The excavations at Leckie broch yielded a rich assemblage of Roman imports,[20] including other high-quality glass of an early date. But whether this material actually represents a pre-Agricolan or later exchange is difficult to ascertain. The wide range of glass vessels unearthed is made up of a cup, a beaker, a minimum of one jug, and bottles. These vessels may have formed parts of a drinking set.

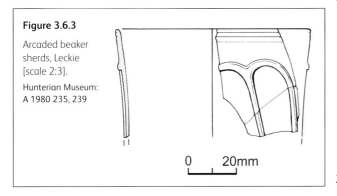

Figure 3.6.3

Arcaded beaker sherds, Leckie [scale 2:3].

Hunterian Museum: A 1980 235, 239

0   20mm

Leckie, Stirlingshire. K:4.

A 1980 235*, A 1980 239*, Hunterian Museum. Two joining fragments, rim and upper body. Rim knocked off and ground. Straight side, applied decoration. Clear, colourless glass. RD 80; PH 38; W 27; WT 1.6.

Finds from other areas beyond the borders of the Roman Empire

To my knowledge no other finds have been made beyond the borders of the Roman Empire.

Notes

1. Isings 1957, 47; Cool & Price 1995, 71; Price 1995a, 163; Price & Cottam 1998a, 83.
2. Berger 1960, 47, Taf. 7 nos 111–13 (arcaded), Taf. 7 nos 110, 114 (elongated ovals).
3. Price & Cottam 1998a, fig. 27a & b.
4. Charlesworth 1979a, 58, fig. 20 no. 2.
5. Berger 1960, 47.
6. Welker 1974, 25.
7. Oelmann 1938–39, Abb. 1.
8. Isings 1957, 47.
9. Berger 1960, 93.
10. Cool & Price 1995, 71.
11. Price 1995a, 163.
12. Price & Cottam 1998a, 83.
13. Price 1995a, 163; Cool & Price 1995, 71; Price & Cottam 1998a, 83–84 with references.
14. Price & Cottam 1998a, 84.
15. Charlesworth 1979c, 166, fig. 84.
16. Charlesworth 1979a, 58, fig. 20.
17. Price & Cottam 1998a, 84.
18. A single fragment was found during the excavations at Nijmegen, **the Netherlands** (Isings 1980, 295, fig. 8.6). **Germany**: Nida-Heddernheim (Welker 1974, 25–27) and Oberstimm (Garbsch 1978, 90, Taf. XII). The type is also known at Conimbriga, **Portugal** (Alarcão & Alarcão 1965, est. III no. 82), and other sites in **Spain** and southern **France** (Cool & Price 1995, 71). For example there are finds from Alicante, Spain (Sanchez de Prado 1984, 88, fig. 6.5).
19. **Switzerland**: One of the most prolific sites when it comes to beakers of Isings Form 33 is Vindonissa where no less than 71 were found (Berger 1960, 77–78). Excavations in Muralto and other sites in the Canton of Ticino have yielded several finds (Simonett 1941, 62, Abb. 41, Taf. 12 no. 2; Biaggio Simona 1991, fig. 10, fig. 47 & fig. 48). Finds of this type have also been made in Baden (Aquae Helveticae) (Berger 1960, 78). Excavations at a number of sites in northern **Italy** have yielded beakers of Isings Form 33: Palazzolo Vercellese, Turin (Isings 1957, 47–48); Claterna (Meconcelli Notarianni 1987, fig. 13 no. 9); Luni (Roffia 1973, 471, tav. 81 no. 13), and Aquileia (Calvi 1968, tav. 5 no. 5).
20. Appendix A, K:4.

3.7 Colourless wheel-cut cups or beakers

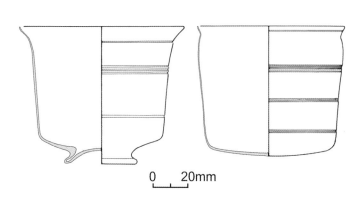

Figure 3.7.1

Colourless wheel-cut cups [scale 1:2].

Left: Stansted, Essex.

After Price & Cottam 1998a, fig. 30a

Right: Skeleton Green, Hertfordshire.

After Charlesworth 1981, fig. 105:3

Figure 3.7.2

Distribution of type 3.7.

0 ___ 100 km

A general description of the type

There is a wide range of related types of colourless wheel-cut cups and beakers of late first to late second-century date. On the basis of fragmented material it is difficult or even impossible to identify the precise types and shapes of these vessels, and therefore they are discussed as a category.

The rims are slightly out-turned, the edge cracked off and ground. The bodies are either cylindrical, carinated (often biconical), or have a slightly rounded to ovoid shape. Three types of bases are found: pushed-in tubular base ring (often thin-walled), separately blown foot, or a flat base.[1] The vessels were decorated with single horizontal wheel-cut grooves or bands of grooves below the rim on the upper and lower body.

In contrast to the Continent, where these types of vessels have attracted relatively little attention, there has been a greater scholarly interest in Britain. In a paper by Michael Baxter, Hilary Cool and Caroline Jackson, convincing arguments based on a chemical analysis of Romano-British material suggest that the colourless wheel-cut cups found in this area were likely to have been produced in the north-western provinces.[2]

Dating the type

The earliest examples of colourless wheel-cut cups and beakers date to the late first century; however, the main period for these types of vessels is the early to mid-second century AD.[3]

The function of the vessels

The shape and size of the vessels suggest that they were drinking vessels.

The finds from Roman contexts

Colourless wheel-cut cups and beakers form one of the most common forms of drinking vessel in use on Romano-British sites in the early and mid-second century AD.[4] In northern Britain they have been found on a number of sites; for example, no less than 32 vessels were unearthed at Castleford, Yorkshire.[5] In the Mid-

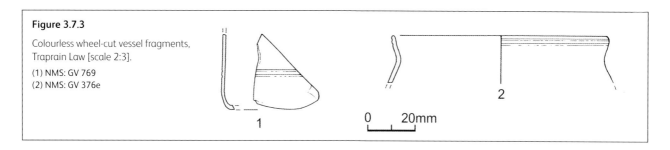

Figure 3.7.3

Colourless wheel-cut vessel fragments,
Traprain Law [scale 2:3].

(1) NMS: GV 769
(2) NMS: GV 376e

lands and southern Britain numerous finds have been made.[6] Finds of this category, and/or related types, have been found in the north-western and western provinces as well as in Italy.[7]

The finds from non-Roman contexts in north Northumberland and Scotland

Two sherds of colourless wheel-cut cups or beakers were found at Traprain Law, East Lothian (fig. 3.7.3). Exactly which types of vessels the Traprain finds derived from could not be established. One of the fragments, a rim, comes from a hemispherical cup with a constriction above the body, and has two wheel-cut grooves below the rim. This type of vessel either had a concave base or a separately blown foot, and is of mid- to late second-century date. Only a small part of the base was preserved of the other vessel, which either comes from a cylindrical cup with a tubular pushed-in base, or a cylindrical cup with a flat base. This find is of late first to mid- to late second-century date.

Traprain Law, East Lothian. N:2

GV 376e* (III 20 104), Area G, Level 2, NMS. Rim fragment. Colourless glass. Curved rim; cracked-off and ground edge. Two wheel-cut horizontal lines below rim edge. Convex-curved body. RD 90; PH 19; W 21; WT 2.1.

GV 769* (V 21 343), Area K, Level 4, NMS. Fragment of lower body and base. Colourless with a yellow-green tinge. Almost straight side, tapering slightly outwards. Two horizontal wheel-cut grooves on lower part of body. Occasional bubbles. PH 29; W 26; WT 1.5.

Finds from other areas beyond the borders of the Roman Empire

To my knowledge no other securely identified vessels of this type have been found beyond the boundaries of the Roman Empire. There is, however, a find from Vorbasse, Ribe Amt, Jutland, Denmark,[8] of a lower body and base of a beaker with a separately blown foot which may either belong to this category of wheel-cut vessels, or to a facet-cut beaker.

Notes

1   For a discussion, see Cool & Price 1995, 79–82; See also Price & Cottam 1998a, 88–89, 91–92, 94–95.
2   Baxter et al. 2005, 60.
3   Cool & Price 1995, 79–80.
4   Cool & Price 1995, 79.
5   Cool & Price 1998, 146–47, fig. 56 & fig. 57.
6   Cool & Price 1995, 79–82; Price & Cottam 1998a, 88–89, 91–92, 94–95 with references.
7   Finds have for example been made in: **Belgium**: Maastricht-Belfort, Limburg (carinated beaker) (Isings 1971, 18, fig. 12:6). **Germany**: Trier (carinated beaker with separately blown foot) (Goethert-Polaschek 1977, 87, 325, Taf. 25:297a.); Köln (Cologne) (cylindrical cup with flat base) (Fremersdorf & Fremersdorf-Polónyi 1984, fig. 30). **France**: Normandy (carinated beaker with separately blown foot, and other types) (Sennequier 1994, fig. 2); Fréjus (cylindrical cup with flat base, carinated beaker with flat base, and carinated beaker with pushed-in tubular base-ring) (Béraud & Gébara 1990, fig. 5 nos 7–10.); Saint-Paul-Trois-Châteaux (cylindrical cup with pushed-in tubular base-ring, carinated beaker with pushed-in tubular base-ring) (Bel 1990, fig. 1:16 & fig. 1:18). **Portugal**: Conimbriga (cylindrical cup, carinated beaker with separately blown foot) (Alarcão & Alarcão 1965, est. II:58, est. XI:270). **Italy**: Monte Gelato (carinated beaker) (Price 1997b, 268, fig. 184:4).
8   Lund Hansen 1987, 110, fig. 49.

3.8 Cylindrical cups with fire-rounded rims and base rings

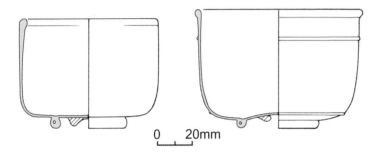

0   20mm

Figure 3.8.1

Cylindrical cups [scale 1:2].

Left: Airlie, Angus.

By Marion O'Neil

Right: Baldock type, from York.

After Price & Cottam fig. 38a

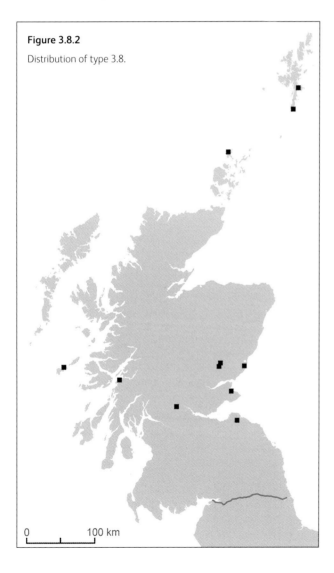

Figure 3.8.2

Distribution of type 3.8.

0   100 km

A general description of the type

Isings 85b is a low blown cylindrical cup with a thick fire-rounded rim. The body has a straight or very slightly concave side. The base is slightly convex and in most cases it has a characteristic double base-ring which makes it easily identifiable. The outer base-ring is tubular and pushed-in, whereas the inner base-ring is an applied thick trail. In the centre of the underside of the base there is often a pontil-scar. The cups vary in size: the rim diameters normally range from *c.* 70 to 140 mm, the height from *c.* 60 to 100 mm.[1] Some finds, however, are considerably smaller.[2] These smaller cups were in most cases part of a set and could be put in one another.[3]

The vast majority of finds are in good quality clear, colourless or greenish colourless glass. However, occasional finds of cups in common blue-green glass have been made,[4] while at the Roman fort at Newstead, Roxburghshire, fragments of deep blue cups have been unearthed. These seem to have been very rare indeed.[5] There are five – or possibly six – varieties of the cylindrical cups with fire-rounded rims:

(a) The first and most common variety is plain and undecorated. In the scholarly literature these are often called Airlie cups after the Scottish find (figs 3.8.1 & 3.8.3).

(b) The second, relatively rare variety is painted.[6] The motifs are either from the arena, with depictions of *venationes* (animal hunts, possibly also animals hunting each other in nature), *munera gladiatoria* (gladiatorial fights; hence the name Gladiator cups), or more peaceful motifs such

Figure 3.8.3

Undecorated cylindrical cup, Airlie, Angus.

NMS: EQ 150

as birds.[7] Both the arena and hunting motifs predominantly depict animals, humans being less frequent (fig. 3.8.4; pls 9–11).[8] All painted cups also display decorative elements, such as dots, lines, and rosettes.

(c) A third, and very rare, variety has applied and flattened threads in contrasting colours, so-called snake-thread decoration. The decoration is either floral or consists of abstract patterns. There are three variations of this sub-type: cups with no applications besides the snake-thread decoration, bucket-shaped cups with two applied handles,[9] and paterae with an applied single handle.[10]

(d) A fourth, and also very unusual type has engraved decoration. The motifs on the vessels are of three kinds. One variety displays motifs from the arena.[11] Another has medallions with portrait-busts.[12] The third type has a decoration consisting of fish in outline, palm leaves (or ferns)[13] and sometimes also inscribed letters.[14]

(e) The fifth variety is the so-called Baldock type, named after a grave-find from Baldock, Hertfordshire, England.[15] This has a shape which differs somewhat from the other varieties, as the rim can either be slightly out-turned or have a vertical rim like other varieties of cylindrical cups. It is decorated with self-coloured threads which run horizontally: one on the upper part of the body, the other on the lower (fig. 3.8.1).[16]

(f) Two finds of cylindrical cups with fire-rounded rims – possibly of Isings Form 85b – may form yet another variety. A cup found in Ilchester, Somerset has abraded horizontal lines below the rim,[17] and a similar find comes from Chichester, Sussex.[18]

In Scandinavian research finds of the painted variety are often called 'Circus cups'. In my view this is a misnomer, and the denomination is best avoided for two reasons. First there is – to the author's knowledge – not a single find of a painted cup with motifs from the circus, i.e. the chariot-racing arena. Second circus-motifs occur on two other types of cups, namely mould-blown ovoid cups and mould-blown cylindrical cups.[19] A more appropriate name, often used in British scholarly works, is 'Gladiator cup'.[20]

Although cylindrical cups are frequent finds in the north-western provinces – not least in Britain – one area appears to stand out: an area along the *Limes*, the Rhineland. Finds have been made on numerous sites here, and of these Köln (Cologne) appears to be particularly prolific.[21] The concentration of finds and the remains of glass-working sites led the German scholar Fritz Fremersdorf to suggest that the major site of production for this specific type was in Köln.[22] Finds have, however, also been made in other areas of the north-western provinces which might suggest that these cups were manufactured on a number of different sites. I am inclined to agree with Fremersdorf, however, that the finds of rare varieties of cups with snake-thread decoration, and the many finds of painted cups in Köln and its surroundings, could imply that these variations were made locally.[23]

Considering the finds of glass-blowing sites in Britain, and the many finds of vessels of this type, a British production of, for example, undecorated cups cannot be excluded. Chemical analysis of undecorated colourless cups from a limited number of Romano-British sites has shown that these were of fairly homogenous composition, reflecting the fact that they were produced in a relatively limited region, the north-west provinces,[24] but do not give any clues as to where in this area.

Figure 3.8.4

Painted cylindrical cups
(a) Nordrup, Zealand.

National Museum, Copenhagen: NM C 4614)
Photo: Roberto Fortuna/Kira Ursem

(b) Nordrup, Zealand (top and right);
Himlingøje 1894, Zealand (left).

National Museum, Copenhagen: NM I C 7672-84)
Photo L. Larsen

Dating the type

In a report on the glass from the Commandant's House, Housesteads, Northumberland, very early dates – AD 128 to 139/42 – for the type were given by Dorothy Charlesworth.[25] This deposit was later shown to contain material from the Antonine period as well.[26] The earliest securely dated finds from Britain are from a rubbish pit in Felmongers, Harlow, Essex, dated to AD 160–170 by samian ware.[27] There is also a find dated to the late Antonine period from Lullingstone Roman villa, Kent.[28] In addition to these sites, the type has been found in deposits at Castleford, West Yorkshire, with an Antonine date.[29]

The latest British finds are from the Roman fort at Vindolanda (Chesterholm), Northumberland. During excavations on the site, cylindrical cups were found in an occupational layer dating from AD 235–250/260.[30] The excavation of a Roman cemetery in Brougham, Cumbria, yielded a number of cylindrical cups, and on the basis of this evidence Cool has argued this vessel type was going out of use in the middle of the third century AD, and they were then replaced by a new form of drinking vessel – the hemispherical cup with a fire-rounded rim.[31]

The function of the vessels

The function of most types of Roman glass vessels can only be ascertained through their general shape.[32] However, in the case of cylindrical cups we have a better understanding of their function, and it is clear these were meant for wine drinking. On one of the Varpelev cups (Zealand, Denmark), the letters *DVBP* are painted.[33] Anton Kisa interpreted this as *D(a) V(inum) B(onum) P(ie)*,[34] 'give the good wine, my good man' – in short 'cheers'. This is also supported by an engraved cup from Trier, Germany, bearing the inscription *BIBAMUS*:[35] 'let us drink'. A unique sarcophagus from Simpelveld, Limburg, the Netherlands depicts – among other things – a drinking set in glass and metal (fig. 6.4). Cool has suggested that the depicted cups are cylindrical cups of the type discussed here.[36]

The finds from Roman contexts

Finds, often in large numbers, have been made on numerous Romano-British sites. In sharp contrast to the finds from beyond the Roman borders – both Scotland and Scandinavia – the lion's share of cylindrical cups found in Roman Britain consists of undecorated vessels. The total number of decorated vessels from Roman Britain

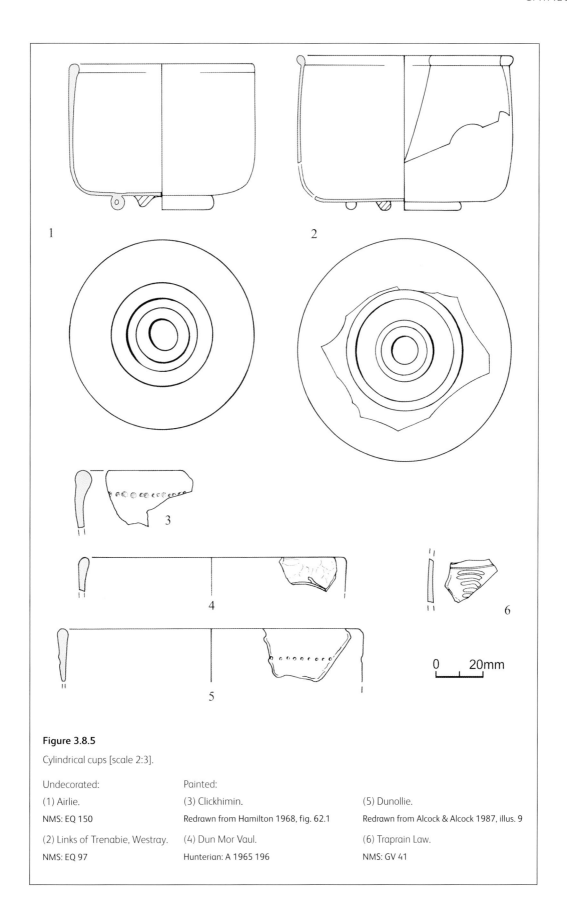

Figure 3.8.5

Cylindrical cups [scale 2:3].

Undecorated:

(1) Airlie.

NMS: EQ 150

(2) Links of Trenabie, Westray.

NMS: EQ 97

Painted:

(3) Clickhimin.

Redrawn from Hamilton 1968, fig. 62.1

(4) Dun Mor Vaul.

Hunterian: A 1965 196

(5) Dunollie.

Redrawn from Alcock & Alcock 1987, illus. 9

(6) Traprain Law.

NMS: GV 41

count to a few dozen, in comparison to several thousands of undecorated vessels.[37] On sites which have yielded finds of decorated vessels, this is reflected in the ratio between undecorated and painted vessels.[38]

Finds of decorated vessels of different types – painted, snake-thread, and engraved – appear to be rather more frequent in the north than in the south of Britain.[39] Although these occur on both military and civilian sites, it may be suggested that this is not mere coincidence. Perhaps the concentration of these – presumably expensive – finds reflects soldiers and officers with their relatively high wages, who could afford them? South of the northern militarised area, the proportions of decorated vessels appear to be considerably lower, whereas undecorated finds are found in large numbers.[40]

Cylindrical cups form one of the most frequent types of drinking vessels of the late second- to mid-third century AD in the north-western provinces, most prominently in the Rhineland, but also in the Netherlands, Belgium, and northern France.[41] There are, however, finds from other parts of the Empire, such as in a shipwreck found off France's Mediterranean coast.[42]

The finds from non-Roman contexts in Scotland and north Northumberland

A minimum of 13 – possibly up to 15 – cylindrical cups with fire-rounded rims have been found on eleven native sites north of Hadrian's Wall. This makes it one of the most common and widely distributed types of Roman glass vessel found in indigenous contexts. They include a remarkably high proportion of decorated vessels: around half of the total number of finds. As is the case in Roman contexts, the majority of vessels were in clear colourless or greenish colourless glass. One single find – a Baldock cup – from Traprain Law, East Lothian, was in blue-green glass.

Two sites on Shetland have yielded cylindrical cups. A fragment of a painted cup was discovered in a wheelhouse during the excavations at Clickhimin (fig. 3.8.5.3). In addition to this find, a cast glass bowl or plate was found.[43] At the recent excavations of Old Scatness, a large number of minute fragments of a painted cup were unearthed in a wheelhouse (fig. 3.8.6b).[44] From Westray, Orkney, there is a single find of an – originally intact – undecorated cup (fig. 3.8.5.2). Unfortunately very little is known about the circumstances of this find. A brief note published in 1831 mentions that it was discovered in a stone cist.[45] It comes from the Links of Trenabie, an area which also produced Viking burials.

There is a single find from the Hebrides; two fragments from a minimum of one painted cylindrical cup were unearthed at the broch and later farmstead of Dun Mor Vaul, Tiree (fig. 3.8.5.4, 3.8.6a; see also pl. 12). Apart from the cylindrical cup/s, other Roman imports include a prismatic bottle and Roman pottery.[46] At Dunollie, Oban, Argyll, one fragment of a painted cup was discovered (fig. 3.8.5.5). This site is generally considered to have been a stronghold in the kingdom of Dál Riata mentioned in the historical sources, and excavations demonstrated that the site belonged to the early Medieval period.[47] The excavator suggested that this find constituted an heirloom[48] and, unless this find represents a hitherto unrecognised Roman Iron Age phase, this seems plausible.

From Angus, no less than three sites have produced cylindrical cups. A workman digging a drain near the school in Airlie found a stone cist. Sadly not much is known about his find, except that it included an undecorated cup (fig. 3.8.3, 3.8.5.1).[49] Five km north-east of Airlie at Kingoldrum, there is another grave with an undecorated cylindrical cup. This was discovered in a stone cist, together with the remains of an inhumation burial. In the original report a number of other finds are mentioned: a bell and a bronze vessel. Whether these finds actually belong to a single burial has, however, been put in question.[50] Some 40 km east of these is yet another Angus findspot, although its precise type could not be determined. Excavations of a souterrain in Redcastle, Lunan Bay, Angus, produced not only this cup but also fragments of a tubular-rimmed bowl and a fragment of Roman pottery.[51]

From Leckie broch, Stirlingshire, there is a unique find of a cylindrical cup with snake-thread decoration (pl. 12). The excavations of this site yielded a wealth of Roman imports, including cups, bottles and jugs, flagons or jars in glass.[52] I argue below that these finds might once have constituted drinking sets employed on the site.[53] In the mid-nineteenth century, 20 stone cists were excavated in Hallowhill, St Andrews, the majority of which were long cists dating to the seventh century AD or later. Among these a short stone cist – an inhumation burial of a child, accompanied by a number of Roman artefacts – was discovered. This grave is reported to have included one or possibly two cylindrical cups, now lost. Another grave of the same kind was unearthed in the extensive excavations that took place on the site more than a century later. Although the excavator argued that these graves were post-Roman, the evidence seems to suggest an earlier Roman Iron Age phase on the site.[54]

Traprain Law, East Lothian, stands out in comparison with all other Roman Iron Age sites north of Hadrian's Wall. No less than four cups have been unearthed on this site: a painted cup (fig. 3.8.5.6, 3.8.6a; pl. 12), an undecorated cup, a cup with an applied self-coloured thread (Baldock type), and one cup of uncertain type.[55] As in the case of Leckie broch, Stirlingshire, I have argued that drinking sets were in use on the site.[56]

Overall there is a marked preference for decorated vessels, which stands in contrast to what is typically found in Roman contexts. A minimum of five painted cups, one cup of Baldock type and one cup decorated in snake-thread technique, have been discovered, plus a minimum of five undecorated cups and two not identified to type. The ratio between decorated and undecorated vessels is thus approximately 1:1. Though decorated cups appear to be somewhat more frequent on Roman sites in northern Britain, finds of decorated vessels in Roman Britain are on the whole rare.[57]

It is noteworthy that no less than four of the native sites that yielded cylindrical cups were burials. Burials were scarce in the Scottish Iron Age, and the number containing imported grave-goods is extremely limited.[58] All these were discovered in the nineteenth century and, unfortunately, we do not know very much about these finds. The remainder of the cylindrical cups come from settlements of different types. It is also interesting to note the strong northern bias. Ten of the eleven sites which have yielded this type are situated north of the Forth-Clyde line, and only one site – Traprain Law, East Lothian – lies south of this line.

Undecorated cups

Airlie, Angus.[59] I:1

EQ 150*, NMS. Intact vessel. Greenish colourless. Vertical rim, fire-rounded edge. Straight side. Tubular base ring, and applied inner ring. Many small bubbles, occasional larger. Strain cracks. Dull surface. RD 74; BD 42; PH 58; WT 3.0.

Hallowhill, Fife.[60] L:2

One, possibly two, cups. Lost.

In an account from 1867 by J. Stuart the find is described in the following way: 'a small circular cup of glass, less than two inches in height, of a pale green colour, and besides it fragments of broken glass of a white colour, which had probably formed another similar vessel'.[61]

Kingoldrum, Angus.[62] I:2

Cylindrical cup, intact when found. Lost.

The find is mentioned by J. Davidson in his paper on the Airlie find: 'a small glass vessel, which was described to me by Rev. Mr Haldane as having upright sides as a tumbler slightly rounded at the bottom, and a low circular foot-stand'.[63]

Links of Trenabie, Westray, Orkney.[64] B:3

EQ 97*, NMS. Intact when found. Fragments of rim and base preserved. Clear, colourless glass. Vertical rim, fire-rounded edge. Cylindrical cup. Bubbly. Dull surface. Very worn on base. RD 90; BD 42; WT 2.0.

Traprain Law, East Lothian. N:2

GV 1625, NMS. Rim fragment. Clear, colourless. Vertical rim, fire-rounded edge. Straight side. Many strain cracks. PH 12; W 11; WT 4.3.

Painted cups

Clickhimin, Shetland.[65] A:1

CLN 76144*, Shetland museum. Rim fragment. Clear, colourless. Straight side. Horizontal line of painted dots in yellow, red and blue. Polished or ground surface on the rim. Very worn, possibly after breakage. PH 22; W 36; WT 4–7.

Dun Mor Vaul, Tiree, Argyll.[66] C:2

A 1965 196*, Hunterian Museum. Rim fragment. Clear, colourless glass, with traces of red painting. RD 110; PH 14; W 30; WT (rim) 4.5.

Unreg., Hunterian Museum. Rim fragment, possibly same vessel as A 1965 196. Clear, colourless glass. PH 8; W 12; WT 3.0.

Dunollie, Oban, Argyll.[67] J:2

A 1990 109*, Hunterian Museum. Rim fragment. Clear, colourless glass. Vertical rim, fire-rounded edge. Straight side. Remains of painted white dots, in a horizontal line. Slightly melted on edge, some dots melted away. PH 20; W 34; WT 2–3.

Old Scatness, Shetland.[68] A:2

Fragments of a painted cylindrical cup*. With the excavator.

Traprain Law, East Lothian.[69] N:2

GV 41* (XI 14 108), Area: unclear, Level: 'lowest level' in 1914, NMS. Body fragment. Clear, colourless. Straight side. Bubbly. Painted horizontal blue band with two red lines; wavy lines in red and yellow. Dims 15 x 19; WT 1.8.

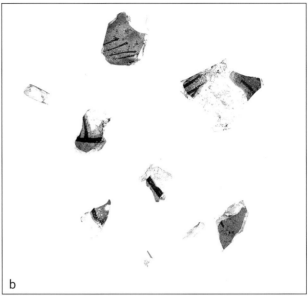

Figure 3.8.6a

Decorated cylindrical cup fragments.

Left: Dun Mor Vaul. Hunterian Museum: A 1965 196

Right: Leckie. Hunterian Museum: A 1980 237

Lower: Traprain Law. NMS: GV 41

Figure 3.8.6b

Old Scatness.

Courtesy of Steve Dockrill

Cups with snake-thread decoration

Leckie, Stirlingshire. K:4

A 1980 237*, Hunterian Museum. Base fragment. Clear colourless glass with an applied thread in white, opaque glass. Dims 21 x 5; WT 1.7.

Cup of Baldock type

Traprain Law, East Lothian. N:2

GV 1801, Area and Level: unknown, NMS. Rim fragment. Blue-green. Vertical rim, edge fire-rounded. An applied, horizontal, self-coloured thread below rim. RD difficult to establish, estimated at ca 70; PH 10; WT 3.1 (rim), 2.5 (body).

Fragments not possible to determine to type

Redcastle, Lunan Bay, Angus. I:3

C. 158, sf.284. Twenty-five or more fragments of base. Colourless with green tinge. Tubular, pushed-in base ring. Extremely fragmented; possibly the result of a short exposure to heat. Largest fragment Dims 7.3 x 2.8, many less than 1 x 1.

Traprain Law, East Lothian. N:2

GV 1231 (R1 1924 95), Area R, Level 1, NMS. Base fragment. Greenish colourless. Tubular base ring, and trailed-on inner ring. Grozed on edge. Bubbly. Surface worn on inside and outside. Several strain cracks. BD 45; PH 8.2. Reused as gaming piece (fig. 2.3b)?

Finds from other areas beyond the borders of the Roman Empire

At least 26 cylindrical cups have been found in Free Germany, most of which come from graves.[70] Eighteen, or almost 70%, of these were of the painted variety; the remaining eight were undecorated. No finds of other types have been made. There is a very strong concentration of finds on the Danish island Zealand.

Even in comparison to other sites from the Roman Iron Age on Zealand, Himlingøje, Præstø Amt, stands out with its exceptionally rich graves. The finds were made as early as 1829 when a gravel pit was dug and a grave was found. Besides an undecorated cylindrical cup, the excavation also yielded a high beaker with snake-thread decoration (Eggers type 246) and a drinking horn in glass. Several bronze utensils, such as a ladle and wine sieve set, a bronze vessel of Hemmoor type, and one of Vængegård type, two silver beakers, and a gold bracelet were unearthed.[71]

In 1894 the owner of the land was digging for gravel, and by accident came upon a painted cylindrical cup as he removed some stones. Realising that he had discovered a grave, he contacted the National Museum in Copenhagen, which conducted an excavation on the site. The grave discovered was an inhumation burial of a man. On his right hand was a gold ring, and on his right arm a gold bracelet. In the deceased's mouth was a piece of gold, presumably intended for Charon. The painted cup is decorated with a panther, a deer and a lion (pl. 10). A fragment of another painted cup was found as well. A bronze ladle and wine sieve and a bronze dish, and a number of other finds were also made. Of particular note was a silver brooch with the name *HARISO* incised in runes on the back.

In 1949 yet another grave with an undecorated cylindrical cup and a snake-thread beaker of Eggers type 189 was found (fig. 3.4.7). This was discovered during an excavation run by professional archaeologists; however, it started as a result of workers uncovering a grave while digging for gravel in 1948. The grave found in 1949 is one of the richest graves in Denmark from this period – an inhumation burial containing a woman. In her mouth was a piece of gold for Charon. She wore two gold bracelets, two golden finger rings, and a silver brooch with an incised name, *WIDUHUDAR*, in runes. Two other silver brooches were also found; as were a necklace with beads in glass, amber and silver, a silver hairpin, and a *denarius* of Titus (AD 80) (pl. 7).[72]

In 1861 a farmer found and partly excavated a grave in Varpelev, Præstø Amt, Zealand, Denmark. There were no visible remains above ground, and the grave consisted of a number of stones forming a cist. In the grave the skeleton of an adult male was found, together with a number of grave gifts. On his right hand was a spiral gold ring. Three painted cylindrical cups were unearthed; one of these was somewhat larger than the others. One of the cups was decorated with a bird and the letters *DVBP*, a second with a lion, a bear and possibly a bull. On the third, two lions flank a cross or rosette. Thirteen gaming pieces in glass, a bronze wine sieve inside a bronze ladle, a bronze vessel, the bronze fittings for a wooden bucket and a fragmented pottery vessel were also found. In addition to these finds, bones from pig and greylag goose were discovered.[73]

In 1939 a stone-circle in Borritshoved, Præstø Amt, Zealand, was excavated. In this the remains of a wooden coffin covered by stones was found. The only skeletal remains still preserved were some teeth. In one end of the coffin stood a set of three undecorated cylindrical cups which fit into another. The largest was placed in the middle and was flanked by the smaller cups on either side. Nearby lay a spiral gold ring, and in the middle of the coffin was a silver brooch. The excavation also yielded a bronze ladle and wine sieve, a bronze kettle of so-called Hemmoor type, and a fragmented pottery vessel. In addition to these finds some skeletal remains of an animal were unearthed.[74]

In 1881 a number of graves were discovered at Nordrup, Sorø Amt, Zealand; the National Museum in Copenhagen was contacted and subsequently excavated the site. In one of these graves (grave A) the skeletal remains of a man were found. On his right hand was a spiral gold ring. Two painted cylindrical cups, one of which was slightly larger than the other, were also unearthed. On one of the cups there are two leopards depicted, one of them chasing a deer. The other cup displays a scene from the arena – *venatio* (an animal hunt) with a bull and a bear being urged on by a man (fig. 3.8.4a; pl. 9). In the grave a bronze wine sieve inside a bronze ladle, a bronze vessel, the bronze fittings for a wooden box, several pottery vessels, intact as well as fragmented, 41 gaming pieces in glass and a silver brooch were also found.[75]

In 1944 workers digging for gravel at Sletteberggård, Stenlille, Holbæk Amt, Zealand, found what must have been a grave; unfortunately not much is known about the context, except that the grave was covered by stones. A bronze kettle of so-called Vestland type was found, and a gold ring. A few fragments of a painted cylindrical cup were also unearthed. On these it can be seen that one or two leopards and two rosettes were painted on the vessel.[76]

In 1870 a grave was discovered in Thorslunde Mark (Præstegårdsmarken), Københavns Amt, Zealand, when a gravel pit was dug. Not much is known about the context of this find, except for a brief account by the archaeologist Conrad Engelhardt. The skeletal remains showed that the buried person was sitting, possibly with outstretched legs. Three cylindrical cups were found, of which two or three are of the painted type. A wolf or a dog chasing a lion is depicted on one of the vessels, whereas two pairs of gladiators in combat are depicted on another. According to Engelhardt all three vessels are painted, though on the plates in the publication one of the vessels seems to be of the plain undecorated type.[77] A bronze vessel, a bronze ladle and wine sieve, a bone comb, pottery vessels, and some silver fittings still attached to leather were also found.[78]

In 2007 yet another very rich site was discovered a mere 1 km east of the aforementioned site, at Ellekilde, Thorslunde Amt, Ishøj. Some 31 graves of Roman Iron Age date were discovered, most of which were centred around a grave-mound. The centrally placed grave contained the remains of a man around 40 years old who was placed in a wooden chamber. He was accompanied by very rich grave gifts, and among the finds were a massive gold ring worn on the right hand, a brooch in silver with inlays in semi-precious stones and glass, a set of Roman gaming pieces in black and white glass, two painted glass cups, a ladle and strainer in bronze, bronze fittings from a drinking horn, and pottery of local manufacture. The cups display rather unusual motifs, including dolphins, to which the author knows no parallels (pl. 11).[79]

In 1977 excavations at Skovgårde, Baarse Amt, Zealand revealed an Iron Age burial-ground with inhumation burials. In two of the graves – nos 209 and 400 – sherds of cylindrical beakers were deposited as *pars pro toto* gifts. Grave 209 appears to be the burial of a wealthy woman. Besides a sherd of an undecorated cylindrical cup, several fibulae were found, one of which had an inscribed name. She wore a necklace with glass beads, and a number of other finds were made too, including a comb and a hairpin. Grave 400, which also appears to be a woman's grave, contained a number of finds besides a sherd of a cylindrical cup of painted type, including a cup of Isings Form 96, and a pear-shaped glass cup with cracked-off rim. A number of fibulae, a hairpin and a comb were discovered as well.[80]

A small number of finds of cylindrical cups have also been found in other parts of Denmark. A large burial ground in Møllegårdsmarken, Gudme, Odense Amt, Funen, was excavated in 1959–66. This lies near the important Iron Age settlement Gudme. Glass was found in a number of graves; however, the custom of cremating the dead dominated and consequently most finds are melted and beyond recognition. In one of the inhumation burials, grave number 1304, a fragment of a cylindrical cup of the painted type was found. On the fragment was the head of a dove and some leaves.

The excavator – Erling Albrechtsen – interpreted this and two other finds as *pars pro toto* grave gifts, i.e. the deposits of fragments were meant to represent the whole: a fragment of a samian bowl of Dragendorff type 37 with a drilled hole worn in a necklace, and a fragment of chain mail. A necklace of glass beads, including several gold foil beads, and a pottery cup were also found. No remains of the skeleton were preserved.[81]

In 1939 a grave was excavated at Enekrogen (Hundsemyre), Bornholm, Denmark. According to Ulla Lund Hansen this was a cremation grave, whereas both Gunnar Ekholm and Hans Norling-Christensen put forward the idea that the finds come from an inhumation burial, the latter on the basis that the sherds were not melted.[82] On the whole there is very little information on the find. A fragmented cylindrical cup with a leopard or panther is all that remains.[83]

In the years 1988 to 1993 the burial-mound Gullhögen, Husby Långhundra, Uppland, Sweden, was excavated. Three graves, one of pre-Roman Iron Age, one of

Roman Iron Age and one of Viking Age date, were covered by a large burial-mould. Grave B – that of Roman Iron Age date – appears to have been the burial of a high-status person, and on the basis of the finds the excavator Birgit Arrhenius suggested that this was a woman.[84] Two, or possibly three, fragmentary glass vessels were found: a painted cylindrical cup, and the melted remains of one or two snake-thread vessels.[85] Other finds include remains of a comb, possibly a silver fibula, beads in glass and amber,[86] and a snake-head ring.[87]

A number of finds have also been made in other parts of Free Germany.[88] A small fragment of colourless glass – possibly of undecorated type – was discovered during the excavations of the Germanic settlement Castrop-Rauxel, Kreis Recklinghausen, Nordrhein-Westfalen, Germany.[89] A base fragment of a cylindrical cup was found in the excavations of the settlement Westick bei Kamen, Kreis Unna, Nordrhein-Westfalen, Germany.[90] From Sieker, Kreisfreie Stadt Bielefeld, Nordrhein-Westfalen, is a single fragment which could have come from a cylindrical cup in colourless glass with a green tinge.[91]

A fragmented cylindrical cup of the rare Baldock type was found in a cremation burial at Westerwanna, Wanna, Landkreis Cuxhaven, Niedersachsen.[92] There is a fragmented painted cup (the head of a male with brown hair is preserved) found in a grave at Bordesholm, Kreis Rendsburg-Eckernförde, Schleswig-Holstein.[93] A number of fragments of a painted cup were inserted in a 'window urn' found in a cremation grave at Kasseedorf, Ostholstein, Schleswig-Holstein.[94] In addition, there is an uncertain find from Bornstein, Neudorf-Bornstein, Schleswig-Holstein, Germany: a base fragment reported as belonging to a cylindrical cup with a double base-ring.[95]

Exavations in the winter of 2001 to 2002 of an Iron Age settlement at Freyburg, Kreis Nebra, Sachsen-Anhalt, yielded a number of Roman imports, among which there is a fragmented painted cup decorated with a bird motif.[96] From Weißenfels, Kreis Weißenfels, Sachsen-Anhalt, there is a rim fragment of a painted cup. The context of this find is uncertain; possibly it comes from the burial ground at Weißenfels-Beudefeld.[97]

There are the two well-known painted cups from an inhumation burial discovered at Jesendorf, Kreis Sternberg, Mecklenburg-Vorpommern, hence the denomination 'Jesendorf cup' sometimes found in the scholarly literature. One displays a lion chasing a gazelle, the other has two birds.[98] An undecorated cup was found in an inhumation burial at Woldegk, Kreis Straßburg, Mecklenburg-Vorpommern.[99] A find of a painted cup has also been made at Polowite, Morag, Poland.[100]

In addition to the material from Free Germany, there are two possible finds of undecorated cups from Ireland.[101] These are from Castletown Tara, Meath and Dalkey Island, Dublin.[102] Despite claims of finds from other areas – for example the Black Sea area and Afghan-istan – there is no evidence for this type of vessel having been found, except in the north-western provinces and the areas beyond these. The finds from Begram, Afgha-nistan, come from tall beakers with a painted decor-ation.[103]

Notes

1 Price & Cottam 1998a, 99–101.
2 Cool & Price 1995, 83.
3 A set of four cups was found in Cologne; see Fremersdorf & Fremersdorf-Polónyi 1984, 9. In Borritshoved, Zealand, Denmark a similar set of three cups was discovered; see Norling-Christensen 1952, 84, fig. 3.
4 Price 1985b, 208–9; Price & Cottam 1998a, 99–103.
5 Cool & Price 1995, 82.
6 Chemical analysis of another type of painted vessel – high conical beakers of the type found at Lübsow (Lubieszewo, Poland) – revealed that they must have been rather costly. For instance the blue colour was made from lapis lazuli imported from Afghanistan (Grieff & Schuster 2008, e31).
7 Schönberger 1956, 41.
8 Norling-Christensen 1953a, 55–60.
9 See Fremersdorf 1955a, Taf. 24:2; Fremersdorf 1959, Taf. 60, 61, 65.
10 See Rütti 1983, Abb. 8.
11 Krüger 1909; Goethert-Polaschek 1977, 48–49, Taf. 37.
12 Fremersdorf 1970a, Abb. 5.
13 Possible Christian associations of the fish and palm leaves motif are discussed by Jennifer Price in a detailed study of all finds made in Britain. She does not reject the idea, but draws attention to the early date of the finds, and the fact that they have been found in contexts lacking any Christian associations (Price 1998, 309). Denise Allen also points to the fact that the finds were manufactured some 100 years before Constantine made Christianity the official religion. She likewise stresses that no intact vessels with anything written on them have been found, and consequently there are no clear connections with Christianity (Allen 1986d, 268). Thus the case remains unsolved.
14 Hope 1902, 31.
15 Westell 1931, 274, fig. 6.
16 Cool & Price 1987, 112; Price & Cottam 1998a, 101–3.
17 Price 1982b, 230.
18 Price & Cool 1989, 134.
19 Price & Cottam 1998a, 61–64, fig. 15 & fig.16; see also Price 1991, pl. XVc, fig. 10. The cylindrical mould-blown cups are known as 'Sports cups' or 'Chariot cups'.
20 Price 1987a, 192.
21 Köln (Cologne): (undecorated, painted, snake-thread and engraved cups) (Fremersdorf & Fremersdorf-Polónyi 1984, 8–10 (undecorated); Fremersdorf 1970a, Abb. 6 (painted); Fremersdorf 1955a, 118, Taf. 24:2; Fremersdorf 1959, Taf. 60, 61, 65; Päffgen 1989, Abb. 6:2 (snake-thread); Fremers-dorf 1970a, Abb. 5 (engraved).
22 Fremersdorf 1970a, 67–68.
23 Welker (1974, 114) and Charlesworth (1959a, 44) are also of this opinion.
24 Baxter et al. 1995, 137–40; Baxter et al. 2005, 60–61. In one case – the Roman-British settlement at Stonea, Cambridge-shire – the analysed cups appear to have come from a single batch or melting pot. It is argued by Jennifer Price, Ian Free-stone and Caroline Cartwright that this group of glass either were the products of a recently made batch from a market or glass house, or blown on-site by a peripatetic glass-blower (Price et al. 2005, 170).
25 Charlesworth 1971, 36–37.
26 Charlesworth 1975b, 24.
27 Price 1987a, 192–93.
28 Cool & Price 1987, 112.
29 Referred to by Price 1998, 307.
30 Price 1985b, 207.
31 Cool 2004, 367–68.
32 See van Lith & Randsborg 1985, 420.
33 *CIL* XIII 3, 10036 no. 45.
34 Kisa 1908, 824; supported by Krüger 1909, 361.
35 Goethert-Polaschek 1977, 48–49, Taf. 37.
36 Cool 2006, 136–37, fig. 15.1; for further discussion of this sarcophagus see ch. 6.3.
37 Cool & Price 1995, 82.
38 This is, for example, the case at Piercebridge, West Yorkshire. The excavations yielded a total of 21.6 EVEs of undecorated vessels, which can be compared with 0.4 EVEs of painted vessels, a ratio of 54:1 (Cool & Price 2008, 238).
39 Le Maho & Sennequier 1996; Cool & Price 2008, 238.
40 Price & Cottam 1998a, 99–101 with references.
41 **The Netherlands**: Esch (undecorated) (van der Hurk 1977, 98–99, fig. 8 & fig. 9; 120, fig. 45); Stein, Houterend (undecorated); Gulpen (undecorated) (Isings 1971, 17, fig. 3). **Belgium**: Lixhe, Luik, Belgium (snake-thread) (Mariën 1984, 65, fig. 5); Embresin (painted) (Fremersdorf 1970a, Abb. 4:7 a–b). **Germany**: Xanten (painted) (Charlesworth 1984, 290); Trier (undecorated, engraved) (Krüger 1909; Goethert-Polaschek 1977, 48–49, Taf. 36–37); Zugmantel (painted, engraved) Fremersdorf 1939a, Abb. 2:4, Abb. 2:6; Schön-berger 1956, 41; Saalburg (engraved with fish motif) (Fremersdorf 1970a, Abb. 1:1-3.); Butzbach (engraved with a fish motif) (Fremersdorf 1970a, Abb. 1:5); Nida-Heddern-heim (undecorated) (Welker 1974, 112–15; Welker 1985, 41–43); Mainz (engraved) (Fremersdorf 1970a, Abb. 2); Osterburken (engraved with fish motif) (Fremersdorf 1970a, Abb. 1:4); Regensburg (undecorated) (von Schnurbein 1977, 74), **France**: Meuilley (undecorated) (Sennequier 1977, 257, fig. 5); Besançon ('Baldock') (Koltes 1982, 50–51, pl. 31); Normandy (undecorated) (Sennequier 1994, 58, fig. 2).

42 Foy et al. 2005.
43 Appendix A, A:1.
44 Appendix A, A:2.
45 Appendix A, B:3.
46 Appendix A, C:2.
47 Appendix A, J:2.
48 See ch. 4.6.
49 Appendix A, I:1.
50 Appendix A, I:2.
51 Appendix A, I:3.
52 Appendix A, K:4.
53 See ch. 6.
54 Appendix A, L:2.
55 Appendix A, N:2.
56 See ch. 6.
57 Cool & Price 1995, 61, 82; Price 1998; Le Maho & Sennequier 1996; Cool & Price 2008, 238.
58 See ch. 4.2.
59 Davidson 1886, 139.
60 Stuart 1867, viii; Proudfoot 1976, 33–34.
61 Stuart 1867, viii.
62 Chalmers 1851–54, 191.
63 Davidson 1886, 139.
64 *Archaeologia Scotica* 3, 1831 – appendix II, 113.
65 Hamilton 1968, 143–44, no. 161, fig. 62.1.
66 MacKie 1974, 148–49.
67 Alcock & Alcock 1988, 131–32.
68 Dockrill et al. 2002, 386.
69 Curle 1915, 180; Curle 1932a, 294, fig. 5.1.
70 See Kisa 1908, 347–53; Eggers 1951, 179–80, Karte 56; Norling-Christensen 1953a; Norling-Christensen 1953b; Fremersdorf 1970a; Lund Hansen 1987, 74–77.
71 Sorterup 1844–45, 363, fig. 113; Engelhardt 1866–71, 262–63, fig. 1:2.
72 Norling-Christensen 1951. See also Lund Hansen 1987, 412–13 with references.
73 Herbst 1861.
74 Norling-Christensen 1952, fig. 3.
75 Petersen 1890–1903; Eggers 1951, 179–80; Lund Hansen 1987, 411.
76 Norling-Christensen 1953a, 50, fig. 8; Fremersdorf 1970a, 67; Lund Hansen 1987, 410.
77 I have not had the chance to study the finds; therefore the problem of identification remains unsolved.
78 Engelhardt 1871; Lund Hansen 1987, 410.
79 Iversen 2008.

80 Ethelberg 2000, 287–319; Lund Hansen 2000, 329–32, fig. 3a & b, fig. 4a & b.
81 Albrechtsen 1968, 293; Albrechtsen 1971, 243–44, tav. 140g (the glass), fig. 56 (the grave); Lund Hansen 1987, 422.
82 Lund Hansen 1987, 418; Ekholm 1937a, 340; Norling-Christensen 1953a, 57.
83 Ekholm 1937a, 340, fig. 9; Norling-Christensen 1953a, 57; Lund Hansen 1987, 418.
84 Arrhenius 2006, 10–11; see also the discussion in Andersson 2001, 226–27.
85 Henricson 2006, 81.
86 Arrhenius 2006, 10–11
87 Andersson 2001, 222.
88 In *CRFB*, apart from the finds mentioned below there are a small number of finds reported as resembling Eggers Type 209/Goethert-Polaschek Form 47a, i.e. Isings Form 85b. In the cases of Südensee, Kreis Schleswig-Flensburg (*CRFB* D5, XXIV-12-20/5.1; Lagler 1989, 109: 83, Taf. 42: 83), and Böhme, Landkreis Soltau-Fallingbostel, Niedersachsen (*CRFB* D4, XXI-08-1/1.1; Schirnig 1969, 72: no. 8), I find nothing in the original publications to support these identifications. Another find which, in my view, is incorrectly identified as a cylindrical cup of Isings Form 85b, was found in Oetinghausen, Kreis Herford, Nordrhein-Westfalen (*CRFB* D7, X-03-4/2.29).
89 *CRFB* D7, XI-06-1/6.14; Fremersdorf 1970c, 90–91.
90 *CRFB* D7, IX-12-5/5.175; Fremersdorf 1970b, 53.
91 *CRFB* D7, X-01-1/23.63.
92 *CRFB* D4, XXI-02-27/1.5; Zimmer-Linnfeld 1960, 36, Taf. 105b.
93 Saggau 1981, 83; Saggau 1985, 63; *CRFB* D5 XXIV-11-1/1.9; Taf. 46.1.
94 *CRFB* D5, XXIV-08-8/1,2, Taf. 17:2c.
95 *CRFB* D5, XXIV-11-11/1.3. Unfortunately the original publication does not give a detailed description of the find, nor does it depict it (Schäfer 1968, 46).
96 *CRFB* D6, VIII-12-2/1.9, Taf. 133: 1a & 1b.
97 *CRFB* D6, VIII-18-8/3.2, Taf. 88:4.
98 Schuldt 1948–49, 225; *CRFB* D3, II-09-7/1.3 & 1.4; Taf. 37.7, 37.8, 56.1 & 56.2.
99 Eggers 1951, 230; *CRFB* D3, III-09-3/1.3; Taf. 37.4.
100 Fremersdorf 1970a, 65; Lund Hansen 1987, 76.
101 I would like to thank Prof. Jennifer Price for this information. E. Bourke (1994) has identified them as other types.
102 Bourke 1994, 194, fig. 20 no. 5; 200, fig. 23 no. 31.
103 Pers. comm. Prof. Jennifer Price.

3.9 Hemispherical cups with cracked-off rims, conical beakers with cracked-off rims or fire-rounded rims

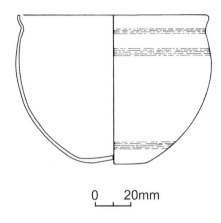
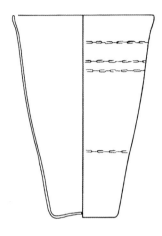

0   20mm

Figure 3.9.1

Left: hemispherical cup with cracked-off rim, Towcester, Northamptonshire.
After Price & Cottam 1998a, fig. 48b

Centre: conical beaker with cracked-off rim, Welford-on-Avon, Warwickshire.
After Cool & Price 1994, fig. 6

Right: conical beaker with fire-rounded rim, Burgh Castle, Norfolk.
After Harden 1983, fig. 37:85
[scale 1:2]

Figure 3.9.2

Distribution of type 3.9.

0   100 km

Hemispherical cups or small bowls of Isings Form 96 and conical beakers of Isings Form 106 are found with a range of different types of decoration. I have chosen to discuss two categories of the decorated vessels in separate chapters: cups with wheel-cut and/or abraded figured decoration (3.10) and cups/beakers with applied blobs (3.11) respectively.[1]

All three types of cups and beakers are commonly found in the north-western provinces. It has been suggested by Cool that much of the glass of fourth-century date found in Britain was made there.[2] Whether or not these types were produced in Britain remains unknown; quite possibly some represent local production whereas others were imported.

A general description of the types

Hemispherical cups with cracked-off rims

Isings Form 96 has cracked-off rim edges which are mostly left unworked, but in the case of vessels of high quality glass they are ground and polished smooth. The rims are either straight or curved. The body is spherical with a flattened or slightly concave base. The rim diameters are c. 70–90 mm, and the vessels are c. 65–80 mm high.[3] Hemispherical cups were produced in yellowish-green, greenish colourless or clear, colourless glass, colours typical of the fourth century.[4] With the exception of the plain Isings 96a[5] – a relatively rare sub-type – most vessels had some sort of decoration.[6]

The most common type of decoration is abraded horizontal bands. The abraded bands are normally just below the rim, on the upper part of the body and on the lower part of the body. A relatively rare group with a similar type of decoration are vessels with wheel-cut horizontal bands.[7] Another rare group is one with wheel-cut or abraded figured decoration with Pagan or with Christian motifs. Clasina Isings also includes vessels with *diatretum* cutting and mould-blown vessels in this form.[8]

Vessels with applied blobs in one or several colours have already been mentioned, and there are those with self-coloured trails in the form of festoons. Zigzag bands in contrasting colours are occasionally combined with applied blobs.[9] A type of decoration which might be added are vessels with applied lion-masks. A type closely related to the hemispherical cups of Isings form 96 is Isings form 107a, hemispherical cups with mould-blown honeycomb patterns.[10] On many vessels decoration such as blobs or festoons are combined with abraded horizontal bands.

Conical beakers with cracked-off rims

Isings Form 106[11] and the closely related Isings Form 109[12] are conical beakers, the difference between the two forms being that the latter have pushed-in base rings; Isings Form 109 is not considered further here. The rim edge was cracked-off and mostly left unworked. Only on high quality vessels was the edge ground. The rims are straight or curved. The body is conical, the base concave.[13] As with hemispherical cups, some were left plain but most are decorated. Conical beakers were normally manufactured in the colours typical of the fourth century: greenish colourless, pale green, yellow-green and clear colourless. However, finds in blue-green glass are occasionally made. The rim diameters are *c.* 70–90 mm and the vessels are *c.* 90–110 mm high.[14]

The variety most frequently found has abraded horizontal bands below the rim, on the upper part of the body and on the lower part of the body.[15] Wheel-cut horizontal bands are less frequent.[16] Beakers with engraved letters are known but rare,[17] as are those with wheel-cut or abraded figured[18] or facet-cut decoration.[19] A limited number of finds with diagonal optic-blown ribs,[20] mould-blown honeycomb pattern[21] and indents[22] have been made. Applied un-marvered trails in the form of festoons and applied blobs are sometimes found.[23]

Conical beakers with fire-rounded rims

Cups and beakers of several types and shapes, including conical beakers, had fire-rounded rims.[24] The body of the latter type have a conical body and a concave base or a tubular pushed-in base ring. They were produced in pale green or yellow-green glass, and are of roughly the same size as conical beakers with cracked-off rims.[25] Most vessels of Roman date are plain, whereas various types of conical beakers of later date often were decorated with applied self-coloured or coloured threads.[26] As the general shape continues for a long period of time, at least six centuries, there is a risk that fragmentary finds have been wrongly identified as beakers of a later date.

Dating the types

Hemispherical cups with cracked-off rims

Hemispherical cups – which were contemporary with conical beakers with cracked-off rims – first appear in the late third or early fourth century, and continue throughout the fourth century.[27] The earliest finds of this type found in Britain were discovered in Verulamium, in Hertfordshire, and date from AD 280–315.[28] A cup found in a grave in Colchester, Essex, dates to AD 360–380.[29] Much of the material of this type found in Colchester is from post-Roman contexts.

Conical beakers with cracked-off rims

Conical beakers with cracked-off rims first appear in the late third or early fourth century.[30] The earliest finds are from Portchester, Hampshire, found in a context in which the latest coins date to AD 308–317,[31] and from Colchester, Essex, dated from *c.* AD 300 and AD 225–275/325.[32] There is a continuation of use, and most likely also of production, throughout the fourth century. At the Romano-British cemetery at Lankhills, Winchester, Hampshire, conical beakers were found in graves dated to AD 370–410.[33]

Conical beakers with fire-rounded rims

Conical beakers with fire-rounded rims are of later date. The evidence from Towcester, Northamptonshire, suggests that production started in the mid-fourth century.[34] The finds from Burgh Castle, Norfolk, date to *c.* AD 400 to 425, and it is argued by Harden that most finds are of fifth-century date (fig. 3.9.3b).[35] This shape continues into the Frankish and Viking periods.[36]

Figure 3.9.3

(a) Hemispherical cup with cracked-off rim, Vedsted, Zealand. National Museum, Copenhagen: NM 8300

(b) Conical beaker with fire-rounded rim, Burgh Castle, Norfolk. British Museum: 2003,0303.4

The function of the vessels

Hemispherical cups

Nothing is known about the function of the hemispherical cups/bowls.[37] However, to my knowledge there is nothing to contradict the assumption that they functioned as drinking vessels in the north-western provinces. Marianne Stern has suggested that in the east – where the production starts considerably earlier – this type of vessel was used for storage. Stern has put forward the idea that the constriction below the rim facilitated the tying of a cloth cover, and points to the fact that some finds had glass lids.[38]

Conical beakers

It is probable that conical 'beakers' had several functions, both as drinking vessels and as lamps, as discussed in 1931 by Grace Crowfoot and Donald Harden. They observe that lamps made in glass for illuminating churches and other buildings are mentioned in ancient literature from the fourth century and later, and that glass lamps were depicted in contemporary mosaics from the eastern Mediterranean area.[39] Moreover, a number of finds from Karanis, Egypt, still had traces of oil left on the surface.[40] Notwithstanding, the function as lamps mainly seems to have been an eastern phenomenon. In the west conical beakers appear to have functioned as drinking vessels. Depictions from a funerary context in Ostia support this view.[41]

The finds from Roman contexts

Hemispherical cups with cracked-off rims

Hemispherical cups of several subtypes – plain, with abraded bands, applied trails, mould-blown honeycomb patterns – have been found at many different sites in northern Britain. In this area they constitute one of the most common types of glass vessel. For example, the excavations at Beadlam Roman villa, Yorkshire, yielded no less than seven hemispherical cups.[42] They are equally frequent in the Midlands and southern Britain.[43] Hemispherical cups with cracked-off rims are very common finds in the north-western provinces, both on settlements and in graves of the late Roman period.[44] Finds of this type have also been made in Italy,[45] Switzerland,[46] and former Yugoslavia.[47]

73

Conical beakers with cracked-off rims

As with hemispherical cups, conical beakers are common finds in northern Britain. For example, a minimum of 16 conical beakers with abraded bands, facet-cut decoration and vertical indents in pale green and yellowish-green glass were found at Beadlam Roman villa, in Yorkshire.[48] Conical beakers with cracked-off rims are equally common finds in other parts of Roman Britain, from both settlements and burials.[49] Beakers of this type are frequently found in other parts of the north-western provinces. These have been found in burials, as well as on settlements of the late Roman period.[50] Conical beakers are also known from sites in Switzerland,[51] Hungary[52] and Montenegro.[53]

Conical beakers with fire-rounded rims

To my knowledge finds of conical beakers with fire-rounded rims in northern Britain have been few. Possibly beakers of this type found in late Roman/post-Roman contexts have not been recognised, or they may simply be rare. Finds have been made at Beadlam Roman villa, Yorkshire,[54] and York.[55] Beakers of this type have been found on a number of late Roman/post-Roman sites in the Midlands and southern Britain. With few exceptions they are all undecorated and in green or yellowish-green glass.[56] Like the closely related conical beakers with cracked-off rims, they appear to be widely distributed in the areas which once constituted the Roman Empire.[57]

The finds from non-Roman contexts in north Northumberland and Scotland

Both hemispherical cups and conical beakers were common finds in Roman contexts, but have only been unearthed on a single native site: Traprain Law. This has produced a minimum of nine hemispherical cups (figs 3.9.4.1–2), a minimum of two, possibly three, conical beakers with cracked-off rims (figs 3.9.4.3–4) and a minimum of six conical beakers with fire-rounded rims (fig. 3.9.4.5). In addition, a hemispherical cup with wheel-cut figured decoration, and two vessels of unknown type – probably hemispherical cups or conical beakers – with applied coloured blobs, were discovered on the same site.[58] These vessels were in all likelihood employed for drinking, rather than as lamps.

The material from this site is highly fragmented, more than on most indigenous sites and markedly more than on the average Roman site. This was particularly

problematic in the case of the late Roman glass, which does not display the same degree of variation as the early material. As a consequence of the high degree of fragmentation, part of the assemblage could not be identified to type, and I have chosen to treat these finds separately.[59] It is therefore important to emphasise that the original assemblage of the types discussed below is likely to have been larger than the minimum estimates given.

Traprain Law, East Lothian. N:2

Hemispherical cups with cracked-off rims

GV 49* (XI 14 116), NMS. Rim fragment. Cracked-off rim. Two bands of abraded lines. Green. Bubbly. PH 23; W 20; WT 1.3–1.8.

GV 174:1 (XII 15 139), Area E, Level 1, NMS. Rim fragment. Cracked-off rim. Two thin bands of abraded lines. Green. Bubbly. PH 20; W 19; WT 2.1–2.2.

GV 176.5, Area Tb, Level 2, NMS. Lower body and base. Green. Bubbly. Convex-curved. Dims 34 x 19; WT 0.9–1.2. Hemispherical cup.

GV 378 (G2 III 20 107), Area G, Level 2, NMS. Rim fragment. Curved rim, edge cracked-off and ground. Two horizontal abraded bands below rim. Pale yellow-green. PH 22; W 24; WT 1.3.

GV 381a (III 20 111), Area H, Level 2, NMS. Fragment of lower body and base? Convex-curved side, flat base. Yellow-green. Very bubbly. Dims 20 x 18; WT 1.0. Same vessel as GV 381b?

GV 381b (III 20 112), Area H, Level 2, NMS. Fragment of rim and upper body. Curved rim, cracked-off and ground edge. Abraded band on upper body. Yellow-green. RD c.80; PH 27; W 21; WT 1.3–1.9.

GV 1280 (1924 177), Area R, Level 2, NMS. Body fragment. Convex-curved body. Abraded band on upper part. Yellowish-green. Purple streak (impurity). Dims 18 x 28; WT 1.3.

GV 1626*, Area R, Level 2, NMS. Rim fragment. Cracked-off rim left unground. Constriction below rim. Convex-curved body (hemispherical). Pale green. Bubbly. Strain cracks. RD 80; PH 25; W 37; WT 1.5.

GV 1627, Area Oa, Level 1, NMS. Rim fragment. Curved rim; cracked-off. Convex-curved side; body tapering in. Decorated with a band of abraded lines. Yellowish-green. Bubbly. PH 28; W 14; WT 1.2.

TLSP find 740. Body sherd of hemispherical cup. Convex-curved body. Fragment rectangular in shape, with traces of grozing on two sides, suggesting possible reuse as a gaming piece. Yellowish-green glass with occasional spherical bubbles. Dims 22 x 23; WT 1.8–2.1.

Conical beakers with cracked-off rims

GV 176:1 (XII 15 141), Area F, Level 3, NMS. Rim fragment. Vertical rim, cracked-off and ground edge. Side tapering slightly inwards. Many strain cracks. Greenish colourless. RD 100; PH 24; W 23; WT 2.3.

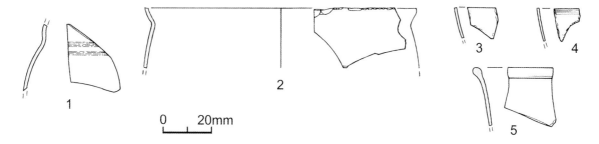

Figure 3.9.4

Hemispherical cups with cracked-off rim.
(1) NMS: GV 49; (2) NMS: GV 1626

Conical beakers with cracked-off rim.
(3) NMS: GV 1628; (4) NMS: GV 1568

Conical beaker with fire-rounded rim.
(5) NMS: GV 381c.

All from Traprain Law [scale 2:3].

GV 1568*, surface collection from summit, near trig point, NMS. Body fragment. Two horizontal abraded bands. Pale green. Bubbly. Dims 15 x 22; WT 1.0

GV 1628*, Area S, Level 2, NMS. Rim fragment. Rim cracked-off; abraded band below. Straight side. Greenish colourless. PH 13; W 10; WT 1.0.

Cups or beakers with fire-rounded rims

GV 109 (XI 14 258), NMS. Rim fragment of conical beaker. Curved rim, fire-rounded edge. RD 90; PH 19; W c. 23; WT 1.3.

GV 381c* (III 20 113), 1919 excavations, Level 2, NMS. Rim fragment of conical beaker. Curved rim, fire-rounded edge. Usage scratches on outside. PH 23; W 20; WT 1.2 (body); 3.4 (edge).

GV 381d (III 20 114), Area H, Level 2, NMS. Rim fragment. Curved rim, fire-rounded edge. Natural green. Bubbly. RD 70; PH 14; W 22; WT 1.4.

GV 1233 (1924 97), Area 1923, Level 1, NMS. (a) Two joining rim fragments. Out-turned rim, fire-rounded edge. Natural green. Occasional black spots. Bubbly. RD 65; PH 17; WT 1.2 (body); 2.7 (edge). (b) Rim fragment. Out-turned rim, fire-rounded edge. Natural green. Occasional black spots. Bubbly. RD 65; PH 14; W 28; WT 1.6 (body); 2.5 (edge).

GV 1282 (1924 179), Area R, Level 2, NMS. Rim fragment. Out-turned rim, fire-rounded edge. Natural green. Bubbly. Distorted by heat. PH 11; W 34; WT 2.8.

GV 1629, Area Q, Level 2, NMS. Rim fragment. Out-turned rim, fire-rounded edge. Blue-green. Bubbly, black specks. PH 10; RD 60; W 29; WT 2.2.

Finds from other areas beyond the borders of the Roman Empire

Hemispherical cups with cracked-off rims

Hemispherical cups with cracked-off rims have been found on a small number of sites in Scandinavia, including finds with applied blobs which are discussed elsewhere.[60]

At Rumpegården, Västergötland, Sweden, a hemispherical cup in pale green glass with a cracked-off rim and abraded bands was discovered in an inhumation burial in a stone cist, below a low cairn. This site was excavated in 1869, and in the same grave other finds, including a silver brooch, were unearthed.[61] A plain, undecorated hemispherical cup was found in a grave mound at Valstad, Nord Trøndelag, Norway. Not much is known about this find, which was excavated before 1879.[62]

During the excavations of a grave at Lille Værløse, Kro's Mark, Zealand, Denmark, in 1844–45, a plain hemispherical cup with a cracked-off rim was found. A wooden bucket with metal mountings and a gold ring were found in same grave.[63] At Skovgårde, Zealand, Denmark, excavations of an Iron Age cemetery yielded a plain hemispherical cup,[64] and from Vedsted, Zealand, there is a plain hemispherical cup.[65]

A most interesting discovery is a cup found during an excavation in 1952 at Højvang, Jutland, Denmark. The hemispherical cup in pale green glass has a cracked-off and ground rim. The vessel is decorated with three abraded horizontal bands – one below the rim, one on the upper part of the body and one on the lower part of the body – and two applied lion masks on opposite sides of the vessel. The finds of pottery in the same grave suggest a late third-century, or more likely a fourth-century date. The grave was found in a low burial mound, and although no remains of the skeleton were discovered, another grave a few metres away indicates that this was originally an inhumation grave.[66] A possible parallel to this find comes from Reims, France: a large, footed beaker with cracked-off rim and applied lion masks is dated to the fourth century.[67]

There are also finds from other parts of Free Germany. A hemispherical cup with abraded bands was found in an inhumation burial at Häven, Kreis Sternberg, Mecklenburg-Vorpommern.[68] Sherds representing a minimum of four hemispherical cups were unearthed at the settlement Castrop-Rauxel, Kreis Recklinghausen, Nordrhein-Westfalen, Germany.[69] A large number of fragments of hemispherical cups were unearthed at the settlement site Westick, Kreis Unna, Nordrhein-Westfalen, Germany.[70]

Conical beakers with cracked-off rims

Conical beakers with cracked-off rims have been found beyond the Empire, but with the exception of beakers with coloured blobs found in the Black Sea region, they seem to be relatively rare. There are, however, a few sites in Free Germany which have yielded finds of this type. A possible find – the base of a beaker – comes from Bochum-Harpen, Kreisfreie Stadt Bochum, Nordrhein-Westfalen.[71] A large number of finds of conical beakers were discovered during the excavation of the settlement Castrop-Rauxel, Kreis Recklinghausen, Nordrhein-Westfalen, Germany.[72] From the settlement Westick, Kreis Unna, Nordrhein-Westfalen, Germany, there are a number of fragmented conical beakers.[73]

At Aksum in Ethiopia, a number of fragments of beakers – or rather lamps – in yellowish-green glass with cracked-off rims were found. Some of these were plain, undecorated, whereas others had applied blobs.[74]

Conical beakers with fire-rounded rims

As far as I know there are no finds of conical beakers with fire-rounded rims of the same type discussed above in the areas beyond the Roman *Limes*.

Notes

1 'Hemispherical cups with wheel-cut figured decoration', ch. 3.10.; 'Vessels with applied blobs', ch. 3.11.
2 Cool 1995b, 14.
3 Price & Cottam 1998a, 117.
4 Cool & Price 1995, 88; Price & Cottam 1998a, 117.
5 Isings 1957, 113.
6 Isings 1957, 114–16, 131–33.
7 Cool & Price 1995, 88.
8 Isings 1957, 132.
9 Lantier 1929, fig. 16 & fig. 17.
10 Isings 1957, 133. For a discussion on vessels with honeycomb patterns, see Price & Cottam 1996b.
11 Isings 1957, 129–32.
12 Isings 1957, 136–38.
13 Price & Cottam 1998a, 121.
14 Price & Cottam 1998a, 122.
15 Cool & Price 1995, 88.
16 Price & Cool 1985, 44, fig. 20 no. 89.
17 Price & Cool 1993, 149–50, fig. 130 no. 49.
18 Painter 1971.
19 Price & Cottam 1996b, 98.
20 Isings 1957, 127–29.
21 Price & Cottam 1995b, 237–38.
22 Price & Cottam 1996b, 98.
23 Cool 1995b, 12, fig. 3.2 & fig. 3.4.
24 Cool & Price 1995, 92.
25 Price & Cottam 1998a, 129.
26 See, for example: Rademacher 1942, Taf. 50–51; Stjernquist 1986, fig. 7, fig. 10 to fig. 16; Campbell 1995, fig. 4; Campbell 2000, fig. 5.
27 Cool & Price 1995, 90.
28 Charlesworth 1972, 210, fig. 79.
29 Cool & Price 1995, 90.
30 Cool & Price 1995, 90.
31 Harden 1975, 371, no. 11, fig. 198.
32 Cool & Price 1995, 90.
33 Harden 1979, 214.
34 Price & Cool 1983, 122, nos 42–44, fig. 47.
35 Harden 1983, 123.
36 Arbman 1937, 34–36.
37 Isings 1957, 113.
38 Weinberg & Stern 2009, 92.
39 Crowfoot & Harden 1931; see also Whitehouse 1997, 213; Fleming 1999, 99–101.
40 Crowfoot & Harden 1931, 197.
41 Weinberg & Stern 2009, 135–36 with references.
42 Price & Cottam 1996b, 99.
43 Cool 1995b; Cool & Price 1995, 88–90; Price & Cottam 1998a, 117–19 with references.
44 **The Netherlands:** Maastricht (van Lith 1987, 51–52). **Belgium:** Spontin, Namur (Dasnoy 1966, 229). **Germany:** Köln (Cologne) (Friedhoff 1989, Abb. 1:12); Trier (Goethert-Polaschek 1977, 50–55); Oberingelheim (Behrens 1925–26, Abb. 21); Hohensülzen, Kr. Alzey-Worms, Wolfsheim, Kr. Mainz-Bingen (Bernhard 1982, 80, Abb. 11; 85, Abb. 16:9). **France:** Normandy (Sennequier 1994, fig. 2); Besançon (Koltes 1982, 53–54, pl. 35); Épiais-Rhus, Val-D'Oise (Vanpeene 1993, 44); Bordeaux (Foy & Hochuli-Gysel 1995, 156, fig. 59).
45 **Italy:** Luni, Liguria (Roffia 1973, 472; Chiaramonte Trerè 1973a, 726; Chiaramonte Trerè 1973b, 778); Ravenna (Sternini 1995, 244); Aquileia (Calvi 1969, tav. 26: 4–5); Temple of Magna Mater, Palatine, Rome (Sternini 2001, 26–27); Cimiterio ad duas lauros, Rome (Sternini 1995, 251); Sardinia (Stiaffini & Borghetti 1994, tav. 88).
46 **Switzerland:** Kaiseraugst (Fünfschilling 2000, 164).
47 **Slovenia** (Petru 1974, tab. 4); **Croatia** (Damevski 1974, tab. 9); **Bosnia** (Paskvalin 1974, tab. 9); **Montenegro** (Cermanović-Kuzmanović 1974, tab. 5).
48 Price & Cottam 1996b, 98, fig. 55 & fig. 56.

49 Cool 1995b; Cool & Price 1995, 88–92; Price & Cottam 1998a, 121–23 with references.

50 **The Netherlands:** Nijmegen (Isings 1957, 129). **Germany:** Köln (Isings 1957, 126–31; Friedhoff 1989, Abb. 1); Trier (Goethert-Polaschek 1977, 69–74); Worms (Isings 1957, 126–31); Mayen (Haberey 1942, 253–54).
France: Normandy (Sennequier 1994, fig. 2); Besançon (Koltes 1982, 57, pl. 37); St-Laurent-des-Combes, Aquitaine (Foy & Hochuli-Gysel 1995, 156).

51 **Switzerland:** Vindonissa (Berger 1960, 85, Taf. 22 nos 104 & 105); Kaiseraugst (Fünfschilling 2000, 164); Martigny, Valais (Martin 1995, 94, fig. 1:1).

52 **Hungary** (Barkóczi 1988, 80–83).

53 **Montenegro** (Cermanović-Kuzmanović 1974, tab. 5).

54 Price & Cottam 1996b, 96, 98–99.

55 Cool 1995a, 1578.

56 Cool 1995b; Cool & Price 1995, 92–93; Price & Cottam 1998a, 130–31 with references.

57 Isings 1957, 126–31. Finds have for example been made in **The Netherlands:** Maastricht (van Lith 1987, 62–64); **Italy:** Mola di Monte Gelato (with horizontal abraded bands) (Price 1997b, 278, fig. 189); **Slovenia:** Ptuj (Subic 1974, tab. vii: 53).

58 See ch. 3.10; ch. 3.11.

59 See 'Miscellaneous fragments (including post-Roman finds)', ch. 3.25.

60 See ch. 3.11.

61 Werner 1873, 3; Sahlström et al. 1931–32, 84–85, fig. 101; Ekholm 1956, fig. 1a; Eggers 1951, 98 no. 482; Lund Hansen 1987, 451.

62 Rygh 1880; Eggers 1951, 96 no. 422; Lund Hansen 1987, 442.

63 Worsaae 1850, 358; Engelhardt 1865, 48; Eggers 1951, 86 no. 188; Ekholm 1956, fig. 5c; Lund Hansen 1987, 430.

64 Ethelberg 1995, 46–49, fig. 5; Lund Hansen 2000, 332–34.

65 Björklund & Hejjl 1996, 104, no. 107.

66 Neumann 1953; Lund Hansen 1987, 430.

67 Harden et al. 1968, 85. Dr Hilary Cool has kindly brought another parallel – a find from Cuijk, Noord-Brabant, the Netherlands – to my attention.

68 *CRFB* D3, II-09-6/1.21; Taf. 37.3.

69 *CRFB* D7, XI-06-1/6.10, 6.15, 6.27 & 6.28.

70 *CRFB* D7, IX-12-5/5.2, 5.50, 5.53, 5.68, 5.72, 5.96–97, 5.100, 5.126, 5.128, 5.162, 5.164, 5.1.166; Fremersdorf 1970c, 55–56.

71 *CRFB* D7, IX-01-1/6.31.

72 *CRFB* D7, XI-06-1/6.48–6.58.

73 *CRFB* D7, IX-12-5/5.25, 5.30, 5.32, 5.47, 5.94, 5.98, 5.99, 5.111, 5.124, 5.129, 5.130, 5.150, 5.156, 5.161, 5.163, 5.172–74; Fremersdorf 1970b, 56.

74 Morrison 1989, 202, fig. on page 203.

3.10 Hemispherical cups with wheel-cut figured decoration

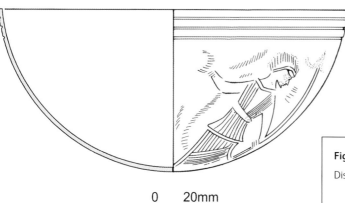

0   20mm

Figure 3.10.1

Hemispherical cup/bowl with wheel-cut figured decoration, Amiens, France [scale 1:2].

After Painter 1971, fig. 2

Figure 3.10.2

Distribution of type 3.10.

0   100 km

A general description of the type

A range of different glass vessels of fourth-century date from the north-western provinces and Italy – hemispherical cups, conical beakers,[1] segmental bowls, and spherical flasks with funnel necks – have cut and abraded figured decoration. There are a number of distinct styles in which different techniques of cutting were used, which either reflect regional variations, or, more probably, are the products of individual workshops.

In 1967 Fritz Fremersdorf suggested a typology for the finds from the north-western provinces.[2] The Traprain find discussed below belongs to Fremersdorf's group IV: *Schwach eingeteifte Umrißlinie und gerauhte Innenfläche*.[3] This style is characterised by short, sharp wheel-cuts forming the outline of the figures, spiky hair, and lozenge-shaped eyes (figs 3.10.1 & 3.10.3). The flesh or clothes of the figures were rendered matt by abrasion, so-called pointillé-technique. The entire surface is normally decorated, all areas that are not covered by figures being filled out with circles, scribbles, etc.

The motifs on these vessels vary. A majority of finds are decorated with pagan scenes, such as the Bacchic dance on a bowl from Colliton Park, Dorchester, Dorset,[4] or Marsyas and Apollo on a bowl from Rodenkirchen, Köln (Cologne), Germany.[5] Scenes from the circus, as on the well-known circus-bowl from Köln,[6] or hunting

scenes, as on a bowl from Köln-Müngersdorf, are also relatively frequent.[7] There are those, however, which had Christian motifs too; for instance a conical beaker from Köln displays four guards, which were identified as Christian.[8]

From Rome and its surroundings a group of bowls in a distinct style, reminiscent of Fremersdorf's group IV but with a 'softer' appearance, have been found.[9] The finds from Rome probably originate from a local workshop; and finds from Turkey and Hungary were executed in a similar style/technique, and in all likelihood originate from the same workshop as those found in Rome.[10] To my knowledge no finds of the latter type have been made in Britain.

Figure 3.10.3

Hemispherical cup with wheel-cut decoration, Amiens, France.

British Museum: BM GR 1886.5-12.3

There are several more or less contemporary styles of cut/abraded figured vessels. The most closely related is a style found in the north-western provinces, Fremersdorf's group V: *Parallele Schliff-Fürchen*.[11] This style is characterised by eyes made up of two parallel lines, and pointillé-infilled surfaces, which gives a cruder impression than Fremersdorf's group IV. The decoration consists of Pagan/mythological motifs, Biblical and Christian motifs.

Fritz Fremersdorf argued that there is much to suggest that a workshop was situated somewhere along the Rhine, quite possibly in Köln itself, on the basis of the concentration in the Rhineland for finds of Fremersdorf group IV and V.[12] In later research a number of differing views concerning the area of manufacture have been put forward. In 1994 Giandomenico De Tommaso put forward the idea that this group of vessels originated from the south of Gaul.[13] In contrast Lucia Saguí has argued that these vessels were in fact manufactured in Rome.[14] Finally, Fabrizio Paolucci has presented the hypothesis that the craftsmen from Köln moved to Rome in AD 390.[15]

Dating the type

The well-known bowl with a circus-motif from Köln was dated by coins found in the grave to AD 320–340.[16] The finds from Frocester Court Roman villa, Gloucestershire, and Lullingstone Roman villa, Kent, have been dated to AD 350–360 and AD 330–350 respectively.[17] Fremersdorf's groups IV and V were more or less contemporary, and a general time span for the finds is AD 330–370.[18]

The function of the vessels

It is likely that both the hemispherical cups of Isings Form 96 and conical beakers of Isings Form 106 were drinking vessels.

The finds from Roman contexts

To my knowledge there are only two possible finds of figure-cut vessels of Fremersdorf's group IV from Roman contexts in northern Britain. A small fragment of a hemispherical bowl in pale greenish colourless glass was found at York Minster. The motif could not be identified, but what was preserved was interpreted as depicting part of a human limb.[19] In addition to this a find made in the legionary fortress at York belongs to either a hemispherical cup or a segmental bowl. All that is preserved is a fragment with six short diagonal wheel-cuts showing that the style of decoration belongs to Fremersdorf's groups IV or V.[20]

A number of finds of vessels with wheel-cut figured design have been made in the Midlands and southern Britain, all settlement finds. The fragmented state of the material makes it impossible to classify much of it.[21] Finds of vessels belonging to Fremersdorf's group IV seem to be very rare; only one positively identified find of this type has been made in the area. A fragmented bowl of which large parts were preserved was found during excavations in Colliton Park, Dorchester, Dorset.[22] It is a bowl with a Bacchic scene. Two Maenads and three Satyrs dance in ecstasy, and in its centre is an emblemata – a bust in a circular frame – interpreted as a Satyr.[23]

There is a concentration of finds in the Rhineland, with Köln being a particularly prolific site,[24] although finds have been made in northern and central France, Switzerland and other neighbouring countries.[25] Whereas most finds in Romano-British contexts are from settlements, including a number of villas, the Continental finds mostly come from graves.

The finds from non-Roman contexts in north Northumberland and Scotland

Three fragments found at Traprain Law belong to the same vessel, a hemispherical cup/bowl of Isings Form 96 in clear, colourless glass. A head with spiky hair and the typical lozenge-shaped eyes[26] shows that it belongs to a small group of vessels produced in the north-western provinces, possibly in Köln, namely Fremersdorf's group IV. Sadly, the fragmented state of the vessel renders it impossible to tell what the original motif was. Roman glass with wheel-cut decoration of this type is very rare in Roman Britain – in particular those identified as belonging to Fremersdorf's group IV – and the finds from Traprain Law demonstrate the indigenous preference for decorated vessels and rare sub-types.

Traprain Law, East Lothian. N:2

GV 173* (XII 15 138), Area and Level: unknown – from the 1915 excavations, NMS.[27] Fragment of rim and upper body. Cracked-off and ground edge. Convex-curved side. The decoration consists of a head with a lozenge eye and part of a circle (?) in sharp wheel-cut lines. The upper part of the rim is rendered matt by abrasion; in addition there are two abraded circles and dots. Clear, colourless. RD 115; PH 37; W 38; WT 2.9 (lower part) – 2.1 (upper part). Same vessel as GV 178:1 (XII 15 143) & GV 1630.

GV 178:1* (XII 15 143), Area and Level: unknown, NMS. Body fragment. Convex-curved body. Wheel-cut decoration. The decoration consists of short, sharp wheel-cut lines and abraded surfaces. Clear, colourless, high quality glass. Strain cracks. Dims 22 x 20; WT 3.0. Same vessel as GV 173 & GV 1630.

GV 1630*, Area F, Level 4, NMS. Rim fragment. Rim cracked-off and ground. Surface below rim rendered matt with abrasion; horizontal abraded band. Clear, colourless. RD 115; PH 15; W 16; WT 2.0. Same vessel as GV 173 & GV 178:1.

Finds from other areas beyond the borders of the Roman Empire

To my knowledge no finds of vessels with wheel-cut decoration of Fremersdorf's groups IV and V have been made outside of the Empire. A bowl in Wint Hill style (Fremersdorf's group III) with a hunting scene has been found at Dalagergård, Sdr. Vissing, Jutland.[28] A hemispherical bowl of a related type – Eggers type 215 – was discovered in an inhumation burial at Leuna, Kreis Merseburg, Sachsen-Anhalt, Germany. This depicts Artemis transforming Actaeon into a deer, suffering death as his own dogs attacked him.[29] From Aksum, Ethiopia, there is a segmental bowl with cut decoration of a different style.[30]

Figure 3.10.4

Left: hemispherical cup sherds with wheel-cut decoration, Traprain Law [scale 2:3].
NMS: GV 173, 178.1, 1630

Figure 3.10.5

Right: hemispherical cup sherd with wheel-cut decoration, Traprain Law.
NMS: GV 173

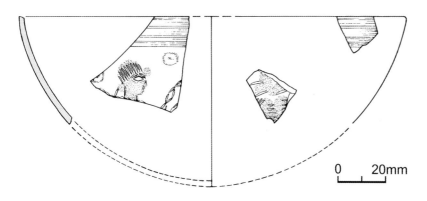

Notes

1 For a discussion on hemispherical bowls and conical beakers, see also 'Hemispherical cups with cracked-off rims, conical beakers with cracked-off rims or fire-rounded rims', ch. 3.9, and 'Vessels with applied blobs', ch. 3.11.
2 Fremersdorf 1967, 21–22.
3 See Fremersdorf 1967, Taf. 230–45.
4 Anonymous 1939, 219, pl. 32; Fremersdorf 1967, Taf. 243.
5 Fremersdorf 1967, Taf. 245.
6 Harden et al. 1988, 210–12.
7 Fremersdorf 1967, Taf. 244.
8 Fremersdorf 1967, Taf. 235.
9 A number of finds have been made in Rome. A small hemispherical cup with men fishing was found in a catacomb (Hayes 1928). Another find, in this case a segmental bowl, with men fishing, is of the same distinct style (Harden et al. 1988, 214–15; De Tommaso 1989, fig. 1). At Isola Sacra, Ostia's cemetery, a deep bowl with Hector and Priam was found in one of the graves (Harden et al. 1988, 216–17). A number of finds with Biblical, Christian and Pagan motifs have been unearthed in Rome (Fremersdorf 1975; De Tommaso 1989; De Tommaso 2000).
10 Two finds, a hemispherical cup with a man and a star from Gorsium, Hungary (Barkóczi 1988, 67 no. 48, Taf. 5 & 71) and a segmental bowl with Apollo and Athena from Bodrum, Turkey (Harden et al. 1968, 74) probably belong to the production of the same workshop as the finds from Rome.
11 See Fremersdorf 1967, Taf. 246–69; Caron 1997, fig. 15 to fig. 20, 28–33.
12 Fremersdorf 1967, 21–23.
13 De Tommaso 1994, 267.
14 Saguí 1996, 354–55.
15 Paolucci 2002, 77.
16 Fremersdorf 1967, 172.
17 Price 1995c, 26–27.
18 Harden et al. 1988, 185.
19 Price 1995d, 348, 357, fig. 142 no. 18.
20 Cool 1995a, 1578, fig. 744 no. 6186.
21 Price 1995c, 25.
22 Anonymous 1939, 219, pl. 32.
23 Painter 1971, 47.
24 **Germany**: there is a concentration of finds belonging to Fremersdorf's group IV. The well-known circus-bowl (for a discussion of the motif, see Frazer 1964; Fremersdorf 1967, 171–72; Harden et al. 1988, 210–12), a conical beaker with Venus and Amor (Fremersdorf 1967, Taf. 236–39), a conical beaker with Christian guards (Fremersdorf 1967, Taf. 235) and a hemispherical bowl with busts (Fremersdorf 1967, Taf. 240; Follmann-Schulz 1992, 69–70), all from burials in Köln (Cologne) and its surroundings. A conical beaker with a Bacchic motif was found in Cobern on the Moselle (Fremersdorf 1967, Taf. 232). A fragmented segmental bowl with a winged figure was discovered in Trier, a similar bowl in Konz, Kr. Trier-Saarburg (Goethert-Polaschek 1977, 26–27, Abb. 6). From Trier there is a fragment of a deep bowl with a circus motif belonging to Fremersdorf's group V (Goethert-Polaschek 1977, 38, Abb. 12). In addition to these finds there are two bowls from a private collection – the Karl Löffler Collection, Köln – one belonging to Fremersdorf's group IV, the other to his group V (La Baume 1976, 80–81, Taf. 23:4 & 23:3).
25 **France**: a group of glass vessels found in Amiens, northern France belong to Fremersdorf's group IV. There is a globular flask with funnel mouth and a decoration of winged cupids, men and women and a series of fish and palm trees (Painter 1971, 44–46, fig. 1, pl. 16); a hemispherical bowl which resembles the Colliton Park find (Harden et al. 1968, 75; Painter 1971, 47, fig. 2, pl. 17a); and a segmental bowl with a bust of Attis wearing a Phrygian cap (Painter 1971, 47, fig. 3, pl. 17b). From Plassac, Aquitaine there is a fragment of a hemispherical cup of Isings Form 96 with a standing figure, possibly from a Thiasos-scene belonging to Fremersdorf's group V (Hochuli-Gysel 1993, Abb. 3; Foy & Hochuli-Gysel 1995, fig. 2:13). A conical beaker of Isings Form 106 with a Bacchic motif belonging to Fremersdorf's group V was unearthed at the Cybele-temple at Vienne, central France (Foy & Nenna 2001, 275, no. 406). **Switzerland**: from Kaiseraugst there are fragments of a conical beaker with wheel-cut decoration of Fremersdorf's group V (Fünfschilling 2000, 167, fig. 3:3), and from Sion, Valais there is a small fragment with a wheel-cut decoration belonging to Fremersdorf's group IV, the motif unclear, but perhaps the head and wings of a cupid (Martin 1995, 101, fig 3:3).
26 Jennifer Price has argued that it probably is a female head (Price 2010, 44).
27 Curle & Cree 1915–16, 111, fig. 27.
28 Fischer 1981, 173; Lund Hansen 1987, 111–12, fig. 53.
29 *CRFB* D6, VIII-10-12/1.21, Taf. 86.
30 Morrison 1989, 194, 197.

3.11 Vessels with marvered applied blobs

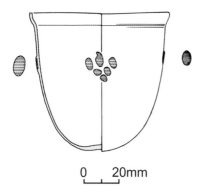

Figure 3.11.1

Hemispherical cup with applied blobs, Chignall, Essex [scale 1:2].

After Allen 1998a, fig. 59:9

A general description of the type

Glass vessels manufactured in the last part of the third century, the fourth and early fifth century AD were often decorated in different techniques, such as abraded or cut decoration, applied threads and applied blobs. These techniques were often combined, for example abraded horizontal lines with applied blobs (fig. 3.11.3). A range of vessel types and forms have applied blobs, such as cups, beakers, bowls, flasks, and drinking horns,[1] with hemispherical cups (Isings Form 96)[2] and conical beakers (Isings Form 106)[3] being the most common.[4] As the material from native Scotland cannot be positively identified to type, I have chosen to discuss all types of vessels with this kind of decoration together.[5]

The blobs are oval or round and vary in size from a few millimetres to more than a centimetre. The decoration is either monochrome or polychrome. As was the case with so-called snake-thread glass there were differences in technique between the centres of production in the western and the eastern parts of the Roman Empire.[6] In the east only monochrome vessels were made, whereas in the west both mono- and polychrome vessels were produced.[7]

Most vessels were manufactured in colourless, greenish colourless or yellowish-green glass, with blobs in a contrasting colour. Deep blue is the most common colour in both the west and the east. Other colours known in the west are dark green, emerald green, yellow,

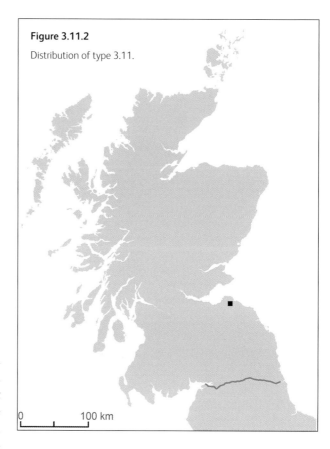

Figure 3.11.2

Distribution of type 3.11.

yellow-brown and purple. Colourless blobs are known, but appear to be very rare.[8] The blobs were often placed in one or several horizontal patterns across the vessel. On other vessels small blobs were placed in groups of three forming triangles, or in four forming lozenges. There are also examples of applied blobs being combined with other types of decoration, for instance an applied horizontal zigzag pattern which is in a contrasting colour.[9]

There seems to have been a production of vessels with this kind of decoration in the west as well as in the east. As so often Köln (Cologne) has been pointed out as one of the main manufacturing centres in the west.[10] However, this is based on the grave-finds rather than evidence from actual manufacturing centres. There is better evidence from the east. In Jalame (Jalamet el Asafna), 10 km south-east of Haifa, Israel, a glass factory has been found, in which beakers or, more probably, lamps with applied blue blobs were produced. The period of manufacture at this site was dated to the mid-fourth century by coins.[11]

Dating the type

Applied blobs appear on vessels from the third century;[12] however, most objects date to the fourth or early fifth centuries.[13] In the east the production continued into the Islamic period.[14]

The function of the vessels

There is a range of vessel types with applied blobs, and there is nothing to contradict the assertion that most of these were tableware. However, there is one exception, conical beakers of Isings Form 106. It is likely that this vessel-type had different functions, as either drinking vessels or lamps, depending on where they were used/manufactured.[15]

This problem was discussed in some detail by Grace Crowfoot and Donald Harden in 1931. Glass lamps for illuminating churches and other buildings are referred to in literary sources from the fourth century AD onward, and they are depicted in mosaics from the same period. This has been confirmed by archaeological evidence. On many fragments of conical vessels with applied blue blobs found in Karanis, Egypt, chemical analysis showed traces of oil.[16] Crowfoot and Harden suggested that most vessels of this type found in Egypt, Syria and Jordan were lamps, whereas most vessels in the west were drinking vessels. However, they pointed out that some of these vessels found in the west may have been lamps.[17] Later finds have confirmed the idea that conical vessels

were employed as lamps in the west, but this seems to have been very rare.[18]

In Anton Kisa's posthumously published work from 1908 convincing arguments were put forward for the idea that vessels with applied blobs were a cheap substitute for the expensive and exclusive *potoria gemmata*, that is a kind of drinking vessel in metal with inlayed semi-precious stone or glass gems.[19]

The finds from Roman contexts

Both hemispherical cups and conical beakers are very common finds in Roman Britain, mostly on settlements, less often in graves. But only a tiny fraction of those are decorated with this specific form of decoration.[20] The only grave-find known to me is from Chignall Roman villa, Essex (fig. 3.11.1). This almost intact vessel is a hemispherical cup in olive green glass with two clusters of six deep blue blobs forming triangles and two single blue blobs.[21] In contrast to Britain, cups and beakers with applied blobs appear to be more common in other parts of the north-western provinces[22] as well as in the central[23] and eastern parts of the Empire.[24]

The finds from non-Roman contexts in Scotland and north Northumberland

Three fragments from two vessels with applied blobs have been unearthed at Traprain Law, East Lothian (figs 3.11.4–5). The fragments are minute and could not be identified to type. One is a yellowish-green vessel with an applied blob in dark green glass, the other a vessel in natural green glass with an applied blob in deep blue. However, considering that the glass in both cases is rather thin, 0.9 mm and 1.6 mm respectively, these fragments must have come from cups or beakers. Hemispherical cups and conical beakers (Isings Forms 96 & 106) occasionally have applied blob decoration, and finds of both types are relatively common on the site.

The colour of the glass, the type of decoration and the likely origin as hemispherical cups or conical beakers suggest a fourth-century AD date. Yellow-green glass is most common in the late part of the fourth century.[25]

Figure 3.11.3

Hemispherical cup with applied blue blobs, Felix Slade collection. British Museum: 1871,1004.3

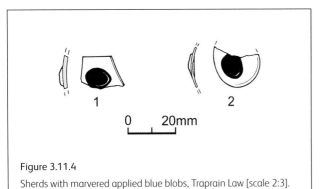

Figure 3.11.4
Sherds with marvered applied blue blobs, Traprain Law [scale 2:3].
(1) NMS: GV 1559 (2) NMS: GV 45

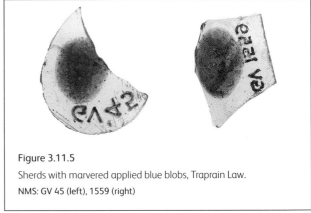

Figure 3.11.5
Sherds with marvered applied blue blobs, Traprain Law.
NMS: GV 45 (left), 1559 (right)

What function these may have had is difficult to tell: drinking vessels seem the most likely, but it cannot be ruled out that they might have been lamps.

Although hemispherical cups and conical beakers with simple abraded decoration[26] were more common than vessels of the same types decorated with blobs or wheel-cut decoration,[27] a significant proportion – one quarter of the identified material – was decorated. As with other categories of material, this implies that the assemblage represents a choice of what was available.

Traprain Law, East Lothian. N:2

GV 45* (XI 14 112), NMS. Body fragment. Yellowish-green. Convex-curved side. Applied blob in green. Bubbly. Usage scratches. Dims 16 x 19; WT 0.9.

GV 1559*, Area: 'fill in', NMS. Two joining body fragments. Curved side. Natural green. Applied blob in blue. Bubbly. Fragment (a) Dims 17 x 13; WT 1.6. Fragment (b) Dims 8 x 4; WT 1.6.

Finds from other areas beyond the borders of the Roman Empire

A few finds of vessels with applied blobs have been made in Scandinavia; of these, only three can definitely be shown to belong to the group. At the Iron Age fort/settlement of Eketorp on the island of Öland, Sweden a hemispherical cup was found, in yellowish-green glass with applied and marvered blobs in brown and green. Larger singular blobs are interspaced with clusters of blobs forming elongated triangles. On the upper part of the body is a decoration of applied green threads, two horizontal ones with a zigzag pattern between. The rim was cut and polished.[28]

A fragment of a vessel in yellowish-green glass with three applied blobs in deep blue was unearthed in a house in the Iron Age settlement Hässelby, also on the island of Öland, excavated in 1970–71.[29] In addition to these finds, there is an uncertain find which Ulf Näsman suggests may have originated from a vessel with applied blobs. This is from Skön, Västland, Medelpad, Sweden – a melted lump with spots in green, blue and brown.[30] Not much is known about the context of this find, except that it may have been found in a stone cist in a burial mound.[31]

A small bowl or large cup in greenish glass of similar decoration was found in Haugstad, Rogaland, Norway.[32] As with the Eketorp find, it has a zigzag border on the upper part of the body, and clusters of blobs forming triangles. The vessel was repaired with a decorated gilded band dating to the Migration period. It was found in a burial mound excavated in 1883 or earlier, and unfortunately little is known about the context. In the same grave a large bronze vessel of Vestland type, a cross-shaped fibula, a gold ring, a bronze ring and a small pottery vessel were uncovered.[33]

From Røra, Telemark, Norway, five fragments forming a vessel of unidentified type in greenish glass with applied blobs in green were found in a grave.[34] This was discovered during construction work in 1936, and only examined by an archaeologist four years later. Thus little is known about the context, although around 100 fragments of coarse pottery of local manufacture from at least four vessels were found at the same site.[35]

A small fragment of a colourless conical beaker with applied blobs in yellowish glass was found during excavations of the settlement Castrop-Rauxel, Kreis Recklinghausen, Nordrhein-Westfalen, in Germany.[36] Excavations of this site yielded a rich assemblage of imported Roman goods, not least glass vessels of various types.[37] From Westick, Kreis Unna, Nordrhein-Westfalen, Germany – another settlement site with a large assemblage of Roman imports – there is a single find of a cup or beaker with applied blobs. The colour of this find is natural-coloured green, with an applied self-coloured blob.[38]

Conical-shaped vessels which in all probability functioned as beakers in a western context may have functioned as lamps in an eastern context. Consequently some of the finds made beyond the Roman border, in Africa and Asia, could have been cups, beakers or lamps.

A large number of glass vessels with applied blobs of eastern production have been found in the Black Sea area, an area which partly falls within the Empire and partly consisted of Client States. These are hemispherical cups, conical beakers with a flat base and true conical beakers. They were in yellowish-green or greenish-yellow, less commonly in clear colourless glass with deep blue blobs. Finds have also been made in neigh-bouring Azerbaijan.[39] Excavations at Nineveh, in northern Iraq have yielded finds of what may have been lamps.[40] A conical lamp (or beaker) now in Berlin was originally found in Amlash, Guilan, Iran, a site on the coast of the Caspian Sea.[41] A small hemispherical cup in greenish colourless glass with two rows of applied blue blobs was discovered in a tomb at Okjeon, Hapcheon, south Gyeongsang, South Korea.[42] This tomb dates to the Era of the Gaya Confederacy, i.e. the first centuries AD.

A minimum of three vessels – conical or hemispherical lamps/beakers – with applied blobs were discovered at Aksum, Ethiopia.[43] These were in colourless or greenish-yellow glass with deep blue blobs, and were discovered around a looted tomb.[44] From Fezzan in the Saharan desert (i.e. Libya), there are grave finds of hemispherical cups and footed conical beakers with applied blobs.[45]

Notes

1 Fremersdorf 1962, Taf. 1–23; Doppelfeld 1966, 59–69; Harden et al. 1988, 114–17.
2 Isings 1957, 113–16, 131–32.
3 Isings 1957, 126–31.
4 Price & Cool 1993, 149.
5 For a discussion on hemispherical bowls and conical beakers, see also 'Hemispherical cups with cracked-off rims, conical beakers with cracked-off rims or fire-rounded rims', ch. 3.9, and 'Hemispherical cups with wheel-cut figured decoration', ch. 3.10.
6 See 'Snake-thread glass', ch. 3.4.
7 Harden et al. 1988, 101–3.
8 Fremersdorf 1962, 10.
9 Lantier 1929, fig. 16B.
10 Fremersdorf 1962, 7–13.
11 Davidson Weinberg 1988, 60.
12 Fremersdorf 1962, 7.
13 Price & Cottam 1998a, 118, 122.
14 Isings 1957, 131.
15 See also ch. 3.9.
16 Crowfoot & Harden 1931, 197.
17 Crowfoot & Harden 1931, 200; See also Stern 1999, 479–80; Fleming 1999, 99–101. Egypt: conical lamp, Karanis (Harden 1936b, pl. 5).
18 Weinberg & Stern 2009, 135 with references.
19 Kisa 1908, 479; see also Fremersdorf 1962, Taf. 118; Weinberg & Stern 2009, 136 with references.
20 Allen 1998a, 96
21 Allen 1998a, 96, fig. 59 no. 9, pl. 10.
22 **Germany:** Köln (Fremersdorf 1955a, 120; Doppelfeld 1966, Taf. 137; Taf. 136, 138–41; Fremersdorf 1962, Taf. 1–23; Harden et al. 1988, 114–17); Nida-Heddernheim (Welker 1985, 50–51); Oberingelheim (Behrens 1925–26, Abb. 20); Brühl (Follmann-Schulz 1992, 61); Ruppertsberg (Bernhard 1982, 78, Abb. 6:11). **France:** Normandy (Sennequier 1994,

fig. 2); Fère-en-Tardenois, Aisne (Lantier 1929, 12, fig. 16); Vienne (Foy & Nenna 2001, 218, no. 396); Aquitaine (Foy & Hochuli-Gysel 1995, 156, fig. 5).
23 **Austria:** Magdalensberg (Czurda-Ruth 1979, 160–61). **Switzerland:** Martigny (Martin 1995, fig.1:5); Kaiseraugst (Fünfschilling 2000, fig. 2). **Italy:** Sevegliano, Friuli (Buora 1998, 168); Sardinia (Stiaffini & Borghetti 1994, tav. 37).
24 **Slovenia:** Ravno brdo (Petru 1974, Taf. 8); Ptuj (Subic 1974, tav. vii: 54). **Croatia:** Sisak; Radovanci (Damevski 1974, Tab. 15: 3 & 4). **Bulgaria:** Novae (Turno 1989, Abb. 3:3). **Greece:** the Agora, Athens (Weinberg & Stern 2009, 136, fig.18); **Cyprus:** unknown location (Harden et al. 1968, 66). **Turkey:** Ephesus (Czurda-Ruth 1989, Abb. 2 & 3). **Jordan:** el-Lejjun (Jones 1987, fig. 133 & fig. 134).
25 Cool 1995b, 11.
26 See ch. 3.9.
27 See ch. 3.10.
28 Näsman 1984, 45–49.
29 Edgren et al. 1976, 35–36, fig. 15.
30 Näsman 1984, 46.
31 Selinge 1977, 262–63.
32 Ekholm 1937b, fig. 10.
33 Bjørn 1929, nos 37 & 142.
34 *Universitetets Oldsaksamling Årbok* 1950, 249.
35 Marstrander 1947.
36 Fremersdorf 1970c, 97.
37 *CRFB* D7, XI-06-1; Fremersdorf 1970c.
38 *CRFB* D7, IX-12-5/5.31; Fremersdorf 1970b, 54, Taf. 15: G1.
39 Sorokina 1972; Sazanov 1995.
40 Simpson 2005, 149.
41 Kunisch 1967, 196, Abb. 38.
42 Korean National Heritage Online: http://211.252.141.88/program/relic/relicDetailEng.jsp?menuID=00200400104&relicDetailID=17798&relicID4450.jsp [Accessed 4 March 2014].
43 Morrison 1989, 200, 202, fig. p. 203.
44 Morrison 1983, 122.
45 Caputo 1951, fig. 86 & fig. 87

3.12 Beakers of late Roman type with zigzag decoration

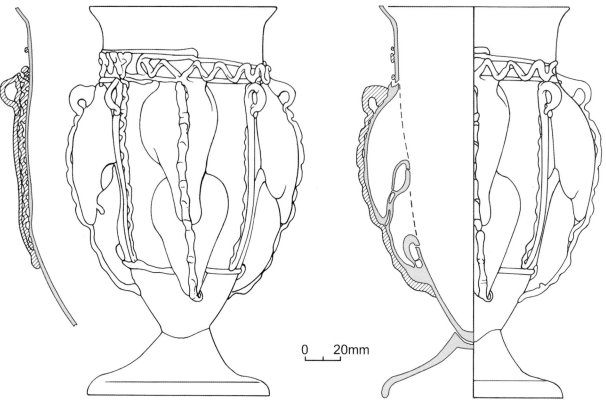

Figure 3.12.1

Claw-beaker, Mucking, Essex [scale 1:2].
After Harden et al. 1988, 258

Figure 3.12.2

Distribution of type 3.12.

A general description of the type

Three finds of beakers of late Roman date with self-coloured trailed-on decoration have been made on two native sites in Scotland, two at Traprain Law, East Lothian,[1] and one at Howe of Howe, Orkney.[2] As it remains uncertain if the finds from Traprain Law and Howe of Howe were of the same type, or if they are of closely related types, they are discussed separately. The latter will be treated in chapter 3.13.

Exactly which type or types the finds from Traprain Law belong to cannot be proven beyond doubt; however, it is clear that they belonged to a group of vessels which have a decoration of trails in a zigzag pattern, sometimes combined with other types of decoration, including 'claws' and claw-shaped blobs.

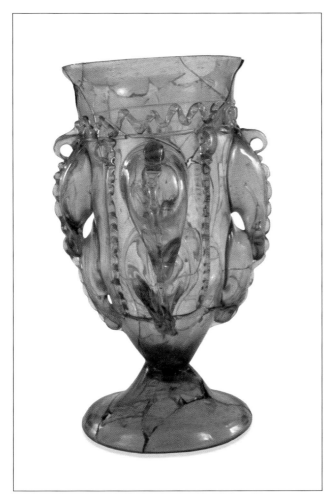

Figure 3.12.3

Late Roman beaker with trailed-on decoration, Mucking, Essex.

British Museum: 1970,0406.1675

A number of different types of drinking vessels were decorated with zigzag trails placed within two horizontal trails: hemispherical cups of Isings Form 96;[3] hemispherical cups with pushed-in base rings of Isings Form 108b (including finds with 'claws');[4] conical beakers of Isings Form 106;[5] conical beakers with small pushed-in base-rings of Isings Form 109c;[6] and glass drinking horns of Isings Form 113.[7] The closest parallel to the two finds from Traprain Law, however, are claw-beakers of late Roman date – Evison Type 1 – and they bear a close resemblance to this type.[8] Nevertheless, it has to be stressed that no remains of 'claws' survive in the finds from Traprain.

Vera Evison based the definition of this type on a beaker from Mucking, Essex (fig. 3.12.3). It is of a relatively broad cylindrical shape with a separately blown foot attached to the body. The rim is slightly out-splayed, and the edge is cracked-off and left unground. Below the rim is a zigzag pattern in self-coloured glass, below which are two rows of 'claws'. Vertical trails run down from the zigzag pattern and form a framing around the claws. The type is very rare; Evison has only identified one single find which positively belongs to the type.[9] The arguments for the Traprain finds belonging to claw-beakers of Evison Type 1 – or some closely related type – are the following:

- The shape. The shape of the vessels is cylindrical, which excludes hemispherical cups (Isings Form 96), hemispherical cups with pushed-in base-rings (Isings Form 108b) and drinking horns. Two vessel forms have straight sides and have a more or less cylindrical upper body: conical beakers of Isings Form 109c and beakers of Evison Type 1 respectively.
- The decoration. Vessel types found on the Continent – Isings Forms 96, 108b, 109c and drinking horns – all have decoration in one or several contrasting colours (green, brown and blue), whereas several of the British finds have self-coloured trails: the conical beaker from High Down, Sussex, the fragments from Silchester, Hampshire and the claw-beaker from Mucking, Essex.
- The colour and quality of the glass. The colour of the Traprain Law finds, pale green, is the same as that of Evison Type 1 from Mucking, Essex.

Claw-beakers constitute a link between the Roman glass-blowing traditions of the late Roman period and the following Merovingian period, and have thus attracted much attention by glass historians. Anton Kisa was the first to discuss this group of vessels in detail – a study posthumously published in 1908[10] – which was followed by a thorough study by Fritz Fremersdorf in 1934.[11] Most scholars still adhere to Fremersdorf's (and to some extent also to Kisa's) general ideas concerning the Roman origins of the Merovingian claw-beakers.[12] To sum up Fremersdorf's views, the claw-beakers derive on the one hand, from beakers with dolphin-shaped appliqués, on the other hand from the type of vessels with zigzag patterns described above.[13] It was suggested by Fremersdorf that the production of vessels with this type of decoration took place in Namur, Belgium.[14] However, the British finds which in several cases have self-coloured trails were probably manufactured in Britain itself.[15]

Dating the type

The claw-beaker from Mucking, Essex (Evison Type 1) was found during the excavations of a Saxon cemetery, in a grave which is thought to have been that of a woman on the basis of the female possessions found, such as Kentish square-headed brooches. The interment took place in the first half of the sixth century or later, but it was suggested by Vera Evison that the claw-beaker was an heirloom dated to *c.* AD 400.[16]

A number of different vessel forms were decorated with the same type of zigzag patterns as the claw-beakers of Evison Type 1, and numismatic evidence suggests a late fourth-century date for those vessels. A hemispherical cup of Isings Form 108b found in Mayen, Rheinland-Pfalz, Germany was discovered in a grave also containing a coin struck between AD 383 and 408,[17] while excavations of a late Roman grave-field at Flavion, Namur, Belgium yielded a claw-beaker (Isings Form 109c) in a grave which also included two coins, one of which was struck between AD 388 and 402.[18]

The function of the vessels

Anton Kisa thought that claw-beakers would be impractical to drink from.[19] However, modern replicas have been tested, and there are no problems whatsoever in drinking wine from them.[20]

The finds from non-Roman contexts in Scotland and north Northumberland

Fragments belonging to two vessels have been discovered at Traprain Law, East Lothian. During the early excavations no less than 26 fragments belonging to a vessel with trailed-on decoration were found.[21] The fragments were in a bubbly pale green glass, which varied in thickness from 1.2 to 1.6 mm. Three horizontal trails encircled the vessel. Between the upper two of these, a zigzag trail was applied. On a few fragments the remains of vertically running trails were still left (fig. 3.12.4–5a).

Excavations in 2003 at the same site unearthed one fragment of yet another vessel of the same or a closely related type. This is also cylindrical in shape, with self-coloured zigzag decoration. As was the case with the fragments discussed above, this fragment is also in pale

green glass, although with considerably fewer bubbles. The thickness of this vessel is 1.6 to 2.0 mm.

As argued above, much evidence points in the direction that one or both of the Traprain Law finds belonging to Evison Type 1. Whether or not this was the case, the finds can be dated to *c.* AD 370–400, and in all likelihood they were produced in the north-western provinces, possibly in Britain itself. They have a parallel from Howe of Howe, Orkney, discussed below. Little survives of the latter find, and it is not clear whether it had a zigzag decoration. These finds are some of the latest finds of glass made at Traprain Law, with the exception of a bowl of post-Roman date and two or three glass vessels of post-Roman Mediterranean type.[22]

Traprain Law, East Lothian. N:2

GV 1075* (1923/79), Area 1922, Level 2, NMS. Twenty-six body fragments, mostly joining. Cylindrical body. Three applied self-coloured vertical trails; between the upper two is a self-coloured zigzag pattern of trails. Remains of two vertical trails on the upper part of the vessel. Pale green. Very bubbly glass. Dims 44 x 53; WT 1.2–1.6.

TLF 03, find 813, NMS. A body fragment. Cylindrical body. Applied self-coloured vertical trail, part of a zigzag trail. Pale green. Occasional bubbles; dull, iridescent surface. Dims 28 x 30; WT 1.6–2.0. Different vessel.

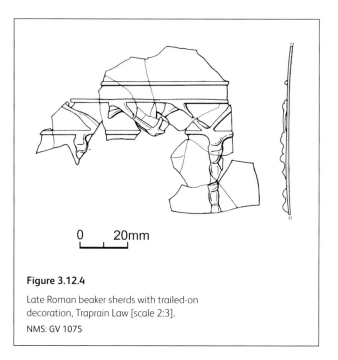

0   20mm

Figure 3.12.4

Late Roman beaker sherds with trailed-on decoration, Traprain Law [scale 2:3].
NMS: GV 1075

Figure 3.12.5

(a) Late Roman beaker sherds with trailed-on decoration, Traprain Law. NMS: GV 1075

(b) Sherd from a similar vessel, found on Traprain in 2003.

The finds from Roman contexts

The claw-beaker from Mucking, Essex, has been discussed above. Fragments of three vessels with applied zigzag decoration have been found in Silchester, Hampshire. Two of these fragments may have come from beakers of Evison Type 1. Rim fragments in green glass are out-turned and have cracked-off rims, and decorated with self-coloured zigzags.[23] As far as I know there no exact parallels from the Continent.

Finds from other areas beyond the borders of the Roman Empire

To my knowledge no vessels of this kind have been found beyond the borders of the Roman Empire.

Notes

1 Appendix A, N:2.
2 Appendix A, B:1.
3 Lantier 1929, 12, fig. 16b; for a general discussion of this type, see Isings 1957, 131–32.
4 Lantier 1929, 12, fig. 17; Dasnoy 1969, 159–60, fig. 10; Follmann-Schulz 1995, 87, fig. 3 & fig. 10; for a general discussion of this type, see Isings 1957, 134–35.
5 Harden 1956, 135; White 1988, 130, fig. 76 no. 1; for a general discussion of this type, see Isings 1957, 126–31.
6 Haberey 1942, Taf. 37:1–2; Dasnoy 1966, 208, fig. 14; Follmann-Schulz 1995, 87, fig. 8; for a general discussion of this type, see Isings 1957, 137–38.
7 Dasnoy 1968, 285, fig. 5.
8 Ingemark 2000, 176; see also: Price 2010, 44–45.
9 Evison 1974; Evison 1982, 45–46, pl. 4.
10 Kisa 1908, 486.
11 Fremersdorf 1933–34.
12 Rademacher 1942; Evison 1982; Follmann-Schulz 1995.
13 See Doppelfeld 1966, Taf. 100; Harden et al. 1988, 256; Follmann-Schulz 1995.
14 Fremersdorf 1933–34.
15 For a discussion concerning the manufacture of glass in Britain in the fourth century, see Cool 1995b, 14.
16 Evison 1982, 45, 52.
17 Haberey 1942, 270–71, Abb. 11b.
18 Dasnoy 1966, 206, 220.
19 Kisa 1908, 352.
20 Follmann-Schulz 1995, 85.
21 Cree 1923, 211, fig. 21.
22 See 'Miscellaneous fragments (including post-Roman finds)', ch. 3.25; Appendix A, N:2.
23 Boon 1959, 81, fig. 41 nos A13–A15.

3.13 Beaker of late Roman type with trailed-on decoration

A general discussion of the type

Two fragments of a beaker of late Roman type were discovered at Howe of Howe, Orkney; however, these could not be classified to type with certainty. Notwithstanding, there are many similarities between this find and the two late Roman beakers with a trailed-on zigzag decoration made at Traprain Law, East Lothian, discussed in the previous chapter.[1] The similarities are:

- The shape. The vessels are cylindrical, which excludes several other types common at the same period, for example hemispherical cups of Isings Forms 96 and 108.

- The decoration technique. The Howe find has an applied slashed thread, similar to that on one of the Traprain finds. All that remains on the Howe find is a single thread, whereas both finds from Traprain Law have applied zigzag decoration. Nevertheless, it is possible that the Howe find might originally have had a zigzag decoration.

- The colour and quality of the glass. The Howe and both the Traprain Law finds were manufactured in a pale green glass typical of the late fourth century.

The Continental finds in almost all cases have an applied decoration in contrasting colours, whereas the majority of British finds – including that from Howe – have self-coloured trails. This may suggest that they were of local production.

Dating the type

The colour and quality of the glass suggests a late fourth-century AD date.

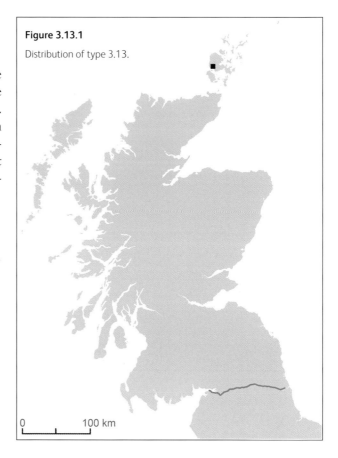

Figure 3.13.1

Distribution of type 3.13.

0   100 km

The function of the vessels

Little can be said about this find; in all probability it was a beaker used for drinking wine or some other liquid.

The finds from non-Roman contexts in Scotland and north Northumberland

The beaker from Howe, Orkney,[2] has its closest parallel in the finds from Traprain Law, East Lothian, but whereas one or both of the latter might have belonged to Evison Type 1, this cannot be demonstrated in the case of the Howe find. It is, however, a notable find, as very little Roman glass reached native sites in the fourth century.

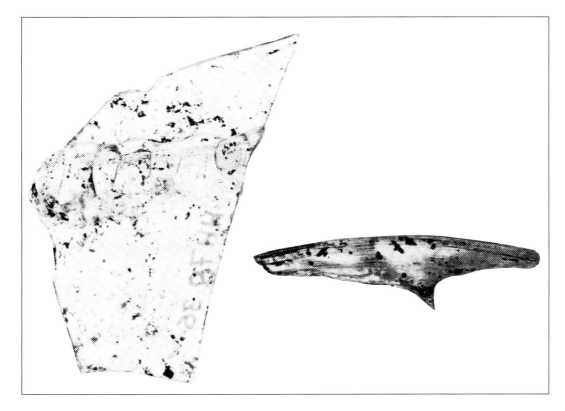

Figure 3.13.2

Late Roman beaker sherds with trailed decoration, Howe (from Ballin Smith 1994, Ill. 137).

Courtesy of Society of Antiquaries of Scotland

Howe of Howe, Orkney.[3] B:1

HH 76 36*, Tankerness House Museum. Two body fragments of cylindrical vessel with an applied trail in the same metal. Pale green, very bubbly glass. Fragment a: PH 23; W 37; WT 1.0; b: PH 7; W 28; WT 1.0.

Notes

1 For a more extensive discussion of parallels, dating and area of production, see 'Beakers of late Roman type with trailed-on zigzag decoration', ch. 3.12.
2 Appendix A, B:1.
3 Henderson 1994, 234, ill. 137.

3.14 Tubular-rimmed bowls

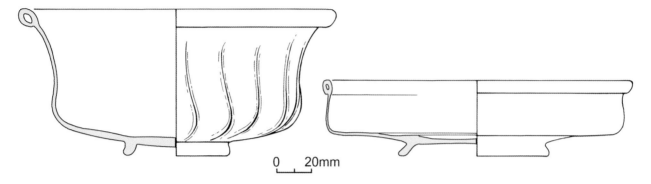

Figure 3.14.1

Tubular-rimmed bowls [scale 1:2].

Left: deep bowl, Chichester, Sussex.

After Charlesworth 1978, fig. 10:22, no. 14

Right: shallow bowl, Sheepen, Colchester, Essex.

After Charlesworth 1985a, fig. 80:37

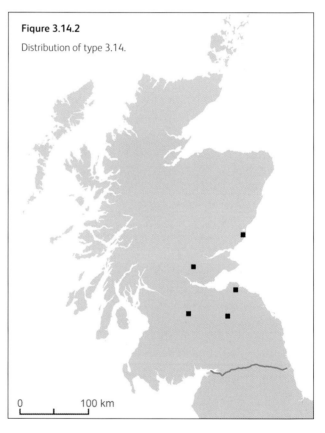

Fiqure 3.14.2

Distribution of type 3.14.

The characteristic and easily identifiable tubular rim is found on both deep bowls of Isings Form 44b and shallow bowls of Isings Form 45, dating to the first and second centuries, as well on deep bowls of the fourth century. The finds of the latter type differ in colour and general appearance, and only two finds which may belong this category have been made in a native context north of Hadrian's Wall.[1]

A general description of the type

Isings Form 44b has a broad vertical tubular rim, the rim edge folded out and down.[2] Occasionally the rim is rolled in, forming a double fold. The rim diameter of the vessels varies from *c.* 100–250 mm.[3] The body is of cylindrical or slightly concave shape, with a smoothly rounded or sharp angle between the body and base. The base is horizontal with an applied vertical or diagonal base ring. The bodies can be plain or have optic-blown diagonal or vertical ribs which occasionally extend to part of the base (fig. 3.14.1, left).[4] Body sherds are more difficult to identify than the rims, in particular if they are plain and undecorated.

Tubular-rimmed bowls of this type were manufactured in both strong colours and common blue-green glass, the latter being the most common.[5] Colourless vessels are known, but are rare finds. Strong colours such as deep blue and purple, and vessels with marvered opaque dots, belong to the Neronian period, whereas colours such as yellow-brown, yellow-green and blue-green were produced in both this period and until the third quarter of the second century.[6]

Isings Form 45 has a narrow vertical tubular rim, the rim edge folded out and down.[7] The rim diameter of the vessels varies between *c.* 130–180 mm. The body is of cylindrical shape, and shallow. The base is horizontal, with an applied diagonal base ring (fig. 3.14.1, right).

Figure 3.14.3

Tubular-rimmed vessel, Faversham, Kent.
British Museum: 1312.70

These were also manufactured in both strong colours and in common blue-green and green glass.[8] Finds of Isings Form 45 appear to be relatively frequent in Italy, and it has been argued that they were produced in that area.[9]

Dating the type

The deep tubular-rimmed bowls date from the late Neronian period (AD 60–65) to the third quarter of the second century. From Long Melford, Suffolk, a bowl was found in a layer with samian of Neronian date.[10] One of the latest securely dated finds is from Felmongers, Harlow, Essex: deep bowls of Isings Form 44b were found in a deposit dated to AD 160–170.[11] Finds are common between the Flavian period and early second century.[12]

Shallow bowls of Isings Form 45 date from the Claudian to the Neronian period in Britain,[13] whereas the earliest Continental finds date to the last decades of the first century BC or the first decades AD. A deposit from the Regia, Forum Romanum, Rome, of this date included fragments of shallow bowls of this type.[14]

The function of the vessels

From still-life wall paintings found in the Bay of Naples area, we know that large deep tubular-rimmed bowls (Isings Form 44b) were used for serving fruit.[15] In the Villa of Publius Fannius Sinistor at Boscoreale a tubular-rimmed bowl is depicted filled with peaches, quinces, green almonds and twigs.[16] A similar fresco was found in the Villa of Iulia Felix, Pompeii.[17]

The finds from Roman contexts

Deep tubular-rimmed bowls have been found on a number of Roman sites in northern Britain. The majority of these were in common blue-green glass, though finds in other shades of green are occasionally found too.[18] In the Midlands and in southern Britain such bowls constitute a common category of find in the glass assemblages, in both strong colours and blue-green glass.[19] In addition to these are rare examples of vessels in strong colours with marved dots, such as a vessel in deep blue with marvered opaque white spots from Kingsholm, Gloucester, Gloucestershire.[20] Deep tubular-rimmed bowls of Isings Form 44b are very frequent finds in the north-western provinces. The majority of these are in common blue-green glass or other shades of green, but vessels in strong colours are occasionally found.[21]

Shallow bowls of Isings Form 45 are relatively rare finds in Britain, and come exclusively from sites in southern Britain.[22] Similarly they appear to be less frequent in the north-western provinces, probably because the type is not as long-lived as the deep tubular-rimmed bowls.[23] In contrast, the shallow bowls are more common in Italy.[24]

The finds from non-Roman contexts in Scotland and north Northumberland

A minimum of five deep tubular-rimmed bowls of Isings Form 44b have been found on four sites: Redcastle, Lunan Bay, Angus; Hyndford, Lanarkshire; Torwoodlee, Selkirkshire; and a recent find from Castle Craig, Perthshire (not in catalogue). All of these bowls are in strong colours apart from Castle Craig which are pale yellow, green and pale blue-green glass; the Redcastle find is in greenish-brown glass, the Hyndford and the Torwoodlee finds are in brown glass (pl. 13).

One find from Culbin Sands, Morayshire, was reported to be of the same type as the Torwoodlee finds in a publication by G. F. Black in 1891.[25] This find was long believed to have been lost, but was rediscovered in the autumn of 2010. Examination shows that it represents a Late Roman type of tubular-rimmed bowl, however; a bowl of Burgh Castle type.[26]

Tubular-rimmed bowls in these colours were produced between AD 60/65 and 160/170. Although the number of finds is limited, it is clear that the native assemblage represents a selection of goods. The finds from Roman sites are predominantly in common blue-green glass, whereas the native were predominantly in strong colours.

In a backfilled souterrain at Redcastle in Lunan Bay, Angus, heavily fragmented Roman vessel glass was unearthed: one tubular-rimmed bowl (fig. 3.14.4.1), and at least one cylindrical cup.[27] Hyndford, Lanarkshire, has yielded a relatively large assemblage of Roman imports. Besides the tubular-rimmed bowl, these include a pillar-moulded bowl, cylindrical and prismatic bottles, and a variety of Roman fine-ware and coarse-ware pottery: platters, bowls, a jar, a flask and fragments of a *mortarium*.[28] Excavations at Torwoodlee, Selkirkshire, a hillfort and a later broch, also yielded a relatively large assemblage of Roman imports, associated with the broch. These included the tubular-rimmed bowl (fig. 3.14.4.2); cylindrical bottles; samian platters; amphorae, and fragments of a *mortarium*.[29]

In addition to the finds of deep tubular-rimmed bowls discussed above, there are a minimum of three tubular-rimmed bowls from Traprain Law in East Lothian.[30] These include a base sherd in brown glass, one sherd with a narrow tubular rim in blue-green glass (fig. 3.14.4.3), and one in pale blue-green (fig. 3.14.4.4). It is not clear if these finds belong to large deep bowls of Isings Form 44b, or to shallow bowls of Isings Form 45. In the case of the blue-green vessel, this might be an Isings 45, which would suggest a Claudian to Neronian date of manufacture. Finds of this type at the Roman fort of Corbridge, Northumberland, however, demonstrate that they were still in use in the Flavian period. The brown bowl could belong to either type, and thus dates between *c.* AD 60 and 170.

Deep tubular-rimmed bowls (Isings Form 44b)

Hyndford, Lanarkshire. O:1

HTA 39, NMS. Rim fragment. Brown. Tubular rim, edge first rolled, then folded out and down. Bubbly. PH 17; W 41; WT 1.1.

HTA 40, NMS. Rim fragment. Brown. Same vessel as HTA 39. PH 14; W 28; WT 1.2.

Redcastle, Lunan Bay, Angus. I:3

SF 024: 1*. Fragment of rim and upper body. Greenish-brown. In-bent tubular rim, edge bent out, down and in. Rounded change of angle to the lower body. RD *c.* 100; PH 17; WT 1.9.

SF 024: 2 & 3*. Two joining fragments of lower body and base. Greenish-brown. Base of flat shape. Many internal cracks. Very little sign of wear. Dims 41 x 32; WT 1.5.

SF 024: 4. Base fragment. Greenish-brown. Base of flat shape. Many internal cracks. Very little sign of wear. Dims 18 x 13; WT 3.4.

SF 024: 5. Base fragment (?). Greenish-brown. Some bubbles. Many internal cracks. Very little sign of wear. Dims 14 x 13; WT 1.5.

SF 041. Fragment of lower body and base. Greenish-brown. Base flat with a slightly raised rib running diagonally; optic-blown (?). Some bubbles. Dims 35 x 45; WT 1.5.

SF 033. Fragment of base. Greenish-brown. Some small bubbles, one large. Internal cracks. Very little sign of wear. Dims 29 x 47; WT 2.2.

SF 051. Fragment of base. Greenish-brown. Small bubbles. Internal cracks. Very little sign of wear. Dims 23 x 28; WT 2.4.

Torwoodlee, Selkirkshire. S:1

GA 372, NMS. Rim fragment. Brown. Slightly out-bent tubular rim, edge bent out and down. Straight side. RD *c.* 200; PH 23; W 33; WT 1.6.

GA 372 (No 54)*, NMS. Rim fragment. Brown. Slightly out-bent tubular rim, edge bent out and down. Straight side. RD *c.* 200; PH 25; W 79; WT 2.5.

GA 372a, NMS. Fragment of lower body and base. Brown. Dims 26 x 26; WT 1.6–2.6.

GA 372a*, NMS. Fragment of lower body and base. Brown. Dims 32 x 17; WT 1.3-2.0.

GA 1254, NMS. Base fragment. Brown. Distorted by heat. Dims 26 x 26; WT 2.5.

GA 1254*, NMS. Base fragment. Brown. Dims 22 x 24; WT 1.5.

GA 1254, NMS. Body fragment. Brown. Dims 10 x 19; WT 1.9.

Unreg., NMS. Body fragment. Brown. Dims 14 x 14; WT 1.9.

Unreg., NMS. Rim fragment. Brown. Slightly out-bent tubular rim, edge bent out and down. PH 17; W 34; WT 2.1–2.6.

Tubular-rimmed bowls (Isings Form 44b or 45)

Traprain Law, East Lothian. N:2

GV 380 (III 20 110), Area G, Level 2, NMS. Base fragment. Brown. Almost flat. Dims 27 x 23; WT 1.9.

GV 687* (V 21 182), Area J, Level 2, NMS. Fragment of rim and upper body. Pale blue-green. Narrow tubular rim; bent out, rim edge first rolled in, then folded out, down and in. Straight side. Bubbly. RD 160; PH 14; W 26; WT 0.8–3.0. Same vessel as GV 734.

GV 734* (V 2 278), Area K, Level 3, NMS. Rim fragment. Blue-green. Narrow tubular rim; rim edge first rolled in, then folded out, down and in. Bubbly. RD 150; PH 8; W 39; WT 2.

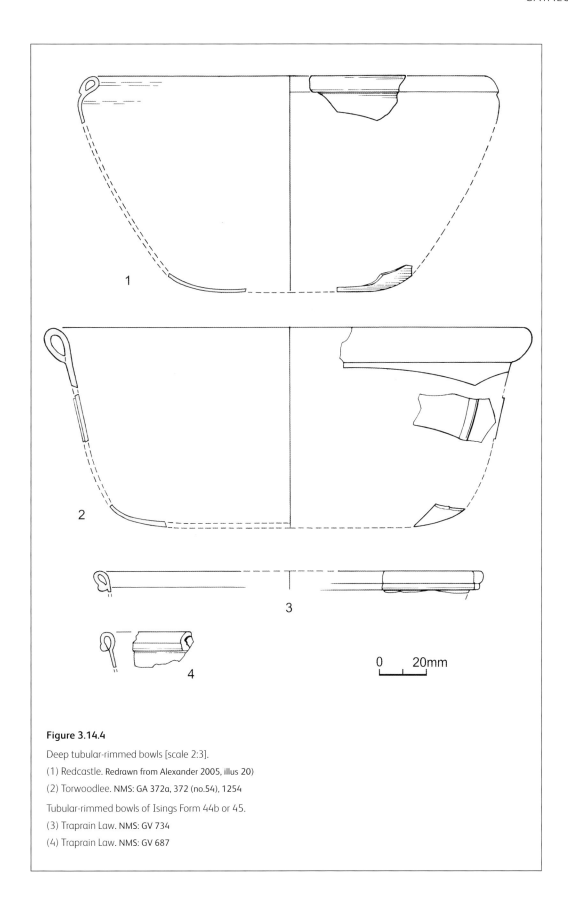

Figure 3.14.4

Deep tubular-rimmed bowls [scale 2:3].

(1) Redcastle. Redrawn from Alexander 2005, illus 20)

(2) Torwoodlee. NMS: GA 372a, 372 (no.54), 1254

Tubular-rimmed bowls of Isings Form 44b or 45.

(3) Traprain Law. NMS: GV 734

(4) Traprain Law. NMS: GV 687

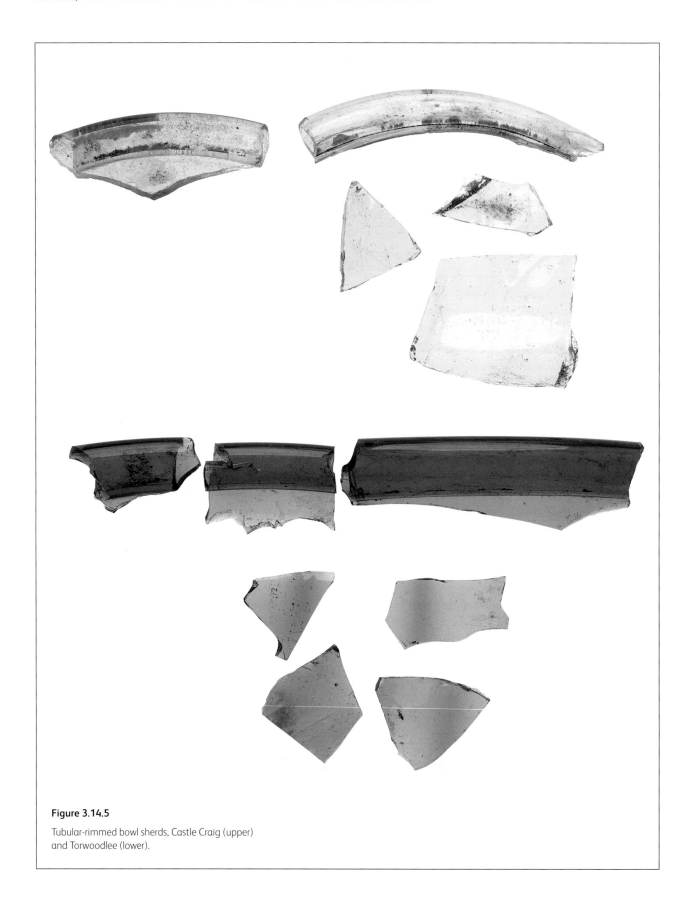

Figure 3.14.5

Tubular-rimmed bowl sherds, Castle Craig (upper)
and Torwoodlee (lower).

Plate 1

Recycling: a bangle made from purple mottled pillar-moulded bowl sherds from Traprain Law.

Plate 2

Polychrome bowl from Espe, Fyn.

National Museum, Copenhagen: NM C 1309

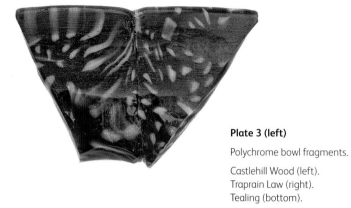

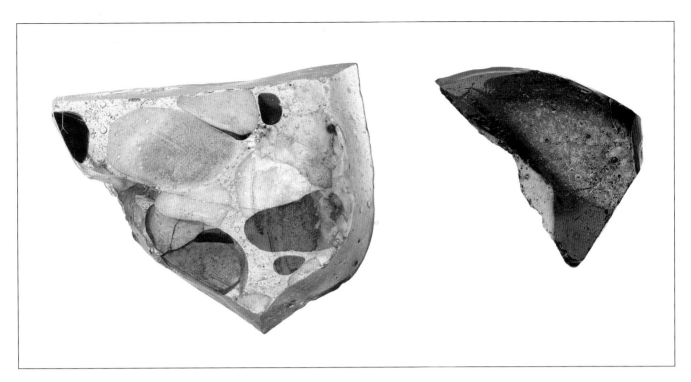

Plate 5

Sherds with marvered blobs.
Culbin Sands (left) and Leckie (right).

Plate 6

Snake-thread beaker: Himlingøje 1949 (grave 2), Zealand.

National Museum, Copenhagen: NM I C 24137 & 6-9/49

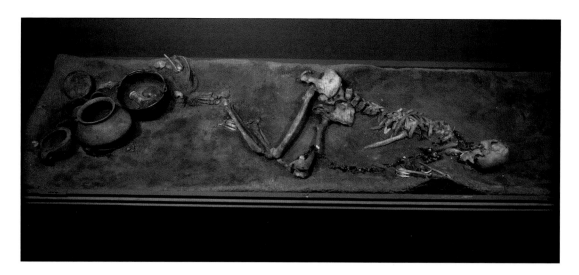

Plate 7

Himlingøje 1949, grave 2. National Museum, Copenhagen

Plate 8

Snake-thread glass sherds.
Mine Howe (left upper).
Culbin Sands (left lower).
Covesea (right).

Plate 9

Painted cylindrical cup from Nordrup, Zealand.

National Museum, Copenhagen: NM C 4614
photo: Roberto Fortuna/Kira Ursem

Plate 10

Painted cylindrical cups from Nordrup, Zealand
(top and right);
Himlingøje 1894, Zealand (left).

National Museum, Copenhagen: NM I C 7672-84
photo: L. Larsen

Plate 11

Two painted cups from a rich grave at Ellekilde, Zealand, excavated in 2007 (see Iversen 2011).

Kroppedal Museum / photo: Line Torup

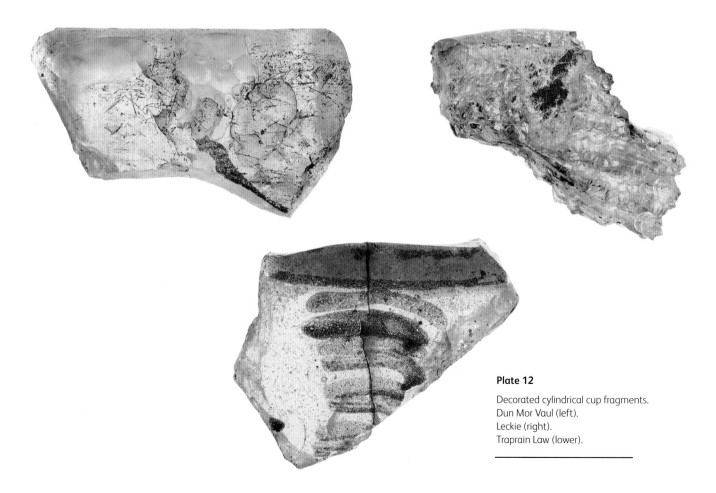

Plate 12

Decorated cylindrical cup fragments.
Dun Mor Vaul (left).
Leckie (right).
Traprain Law (lower).

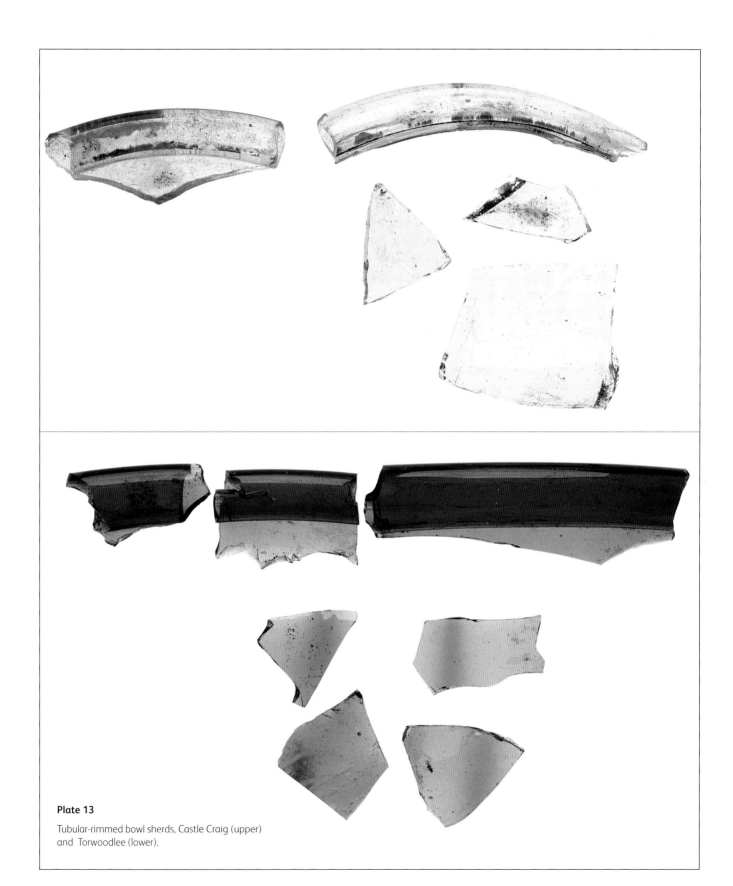

Plate 13

Tubular-rimmed bowl sherds, Castle Craig (upper)
and Torwoodlee (lower).

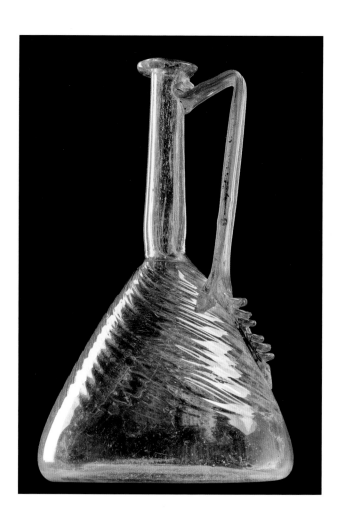

Plate 14 (above)

Globular jar in deep blue glass, Chettle.

(British Museum: 2009,8006.7)

Plate 15 (right)

Conical jug, Turriff, Aberdeenshire.

Plate 16 (above)

Base sherd from a cast vessel, Leckie.

Plate 17 (right)

Waulkmill grave group.

Finds from other areas beyond the borders of the Roman Empire

In Ulla Lund Hansen's study of Roman imports in Scandinavia one find of a bowl of Goethert-Polaschek type 22 (i.e. Isings Form 44a) is reported to have come from a grave excavated in 1977 at Himlingøje, Zealand, Denmark.[31] I do not know of any finds of tubular-rimmed bowls of Isings Forms 44b or 45 made in other areas beyond the borders of Rome.

Notes

1 See 'Tubular-rimmed bowls of late Roman type', ch. 3.15.
2 Isings 1957, 60.
3 Price & Cottam 1998a, 78.
4 Cool & Price 1995, 94–95; Price & Cottam 1998a, 78.
5 Price & Cottam 1998a, 78
6 Price 1995a, 166; Price 1996, 382.
7 Isings 1957, 60–61.
8 Price & Cottam 1998a, 77.
9 Grose 1977, 18–20.
10 Avent & Howlett 1980, 246.
11 Price 1987a, 202.
12 Price & Cottam 1998a, 78.
13 Price & Cottam 1998a, 77.
14 Grose 1977, 18–20.
15 van Lith & Randsborg 1985, 417.
16 Naumann-Steckner 1991, 87, pl. xxi a & b.
17 Welker 1985, 20–21.
18 See, for example Price 1985b, 206, fig. 77:3; Price 1990a, 172–74, fig. 162 no. 39; Price & Cottam 1997a, 341–42, 347, 349, fig. 248; Price & Cottam 2000b, fig. 66:16.
19 Cool & Price 1995, 94–95; Price & Cottam 1998a, 78–80 with references.
20 Price & Cool 1985, 43–44, fig. 17 no. 17.
21 **The Netherlands**: Nijmegen (Isings 1980, 310–15, fig. 20 & fig. 21); Stein, Limburg (Isings 1971, 20–21); Valkenburg, Zuid-Holland (van Lith 1978–79, 68–71). Hoedeng-Goegnies (deep blue with marvered opaque white spots) (Faider-Feytmans 1940, 218, pl. III:1). **Germany**: Trier (Goethert-Polaschek 1977, 35); Remagen (Funck 1912, 265, Taf. 22:8); Nida-Heddernheim (Welker 1985, 20–21); Asberg (van Lith 1984, 248–49); Kretz, Kr. Mayern (Oelmann 1938–39, 404, Abb. 36:4). **France**: Boulogne-sur-Mer (Morin-Jean 1913, fig. 180); Fréjus (Béraud & Gébara 1988, 157, fig. 7); Meuilley (Sennequier 1977, 259–60, fig. 7); Orange (Foy & Nenna 2001, 167).
22 Price 1995a, 166; Price & Cottam 1998a, 77–78 with references.
23 **Belgium**: Vervoz (Gueury & Vanderhoeven 1989, 119, fig. 4:8 to fig. 10; 120–21, fig. 5:11); **France**: Lucciana, Corsica (Foy & Nenna 2001, 137).
24 Isings 1957, 60–61. **Italy**: Cosa (Grose 1974, 39, fig. 3:10; Grose 1977, fig. 3c); the Regia, Forum Romanum, Rome (Grose 1977, 18–20, fig. 1:10 & fig. 3b); the House of Sallust, Pompeii, Italy (Grose 1977, fig. 3a).
25 Black 1891, 510.
26 See ch. 3.15.
27 Appendix A, I:3.
28 Appendix A, O:1.
29 Appendix A, S:1.
30 Appendix A, N:2.
31 Lund Hansen 1987, 110, 413.

3.15 Tubular-rimmed bowls of late Roman type

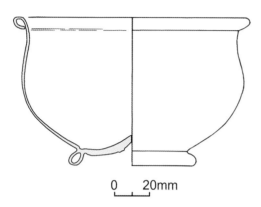

0   20mm

Figure 3.15.1

Tubular-rimmed bowl of late Roman type,
Burgh Castle, Norfolk [scale 1:2].

After Harden 1983, fig. 37:81

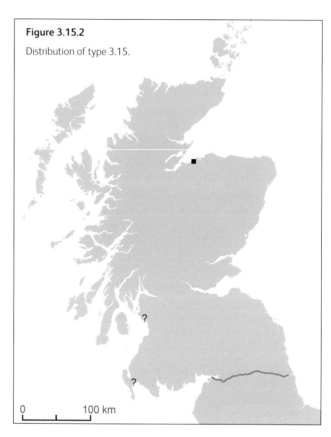

Figure 3.15.2

Distribution of type 3.15.

0   100 km

A rim fragment of a tubular-rimmed vessel was found at Ardeer, Ayrshire or Luce Sands, Wigtownshire (records are unfortunately confused). This fragment either belonged to a small bowl or to a cup with an out-splayed tubular rim in colourless glass with a green tinge. The colour and quality of the glass implies a fourth-century date for this find. Although it cannot be proven beyond doubt, it is suggested that this find either belongs to a type known as 'tubular-rimmed bowls of Burgh Castle type', or some related type of vessel.

A find from Culbin Sands, Morayshire, was reported to be of the same type as the Torwoodlee finds in a publication by G. F. Black in 1891.[1] This find was long thought to have been lost, but was rediscovered in the autumn of 2010.[2] The colour – greenish colourless – and the shape of the object suggests that this fragment is actually from a tubular-rimmed bowl of a different type than those from Torwoodlee, namely from a tubular-rimmed bowl of Burgh Castle type.

In addition to these finds there are two base fragments – one in blue-green glass (a rare colour for this type of vessel), and one in yellow-green glass – representing two bowls from Traprain Law, East Lothian. As the identification of these fragments is uncertain, I have chosen not to include them in this chapter.[3]

A general description of tubular-rimmed bowls of Burgh Castle type

Bowls – or cups, as some vessels are relatively small – of Burgh Castle type have vertical or slightly out-bent tubular rims. The edge is bent out and down. The body has a rounded, or in some cases cylindrical, shape. The base is concave, with a tubular pushed-in base ring (figs 3.15.1, 3.15.3).[4] Both plain and decorated bowls are found. The latter are of two types, either with optic-blown decoration or applied self-coloured spiral trails.[5] The rim diameters vary between c. 90 and 140 mm; the heights are c. 70–80 mm. The colours are typical of the late Roman period: greenish colourless, yellow-green, and pale green; however, finds in blue-green are also known.[6]

The date of tubular-rimmed bowls of Burgh Castle type

These bowls date to the later half of the fourth century, and it is possible that manufacture continued into the fifth century.[7] A well-known find from High Down, Sussex comes from a grave of post-Roman date.[8]

Figure 3.15.3

Tubular-rimmed bowl, Burgh Castle, Norfolk.

British Museum: 2003,0303.9

The function of the vessels

Although the rim diameter of these vessels is somewhat larger than that of other contemporary drinking vessels, the relatively small size implies that they belong to the same category of objects.

The finds from Roman contexts

There is a concentration of finds of this type in southern England,[9] which may reflect the area of production. Single finds of related types have been made on the Continent.[10] There is, as argued by Cool, much to suggest that a large part of the fourth-century glass found in Britain was of local manufacture.[11]

The finds from non-Roman contexts in Scotland and north Northumberland

The find from Ardeer or Luce Sands comes from one of these sand dune sites, but museum records are unfortunately confused over this specific collection. Apart from some Roman blue-green bottle glass, including a cylindrical bottle, the glass from this specific collection is of late Roman or post-Roman date. In addition to the tubular-rimmed cup/bowl, a fragment of post-Roman window glass and a sherd of an engraved eastern Mediterranean vessel were discovered.[12] The find differs somewhat from a typical Burgh Castle bowl as it is of smaller size, and probably functioned as a drinking vessel. The general shape, the colour and quality of the glass, however, are of the same type (fig. 3.15.4.1). It is of mid- to late fourth-century AD date.

Culbin Sands, Morayshire, is an area with sand dunes where many casual finds have been made over the years, and the exact find spot of these items is unknown.[13] They appear, however, to have come from the Reverend John MacEwan's collections, which were sold to the Marischal Museum in 1919. The base of the Culbin Sands find is probably a tubular-rimmed bowl of Burgh Castle type, as it has a diagonal tubular pushed-in base ring. It is of mid- to late fourth-century AD date.

?Ardeer, Ayrshire or ?Luce Sands, Wigtownshire. P:1 or Q:1

Unreg*., NMS. Rim fragment. Poor quality colourless glass with a slight green tinge. RD c. 80–85; PH 17; W 34; WT 1.3.

Culbin Sands, Morayshire. F:2

15790*, Marischal Museum, University of Aberdeen. Tubular pushed-in base ring from a domed base. Greenish colourless glass. BD c. 90. W 34; H c. 10; WT 1.1.

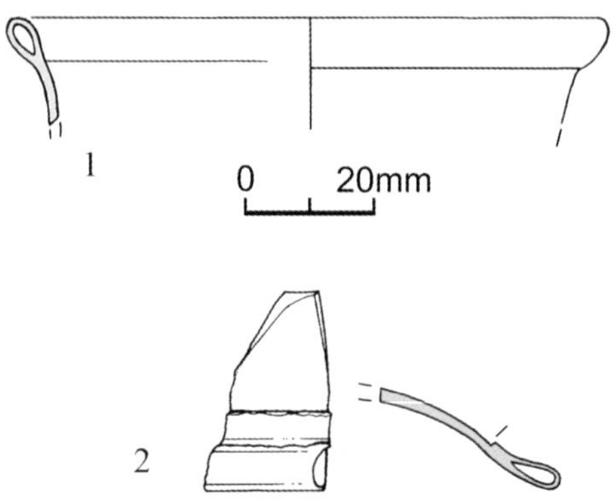

Figure 3.15.4

Late Roman tubular-rimmed bowl sherds [scale 2:3].

(1) Ardeer or Luce Sands

NMS

(2) Culbin Sands

Aberdeen University Museum: 15790

Finds from other areas beyond the borders of the Roman Empire

To my knowledge no other finds of this type have been made beyond the borders of the Roman Empire.

Notes

1. Black 1891, 510.
2. I would like to thank Trevor Cowie, Curator at the National Museum of Scotland, who made this rediscovery.
3. See ch. 3.25 under 'Miscellaneous bases – cups, beakers, bowls and jugs'.
4. Cool & Price 1995, 95; Price & Cottam 1998a, 131.
5. Harden 1983, 81–82, fig. 37 (plain, Burgh Castle, Norfolk); Price & Cottam 1998a, 131–32, fig. 55 (optic-blown decoration, Burgh Castle, Norfolk); Price 1993a, 214, fig. 158:25 (applied spiral thread, Uley, Gloucestershire).
6. Price & Cottam 1998a, 131–32.
7. Cool 1995b, 13; Price & Cottam 1998a, 132.
8. White 1988, 130.
9. Price & Cottam 1998a, 131–33 with references.
10. **Belgium**: Spontin, Namur (Dasnoy 1966, 229); **Germany**: Trier (Goethert-Polaschek 1977, 35).
11. Cool 1995b, 14; Cool 2003, 141–42.
12. Appendix A, P:1.
13. Appendix A, F:2.

3.16 Jars with globular bodies and collared rims

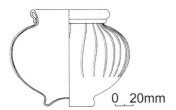

Figure 3.16.1

Globular jar, Verulamium (St Albans),
Hertfordshire [scale 1:4].

After Charlesworth 1972, fig. 76:26

Globular jars of Isings Form 67c – or 'Convex jars with collared rims', as they are termed by Price and Cottam – are a common type in Romano-British contexts.[1] Although they have very characteristic features, identification of fragmentary material is rendered difficult by the fact that they share these with other types of vessels. The bodies and bases of jars of Isings Form 67c are similar to those of jugs of Isings Form 52.[2] To complicate matters further, the rims of Isings Form 67c resemble those of square jars of Isings Form 62.[3] The latter is normally a sturdier vessel manufactured in thicker glass,[4] and is treated separately in chapter 3.17.

A general description of the type

Globular jars have vertical or slightly out-bent rims. The edge was bent out and down, forming a 'tube' of ovular shape (figs 3.16.1, 3.16.3). In many cases the edge was rolled in before it was bent, which gave a double fold forming two horizontal ridges (the 'collared' rim). These vessels lack neck and shoulder; instead the body expands out below the collared rim.[5] The body is of globular shape and decorated with optic-blown or tooled ribs, which either run vertically or slightly diagonally. The bases are concave with open pushed-in base rings. Rim diameters vary from c. 80–130 mm, heights c. 120–180 mm.[6] The shape of the vessel resembles an enlarged poppy-seed capsule, and is also found in contemporary pottery.[7]

Although most were manufactured in common blue-green glass, a wide range of other colours were used up until the Flavian period: deep blue, yellow-brown and yellow-green. After this period they were produced in blue-green and other shades of naturally coloured green. Occasional finds of polychrome vessels with marvered opaque white spots have been made.[8] In most cases a strong colour was combined with white spots, although there is a rare example of a blue-green jar with white spots from Colchester, Essex.[9] A generally held – and in all probability correct – view is that these vessels were manufactured in the areas in which they have been found, i.e. the north-western provinces.

Dating the type

Jars of Isings Form 67c date from the mid- to late first century to the early to mid-second century. The earliest find known to myself is a polychrome jar from a pre-Boudican context in Colchester, Essex, dating to AD 49/55–60/61.[10] There is another early find from Verulamium (St Albans), in Hertfordshire, which dates to c. AD 60–75.[11] The bulk of the material, however, both in Britain and on the Continent dates from the Flavian to the Trajanic/Hadrianic period (i.e. the last third of the first to the first third of the second century AD).[12]

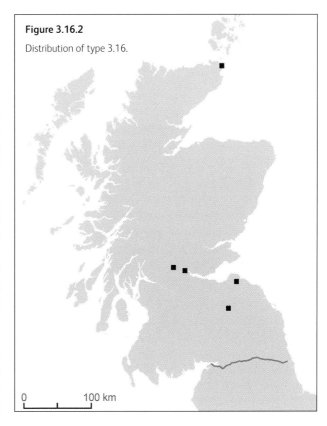

Figure 3.16.2

Distribution of type 3.16.

The function of the vessels

Not much is known about the function of decorated globular jars with collared rims (Isings Form 67c), but they are often – and in my view rightfully – regarded as some form of tableware.[13] Price has put forward the idea that they were employed for presenting and serving liquids and fruit.[14] In my view, this type of vessel appears inherently impractical for this kind of use. On the basis of the iconographical record we know that fresh fruit was normally presented in open vessels such as bowls, and that a liquid such as wine was sometimes served from bottles.[15]

Two closely related vessel types may give an indication of their function, namely plain jars with flat rims of Isings Form 67a and plain jars with collared rims of Isings Form 67b. As argued by Gabriele Harter – on the basis of two pas-sages in Apicius' *De re coquinaria* (an ancient collection of recipes) – jars of Isings Form 67a were used for storing pickled fruit in, as well as spices.[16] On the Continent, plain globular jars of Isings Form 67b have been discovered with a lid,[17] which suggests that some foodstuff was stored in such vessels.

It could be suggested that similar types of foodstuffs were served in decorated globular glass jars (Isings Form 67c). Pickled and preserved fruits and vegetables appear to have been an important part of Roman cuisine, demonstrated by numerous passages in the Roman agricultural writers Cato the Elder, Varro, Columella and Palladius, and the encyclopaedia author Pliny the Elder.[18] It is also possible that semi-liquids such as honey and *defrutum* were served in the vessels, perhaps in combination with a spoon, though *defrutum* was relatively rare in Roman Britain.[19]

The finds from Roman contexts

Globular jars of Isings Form 67c are frequent finds in Romano-British contexts.[20] One has to bear in mind, however, that these are very visible and easily identifiable in the glass assemblages, first because of the characteristic ribbed design, and second as a result of many vessels being manufactured in strong colours (pl. 14). Finds of this type are also common on the Continent, predominantly in the north-western and western provinces.[21]

Figure 3.16.3

Globular jar in deep blue glass, Chettle.

British Museum: 2009,8006.7

The finds in non-Roman contexts in Scotland and north Northumberland

Jars constitute a relatively small category of Roman glass vessels discovered on indigenous sites north of Hadrian's Wall. A minimum of four vessels have been unearthed on three sites: Everley, Caithness; Traprain Law, East Lothian; and Torwoodlee, Selkirkshire. There is also a minute sherd from Leckie, Stirlingshire, which either comes from a globular jar, a globular jug or a conical jug. In addition to the finds included in the catalogue, there is a recent find from Easter Moss, Cowie/Cowiehall Quarry, Stirlingshire: two body sherds in light yellow-brown glass.[22]

It is noteworthy that three of these five or six vessels were in strong colours, whereas the majority of such finds on Roman sites in northern Britain are in blue-green glass.

Everley, Caithness – a broch – has yielded a small assemblage of Roman imports. These include a single rim fragment of a yellow-brown jar and a few sherds of Roman pottery.[23] Strong colours were rarely used for plain ovoid jars, suggesting that this find represents a globular jar (Isings Form 67c) (fig. 3.16.4.1). This colour indicates an early date of manufacture – Neronian or early Flavian. Single finds of this type have been made in northern Britain, and we cannot demonstrate that it pre-dates the Agricolan invasion.

Excavations at Traprain Law, East Lothian have yielded two fragments, representing a minimum of two jars. One is in pale natural green, the other in common blue-green glass. A first to second-century AD date is suggested for these finds.

Torwoodlee, Selkirkshire – a hillfort and a later broch – yielded a relatively rich assemblage of Roman imports. These finds include: four sherds from a globular jar with tooled vertical ribs in blue-green, poor quality glass of early to mid-second-century date (fig. 3.16.4.2); amphorae; a *mortarium*, and samian.[24]

Leckie, Stirlingshire – a timber-built roundhouse later replaced by a broch – yielded a rich and varied assemblage of Roman goods.[25] A minute body fragment of a deep blue vessel with optic-blown decoration was discovered at the site. Due to its small size the exact type of the vessel could not be established; it comes from either a globular jar (Isings Form 67c), a globular jug (Isings Form 52b), or a conical jug (Isings Form 55). The strong colour indicates a Neronian to early Flavian date. It is notable that a substantial part of the Roman vessel glass unearthed on this site was manufactured in the Neronian to early Flavian period, and in one case even earlier. These types are, however, represented on Roman sites in northern Britain of Flavian date, and thus one cannot presuppose a Roman–native exchange before the Agricolan invasion in AD 79 to 83.

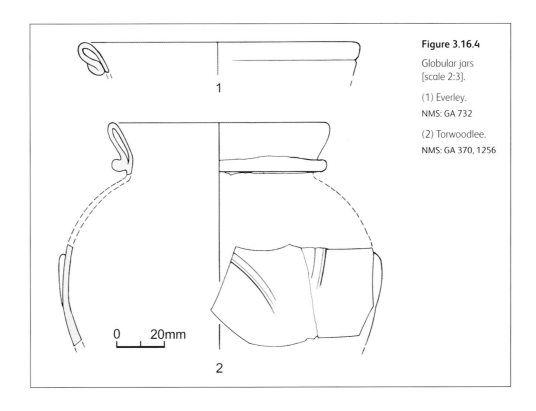

Figure 3.16.4

Globular jars [scale 2:3].

(1) Everley. NMS: GA 732

(2) Torwoodlee. NMS: GA 370, 1256

Everley, Caithness. D:2

GA 732*, NMS. Rim fragment of a globular jar. Vertical double tubular rim, edge first rolled in, then bent out and down. Yellow-brown. RD 90; PH 14; WT 2.0.

Leckie, Stirlingshire. K:4

A 1980 338, Hunterian Museum. Body fragment. Remains of a raised rib. Deep blue. Dims 8 x 14; WT 2.0.

Torwoodlee, Selkirkshire. S:1

Four fragments from one globular jar, with vertical ribs:

Unregistered (no 8), NMS. Two joining fragments of lower body and base. Convex-curved side. Two tooled vertical ribs. Blue-green. Extremely bubbly; brown/red spots. PH c. 35; W 72; WT 4.2 (base), 2.1 (body).

GA 370* (no. 53), NMS. Rim fragment. Out-bent rim, edge first bent to form a roll, then bent out and in. Blue-green. Very bubbly; brown/red spots. RD 90; PH 20; WT 2.2.

GA 1256*, NMS. Body fragment. Convex-curved side. Remains of tooled rib. Blue-green. Extremely bubbly. Dims 20 x 21; WT 3.6.

Traprain Law, East Lothian. N:2

GV 374 (III 20 97), Area H, Level 2, NMS. Rim fragment. Out-turned rim; bent out, down and in. Pale natural green. Bubbly glass. RD 105; W 41; WT 3.

GV 1797, Area Q, Level 2, NMS. Rim fragment. Vertical tubular rim, edge rolled in, bent out and down. Blue-green. RD c. 65. PH 11; Thickness of the rim 5.8; WT not possible to establish.

Finds from other areas beyond the borders of the Roman Empire

There is one find of a related type – an ovoid, plain jar of Isings Form 67b, in deep blue glass – from Borre Mark, Viborg Amt, Jutland, Denmark. It was registered at the local museum in Viborg in 1885, but little else is known about this find.[26] Two finds of globular, ribbed jars of Isings Form 67c are known from Free Germany. A fragmentary find in green glass comes from a funerary context in Veltheim, Kreis Minden-Lübbecke, Nordrhein-Westfalen, Germany.[27] The identification of the second find – a single sherd – is less certain. This comes from Sieker, Stadt Bielefeld, Nordrhein-Westfalen, in Germany.[28]

Notes

1 Price & Cottam 1998a, 137–38.
2 Isings 1957, 69–70.
3 Isings 1957, 81, 88.
4 Price & Cottam 1998a, 135–36.
5 Price & Cottam 1998a, 137–38.
6 Follmann-Schulz 1992, 27–31; Cool & Price 1995, 106.
7 See, for example Liversidge 1977, 16, pl. 3; Cüppers et al 1983, 94.
8 Cool & Price 1995, 106; Price & Cottam 1998a, 137.
9 Cool & Price 1995, 106.
10 Cool & Price 1995, 107.
11 Charlesworth 1972a, 204.
12 Price & Cottam 1998a, 137; Welker 1974, 39.
13 See, for example Harter 1999, 35.
14 Price 1995a, 170.
15 Bowls, see for instance: Naumann-Steckner 1991, pls 20a; 21.a; 24b. Bottles, see for example: Holwerda 1931, afb. 20–21; Ceselin 1998, fig. 11; Cool 2006, 136–38.
16 Harter 1999, 34; Apicius, *De re coquinaria*, 1.12.6; 1.10.
17 Harter 1999, Abb. 1.
18 See, for instance, [fruit preserves]: Cato the Elder, *De agricultura*, 7.2; 7.4; Varro, *De re rustica*, 1.58; Columella, *De re rustica*, 12.10.4; Palladius, *Opus agriculturae*, 3.25.8–10; [pickled fruits]: Palladius, *Opus agriculturae*, 12.7.8; [pickled vegetables]: Pliny the Elder, *Historia Naturalis*, 19.24; 19.43.
19 Cool 2006, 67–68.
20 Cool & Price 1995, 106–9; Price & Cottam 1998a, 137–38.
21 **The Netherlands:** Valkenburg, Zuid-Holland (van Lith 1978–79, 94–97, Abb. 46; **Germany:** Köln (Cologne) (Fremersdorf 1958b, 25, Taf. 16; 48, Taf. 106); Kretz (Oelmann 1938–39, 401–4, Abb. 35 & 36, Taf. 1; Follmann-Schulz 1992, 30–31, Taf. 15); Gutenberg (Behrens 1925, 20, Abb. 4); Wiesoppenheim; Mainz-Kastel; Worms (Behrens 1925–26, 67, Abb. 9:3); Trier (Goethert-Polaschek 1977, 237–40). **France:** Normandy (Sennequier 1994, fig. 3); Meuilly (Sennequier 1977, 255, figs. 1 & 2); Poitiers (Simon-Hiernard 2000, 87–91); Aoste (Foy & Nenna 2001, 142–43); Montmerle (Foy & Nenna 2001, 204). **Luxemburg:** Wilhelm 1979, 19, 61.
22 Pers. comm. Dr Hilary Cool.
23 Appendix A, D:2.
24 Appendix A, S:1.
25 Appendix A, K:4.
26 Lund Hansen 1987, 92, 398, 405–6, fig. 33.
27 Eggers 1951, 179; *CRFB* D7, X-06-7/10.7, Taf. 25:6 (erroneously quoted as an example of a glass vessel of Eggers type 209).
28 *CRFB* D7, X-01-1/23.6.

3.17 Square jar

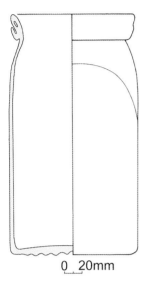

Figure 3.17.1

Square jar, Cirencester, Gloucestershire [scale 1:4].

After Price & Cottam 1998a, fig. 57

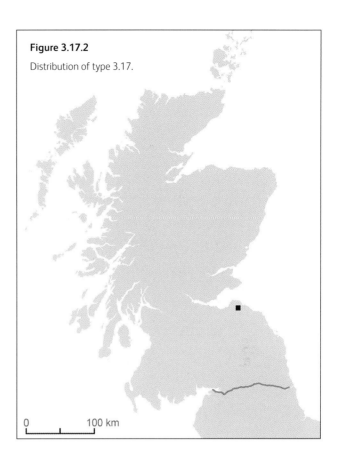

Square jars of Isings Form 62 are regarded as a relatively rare category of finds in Romano-British contexts.[1] This may, however, be a result of the difficulty in identifying fragmented material. The rims of square jars are similar to those of globular jars of Isings Form 67b and 67c, but the former were only manufactured in blue-green or other shades of green, and, more importantly, in thicker glass.[2] To complicate things further they have bodies and bases which are identical to those of square, i.e. prismatic, bottles of Isings Form 50, a very common category of finds in both Roman Britain and in non-Roman contexts in Scotland and north Northumberland.[3]

A general description of the type

Square jars have vertical or slightly out-bent collared rims. The edge was bent out and down. In many cases the edge was rolled in before it was bent, which gave a double fold/two horizontal ridges. The same type of rim is found on globular jars of Isings Form 67c,[4] but the rims of square jars are mostly in somewhat thicker glass than those of globular jars of Isings Form 67c.[5] The neck is wide and short; the shoulder expands out to the body (fig. 3.17.1).

The body could either be free blown, with the sides flattened on a marver (these sometimes have pontil marks on the base), or they were blown in moulds of the same type as those for square bottles. As was the case with square bottles, these bases were decorated with different raised designs.[6] Some of these were purely functional, such as concentric circles, others were maker's marks. Rim diameters vary from *c.* 50 to 120 mm and heights from *c.* 100 to 260 mm. The only colour used was common blue-green.[7] The simple manufacture of these jars makes it probable that they were made on many sites in the north-western provinces, quite possibly including Romano-British glass working sites.[8]

Dating the type

Due to the difficulty in identifying square jars in military and civilian settlements, and their scarcity in funerary contexts, it is very hard to give a date range for these objects.[9] The earliest British finds date to around AD 65 to 75,[10] and it seems that they became common from this period onwards on the Continent.[11] For example, frequent finds have been made in Pompeii and in Herculaneum.[12] On the basis of a number of grave-finds from the Continent, it has been suggested that the manufacture of square jars continued up to the late second and probably into the early or mid-third century AD.[13] For example, a jar of this type was found in a cremation grave in Poitiers, Vienne, France, dated by a coin of Septimius Severus (AD 193–211).[14]

The function of the vessels

The design of square jars is purely functional, and they must have been used for storing and transporting foodstuffs. The relatively wide mouth implies that they could be used for preserving food in, such as fruits and vegetables. This was probably also the case with the plain, blue-green ovoid jars. An often-quoted passage in Columella's *On agriculture*, written *c.* AD 60–65, concerns the usage of glass storage vessels:

> Vessels should be either of earthen-ware or glass and should be numerous rather than large, and some of them should be properly treated with pitch but some in their natural state as the condition of the material demands. Great care ought to be taken in the making of these vessels that they have a wide mouth and that they are of the same width right down to the bottom and not shaped like wine-jars, so that, when the preserved food is removed for use, what remains may be pressed with equal weight to the bottom, since the food is kept fresh when it does not float on the surface but is always covered by liquid. This can scarcely happen in the globular shape of a wine-jar, because of the irregularity of its form.

Columella, *De re rustica*, 12.4.4–5

In the text Columella uses the word *vasa*, which denotes a wide range of vessels ranging from plates and bowls to bottles.[15] Yet, he specifies that they '… have a wide mouth and that they are of the same width right down to the bottom … .' It remains unclear if he speaks of jars or wide-mouthed bottles; possibly the distinction between the two forms is a modern concept. Jars in common blue-green glass must primarily have been intended for storing foodstuffs, which is supported by finds from Pompeii.[16]

The primary function of the square jars must have been storage of foodstuffs, but as with other types of jars they also had a secondary function as ash-urns. Finds of this type have been made in Roman Britain, as well as on the Continent.[17]

The finds from Roman contexts

Finds of square jars have been made in a limited number of funerary contexts in Roman Britain. In Lincoln, Lincolnshire a jar containing a *stylus* was found in an inhumation burial.[18] In a grave unearthed in Mancetter, Warwickshire, a square jar served as a cinerary urn for a cremation.[19] And yet another cremation grave with a square jar was discovered in Cirencester, Gloucestershire (fig. 3.17.1).[20] In reports on the fragmented glass assemblages from settlements and forts in Roman Britain, one rarely finds references to square jars, though these have (for example) been reported from Fishbourne, Sussex,[21] Richborough, Kent,[22] and Usk, Gwent.[23] Either the few finds reflects their relative scarcity,[24] or they were more frequent but have not been recognised, the fragments being identified as the rims of collared ovoid/globular jars or as body and base sherds of square bottles.

Due to the difficulties in identifying fragmented material, little is known of how frequent these finds were on settlement sites in other parts of the Roman Empire. As may have been the case in Roman Britain, it seems likely that many fragments of square jars have been mistaken for other types. The majority of positively identified finds come from burial contexts, sometimes deposited as grave-gifts, sometimes functioning as grave-urns. Square jars were widely distributed in the Roman world, and have been found in the north-western provinces, in Switzerland and Italy, as well as the eastern provinces.[25]

The finds from non-Roman contexts in Scotland and north Northumberland

Only one single find has been tentatively identified as a square jar: a fragment of a collared rim in thick blue-green glass (fig. 3.17.3). This comes from Traprain Law, East Lothian, a native site which is exceptionally rich in Roman imports.[26] Close contacts with Romans upheld by the inhabitants of this site is reflected not only in a wealth of imported items, but also in the wide variety of these.

Traprain Law, East Lothian. N:2

GV 175:5* (XII 15 140), Area Fb, Level 1a, NMS. Rim fragment. Out-bent rim, bent out, down, in and up. Blue-green. RD 90; PH 22; W 37; WT 4.0.

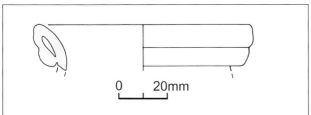

Figure 3.17.3

Rim sherd, probably from a square jar, Traprain Law [scale 2:3].
NMS: GV 175.5

Finds from other areas beyond the borders of the Roman Empire

To my knowledge no finds of square jars of Isings Form 62 have been made outside of the Roman Empire, besides the possible find from Traprain Law.

Notes

1 Price & Cottam 1998a, 135–36.
2 Price & Cottam 1998a, 135.
3 Isings 1957, 63–67. See 'Cylindrical and prismatic bottles', ch. 3.23.
4 Isings 1957, 81.
5 Price & Cottam 1998a, 135.
6 See, for example Foy & Nenna 2001, 82–83.
7 Cool & Price 1995, 185; Price & Cottam 1998a, 135–36.
8 One such Romano-British production site could have been Mancetter, Warwickshire. Among the glass-working debris from this site is a rim that could have come from a square jar (Price & Cool 1991, fig. 2.9). I would like to thank Dr Hilary Cool for making me aware of this find.
9 Price & Cottam 1998a, 135.
10 Price & Cottam 1998a, 136.
11 Isings 1971, 39.
12 Scatozza Höricht 1986, 68.
13 Isings 1971, 39–40; Isings 1980, 288.
14 Simon-Hiernard 2000, 93.
15 'Vas' in Lewis & Short 1962 (1879).
16 van Lith & Randsborg 1985, 424.
17 Behrens 1925–26, 67.
18 Carter 1796, 108, pl. XIII, no. 1.
19 Booth 1982, 134, fig. 2.
20 Lysons 1792, 131, p. IX, fig. 1.
21 Harden & Price 1971, 356.
22 Bushe-Fox 1949, 159, pl. LXIX, no. 377.
23 Price 1995a, 184.
24 Price & Cottam 1998a, 135.
25 **The Netherlands:** possible finds from Nijmegen (Isings 1980, 288, 319, fig. 26); Stein, Houterend (Isings 1971, 39–40, fig. 10:126). **Germany:** Hofheim (Ritterling 1913, 376); Laurenzberg (Follmann & Piepers 1963, 541, Abb. 28:6); Trier; Mainz (Behrens 1925–26, 67, Abb. 8:1); Köln (Cologne) (Fremersdorf 1958b, Taf. 122). **France:** Marseilles (Foy & Nenna 2001, 83); Aoste, Rhone-Alpes (Foy & Nenna 2001, 221); d'Épiais-Rhus, Val d'Oise (Vanpeene 1993, 28); Normandy (Sennequier 1994, fig. 3); Besançon (Koltes 1982, 37–39, pl. 15–18). **Switzerland:** Muralto, Tessin (Ticino) (Simonett 1941, Abb. 142:8). **Italy:** Bologna (Meconcelli-Notarianni 1979, 88–89); Herculaneum, Pompeii and other sites in the Bay of Naples area (Scatozza Höricht 1986, 68, tav. xvi & xxxviii; Ziviello 1998, 67). **Croatia:** Starigrad (Abramić & Colnago :1909, 75–77); Montenegro (Cermanovi-Kuzmanović 1974, Taf. 1:16). **Hungary:** Intercisa (Barkóczi 1988, 155). **Greece:** Corinth (Isings 1957, 81).
26 Appendix A, N:2.

3.18 Jugs or flagons with globular or conical bodies

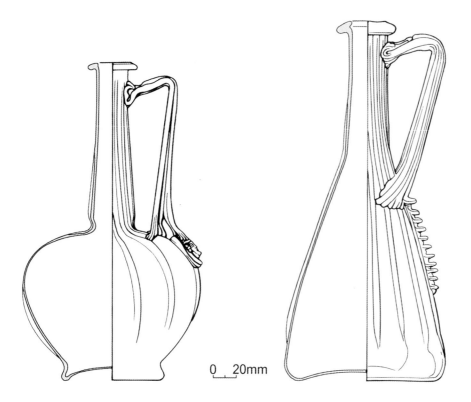

Figure 3.18.1

Left, globular jug, Köln (Cologne), Germany.
After Harden et al. 1988, 119

Right, conical jug, Radnage, Buckinghamshire.
After Harden et al. 1988, 140

[scale 1:3]

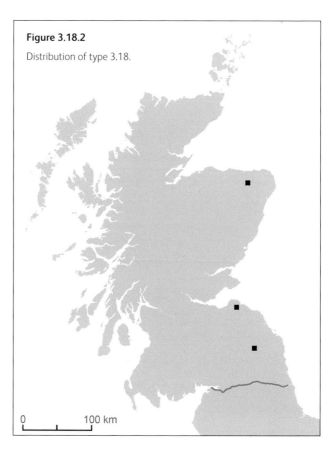

Figure 3.18.2

Distribution of type 3.18.

Globular jugs of Isings Form 52 and conical jugs of Isings Form 55 have similar or identical rims, necks and handles.[1] These parts of the vessels are relatively thick, and thus are preserved to a greater extent than the body sherds.[2] On many military and civilian sites the fragmented state of the vessels sometimes renders it impossible to tell which of the types were present. For this reason I have chosen to discuss the two types together.

The general description of the types is primarily based on intact vessels found in funerary contexts. Parts of the bodies of the globular jugs are identical to those of globular ribbed jars of Isings Form 67c, and those of the rare flasks of Isings Form 71.[3] However, in Scottish contexts body sherds of this type have been found together with rim fragments showing that they originated from jars. Therefore the latter are discussed separately.[4]

A general description of the types

Globular jugs

Globular jugs have rims that are horizontal or diagonal, edges bent out, up, in and flattened. Most finds of this type have long, slender cylindrical necks. However, examples with short necks are known, albeit less common. The neck is somewhat wider at its lower part, and often constricted just above the shoulder of the jug. Sometimes the optic-blown decoration extends up to the lower part of the neck.

The handles are angular; in most cases a single ribbon with a central rib, or reeded, i.e. with several narrow ridges. The handle joins the underside of the rim or the upper neck with a folding, and the lower part of the handle is attached to the body. Either the ribs are drawn down into small prongs, or – less commonly – it terminates in a 'claw' with three prongs. In some cases the middle 'claw' continues in a vertical trail with pinched projections or 'teeth'.[5] In some cases a medallion in the shape of a so-called Medusa or a Bacchus mask was attached to the lower end of the handle (fig. 3.18.1, left). In Britain these are often called Medusa medallions, but as pointed out by Cool and Price it is more likely that these depict Bacchus or Silenus.[6] Many of these medallions have been reused when the vessel was broken.[7] The bodies are either spherical, as one from Baldock, Hertfordshire,[8] or discoid like a jug from Lincoln Road, Enfield, London.[9] They were decorated with diagonal or vertical ribs, accomplished by either optic-blowing, tooling or trailing. Globular jugs have open or closed pushed-in base rings, with concave bases.[10]

With few exceptions globular jugs were produced in monochrome glass, and it has been argued that these were manufactured in north-western provinces. However, a handful of polychrome jugs with marvered opaque white spots have been found, for example in the annexe ditch of the Flavian fort at Carlisle, Cumbria,[11] and at Muralto, Tessin, Switzerland.[12] The colours used are of chronological significance, and can sometimes be employed to date the finds. Many of the early finds were made in the strong colours which fell out of use in the Flavian period; colours such as deep blue, dark yellow-brown, and claret red. Colours like blue-green, pale green and light yellow-brown continued to the second century.[13] There is surprisingly little variation in the size of these vessels. The rim diameters are c. 30–40 mm; heights c. 250–300 mm.[14]

Conical jugs

The rims of conical jugs are identical to those of globular jugs: horizontal or diagonal, edges bent out, up, in and flattened. Most finds of conical jugs have long, slender cylindrical necks. However, examples with short necks are known too, such as a find from Tessin, Switzerland.[15] The neck is somewhat wider at its lower part, and often constricted just above the shoulder of the jug.[16]

The handles are angular, and are attached either just below the rim or halfway up the neck. The lower attachment is on the body, and is shaped like a 'claw' with three tooled prongs. In most cases the central prong is longer, and has tooled 'teeth'. This can be seen on a well-known find from Radnage, Buckinghamshire (fig. 3.18.1, right).[17] Less frequently the central trail is without 'teeth', as for example on a find from Barnwell in Cambridgeshire.[18] Finds of conical jugs with two handles are known. One of these rare finds was made in Bayford, Kent.[19] Like the globular jugs, the conical jugs are sometimes decorated with applied medallions.[20] In most cases these were applied where the lower part of the handle terminates. Very rarely, these medallions were placed elsewhere on the body. An example of this comes from Bex Hill, Milton-next-Sittingbourne, Kent.[21]

There is considerable variation in the body shapes of conical jugs, from a true conical shape to pyriform. An example of the former is the find from Radnage, Buckinghamshire.[22] Examples of the latter sub-type have been found at Church Field, Northill, Bedfordshire,[23] and Bartlow Hills, Ashdon, Essex.[24] The shape of the base also varies. It is either plain with a convex base (Isings Form 55a), as on an example from Giesenkirchen, Rheyt, Germany;[25] or it has an open pushed-in base ring (Isings Form 55b), as one from Huntingdon, Surrey.[26] This find also has an unusual cut-out flange around the lower body.

Like the globular jugs, there are both plain and ribbed conical jugs. Plain jugs have been found on several sites, e.g. Kröv, Bernkastel-Wittlich, Germany;[27] Gors-Opleeuw, Belgium;[28] and Castleford, West Yorkshire.[29] The ribbed jugs have diagonal or vertical ribs which were optic-blown or tooled. A very rare specimen from Grange Road, Winchester, Hampshire, has a ribbed design commonly known as nipt' diamonds.[30]

The majority of conical jugs were produced in monochrome glass. However, a handful of polychrome jugs with marvered-flush opaque white spots or 'pebbles' have been found. An example of the former was discovered at Locarno, Tessin, Switzerland.[31] Many of the early finds were made in strong colours which fell out of use in the Flavian period; colours such as deep blue, dark yellow-brown, and claret red. Thus the colour can be used to date some finds. Colours like blue-green, pale green, and light yellow-brown continue to the second century.[32] The same range of colours was utilised for globular jugs. The sizes of the conical jugs fall within same range as that of globular jugs, i.e. rims are c. 30–40 mm, and the heights c. 250–300 mm.[33]

Dating the types

Globular jugs

The earliest finds of globular jugs are of the plain, undecorated type, and were found in Tiberian contexts at Vindonissa, Switzerland.[34] In Britain the earliest finds, also of the plain type, have been made at the Lunt, Baginton, Warwickshire, dating to the Claudian-Neronian period,[35] and Fishbourne, Sussex, dating to c. AD 55–75.[36] It is unclear when the production of globular jugs ceased; however, they continued at least to the first quarter of the second century AD.[37]

Conical jugs

There is some evidence to imply that conical jugs were in production and use during a longer time span than globular jugs.[38] The earliest dated conical jugs are of Claudian date, and were found in Hofheim, Germany.[39] As is the case with the globular jugs, the earliest finds of conical jugs are plain. From Britain finds from Neronian contexts have been made at the Lunt, Baginton, Warwickshire,[40] and Kingsholm, Gloucestershire.[41] The latest finds date from c. AD 150–170, and have been made in rubbish pits in Park Street, Towcester, Northamptonshire; Felmongers, Harlow, Essex; and Alcester, Warwickshire.[42] The majority of vessels were produced between AD 65 and 125.[43]

The function of the vessels

There is much to suggest that conical – and in all probability also globular – jugs formed parts of drinking sets. Cool has convincingly argued this based on a find from a funerary context at Grange Road, Winchester, Hampshire.[44] Besides the conical jug, the drinking set included eight samian cups (two small and six somewhat larger vessels). Among the many funerary gifts were also a bronze jug and one in coarse-ware pottery, vessels which may have formed part of this drinking set, perhaps to pour hot or cold water from.[45]

The finds from Roman contexts

Globular and conical jugs

As has been stressed several times already, fragmentary material of these two related jug types is difficult to differentiate, and they are treated together. They are the commonest form of jugs found on Romano-British sites of the later first and early second century AD in all parts of Roman Britain, from the civilian south to the militarized north.[46] Their frequency is reflected in the glass assemblage from the Colchester 1971–85 excavations: 139 fragments representing a minimum of 52 vessels.[47]

These two types have predominantly been found in the north-western provinces, and finds are particularly prolific in the areas around the Rhine.[48] They were predominantly manufactured in monochrome glass, either in strong colours such as yellow-green (olive), yellow-brown (amber), and deep blue, or in common blue-green glass. Occasional finds are bichrome in deep colours – deep blue being the most frequent colour –with marvered spots in contrasting opaque white. In addition, there is a group of globular and conical jugs in bichrome or polychrome glass in strong colours with marvered spots in opaque white, red or yellow. These finds come from an area outwith the north-western provinces: Austria, Switzerland, northern Italy and the northern Adriatic region.[49]

The finds from non-Roman contexts in Scotland and north Northumberland

An intact conical jug was accidentally discovered after construction of a railway between Turriff and Banff in Aberdeenshire in the mid-nineteenth century. Unfortunately, very little is known about the circumstances of this find. Although no ashes or bones were reported to have been found, the intact state of the vessel suggests that it came from a burial. A number of beads, now lost, unearthed on the same site support this view.[50]

Burials, particularly those including imported Roman grave-goods, are exceedingly rare in a native context. If the identification of this find as an indigenous burial of Roman Iron Age date is correct, it is unique in that a jug rather than a cup or beaker was deposited.

The Turriff find, a tall conical jug in pale green glass with optic-blown decoration, was of late first- or early to mid-second-century AD date (fig. 3.18.3; pl. 15).

At Traprain Law, East Lothian, no less than seven fragments from a minimum of seven jugs have been unearthed to date. One find was in deep blue (fig. 3.18.4.2), the others in various shades of green. In at least two cases they come from conical jugs; the identification of the remainder is less certain. In the case of the fragment of a deep blue conical jug, the colour suggests an early date for manufacture: Neronian or early Flavian. When it reached native hands is not clear, but there is an example of this type and colour from the Flavian site of Strageath in Perthshire.[51] The remaining finds from Traprain Law are difficult to date more exactly than between AD 65 and AD 170. A wide range of Roman glass has been found on this site, including cups, beakers and bottles that are more or less contemporary with these jugs. It is possible that these might once have formed imported Roman drinking sets, as discussed below.

Crock Cleuch, Roxburghshire, consisted of two closely adjacent and probably contemporary settlements with roundhouses. The only Roman import discovered on the site is a fragment of a brown conical jug (fig. 3.18.4.1).[52] This find was manufactured in the Neronian to the early Flavian period, and as with the find from Traprain Law discussed above, it could have reached native hands around the time of the Agricolan invasion of northern Britain.

In addition to these finds, there is a body

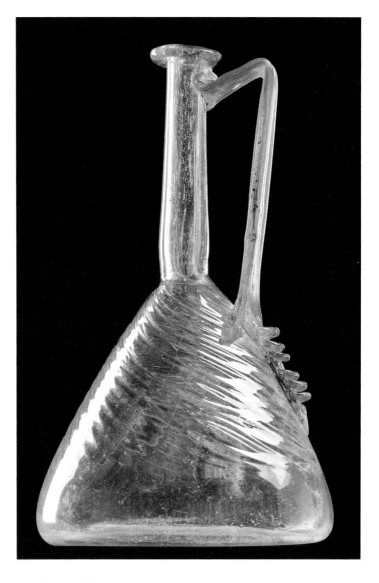

Figure 3.18.3

Conical jug, Turriff, Aberdeenshire.

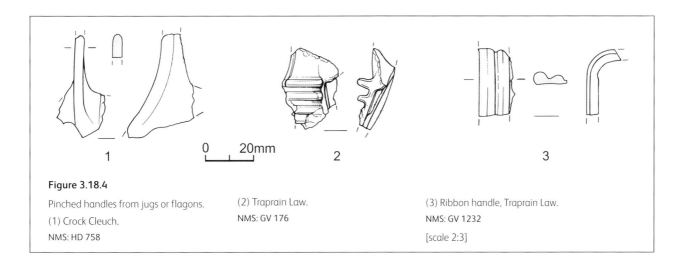

1

0 20mm

2

3

Figure 3.18.4

Pinched handles from jugs or flagons.

(1) Crock Cleuch.

NMS: HD 758

(2) Traprain Law.

NMS: GV 176

(3) Ribbon handle, Traprain Law.

NMS: GV 1232

[scale 2:3]

sherd in deep blue glass of an optic-blown globular jar (Isings Form 67c), or a globular or conical jar (Isings Forms 52b or 55) from Leckie, Stirlingshire; this is discussed elsewhere.[53] (One find which I have not been able to study myself and where the identification remains uncertain comes from Chapleton, Haugh of Urr, Kirkcudbrightshire. This find is thus neither included in the catalogue nor on the distribution map.)[54]

Brackenbraes, Turriff, Aberdeenshire. G:3

FR 484*, NMS. Intact vessel. Pale green. Folded, horizontal rim. A tall, narrow neck with a constriction at its base. Angular ribbon handle with a central rib, applied on the neck, below the rim. The handle terminates in a three-pronged 'claw', which continues in a vertical trail with six tooled 'teeth'. The body has optic-blown diagonal decoration. The base is plain and concave. This intact vessel is 227mm high, of which the body is 125mm high and the neck 102mm. The base diameter is 133mm.

Crock Cleuch, Roxburghshire. T:2

HD 758*, NMS. Lower part of handle from conical jug. Brown. Very bubbly. Dims 33 x 20; WT 4.0.

Traprain Law, East Lothian. N:2

GV 47 (XI 14 114), NMS. Fragment of handle. Angular ribbon handle, with central rib. Blue-green. Very bubbly. Worn (after breakage?). Dims 22 x 24; WT 4.9–8.2.

GV 176:3* (XII 15 141), Area: unknown, Level 3, NMS. Fragment of handle and body. Lower part of handle. Three pinched projections. Deep blue glass. Dims 32 x 21; WT 7.0 (body 1.0).

GV 602 (V 21 59), Area J. Level 1, NMS. Fragment of handle. Part of angular ribbon handle, only one rib remains. Natural green with yellow streaks. Deliberately reworked; knapped to form an oblong gaming piece? Dims 46 x 12; WT 6.

GV 1232* (1924 96), Area T, Level 1, NMS. Fragment of handle. Angular ribbon handle. Originally three ribs, of which two are preserved. Yellow-green. Very worn. Dims 26 x 14; WT 4.3.

GV 1633, Area P, Level 2, NMS. Body fragment and lower part of handle. Straight-sided body. Remains of claw; elongated central rib. Pale green. Many elongated bubbles. Dims 40 x 19; WT 4.0.

GV 1794, Area I, Level: illegible, NMS. Fragment of ribbon handle. Natural green. Very bubbly. Dims 17 x 21; WT 3.7.

GV 1715, Area R, Level 1, NMS. Fragment of handle – ribbon handle? Pale blue-green. Dims 11 x 11; WT 3.6.

Finds from other areas beyond the borders of the Roman Empire

With the exception of a possible find of a conical jug from Ireland, no other finds of this type – save the Scottish finds – have been made outside the Empire. The Irish find, a handle in blue-green glass, is unfortunately without provenance, and may or may not have been found on Ireland.[55]

Notes

1 Isings 1957, 69–73.
2 Harden 1967, 238.
3 Isings 1957, 88, 91.
4 See 'Jars with globular bodies and collared rims' ch. 3.16.
5 Isings 1957, 69–73; Harden 1967, 238–41; Cool & Price 1995, 120–21; Price & Cottam 1998a, 150–53.
6 Cool & Price 1995, 119.
7 Price 1995a, 178; see for example Roach-Smith 1859, 121.
8 Price & Cottam 1998a, fig. 66b.
9 Price 1977, fig. 27.2; Price & Cottam 1998a, pl. 2. 1.
10 Cool & Price 1995, 120.
11 Cool 1992, 67, fig. 10 no. 5.
12 Biaggio Simona 1990, 101, Abb. 6.
13 Cool & Price 1995, 120.
14 Price & Cottam 1998a, 150.
15 Berger 1960, Taf. 16. 7.
16 Harden 1967, 238.
17 Skilbeck 1923, Fig. 2a; Harden et al. 1988, 140.
18 Harden et al. 1968, 59, no. 73; Liversidge 1977, pl. 8.
19 Harden et al. 1968, 82, no. 108.
20 For a discussion of applied medallions, see Cool & Price 1995, 118–20; Price & Cottam 1998a, 32.
21 Payne 1874, plate facing page 170.
22 Skilbeck 1923, fig. 2a; Harden et al. 1988, 140.
23 Inskip 1846, 52.
24 Gage 1834, pl. II, fig. 1.
25 Goethert-Polaschek 1977, Abb. 45.
26 Harden 1968d, 308, pl. LXXX a.
27 Goethert-Polaschek 1977, Taf. 7, 79b.
28 Lux & Roosens 1971, fig. 22, no. 23.
29 Price & Cottam 1998a, fig. 68.
30 Harden 1967, fig. 7.17, pl. XLIIIa.
31 Biaggio Simona 1990, 97–98, Abb. 2.
32 Cool & Price 1995, 120.
33 Price & Cottam 1998a, 153.
34 Berger 1960, Taf. 20 no. 89.
35 Charlesworth 1973, 78.
36 Harden & Price 1971, 360.
37 Cool & Price 1995, 123.
38 Price & Cottam 1998a, 151–53.
39 Ritterling 1913, 374 Form 13, Taf. XXXVIII, 13.
40 Harden 1971–73, 78.
41 Price & Cool 1985, 46 no. 27.
42 Cool & Price 1995, 123.

43 Price 1989a, 195.

44 Cool 2006, 195–97.

45 See also the original reports: Biddle 1967, 230–37, pl. xlii–xliv, fig. 5 & fig. 7; Harden 1967; Toynbee 1967.

46 Cool & Price 1995, 120–30; Price & Cottam 1998a, 150–57, with references.

47 Cool & Price 1995, 120.

48 Isings Form 52: **The Netherlands**: Valkenburg (van Lith 1978–79, 85–86; Sablerolles 1996, 144–145); Nijmegen (Isings 1980, 302). **Belgium**: Vervoz (Gueury & Vanderhoeven 1989, 122, fig. 5:13). **Germany**: Köln (Cologne) (Fremersdorf 1958b, Taf. 13; Doppelfeld 1966, Taf. 21); Asberg (van Lith 1984, 255–58); Kretz (Oelmann 1938–39, 401–4, Abb. 1, 35 & 36; Follmann-Schulz 1992, 27–30); Planig (Behrens 1925–26, Abb. 6.4). **France**: Caudebec-les-Elbeuf, Normandy (Arveiller-Dulong et al. 2003, 149, fig. 6.3; see also Sennequier 1994, fig. 4).

Isings Form 55: **The Netherlands**: Valkenburg (van Lith 1978–79, 86–90; Sablerolles 1996, 144–45); De Woerd (van Lith & Randsborg 1985, 494); Esch (van den Hurk 1977, 118–19, fig. 42); Nijmegen (Isings 1980, 302–3, fig. 12); Stein, Houterend (Isings 1971, 35, fig. 8:113). **Belgium**: Gors-Opleeuw (Lux & Rosens 1971, 30, fig. 22:23); Haulchin (Faider-Feytmans 1940, pl. i). **Germany**: Hofheim (Ritterling 1913, 374, Taf. xxxviii); Köln (Cologne) (Fremersdorf 1955a, Taf. 30 no. 1; Fremersdorf 1958b, Taf. 8–10; Doppelfeld 1966, Taf. 28 & 29); Bonn (Follmann-Schulz 1990, Abb. 2); Xanten (Charlesworth 1984, 292–93); Nida-Heddernheim (Welker 1974, 84–85; Welker 1985, 33); Asberg (van Lith 1984, 255–58); Planig (Behrens 1925–26, Abb. 6:4). **France**: Harfleur, Normandy (Arveiller-Dulong et al. 2003, 149, fig. 6.2; see also Sennequier 1994, fig. 4); the Port-Vendres II wreck, found off the French Mediterranean coast (Colls et al. 1977, 121, fig. 42:11).

49 Isings Form 52: **Austria**: Magdalensberg (Czurda-Ruth 1979, 139–40). **Switzerland**: Locarno, Tessin (blue with marvered spots in white, red and yellow) (Biaggio Simona 1990, Abb. 6). **Italy**: Pompeii (Scatozza Höricht 1990, Taf. 1, no. 12489). **Slovenia**: Emona (Petru 1974, tab. v:4); Ljubljana (with marvered spots) (Fremersdorf 1938, 116, Taf. 14:6).

Isings Form 55: **Austria**: Magdalensberg (Czurda-Ruth 1979, 139–40). **Switzerland**: Muralto, Tessin (blue glass with marvered spots in white, red and yellow) (Biaggio Simona

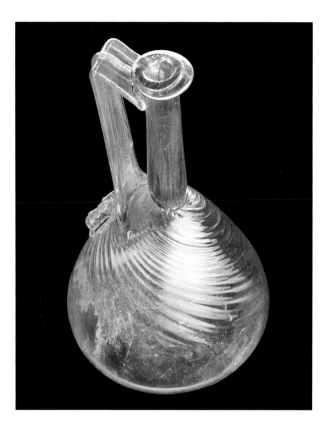

1990, 97–98, fig. 2). **Italy**: Luni (Roffia 1973, 475); Bologna (brown with marvered spots) (Meconcelli Notarianni 1979, 54–55). **Slovenia**: Emona (DeMaine 1990, fig. 2A:4).

50 Appendix A, G:3.

51 Price 1989a, 195.

52 Appendix A, T:2.

53 See 'Jars with globular bodies and collared rims', ch. 3.16.

54 This find was not identified in the original publication (Simpson 2004). Having studied the published illustration of the find it is clear that it is reeded handle, but unfortunately the scale is not given nor are any measurements mentioned. If the scale is 1:1 it may have originated from a globular jug of Isings Form 52 or a conical jug of Isings Form 55; ch. 3.26.

55 Bourke 1994, 166.

3.19 Globular or ovoid jug with chain-handle

Figure 3.19.1

Ovoid jug with chain-handle, Wimborne, Bucknowle Farm, Dorset [scale 1:3].

After Price & Cottam 1998a, fig. 71b

0   20mm

Figure 3.19.2

Distribution of type 3.19.

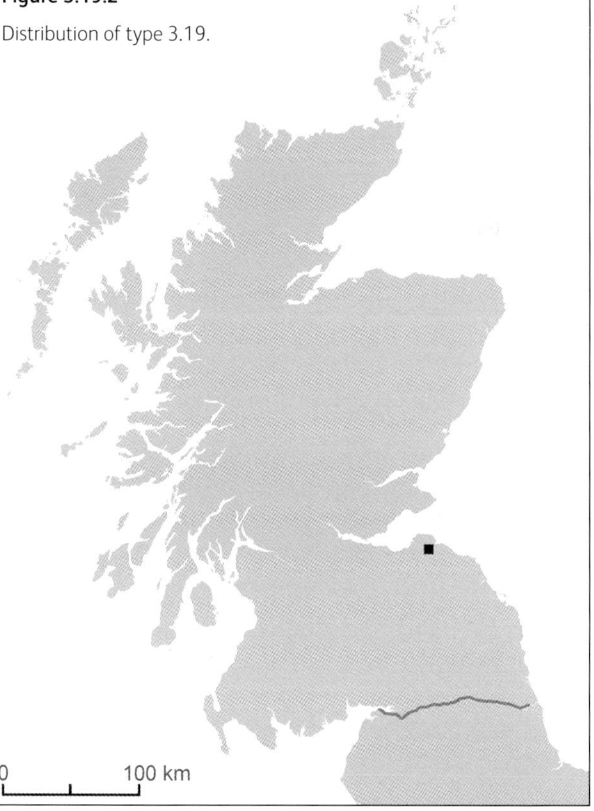

0   100 km

A general description of the type

Chain-handles, consisting of two parallel rods pinched together at intervals to form loops or a 'chain', were used on globular, ovoid, discoid and conical jugs of second- to fourth-century date,[1] such as spouted jugs of Isings Form 88 and funnel-mouthed jugs of Isings Form 120.[2] Due to this variation in form and manufacture, the strongly fragmented material from settlements and forts is often difficult to identify to precise type or even shape.

Isings Form 88 is globular or discoid in shape and has a spout mouth with rolled-in or fire-rounded rim. The base is concave or has a tubular ring base. Both Form 88 and 120 have a range of different handles: ribbon, rod and chain, the latter two variations being less common. There is a wide variety of spouted jugs of different shapes and decorations from the first to the fourth centuries AD.[3] However, Isings Form 88 is the only one of these with a chain-handle.[4] The jugs are dec-

orated with horizontal self-coloured trails and optic-blowing, and were produced in colourless, blue-green and pale green glass. This type is smaller than Isings Form 120; the heights are generally c. 100–150 mm, sometimes less.[5]

Isings Form 120c is ovoid or globular in shape and has a funnel mouth with fire-rounded or rolled-in edge. The bases are concave, have applied base rings or pushed-in tubular rings. Below the rim is a horizontal or spiral trail in self-coloured glass. The body is decorated with optic-blown vertical ribs or applied trails, which sometimes are tooled to form so-called nipt' diamonds.[6] The rim diameters are c. 55–70 mm, the heights c. 150–250 mm.[7] The jugs were produced in colourless, greenish colourless, blue-green and pale green glass (fig. 3.19.1).

Dating the type

Both spouted jugs of Isings Form 88 and funnel-mouthed jugs of Isings Form 120 have imprecise date ranges. The former dates roughly to the late second to the third century, the latter from the second to the fourth century.[8] Although the time span covered by the different variations of jugs is fairly long, the colour of the glass can give an indication of the date of the specific vessel: typical of fourth-century objects is bubbly, greenish glass of poor quality.

The function of the vessels

In an interesting study on the glass from a Roman cemetery at Emona, Slovenia, Mary DeMaine discusses how the depictions on grave stelae and wall paintings can reveal the function of the objects found in the graves. There is much to suggest that jugs of both metal and glass were used for serving wine, as shown in these depictions.[9]

The finds from Roman contexts

Although the number of intact or well-preserved vessels with chain-handles from Roman Britain is relatively few, they are known, for instance, from Kingsbury Manor, St Albans (Verulamium), Hertfordshire;[10] Colchester, Essex,[11] and Wimborne, Bucknowle Farm, Dorset (fig. 3.19.1).[12] Fragmentary finds suggest they were by no means uncommon in Romano-British contexts.[13] Globular, ovoid, discoid and conical jugs with chain-handles have been found in the north-western provinces, the area along the river Rhine being particularly prolific.[14]

The finds from non-Roman contexts in Scotland and north Northumberland

Although there is only one certainly identified jug with a chain-handle found in native context north of Hadrian's Wall – from Traprain Law, East Lothian[15] – other fragments of jugs found in non-Roman contexts may have belonged to the same type, such as spouted jugs from Traprain Law and Witchy Neuk, Hepple, Northumberland.[16]

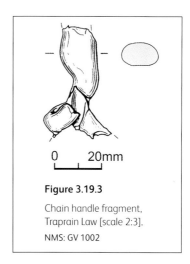

Figure 3.19.3

Chain handle fragment, Traprain Law [scale 2:3].

NMS: GV 1002

The find from Traprain Law is in green, very poor quality glass, which implies a late date, third or fourth century AD (fig. 3.19.4). Which type of vessel the handle once belonged to is impossible to tell with any certainty. Nevertheless, the late date indicated by the colour suggests that it could have been an ovoid jug of Isings Form 120c. Regardless of its precise type, the late date of this find is noteworthy.

Traprain Law, East Lothian. N:2

GV 1002* (1922 336), Area N, Level 3, NMS. Fragment of handle. Pale olive-green, nearly opaque. The opaque colour is not the result of deliberate colouring, but due to a very bubbly glass. Dull surface. Dims 46 x 16; WT 9.6.

Figure 3.19.4

Chain handle fragment, Traprain Law.

NMS: GV 1002

Finds from other areas beyond the borders of the Roman Empire

To my knowledge there are no other finds of vessels with chain-handles from beyond the borders of the Roman Empire.

Notes

1   Price & Cottam 1998a, 25; globular & ovoid: Zobel-Klein 1999, Abb. 1; conical: Zobel-Klein 1999, Abb. 21a.
2   Isings 1957, 104, 149–51; see Zobel-Klein 1999, Abb. 1.
3   See 'Spouted jug', ch. 3.20.
4   Cool & Price 1995, 131–34.
5   Price & Cottam 1998a, 159; Fremersdorf & Fremersdorf-Polónyi 1984, 86.
6   See Follmann-Schulz 1992, 52–53 no. 29.
7   Price & Cottam 1998a, 161.
8   Isings 1957, 104, 151; Isings 1971, 36; Cool 1995b, 12; Price & Cottam 1998a, 163.
9   DeMaine 1990, 133, fig. 3a.
10 Allen 1998b, cover, 2.
11 Harden et al. 1968, 84.
12 Price & Cottam 1998a, 161, fig. 71b.
13 Cool & Price 1995, 139–40; Price & Cottam 1997a, 345 with references.
14 The Netherlands: Stein, Limburg (Isings Form 120c) (Isings 1971, 36–37, pl. 3; Fremersdorf & Fremersdorf-Polónyi 1984, 84); Maastricht, Limburg (Isings 1971, 37). Germany: Mainz is one of the most prolific sites when it comes to vessels with chain-handles. No less than twenty have been found, including both globular jugs of Isings Form 88 and ovoid jars of Isings Form 120 (Behrens 1925, Abb. 8; Behrens 1925–26, 70, Abb. 11:1–3; Fremersdorf & Fremersdorf-Polónyi 1984, 84; Zobel-Klein 1999); Budenheim, Mainz-Bingen (Isings Form 120c) (Behrens 1925–26, Abb. 18:4); Köln (Cologne) (Isings Form 88c, Isings Form 120c (Behrens 1925–26, 70; Fremersdorf 1939a, 19; Doppelfeld 1966, 48, Taf. 80; Fremersdorf & Fremersdorf-Polónyi 1984, 82); Bonn (Isings Form 120c) (Zobel-Klein 1999, Abb. 16); Xanten (fragment of handle) (Charlesworth 1984, 293); Kandel, Pfalz (Isings Form 88) (Zobel-Klein 1999, Abb. 19), Grafschaft-Gelsdorf (Isings Form 120c) (Follmann-Schulz 1992, 52); Saalburg (Fremersdorf 1939a, 19); Zugmantel (fragment of handle) (Fremersdorf 1939a, 19). France: Normandy (Sennequier 1994, fig. 4).
15 Appendix A, N:2.
16 Appendix A, U:8. See 'Spouted jug', ch. 3.20.

3.20 Spouted jugs

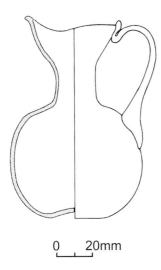

0   20mm

Figure 3.20.1

Spouted jug, Dieppe, France [scale 1:2].
After Sennequier 1985, fig. 292

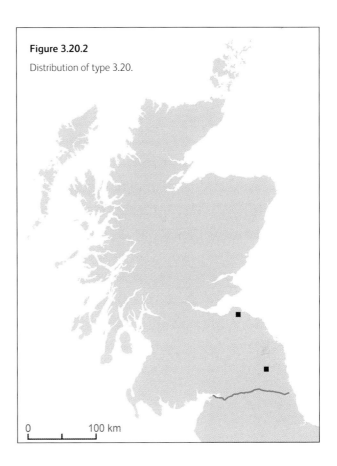

Figure 3.20.2

Distribution of type 3.20.

0   100 km

A general description of the type

Such jugs have rolled-in or fire-rounded edges, and, as their name suggests, a pulled-out spout. The spout is either in alignment with the handle, or it is turned 90 degrees. The curved or angular ribbon handle is attached to the rim and upper body. The neck is cylindrical and relatively short; the body is globular, or squashed spherical to discoid. An example of the latter variant was discovered at Silchester.[1] The base is either concave, or has a tubular pushed-in base ring. Spouted jugs were produced in blue-green, pale green or colourless glass.[2] These jugs are of relatively small size, *c.* 100–150 mm in height. Occasionally these vessels were decorated, in most cases a simple decoration with one or two self-coloured horizontal trails on the body. Finds with spiral trails on the body are also known,[3] and from Black-friar's Street, Carlisle, Cumbria, there is a very rare find with a network of fine trails inside the funnel mouth.[4]

In earlier scholarly work, the Seine-Rhine area was considered the most likely area of manufacture for spouted jugs,[5] and there is nothing to contradict the idea that they were produced somewhere in the north-western provinces.

Dating the type

It is not entirely clear exactly when these jugs were produced. Jugs with pulled-out spouts seem to have been roughly contemporary with jugs with pinched-in spouts, although the latter appear to have a slightly earlier date range – late first to early third century. The jugs with pulled-out spouts are found in second- and third-century contexts.[6] There is, however, new evidence that may suggest this type was in use, and perhaps also in manufacture, later than previously thought.[7] Fragments making up an almost intact jug of discoid shape with a pulled-out spout were discovered in a late Roman rubbish pit in Silchester, Hampshire, containing material of mid-third to fourth century AD date. The material from these contexts is difficult to interpret, however, and it is possible that some of the glass assemblage was residual.[8]

The function of the vessels

Jugs of similar shape in metal were depicted on still lifes in Pompeii and Herculaneum, and it is apparent from these that the jugs were used for serving liquids – presumably wine.

The finds from Roman contexts

To my knowledge relatively few finds of spouted jugs have been made in northern Britain: for example at Blackfriar's Street, Carlisle, Cumbria;[9] Aldborough, North Yorkshire;[10] and at the legionary fortress, York.[11] In the Midlands and southern Britain they appear to be relatively frequent, although never as common as jugs with circular mouths.[12] Finds have, for instance, been made at Stonea, Cambridgeshire, where excavations yielded a minimum of five spouted jugs, four in blue-green and one in colourless glass.[13] At Colchester, Essex, no less than nine spouted jugs were discovered; three of these had pulled-out spouts, three pinched-in spouts and three were indeterminate. Those with pulled-out spouts were in pale green and blue-green glass.[14] Spouted jugs of this type are distributed in the north-western provinces and also in the central area of the Empire.[15]

The finds from non-Roman contexts in Scotland and north Northumberland

A minimum of two finds of spouted jugs are known from native sites north of Hadrian's Wall – a rim fragment from Traprain Law, East Lothian, and a rim fragment from Witchy Neuk, Hepple, Northumberland.

A small fragment of the rim of a spouted jug was found during the excavations at Witchy Neuk, Hepple, Northumberland, in 1936. Unfortunately this fragment can no longer be traced. The fragment had, however, been examined by W. A. Thorpe, a scholar specialising in glass from the Victoria & Albert Museum, London. On the basis of the information in the published excavation report, it remains unclear exactly which type of spouted jug the Witchy Neuk find belonged to, and what colour it was. The published information is thus worth quoting *in extenso*:

> The fragment of glass has been examined by Mr. W. A. Thorpe, of the Victoria and Albert Museum, who is of the opinion that it is of Seine-Rhine manufacture of the third century AD. He suggests that it belongs to the rim and neck of one of the small one-handled globular jugs with short neck and beaky spout. In the fragment, which is very small, the narrow end of the rim is approaching the beaky lip.[16]

Price and Cottam differentiate between two types of spouted jugs found in Romano-British contexts: those with pinched-in spouts and those with pulled-out spouts.[17] The use of the word 'beaky' in the description of the Witchy Neuk find, rather than describing it as trefoil, suggests to me that it was a jug with a pulled-out spout. Admittedly this is an educated guess, but as these types are closely related and roughly contemporary, the difference is of relatively minor importance. In Clasina Isings' typology, for example, these are treated as one Form (88 a–c).[18] The site was a fortified enclosure with two roundhouses. Excavations yielded very few artefacts, and no other Roman imports except the jug.[19]

Recent excavations at Traprain Law, East Lothian, brought a further fragment of a spouted jug to light. The minute size of this fragment renders it impossible to determine the exact type. The quality of the glass is high – in stark contrast to the find of a chain handle from the same site – but these finds may have originated from the same type of vessel: globular jugs with spouted mouths. As with the Witchy Neuk find, a second or third century date might be suggested.

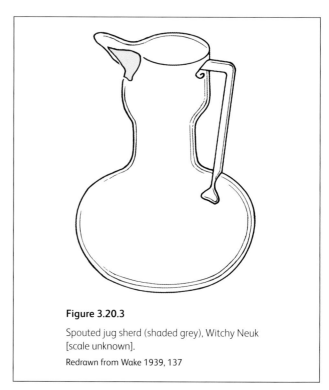

Figure 3.20.3

Spouted jug sherd (shaded grey), Witchy Neuk [scale unknown].

Redrawn from Wake 1939, 137

Witchy Neuk, Hepple, Northumberland. U:8
Lost*.

Traprain Law, East Lothian. N:2
TLF 04, find 352, NMS. Rim fragment. 'Tubular' rim rolled-in, from a funnel mouth. Clear, colourless glass. Dims 22 x 14; PH ca. 9; WT 1.4.

Finds from other areas beyond the borders of the Roman Empire

To my knowledge, no other finds of spouted jugs have been made beyond the boundaries of the Roman Empire.

Notes

1 Allen 2006, 118, 317–18, fig. 74.4.
2 Isings 1957, 104–6; Welker 1974, 102–6; Cool & Price 1995, 131–4; Price & Cottam 1998a, 159–61.
3 Price & Cottam 1998a, 159.
4 Price 1990a, 170, fig. 160:20.
5 See, for example Welker 1974, 104.
6 Price & Cottam 1998a, 159.
7 I would like to thank Dr Hilary Cool for bringing a relatively recent discovery to my attention, namely the material from late Roman deposits discovered at Silchester.
8 Allen 2006, 118; for the dating of the deposited material, see Timby 2006, 95–96; Eckardt 2006, 239.
9 Price 1990a, 170, fig. 160:20.
10 Ecroyd Smith 1852, 48 no. 5, pl. 24 quoted by Price & Cottam 1998a, 160.
11 Cool 1995a, 1576, fig. 743 no. 6002.
12 Cool & Price 1995, 131–34; Price & Cottam 1998a, 159–61 with references.
13 Price 1996, 390, 402, fig. 131.
14 Cool & Price 1995, 131–32, 140–41, fig. 8.8 & fig. 8.9.
15 **The Netherlands:** Maastricht, Limburg (Isings 1971, 37, fig. 11:119). **Germany:** Köln (Cologne) (Fremersdorf & Fremersdorf-Polónyi 1984, 81, Fig. 185; Fremersdorf 1958a, Taf. 61; Doppelfeld 1966, Taf. 80; Päffgen 1989, Abb. 3); Xanten (Charlesworth 1984, 293); Nida-Heddernheim (Welker 1974, 102–6; Welker 1985, 37–39). **France:** Normandy (Sennequier 1994, fig. 4); three spouted jugs were found in the Roman cemetery at d'Épiais-Rhus, Val-d'Oise, France, one of which was decorated with a spiral thread (Vanpeene 1993, 36–38, pl. 13). **Italy:** Angera (Facchini 1990, 106, fig. 3.1); Luni (Chiaramonte Trerè 1973b, 785, tav. 217 no. KA 321); the cemetery at the Ancient Cornus (Santa Caterina di Pitenuri), Sardinia (Fortuna Canivet 1969, 24, fig. 24). **Slovenia:** Ptuj (Subic 1974, Taf. 3:22; Petru 1974, Taf. 8:1).
16 Wake 1939, 137.
17 Price & Cottam 1998a, 157–61.
18 Isings 1957, 104–6.
19 Appendix A, U:8.

3.21 Unguent bottles

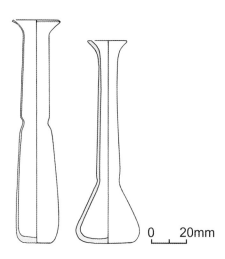

Figure 3.21.1

Left: tubular unguent bottle, York.
After Harden 1962, fig. 89: H.G. 32

Right: conical unguent bottle, York.
After Price & Cottam 1998a, fig. 77

[scale 1:2]

Figure 3.21.2

Distribution of type 3.21.

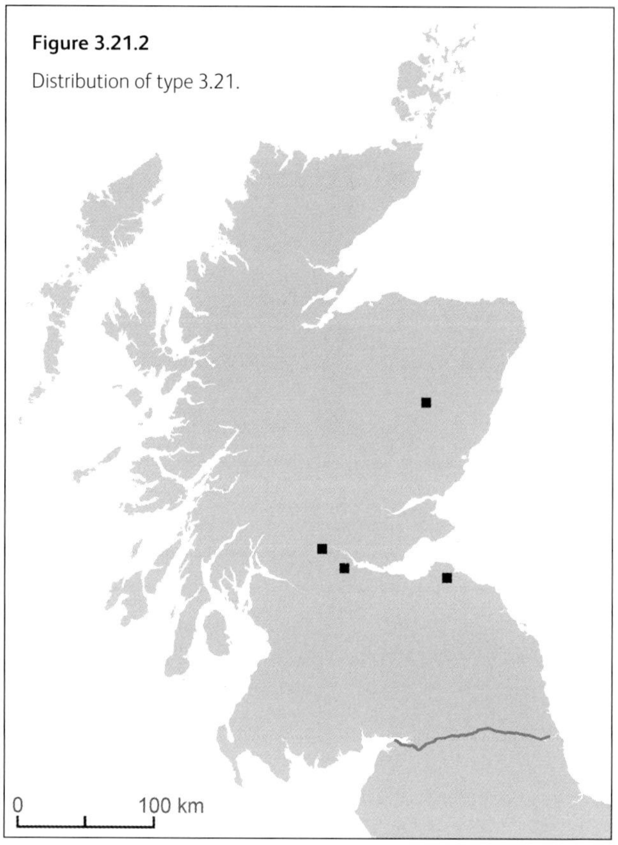

A general description of the type

Unguentaria, or perfume bottles, were produced in a wide variety of shapes and types, particularly in the first and second centuries, but also later. Clasina Isings and others have made attempts to place these within a typology.[1] It must, however, be stressed, as pointed out by Cool and Price, that these divisions between different forms or types are not sharp, but rather points in a continuum.[2] This makes any attempt to classify fragmentary material very difficult. The most common shapes/types in Britain and on the Continent are:

(a) Tubular unguent bottles, which have out-turned, sheared or rolled-in rims; a cylindrical neck, with a constriction above the body; a slightly convex body, and a small flattened area on the base (fig. 3.21.1, left). These are *c.* 60–120 mm high,[3] and the majority were produced in blue-green glass, although examples in pale yellow-green and strong colours are also known.[4]

(b) Conical unguent bottles have out-turned rims, the edge sheared or rolled-in. The neck is tall and cylindrical, and the body is of conical shape (fig. 3.21.1, right). These are *c.* 90–130 mm high, and manufactured in common blue-green glass.[5]

(c) Convex flasks have rims folded out, up, in and flattened. The neck is short and cylindrical, the body ovoid or globular. These are *c.* 150–220 mm high, and were made in blue-green glass.[6]

(d) Indented unguent bottles have out-turned rims sheared or bent out, a cylindrical neck, and a long body with indents. These are *c.* 135–160 mm high, and produced in blue-green, pale green and greenish colourless glass.[7]

(e) Pipette-shaped bottles have rolled-in or folded out rims. The body is long and slightly bulbous on the middle – hence the name. These are *c.* 150–370 mm high, and were manufactured in pale green, greenish colourless and blue-green glass.[8]

Dating the type

Tubular unguent bottles have an extended period of production and use: British finds date from the Claudian period to the early third century AD. It is, however, possible to give a more precise dating if the rim is preserved. Sheared rims were in use from the Claudian to the early Flavian period, whereas rolled rims were in use from the Flavian period to the early third century, while conical unguent bottles are found in Flavian to Hadrianic contexts. Convex flasks were in use from the Claudian to the Neronian period in Britain. Indented flasks date from the late second to the third century AD, and pipette-shaped flasks are fourth century in date.[9]

The function of the vessels

Unguentaria have been demonstrated to be containers for scented oils, cosmetics, skin emollients or medical preparations. Gas chromographic and mass spectrometric analysis of the contents of a number of glass *unguentaria* of Isings Form 82 (so-called 'candlestick' *unguentaria*) found at Oplontis in the Bay of Naples area showed that these contained remains of beeswax, *Pinaceae* resin, and waxes from flowers or leaves.[10]

On the basis of historical sources, we know that fragrant components in perfumes and skin emollients were extracted from resins, woods, spices, and flowers, using vegetable oils, waxes or animal fats as a base.[11] Theophrastus (*c.370–c.285* BC) mentions the use of different oils as a basis for perfumes – almond oil, balanos oil, sesame oil and olive oil – in his work *De Odoribus* (*On Odours*).[12] For example, analysis of the remains in two *unguentaria* of Isings Form 82, reported to have been found in the vicinity of Jerusalem, contained a substance based on olive oil.[13]

An unguent bottle discovered in a burial at Stoneyford, Co. Kilkenny, Ireland, still contained what is described as 'a hard white substance',[14] in all probability some sort of cosmetic. A number of glass vessels found in different parts of the Roman Empire containing white make-up (*pyxides*, *unguentaria* of different types, including bird-shaped bottles of Isings Form 11), were analysed employing electron microscopy and X-ray diffraction. These analyses detected not only lead white, but also gypsum or calcite.[15]

Occasionally these *unguentaria* have been found at baths: for example the legionary bathhouses at Exeter, Devon,[16] and Caerleon, Gwent.[17] This emphasises their link to hygiene and bathing.

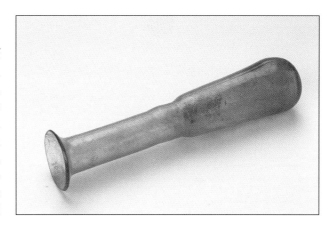

Figure 3.21.3

Intact unguent vessel, Loch Kinnord, Aberdeenshire.

University Museums, University of Aberdeen: ABDUA 36857

The finds from Roman contexts

Tubular unguent bottles – that is, the same type as the Loch Kinnord find – are common finds in Roman Britain,[18] and a number of other types (conical,[19] tall discoid,[20] and indented unguent bottles[21]) are relatively frequent finds. In contrast, finds of the late Roman pipette-shaped unguent bottles are relatively sparse.[22] Although there was a decline in the late Roman era, *unguentaria* are on the whole a very widely spread category of find.

If we look elsewhere in the Roman world, unguent bottles of different types are found in abundance all over the Empire, on civilian settlements and military forts, and in particular in funerary contexts.[23] Although local production cannot be excluded, there is much to suggest that they were imported with their contents from different areas. To prevent the bottles from breaking during transport, they were sometimes wrapped in papyrus or other plant materials, and finds of this type have been made in Egypt.[24]

The finds from non-Roman contexts in Scotland and north Northumberland

An intact tubular-shaped unguent flask (Isings Form 8) was found in Loch Kinnord, Aberdeenshire (fig. 3.21.3).[25] The colour and shape of the vessel suggest a mid-first-century date. Very little is known about the circumstances of this find, and it remains unclear whether it represents an ancient loss or some form of ritual deposition. There is a crannog in the same loch, and settlements with roundhouses and souterrains around it, demonstrating Iron Age activity in the area.[26]

Camelon native site, Stirlingshire – a palisaded settlement with roundhouses – was the object of a rescue excavation. This indigenous site is situated in the vicinity of an area where a number of temporary Roman camps and two Roman forts have been discovered. A fragmentary unguent flask in colourless glass with a yellowish tinge, probably of first- to second-century date, was found, but the type could not be established. In addition to this, two gaming pieces in glass and a small assemblage of Roman pottery were found.[27]

Excavations at Keir Hill, Gargunnock, Stirlingshire, unearthed a roundhouse and a small assemblage of Roman goods. Three body sherds in blue-green glass from a convex-curved vessel were unearthed. A first- to second-century date is suggested for this find.[28]

The exceptionally rich and varied assemblage of Roman imports from Traprain Law, East Lothian,[29] includes a small number of finds that were associated with personal hygiene in their original Roman context: the fragment of an unguent flask in pale purple glass, possibly of first- or second-century date (fig. 3.21.4); a fragment of an *aryballos*, (i.e. an oil flask), tweezers, nail-cleaners and an ear-scoop.[30]

Finds linked to hygiene are rare in native contexts of Roman Iron Age date, which stands in contrast to the many finds made in Roman contexts. It has to be stressed, however, that unguent bottles are less frequent in military than in civilian contexts, which might have had an influence on the availability of these vessels in northern Britain.[31] It is also noteworthy that two out of four finds – admittedly a small assemblage – were in rare colours, such as pale purple and colourless glass. This suggests a selection of particularly valuable objects.

Camelon, Stirlingshire. K:1

C61 149. NMS. Fragment of neck and body of unguent flask. Colourless with a yellow tinge. Body convex-curved. PH 15; WT 1.2.

Keir Hill, Gargunnock, Stirlingshire. K:5

L.1961.5, NMS. Three body fragments of an unguent bottle. Blue-green glass with few bubbles. (a) Dims 16 x 22; WT 0.8. (b) Dims 18 x 31; WT 1.1. (c) Dims 14 x 21; WT 1.0.

Loch Kinnord, Aberdeenshire. G:1

ABDUA 36857*, University Museums, University of Aberdeen. Intact unguent flask in blue-green glass; tubular-shaped in blue-green glass. Out-turned sheared rim. Long cylindrical neck, with a tooled constriction between neck and body. Body almost cylindrical, the lower part slightly rounded. Flattened base. PH 127; RD 25.

Traprain Law, East Lothian. N:2

GV 110* (XI 14 259), NMS. Fragment of neck. Unguent flask. Pale purple. Narrow neck. Elongated bubbles. Diameter c.15; PH 15; WT 2.2.

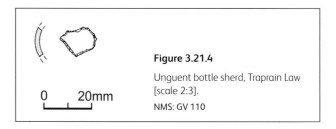

Figure 3.21.4

Unguent bottle sherd, Traprain Law [scale 2:3].

NMS: GV 110

0   20mm

Finds from other areas beyond the borders of the Roman Empire

In contrast to the situation within the Roman Empire where finds have been made in abundance, unguent bottles are very rare beyond its boundaries. A limited number of finds are known from Free Germany. A cremation grave excavated in 1872 at Pritzier, Kreis Hagenow, Mecklenburg-Vorpommern contained a somewhat melted conical unguent flask (Isings Form 28a).[32] Another cremation grave excavated before 1880 at Brandenburg-Görden, Stadtkreis Brandenburg, Brandenburg, contained a small unguent flask which was slightly affected by heat. This was identified as an Isings Form 6 or 8 (it is closer to Isings Form 6 in shape).[33]

A grave excavated in 1832 or 1852 at Stoneyford, Co. Kilkenny, Ireland, was Roman in character: a large convex jar of Isings Form 67a with the remains of a cremation was found together with a tubular unguent bottle (Isings Form 8). This appears to have contained some sort of cosmetic.[34]

A number of finds have been made in the Black Sea region of tubular, ovoid/conical, conical and indented unguent flasks (Isings Forms 6, 8, 82, 83 and other types).[35] Excavations at Aksum, Ethiopia, yielded a number of colourless tubular unguent bottles.[36] An unguent bottle of Isings Form 6 was found in Heïs, Somalia.[37] At ed-Dur, Umm al-Qaiwain, United Arab Emirates, globular, ovoid, and possibly also conical-shaped (Isings Form 28?) unguent bottles were discovered in graves;[38] and in Ter, Deccan, India, an unguent bottle with marvered opaque white threads was found.[39]

Notes

1 Isings 1957.
2 Cool & Price 1995, 161. Despite the drawbacks in Clasina Isings' typology, however, it still maintains the advantage of being widely understood and accepted; and rather than attempting to reclassify material studied by other scholars – the majority of which employ Isings – I have chosen to refer to her typology in the catalogue.
3 Isings Form 8; see Cool & Price 1995, 159–60; Price & Cottam 1998a, 169–71.
4 Harden 1947, 304–5; Price & Cool 1985, 44.
5 Isings Form 82b; see Cool & Price 1995, 161; Price & Cottam 1998a, 172–74.
6 Isings Form 16; see Price & Cottam 1998a, 171–72.
7 Isings Form 83; see Price & Cottam 1998a, 177–79.
8 Isings Form 105; see Price & Cottam 1998a, 187–88.
9 Price & Cottam 1998a, 169–74, 177–79, 187.
10 Ribechini et al. 2008, 158–59, 168.
11 Brun 2000, 277. See, for instance: Theophrastus, *De Odoribus*, 14.67.
12 Theophrastus, *De Odoribus*, 4.14–16. See also Mattingly 1990, 80–81.
13 Barag 1972; Basch 1972.
14 Bateson 1973, 72.
15 Welcomme et al. 2006, 552–53.
16 Charlesworth 1979b, 229.
17 Allen 1986b, 98, 100.
18 Cool & Price 1995, 159–60; Price & Cottam 1998a, 169–71 with references.
19 Cool & Price 1995, 161–62; Price & Cottam 1998a, 172–74 with references.
20 Price & Cottam 1998a, 175–77 with references.
21 Cool & Price 1995, 162–63; Price & Cottam 1998a, 177–79 with references.
22 Price & Cottam 1998a, 187–88 with references.
23 **The Netherlands:** Maastricht (Isings Forms 8, 28) (Isings 1971, 6–9, fig. 1); Valkenburg (Isings Forms 8, 28) (van Lith 1978–79, 37, 56); Nijmegen (Isings Form 8) (Isings 1980, 307–10, fig. 16:26). **Belgium:** Vervoz (Isings Form 8) (Gueury & Vanderhoeven 1989, 116–17, fig. 4:5). **Luxembourg:** Hellingen (Isings Form 26?) (Thill 1975, Taf. 20:2). **Germany:** Oberstimm (Isings Forms 6, 27) (Garbsch 1978, 280, Taf. 109); Hofheim (Isings Form 8) (Ritterling 1913, 376, Taf. 38); Nida-Heddernheim (Isings Forms 27, 28, 82) (Welker 1985, 23–24); Asberg (Isings Forms 6, 8) (van Lith 1984, 230–31); Köln (Cologne) (Isings Forms 8, 28, 82?) (Fremersdorf 1955a, Abb. 1:13; Päffgen 1989, Abb. 2:1–2); Weisenau bei Mainz (Isings Form 8) (Behrens 1925, Abb. 3:4; Behrens 1925–26, Abb. 2:4); Mainz (Isings Forms 27, 105) (Behrens 1925, Abb. 13, 18, 20; Behrens 1925–26, Abb. 10, 12). **France:** Normandy (Isings Forms 6, 8, 82) (Sennequier 1994, fig. 3); the necropolis at d'Épiais-Rhus, Val-d'Oise (Isings Form 82) (Vanpeene 1993, 32); the shipwreck Saint-Gervais 3, Golfe de Fos (Isings Form 82) (Foy & Nenna 2001, 109); Saint-Paul-Trois-Châteaux (Isings Forms 6, 8, 28, 82) (Bel 1990, 145–48, fig. 1; Foy & Nenna 2001, 125); Fréjus (Isings Forms 6, 8, 9 28, 82) (Béraud & Gébara 1990, 156–57, fig. 4). **Austria:** Magdalensberg (Isings Forms 6, 8, 10, 26, 28) (Czurda-Ruth 1979, 103–25). **Switzerland:** Locarno (Simonett 1941, *passim*). **Italy:** Angera (Isings Form 105) (Facchini 1990, fig. 1:5); Luni (Isings Forms 6, 8, 26 (Roffia 1973, 468; Chiaramonte Trerè 1973b, 776–78); Claterna (Maggio, Ozzano dell'Emilia) (Isings Forms 6?, 82) (Meconcelli Notarianni 1987, 53–56, fig. 14:16 & fig. 14:13); Bologna (Isings Forms 6, 8, 82) (Meconcelli Notarianni 1979, 96–133); the Necropolis at 'Le Palazzette', Classe, Ravenna (Isings Forms 6, 8, 82) (Maioli 1974, *passim*, fig. 1 to fig. 11, fig. 17 to fig. 20); Aquileia (Isings Forms 6, 8, 26, 82) (Calvi 1969, tav. 3–6); Monte Gelato (Isings Form 82) (Price 1997b, 271, fig. 186:34); Ostia (Isings Forms 8, 28, 82) (Moriconi 1969–72, 365–67; Capo 1972–76, tab. 1); Herculaneum (Isings Forms 6, 8, 82, 26, 28, 105 (Scatozza Höricht 1986, 57–66, tav. 19–20; Scatozza Höricht 1990, fig. 1); the cemetery at the Ancient Cornus (Santa Caterina di Pitenuri), Sardinia (Isings Forms 8, 82) (Fortuna Canivet 1969, 24, fig. 9 to fig. 11). **Slovenia:** Ljubljana (Isings Forms 8, 82, 105) (Petru 1974, Taf. V:3, VI:1, VIII:2 & VIII:3); Emona (Isings Forms 6, 82) (DeMaine 1990, fig. 1A:1, fig. 4A:2 & fig. 8A:12); Ptuj (Isings Forms 8, 28, 82) (Subic 1974, Taf. II). **Croatia:** Bakar (Isings Forms 6, 82) (Damevski 1974, Taf. III & IV); Osijek (Isings Form 82) (Bulat 1974, Taf. V); Solin (Isings Form 8) (Damevski 1974, Taf. III); Starigrad (Isings Forms 82, 105) (Abramić & Colnago 1909, Abb. 20, 36). **Montenegro** (Isings Forms 27, 28, 82, 105) (Cermanović-Kuzmanović 1974, Taf. II–V). **Bosnia & Herzegovina** (Isings Forms 6, 8, 27, 28, 82) (Paskvalin 1974, Taf. I–IV). **Greece:** Monasteiaki Kephala, Knossos, Crete (Isings Forms 6, 8, 27, 28) (Carington Smith 1982, 274–77); Tarrha, Crete (Isings Form 28?) (Buechner 1960, 110). **Libya:** Forte della Vite, Tripolitana (Price 1985c, 70, 96, fig. 6:1, no. 6). **Egypt:** Quseir al-Qadim (Isings Form 82) (Meyer 1992, 29–30).
24 Foy & Nenna 2001, 114–15.
25 Ingemark 2006a, 211.
26 Appendix A, G:1.
27 Appendix A, K:1.
28 Appendix A, K:5.
29 Appendix A, N:2.
30 For a discussion, see 'Small globular flasks with looped handles – *aryballoi*', ch. 3.22.
31 For a discussion, see ch. 4.3.
32 *CRFB* D3 II-04-17/1.7.
33 *CRFB* D1 IV-17-3/1.1; Taf. 10.1.
34 Bateson 1973, 72; Rafterty 1981, 194; Bourke 1994, fig. 19:3.
35 Sorokina 1967, Abb. 1 & 3.
36 Morrison 1989, 195–96, fig. 14.
37 Stern 1993, 56.
38 Whitehouse 1998, 26, 28–32, fig. 7; Whitehouse 2000, 100–1, fig. 17.
39 Stern 1992, 115, fig. 6.4.

3.22 Small globular flasks with looped handles – *aryballoi*

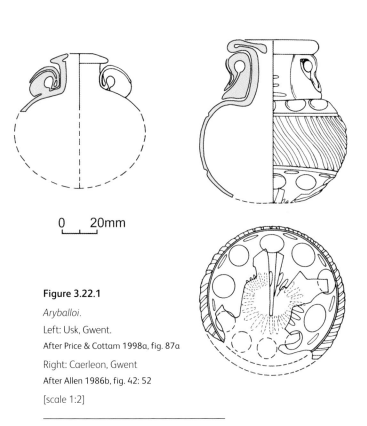

Figure 3.22.1

Aryballoi.

Left: Usk, Gwent.

After Price & Cottam 1998a, fig. 87a

Right: Caerleon, Gwent

After Allen 1986b, fig. 42: 52

[scale 1:2]

0   20mm

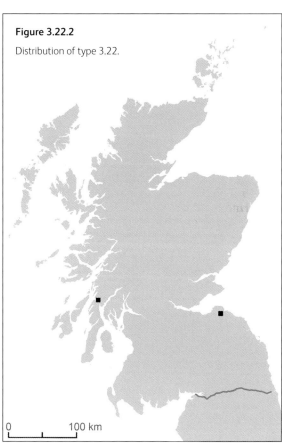

Figure 3.22.2

Distribution of type 3.22.

0   100 km

A general description of the type

The bath flask or *aryballos* is a small globular flask,[1] *c.* 50–100 mm high. It has a folded rim, edge bent out, up and in. Early – first century AD – examples often have rims with a triangular profile (fig. 3.22.1; left), whereas later examples are more or less flat (fig. 3.22.1; right). The neck is short and cylindrical. The body is globular with a flattened base, entirely flat or slightly concave. In many cases the pontil-scar is still visible on the base. The handles are attached to the shoulder and the rim, and most have so-called dolphin handles, i.e. a handle beginning on the shoulder, drawn up to the underside of the rim and then back. There are also simple loop handles, which are of early date.[2] The overwhelming majority of finds are in common blue-green glass.

Decoration is quite common on bath flasks of this type; the most common variant has a simple self-coloured trailed-on thread decoration. Less common are wheel-cut decorations; among the British finds, those from Caerleon, Gwent, stand out (fig. 3.22.1, right).[3] A handful of vessels in strong colours, and with marvered splashes in opaque glass, have been found both in Britain and on the Continent. From Carmarthen, Carmarthenshire, there is a deep blue *aryballos* with marvered opaque white and yellow splashes;[4] and from Richborough, Kent, a deep blue *aryballos* with marvered opaque white splashes.[5]

Dating the type

Blown bath flasks are a long-lived type both on the Continent and in Britain. There are no finds which positively can be shown to belong to the Claudian period, the earliest finds being of Neronian date, from Kingsholm, Gloucestershire,[6] and Usk, Gwent.[7] From Colchester, Essex, one flask was found in a layer dating from AD 60–100.[8] Most finds belong to the first and the second centuries. However, there are sporadic finds from the

124

third century. The latest dated finds – AD 240–270 – come from the Roman cemetery at Brougham, Cumbria.[9]

The function of the vessels

These small globular flasks with looped handles are denominated bath flasks or *aryballoi*. The latter name was used for a vessel of the same general shape and size in pottery or bronze used by athletes in the bath and *palestra*, and by women in the bath in Classical Greece. Vase paintings, as well as carvings on tomb-stones of the Classical period, depict scenes with young athletes with an *aryballos* on a thin chain hanging from the wrist, or together with a strigil and sponge on the wall. Finds of pottery *aryballoi*, of Corinthian origin in particular, are relatively common.[10]

Although there are finds of core-formed glass *aryballoi* from Egypt contemporary with the Greek finds mentioned above,[11] the blown *aryballoi* of the Roman period do not constitute a continuation of this tradition. Rather, it seems the Roman *aryballoi* in blown glass are copies of contemporary vessels made in pottery or bronze.[12] In Roman Britain, as well as on the Continent, finds come predominantly from baths or, less commonly, burials.[13] The finds from baths, for example in Caerleon[14] and York,[15] confirm an association with bathing.

In burial contexts the flasks have been found with strigils and other objects associated with bathing,[16] and several finds still have the thin chains on which they were carried attached to the handles.[17] Literary evidence shows that bathers, regardless of whether they exercised before bathing or not, were massaged and used oil and a strigil to clean themselves with.[18] And Pliny the Elder argued, 'there are two liquids that are especially agreeable to the human body, wine inside and oil outside'.[19]

Although baths and bathing formed a fundamental part of Roman culture,[20] these finds may not only reflect how they were used in life. Cool has suggested that the presence of *aryballoi* in cremation burials reflects the preparation of the body prior to being put on the funerary pyre, or the anointing of the burnt bones before placing them in the grave.[21]

The finds from Roman contexts

In northern Britain finds of bath flasks or *aryballoi* are frequent, and this is also the case in the Midlands and southern Britain.[22] Bath flasks are common finds in the area which once was the Roman Empire, not least in the north-western provinces. Many of the finds come from Roman forts, and they are particularly prolific in the baths. Similarly the majority of finds in civilian contexts come from baths, with occasional finds from funerary contexts.[23]

The finds from non-Roman contexts in Scotland and north Northumberland

Two finds of bath flasks or *aryballoi* have been made in non-Roman/native contexts north of Hadrian's Wall: one comes from Dunadd, Argyll; the other from Traprain Law, East Lothian.

The find from Dunadd is a reworked rim of a bath flask, probably used as a gaming piece or as a bead (fig. 3.22.3.1). The rim is flat which indicates a late first to third century AD date. Dunadd is primarily an early Medieval site; there are, however, clear indications of a Roman Iron Age phase.[24] The assemblage of Roman imports discovered on this site is, however, very limited. Besides the bath flask, there is a single sherd of blue-green bottle glass, a glass bead of Roman date, and four fragments of samian ware (including a platter of second-century date). In addition to these there is a fragment of a glass bangle.[25] Whether or not these objects belong to the Iron Age phase, or represent reuse in the early Medieval phase, is not clear. Both Alan Lane and Ewan Campbell have suggested that the latter may be the case.[26]

Turning to the find from Traprain Law in East Lothian – a looped handle in natural green glass of first-century type, reworked to form a bead (fig. 2.3a, 3.22.3.2) – it is the only such find certainly from a Roman Iron Age site. One question that arises from this is whether the find reached Traprain Law as a bead, or as an intact vessel which was later broken and then reused as a bead? The assemblage of Roman imports on this site is exceptionally large with material from the first to the early fifth centuries AD, encompassing an unusually wide range of objects.[27] Hence it is quite possible that the object reached the site as an intact vessel, an interpretation which, of course, is open to debate. The Traprain assemblage includes an – admittedly very small – group of vessels and objects that were associated with personal hygiene in their original Roman context: the aforementioned *aryballos*, at least one perfume bottle, tweezers, nail-cleaners and an ear-scoop. All evidence seems to indicate that there were close contacts between Rome and the Votadini tribe who inhabited the site; in the light of this, it could be suggested that some individuals at the site had an acquaintance with this aspect of Roman culture.

Hygiene and bathing can be said to constitute a fundamental aspect of Roman culture, and it was a part of daily life, not least in the Roman forts of Britain.[28] If these objects from Traprain Law were linked to Roman hygienic practices, it would be a rare, but far from unique, example of how this aspect of Roman culture came to influence the peoples beyond the borders of the Empire. J. D. Hill has pointed to a number of finds of toilet instruments – such as tweezers and ear scoops – found on late pre-Roman Iron Age sites in southern Britain, indicating the adoption of Roman practices.[29]

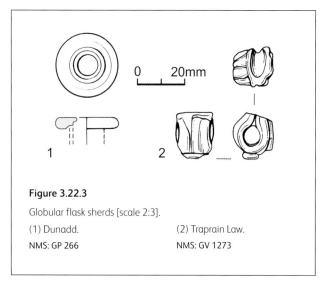

Figure 3.22.3

Globular flask sherds [scale 2:3].

(1) Dunadd.   (2) Traprain Law.
NMS: GP 266   NMS: GV 1273

Dunadd, Argyll.[30] J:1

GP 266*, NMS. Folded rim, reused as gaming piece. Blue-green. Worn on both sides. Diameter 25; WT 3.4.

Traprain Law, East Lothian.[31] N:2

GV 1273* (1924 170), Area S, Level 2, NMS. Looped handle, with remains of the neck to which it was attached. Reused as bead. Green. Bubbly. Worn as a result of secondary usage. PH 17; WT 3.5.

Finds from other areas beyond the borders of the Roman Empire

Bath flasks seem to be very rare finds outside the Roman Empire. From the Germanic settlement Castrop-Rauxel, Kreis Recklinghausen, Nordrhein-Westfalen, Germany, there is a single sherd of an *aryballos*.[32] Another reported find from Free Germany – a base fragment of a pale blue *aryballos* – comes from Westerwanna, Wanna, Kreis Cuxhaven, Niedersachsen, Germany.[33] There are also a number of finds from the Black Sea region, including finds with cut decoration and applied self-coloured trails.[34]

A number of finds come from the Kingdom of Meroë – a kingdom situated in Lower Nubia, present-day Egypt and Sudan – and finds have been made on a number of the major sites such as Karanóg, Faras, Semna and Sedeinga. Many of these are facet-cut: for example, those from Semna,[35] Karanóg,[36] and a find which possibly comes from Maharraka (a settlement on the border between the Roman Empire and Kingdom of Meroë).[37] Whether or not these represent Roman imports, or in fact were the results of an indigenous manufacture, is unclear. Finds of glass are relatively rich in this area, and a number of types differ from finds within the borders of Rome, which has led Cool to suggest that an indigenous manufacture may have existed.[38]

A small number of finds come from the United Arab Emirates. A very rich tomb of the Roman-Parthian period at Dibba Al Hisn, Sharjah, included a find of a greenish colourless *aryballos*. From ed-Dur, Umm al-Qaiwain, there is a fragmented *aryballos*, in thin yellow-brown to yellow-green glass of a different type than those typical of the north-western provinces. This find has two strap handles, attached below the rim and at the shoulder of the vessel.[39]

Notes

1   Isings Form 61.
2   Cool & Price 1995, 156; Price & Cottam 1998a, 188–89.
3   Allen 1986b, 104–9, fig. 41 & fig. 42, pl. III.
4   Unpublished, referred to by Cool & Price 1995, 157.
5   Harden et al. 1968, 58.
6   Price & Cool 1985, 44.
7   Price 1995a, 172.
8   Cool & Price 1995, 158.
9   Cool 2004, 365–66.
10 C. Robert, s.v. 'Aryballos', *RE* II (1896) col. 1495; Richter & Milne 1935, 16.
11 Harden et al. 1968, 22.
12 Allen 1986b, 104; see also Price 1995a, 172.
13 van Lith & Randsborg 1985, 424; Price & Cottam 1998a, 189.
14 Allen 1986b, 104.
15 Charlesworth 1976b, 18.
16 Kisa 1908, 323.
17 See Fremersdorf 1958b, Taf. 41.
18 Galenos, *de sanitate tuenda*, 3.13
19 Pliny the Elder, *Historia Naturalis*, 14.150.
20 Fagan 1999.
21 Cool 2004, 366.
22 Cool & Price 1995, 156–58; Price & Cottam 1998a, 188–90 with references.
23 **The Netherlands**: Hoensbroek (Isings 1971, 14, fig. 2); Ubach over Worms (Isings 1971, 14, fig. 2); Nijmegen (Isings 1957, 79; Isings 1968, 10; Isings 1980, 316–19). **Belgium**: Opgrimby (Isings 1971, 14, fig. 2); Gors-Opleew (Lux & Roosens 1971, 37, fig. 26). **Germany**: Köln (Cologne) (Kisa 1908, 322, Abb. 60–63a, Fremersdorf 1926, Abb 1.4, 1.5, 13.5; Fremersdorf 1955a, Abb 2–3, Taf. 24 & 27; Doppelfeld 1966, Abb. 104; Fremersdorf 1967, 118; Fremersdorf & Fremersdorf-Polónyi 1984, 101–2; Friedhoff 1989, Abb. 2:17; Päffgen 1989, Abb. 2); Laurenzberg (Follmann & Piepers 1963, 540, Abb. 28:5); Asberg (van Lith 1984, 260); Trier (Goethert-Polaschek 1977, 227–30); Regensburg (von Schnurbein 1977, 74–75); Nida-Heddernheim (Welker 1974, 30–34; Welker 1985, 14–16); Xanten (Charlesworth 1984, 294). **France**: Normandy (Sennequier 1994, fig. 3); the cemetery at d'Épiais-Rhus, Val-d'Oise (Vanpeene 1993, 39, pl. 16); Fréjus (Béraud & Gébara 1990, 159, fig. 4:23). **Portugal** (Alarcão & Alarção 1965, est. 3.). **Italy**: Aquileia (Calvi 1969, tav. 2); Luni (Roffia 1973, 478); the Mithraeum of the Church of Santa Prisca, Rome (Isings 1965, 527, fig. 466); Ostia (Moriconi 1969–72, 371–72); Herculaneum & Pompeii (Scatozza Höricht 1986, 55–56); the cemetery at the Ancient Cornus (Santa Caterina di Pitenuri) (Fortuna Canivet 1969, fig. 29). **Croatia**: Senj (Damevski 1974, 71, tab. 7:1); Starigrad (Abramić & Colnago 1909, 82, Abb. 42). **Greece**: Samothrace (Dusenbery 1967, 47, fig. 48); Monasteriki Kephala, Knossos, Crete (Carington-Smith 1982, 278). **Cyprus** (Vessberg & Westholm 1956, 167, fig. 50; Åström 1964, fig. 2). **Egypt**: Quseir al Qadim (Meyer 1992, 31); Krokodilo (al-Muwayh) (Brun 2003, 383).
24 Lane & Campbell 2000, 87–90.
25 Appendix A, J:1.
26 Lane & Campbell 2000, 90.
27 Appendix A, N:2.
28 Alcock 1996, 101–2.
29 Hill 1997.
30 Christison, & Anderson 1905, 315, fig. 44.
31 Cree 1924, 268.
32 *CRFB* D7, XI-06-1/6.11; Fremersdorf 1970c, 89.
33 *CRFB* D4, XXI-02-27/1.6.
34 Sorokina 1987, 40–46.
35 Cool 1996, fig. 5.1.
36 Fleming 1996, 25.
37 Harden et al. 1968, 81; Harden et al. 1988, 201.
38 For a discussion, see Cool 1996.
39 Whitehouse 1998, 35, fig. 8:79.

3.23 Cylindrical and prismatic bottles

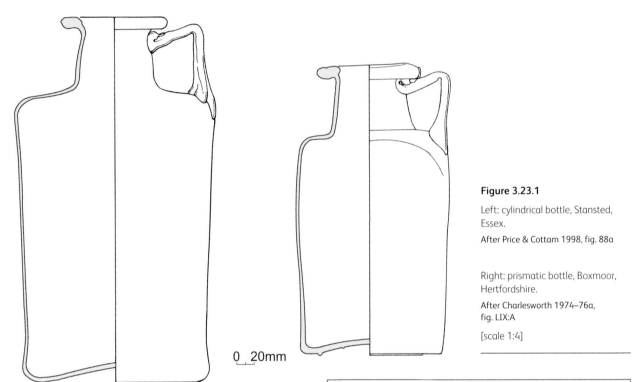

0 20mm

Figure 3.23.1

Left: cylindrical bottle, Stansted, Essex.

After Price & Cottam 1998, fig. 88a

Right: prismatic bottle, Boxmoor, Hertfordshire.

After Charlesworth 1974–76a, fig. LIX:A

[scale 1:4]

The rims, necks and shoulders of cylindrical bottles (Isings Form 51) are identical to those of all types of prismatic bottles: square, hexagonal, octagonal (Isings Form 50), and rectangular bottles (Isings Form 90).[1] For this reason I have placed all finds of blue-green bottle glass in one chapter. Although most of the blue-green glass comes from bottles, however, it is important to note that the bodies and bases of square bottles are similar or identical to those of collared square jars (Isings Form 62; see chapter 3.17).

A general description of the types

Cylindrical bottles

Cylindrical bottles of Isings Form 51 are, with few exceptions, purely functional in design. The bottle is thick-walled and robust, made to withstand continuous use as a storage vessel or transport container for liquids, semi-liquids and possibly also solids.[2] Most bottles have rims that are folded out, up and in. They are flat or diagonal

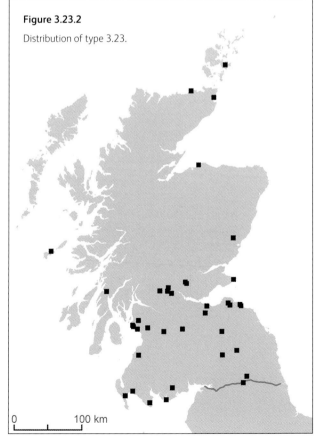

Figure 3.23.2

Distribution of type 3.23.

0 100 km

in profile, and wider than the neck. The necks are short, cylindrical and vary in breadth from narrow to wide. The shoulder is almost flat and horizontal (fig. 3.23.3a).

Several types of handles occur, all of which are broad and angular. The most frequent type of handle is reeded, i.e. has multiple tooled narrow ribs. This kind of handle has been appropriately termed *Selleriehenkel*, i.e. *celery-handle*, in German scholarly research. However, ribboned plain handles and handles with two or more broad ribs also occur. The handles have a lower attachment to the shoulder and a folded upper attachment just below the rim, somewhat drawn in;[3] this is to protect it against blows and prevent damage.

The body has a vertical side and is cylindrical in shape, often with a slight bulge at the upper part just below the shoulder. The base is slightly concave, and pitted or dimpled on the outer surface. In contrast to prismatic bottles, the bases never have any form of maker's mark or decoration. Cylindrical bottles are either free-blown or blown in a one-piece mould.[4] With the exception of a group of wheel-cut bottles not discussed here, all such bottles were produced in blue-green glass.

There is considerable variation in size: rim diameters vary from *c.* 40–160 mm, heights from *c.* 150–400 mm, and body diameters from *c.* 80–250 mm. The capacity of the bottles is up to *c.* 8 litres.[5] This variation in size and shape probably reflects different functional uses.

Cylindrical bottles must have been relatively simple to manufacture. Most vessels were free-blown and needed no moulds, and in most cases they were made in common blue-green glass.[6] This, and the very large number of finds made predominantly in the north-western provinces and North Africa, implies that they were produced on many sites in those areas, including Britain. Unlike the contemporary prismatic bottles, cylindrical bottles lack makers' marks; therefore it is impossible to tell where these might have been made.

Prismatic bottles

I have chosen to use the wider term 'prismatic' bottles for square, rectangular, hexagonal and octagonal bottles (the terms describe the varying base shapes). However, in native contexts north of Hadrian's Wall there is no evidence for any other type of prismatic bottles than the square ones, but as these can only be identified from larger body sherds or base sherds, it cannot be excluded that single rectangular, hexagonal, or octagonal bottles were brought to the area. Therefore prismatic bottles as a whole are discussed, with a primary focus on square bottles.

Prismatic bottles are thick-walled and robust vessels, designed to withstand continuous usage. Most bottles have rims that are folded out, up and in. They are flat or diagonal in profile, and wider than the neck. The necks are short, cylindrical and vary in breadth from narrow to wide. The shoulder is almost flat and horizontal (fig. 3.23.3b).

Several types of handles occur, all of which are broad and angular. The most frequent type of handle is reeded. However, ribboned plain handles and those with two or more broad ribs are also known. The handles have a lower attachment to the shoulder, and a folded upper attachment just below the rim, somewhat drawn in;[7] these parts of the bottle were made by free manipulation. The bodies and bases of prismatic bottles could be manufactured in two ways.

(a) They were blown freehand and flattened on a marver block.[8] Finds of this category have predominantly been made in the Mediterranean area,[9] and they are very rare in Britain.[10]

(b) They were blown in a multi-part mould. Bottles of this type have sharp right angles on the bodies, and flat or slightly concave bases with raised designs.[11] Here yet another problem of identifying the sherds arises. The bodies and bases of prismatic bottles are identical to those of collared square jars (Isings Form 62).[12] It has generally been assumed that these are comparatively rare, but it may well be that finds have wrongly been identified as bottles.[13]

The majority of prismatic bottles have simple base designs, with raised concentric circles in the centre enclosed by L-shaped angles in the corners.[14] Sometimes these base designs are accompanied by letters.[15] The letters are mostly Latin, though in the eastern Mediterranean bottles which bore Greek letters have also been found.[16] Normally it is abbreviated names, full names being considerably less common.

On many bases concentric circles are combined with other types of geometrical designs, such as dots, small circles, and lozenges. Less common in the north-western provinces are simple figures or scenes.[17] One of the few British finds of this kind is the base of a prismatic bottle from Caersws *vicus*, Powys, Wales, that depicts a helmeted gladiator.[18]

As is the case with cylindrical bottles, prismatic bottles vary considerably in size. Dorothy Charlesworth was of the opinion that the bottles could not be divided by size,[19] but a detailed study by Cool and Price shows that there were three main sizes: small bottles, large bottles, and tall narrow bottles.[20] Rim diameters varied from 40–160 mm or more, heights 120–350 mm or more, and body widths 50–150 mm.[21]

Prismatic bottles are most frequent in the western and north-western provinces, even though they also occur in North Africa and the eastern Mediterranean area. Considering the very large numbers of finds of this type, and the widespread distribution, it is likely that they were produced on a multitude of sites in the Roman Empire. It has been suggested that the manufacturing centres were placed in the wine- and oil-producing areas, in order to supply the army with these goods.[22] I am inclined to disagree with this suggestion, given the practical difficulties in transporting and handling large numbers of bottles. A more likely scenario, is that the bottles normally were used for regional distribution.

The raised designs on the bases of prismatic bottles have attracted much attention in scholarly research, as these might yield information about where the bottles and/or their contents originated. Base-moulds were made in wood, terracotta and marble.[23] Finds of the latter two types have been made at number of sites across the Empire,[24] for example at Köln (Cologne), Germany;[25] Augst, Switzerland;[26] Lyon, France;[27] Saintes, France;[28] Augustobriga (Ciudad Rodrigo), Spain;[29] and Apulium, Romania.[30] But these are all of common designs, and thus add little to our knowledge of their distribution.

Many bottles have raised letters on the bases, but whether these refer to the manufacturer of the bottle, the producer of its content, those who traded it, or the origin of the content, remains unclear. For example, it has been suggested that the letters CCV on several British finds were produced at *Colonia Claudia Victricensis*, i.e. Colchester, Essex,[31] or that bottles with the stamp *CCAA* discovered in Germany were made in *Colonia Claudia Ara Agrippinensis*, that is Köln (Cologne).[32] A very interesting and indeed rare find comes from Linz, Austria; a bottle bearing the mark: *Sentia Secunda facit Aq(uileiae) vitr(earia)*. This is a most unusual find, which names a woman as glass-blower at, or the owner of, a glass-working plant in Aquileia, Italy.[33]

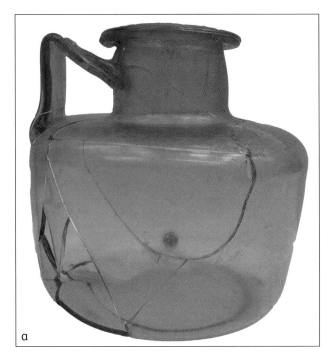

a

Figure 3.23.3

(a) Cylindrical bottle, Boards Farm, Suffolk.	(b) Prismatic bottle, Faversham, Kent.
British Museum: 1912,0528.2	British Museum: 1299.70

b

Dating the types

Cylindrical bottles

Considering that cylindrical bottles were predominantly functional in design, the type is surprisingly short-lived: their production lasted around 70 to 100 years. The reason for this is probably that the type was regarded as less practical than the prismatic bottles of Isings Form 50 when it came to storing and transporting liquids and semi-liquids.

The oldest dated finds on the Continent are from Magdalensberg, Austria, considered to be of Tiberian date.[34] Hofheim, a Roman military site in the Rhineland, Germany, founded in the Claudian period, has also yielded finds of this type.[35] Several finds have also been unearthed in layers dated to *c.* AD 15–55 at Velsen, Noord-Holland, the Netherlands.[36] In Britain the earliest finds are of similar dates: Colchester, Essex, dating to the Claudian-Neronian period;[37] and Fishbourne, Sussex, dating to AD 43–75.[38] In earlier scholarly publications, e.g. those by Dorothy Charlesworth, it was argued that the production of cylindrical bottles continued to *c.* AD 150.[39] However, today it is generally accepted that production ended well before that date – *c.* AD 110.[40]

Cool and Price have pointed out the main reasons why it is so hard to establish when the production ended. First, the very large scale of production meant that there are very great quantities of fragments on sites which have sometimes been redeposited. Second, the bottles were robust and could have been in use a long time after production had ceased.[41] Although the earliest British finds date to the Claudian or Neronian periods, the majority of finds are of Flavian date.[42]

Prismatic bottles

The earliest dated finds of prismatic bottles on the Continent belong to the late Augustan period, and were found in Magdalensberg, Austria.[43] This is still the only find of this early date. Other finds belong to the Gaian/Claudian period. In Cosa, Tuscany finds of prismatic bottles were made under a wall which collapsed in AD 40–45.[44] A shipwreck that sank off the French coast in AD 41–42, *Port-Vendres II*, is another early example.[45] Finds of Claudian date have also been made in Hofheim, Germany.[46] The earliest British finds are of Claudian date:[47] for example, from Sheepen, near Colchester, Essex.[48]

There are several difficulties in trying to establish when the production of prismatic bottles ceased. The bottles were designed to withstand rough handling, and in many cases intact bottles must have been in circulation long after they were made. Another problem is that of redeposition. Due to the very high numbers of fragments of prismatic bottles on sites, much of it was redeposited as a result of later construction work during antiquity.

In 1966 Dorothy Charlesworth suggested that the production of prismatic bottles ended *c.* AD 120–130.[49] Cool and Price have put forward the idea that production continued to the late second or possibly early third century.[50] This is supported by a number of late finds. A pit excavated at Felmongers, Harlow, Essex, contained material dated to AD 160–170.[51] From a late second-century pit in Thomas Street, Southwark, London, there was a tall prismatic bottle.[52] Finds from funerary contexts – a Roman cemetery at Brougham, Cumbria – demonstrate that prismatic bottles were still in use in the mid- to late third century AD, while at Frocester Court Roman villa, Gloucestershire, bottles seem to have been in use as late as the late third or early fourth century.[53]

The function of the vessels

When discussing the function of bottles, it has to be emphasised that they could have several functions during their 'life-span', and it is important to differentiate between their primary, secondary and possibly even tertiary use.

Both cylindrical and prismatic bottles are thick-walled and robust, made to withstand continuous employment as transport containers or storage vessels. Wear-patterns on much of the material bear evidence of a long period of use,[54] and there is both archaeological and iconographic evidence to show how they were stored and transported in boxes and crates.[55] There is much to suggest that bottles could carry a wide range of different liquids, semi-liquids, and in some cases even solid foodstuffs.

Residues found in bottles have rarely been analysed, but from a limited sample we know that they functioned as containers for olive oil.[56] Iconographic evidence demonstrates that bottles were used as containers for wine (see below), and in all probability also a range of different foodstuffs. The bottles with wide necks may have been used for storing semi-liquids such as *defrutum* or solid foodstuffs such as honey, whereas those with narrower necks could have been used for liquids such as wine or olive oil.

Bottles are simple to manufacture and are likely to have been relatively inexpensive. Thus there is little to indicate that they were traded in their own right; rather it must have been the contents that were important. Our knowledge as to what extent bottles were used for the transport of different alcoholic beverages or foodstuffs is limited, however, due to the difficulties in determining the provenance of bottles. Cylindrical bottles are more or less identical regardless of where they are found in the north-western provinces; and our understanding of the so-called maker's marks on the bases of some prismatic bottles is deficient.

With the possible exception of exclusive wines and foodstuffs, there would be little point in the employment of bottles for long-distance trade. Here amphorae and barrels would be inherently more practical as transport containers.[57] Although no certain evidence can be presented, it might be suggested that bottles were used in the regional and local distribution of, for instance, wine. This might be supported by iconographic evidence. A carved representation of what might be the interior of a shop discovered in Langres, Champagne-Ardenne, France, depicts a pair of shoes and a pair of sandals hanging suspended, as well as two bottles.[58] Perhaps one went to the local wine-merchant to have the bottle refilled once it was empty; the wear patterns demonstrate an extended period of usage.

It was not only in civilian contexts that bottles were employed as transport containers in regional and local distribution. In a study of the uses of glass vessels in Roman Britain, Hilary Cool and Michael Baxter have highlight the fact that bottles form a proportionally larger component at military sites than at civilian sites. They argue that this demonstrates the army's greater need for transport and storage vessels.[59] We know that wine, olive oil and a number of other types of foodstuffs were transported to the Roman army units based in Britain in large transport vessels such as amphorae and barrels, and it is possible that this was drawn off into individual bottles.

In addition to serving as transport and storage vessels, bottles were employed as tableware. On the basis of iconographic evidence – mosaics, tombstones and sarcophagi – it is evident that bottles were employed as part of drinking sets.[60] Cylindrical bottles are sometimes depicted on tombstones, demonstrating that they were employed in funerary banquets.[61] A unique sarcophagus from Simpelveld, Limburg, the Netherlands, is carved on the inside. This shows the interior (and exterior) of a Roman villa (fig. 6.4). On either side of a three-legged table stand two prismatic and one cylindrical bottle

placed on a low cupboard, and a low cupboard with three cylindrical glass cups, two 'mixing-bowls' and two metal jugs.[62] The cups, bowls and jugs on the right-hand side of the table clearly constitutes a drinking set, but do the bottles on the other side of the table belong to this? I would argue that this is very likely, for other iconographic evidence seems to support the idea that they often were wine bottles. A mosaic from Tunisia shows a cylindrical bottle and beaker filled to the brim with a dark liquid, presumably wine; another mosaic depicts a cylindrical bottle, a *skyphos* and a ladle.[63]

The vast majority of intact bottles discovered come from funerary contexts, containing the cremated remains of the deceased. Bottles used as ash-urns have been found in many parts of the Roman Empire: for example in Britain,[64] France, Italy,[65] and Algeria.[66] It was also not uncommon that broken glass, particularly bottles, was reused. On many Roman sites, fragments of bottles were knapped or chipped into gaming pieces. From Prestatyn, Clwyd, Wales, there are examples of knapped fragments of cylindrical bottles utilised as tools or blades, although these are very rare indeed.[67] Broken bottles, like most other Roman glass, were recycled and used as cullet.[68] An example of blue-green vessel glass being imported as cullet comes from the excavations of a high status site in north-west Wales: Cefn Cwmwd, Anglesey. The evidence from this recently excavated site seems to suggest that this cullet was intended for bead-working.[69]

The finds from Roman contexts

Cylindrical bottles

Cylindrical bottles are outnumbered by prismatic bottles, not just in terms of fragments, but also the number of sites on which they are represented. The number of Roman sites in northern Britain that have yielded cylindrical bottles is relatively limited. Although prismatic bottles dominate on Romano-British sites in general, there are indications that some Flavian military sites were supplied with liquids and foodstuffs in cylindrical rather than prismatic bottles, as at Inchtuthil, Perthshire, a legionary fortress north of the Antonine Wall, occupied in AD 83–86.[70] In the Midlands and southern Britain, finds are relatively sparse from contexts earlier than the Flavian period. On the other hand, they are very common in the last quarter of the first century.[71] In most cases, however, they are outnumbered by prismatic bottles.

Cylindrical bottles are mainly found in the north-western and western provinces, as well as in Italy.[72] However, a related type of cylindrical bottle with a 'collar' rim, which is of a later date, is found in the eastern Mediterranean.[73] As is the case in Britain, most Continental sites have considerably more prismatic than cylindrical bottles. An exception to this rule is Hofheim, Germany.[74]

Prismatic bottles

A majority of Roman military sites in northern Britain have yielded blue-green bottles; they constitute substantial parts of the total assemblages of the vessel glass. For example, in Strageath, Perthshire, no less than 64.5% of the assemblage was blue-green bottle glass.[75] As pointed out above, bottles appear to be more frequent finds on military than on civilian sites.[76]

In the Midlands and southern Britain, finds of prismatic, predominantly square, bottles are exceedingly common,[77] and a large proportion of late first and early second-century sites have finds of prismatic bottles. An interesting fact is that bottles are often the only type of Roman vessel glass found on rural sites.[78]

Although prismatic and cylindrical bottles were only produced during half the Roman period, blue-green bottle glass constitutes substantial parts of the total assemblages of Roman glass on many sites. It is not uncommon that this category of glass accounts for 15–30% of the assemblages. Nevertheless, finds are relatively scarce until Flavian times. With few exceptions the early finds are of the low, squat type of bottle.[79]

Prismatic bottles of Isings Form 50 are exceedingly common in the Roman Empire. Yet the types discussed above are chiefly found in the western and the north-western provinces, Italy and North Africa.[80] In the eastern Mediterranean, many of the prismatic bottles are free-blown, and/or have collared rims.[81]

The finds from non-Roman contexts in Scotland and north Northumberland

Blue-green bottle glass constitutes the single largest category of imported Roman glass found in non-Roman/native contexts north of Hadrian's Wall, and to date 37 sites have yielded glass of this type. (The bottle glass is predominantly blue-green in colour; however, there are finds in pale green glass too.) Thirty-one of these sites are included in the catalogue. In addition to these there are six recent finds: Clarkly Hill, Morayshire;[82]

Castle Craig, Perthshire;[83] Kay Craig, Perthshire;[84] Gilmerton House, Athelstaneford, East Lothian;[85] Broxmouth, East Lothian;[86] and Whitefield Loch, Wigtownshire.[87] The bulk of the material was found in the south – both in terms of quantity and geographical distribution – whereas finds are fewer north of the Forth-Clyde isthmus. Blue-green bottle glass has been discovered on 14 sites north of the Forth-Clyde isthmus, and on 23 sites south of this line. A significant proportion of the finds come from a single site south of the Forth-Clyde line, Traprain Law; but even if we exclude this site, the estimated minimum number of vessels is more than twice as large in the south as in the north. The underlying reasons for this regional imbalance may be a reflection of a 'filter effect', with a high proportion of low value goods closer to the border.

Undeniably the bottles must have been very practical containers; many vessels are worn, indicating an extended period of use. In addition there are a number of cases of broken vessels being reused as gaming pieces. However, as in the case of amphorae and barrels, it must have been the contents rather than the container that was of primary interest. As there are no analyses of possible remaining residues on these bottles, we cannot be certain what they once contained. As argued above, there is a much evidence to demonstrate that bottles were used for the transport and storage of wine, as well as being parts of drinking sets, in a Roman context. We also know bottles were used in the transport and storage of olive oil, and other liquid foodstuffs, in the Roman world. One of the main arguments in this work is that the Iron Age elites tried to imitate Roman drinking customs – and to some extent even drank wine – but possibly there also was some influence from Roman culinary practices.

North of the Forth-Clyde isthmus

Bottles have been discovered on the following sites north of the isthmus (including only the finds in the catalogue). The northernmost find of bottle glass comes from Mine Howe, Tankerness, Orkney. The site was first discovered just after the end of the Second World War, but subsequently refilled and thereafter forgotten until its rediscovery in 1999. This enigmatic site consists of a mound in the centre of which is drystone masonry staircase which leads down to an underground chamber. It is surrounded by a massive ditch, with a range of activities taking place outwith this. Fragments of other glass objects, including a fragment of snake-thread glass vessel, were discovered, along with Roman pottery and brooches.[88]

Excavations at Crosskirk, Caithness – a promontory enclosure with a broch – yielded one fragment from a minimum of one cylindrical bottle, an unidentified glass beaker, and some Roman pottery.[89] Keiss Harbour broch, Caithness, was dug in the late 1800s and in 2006, and a rim sherd in blue-green bottle glass was discovered, although not recognised as such but instead identified as a fragmented glass bangle. A small body sherd of Roman pottery was also unearthed.[90]

Only a single site in the Hebrides has yielded bottle glass: one fragment from a minimum of one prismatic bottle was found at Dun Mor Vaul, Tiree. In addition to this there were six fragments of blue-green bottle glass of uncertain type. This site, a broch and later farmstead fig. 8.5), yielded a small assemblage of Roman goods: the bottle glass, a cylindrical cup, and a few sherds of Roman pottery including samian.[91]

A rescue excavation of Dalladies, Kincardineshire, showed that it was an open settlement with souterrains. Unfortunately the site was partly destroyed due to gravel-extraction, and it is rather difficult to interpret. Nevertheless, a small body of Roman imports was recovered: one sherd representing a minimum of one prismatic bottle, a piece of samian and a fragmented flagon in Roman coarse-ware.[92]

Dunadd, Argyll, has been the object of several excavations. As a consequence of the poorly executed early excavations, however, relatively little is known about the earlier – Roman Iron Age – occupation of the site. One fragment of unidentified bottle glass was found, as well as a reworked rim of a bath flask and four sherds of Roman pottery (samian).[93]

Two fragments from a minimum of one cylindrical bottle were discovered at Castlehill Wood, Stirlingshire, a dun/fort excavated in 1955. One sherd of a pillar-moulded bowl was found on the same site.[94]

Excavations of a wooden roundhouse and a later broch at Fairy Knowe, Stirlingshire, yielded a rich and varied assemblage of Roman goods of first-century AD date, including twelve fragments from a minimum of one, probably more, cylindrical bottles; three fragments of unidentified blue-green bottle glass (fig. 3.23.4.1); pottery flagons, oil amphorae, *mortaria* and bowls.[95] But while this may indicate an acquaintance with Roman cuisine, there is no conclusive evidence for Roman drinking customs, since while the bottles might have contained wine, there are no drinking vessels in glass, although vessels in other materials could have been used.

The excavations of Leckie, Stirlingshire – a wooden roundhouse and a later broch – yielded an assemblage of imported Roman goods, which is not only unusually

rich and varied, but also of notable quality.[96] Six fragments from a minimum of one cylindrical bottle, 14 fragments from a minimum of one, probably more prismatic bottles, and 15 fragments that could not be determined to type, were discovered on the site. Jugs, cups and beakers, possibly contemporary with the bottles, were also unearthed. This assemblage might once have constituted Roman drinking sets employed on the site.

Excavations at East Coldoch – a defended roundhouse – unearthed a number of sherds of prismatic bottles. No great quantities of Roman material were found, but finds included a piece of samian of Antonine date.[97]

Constantine's Cave, Fife, was excavated in 1914, and a small assemblage of Roman goods indicating a Roman Iron Age phase was discovered. This consisted of a single sherd from a cylindrical bottle, and fragments of three amphorae.[98]

South of the Forth-Clyde isthmus

A wide range of sites south of the isthmus have yielded Roman bottle glass.

The excavations of Castlelaw, Midlothian, yielded a small body of Roman goods: a single sherd of a bottle, probably a cylindrical bottle, and a few sherds of samian.[99] Excavations at Edinburgh Castle were only partial as the present castle covers much of the area. A refuse heap, probably from a hillfort of the Roman Iron Age period, was excavated. Despite the small scale of these excavations, a fairly substantial assemblage of Roman imports was discovered, including a fragment of a prismatic bottle, a fourth-century jug or flask, and a wide array of Roman fine-ware and coarse-ware.[100]

Dryburn Bridge, East Lothian – a palisaded homestead with timber roundhouses – has generally been considered as an early Iron Age site. Radiocarbon dates and a single fragment of blue-green bottle glass, however, suggest some Roman Iron Age activity at the site.[101]

Excavations have taken place at Traprain Law, East Lothian, over almost a century, and these have yielded an assemblage of Roman goods which surpasses that of any other native site in terms of size.[102] Therefore it is hardly surprising that it includes a substantial number of bottles (fig. 3.23.7): 24 fragments from a minimum of seven, probably more, cylindrical bottles (fig. 3.23.4.3); 66 fragments from a minimum of 16 prismatic bottles (figs 3.23.4–6); and 67 fragments not possible to determine to type. Cups, beakers and jugs, which are roughly contemporary, have also been discovered, implying that these might once have constituted imported Roman drinking sets.

Hyndford crannog, Lanarkshire, was dug in 1898, unearthing a body of first- and second-century Roman artefacts. These included 14 fragments from a minimum of one cylindrical bottle, two fragments from a minimum of two prismatic bottles (fig. 3.23.5.1), and six fragments of blue-green bottle glass not possible to determine to type. Two glass bowls and a variety of Roman fine-ware and coarse-ware were also discovered.[103]

A unique find – a prismatic bottle containing a coin hoard with some 400 Roman silver coins – was discovered in 1803 at Torfoot, Lanarkshire. The latest coins date to Commodus (AD 180–192),[104] implying it was deposited in the last few years of the second century. One fragment of a cylindrical bottle, and two fragments of blue-green bottle glass not possible to identify to type, were found at ?Ardeer, Ayrshire or ?Luce Sands, Wigtownshire. A few sherds of late Roman, or more probably post-Roman, glass were also recovered from this collection.[105]

Buston crannog, Ayrshire, was excavated in 1880 to 1881, and again in 1989–90. Only a very small assemblage of Roman goods was unearthed: two fragments from a minimum of one prismatic bottle; one unidentified fragment of bottle glass (possibly from the same vessel); and fragments of a samian platter.[106]

Excavations at Castlehill, Dalry, Ayrshire – a fort – yielded a small body of Roman imports: one fragment of a cylindrical bottle; two fragments from a minimum of one prismatic bottle; one sherd of blue-green glass not possible to determine to type; and fragments of samian platters.[107]

At Glenhead, Ayrshire – a 'fort' with wooden roundhouses – excavations yielded two fragments of a prismatic bottle, one fragment of unidentified bottle glass, and fragments of a samian bowl and a platter.[108]

A small body of Roman goods was unearthed during the excavation of a crannog at Lochspouts, Ayrshire: a fragment of blue-green bottle glass reused as a gaming piece, fragments of a samian platter and a bowl, and fragments of a white jar.[109]

The small fort at Seamill, West Kilbride, Ayrshire, was dug in 1840 and 1880. Two fragments from one, possibly two cylindrical bottles, along with fragments of Roman coarse-ware, were unearthed.[110]

Numerous casual finds have been made in the area of Luce Sands, the coastal dunes at the head of Luce Bay, Wigtownshire, but whether these relate to each other is unclear. These include a fragment of a prismatic bottle.[111]

It is argued elsewhere that the finds of Roman glass at Whithorn, Wigtownshire – an early monastic site – represent loot from abandoned Roman forts, rather than a Roman Iron Age phase on the site.[112] The assemblage of Roman glass includes: two fragments from a minimum of one cylindrical bottle, and four fragments of prismatic bottles or late Roman double-glossy window glass.[113]

In 1866 two fishermen dredged up a cauldron in Carlingwark Loch, Kirkcudbrightshire. This hoard – mainly consisting of metal tools, and a few pieces of weapons and armour – is unique in that it is the only such hoard that includes glass of any kind. Three fragments of the base of a prismatic bottle were discovered, and subsequently lost, the only find so far in a native context of a bottle with maker's marks.[114]

A few Roman objects have been unearthed at Torrs Cave, Kirkcudbrightshire – a natural cave – including a fragment of a prismatic bottle (fig. 3.23.5.2), and fragments of two samian vessels.[115]

Excavations at Torwoodlee, Selkirkshire – a hillfort and later broch – yielded a fairly large assemblage of Roman imports.[116] This assemblage from the broch includes: 43 fragments representing a minimum of three, probably more cylindrical bottles (fig. 3.23.4.2);14 fragments of unidentified blue-green bottle glass;[117] a tubular-rimmed glass bowl; a globular glass jar; fragments of a mortarium; a minimum of two amphorae; samian platters; and fragments of flagons and jars.

Edgerston, Roxburghshire – a multivallate fort and later enclosed settlement – is a relatively poorly understood site. The assemblage of Roman goods from the site included one fragment of unidentified blue-green bottle glass; a rim fragment of a bronze vessel; and a variety of Roman pottery.[118]

At the Dod, Roxburghshire – a settlement consisting of roundhouses, a souterrain and other structures, surrounded by a system of earthworks – three sherds representing a minimum of one prismatic bottle were discovered during archaeological excavations. Other finds include five fragmented glass bangles and two broken annular beads.[119]

Milking Gap, High Shield, Northumberland, was a settlement with timber roundhouses. Fragments of blue-green bottle glass were reported to have been recovered at the site, but unfortunately they have since been lost. Roman fine- and coarse-ware was also found.[120]

Little is known about West Longlee, Northumberland, except that a stone-paved roundhouse was uncovered at the site. Blue-green bottle glass, now lost, and a fragment of a Roman flagon and a cooking pot were also discovered.[121]

The following finds are listed site by site, in alphabetical order:

?Ardeer Sands, Ayrshire or ?Luce Sands, Wigtownshire. P:1 or Q:1

Cylindrical bottle

Unreg., NMS. Base fragment? Pale blue-green. Reused as gaming piece? Dims 36 x 20; WT 1.8.

Unidentified blue-green bottle glass

Unreg., NMS. Body fragment? Blue-green. Reused as gaming piece? Dims 26 x 14.5; WT 1.4.

Unreg., NMS. Body fragment? Blue-green. Dims 22 x 19; WT 1.4.

Buston, Ayrshire. P:2

Prismatic bottle/s

HV 98*, NMS. Base fragment. Blue-green. Remains of raised, moulded circle. Dims 28 x 21; WT 6.7.

HV 100, NMS. Body fragment. Blue-green. Dims 19 x 25; WT 4.6.

Neck

HV 99, NMS. Fragment of neck? Blue-green. Dims 22 x 17; WT 9.0.

Carlingwark Loch, Kirkcudbrightshire. R:1

Prismatic bottle

Lost. A few fragments of the base of a prismatic bottle, with the letters A, I and possibly M.[122]

Castlehill, Ayrshire. P:3

Cylindrical bottle

HH 363 A, NMS. Body fragment. Blue-green. Bubbly. Dull, very worn surface. Dims 61 x 34; WT 3.5.

Prismatic bottle/s

HH 363 B, NMS. Body fragment. Blue-green. Dims 24 x 28; WT 5.0.

HH 363 D, NMS. Base fragment. Concentric circle in relief. Blue-green. Dims 19 x 15; WT 9.3.

Neck

HH 363 C, NMS. Fragment of neck. Blue-green. Bubbly. Brown speck. H 20; W 23; WT 4.1.

Castlehill Wood, Stirlingshire. K:2

Cylindrical bottle/s

HH 583, NMS. Fragment of base and lower body. Blue-green. Usage scratches on base. Dims 39 x 34; WT 3.5.

HH 584, NMS. Body fragment. Blue-green. Dims 12 x 21; WT 5.9.

Castlelaw, Midlothian. M:1

Cylindrical bottle

HH 439, NMS. Body fragment. Shoulder? Blue-green. Dull surface, many strain cracks. Dims 23 x 22; WT 6.0.

Constantine's Cave, Fife. L:1

Cylindrical bottle

Lost. 'Part of the shoulder and the ribbed end of the handle of a rounded glass bottle.'[123]

Crosskirk, Caithness. D:1

Cylindrical bottle?

A 1979 78, Hunterian Museum. Base fragment. Blue-green. Usage scratches. Dims 19 x 22; WT 9.0.

Dalladies, Kincardineshire. H:1

Prismatic bottle

HD 2116, NMS. Find 288, context f. 18. Body fragment. Blue-green, almost blue. Dims 25 x 22; WT 7.0.

The Dod, Roxburghshire. T:3

Prismatic bottle

HHE 256, NMS. Lower body and base. H 11; WT 11.

HHE 257, NMS. Body fragment. Dims 17 x 10; WT 5.5.

HHE 258, NMS. Shoulder fragment. Dims 19.5 x 12.5; WT 6.5.[124]

Dryburn Bridge, East Lothian. N:1

Rim

HDD 26., NMS. Rim fragment. Blue-green. Usage scratches. Unidentified. PH 14; WT 6.0.

Dun Mor Vaul, Tiree, Argyll. C:2

Prismatic bottle

A 1965 318, Hunterian Museum. Base fragment. Blue-green. Dims 28 x 14; WT 3.8.

Rims

A 1965 312, Hunterian Museum. Rim fragment. Blue-green. Bubbly. PH 16; WT 3.0.

A 1965 319, Hunterian Museum. Rim fragment. Blue-green. Bubbly. Dims 14 x 7; WT 4.0.

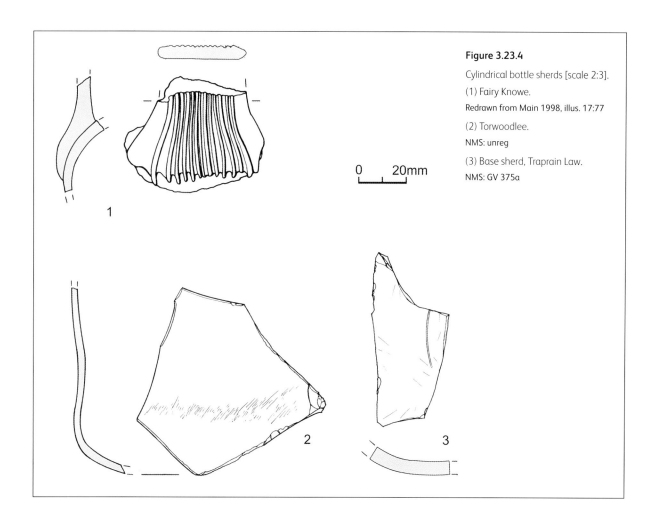

Figure 3.23.4
Cylindrical bottle sherds [scale 2:3].
(1) Fairy Knowe.
Redrawn from Main 1998, illus. 17:77
(2) Torwoodlee.
NMS: unreg
(3) Base sherd, Traprain Law.
NMS: GV 375a

0   20mm

Handle

A 1965 398/1, Hunterian Museum. Fragment of reeded handle. Blue-green. Dims 32 x 7.*Unidentified blue-green bottle glass*

Unidentified blue-green bottle glass

A 1965 242, Hunterian Museum. Fragment. Blue-green. Distorted by heat. Dims 12 x 8.

A 1965 398/2, Hunterian Museum. Blue-green. Distorted by heat. Dims 6 x 12.

A 1965 532, Hunterian Museum. Fragment. Blue-green. Dims 4 x 7.

Dunadd, Argyll. J:1

Unidentified blue-green bottle glass

Not seen

Edgerston, Roxburghshire. T:1

Unidentified blue-green bottle glass

Unreg., NMS. Body fragment? Blue-green. Dims 16 x 11; WT 1.9.

Edinburgh Castle, Midlothian. M:3

Prismatic bottle

SF 415, Edinburgh Castle. 'Small, flat fragment of blue-green glass, both surfaces glass, but one showing slight pitting, as though from contact with a mould. Small elongated bubbles within the metal, indicating that it had been blown. *c.*4mm thick.'[125]

East Coldoch, Stirlingshire. K:6

Prismatic bottle/s

SMR 922.00, (with excavator). 'Fragments of … Roman square bottles…'[126]

Fairy Knowe, Stirlingshire. K:3

Cylindrical bottle/s

FK SF 8, Smith Museum, Stirling. Base fragment. Blue-green, heavily worn. Dims 17 x 28; WT 3.

FK SF 38, Smith Museum, Stirling. Rim fragment. Blue-green, slightly distorted by heat. Dims 16 x 15; WT 4.

FK SF 102, Smith Museum, Stirling. Base fragment of a cylindrical bottle (?). Blue-green bottle glass. Usage scratches. Dims 13 x 17; WT 4.

FK SF 146, Smith Museum, Stirling. Base fragment. Blue-green, which was heavily worn before breaking. Dims 25 x 37; WT 6.0. Same vessel as FK 321.

FK SF 224, Smith Museum, Stirling. Base fragment. Blue-green. Dims 8 x 28; WT 5.

FK SF 321, Smith Museum, Stirling. Fragment of the base of a cylindrical bottle, belonging to the same vessel as FK SF 146. Blue-green bottle glass, which was heavily worn before breaking. Dims 12 x 49; WT 6.0.

FK SF 324, Smith Museum, Stirling. Body fragment? Dims 15 x 18; WT 2.

FK SF 344, Smith Museum, Stirling. Base fragment. Blue-green. The fragment was slightly distorted by heat. Dims 38 x 23; WT 3.

FK SF 362, Smith Museum, Stirling. Body fragment. Blue-green. Dims 14 x 32; WT 4.

Handle

FK SF 77*, Smith Museum, Stirling. Fragment of the lower part of a reeded handle. Blue-green, bubbly glass. Dims 61 x 40; WT 19.

Unidentified blue-green bottle glass

FK SF 76, Smith Museum, Stirling. Unidentified fragment of blue-green bottle glass. Dims 7 x 8; WT 1.5.

FK SF 160, Smith Museum, Stirling. Unidentified fragment of blue-green bottle glass. Dims 7 x 13; WT 5.

FK SF 384, Smith Museum, Stirling. Blue-green. Dims 21 x 17; WT 2.

FK SF 405, Smith Museum, Stirling. Blue-green. Distorted by heat, and therefore impossible to identify to type. Dims 33 x 17; WT 2.5.

FK SF 410, Smith Museum, Stirling. Blue-green, distorted by heat. Neck? Dims 22 x 10; WT 3.

Glenhead (Gourock Burn), Ayrshire. P:4

Prismatic bottle/s

Unreg., with excavator Alastair Hendry. Body fragment of prismatic bottle (?). Blue-green glass. Dims c. 17 x c. 20 (from photo).

Unreg., with excavator Alastair Hendry. Body fragment of prismatic bottle (?). Blue-green glass. Dims c. 30 x c. 45 (from photo).

Neck

Unreg., with excavator Alastair Hendry. Fragment of bottle neck. Blue-green glass. Dims c. 30 x c. 40 (from photo).

Hyndford, Lanarkshire. O:1

Cylindrical bottle/s

HTA 42, NMS. Base fragment. Blue-green. Dims 28 x 23; WT 3.5–6.3.

HTA 42, NMS. Body fragment. Blue-green. Usage scratches. Dims 31 x 14; WT 5.3.

HTA 42, NMS. Base fragment. Blue-green. Dims 30 x 19; WT 4.9.

HTA 43, NMS. Base fragment. Blue-green. Usage scratches. Dims 42 x 14; WT 5.7.

HTA 43, NMS. Body fragment. Blue-green. Lower body. Extremely worn. Dims 40 x 30; WT 3.7.

HTA 43, NMS. Body fragment. Blue-green. Usage scratches. Dims 39 x 40; WT 2.9.

HTA 43, NMS. Body fragment. Blue-green. Usage scratches. Dims 36 x 28; WT 3.4.

HTA 43, NMS. Body fragment. Blue-green. Affected by heat, giving a pitted surface. Dims 26 x 30; WT 2.8.

HTA 43, NMS. Fragment of lower body and base? Blue-green. Dims 22 x 13; WT 4.3.

HTA 43, NMS. Body fragment. Blue-green. Extremely worn. Dims 32 x 24; WT 2.8.

HTA 43, NMS. Body fragment. Blue-green. Dims 26 x 8; WT 3.8.

HTA 43, NMS. Body fragment. Blue-green. Dims 23 x 10; WT 2.5.

HTA 43, NMS. Body fragment. Blue-green. Dims 26 x 15; WT 2.9.

HTA 43, NMS. Body fragment. Blue-green. Heavily worn. Dims 40 x 30; WT 3.7.

Prismatic bottle/s

HTA 42*, NMS. Fragment of base and lower body. Blue-green. Two concentric circles in relief. Occasional small bubbles. Worn on base. Dims 32 x 42; WT 3.7–9.2.

HTA 42, NMS. Base fragment. Blue-green. Two concentric circles in relief. Bubbly. Worn on base. Dims 28 x 17; WT 6.6–8.0.

Rims and necks

HTA 42*, NMS. Fragment of rim and neck. Blue-green. Rim edge bent out, up, in and flattened. Occasional bubbles. Worn on inside of rim and on edge. PH 48; WT 8.5.

HTA 42, NMS. Fragment of rim and neck. Blue-green. Rim edge bent out, up, in and flattened. Bubbly. Worn on inside of rim and on edge. PH 23; WT 7.1. Same vessel as above.

HTA 42, NMS. Fragment of neck. Blue-green. Worn. Dims 38 x 29; WT 6.8. Same vessel as above.

Unidentified blue-green bottle glass

HTA 43, NMS. Fragment. Blue-green. Distorted by heat. Dims 27 x 19; WT 5.1.

HTA 43, NMS. Fragment. Blue-green. Dims 34 x 9; WT 3.0.

HTA 43, NMS. Fragment. Blue-green. Distorted by heat. Dims 21 x 16; WT 5.2.

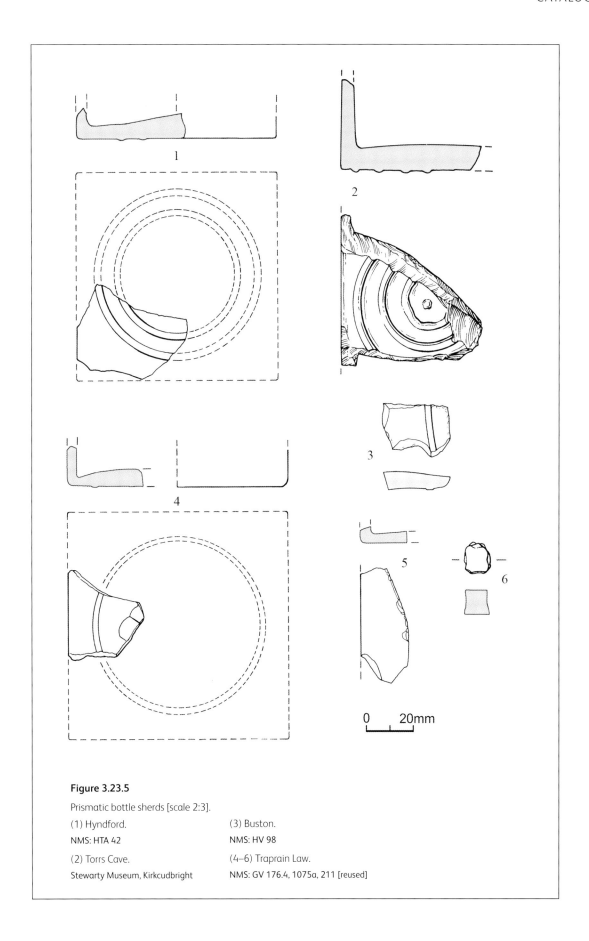

Figure 3.23.5

Prismatic bottle sherds [scale 2:3].

(1) Hyndford.

NMS: HTA 42

(2) Torrs Cave.

Stewarty Museum, Kirkcudbright

(3) Buston.

NMS: HV 98

(4–6) Traprain Law.

NMS: GV 176.4, 1075a, 211 [reused]

Keiss Harbour, Caithness. D:3

Rim

GA 493, NMS. Fragment of horizontal rim in blue-green glass. Folded out, up and in. Very worn after breakage. RD 100; PH 13; W 24; WT 4.0.

Leckie, Stirlingshire. K:4

Cylindrical bottle/s

A 1980 180, Hunterian Museum. Base fragment. Usage scratches. Blue-green. Dims 47 x 15.

A 1980 181, Hunterian Museum. Base fragment. Blue-green. Very bubbly. Dims 50 x 18; WT 5.1.

A 1980 185, Hunterian Museum. Fragment of body and base. Blue-green. Dims 39 x 37; WT 6.5.

A 1980 190, Hunterian Museum. Base and body fragment. Blue-green. Dims 31 x 22.

A 1980 193, Hunterian Museum. Base fragment. Blue-green. Very worn. Dims 27 x 20.

A 1980 204, Hunterian Museum. Base fragment. Usage scratches. Blue-green. Dims 20 x 10; WT 3.2.

Prismatic bottle/s

A 1980 176, Hunterian Museum. Base fragment. Blue-green. Remains of two raised concentric circles. Dims 64 x 34; WT 4.6.

A 1980 178, Hunterian Museum. Base fragment. Blue-green. Dims 34 x 22; WT 5.3.

A 1980 187, Hunterian Museum. Body fragment. Blue-green. Dims 34 x 14; WT 4.0.

A 1980 188, Hunterian Museum. Base fragment. Blue-green. Dims 38 x 30.

A 1980 189, Hunterian Museum. Base fragment. Blue-green. Dims 47 x 30.

A 1980 191, Hunterian Museum. Fragment of body or base. Blue-green. Bubbly. Dims 33 x 26.

A 1980 192, Hunterian Museum. Base fragment. Blue-green. Dims 24 x 23; WT 2.8.

A 1980 196, Hunterian Museum. Base fragment. Blue-green. Dims 13 x 19; WT 2.2.

A 1980 197, Hunterian Museum. Base fragment. Blue-green. Dims 13 x 18; WT 2.0.

A 1980 200, Hunterian Museum. Body fragment. Blue-green. Dims 20 x 13; WT 4.5.

A 1980 201, Hunterian Museum. Body fragment. Reused as gaming piece? Blue-green. Worn surface. Dims 10 x 9.

A 1980 202, Hunterian Museum. Body fragment. Blue-green. Dims 26 x 7; WT 1.6.

A 1980 209/1, Hunterian Museum. Base fragment. Blue-green. Dims 26 x 13; WT 3.9.

A 1980 217, Hunterian Museum. Body fragment. Blue-green. Dims 17 x 11; WT 2.5.

Necks

A 1980 177, Hunterian Museum. Neck fragment. Blue-green. Affected by heat. 45 x 23; WT 6.1.

A 1980 182, Hunterian Museum. Neck fragment. Blue-green. Dims 17 x 22; WT 6.2.

Handles

A 1980 179, Hunterian Museum. Fragment of handle. Blue-green. Dims 22 x 20; WT 5.0.

A 1980 183, Hunterian Museum. Two joining fragments of a reeded handle. Blue-green. Dims 23 x 18; WT 4.5.

Unidentified blue-green bottle glass

A 1980 184, Hunterian Museum. Fragment. Blue-green. Dims 23 x 17.

A 1980 186, Hunterian Museum. Fragment. Blue-green. Dims 30 x 31.

A 1980 194, Hunterian Museum. Base fragment? Blue-green. Somewhat distorted by heat. Dims 34 x 12 x 3.5.

A 1980 195, Hunterian Museum. Fragment. Blue-green. Dims 28 x 14; WT 2.5.

A 1980 198, Hunterian Museum. Fragment. Blue-green. Dims 13 x 11; WT 4.6.

A 1980 199, Hunterian Museum. Fragment. Blue-green. Dims 20 x 13.

A 1980 203, Hunterian Museum. Fragment. Blue-green. Dims 18 x 7; WT 3.6.

A 1980 205, Hunterian Museum. Fragment. Blue-green. Affected by heat. Dims 17 x 8 x 7.

A 1980 207, Hunterian Museum. Fragment. Blue-green. Dims 10 x 4 x 3.

A 1980 208, Hunterian Museum. Fragment. Blue-green. Dims 9 x 9 x 3.

A 1980 209/2, Hunterian Museum. Fragment. Blue-green. Dims 15 x 7; WT 3.5.

A 1980 213, Hunterian Museum. Fragment. Blue-green. Dims 14 x 10; WT 2.0.

Lochspouts, Ayrshire. P:5

Unidentified blue-green bottle glass

HW 21, NMS. Base fragment. Bottle. Blue-green. Reused as gaming piece. Dims 24 x 15; WT 7.0.

Luce Sands, Wigtownshire. Q:1

Prismatic bottle

JBC 10/5/04, Kelvingrove Museum. Prismatic bottle? Green glass, poorly preserved. Dims 23 x 22; WT 3.0.

Milking Gap, High Shield, Northumberland. U:5

Unidentified blue-green bottle glass

Lost? 'numerous fragments of pale green Roman bottle glass.'[127]

Mine Howe, Tankerness, Orkney. B:2

Prismatic bottle

MH02: find 102 (with excavator). Lower body and base. Pitted surface on base. Heavy traces of wear, and occasional cracks in the glass. Blue-green. Dims 10 x 10; WT 4.8.

Seamill, Ayrshire. P:6

Cylindrical bottle/s

HR 477, NMS. Base fragment. Blue-green. Very worn. Dims 30 x 22; WT 3.4–5.8.

HR 477, NMS. Base fragment. Blue-green. Usage scratches. Dims 34 x 16; WT 3.3.

Torfoot, Lanarkshire. O:2

Prismatic bottle

Lost. 'March 26, 1803. "A few days ago, at Torfoot, about seven miles south-west of Strathaven in the shire of Lanark, a boy, cleaning out a drain, at the foot of a rising ground, struck upon a glass bottle, which contained about 400 silver Roman coins of Trajan, Antonius Pius, Faustina, wife of Antoninus, and various other emperors and empresses, &c. …. The bottle was an oblong square".'[128]

Torrs Cave, Kirkcudbrightshire. R:3

Prismatic bottle

Unreg*., the Stewarty Museum, Kirkcudbright. Fragment of base and body. Blue-green. Three concentric circles in relief on base. Usage scratches. PH 35; W (body) 65; W (base) 55.

Torwoodlee, Selkirkshire. S:1

(all unregistered unless prefixed with GA)

Cylindrical bottle/s

No. 1*, NMS. Fragment of lower body and base. Blue-green. Worn on base. PH 73; W 78; WT 3.7. Same vessel as GA 1257.

No. 2, NMS. Fragment of lower body and base. Blue-green. Body tapering out. Very worn. PH 54; WT 3.5 (body), 5.0 (base).

No. 3, NMS. Body fragment. Blue-green. Dims 57 x 41; WT 2.7.

No. 6, NMS. Base fragment. Blue-green. Dims 60 x 25; WT 3.5.

No. 7, NMS. Three joining base fragments. Blue-green. Worn. Dims 51 x 49; WT 4.9.

No. 9, NMS. Base fragment. Blue-green. Dims 14 x 23; WT 6.1.

No. 10, NMS. Base fragment. Blue-green. Dims 42 x 36; WT 4.2.

No. 11, NMS. Body fragment. Blue-green. Dims 50 x 34; WT 2.5.

No. 12, NMS. Body fragment. Blue-green. Dims 49 x 30; WT 2.8.

No. 13, NMS. Body fragment. Blue-green. Dims 31 x 33; WT 3.1.

No. 14*, NMS. Fragment of base and lower body. Blue-green. Pitted surface. Dims 47 x 37; WT 3.8.

No. 15, NMS. Base fragment. Blue-green. Dims 30 x 26; WT 2.8.

No. 16, NMS. Body fragment. Blue-green. Dims 30 x 30; WT 2.5.

No. 17, NMS. Base fragment. Blue-green. Dims 36 x 30; WT 6.1.

No. 18, NMS. Base fragment. Blue-green. Dims 19 x 18; WT 6.2. Same vessel as no. 17.

No. 19, NMS. Body fragment. Blue-green. Dims 51 x 14; WT 5.5.

No. 20, NMS. Body fragment. Blue-green. Strain cracks. Dims 34 x 31; WT 2.7.

No. 21, NMS. Body fragment. Blue-green. Worn on lower body. Dims 68 x 30; WT 2.9.

No. 22, NMS. Fragment of lower body and base. Blue-green. Dims 43 x 25; WT 3.0.

No. 23, NMS. Body fragment. Blue-green. Dims 30 x 21; WT 3.4.

No 24, NMS. Fragment of lower body and base. Blue-green. Worn. PH 42; W 24; WT 2.1.

No. 25, NMS. Base fragment. Blue-green. Dims 37 x 28; WT 2.6.

No. 26, NMS. Base fragment. Blue-green. Dims 26 x 23; WT 4.8.

No. 27, NMS. Body fragment. Blue-green. Dims 21 x 25; WT 2.8.

No. 28, NMS. Base fragment. Blue-green. Pitted surface. Dims 30 x 24; WT 4.3.

No. 29, NMS. Body fragment. Blue-green. Dims 42 x 13; WT 2.6.

No. 30, NMS. Body fragment. Blue-green. Dims 28 x 22; WT 2.8.

No. 31, NMS. Body fragment. Blue-green. Dims 58 x 31; WT 3.0.

No. 32, NMS. Base fragment. Blue-green. Dims 43 x 25; WT 3.7.

No. 33, NMS. Body fragment. Blue-green. Dims 46 x 17; WT 3.5.

No. 34, NMS. Body fragment. Blue-green. Dims 28 x 26; WT 2.4.

No. 35, NMS. Body fragment. Blue-green. Dims 23 x 10; WT 4.1.

No. 36, NMS. Base fragment. Blue-green. Dims 23 x 19; WT 3.0.

No. 37, NMS. Body fragment. Blue-green. Dull surface, worn. Dims 21 x 28; WT 2.6.

No. 38, NMS. Body fragment. Blue-green. Dims 33 x 22; WT 2.9.

No. 39, NMS. Body fragment. Blue-green. Dims 19 x 27; WT 2.8.

No. 40, NMS. Body fragment. Blue-green. Dims 25 x 24; WT 2.6.

No. 41, NMS. Body fragment. Blue-green. Dims 27 x 33; WT 3.0.

No. 44, NMS. Body fragment with parts of attached handle. Blue-green. Dims 21 x 17; WT 10.4.

No. 45, NMS. Base fragment. Blue-green. Usage scratches. Dims 51 x 24; WT 5.3.

No. 47B, NMS. Five joining fragments of lower body and base. Blue-green. Dims 56 x 31; WT 3.4.

No. 50, NMS. Body fragment. Blue-green. Dims 11 x 16; WT 1.

No. 51, NMS. Body fragment. Blue-green. Dims 31 x 30; WT 2.9.

No. 52, NMS. Body fragment. Blue-green. Dims 67 x 42; WT 3.6.

GA 1255, NMS. Base fragment. Blue-green. Very worn on edge. Dims 64 x 31; WT 8.8.

GA 1257, NMS. Body fragment – lower part of body. Blue-green. Very worn. Dims 48 x 62; WT 3.0. Same vessel as no. 1.

Rims, necks and handles

No. 4, (GA 371), NMS. Fragment of rim, neck and handle. Blue-green. Bubbly. Dims 33 x 29; WT 7; WT (including handle) 14.

No. 5 (GA 371)*, NMS. Fragment of rim and neck. Blue-green. Rim edge bent out, up, in and flattened. Dims 17 x 33; WT 5.8.

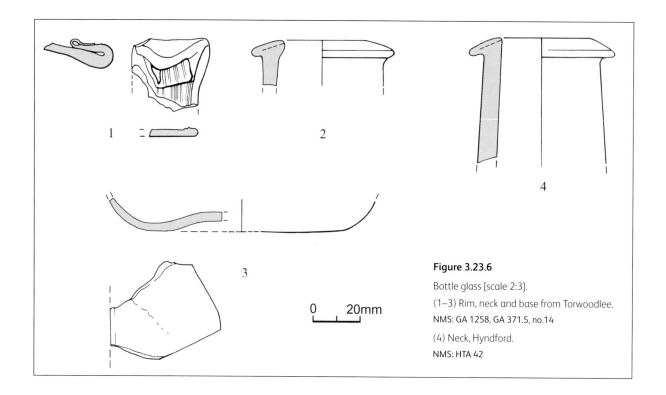

Figure 3.23.6

Bottle glass [scale 2:3].

(1–3) Rim, neck and base from Torwoodlee.
NMS: GA 1258, GA 371.5, no.14

(4) Neck, Hyndford.
NMS: HTA 42

0   20mm

GA 368, NMS. Neck fragment. Blue-green. Dims 26 x 43; WT 5.6. Joins no. 57.

GA 369, (No. 57) NMS. Two joining fragments of neck and upper body. Blue-green. Very bubbly. Diameter c. 50; PH 44; W 50; WT 6.9.

GA 1255, NMS. Bottle neck. Blue-green. H 51; W 24; WT 5.9.

Handles

No 46, NMS. Fragment of reeded handle. Blue-green. Dims 33 x 23; WT 6.0. Same vessel as GA 1258?

GA 1258*, NMS. Fragment of reeded handle. Blue-green. Bubbly. Dims 28 x 32; WT 2.8. Same vessel as no. 46?

GA 367, (No. 55) NMS. Three joining fragments of angular reeded handle with simple attachment. Blue-green. Very bubbly glass with black specks. Dims 64 x 70; WT 8.3–20.0.

GA 367, (No. 56) NMS. Fragment of lower part of reeded handle. Blue-green. Very bubbly glass with black specks. Dims 56 x 103; WT 26 (lower part), 9.2 (upper part).

Unidentified blue-green bottle glass.

No. 42; NMS. Fragment. Distorted by heat. Blue-green. Dims 26 x 24; WT 5.2.

No. 43, NMS. Fragment. Distorted by heat. Blue-green. Dims 30 x 7; WT 3.3.

No. 47A, NMS. Fragment. Blue-green. Dims 13 x 21; WT 12.3.

No. 48, NMS. Fragment. Blue-green. Distorted by heat. Dims 46 x 17; WT 5.6.

No. 49, NMS. Fragment. Blue-green. Distorted by heat. Dims 51 x 29; WT 6.2.

Traprain Law, East Lothian. N:2

Cylindrical bottle/s

GV 50 (XI 14 117), 1914 excavations, Area and Level: unknown, NMS. Base fragment. Blue-green. Dims 23 x 17; WT 2.5–5.5.

GV 51 (XI 14 118), 1914 excavations, Area and Level: unknown, NMS. Body fragment. Blue-green. Dims 25 x 20; WT 4.3.

GV 375a* (III 20 98), Area H, Level 2, NMS. Base fragment. Blue-green. Usage scratches. Dims 33 x 69; WT 4.8.

GV 375b (III 20 99), Area G, Level 2, NMS. Base fragment? Pale blue-green. Usage scratches. Dims 58 x 37; WT 5.3.

GV 454 (III 20 227), 1919 excavations, Level 3, NMS. Body fragment. Blue-green. Dims 23 x 46; WT 4.7.

GV 1634, Area and Level: unknown, NMS. Body fragment. Slightly curved side. Blue-green. Worn. Dims 25 x 14; WT 2.5.

GV 1723, Area and Level: unknown, NMS. Body fragment. Pale green. Worn. Dims 16 x 18; WT 2.6.

GV 1724, Area and Level: unknown, NMS. Body fragment. Blue-green. Bubbly. Dims 14 x 19; WT 5.3.

GV 1725, Area and Level: unknown, NMS. Body fragment. Blue-green. Dims 15 x 18; WT 3.6.

GV 1726, Area L, Level unknown, NMS. Body fragment. Pale blue-green. Dims 23 x 7; WT 3.2.

GV 1727, Area P, Level 3, NMS. Body fragment. Blue-green. Bubbly. Dims 13 x 15; WT 4.9.

GV 1728, Area P, Level 3, NMS. Body fragment. Pale blue-green. Dims 16 x 16; WT 3.6.

GV 1729, Area J, Level 4, NMS. Base fragment. Pale blue-green. Dims 12 x 25; WT 4.0.

GV 1730, Area K, Level 1, NMS. Base fragment. Pale blue-green. Dims 23 x 34; WT 2.2.

GV 1731, Area K, Level 3, NMS. Base fragment. Pale blue-green. Dims 20 x 40; WT 3.7.

GV 1732, Area L. Level 1, NMS. Fragment of lower body and base. Blue-green. Very worn. Dims 23 x 18; WT 5.7.

GV 1733, Area P, Level 3, NMS. Fragment of lower body and base. Blue-green. Worn. PH 15; W 24; WT 4.3.

GV 1734, Area P, Level 3, NMS. Base fragment. Blue-green. Worn. Dims 16 x 26; WT 4.7.

GV 1735, Area Q, Level 3, Q3, NMS. Base fragment. Blue-green. Worn. Dims 18 x 26; WT 3.1.

GV 1736, Area T, Level 2, NMS. Base fragment. Green. Bubbly. Dims 13 x 12; WT 3.6.

GV 1737, Area and Level: unknown, NMS. Fragment of base and lower part of body. Blue-green. Heavily worn. Dims 18 x 19; WT 4.5.

GV 1738, Area and Level: unknown, NMS. Fragment of lower body and base. Blue-green. Worn. Dims 12 x 11; WT 3.7. Same vessel as GV 1737.

GV 1832, Area T, Level 1, NMS. Base fragment. Blue-green. Dims 18 x 11; WT 2.8–3.6.

GV 1839, Area I, Level unknown, NMS. Fragment of shoulder? Blue-green. Convex-curved. Dims 18 x 23; WT 3.1.

Prismatic bottle/s

GV 42 (XI 14 109), Area and Level: unknown, NMS. Body fragment. Blue-green. Dims 26 x 23; WT 5.0.

GV 174:3 (XII 15 139), Area F, Level 1, NMS. Body fragment. Bluish-green. Dims 18 x 22; WT 4.

GV 174:4 (XII 15 139), Area F, Level 1, NMS. Base fragment. Blue-green. Two concentric circles in moulding; remains of L-shaped moulding in corner. Somewhat affected by heat. Dims 20 x 23; WT 8.

GV 176:4* (XII 15 141), Area Fe, Level 3, NMS. Fragment of lower body and base. Straight side. Flat base, pitted surface. Blue-green. Remains of low moulded circle. Worn on underside. PH 16; Dims 36 x 31; WT 4.2–7.1.

GV 176:5 (XII 15 141), Area Fb, Level 2, NMS. Base fragment. Pitted surface. Blue-green. Bubbly. Dims 34 x 45; WT 4.0.

GV 177.1 (XII 15 142), Area F, Level 4, NMS. Base fragment. Blue-green. Flat. Pitted surface. Dims 34 x 23; WT 3.8.

GV 177:2 (XII 15 142), Area H, Level 3, NMS. Base fragment. Blue-green. Circular moulding. Bubbly. Dims 43 x 18; WT 8.3.

GV 211* (XII 15 181), Area F, Level 3, NMS.[129] Base fragment. Blue-green. Reused as gaming piece (fig. 2.3a). Dims 12 x 11; WT 8.9.

GV 331:1 (III 20 25), Area 1919, Level 1, NMS. Base fragment. Blue-green. Worn. Dims 17 x 28; WT 7.6.

GV 331:2 (III 20 26), Area 1919, Level 1, NMS. Base fragment. Blue-green. Dims 35 x 35; WT 3.5.

GV 331:3 (III 20 27), Area 1919, Level 1, NMS. Base fragment. Blue-green. Worn. Dims 23 x 29; WT 5.7.

GV 379a (III 20 108/2), Area G, Level 2, NMS. Base fragment.

Blue-green glass with yellow/black impurities. Very worn. Dims 19 x 33; WT 6.6.

GV 452 (III 20 225), Area G, Level 3, NMS. Body fragment. Pale blue-green. Dims 24 x 20; WT 3.0.

GV 536a (III 20 398), Area 1919, Level 4, NMS. Base fragment. Blue-green. Dims 16 x 33; WT 4.8.

GV 536d (III 20 401), Area 1919, Level 4, NMS. Base fragment. Blue-green. Dims 13 x 19; WT 6.2.

GV 603 (V 21 60), Area K, Level 1, NMS. Base fragment. Blue-green. Reused as gaming piece? Worn. Dims 11 x 21; WT 11.

GV 864 (1922 102), Area M, Level 1a, NMS. Fragment of base and lower body. Blue-green. Dims 32 x 23; WT 8.7.

GV 1073 (1923 77), Area Q, Level 2, NMS. Base fragment. Prismatic moulding parallel to edge. Blue-green with streaks in black, reddish-brown and yellow. Pitted surface, worn. Dims 43 x 28; WT 9.2.

GV 1074 (1923 78), Area P, Level 2, NMS. Fragment of lower body and base. Base design: moulded square and circle. Blue-green. Bubbly. Very worn. Dims 14 x 24; WT 9.

GV 1075a* (1923 79), Area Q, Level 2, NMS. Base fragment. Pale green. Bubbly. Dims 20 x 45; WT 4.3–4.9.

GV 1560, Area and Level: unknown, NMS. Base fragment. Blue-green. Very bubbly. Usage scratches. Dims 42 x 75; WT 5.9.

GV 1635, Area and Level: unknown, NMS. Base fragment. Flat. Blue-green. Bubbly. Dims 17 x 20; WT 5.0.

GV 1636, Area F, Level 4, NMS. Base fragment. Blue-green. Flat. Pitted surface. Dims 23 x 36; WT 2.4.

GV 1637, Area Ga, 'fill in', NMS. Base fragment. Reworked to gaming piece of triangular shape. Blue-green. Worn on both sides. Dims 24 x 35; WT 8.7.

GV 1739, Area J, Level 1, NMS. Base fragment. Blue-green, bubbly glass with green streak. Dims 18 x 20; WT 4.0.

GV 1740, Area J, Level 3, NMS. Base fragment. Blue-green. Bubbly. Usage scratches. Dims 42 x 52; WT 3.3–8.0.

GV 1741, Area K, Level 1, NMS. Base fragment. Pale green. Usage scratches. Dims 22 x 26; WT 5.7.

GV 1742, Area K, Level 3, NMS. Base fragment. Two very low circles in relief. Pale green. Dims 31 x 35; WT 7.4.

GV 1743, Area Q, Level 2, NMS. Base fragment. Blue-green. Dims 19 x 29; WT 4.9.

GV 1744, Area Q, Level 3, NMS. Base fragment. Very low circles in relief. Blue-green. Dims 17 x 30; WT 3.8.

GV 1745, Area R, Level 2, NMS. Base fragment. Blue-green. Dims 14 x 18; WT 2.9.

GV 1746, Area I, Level 1, NMS. Base fragment. Two concentrical circles in relief. Affected by heat. Pale green. Dims 29 x 35; WT 6.1.

GV 1747, Area X, Level 2, NMS. Base fragment. Two concentrical circles and a dot within a square in relief. Pale green. Bubbly. Dims 30 x 25; WT 8.0.

GV 1748, Area T, Level 1, NMS. Base fragment. Pale green. Worn on inside. Dims 20 x 23; WT 3.2–3.8.

GV 1749, Area and Level: unknown, NMS. Base fragment. Two very low circles in relief. Blue-green. Bubbly. Dims 34 x 44; WT 8.0.

GV 1750, Area and Level: unknown, NMS. Base fragment. Blue-green glass with black-green speck. Dims 17 x 47; WT 7.8. Same vessel as GV 1749?

GV 1751, Area and Level: unknown, NMS. Base fragment. Blue-green. Dims 10 x 23; WT 4.3.

GV 1752, Area J, Level 2, NMS. Base fragment. Blue-green. Usage scratches. Dims 24 x 17; WT 5.4.

GV 1753, Area and Level: unknown, NMS. Body fragment. Blue-green. Dims 15 x 30; WT 4.0.

GV 1754, Area and Level: unknown, NMS. Body fragment. Blue-green. Dims 8 x 13; WT 4.6.

GV 1755, Area H, Level 0, NMS. Body fragment. Pale blue-green. Usage scratches. Dims 11 x 13; WT 3.5.

GV 1756, Area J, Level 1, NMS. Body fragment. Pale blue-green. Dims 15 x 19; WT 4.7.

GV 1757, Area J, Level 1, NMS. Body fragment. Pale blue-green. Dims 15 x 16; WT 4.6.

GV 1758, Area J, Level 1, NMS. Body fragment. Blue-green. Dims 15 x 22; WT 1.9.

GV 1759, Area J, Level 1, NMS. Body fragment. Blue-green. Dims 15 x 28; WT 3.5.

GV 1760, Area J, Level 2, NMS. Body fragment. Blue-green. Dims 18 x 20; WT 6.7.

GV 1761, Area K, Level 1, NMS. Body fragment. Pale green. Dims 13 x 15; WT 8.8.

GV 1762, Area K, Level 3, NMS. Body fragment. Blue-green. Worn on both sides. Dims 12 x 26; WT 3.7.

GV 1763, Area P, Level 2, NMS. Body fragment. Pale blue-green. Dims 13 x 25; WT 3.8.

GV 1764, Area R, Level 3, NMS. Body fragment. Pale blue-green. Dims 11 x 19; WT 4.3.

GV 1765, Area S, Level 1, NMS. Body fragment. Blue-green. Dims 13 x 12; WT 2.0.

GV 1766, Area X, Level 2, NMS. Body fragment. Blue-green. Dims 16.5 x 32; WT 7.3.

GV 1767, Area T, Level 1, NMS. Body fragment. Blue-green. Dims 13 x 22; WT 3.0.

GV 1768, Area T, Level 1, NMS. Body fragment. Blue-green. Dims 18 x 15; WT 2.5.

GV 1769, Area T, Level 2, NMS. Body fragment. Blue-green. Dims 16 x 31; WT 5.0.

GV 1770, Area T, Level 2, NMS. Body fragment. Blue-green. Worn. Dims 12 x 41; WT 4.0.

GV 1771, Area T, Level 2, NMS. Body fragment. Blue-green. Dims 14 x 16; WT 7.4.

GV 1772, Area T, Level 2, NMS. Base fragment. Usage scratches. Blue-green. Dims 10 x 5; WT 7.4.

GV 1773, Area P, Level 3, NMS. Base fragment. Blue-green. Very worn. Dims 17 x 23; WT 3.8.

GV 1785, Area and Level: unknown, NMS. Body fragment. Pale green. Usage scratches. Dims 8 x 10; WT 2.7.

GV 1788, Area A1, Level 2, NMS. Body fragment. Blue-green. Dims 23 x 16; WT 4.3.

GV 1835, NMS. Body fragment. Blue-green. Dims 18 x 12; WT 3.7.

GV 1836, NMS. Fragment of lower body and base. Blue-green. Worn. H 7.5; Dims 22 x 18; WT 5.2.

GV 1837, NMS. Base fragment. Blue-green. One edge of the base. Dims 17 x 17; WT 2.3. Area R2.

GV 1838, NMS. Base fragment. Blue-green. Dims 18 x 16; WT 5.0. Area T2.

TLSP 1999, find 210, NMS. Body fragment. Blue-green. Dims 11 x 8.

Rims, necks and handles

GV 175:3 (XII 15 140), 1914 excavations, Level 2, NMS. Neck fragment. Cylindrical neck. Blue-green. Very worn. Diameter c. 35; H 35; WT 3.0.

GV 178:2 (XII 15 143), NMS. Neck fragment. Pale blue-green. Dims 18 x 13; WT 5.

GV 379b (III 20 109), Area G, Level 2, NMS. Neck fragment. Blue-green. Dims 19 x 25; WT 4.8.

GV 534 (III 20 396), Area H, Level 4, NMS.[130] Fragment of rim and neck. Rim folded up and in. Cylindrical neck. Blue-green. Usage scratches on rim. RD 60; PH 15; WT 7.2.

GV 535 (III 20 397), Area H, Level 4, NMS. Neck fragment. Blue-green. Very bubbly. Dims 19 x 21.

GV 536b (III 20 399), Area G, Level 4, NMS. Neck fragment. Blue-green. Dims 19 x 23; WT 7.2.

GV 732 (V 21m271), Area K, Level 3, NMS. Fragment of rim, neck and handle. Remains of attached handle below rim. Blue-green. PH 21; W 23; WT 8.

GV 1072 (1923 76), Area Q, Level 2, NMS. Rim fragment. Rim folded out, up, in and flattened. Pitted surface. Blue-green. RD 60; H 20; W 46; WT 5.8.

GV 1277 (1924 174), Area T, Level 2, NMS. Fragment of rim and neck. Rim edge bent out, up and in, leaving a ridge along the inner side of the neck. Cylindrical neck. Very heavy wear. Diameter ca 50; H 21; WT 3.5.

GV 1713, Area J, Level 1, NMS. Rim fragment. Rim folded out, up, in and flattened. Blue-green. RD 45; PH 13.

GV 1714, Area S, Level 2, NMS. Rim fragment. Blue-green. Very worn. Dims 9 x 10; WT 6.5.

GV 1718, Area G, Level 2, NMS. Neck fragment? Blue-green. Dims 15 x 17; WT 5.0.

GV 1719, Area H, Level 1, NMS. Neck fragment. Blue-green glass with a large, elongated bubble. Dims 11 x 11; WT 3.5.

GV 1720, Area H, Level 2, NMS. Neck fragment. Blue-green. Dims 18 x 23; WT 5.5.

GV 1721, Area Oa, Level 3, NMS. Neck fragment. Blue-green. Very bubbly. Dims 19 x 27; WT 4.6.

GV 1722, NMS. Neck fragment. Blue-green. Dims 25 x 14; WT 2.5.

GV 1789, Area A, Level 2, NMS. Fragment of neck. Blue-green. Very worn after breakage. Diameter c.50; H 11; W 21; WT 5.0.

GV 1830, Area and Level: unknown, NMS. Fragment of rim. Blue-green. Dims 12 x 6.5 x 3.5.

GV 1831, Area and Level: unknown, NMS. Fragment of rim. Pale blue-green. Dims 9 x 7 x 4.

Handles

GV 176:7 (XII 15 141), Area Fa, Level 3, NMS. Fragment of reeded handle. Pale green. Bubbly. Usage scratches. Dims 28 x 32; WT 5.2.

GV 451 (III 20 224), Area G, Level 3, NMS. Fragment of reeded handle. Pale blue-green. Reused as gaming piece. Worn. Dims 24 x 27; WT 4.8.

GV 537 (III 20 402), Area H, Level 4, NMS. Fragment of reeded handle. Blue-green, bubbly glass with yellow impurities. Dims 25 x 17; WT 3.9.

GV 782 (V 21-372), Area X, Level 4, NMS. Fragment of reeded handle. Blue-green. Worn. Dims 21 x 18; WT 7.7.

GV 784 (N-21-378), Area K, Level 2, NMS. Fragment of reeded handle. Pale blue. Dims 33 x 34; WT 8.2.

GV 1638, Area F, Level 1, NMS. Fragment of reeded handle. Blue-green. Dims 32 x 22; WT 3.0.

GV 1710, Area K, Level 1, NMS. Fragment of reeded handle. Blue-green. Bubbly. Dims 13 x 17; WT 4.0.

GV 1711, Area I, Level 1, NMS. Fragment of angular reeded handle. Blue-green. Very bubbly. Dims 26 x 29; WT 5.0.

GV 1712, Area S, Level 2, NMS. Fragment of reeded handle. Pale blue-green. Bubbly. Dims 8 x 29; WT 3.8.

FR 520 (1939 110), (found at Traprain April 1910), NMS. Fragment of reeded handle. Blue-green. Dims 31 x 19; WT 3.8.

Unidentified blue-green bottle glass.

GV 174:6 (XII 15 139), Area Ga, Level 1, NMS. Base fragment? Blue-green. Linear moulding. Distorted by heat? Dims 14 x 10.

GV 174:8 (XII 15 139), Area F, Level 1, NMS. Body fragment. Blue-green. Dims 30 x 25; WT 5.1.

GV 456, 1919 excavations, Level 3, NMS. Fragment. Distorted by heat. Blue-green. Dims 17 x 15; WT 4.2.

GV 536c (III 20 400), Area G, Level 4, NMS. Base fragment? Blue-green. H 8; W 41; WT 7.3–8.5.

GV 538 (III 20 403), 1919 excavations, Level 4, NMS. Fragment of base? Blue-green. Reused as gaming piece (fig. 2.3a). Dims 9 x 8 x 5.

GV 1541 (1974-131), Area and Level: unknown, NMS. Fragment. Blue-green. Dims 15 x23; WT 8.3.

GV 1639, Area and Level: unknown, NMS. Fragment. Blue-green. Distorted by heat. Dims 22 x 35; WT 4.9.

GV 1640, Area and Level: unknown, NMS. Fragment. Blue-green. Distorted by heat. Dims 15 x 8 x 3.

GV 1642, Area Ga, Level 1, NMS. Fragment. Blue-green. Dims 13 x 10; WT 6.9.

GV 1643, Area Q, Level 1, NMS. Fragment. Distorted by heat. Blue-green. Dims 16 x 9 x 4.

GV 1644, Area R, Level 1, NMS. Melted Roman glass; from intentional recycling? Drop-shaped. Blue-green. Dims 23 x 14; WT 9.

GV 1774, Area Oa, Level 3, NMS. Fragment. Totally distorted by heat. Blue-green. Discoloured with yellow-green and small red specks. H 18; W 35; WT 11.

GV 1775, Area P, Level 3, NMS. Fragment. Blue-green. H 7; W 13; WT 8.1.

GV 1776, Area P, Level 3, NMS. Fragment. Totally distorted by heat, from intentional recycling? Blue-green. Small red specks on surface. H 21; W 16; WT 11.

GV 1777, Area Q, Level 2, NMS. Fragment. Blue-green. Dims 9 x 11; WT 5.3.

GV 1778, Area S, Level 2, NMS. Fragment. Blue-green. Dims 10 x 9; WT 2.7.

GV 1780, Area and Level: unknown, NMS. Fragment. Blue-green. Dims 7 x 17; WT 2.9.

GV 1781, Area and Level: unknown, NMS. Fragment. Blue-green. Dims 22 x 8; WT 3.4.

GV 1782, Area and Level: unknown, NMS. Fragment. Blue-green. Dims 7 x 9; WT 3.8.

GV 1783, Area and Level: unknown, NMS. Fragment. Blue-green. Dims 5 x 7; WT 4.3.

GV 1784, Area and Level: unknown, NMS. Fragment. Blue-green. Dims 4 x 9; WT 7.5.

GV 1795, Area S, Level 1, NMS. Fragment. Totally distorted by heat, from intentional recycling? Pale blue-green. Dims 13 x 18; WT 2.2.

GV 1797, Area I, Level 2, NMS. Fragment. Blue-green. H 10; W 11; WT 6.8.

GV 1804, Area P, Level 3, NMS. Body fragment. Blue-green. Curved. Heavy wear after breakage – used as a polishing tool? Dims 19 x 10; WT 3.0.

GV 1842, Area R, Level 2, NMS. Splinter. Pale blue-green. Dims 13 x 4 x 9.

GV 1828, NMS. Fragment. Totally distorted by heat. Dims 11 x 8; WT 3.6.

GV 1840, NMS. Distorted by heat. Blue-green. Dims 16 x 11 x 8.

GV 1841. Area P, Level 2, NMS. Fragment. Totally distorted by heat. Blue-green. Dims 20 x 11 x 7.

GV 1843, Area S, Level 2, NMS. Fragment. Distorted by heat. Blue-green. Dims 34 x 31; WT 4.0.

GV 1844, Area T, Level 1, NMS. Fragment. Totally distorted by heat. Blue-green. Dims 19 x 24.

GV 1845, Area T, Level 2, NMS. Splinter. Blue-green. Dims 12 x 7 x 4.

GV 1846, Area T, Level 3, NMS. Splinter. Blue-green. Dims 10 x 7 x 4.

GV 1847, Area T, Level 3, NMS. Fragment. Distorted by heat. Blue-green. Dims 24 x 13 x 8.

GV 1848, NMS. Splinter. Blue-green. Dims 14 x 15.

Figure 3.23.7

Prismatic bottle fragments, Traprain Law.

GV 1849, NMS. Three splinters. Pale blue-green
Dims 9 x 2; WT 5.5; Dims 8 x 4; WT 5.5; Dims 11 x 5 x 3.

GV 1850, NMS. Two joining fragments. Pale blue-green.
Dims 13 x 13; WT 2.5.

GV 1851, NMS. Splinter. Blue-green. Dims 8 x 4 x 1.5.

GV 1852, NMS. Splinter. Blue-green. Dims 9 x 5 x 3.5.

West Longlee, Northumberland. U:6

Unidentified blue-green bottle glass.

Lost? 'Small fragment of Roman bottle glass, too small to restore type.'[131]

Whithorn, Wigtownshire. Q:2

Cylindrical bottle/s

Small, thick body fragment. Bluish green. Slight evidence for convex curve, possibly cylindrical side. Dims 5 x 7.

Base fragment, cylindrical bottle?. Bluish green. Edge of concave base. Ring of heavy wear on base edge, surfaces worn. Dims 22 x 20.5.

Square bottle/s

Approximately D-shaped body fragment, prismatic vessel. Bluish green, straight side. Broken edges reworked and carefully smoothed for secondary use. Surfaces heavily worn. Dims 26 x 23.5; T 4.5–6, 5.

Flat fragment, prismatic vessel. Bluish green. Dull. Dims 11.5 x 12.5; T 6.0.[132]

Finds from other areas beyond the borders of the Roman Empire

Cylindrical bottles

With the exception of the Scottish and Northumbrian finds, only one certain find of a cylindrical bottle of the type discussed above has been made in the area beyond the borders of Rome. An intact bottle was discovered in the spring or summer of 1859 in Herlufmagle, Præstø Amt, Zealand, Denmark. The bottle, two glass bowls and a bronze object of unknown function, were discovered in what must have been an inhumation grave. One of the bowls was deliberately broken and cast aside. The other, which is still preserved in King Frederik VII's collection at Fredensborg castle, is a spherical facet-cut cup. The bottle is a typical specimen of Isings Form 51b, in blue-green glass with a reeded handle, 285 mm high.[133]

In the Black Sea region, finds of wheel-cut cylindrical bottles with collared rims have been made.[134] An example of this is a bottle with horizontal wheel-cut lines found in an exceptionally rich grave in the Samtavro cemetery outside of Mtskheta (north of Tbilisi, Georgia), the ancient capital of the Caucasian kingdom of Iberia. This was discovered in a stone cist containing an inhumation burial, a cylindrical bottle, two prismatic bottles, jewellery, silver and bronze vessels of Roman origin, and coins.[135]

Prismatic bottles

Finds of the eastern variety of prismatic bottles, with collared rims, have been made in the Black Sea region.[136] The find from Mtskheta, Georgia, mentioned above, includes a pair of prismatic bottles. One of the bottles has a base decorated with concentric circles, and small circles in each corner; the other bottle's base has a 'flower' in a circle.[137] A number of finds have been made in the area which once constituted the Kingdom of Meroë, situated in Lower Nubia, present-day Egypt and Sudan. A mould-blown rectangular bottle in yellowish green was discovered at Melik Elndsay, a blue-green hexagonal bottle at Karanóg, and a square bottle at Faras.[138]

Unidentified bottle glass

In the *Corpus der römischen Funde im europäischen Barbaricum* a few objects are listed as possible finds of cylindrical bottles of Isings Form 51 or prismatic bottles of Isings Form 50 in Germany. A base fragment which may have come from a prismatic bottle of Isings Form 50b was found in Sieker, Kreisfreie Stadt Bielefeld, Nordrhein-Westfalen;[139] a rim was discovered in Oldendorf, Melle, Landeskreis Osnabrück, Niedersachsen;[140] a handle was unearthed in Jeinsen, Pattensen, Landkreis Hannover, Niedersachsen;[141] and similarily a handle from Altenwalde, Stadt Cuxhaven, Landkreis Cuxhaven, Niedersachsen.[142] The identifications of these finds, however, remain uncertain.

At Aksum, Ethiopia, two reeded handles were found during excavation: one in greenish colourless glass, the other in dark green glass.[143] A reeded handle has also been discovered in Taxila-Sirkap, Punjab, Pakistan.[144] They could either have come from prismatic or cylindrical bottles.

Notes

1 Isings 1957, 63–69, 108.
2 Isings 1957, 67–69; Charlesworth 1966, 26.
3 Cool & Price 1995, 179; Price & Cottam 1998a, 191.
4 Price 1995a, 185.
5 Price & Cottam 1998a, 191.
6 Cool & Price 1995, 179.
7 Cool & Price 1995, 179; Price & Cottam 1998a, 191.
8 Price 1995a, 185.
9 Isings 1957, 64.
10 Cool & Price 1995, 179.
11 Price & Cottam 1998a, 194.
12 Isings 1957, 81.
13 Cool & Price 1995, 185.
14 Price & Cottam 1998a, 194.
15 See for example Stern 1999, 468–69; Rotloff 1999, 42–47.
16 Lehrer Jacobson 1987, 35; Barag 1987, 111.
17 For examples, see Gudiol Richart 1936, 21; Charlesworth 1959a, 53; Price & Cottam 1998a, fig. 89d.
18 Cool & Price 1989, 34, fig. 22 no. 89.
19 Charlesworth 1966, 28.
20 Cool & Price 1995, 180.
21 Price & Cottam 1998a, 194.
22 Lehrer Jacobson 1987, 43.
23 Cool & Price 1995, 180.
24 Aguilar-Tablada Marcos & Sánchez de Prado 2006, 182–88.
25 Fremersdorf 1965–66, 29, Abb. 2.9; Price 1976b, 119, fig. 212.
26 Rütti 1991b, 163–64, fig. 103.
27 Motte & Martin 2003, 316, fig. 21.5.
28 Hochuli-Gysel 1993, 87, fig. 5 to fig.7; Hochuli-Gysel 2003, 184, fig. 12 & fig. 13.
29 Aguilar-Tablada Marcos & Sánchez de Prado 2006, 182–84.
30 Baluta 1981, 111, fig. 1 & fig. 2.
31 Price 1978a, 70.
32 Fremersdorf 1965–66, 28.
33 Stern 1999, 457.
34 Czurda-Ruth 1979, 140.
35 Ritterling 1913, 373.
36 van Lith 1977, 41.
37 Harden 1947, 306.
38 Harden & Price 1971, 361–63.
39 Charlesworth 1968, 6.
40 Price & Cottam 1998a, 191.
41 Cool & Price 1995, 184.
42 Price & Cottam 1996a, 168.
43 Czurda-Ruth 1979, 136.
44 Grose 1974, 32, 45–46, fig. 5 no. 39.
45 Colls et al. 1977, 120.
46 Ritterling 1913, 374, Abb. 96.
47 Price & Cottam 1998a, 195.
48 Harden 1947, 306.
49 Charlesworth 1966, 30.
50 Cool & Price 1995, 184.
51 Price 1987a, 206.
52 Townend & Hinton 1978, 389, fig. 176 no. 116.
53 Price 1980, 45.
54 Boon 1969, 95; Cool & Price 1995, 179.
55 See Masseroli 1998, fig. 7.
56 Cool 2006, 62–64 with references.
57 Highly exclusive wines, such as Falernian, was stored in glass bottles, see Petronius, *Satyrica*, 34; Martial, *Epigrammata*, 2.40.6. For a discussion of amphorae and barrels as transport vessewls, see ch. 6.4.
58 Espérandieu 1911, 311, no. 3317.
59 Cool & Baxter 1999, 84.
60 Kisa 1908, Abb. 14; Holwerda 1931, Afb. 20 & 21; Charlesworth 1968, 7; DeMaine 1990, fig. 3A; Ceselin 1998, fig. 11.
61 Holwerda 1931, afb. 20, 21, 35.
62 Holwerda 1931, afb. 18b; see the discussion in Cool 2006, 136–38.
63 Masseroli 1998, fig. 6 & fig. 7.
64 Harden 1962, 136.
65 Calvi 1968, 80.
66 Lancel 1967, 44.
67 Allen 1989, 120–21, fig. 55.
68 Price 1978a, 70–71.
69 Cool 2003, 140.
70 Price 1985a, 308.
71 Cool & Price 1995, 179–99; Price & Cottam 1998a, 191–94 with references.
72 **The Netherlands**: Velsen (van Lith 1977, 41); Nijmegen (Isings 1980, 285, 290); Obbicht (Isings 1971, 33, fig. 7); Valkenburg (van Lith 1978–79, 78–80). **Germany**: Köln (Cologne) (Fremersdorf 1958b, 31–32, Taf. 42–45); Xanten (Charlesworth 1984, 295–97); Nida-Heddernheim (Welker 1985, 32); Asberg (van Lith 1984, 252–53); Hofheim (Ritterling 1912, 373–74, taf. 37); Oberstimm (Garbsch 1978, 281). **France**: Normandy (Sennequier 1994, 59); Saint-Paul-Trois-

Châteaux (Bel 1990, 148–49); Arles (Foy & Nenna 2001, 193); Aoste (Foy & Nenna 2001, 193). **Austria**: Magdalensberg (Czurda-Ruth 1979, 137–38). **Switzerland**: Vindonissa (Berger 1960, 80). **Italy**: Aquileia (Calvi 1969, tav. 14); Settefinestre (De Tommaso 1985, 192); Herculaneum and Pompeii (Scatozza Höricht 1986, 48).

73 **Cyprus**: (Vessberg & Westholm 1956, 148–49, fig. 46 nos 21–23). **Israel**: Cave of Letters (Barag 1963, 102).
74 Ritterling 1913, 273–74.
75 Price 1989a, 195–96.
76 Cool & Baxter 1999, 84.
77 Cool & Price 1995, 179–99; Price & Cottam 1998a, 194–98 with references.
78 For a general discussion, see Cool & Baxter 1999.
79 Price 1995a, 186.
80 **The Netherlands**: Nijmegen (Isings 1980, 290); Valkenburg (van Lith 1978–79, 71–80); Esch (van den Hurk 1977, 97). **Germany**: Hofheim (Ritterling 1913, 374); Nida-Heddernheim (Welker 1974, 67–71; Welker 1985, 29–32); Oberstimm (Garbsch 1978, 281–82); Asberg (van Lith 1984, 249–51); Xanten (Charlesworth 1985, 295–97); **France**: Normandy (Sennequier 1994, 59); Besançon (Koltes 1982, 30); Les Arcs-sur-Argens (Foy & Nenna 2001, 193); the cemetery at Cimiz, Nice (Foy & Nenna 2001, 119). **Switzerland**: Vindonissa, Switzerland (Berger 1960, 78). **Italy**: Pavia (Grazia Diani 2000, 78–81, fig. 5 to fig. 7); the cemetery at the Catholic University at Milano (Paternoster 2000, 106, fig. 3); Bassa Modenese (Tarpini 1998, 56, fig. 9 & fig. 10); Aquileia (Calvi 1969, tav. 12); Bologna (Meconcelli Notarianni 1979, 58); Luni (Roffia 1973, 473; Chiaramonte Trerè 1973b, 782); Ostia (Moricone 1969–72, 371; Capo 1972–76, 337); Herculaneum and Pompeii (Scatozza Höricht 1986, 43). **Romania**: Tibiscum (Caransebes) (Benea 2000, 178, fig. 1). **Greece**: Knossos, Crete (Carington-Smith 1982, 277–78). **Cyprus** (Vessberg & Westholm 1956, 149). **Egypt**: Quseir Al-Qadim, Egypt (on the Red Sea coast) (Meyer 1992, 31).
81 Carington-Smith 1982, 277–78.
82 Three fragments and a melted piece of glass from a prismatic bottle, ch. 3.26. Identified by the present author.
83 Two fragments from two prismatic bottles; ch. 3.26. Identified by the present author.
84 One fragment of blue-green bottle glass, from a cylindrical or a prismatic bottle; ch. 3.26. Identified by the present author.
85 Two fragments of a cylindrical bottle (Price 2009); ch. 3.26.
86 One fragment of blue-green bottle glass from a prismatic bottle; ch. 3.26. Identified by Dr Hilary Cool.
87 A body fragment from a prismatic bottle; ch. 3.26. Identified by Dr Fraser Hunter (pers. comm.)
88 Appendix A, B:2.
89 Appendix A, D:1.
90 Appendix A, D:3.
91 Appendix A, C:2.
92 Appendix A, H:1.
93 Appendix A, J:1.
94 Appendix A, K:2.
95 Appendix A, K:3.
96 Appendix A, K:4.
97 Appendix A, K:6.
98 Appendix A, L:1.
99 Appendix A, M:1.
100 Appendix A, M:3.
101 Appendix A, N:1.
102 Appendix A, N:2.
103 Appendix A, O:1.
104 Appendix A, O:2.
105 Appendix A, P:1.
106 Appendix A, P:2.
107 Appendix A, P:3.
108 Appendix A, P:4.
109 Appendix A, P:5.
110 Appendix A, P:6.
111 Appendix A, Q:1.
112 See 'Matt/glossy cast window glass', ch. 3.24.
113 Appendix A, Q:2.
114 Appendix A, R:1.
115 Appendix A, R:3.
116 Appendix A, S:1.
117 Donald B. Harden argued that the reeded handles come from large rectangular bottles (1950–51, 112). I have chosen another line of interpretation. In my view these handles were attached to a horizontal or somewhat diagonal shoulder of a cylindrical bottle (see Cool & Price 1995, 192), and indeed all other identified material comes from cylindrical bottles. When broken off, the result is an almost straight edge, hence Harden's interpretation.
118 Appendix A, T:1.
119 Appendix A, T:3.
120 Appendix A, U:5.
121 Appendix A, U:6.
122 Skene 1866, 9; Curle 1932a, 373–74; Piggott 1952–53, 2; *RIB* II:2, 2419.82.
123 Wace & Jehu 1914–15, 239.
124 Identifications and measurements made by Sally Worrell (2000, 319).
125 Allen 1997, 133.
126 D. J. Woolliscroft & B. Hoffmann, *The Roman Gask Project: Annual Report 2002*. Retrieved from The Roman Gask Project's homepage at: www.theromangaskproject.org.uk [accessed 2 March 2014].
127 Kilbride-Jones 1938b, 346.
128 Annual Register (1803), 378. Quoted from Robertson 1978, 203. I would like to thank Prof. Michael Erdrich for drawing my attention to this find.
129 Curle & Cree 1915–16, 128, fig. 38:11.
130 Curle 1920, 71, fig. 7: 44.
131 Jobey 1960, 30. Identified by D. Charlesworth.
132 Quoted from Price 1997a, 295.
133 Norling-Christensen 1953b, 87; Lund Hansen 1980, 88–101, fig. 1; Lund Hansen 1987, 103.
134 Sorokina 1967, Abb. 1.
135 Apakidze & Nikolaishvili 1994, 16–18, 46, fig. 30.
136 Sorokina 1967, Abb. 2.
137 Apakidze & Nikolaishvili 1994, 6–18, 46, fig. 5 (the grave), fig. 6 (the bottles *in situ*), fig. 30.
138 I would like to thank Dr Hilary Cool for making me aware of these finds.
139 *CRFB* D7, X-01-1/23.37.
140 *CRFB* D4, XIX-14-13/3.2.
141 *CRFB* D4, XX-04-5/2.2.
142 *CRFB* D4, XXI-02-6/2.18.
143 Morrison 1983, 119, fig. 4.1; Morrison 1989, 198–99, fig. 86 & fig. 87.
144 Marshall 1951, pl. 210.

3.24 Matt/glossy cast window glass

A general description of matt/glossy and other types of window glass

There are three types of window glass from the Roman period: cast matt/glossy glass, double-glossy (i.e. blown window glass), and crown-glass. However, the latter has only been found on one Roman site in northern Britain, and not a single native site north of Hadrian's Wall. Due to the difficulties in dating double-glossy glass – which is post-Roman or very late Roman in date – I have chosen not to include this in the catalogue.

The matt/glossy window glass is easily identifiable: all panes are matt on the underside and glossy on the upper side. The corners are rounded and the upper surface often bears marks of tools. Around half of all fragments were ground on the underside, to remove the rough surface.[1] This glass is normally comparatively thick, 2–5 mm;[2] however, there are finds from the Mediterranean area which were ground on both sides, resulting in thinner panes.[3] In 1966 George Boon put forward convincing arguments for how this glass was manufactured, by pouring molten glass onto a tray of stone, clay, mortar or wood. Boon argued the tool-marks that often occur on the finds were the result of pushing molten glass into the corners of the tray.[4] Until relatively recently this view was widely held in scholarly research,[5] but experimental archaeology has proven that these views no longer can be upheld.

Attempts to follow Boon's hypothesis by Mark Taylor and David Hill proved that it was impossible to manufacture window glass in the manner suggested. In an attempt to produce panes with similar surfaces, edges and tool-marks, another method of manufacture was suggested. Molten glass was probably poured onto a flat surface of terracotta tile or damp sandstone (not wood, as this would have charred) and flattened by a large cylindrical block of damp wood to form a round disc. This glass was reheated from one side, and pincers and hooks were used to pull the glass into the required shape. The pane was turned 180 degrees and the same procedure repeated.[6]

The majority of fragments found in Britain are in different shades of blue-green. However, there are examples showing that the glassmaker tried to decolourise the glass, giving it a dull greyish to an almost colourless tone. Examples of this have, for example, been found at three

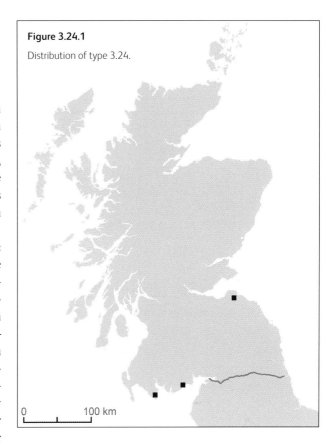

Figure 3.24.1

Distribution of type 3.24.

0   100 km

Welsh sites: Llantwit Major Roman villa, Glamorgan;[7] Cowbridge, Glamorgan;[8] and Caerleon, Gwent.[9] There are also very rare finds of coloured window glass: the bathhouse at the Roman villa at Gorhambury near Verulamium (St Albans) had dark blue windows.[10]

Very few matt/glossy window panes can be reconstructed, but some give us an idea of the size. At Garden Hill, Hartfield, Sussex, a pane of 255 x 235 mm was found[11] and at the bath in Corbridge, Northumberland, there are fragments of a pane that measure 600 x 600 mm.[12] From Pompeii and Herculaneum there are windows varying from 300 x 400 to 300 x 600 mm (fig. 3.24.2).[13] The Forum Baths at Pompeii had comparatively small windows. In contrast, the Central Baths, which were not yet complete at the time of Vesuvius' eruption in AD 79, had larger windows in all probability designed for glass panes. These window panes were to be inserted in wooden or metal frames.[14] An inscribed tombstone from Rome[15] depicts how several window panes were fitted together in a larger frame.[16] On several fragments from Stonea, Cambridgeshire traces of mortar show how they were fixed in the frame.[17]

In the late third century AD, matt/glossy window glass began to be replaced by double-glossy glass. The blown glass is considerably much thinner than its cast counterpart, 0.5–2 mm. This glass was blown into a cylinder, which was cut open and flattened.[18] The colour of double-glossy glass differs from the matt/glossy glass in that it is more greenish. From the late Roman or post-Roman periods it is not uncommon, with discolourations in the form of dark red streaks.[19]

Both cast and blown window glass show evidence of being cut into smaller pieces.[20] Occasional finds of panes knapped into different shapes have been made. Diamond-shaped panes come from the Romano-British industrial settlement at Prestatyn, Clwyd;[21] Gadebridge Roman villa, Hemel Hempstead, Hertfordshire; and Winterton Roman villa, North Lincolnshire.[22] Triangular-shaped panes are known from Lullingstone Roman villa, Kent;[23] Exeter, Devon;[24] and Xanten, Germany.[25]

Matt/glossy window glass was relatively simple to manufacture,[26] and difficult to transport. Thus most window panes are likely to have been produced locally,[27] and the quality of these varies considerably.[28] Epigraphic evidence demonstrates that units within the Roman army sometimes had a *specularius*: i.e. a craftsman who manufactured window glass, and who also worked as a glazier.[29] There were also *specularii* who were not attached to the army; however, some of these might have been glaziers rather than makers of window panes.[30]

Diocletian's *Edict on maximum prices* – i.e. in the period when cast, matt/glossy window glass was replaced by blown, double-glossy window glass – mentions the cost of these:[31]

> Window glass best (quality) one pound denarii 8
> Window glass second (quality) one pound denarii 6
> Diocletian, *Edictum de Maximis Pretiis*,
> 16.5–6, (col. III, 40–41)

Fragments of Diocletian's *Edict on maximum prices* have been found on several sites; this specific passage was found in Aphrodisias, Turkey, and also mentions other prices of glass. Nevertheless, the prices of glass vessels specify where they were manufactured, whereas it does not do this in the case of window glass. In my view this implies that window glass was still made locally around AD 300. The low price of the window glass in comparison to other types of glass led Francesca Dell'Acqua to suggest that what was meant was not actual glass windows, but rather windows made of mica.[32] Marianne Stern has put forward convincing

arguments for this not being the case. First, the section is headed *De vitro*, that is 'On glass'. Second, she points to the fact that window glass is usually of relatively poor quality, which would explain the low price.[33]

Dating the type

When the manufacture of windows in glass first started is a matter of debate. David Grose has argued that a thin, flat piece of glass in marbled purple and opaque white from the Regia, Forum Romanum, Rome is a very early glass-pane. This find dates to the first decade of the first century.[34] Price has contended that this find does not represent a window pane at all, but rather a decorative glass inlay from a piece of furniture.[35] If Grose's interpretation is correct, however, it would constitute the oldest find of cast Roman window glass, and would thus represent an interesting link between the earlier use of thin slabs of stone, such as alabaster or marble,[36] and the later blue-green or colourless cast glass. It was made in a period when much of the vessel glass was created in colours imitating semi-precious stones.[37] Although glass came to replace stone as window panes to a large extent, the use of the latter continued throughout the Roman period.[38]

The first finds of the normal blue-green matt/glossy window glass are from the Claudian-Neronian period, and were found in Colchester, Essex.[39] In Britain and the other north-western provinces, where the usage of window glass was more widespread, the production of this type of glass seems to have continued to c. AD 300.[40]

In the late third century cylinder-blown glass began to replace the cast window glass.[41] It is only in recent times that this method of production has been replaced by the float-glass technique. The very few pieces of crown-glass discovered in the north-western provinces are also of the same late date, third to fourth centuries AD.[42]

The function of the glass

As touched upon above different materials – such as mica or glass – were used for windows. In general windows were used to keep the cold out and the heat in, as one of Symphosius' (possibly 4th–5th century AD) enigmas demonstrates:

Figure 3.24.2

Window pane from Herculaneum.
British Museum: 1772,0317.21

Window-Pane
I am looked clear through
and do not check the eyesight,
transmitting the wandering glance
within my parts;
nor does the cold pass through me,
but yet the sun flashes forth from within me.

> Symphosius, *Aenigmata*, 68

There is some literary evidence as to how specifically window glass was used, for example in the works of Pliny the Elder (AD 23–79) and his nephew Pliny the Younger (AD 61–*c*. 114). In his *Natural History*, Pliny the Elder tells us that window glass was used for buildings in which the well-to-do stored their fruit:

> In regard to keeping fruit it is universally recommended that fruit-lofts should be constructed in a dry and cool place, with boarded floors and windows facing north that are left open on a fine day, and with glazed windows to keep out south winds.
>
> Pliny the Elder, *Historia Naturalis* , 15.59

Pliny the Younger speaks of a *heliocaminus*, i.e. a sun-parlour in his villa:

> At the far end of the terrace, the arcade and the garden is a suite of rooms which are really and truly my favourites, for I had them built myself. Here is a sun-parlour facing the terrace on one side, the sea on the other, and the sun on both. There is also a bedroom which has folding doors opening on to the sea. Opposite the intervening wall is a beautifully designed alcove which can be thrown into the room by folding back its glass doors and curtains.
>
> Pliny the Younger, *Epistulae*, 2.17.20–21

The archaeological evidence seems to indicate that window glass was less extensively used in the Mediterranean area. Window glass has mainly been found on two types of edifices: the villas of the well-to-do, for example at Livia's villa at Prima Porta near Rome, Italy;[43] and in baths, both private as at Casa di Diomede, Pompeii,[44] and public.[45]

There was much more extensive use of window glass in the north-western provinces with their poorer climate. Virtually all baths – the small *balnea* and the large *thermae* – had windows for instance: the legionary baths at Caerleon, Gwent.[46] Many villas had windows, as did a significant number of military buildings, the commandant's quarters in the different forts, and the watchtowers along the Roman border.[47] Anton Kisa has suggested that window glass was also utilised for lanterns.[48]

The finds from Roman contexts

Window glass constitutes one of the most frequently found types of Roman glass on both military and civilian sites in northern Britain. In most cases it is difficult to link this fragmentary material to specific contexts, but both the number of sites which have yielded it, as well as the quantities found, clearly show that window glass was widely used. In contrast to the core of the Roman Empire, there is much to suggest that many types of edifices in northern Britain – ranging from watch-towers to the villas of the wealthy – had glass windows. This is probably a reflection of the fact that it was cheaper to try to keep the cold weather out by using windows, rather than spending large sums on heating. A good example comes from Strageath, Perthshire, where about one-quarter of the total assemblage of Roman glass consisted of matt/glossy window glass.[49]

Finds appear to be equally frequent in other parts of Britain, and come from a wide range of sites, both urban and rural. For example, the considerable quantities of matt/glossy window glass from Stonea, Cambridge-shire included not only the usual blue-green glass, but also greenish colourless and colourless glass.[50] At Fish-bourne, Sussex, no less than 18 kilos of matt/glossy window glass was found, the largest assemblage in Britain.[51] Window glass constitutes a relatively common find in the north-western provinces – military sites and baths being particularly prolific – whereas finds appear not to be as frequent in the Mediterranean area.[52]

The finds from non-Roman contexts in Scotland and north Northumberland

Roman matt/glossy window glass has been found on only a single native site of Roman Iron Age date north of Hadrian's Wall: Traprain Law, East Lothian. In addition to this find, however, two sites of early Medieval date – Whithorn, Wigtownshire, and Mote of Mark, Kirkcudbrightshire – have produced it.

Four or five fragments from a minimum of two, and perhaps four different panes were unearthed at Traprain Law (fig. 3.24.3.2–3). We must study these finds in the light of the close contacts between Rome and the people of this site over almost three and a half centuries, but what these window panes convey is hard to tell. Large parts of this site were dug in the 1910s and 1920s, and unfortunately the excavators had a very poor under-standing of the stratigraphy and structures on the site. Nevertheless, given the close connections with the Roman world and the adoption of various Roman habits, it is entirely plausible that these finds maintained their function as windows, and were part of some edifice on the site. Another possible – but in my view less plausible – explanation is that the glass was intended as raw material for the manufacture of glass bangles. But if there was an import of glass cullet, the main interest of the craftsman making these bangles would have been the quality and colour of the glass, not the type of objects or vessels from which it originated. In other words, had this been the case, one would expect the assemblage of Roman glass found on this site to mirror that of a Roman site.[53]

Roman matt/glossy window glass has been dis-covered on two sites of the early Medieval period. Whithorn, Wigtownshire, is an early monastic site. One fragment from a minimum of one matt/glossy window pane was found on this site. A small assemblage of Roman goods and objects – including glass and glass tesserae, pottery and a coin – was discovered scattered in the earliest Medieval phase on the site, which has caused

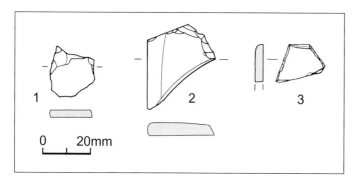

0   20mm

Figure 3.24.3

Window pane fragments [scale 2:3].

(1) Mote of Mark. **NMS:** HH 262

(2) & (3) Traprain Law. **NMS:** GV 1283, 175.2

some scholarly debate.[54] Several academics have asserted that there was a Roman Iron Age phase settlement either on the same location, or in the vicinity. However, Price has convincingly argued that this material represents the looting of an abandoned Roman fort in the Scottish lowlands, as it mirrors what could typically be found on these.[55] Besides the one positively identified example of matt/glossy window glass from Whithorn, Price mentions four fragments that were either prismatic bottles of first- to second-century date, or double-glossy window glass of late Roman/post-Roman date from the site.[56]

One fragment of matt/glossy window glass was unearthed during the 1913 excavations at Mote of Mark, Kirkcudbrightshire (fig. 3.24.3.1), as well as fragments of samian ware. No Roman Iron Age phase is documented on this site,[57] and the evidence implies that this small assemblage of Roman goods represents the loot from an abandoned Roman fort. Window glass is typical for a Roman fort, but exceedingly rare on native Roman Iron Age sites.

In addition to these finds there is some double-glossy window glass with the typical red streaks of the late Roman/post-Roman period from ?Ardeer, Ayrshire or ?Luce Sands, Wigtownshire. This is a type of window glass which also occurs on some of the early monastic sites in northern Britain, such as Monkwearmouth, Co. Durham and Jarrow, Northumberland.[58]

Mote of Mark, Kirkcudbrightshire. R:2

HH 262*, NMS. Fragment. Blue-green/green. Dims 20 x 19; WT 2.5.

Traprain Law, East Lothian. N:2

GV 175:2* (XII 15 140), Area Ff, Level 2, NMS. Fragment. Pale blue-green. Usage scratches on all sides. Dims 14 x 21; WT 3.6.

GV 176:9 (XII 15 141), Area Ga, Level 3, NMS. Fragment. Pale blue-green. Dims 21 x 27; WT 2.8.

GV 1717, Area J, Level 1, NMS. Fragment. Pale green. Dims 19 x 13; WT 3.9.

GV 1283* (1924 180), Area T, Level 2, NMS. Fragment. Pale blue-green. Dims 28 x 34; WT 4.7.

TLF 03, find 802. Fragment of window glass? Pale green. Dims 29 x 26; WT 4.0.

Whithorn, Wigtownshire. Q:2

Fragment. Bluish-green. Flat, one surface matt and slightly pockmarked, the other glossy and slightly uneven. Two edges worn, two new breaks. Dims 21 x 14.5; T 3.5–4.5.[59]

Finds from other areas beyond the borders of the Roman Empire

To my knowledge no finds of Roman window glass – cast or blown – have been made beyond the Roman Empire's borders, with the exception of these Scottish finds.

Notes

1   Boon 1966, 45.
2   Harden 1974, 280.
3   I have found examples of this type of window glass in the Poseidon Sanctuary at Kalaureia (Poros), Greece.
4   Boon 1966.
5   See for instance Haevernick 1981b, 24; Haevernick & Hahn-Weinheimer 1981, 34; Price 1996, 396.
6   For a discussion of this manner of manufacture, see Allen 2002 with references.
7   Nash-Williams 1953, 151.
8   Allen 1996, 214.
9   Allen 1986b, 116.
10   Neal et al. 1990, 74.
11   Harden 1974, 280.
12   Charlesworth 1959b, 166.
13   Kisa 1908, 363.
14   Blake 1947, 61.
15   CIL VI. 33911.
16   Haevernick & Hahn-Weinheimer 1981, Abb. 4.
17   Price 1996, 396.
18   Harden 1961.
19   Price 1993a, 189.
20   Harden 1974, 280; Price 1981, 116.
21   Allen 1989, 124.
22   Charlesworth 1976a, 249.
23   Middleton 1950, 27, fig. 9.43.
24   Charlesworth 1979b, 229.
25   Charlesworth 1984, 300.
26   Boon 1966, 45.
27   Isings 1980, 283.
28   Allen 1989, 124.

29 Haevernick & Hahn-Weinheimer 1981, 38.
30 *CIL* VI. 5202; *CIL* VI. 5203; *CIL* VI. 8659; *CIL* VI. 8660; *CIL* VI. 9044; *CIL* VI. 33911.
31 Erim et al. 1973; Barag 1987, 113–16.
32 Dell'Acqua 2004, 113.
33 Stern 2007, 385–86.
34 Grose 1977, 17–18, fig. 1 no. 12.
35 Pers. comm. Prof. Jennifer Price.
36 Pliny the Elder mentions the use of stone as windows during Nero's time, a period when cast matt-glossy window glass was used (*Historia Naturalis*, 36.46.163).
37 Kisa 1908, 512; Grose 1989, 243.
38 Pers. comm. Dr Lena Landgren.
39 Harden 1947, 306.
40 Boon 1966, 41.
41 Price 1993a, 189.
42 Price 1990a, 179.
43 To be published by the present author.
44 Blake 1947, 61.
45 Herbig 1929; Haevernick 1981b, 24–25; Baatz 1991, 7.
46 Ilen 1986b, 116.
47 Boon 1966, 41; Haevernick 1981b, 25; van Lith 1978–79, 118; Price 1989a, 196.
48 Kisa 1908, 366. The sides of the lanterns were usually made of a stretched bladder or in horn (Martial, *Epigrammata*, 14.62; Symphosius, *Aenigmata*, 67).
49 Price 1989a, 193.
50 Price 1996, 396.
51 Harden & Price 1971, 367; Price & Cottam 1996a, 169.
52 Finds have been made on numerous sites, for example, the **Netherlands**: Valkenburg Z. H. (van Lith 1978–79, 117–19); Nijmegen (Isings 1980, 323–24). **Germany**: Hofheim (Ritterling 1913, 365); Xanten (Charlesworth 1984, 300); Oberstimm (Garbsch 1978, 282); **Italy**: Pompeii (Blake 1947, 61); Cosa (Grose 1973–76, 181); San Lorenzo in Lucina, Rome (Ingemark 2012, 324), and Livia's villa at Prima Porta, outside of Rome (to be published by the present author).
53 For a discussion, see ch. 4.6.
54 Appendix A, Q:2.
55 Price 1997a, 294.
56 Price 1997a, 295, nos 8–11.
57 Appendix A, R:2.
58 Cramp 1968, 16.
59 Price 1997a, 295.

3.25. Miscellaneous fragments (including post-Roman finds)

When dealing with fragmentary material, it is inevitable that there are pieces which lack diagnostic features, making identification to type impossible.[1] Nevertheless, in most cases it is possible to obtain some information from these sherds. This section covers a total of 161 sherds from 18 sites in Scotland and Northumberland which are categorised as closely as possible. Also included are a small number of finds – four fragments in total – of Roman Mediterranean and other early Medieval glass manufactured after AD 400.

The material in this section could have come from a variety of vessels – cups, beakers, flasks, bottles, etc. – but the evidence at hand suggests that the lion's share of it was probably cups or beakers. It is also notable that the unidentified material includes a comparatively high proportion of late Roman glass, most of which has been discovered at one single site: Traprain Law, East Lothian. (No museum is listed in the catalogue for the Traprain finds, which are in the National Museum of Scotland.)

Unidentified cast vessel

From Traprain Law, East Lothian, there is a splinter of greenish colourless glass which is shiny on the outside and ground on the inside. Not enough of the vessel was preserved to establish what type of vessel it belonged to. Possibly this fragment comes from a cast and ground vessel; however, it neither resembles cast and lathe-turned vessels, which were ground on both sides,[2] nor pillar-moulded bowls, as these were in other colours.[3]

Traprain Law, East Lothian. N:2

GV 1645. Body fragment in cast glass? Greenish colourless. Curved. Shiny on outside; ground on inside. Dims 14 x 5; WT 2.9.

Miscellaneous sherds of cups or beakers with abraded and cut decoration

In the assemblage from Traprain Law there are 15 body sherds with abraded horizontal bands which were not sufficiently diagnostic to indicate the precise type. Horizontal abraded bands are one of the most common forms of decoration from the first to the fourth century, and they were used on a wide range of different types of cups and beakers.[4] These include sherds in colourless and blue-green glass of the first to early to mid-fourth century AD. There is a minimum of five colourless cups or beakers, two blue-green cups or beakers, and one cup in late Roman yellow-brown glass.

Hartburn, Northumberland, an enclosed settlement with a large number of roundhouses, was excavated in 1971. A sherd in thin colourless glass with abraded bands, now lost, was discovered on this site. In all probability this was a cup or beaker. A small assemblage of Roman pottery, including jugs, flagons and cooking pots, was found on the site.[5]

Excavations of a scooped settlement with the remains of around ten roundhouses at Hetha Burn, Hethpool, Northumberland, yielded very few Roman imports. The only finds definitely of Roman origin were two sherds of a greenish colourless cup.[6]

Traprain Law, East Lothian. N:2

GV 44 (XI 14 111). Body fragment. Cup/beaker? Blue-green. Straight side. Four horizontal abraded bands. Diameter c. 70; PH 12; W 21; WT 1.7.

GV 48 (XI 14 115). Body fragment. Colourless. Cup/beaker. Straight side. Four horizontal abraded lines. PH 17; W 16; WT 1.7.

GV 174:2 (XII 15 139). Body fragment. Beaker/flask. Clear, colourless. Straight side. Four abraded bands on upper part. Many strain cracks. D c. 80; PH 32; WT 1.8.

GV 175:1 (XII 15 140), Area F or G, Level: unknown. Body fragment. Late Roman yellow-brown. Convex-curved. Horizontal wide wheel-cut groove; horizontal abraded band. Many small bubbles. Dims 20 x 19; WT 2.2.

GV 376b (III 20 101), Area G, Level 2. Body fragment. Colourless with yellow tinge. Straight side. Two horizontal abraded bands, one on upper part of fragment, one on lower. Occasional small bubbles. Many strain cracks. BD 90; PH 38; W 21; WT 2.2.

GLASS, ALCOHOL AND POWER IN ROMAN IRON AGE SCOTLAND

GV 376d (III 20 103), Area H, Level 2. Body fragment. Colourless with a yellow tinge. Straight side. One, thin, horizontal abraded band. Occasional small bubbles. Strain cracks. Dims 16 x 15; WT 1.5. Same vessel as GV 376b?

GV 1646. Body fragment. Clear, colourless. Cup/beaker. Straight side. Two abraded bands. Many small bubbles. BD c.80; Dims 25 x 8; WT 2.5.

GV 1647, Area S, Level 2. Body fragment. Clear, colourless. Cup/beaker. Straight side. Abraded band on upper part. Occasional bubbles. Diameter c.70; PH 20; W 19; WT 2.2.

GV 1648, Area T, Level 2. Body fragment. Colourless. Cup/beaker. Abraded horizontal band. Dims 13 x 8; WT 1.2.

GV 1649, Area H, Level 2. Body fragment. Blue-green. Beaker. Convex-curved body. Horizontal abraded band. Many small bubbles. Dims 21 x 11; WT 1.3.

GV 1650, Area H, Level 2. Body fragment. Blue-green. Beaker. Convex-curved body. Two horizontal abraded bands. Bubbly. PH 14; W 15; WT 1.1. Same vessel as GV 1649?

GV 1651, Area H, Level 2. Body fragment. Blue-green. Beaker. Convex-curved body. Horizontal abraded band. Many small bubbles. Dims 14 x 11; WT 1.1. Same vessel as GV 1649?

GV 1787, Area A, Level 1. Body fragment. Cup/beaker. Natural green. Curved side. Horizontal abraded band. PH 30; W 6; WT 1.5.

GV 1791. Rim fragment. Colourless with yellow tinge. Beaker. Rim cracked off. Abraded band below rim. RD 70; PH 11; W 10; WT 1.5.

GV 1792. Body fragment. Cup/beaker. Clear, colourless. Straight side. Five abraded bands. Many strain cracks. Diameter c. 80; PH 19; W 15; WT 1.4.

Hartburn, Northumberland. U:2

Missing; the published account of this material is as follows: 'A very small fragment of almost colourless glass only 1 mm thick, showing little curvature. Two thin converging lines are engraved on the surface. It is possibly Roman.'[7]

Hetha Burn, Hethpool, Northumberland. U:3

Missing; the published account of this material is as follows:

'Rim fragment of glass vessel, 15 mm x 8 mm, nearly 2 mm thick. Of fine, clear glass with slight bubbling and a greenish tinge. Decorated on the outside with very fine engraved horizontal lines in a zone 1 mm thick, 7 mm below the rim. Roman. .... As above, but a triangular body fragment 15 mm x 10 mm, showing a further zone of engraved lines.'[8]

Miscellaneous sherds of vessels with applied threads (including a spiral base)

The following finds with applied threads all come from Traprain Law. Applied self-coloured trails are found on a number of different types of vessels: cups, beakers, flasks, and jugs, of the first to the fourth century AD.

Two very small fragments in colourless and green glass respectively may have come from cups or beakers. Three sherds – GV 376a, GV 376c, and GV 376f – come from a cup or beaker in colourless glass with a spiral-trail base and horizontal applied thread. Despite several sherds being preserved, this vessel could not be identified.

One fragment – GV 1279 – in late Roman yellow-green, bears close resemblance to ovoid jugs with funnel mouths of the fourth century with closely set spiral trails. However, on the basis of a body sherd alone it cannot be attributed to a specific type.[9] One fragment, an unidentified vessel, in blue-green glass, had a thin self-coloured thread.

Traprain Law, East Lothian. N:2

GV 176:8 (XII 15 141), Area F, Level 3. Body fragment. Blue-green. Unidentified vessel. Thin applied self-coloured thread. Dims 20 x 9; WT 0.7.

GV 376a (III 20 100), Area G, Level 2. Lower body and base. Cup/beaker. Greenish colourless. Side tapering out. Applied base ring in the form of a thick spiral trail. Flat base. Many small bubbles. Strain cracks. BD 60; PH 17; W 36; WT 1.1. Same vessel as GV 376c.

GV 376c (III 20 102), Area 1919, Level 2. Body fragment. Cup/beaker. Greenish colourless. Upper part tapering out, straight side. Applied horizontal trail. PH 14; WT 1.2. Same vessel as GV 376a.

GV 376f (III 20 105), Area G, Level 2. Body fragment. Cup/beaker. Colourless. Straight side. Applied thick thread. Thread 2.9; PH 14; WT 1.2.

GV 1279 (1924 176), Area R, Level 2. Body fragment. Yellow-green. Convex-curved. Five horizontal, applied trails. Very bubbly. Ovoid jug? Diameter c. 140; PH 20; W 22; WT 1.0.

GV 1676. Body fragment. Colourless with yellow tinge. Cup/beaker? Applied thick thread. Many strain cracks. Dims 7 x 9; WT 1.1; Thread 3.6.

GV 1677, Area S, Level 1. Body fragment. Natural green. Cup/beaker? Slightly curved. Applied thick thread. Dims 11 x 21; WT 2.9.

GV 1678, Area S, Level 1. Body fragment. Yellow-green. Cup/beaker. Convex-curved body. Two thin applied horizontal threads. Occasional bubbles. PH 11; W 10; WT 0.7.

Miscellaneous undecorated body sherds of cups and beakers

Undecorated body fragments of cups and beakers are very difficult to classify/identify. The following fragments can be only dated broadly to the first to the fourth century AD, but colour allows a few to be more closely dated.

Crosskirk, Caithness, was a promontory fort later replaced by a broch. A fragment of a cup or beaker in pale green glass, and a fragment of a cylindrical bottle, were discovered on the site. In addition to these, a small number of Roman pottery sherds were unearthed – a samian bowl, unidentified samian, and a Castor Ware beaker.[10]

Most finds from Culbin Sands, Morayshire – a large area of sand dunes along the coast – have been casual, and thus need not be directly linked to each other. A small number of Roman glass vessels have been discovered: an unidentified cup or beaker in colourless glass with a slight yellow tinge; a vessel with marvered blobs; a vessel decorated with snake-thread technique; and possibly a tubular-rimmed bowl. It has been suggested that there was a production of glass beads at Culbin Sands,[11] but this need not relate to the finds of vessel glass; two of four sherds were polychrome, and they would have been of little use in the manufacture of beads.

Dun Ardtreck, Skye, is a galleried dun. The only find of Roman vessel glass is a cup or beaker in bluish-green glass. A small assemblage of Roman pottery was also discovered: a samian cup or platter, unidentified Central Gaulish samian, and fragments of a Severn Valley jug.[12]

Eight fragments of a cup or beaker in green glass were found at Keir Hill, Gargunnock, Stirlingshire, during excavation of a roundhouse. Fragments from a few Roman objects were discovered. In addition to the cup, fragments of an unguent bottle were unearthed and a single sherd of decorated Roman pottery.[13]

From Traprain Law, East Lothian there are 49 fragments from a minimum of ten vessels in colourless, blue-green, late Roman yellow-green, brown-green and green glass. One find worthy of particular mention is a small gaming piece in late Roman glass, made from a vessel of unidentified type (fig. 3.25.1.3).

Crosskirk, Caithness. D:1

A 1979.490, Hunterian Museum. Body fragment. Cup/beaker. Pale green. Straight side. Dims 30 x 20; WT 1.5.

Culbin Sands, Morayshire. F:2

DDCCM ARC 266, Dunrobin Castle. Body fragment. Cup/beaker. Colourless with slight yellow tinge. Dims 4 x 20; WT 3.5.

Dun Ardtreck, Skye, Hebrides. C:1

A 1965 755 (125 ARBX), Hunterian Museum. Body fragment. Cup/beaker. Blue-green/greenish glass, with occasional bubbles. H 13; W 7; WT 1.5.

Keir Hill, Gargunnock, Stirlingshire. K:5

L.1961.4–11, NMS. Eight body fragments of cup/beaker? Green glass with dull surface. WT c.1.0.

Traprain Law, East Lothian. N:2

GV 174:7 (XII 15 139), Area Fe, Level 1. Body fragment. Curved. Pale green. Cup/beaker? Dims 12 x 9; WT 1.8.

GV 175:4 (XII 15 140). Body fragment. Yellow-green. Cup/beaker? Curved. Dims 25 x 17; WT 1.8.

GV 176:2 (XII 15 141), Area Fe, Level 3. Rim fragment. Pale natural green. Cup/beaker. Rim folded out, down and in, leaving trapped air-bubble. RD 70; PH 5; W 22; WT 3.5.

GV 178:3 (XII 15 143). Body fragment. Greenish colourless. Cup/ beaker? Curved. Dims 19 x 11; WT 1.0.

GV 332 (III 20 28). Body fragment. Curved. Pale green. Cup/beaker? Dims 15 x 12; WT 1.2.

GV 333 (III 20 29), Area H, Level 0. Body fragment. Cup/beaker? Yellowish-green. Curved. Occasional bubbles. Dims 19 x 13; WT 1.0.

GV 684* (V 21 179), Area H, Level: unknown. Fragment of unidentified vessel. Late Roman greenish-brown (olive coloured). Flat with raised roundel. Reused, knapped into a small gaming piece. Dims 18 x 19; WT 4.1.

GV 1652. Body fragment. Colourless. Cup/beaker? Curved. Dims 10 x 5; WT 2.0.

GV 1653. Fragment. Colourless with yellow tinge. Beaker? Slightly curved. Dims 10 x 9; WT 3.2.

GV 1654. Body fragment. Colourless with yellow tinge. Cup/beaker? Dims 15 x 7; WT 1.6.

GV 1655, Area G, Level 2. Body fragment. Greenish colourless. Cup/beaker. Convex-curved. Strain cracks. Dims 18 x 11; WT 2.0.

GV 1656, Area H, Level 4. Body fragment. Greenish colourless. Cup/beaker? Convex-curved. Dims 11 x 12; WT 1.0.

GV 1657, Area M, Level 3. Body fragment. Colourless with yellow tinge. Cup/beaker? Curved side. Dims 12 x 17; WT 7.3.

GV 1658, Area P, Level 2. Body fragment. Clear, colourless. Beaker? Curved. Very few bubbles. Dims 12 x 25; WT 1.7.

GV 1659, Area P, Level 3. Body fragment. Clear, colourless. Beaker? Curved. Dims 34 x 10; WT 2.0–3.4. Same vessel as GV 1658 and GV 1657?

GV 1660, Area S, Level 2. Body fragment. Greenish colourless. Cup/beaker? Curved. Dims 15 x 7; WT 1.3.

GV 1661, Area T, Level 2. Body fragment. Colourless. Cup/beaker. Slightly curved. Bubbly. Dims 14 x 11; WT 1.1.

GV 1662, Area T, Level 2. Body fragment. Colourless. Cup/beaker. Convex-curved. Bubbly. Dims 23 x 10; WT 0.9. Same vessel as GV 1661.

GV 1663, Area H, Level 3. Body fragment. Blue-green. Cup/beaker. Convex-curved side. Many small bubbles. Dims 15 x 17; WT 0.9.

GV 1664, Area T, Level 2. Body fragment. Blue-green. Cup/beaker. Curved. Dims 15 x 10; WT 1.7.

GV 1665, Area H, Level: unknown. Body fragment. Cup/beaker? Yellowish-green. Convex-curved. Occasional bubbles. Dims 15 x 10; WT 1.1.

GV 1666, Area H, Level 1. Body fragment. Yellow-green. Cup/beaker. Convex-curved. Dims 11 x 12; WT 0.9.

GV 1667, Area S, Level 1. Body fragment. Yellow-green. Cup/beaker. Convex-curved. Dims 22 x 15; WT 1.5.

GV 1668, Area R, Level 2. Body fragment. Yellow-green. Cup/beaker. Convex-curved. Dims 15 x 10; WT 0.7.

GV 1669, Area T, Level 2. Body fragment. Yellow-green. Cup/beaker. Convex-curved. Dims 12 x 17; WT 0.9.

GV 1670, Area R, Level 2. Body fragment. Yellow-brown. Cup/beaker? Curved. Dims 11 x 9; WT 1.6.

GV 1671. Body fragment. Pale green. Cup/beaker? Straight side. Elongated bubbles. Dims 14 x 7; WT 1.1.

GV 1672. Body fragment. Pale green. Cup/beaker. Straight side. Elongated bubbles. Dims 11 x 10; WT 1.7.

GV 1673. Body fragment. Pale green. Cup/beaker. Dull surface. Dims 12 x 5; WT 0.9.

GV 1674, Area R, Level 2. Body fragment. Natural green. Cup/beaker? Straight side. Elongated bubbles. PH 22; W 9; WT 1.3.

GV 1675, Area R, Level 2. Body fragment. Pale green. Cup/beaker. Curved. Dims 11 x 5; WT 1.3.

GV 1790, 1935 excavations Section A1, 2nd level. Body fragment. Curved. Blue-green. Cup/beaker. Dims 16 x 12; WT 0.6.

GV 1798. Unidentified fragment. Colourless with a green tinge. Totally distorted by heat. Dims 19 x 15 x 3.7.

GV 1802, Area T, Level 2. Body fragment. Clear, colourless glass with many bubbles. Cup or beaker? Convex-curved. Dims 25 x 12; WT 1.0.

GV 1803. Body fragment of a vessel of cylindrical shape. Blue-green glass with elongated bubbles. Cup or beaker? Dims 17 x 18; WT 1.4.

GV 1806. Body fragment. Very pale blue-green. Cup/beaker? Curved. Dims 16 x 4.5; WT 0.7.

GV 1807. Body fragment. Very pale blue-green. Curved. Dims 12 x 10; WT 1.1.

GV 1811, Area S, Level 1. Fragment. Green. Cup or beaker? Convex-curved. Dims 15 x 14; WT 1.5.

GV 1814, Area T, Level 2. Body fragment. Blue-green. Cup or beaker? Curved. Dims 7 x 7; WT 1.5.

GV 1815, Area S, Level 1. Body fragment. Pale green. Cup or beaker? Curved. Dims 14 x 8; WT 1.1.

GV 1817, Area R, Level 1. Body fragment. Colourless with a yellow-green tinge. Cup or beaker? Dims 11 x 11; WT 0.8.

GV 1818, Area R, Level 1. Body fragment. Late Roman yellow-green. Cup or beaker? Curved. Dims 13 x 8; WT 0.7.

GV 1819, Area S, Level 1. Body fragment. Late Roman yellow-green. Bubbly. Cup or beaker? Curved. Dims 9 x 8; WT 0.8.

GV 1821, Area R, Level 3. Body fragment. Blue-green. Cup or beaker? Curved. Dims 12 x 16; WT 12.6.

GV 1823, Area S, Level 1. Body fragment. Blue-green. Cup or beaker? Curved. Dims 15 x 9; WT 1.2.

GV 1825. Body fragment. Late Roman yellow-green. Very bubbly. Cup or beaker? Curved. Dims 19 x 12. WT 0.8.

GV 1826, Area R, Level 2, NMS. Body fragment. Blue-green. Cup or beaker? Curved. Dims 11 x 9; WT 1.0.

GV 1827, Area I, Level 4, NMS. Body fragment. Pale blue-green. Cup or beaker? Curved. Dims 16 x 14; WT 1.5.

TLSP 99, Context 003, sf. 408. Body sherd of unidentified vessel. Pale greenish, bubbly glass. Slightly convex-curved. Dims 12 x 7; WT 1.8. Cup or beaker?

Miscellaneous bases – cups, beakers, bowls and jugs

Whereas most vessel types have diagnostic and readily identifiable rim sherds, the bases are more rarely diagnostic. The same type of base, e.g. tubular pushed-in base rings, is shared by a wide range of vessels: cups, beakers, bowls and jugs of first- to fourth-century AD date. There are, of course, exceptions to this rule; a number of vessels have very specific types of bases, which are discussed in their respective chapters. Applied pad bases are found on bowls and jugs of first- to fourth-century date, and applied spiral trails are found on cups of second to fourth century date.[14]

Vessels with tubular base rings have been found at four non-Roman/native sites: Fendom Sands, Ross & Cromarty, the Sculptor's Cave, Covesea, Morayshire, Dalmeny Park, South Queensferry, Midlothian and Traprain Law, East Lothian. Very little can be said about Fendom Sands – it is an extensive area of sand dunes along the coast. To my knowledge only one find of Roman origin has been made here: a fragment of a base from a blue-green vessel.[15]

The Sculptor's Cave, Covesea, Morayshire, is a sea cave which was excavated around 80 years ago. These excavations yielded a small assemblage of Roman im-ports, and it is noteworthy that a number of these were reused. The base discussed here was reworked to form a bead (fig. 3.25.1.1), and it is possible that it belonged to the same necklace/s as a number of Iron Age glass beads found on the site. The size of the find could sug-gest that this find originates from a cup or beaker. Five reused fragments of samian were also unearthed at this site, as well as a number of other Roman finds.[16]

Dalmeny Park, South Queensferry, Midlothian, is an early Medieval burial discovered incidentally when the British army were building fortifications along the coast during the First World War. A bead necklace (fig. 3.25.2) and some teeth was all that remained. There has been some debate as to the date of this find. Some have argued that the beads were Anglo-Saxon, whereas others have contended that the beads were of Roman date but found in a context of later date.[17] This particular find was originally produced in the Roman period (fig. 3.25.1.4), but whether it represents an intact vessel that once had reached a native site, or it was picked off the ground of an abandoned Roman fort, is impossible to ascertain.

From Traprain Law, East Lothian there is a min-imum of five vessels in blue-green and green glass. In addition to these are fragments of two vessels with out-turned tubular bases and high concave bases from Traprain Law, East Lothian. One is in blue-green, the other in yellow-green glass. The shape of these frag-ments is similar to the bases of late, deep tubular-rimmed bowls of fourth-century date,[18] but a positive identifi-cation cannot be made. A minimum of two vessels with applied pad bases were also found at Traprain Law. These come from jugs or bowls.

Gubeon Cottage, Northumberland was an enclosed settlement with a roundhouse. A small assemblage of Roman imports was discovered on the site: two frag-ments from two bases, which unfortunately are missing, although one might have come from a cup or beaker (possibly Morin-Jean's Base Type 19, a high domed base); a piece of samian; a rim of a coarse-ware vessel; and an intact *mortarium*. The identification made by W. Bulmer may suggest that the other find was a base with a beaded stem – but this is not specifically said – instead he refers to an illustration in Morin-Jean's work on Gaulish glass: fig. 281. This is a tall cylindrical beaker with snake-thread decoration, but it remains unclear what this find represents.[19]

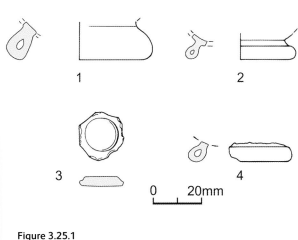

Figure 3.25.1

Miscellaneous fragments [scale 2:3].

(1) Fragent reused as beads, Covesea.
NMS: HM 215

(2) Traprain Law.
NMS: GV 1076

(3) Fragment reused as gaming piece, Traprain Law.
NMS: GV 684

(4) Fragment reused as bead, Dalmeny Park.
NMS: EQ 340

Fendom Sands, Ross & Cromarty. E:1

BK 37, NMS. Base fragment. Blue-green. Pushed-in tubular base-ring. BD c.60; PH 15; WT 3.9.

Covesea, Morayshire. F:1

HM 215*, NMS. Base fragment of a vessel with a tubular pushed-in base ring. Pale green, occasional bubbles. Deliber-ately reworked. H 15; W 8; WT 2.7.

Dalmeny Park, South Queensferry, Midlothian. M:2

EQ 340*, NMS. Base fragment of a vessel with a pushed-in tubular base-ring. Blue-green glass. Reworked and reused as a necklace bead. Very worn on the broken edges. H 11; W 26; WT 2.1.

Traprain Law, East Lothian. N:2

GV 46 (XI 14 113). Base fragment. Jug/bowl. Yellow-brown. Fragment distorted by heat. Base of vessel, which originally had an applied pad base. Dims 22 x 26; WT 2.2.

GV 455 (III 20 228), Area G, Level 3. Base fragment. Pale blue-green. Tubular pushed-in base ring. Slightly convex base. BD 40; Dims 15 x 5.

GV 688 (V 21 183), Area J, Level 2. Lower body and base. Pale green. Bowl/jug. Convex-curved side. Out-splayed base ring formed from applied pad. Very bubbly. BD 80; PH 14; WT 2.5.

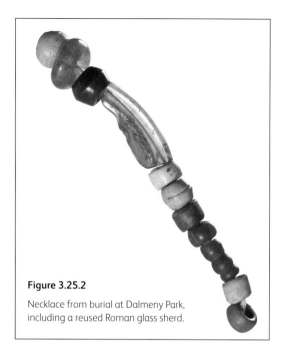

Figure 3.25.2

Necklace from burial at Dalmeny Park, including a reused Roman glass sherd.

GV 1076* (1923 80), Area P, Level 2. Two joining fragments of lower body and base. Green. Cup/beaker. Body tapering out; tubular pushed-in base ring. BD 45; PH 10; WT 2.0.

GV 1679. Base fragment. Blue-green. Tubular pushed-in base ring. Slightly convex base. Many small bubbles. BD 40; PH 12; WT 3.0.

GV 1680, Area and Level: unknown. Base fragment. Tubular pushed-in base ring. Blue-green. Dims 15 x 9; WT 1.2.

GV 1681, Area K, Level 3. Base fragment. Blue-green. High concave base. Dims 12 x 14; WT 1.4.

GV 1716, Area K, Level 1. Base fragment. Blue-green. Pushed-in tubular base-ring; flat base. Dims 15 x 12; WT 1.9.

GV 1799, Area T, Level 2. Base fragment of a cup. Blue-green. Cup or beaker? Almost flat with curved ripples. Dims 27 x 17; WT 1.3.

GV 1805, Area P, Level 2. Base fragment. Green/blue-green, occasional bubbles. Cup/beaker. Concave base with a central kick. Dims 22 x 13; 2.0.

GV 1810, Area R, Level 3. Fragment of lower body and base. Pale green. Cup or beaker? Body curving down to base. Dims 20 x 12; WT 2.1.

TLF 03, trench 8 find 22. Yellow-green. Base of a vessel with a diagonal tubular base. Pushed-in base-ring, domed base, possibly from a bowl. BD ca 60; H 9.5; WT 2.2.

Gubeon Cottage, Northumberland. U:1

Missing; the published account of this material is as follows: 'These two fragments are from bases of glass vessels of the Roman period. No. 2 varies only in minor detail from Morin-Jean's Base Type no. 19. [Morin-Jean 1913] No. 1 is of the same type and, except for its diameter, is exactly comparable with the glass cup from Besançon illustrated in Morin-Jean's figure no. 281. These bases belong to rather tall cylindrical bases with domed footstands.'[20]

Miscellaneous unidentified fragments

A number of fragments could not be identified: in some cases because they were melted, others simply were not diagnostic.

Mine Howe, Tankerness, Orkney, produced fragments of a vessel in snake-thread glass, a prismatic bottle, and 16 fragments representing a minimum of three unidentified glass vessels. Two of these were in common blue-green glass and cannot be given a close date. The last vessel, however, was in pale green glass, a colour suggesting a late Roman date.[21]

There are two unidentified sherds in late Roman green glass from ?Ardeer, Ayrshire or ?Luce Sands, Wigtownshire. With the exception of a cylindrical bottle of first- or early second-century AD date, all the glass from this collection was late-Roman or post-Roman. This small assemblage included an engraved eastern Mediterranean vessel, post-Roman window glass, a tubular-rimmed bowl of Burgh Castle type, and the sherds discussed here.[22]

From Hyndford, Lanarkshire – a crannog – there is a relatively large assemblage of Roman imports.[23] Among this were two unidentified pieces of glass. One is a melted lump of deep blue glass, suggesting a Flavian or earlier date. The other is a thick vessel in yellow-green; no closer dating could be provided for this.

Torwoodlee, Selkirkshire – a hillfort and later broch – yielded a varied and relatively rich assemblage of Roman goods. This included three melted and thus unidentifiable pieces of colourless glass.[24]

From Traprain Law there are no fewer than 45 unidentified sherds in colourless, blue-green, green and pale yellow glass.

Middle Gunnar Peak, Barrasford, Northumberland – a stone-built enclosure with five roundhouses – was excavated in 1978. These excavations yielded samian, amphorae, cooking pots, a *mortarium*, a Castor Ware beaker and Castor Ware cup. Unfortunately the glass is missing, and very little can be said on the basis of the published description, other than that there must have been several vessels in blue-green and blue glass.

Mine Howe, Tankerness, Orkney. B:2

MH04, find 8882. Splinter of unidentified blue-green glass, possibly from a glass vessel. Dims 5 x 6 x 3.

MH03, find 10409. Splinter of unidentified blue-green vessel glass. Dims 5 x 2; WT 1.2.

MH02, find 3341. 14 small fragments of unidentified Roman vessel glass. Pale – natural – green glass. Many cracks in the glass; exposed to heat? Size of fragments ranging from 10 x 7 to 2 x1. Probably from one single vessel.

?Ardeer, Ayrshire or ?Luce Sands, Wigtownshire. P:1 or Q:1

Unreg., NMS. Two fragments in late Roman green. Curved. Dims 15 x 15; WT 0.5; Dims 15 x 9; WT 0.8.

Hyndford, Lanarkshire. O:1

HTA 38, NMS. Melted lump of deep blue glass. Dims 20 x 15 x 6.

HTA 41, NMS. Body fragment. Convex-curved. Yellow-green. Cup/beaker/bowl? Dims 23 x 13; WT 3.0.

Torwoodlee, Selkirkshire. S:1.

GA 1260, NMS. Melted fragment. Colourless. Dims 18 x 14 x 7.

GA 1260, NMS. Two melted fragments – body sherds? Colourless. Dims 20 x 14 x 1.

Traprain Law, East Lothian. N:2

GV 174:5 (XII 15 139), Body fragment. Natural green. Convex-curved. PH 22; W 24; WT 1.0.

GV 175:6 (XII 15 140), Fragment. Flat. Yellowish-green. Dims 17 x 9; WT 1.9.

GV 377 (III 20 106), Area G, Level 2. Body fragment. Cup/flask. Blue-green. Straight side. Occasional bubbles. Dims 21 x 14; WT 1.7.

GV 453 (III 20 226), Area G, Level 3. Body fragment. Curved. Very pale yellow. Elongated bubbles. Usage scratches. Diameter c.40; PH 21; WT 4.

GV 1641 (Rampart): 7 fragments in thick, greenish colourless, crazed glass. This glass was exposed to heat. Dims 17 x 16; WT 4.4–4.6; Dims 18 x 10; WT 4.8; Dims 11 x 15, WT 4.9; Dims 16 x 10, WT 4.2; Dims 9 x 6; WT 5.2; Dims 8 x 7; WT 4.2; 11 x 6; WT 4.2.

GV 1682, Area P, Level 3. Body fragment. Greenish colourless. Dims 19 x 11; WT 3.5.

GV 1683, Area K, Level 1. Body fragment. Greenish colourless. Cup/beaker/flask? Convex-curved. Dims 24 x 15; WT 1.0.

GV 1684, Body fragment. Pale blue-green. Cup/beaker/flask. Convex-curved. Dims 14 x 5; WT 0.9.

GV 1685, Body fragment. Pale blue-green. Cup/beaker/flask. Convex-curved. Dims 11 x 10; WT 1.0.

GV 1686, Area H, Level 4. Base fragment. Blue-green. Cup/flask? Convex-curved. Very bubbly. Dims 20 x 20; WT 1.5.

GV 1687, Area I, Level 3. Body fragment. Pale blue-green. Cup/beaker/flask. Dims 17 x 10; WT 1.4.

GV 1688, Area J, Level 1. Body fragment. Blue-green. Cup/beaker/flask. Curved side. Many small bubbles. Dims 18 x 15; WT 1.1.

GV 1689, Area J, Level 4. Body fragment. Pale blue-green. Cup/beaker/flask? Slightly curved. Dims 15 x 12; WT 1.5.

GV 1690, Area L, Level 1. Fragment of lower body and base. Blue-green. Cup/beaker/flask? Curved side; flat base. Many small bubbles. Dims 22 x 14; WT 1.3.

GV 1691, Area P, Level 1. Base fragment? Blue-green. Cup/beaker/flask? Almost flat. Dims 14 x 16; WT 1.9.

GV 1692, Area P, Level 1. Body fragment. Blue-green. Cup/beaker/flask. Convex-curved side. Dims 17 x 13; WT 1.3.

GV 1693, Area R, Level 2. Body fragment. Pale blue-green. Cup/beaker/flask. Straight side. Dims 17 x 10; WT 2.1.

GV 1694, Area R, Level 2. Fragment. Blue-green. Cup/beaker/flask? Slightly distorted by heat. Dims 9 x 10; WT 2.3.

GV 1695. Base fragment. Blue-green. Flask? Almost flat. Dims 14 x 16; WT 1.5.

GV 1696. Base fragment. Blue-green. Flat. Dims 9 x 23; WT 1.6.

GV 1697. Base fragment. Blue-green. Flat. Dims 11 x 7; WT 1.7.

GV 1698, Area H, Level 4. Base fragment? Blue-green. Almost flat. Bubbly. Dims 26 x 10; WT 1.4.

GV 1699, Area K, Level 3. Fragment of lower body and base. Blue-green. Flat base, curved side. Very worn on edge. PH 15; WT 1.6.

GV 1700, Area I, Level 2. Body fragment. Pale blue-green. Cup/beaker/flask. Convex-curved. Dims 20 x 10; WT 1.0.

GV 1701, Area K, Level 1. Base fragment. Pale yellow-green. Cup/beaker/flask? Almost flat. Many strain cracks.

GV 1702, Area K, Level 1. Base fragment. Yellow-green. Cup/beaker/flask? Curved. Usage scratches. Dims 19 x 22; WT 1.2.

GV 1703, Area L, Level 2. Base fragment. Yellow-green. Cup/beaker/flask? Convex-curved. Worn. Dims 18 x 17; WT 2.0.

GV 1704, Area R, Level 1. Body fragment. Yellow-green. Convex-curved. Dims 18 x 18; WT 0.8–1.8.

GV 1705, Area S; level 1. Body fragment. Yellow-green. PH 12; W 18; WT 1.3.

GV 1706, Area K, Level 1. Base fragment. Yellow-green. Curved. Usage scratches. Dims 16 x 13; WT 1.1.

GV 1707, Area G, Level 2. Fragment of lower body and base? Pale green. Cup/beaker/flask? Curved side; flat base. Dims 18 x 16; WT 1.0.

GV 1708, Area J, Level 3. Body fragment. Pale green. Cup/beaker/flask? Convex-curved side. Dims 16 x 22; WT 1.3.

GV 1709, Area R, Level 2. Body fragment. Natural green. Curved. Many strain cracks. Dims 17 x 14; WT 4.1.

GV 1786, Base fragment. Blue-green. Dims 15 x 21; WT 1.9.

GV 1808. Fragment. Distorted by heat. Pale yellow-green. Dims 12 x 7; WT 1.8.

GV 1809. Fragment. Pale green. Almost flat. Heavy wear on one side. Dims 22 x 18; WT 3.4.

GV 1812. Fragment. Clear, cracked glass (exposed to heat). Dims 13 x 14; WT 8.5.

GV 1813. Body fragment. Colourless with a slight green tinge. Almost flat. Dims 9 x 4; WT 1.0.

GV 1816. Body fragment. Pale blue-green. Convex-curved. Dims 8 x 7; WT 0.8.

GV 1820, Area T, Level 1. Body fragment. Blue-green. Almost flat. Dims 12 x 8; WT 1.6.

GV 1822, Area S, Level 1. Body fragment. Blue-green. Curved. Dims 20 x 11; WT 1.3–2.9.

GV 1824, Area R, Level 1. Body fragment. Blue-green. Curved. Dims 15 x 11; WT 1.8.

TLF 03, find 2. Flat fragment. Very pale natural green. Dims 41 x 21; WT 4.3.

TLF 04, find 345. Splinter. Blue-green. Dims 7 x 3; WT 2.5. F/W zone 20.

TLF 05, find 605. Body fragment. Greenish colourless. Convex-curved. Dims 15 x 13; WT 0.8.

Middle Gunnar Peak, Barrasford, Northumberland. U:4

Missing; the published account of this material is as follows: 'Fragment of bluish-green glass …. Very small fragment of blue glass …. Two fragments of blue tinted glass.'[25]

Late Roman bottle?

Too little of this vessel is preserved to make a positive identification, but this find from Traprain Law, East Lothian, may have come from a late Roman bottle. Tall cylindrical bottles were manufactured in this colour of glass in the late third to fourth century AD.[26]

Traprain Law, East Lothian. N:2

GV 1829, Area E, Level 1. Fragment of neck? Late Roman yellow-green. Diameter not possible to establish, but the curve suggests that this is a neck fragment. Dims 19 x 9; WT 4.0.

Rod handle of late Roman date

Rod handles are found on several types of vessels,[27] and very little can be said about this fragment. The colour, however, suggests a late Roman date for this find from Traprain Law.

Traprain Law, East Lothian. N:2

GV 1796, Area Q, Level 2. Fragment of handle. Pale green with yellow and black streaks. Jug/flask? D-sectioned rod handle. PH 22; W 15; WT 5.5.

Late Roman flask or jug with applied horizontal trail

From Edinburgh Castle[28] came a fragment of a flask or jug with an applied thread. Such applied spiral threads are a common type of decoration on flasks and jugs of the third and fourth centuries AD. The colour of the thread – deep blue – suggests that it does not come from

a vessel with so-called snake-thread decoration, as these had threads in opaque colours. Denise Allen, who published this find, is of the opinion it is a vessel of fourth-century AD date.[29]

Edinburgh Castle, Midlothian. M:3

The published account[30] of this material is as follows:

'SF 68. Rim fragment of a flask or jug of greenish-colourless glass; surfaces pitted, and many pinhead bubbles within the metal. Rim flared out, and folded inward and downward, beneath which part of a horizontal trail of dark glass still adheres. Rim diam. = 45 mm.'[31]

A late Roman or post-Roman bowl

From Traprain Law there is a sherd of a low bowl with applied self-coloured threads forming a 'ribcage' pattern (fig. 3.25.3).[32] Although I have found no parallels to this vessel type in the literature concerning glass from the fifth to eighth centuries,[33] the colour and quality of the glass, suggests a late Roman or post-Roman date – probably after AD 400 – as does the type of decoration. This find is not included in the overall analysis and discussion of the glass assemblage from native sites, but as this may be one of the latest finds of glass from Traprain Law, I have chosen to include it in this section.

Traprain Law, East Lothian. N:2

GV 1278* (1924 175), Area T, Level 2. Convex-curved body sherd from a low bowl? Green, very bubbly glass. Applied self-coloured broad threads forming a 'ribcage' pattern. Dims 46 x 24; WT 1.9.

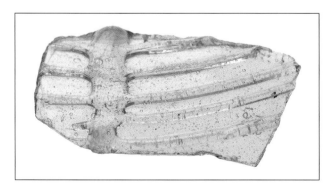

Figure 3.25.3

Ribbed sherd from Traprain Law.

NMS: GV 1278

Late Roman Mediterranean glass – vessels with abraded decoration

Three fragments from a minimum of two – possibly three – hemispherical cups with abraded decoration in the form of circles and lines were discovered at Traprain Law. Two of the fragments are in pale blue-green and one is in pale green glass. Price has argued that these were manufactured in the Mediterranean area, and that they date to the late fifth or early sixth century AD.[34] Glass vessels with this type of decoration are known from a small number of British sites, for example Trethurgy, Cornwall;[35] Cadbury Congresbury, Somerset;[36] High Down, Sussex;[37] Holme Pierrepoint, Nottinghamshire;[38] and Whithorn, Wigtownshire.[39]

A possible addition to these finds comes from ?Ardeer, Ayrshire or ?Luce Sands, Wigtownshire. Due to the fact that the colour of the glass and the style of abrasion differs somewhat from the above finds, this identification remains uncertain. Rather than the typical yellow-green, yellow colourless, pale green or blue-green,[40] this find is a pale purple typical of glass de-coloured with manganese. The abraded decoration forms a floral pattern, which resembles Roman Mediterranean glass in its execution but not in style, as we do not find the typical circles, lines and 'S'-patterns of Roman Mediterranean glass. A number of Roman, late Roman and post-Roman/early Medieval finds are known from this sand dune collection.[41]

Traprain Law, East Lothian. N:2

GV 1281 (1924 178), Area T, Level 2. Body fragment. Convex-curved side. Abraded decoration in the form of one or possibly two circles and a short line. Pale green. Bubbly. Dims 25 x 20; WT 1.6.

GV 1631, Area T, Level 1. Body fragment. Slightly curved side. Part of abraded circle. Pale blue-green. Occasional bubbles. Dims 10 x 19; WT 1.4.

GV 1632, Area T, Level 1. Body fragment. Curved side. Part of short abraded vertical line. Pale blue-green. Occasional bubbles. Dims 13 x 15; WT 1.6. Same vessel as GV1631?

?Ardeer, Ayrshire or ?Luce Sands, Wigtownshire. P:1 or Q:1

Unreg., NMS. Body fragment. Convex-curved side. Cup/beaker/bowl? Abraded decoration in a floral pattern. Very pale purple. Glass worn after breakage. Dims 26 x 15; WT 1.5.

Notes

1 In comparison to the glass material from Roman sites, both Romano-British and Continental, the average size of the fragments is generally smaller on the native sites in Scotland and north Northumberland. This renders identification somewhat more difficult, and lowers the percentage of positively identified material.
2 For a discussion, see 'Cast and lathe-turned vessel', ch. 3.2.
3 For a discussion, see 'Pillar-moulded bowls', ch. 3.1.
4 See Cool & Price 1995; Price & Cottam 1998a.
5 Appendix A, U:2.
6 Appendix A, U:3.
7 Jobey 1973, 44.
8 Burgess 1970, 24, fig. 13 nos 2 & 3.
9 See Cool & Price 1995, 134–35, fig. 8.11, 175, fig. 10.5.
10 Appendix A, D:1.
11 Appendix A, F:2.
12 Appendix A, C:1.
13 Appendix A, K:5.
14 For a discussion, see Cool & Price 1995, 167–69; Price & Cottam 1998a, 25–29.
15 Appendix A, E:1.
16 Appendix A, F:1.
17 Appendix A, M:2.
18 Price & Cottam 1998a, 131–32, fig. 55.
19 Appendix A, U:1.
20 Jobey 1957, 179; identification made by W. Bulmer, Black Gate Museum, Newcastle. Morin-Jean 1913, figs 9 & 281.
21 Appendix A, B:2.
22 Appendix A, P:1.
23 Appendix A, O:1.
24 Appendix A, S:1.
25 Jobey 1981, 70.
26 Price & Cottam 1998a, 204.
27 Price & Cottam 1998a, 25.
28 Appendix A, M:3.
29 Allen 1997, 131–32.
30 I have only had the opportunity to study this sherd in its case at Edinburgh Castle, but never actually handled it. Therefore I have had to rely on the results in the published report.
31 Allen 1997, 133.
32 Cree 1924, 268, fig.17:1.
33 See for example: Haberey 1942; Harden 1956; Evison 1983 & 2000; Price 1992a; Campbell 1995; 2000; 2007.
34 Price 2010, 45; see also: Price 2000a, 26.
35 Price 2004, 88, fig. 51:2.
36 Price 1992a, 134, fig. 97:10.
37 Harden 1956, 134–35, pl. 15d; Harden 1959; Price 2000, 24, fig. 9:1.
38 Harden 1956, 134–35, pl. 15g; Price 2000a, 24–25, fig. 9:3.
39 Campbell 1997, 300–1.
40 Price 2000a, 24.
41 See Appendix A, P:1 for a discussion.

3.26. Lost, missing and dismissed material, and recent finds

For various reasons it has not been possible for me to examine the glass from all sites discussed in this work. The material from 13 sites is reported missing. In twelve of these cases, however, the types of glass are known through published reports with descriptions or drawings, and in some cases the reports include specialist identifications. So although the rather lengthy list below may give the impression that lots of material has been left out of the study, this is not the case. Most of the lost finds are discussed in the catalogue, and are included on the distribution map of Roman glass found in non-Roman/native contexts.

In the case of four recent excavations, the material was still with the excavators at the time of writing. Unfortunately, the glass from one of the recent excavations has been lost. These finds are included on the distribution map of all Roman glass found in non-Roman/native contexts. In addition to these, there may be Roman glass from three sites excavated some time ago that I have not had the opportunity to study, as I only became aware of these at a late stage in the writing of this work. As next to nothing is known about the glass from these sites, they are neither included in the catalogue nor indicated on the distribution maps.

There are a number of finds that have been reported as Roman glass found on non-Roman/native sites, but which should be dismissed. In some cases specialist study revealed that the glass did not belong to the Roman period; in other cases it could be shown that these sites were Roman rather than native; and in one case the find is unlikely to represent an ancient loss.

Finally, I list recent finds which have been discovered since the closing date of the catalogue, or which came to my knowledge at a late stage of editing the manuscript. These new finds confirm the existing picture, with a dominance of bottles. A number of these finds have been identified to type and are therefore both mentioned briefly in the respective chapters and included on the distribution maps.

Lost/missing

Loch na Berie, Lewis, Hebrides.[1] C:4
A find of glass, possibly of Roman date, was made on this site but has subsequently been misplaced by the excavator.[2]

Kingoldrum, Angus.[3] I:2
Cylindrical cup with fire-rounded rim and base ring.[4] Ch. 3.8.

Constantine's Cave, Fife.[5] L:1
Cylindrical bottle.[6] Ch. 3.23.

Hallowhill, St Andrews, Fife.[7] L:2
One or two cylindrical cups with fire-rounded rims and base rings.[8] Ch. 3.8.

Torfoot, Lanarkshire.[9] O:2
Prismatic bottle.[10] Ch. 3.23.

Carlingwark Loch, Kirkcudbrightshire.[11] R:1
Prismatic bottle.[12] Ch. 3.23.

Gubeon Cottage, Northumberland.[13] U:1
Two bases, possibly cups or beakers.[14] Ch. 3.25.

Hartburn, Northumberland.[15] U:2
Colourless fragment with two abraded bands.[16] Ch. 3.25.

Middle Gunnar Peak, Barrasford, Northumberland.[17] U:4
Possible fragments of vessel glass in blue-green and blue glass.[18] Ch. 3.25.

Milking Gap, High Shield, Northumberland.[19] U:5
Blue-green bottle glass (cylindrical or prismatic bottles).[20] Ch. 3.23.

West Longlee, Northumberland.[21] U:6
Blue-green bottle glass (cylindrical or prismatic bottles).[22] Ch. 3.23.

West Whelpington, Northumberland.[23] U:7
Pillar-moulded bowl.[24] Ch. 3.1.

Witchy Neuk, Hepple, Northumberland.[25] U:8
Spouted jug.[26] Ch. 3.20.

With the excavator

Old Scatness, Shetland.[27] A:2

Cylindrical cup with a fire-rounded rim and base ring.[28] Ch. 3.8. One fragment of a fourth-century vessel.[29]

Dun Vulan, South Uist, Hebrides.[30] C:3

One unidentified fragment of clear, colourless glass believed to be Roman.[31]

East Coldoch, Stirlingshire. K:6

Fragments of a prismatic bottle.[32] Ch. 3.23.

Hillhead, Lilliesleaf, Roxburghshire. Z:5

Unidentified glass vessel fragments, possibly Roman.[33]

Figure 3.26.1

Sherd of a colourless cast glass vessel from Fiskavaig, Skye.

Finds since the catalogue closed in 2007

Mine Howe, Tankerness, Orkney. B:2

Blue-green bottle-glass

MH 05 SF 9516, Tr. K, context 1609. Fragment of a reeded handle. Blue-green, very bubbly glass. This fragment was clearly reused – or in the process of being reused – as it is partly melted. The reeded surface is flattened with some sort of implement. PH 31; W 27; WT 6.3.

The function of this reworked handle is not clear: it may have been intended as a crude gaming piece, counter or as a pol-isher. Handles of this type were used for both cylindrical and prismatic bottles, but given that one other sherd from the site originates from a prismatic bottle, this fragment may have the same origin. The dating and distribution of such vessels is discussed in chapter 3.23.

What makes this object particularly interesting are the attempts to rework it. It is one of a number of examples of high-temperature manufacture at the site. The glass assemblage from Mine Howe includes five objects which were clearly made out of recycled Roman glass: the aforementioned object, a triangular-shaped inlay in blue-green glass, an intact gaming piece or counter of spherical shape, a flat base in blue-green glass, and a fragmented spherical object (possibly debris from glass-working). Two of the glass fragments are partly melted, and other sherds show signs of being exposed to heat as they are cracked. This and other evidence may suggest that simple glass-working was taking place at Mine Howe.

Fiskavaig, Skye, Hebrides. Z:9

Colourless, cast vessel

FISK 11 T3, find 3.307*. Rim of a colourless cast vessel (plate or bowl). Surface slightly pitted with a wheel-cut oval facet. Almost flat. Fragment very worn after breakage.
Dims 24 x 13; WT 2.5.

The Fiskavaig find is a cast, carinated vessel, a vessel which probably belongs to a class of cast and lathe-turned wide-rimmed bowls and plates.[34] This find differs from these in one important respect, however: it does not have the dull, ground surface these vessels normally have, but retains its original pitted surface. The wheel-cut decoration of this vessel is crudely executed, suggesting that it originated from an object of not such high quality. The identification of the object is based on three features:

(a) The manufacturing technique, in that it was cast.

(b) The flat shape of this fragment, most likely a rim, supports identification as a wide-rimmed bowl or plate.

(c) Cast and lathe-turned vessels of this type sometimes display wheel-cut decoration of this type.[35]

This find dates from the Flavian – Antonine period.

Culduthel Mains Farm, Inverness, Inverness-shire. Z:1

Two body sherds of an unidentified vessel in blue-green glass and strain cracked granules from an unidentified vessel also in blue-green glass.[36]

Clarkly Hill, Morayshire. Z:10

Prismatic bottle

CH12 SF 1184*. Base fragment of prismatic bottle. Slightly pitted surface. Blue-green, some wear after breakage. Dims 33 x 21; WT 5.0.

CH12 TR E (unnumbered)*. Fragment of bottle; base fragment? Blue-green, very worn after breakage. Dims 23 x 16; WT 6.0.

CH12 SF 934*: Base fragment of prismatic bottle. Slightly pitted surface. Blue-green, very worn after breakage. Dims 31 x 24; WT 4.0.

CH11 SF 576*. Melted lump of blue-green bottle glass. Dims 33 x 35.

At Clarkly Hill three fragments representing a minimum of one prismatic bottle were discovered (although their dispersed locations suggest more than one bottle is present). In addition to these there was a melted piece of blue-green glass, most likely originating from the same or a similar bottle. The dating and distribution of this type of vessel is discussed in chapter 3.23.[37]

Figure 3.26.2

Sherds of bottle glass from Clarkly Hill, Moray.

Castle Craig, Perthshire.[38] Z:11

Tubular-rimmed bowls

CC11 SF 6125*. Lower body of tubular-rimmed bowl? Pale yellow-green, bubbly glass. Bubbles of oval shape. One vertical raised rib.

CC11 SF 6187. Body fragment of vessel, probably tubular-rimmed bowl. Pale yellow-green, bubbly glass. Dims 17 x 5; WT 1.8.

CC12 SF 6623*. Body fragment of vessel, probably tubular-rimmed bowl. Pale yellow-green, bubbly glass. Dims 25 x 23; WT 3.1.

CC12 SF 6227*. Body fragment of tubular-rimmed bowl – lower body. Pale yellow-green, bubbly glass. Two raised ribs. Dims 30 x 13; WT 2.1.

CC11 SF 616*3. Rim of tubular-rimmed bowl. Pale yellow-green, slightly bubbly glass. Rim slightly out-bent, edge bent out and down. RD 160; WT 2.0.

CC11 SF 6179*. Rim and upper body of tubular-rimmed bowl. Pale blue-green glass. Rim slightly out-bent, edge bent out and down. RD 190; WT 2.0.

At Castle Craig, Perthshire, a minimum of two deep, tubular-rimmed bowls of Isings Form 44b were discovered. Six fragments represent a minimum of one bowl in pale yellow-green with ribbed decoration, and one sherd in pale blue-green represents a minimum of one bowl. Vessels in these colours were common in Romano-British contexts, and date from the Neronian period to the third quarter of the second century AD. Their dating and distribution is discussed in chapter 3.14.

Prismatic bottle

CC11 SF 6183*. Base of a prismatic bottle. Blue-green glass. Remains of three concentric circular moulding. Dims 31 x 23; WT 5.9.

CC12 SF 6508*. Base of a prismatic bottle. Blue green glass, with small circular bubbles. Slightly pitted surface. Dims 30 x 12; WT 4.0.

Two sherds representing a minimum of two prismatic bottles were also discovered at Castle Craig. The dating and distribution of this type of vessel is discussed in chapter 3.23.

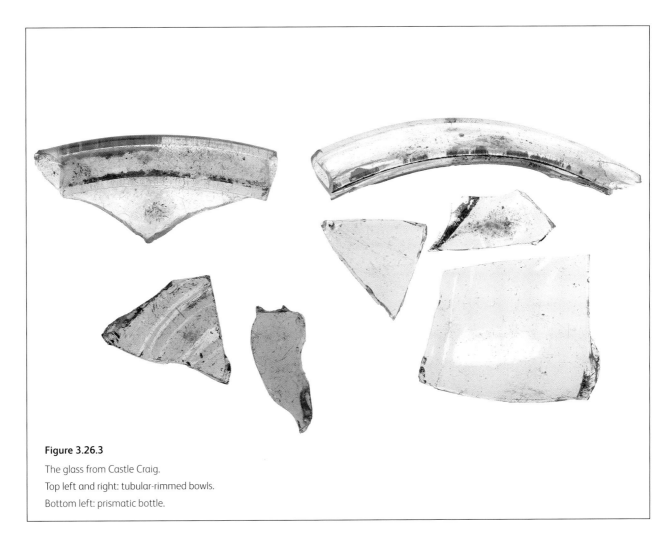

Figure 3.26.3

The glass from Castle Craig.

Top left and right: tubular-rimmed bowls.

Bottom left: prismatic bottle.

Kay Craig, Perthshire.[39.] Z:12

Cylindrical or prismatic bottle

KC 13-02, SF 237. Shoulder of a bottle, cylindrical or prismatic. Blue-green glass with occasional bubbles. Affected by heat and partly melted. PH 39; W 18; WT 6.8.

At Kay Craig, Perthshire the shoulder of a blue-green bottle, cylindrical or prismatic, was unearthed in an Iron Age enclosed site.

Colourless cup or flask with opaque yellow trail

KC 13-02, SF 239. Body fragment of convex-curved shape from an unidentified vessel, possibly a cup or small flask. Clear, colourless glass with occasional round bubbles. Decorated with a horizontal, thin opaque yellow glass trail. PH 12; W 19; WT 1.0.

The fragment of a convex-curved vessel from Kay Craig – a small cup, or possibly a thin unguent flask – in clear, colourless glass with a simple horizontal opaque yellow trail cannot be dated precisely. A first- to third-century AD date is suggested on the basis of its colour and quality. Although it cannot be identified to type or function, it clearly comes from a vessel of relatively high quality.

Leckie, Stirlingshire. K:4

Constricted convex cup

A 1980 167*, Hunterian Museum. Base of a constricted convex cup. The form is typical of ceramics, and the opaque red strongly resembles terra sigillata/samian. Dull, ground surface. Slightly out-splayed base ring, flat base. Diameter of base ring ca. 80; PH 8; WT 3.9.

Since completion of the catalogue, it was discovered that a fragment unearthed during excavations at Leckie broch, and originally believed to be samian pottery, was in fact glass. Its appearance is strikingly similar to samian both in colour (i.e. a rich red colour), and in shape. It belongs to a 'family' of high-quality cast and lathe-turned vessels characterised by angular, carinated shapes.[40]

Only part of the base has survived, but the shape and colour suggest the specific type: a constricted convex cup. These cups are of the same shape as samian bowls of type Dragendorff 27, which in turn closely resemble the forms of metal vessels in silver and bronze. Constricted convex cups are found in a range of strong colours: opaque monochrome colours such as red, orange, and white, opaque polychrome mosaic glass of millefiore type with a range of colours, and translucent monochrome strong colours such as dark green and dark blue.[41]

In Romano-British contexts finds of this specific type are relatively rare. Finds have been made in southern Britain in Claudian to Neronian contexts (AD 43–65).[42] A parallel to the Leckie find, a cup in monochrome opaque red glass, comes from the Marlow Cark Park, Canterbury, Kent.[43] In a native context the Leckie find is in one sense unique, as it is the only find of a constricted convex cup, and it is in a rare colour: brick-coloured opaque red. But, as mentioned, this type or class of glass vessel belongs to a larger 'family' of cast glass vessels (discussed in chapter 3.2), and there are two finds of related types. There is a colourless vessel belonging to a later class of such vessels from Clickhimin broch, Shetland,[44] and a find of a colourless vessel, probably a wide-rimmed bowl or plate, from Fiskavaig, Skye, Inner Hebrides (discussed in this chapter).

Easter Moss, Cowiehall/Cowiehall Quarry, Stirlingshire. Z:2

Jar of Isings Form 67c.[45]

Broxmouth, East Lothian. Z:13

SF 1244. The shoulder of a prismatic bottle.[46]

One sherd representing a minimum of one prismatic bottle was discovered at Broxmouth. The dating and distribution of this type of vessel is discussed in chapter 3.23. It comes from a small cache of unusual items in a house.

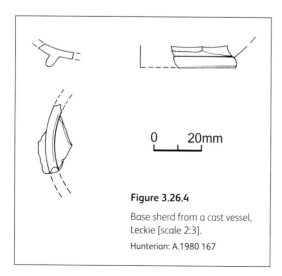

Figure 3.26.4

Base sherd from a cast vessel, Leckie [scale 2:3].

Hunterian: A.1980 167

Figure 3.26.5

Base sherd from a cast vessel, Leckie.

Knowes, East Lothian. Z:3

A splinter of late Roman yellow-green glass.[47]

Gilmerton House, Athelstaneford, East Lothian. Z:4

Blue-green bottle-glass, probably from a cylindrical bottle.[48]

Whitefield Loch, Wigtownshire. Z:6

Blue-green bottle-glass, probably from a prismatic bottle.[49]

Buittle, Kirkcudbrightshire. Z:7

'A piece of melted material which may be glass.'[50]

Chapelton, Haugh of Urr, Kirkcudbrightshire. Z:8

Reeded handle in blue-green glass which may have come from a jug.[51]

Finds not studied

Wester Craiglockhart, Midlothian.

Unknown type and dating.[52]

Castle Dykes, Bilsdean, East Lothian

Unknown type and dating.[53]

Finds not included

Broch of Burrian, Orkney.[54]

Glass of later date.

Ardestie, Monikie, Angus.[55]

Glass possibly of early Medieval date.

Ardownie, Angus.

Glass cannot be classified as Roman with certainty.[56]

Hurly Hawkin, Angus.[57]

The report mentions two sherds of vessel glass believed to be Roman. These could not be traced, and as other fragments of glass are reported as being of seventeenth-century date it was not included.

Black Hill, Meikleour, Perthshire.

Roman site/modern glass.

Barochan Hill, Renfrewshire.[58]

Roman site.

York Hill, City of Glasgow, Lanarkshire.[59]

Probably a Roman site.

Castle Loch, Mochrum, Wigtownshire.[60]

Glass of later date.

Closeburn, Dumfriesshire.[61]

May not be an ancient loss.

Notes

1 Appendix A, C:4.
2 Pers. comm. Dr Fraser Hunter.
3 Appendix A, I:2.
4 Chalmers 1851–54, 191.
5 Appendix A, L:1.
6 Wace & Jehu 1914–15, 239.
7 Appendix A, L:2.
8 Stuart 1867, viii; Proudfoot 1976, 33–34.
9 Appendix A, O:2.
10 Robertson 1978, 203.
11 Appendix A, R:1.
12 Skene 1866, 9.
13 Appendix A, U:1.
14 Jobey 1957, 178–79. Identification by W. Bulmer.
15 Appendix A, U:2.
16 Jobey 1973, 44.
17 Appendix A, U:4.
18 Jobey 1981, 70.
19 Appendix A, U:5.
20 Kilbride-Jones 1938b, 346.
21 Appendix A, U:6.
22 Jobey 1960, 30.
23 Appendix A, U:7.
24 Jarrett 1962, 219. Identified by R. J. Charleston as possibly being a pillar-moulded bowl.
25 Appendix A, U:8.
26 Wake 1939, 137. Identified by W. A. Thorpe.
27 Appendix A, A:2.
28 Pers. comm. Dr Fraser Hunter.
29 Pers. comm. Dr Hilary Cool.
30 Appendix A, C:3.
31 Parker Pearson & Sharples 1999, 88.
32 Pers. comm. Dr Birgitta Hoffmann.
33 Wise 1998. This find was excavated in 1998, but came to my knowledge at a very late stage of the editing.
34 Vessels of this and related classes are discussed in greater detail in ch. 3.2.
35 Jennifer Price discusses finds of this wheel-cut variant from Spain; see Price 1987c, 72–80, figs 4 & 5.
36 Pers. comm. Dr Hilary Cool.
37 Pers. comm. Dr Fraser Hunter. For a summary of work on this unenclosed settlement, see *Discovery and Excavation in Scotland* 13 (2012), 122–23.
38 I am grateful to Dr Tessa Poller for access to this material. See *Discovery and Excavation in Scotland* 12 (2011),

144–45; *Discovery and Excavation in Scotland* 13 (2012), 142.
39 Examined by courtesy of Dr Tessa Poller.
40 In classifying the wide range of cast vessels, David Grose has suggested the word 'family' as an overarching description of several closely related 'classes' manufactured in the same technique and general style. The classes in turn include different shapes and variations (Grose 1989, 241).
41 Price & Cottam 1998a, 48–50.
42 Price & Cottam 1998a, 48–50.
43 Shepherd 1995, 1228 no. 24, fig. 544. Weathering has, however, given the surface of this vessel a green colour (due to its high copper content). In this respect it differs from the Leckie find, which has retained its rich red colour (and may have contained another colour agent).
44 Ch. 3.2; Appendix A, A:1.
45 Pers. comm. Dr Hilary Cool; see ch. 3.16.
46 Identified by Dr Hilary Cool; see Armit & McKenzie 2013.
47 Identified by Prof. Jennifer Price: Hunter, Lowther & MacSween 2009, 138.
48 Price 2009.
49 Cavers et al. 2011, 97–98.
50 Verfied as Roman glass by Robin Birley (Penman 1997, 17. See also Penman 1995, 13).
51 This find was not identified in the original publication (Simpson 2004). Having studied the published illustration it is clear that it is a reeded handle, but unfortunately the scale is not given nor are any measurements mentioned. If the scale is 1:1 it may have originated from the same types of vessels discussed in ch. 3.18, that is, either a globular jug of Isings Form 52 or a conical jug of Isings Form 55.
52 *Discovery and Excavation in Scotland* (1971), 29.
53 Hogg 1944–45, 172–73.
54 The report refers to one or two beads (MacGregor 1972–74, 100). Identification of vessel glass by the present author.
55 Wainright 1963, 135. Identified by D. B. Harden. The find is not listed in the NMS catalogue, and is possibly lost.
56 The glass colour gives no indication of age and cannot be unambiguously dated to the Roman period, despite the fact that it comes from a well-sealed layer (Ingemark 2006b, 33).
57 Taylor 1982, 232.
58 Robertson 1970, 224.
59 Curle 1932a, 381.
60 Ralegh Radford 1949–50, 56–57. Identification by the present author.
61 Robertson 1970, 223; Canmore ID65251 (NX89SE 18) (www.rcahms.gov.uk) [accessed 2 March 2014].

Analysis:
the glass as a symbol of status
and as an instrument of power

Polychrome bowl fragment from Castlehill Wood in Stirlingshire (see fig. 3.1.5).

4

Glass and exchange

DUE to an almost total absence of graves of Roman Iron Age date in Scotland and north Northumberland, the bulk of the material under study derives from settlement sites, and is hence fragmentary. The fragmented state of the material and the general lack of in-depth studies of the artefactual record have had a profound influence on scholarly views concerning the quantity and quality of imported Roman goods, and indeed on Roman–native exchange and relations in general.

The aim of this chapter is twofold. Firstly, it is to bring together the evidence of the quantity, quality, date and spatial distribution of Roman vessel (and window) glass in order to shed light on Roman–native exchange and to discuss how these results relate to previous research. Secondly, arguing that the glass found on indigenous sites represents some sort of peaceful enterprise such as trade or exchange, I endeavour to demonstrate – by using anthropological, archaeological and sociological theory – how the native elite employed imported goods as a means to achieve and sustain power.

4.1 A brief history of earlier research on Roman–native exchange in Scotland and north Northumberland

A fundamental problem in the study of Roman–native relations is whether the Roman imports found on native sites should be regarded as exchange in the true sense of the word, or whether they actually represent loot, pilfer or plunder. The topic will be considered in general here, and specifically for glass in chapter 4.6. It is important to differentiate between the finds on sites of Roman Iron Age date and early Medieval date respectively.

Although relatively little has been written about the Roman finds on early Medieval sites, the notions put forward in this field of research have had an important influence on research concerning the Roman Iron Age period; let us therefore commence with this. Leslie Alcock has called attention to the problems associated with the lack of independent dating evidence for indigenous sites. Alcock's argument is that one cannot presuppose that finds of Roman goods on sites otherwise known to be of early Medieval date represent an earlier Roman Iron Age phase without sound archaeological evidence to substantiate such claims. He advances the notion that a significant proportion of these imports were in fact brought to the early Medieval sites as raw materials or curios from long-deserted Roman sites in Britain and on the Continent.[1]

Turning to the debate concerning Roman Iron Age sites, Euan MacKie argued in 1965 that 'it seems probable that most of the fragments of Roman pottery and glass and coins which found their way into the possession of the tribes north of the Antonine Wall did so as loot from abandoned camps and forts after the two Roman withdrawals to Hadrian's Wall in about 100 and 180'.[2] In a later work, however, MacKie reasons that the most plausible explanation for the movement of Roman goods was exchange of some kind.[3]

MacKie's, and indeed many other scholars', use of the word 'loot' can be somewhat misleading. What is meant is that the Roman objects were picked off the ground or possibly dug up on long-abandoned Roman forts, and not that they constituted war booty or pillage. Relatively few scholars have considered plunder in the true meaning of the word as the underlying reason for finds of Roman goods on native sites. However, in discussing the material from Northumberland, Lindsay Allason-Jones has advocated the idea that the Roman imports constituted 'booty of guerrilla raids, stolen property'.[4]

In fact, the overwhelming majority of scholars have viewed the material chiefly as the outcome of exchange rather than representing loot or pilfer and plunder. In one of the most influential papers written concerning Roman–native exchange in Scotland, James Curle argued that although looting of abandoned Roman forts undeniably did occur, it does not account for more than a fraction of the wealth of Roman goods on native sites.[5] This argument has been strengthened by Anne Robertson, who has pointed to the fact that many Roman forts were deliberately dismantled, and that materials such as pottery and glass were concealed in pits so as not to fall into enemy hands.[6] However, as pointed out by Lesley Macinnes, a limited number of finds derive beyond doubt from abandoned forts, namely dressed Roman stones reused in souterrains.[7]

Thus there appears to be a widely shared agreement that the Roman imports reflect exchange. The scholarly views as to the nature of this exchange, however, differ quite significantly, largely as a result of diverging thoughts on the quantity and quality of the imports. In a paper published in 1970, Robertson stresses the generally high quality of the imports and the scarcity of mundane Roman objects in the native assemblages.[8] A study of the numismatic evidence reinforces her earlier argument, as there seems to have been a preference for silver, or in rare cases gold, coins among the indigenous societies.[9] Lawrence Keppie has even claimed that 'in fact the standard of living seems higher in some native sites than in Roman forts themselves'.[10]

In sharp contrast, other scholars have maintained that the Roman goods were essentially mundane. In a paper published in 1985, Michael Fulford postulated that the objects were predominantly low-grade and – following the work of Hans-Jürgen Eggers and Lotte Hedeager on the Roman imports in Free Germany – put forward the idea that Lowland Scotland represents a buffer-zone similar to that attested in the areas adjacent to the Limes.[11] Following Fulford's minimalist argu-ments, Macinnes claimed that '[the] Roman goods may indeed have been no more than insignificant, though interesting, trinkets'.[12]

This debate has not merely concerned itself with the quality of the imports, but has equally dealt with diverging notions as to the scale of the Roman–native exchange. Some scholars, such as Robertson, and most recently Fraser Hunter, have argued that the amount of Roman material is far from insubstantial,[13] whereas others – most importantly Fulford, Macinnes and Allason-Jones, have voiced the opinion that the volume of imports was low. In fact, Hunter is able to show that no less than 40% of Iron Age sites in Lowland Scotland have yielded Roman artefacts, and 25% of sites in the Western Isles and Orkney.[14]

A paper by Michael Erdrich, Kristina Giannotta and William Hanson takes the Roman imports – in particular the samian – from Traprain Law as a point of departure. They argue that the finds represent commercial exchange or barter with Roman forts in the vicinity, and that diplomatic contacts between the Votadini and the Romans facilitated this exchange. Most important, however, is the argument that the material reached this site only during the periods of Roman military occupation. The authors claim that this 'is a strong argument against the existence of any well-established, extensive and long-term Roman–native trade relations. More specifically, it militates against the establishment of regular trading contacts beyond the frontier.'[15]

Fraser Hunter has taken a different position on this matter in a paper published in 2001, and has put forward the following view: 'We must imagine a varying picture. Much material entered circulation within and beyond the frontier while southern Scotland was occupied, but artefacts continued to move north in lower numbers between and after the occupations.'[16] In this paper, Hunter points to the difficulties in providing the material with exact dates, and moreover to the fact that much of the Roman material from indigenous sites has still not been examined by specialists.

The primary focus of research has been on Roman goods discovered on native sites, whereas the possibility of indigenous objects having reached Roman sites has received relatively limited attention. In one of the earliest papers on Roman–native exchange, however, Curle discussed a group of finds which evidently were not Roman – weaving-combs, querns, and pottery – but which were nevertheless discovered in occupation layers of the Roman forts.[17] On the basis of this body of evidence, he later argued that the exchange between Roman and native was bilateral, predominantly in the

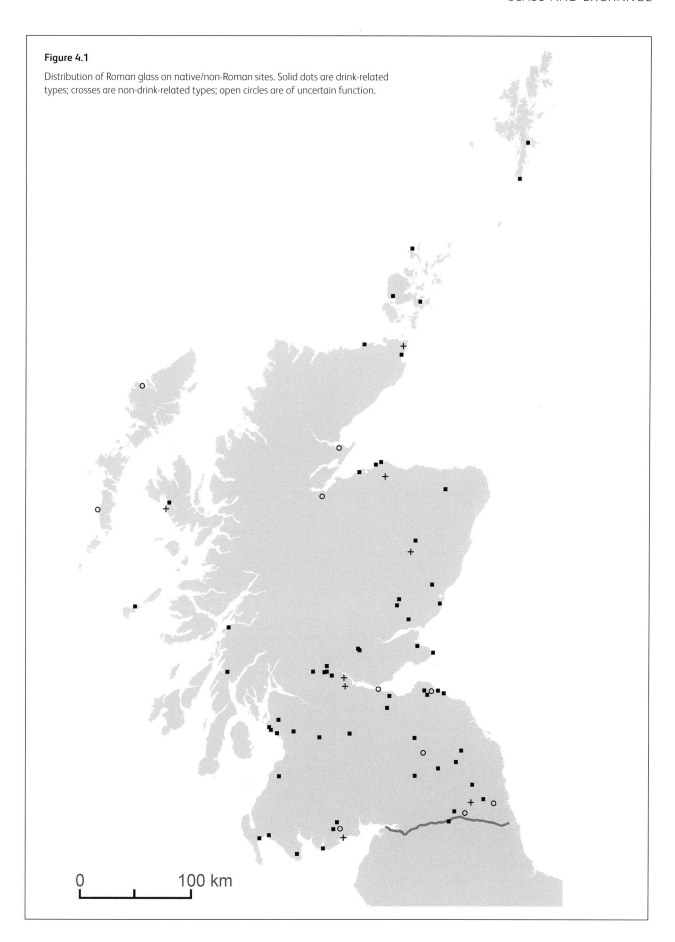

Figure 4.1

Distribution of Roman glass on native/non-Roman sites. Solid dots are drink-related types; crosses are non-drink-related types; open circles are of uncertain function.

0   100 km

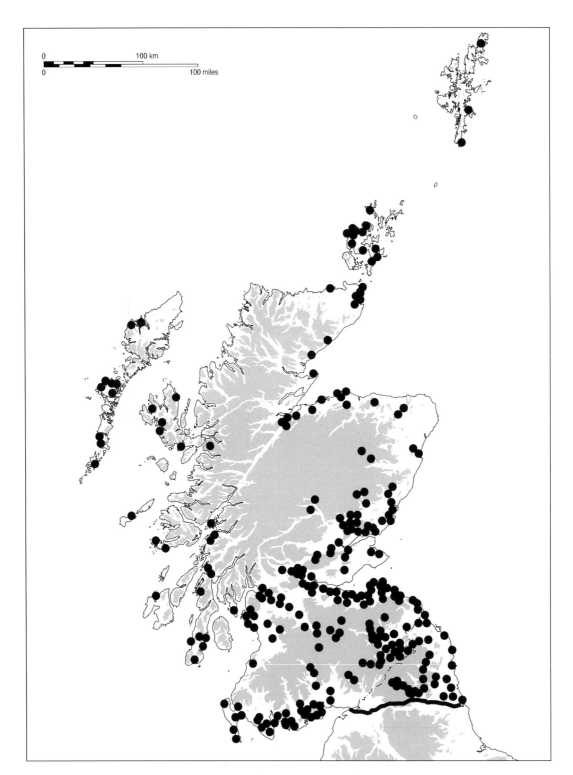

Figure 4.2

Roman finds from non-Roman sites.

F. Hunter

form of trade or barter.[18] Many other scholars have come to share Curle's views, amongst others Robertson, Macinnes and Allan Wilson.[19]

Allason-Jones has claimed it was predominantly native goods that reached Roman sites, whereas very few Roman goods reached native sites; and that these few scattered finds represent bribes, booty or theft, whereas the native goods found in Roman contexts were the result of a brisk trade.[20] In an attempt to explain the small quantity of Roman goods beyond the Roman border, Fulford – in all probability influenced by a passage in Tacitus' *Agricola* where the native chieftain Calgacus speaks of the burdens of taxation[21] – has suggested that the Romans imposed taxes on the Lowlands.[22]

Other scholars, though not necessarily sharing the opinion that only small quantities of Roman goods reached indigenous contexts, have nevertheless proposed that the area was taxed in kind, which could have included dairy products, grain,[23] or hides,[24] commodities leaving no trace in the archaeological record.

Most scholars have put a primary focus on the exchange of material goods, and left the possibility of the exchange of services largely unheeded. However, in a paper published in 1989, C. R. Whittaker argued that Roman imports were the result of native troops having been recruited in the area, and that these objects were later brought back by soldiers returning home or retiring.[25] Several scholars have discussed whether or not troops were recruited in the area, but as yet no definitive evidence to support this has been presented.[26]

In contrast to the conflicting views concerning exchange of goods, taxation and possibly also services, there appears to be a generally accepted conviction that the finds of coin hoards relate to a passage in Dio Cassius mentioning that the Romans had to 'buy peace from the Maeatae for a large sum' in the reign of Septimius Severus (AD 193–211).[27] Robertson has pointed to the fact that the bulk of many of these hoards roughly date to this period,[28] and Malcolm Todd has suggested that the largest coin hoard discovered so far, a hoard of more than 1900 *denarii* from Falkirk, Stirlingshire, is directly linked to the Maeatae.[29]

In a recent paper Fraser Hunter has convincingly argued that the Scottish hoards should not be tied solely to specific historic events; rather he argues they are to be seen as a long-lived Roman policy of paying tributes running from the 160s to the 230s. Moreover, he contends that this is not an isolated phenomenon but rather a general Roman policy, as demonstrated by contemporary finds of Roman coin hoards stretching over

Ireland, the Netherlands, Germany, Scandinavia, Poland and the former USSR.[30]

Recent years have seen increasing discussion of the nature of Iron Age societies and the validity of concepts such as chieftains and elites.[31] By the Roman Iron Age, there does however seem to be good evidence of increasingly marked social differences, and I use the term elite to differentiate groups with greater access to Roman and other goods.

4.2 The quantity and spatial distribution of the finds

Roman vessel glass has been found on 77 non-Roman/native sites in Scotland and north Northumberland, covering most of the area which was inhabited during the Roman Iron Age (fig. 4.1). This can be compared to around 200 settlement sites, 40 votive or burial sites (fig. 4.2) and 100 stray finds – in Scotland alone – which have yielded Roman finds.[32] As touched upon already, the bulk of the glass, as indeed most artefacts, is in a fragmented state, and very little material has survived intact: a mere seven, or possibly eight, vessels from seven sites. Unfortunately only three of these survive today; of the remainder, three or four have been lost and one broken.[33] One find comes from a loch, one contained a coin hoard, whereas the others are certainly or probably from funerary contexts.

The total estimated sum of the vessels found may appear relatively limited – a mere 210 to 215 vessels – but a number of arguments indicate that the original import was considerably larger. First, these are the estimated *minimum* number of vessels. Second, a number of vessels are represented by only one or two sherds, and as I have argued elsewhere this in all probability has a practical explanation.[34] If a glass vessel was accidentally broken, it was necessary to sweep up the sharp sherds. It is, in my view, likely that many vessels that were broken have left no trace at all, all fragments having been swept up.

This brings us to my third argument, that much glass may have been remelted in the manufacture of beads and bangles. There is very little evidence for glass-working on native sites in the form of glass-working debris, but recent excavations at Culduthel Mains Farm, Inverness, Inverness-shire clearly demonstrate that such production indeed existed in native contexts. On this site waste from the production of glass beads and enamelling metal objects was found.[35] Radiocarbon dates shows that this craft was executed in the period 150 BC to AD 60. No recycling of Roman glass took

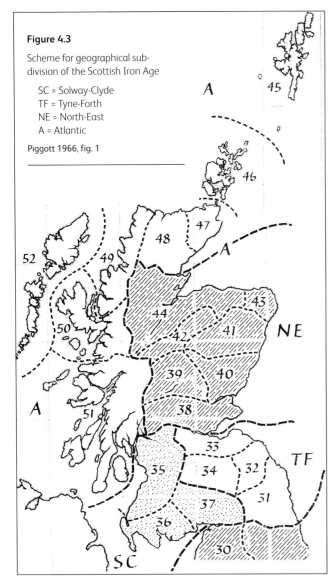

Figure 4.3

Scheme for geographical sub-division of the Scottish Iron Age

SC = Solway-Clyde
TF = Tyne-Forth
NE = North-East
A = Atlantic

Piggott 1966, fig. 1

place at the site; instead glass ingots were used as raw material.[36] The Culduthel material thus demonstrates that the craft was known in the native societies, but it does not prove that Roman glass was recycled. There are, however, a number of objects from native sites which were clearly made of recycled Roman glass.[37]

The present study clearly demonstrates that the minimalist view, advocated amongst others by Fulford and Macinnes, can no longer be upheld. Moreover, it may be suggested that there was a certain psychological element underlying the perception that only small quantities of Roman goods reached indigenous sites. If the material had remained intact and been put on display in the National Museum of Scotland rather than being minuscule fragments kept in dusty cigar boxes and tucked away in storage, scholarly views on Roman–native relations and exchange would in all likelihood have been markedly different. In contrast, in Free

Germany the practice of deposition has yielded rich grave material, some of which is on lavish display in the National Museum in Copenhagen. Few scholars have doubted the existence of extensive trade between the Romans and natives in this area.

There was an almost equal distribution south and north of the Antonine Wall in the number of sites which have yielded Roman glass: following Piggott's division of the Scottish Iron Age (fig. 4.3),[38] 40 are situated in the Atlantic and north-eastern provinces, and 37 in the Tyne-Forth and Solway-Clyde provinces. The greater part of the Roman glass – around three-quarters of the estimated number of glass vessels – comes from the south (the Tyne-Forth and Solway-Clyde provinces), but this bias is due to the fact that one site – Traprain Law, East Lothian – is exceptionally rich. In fact, almost half the total assemblage of glass found north of Hadrian's Wall comes from this single site (an estimated minimum of 105 vessels). If we do not include this material, a different picture emerges, with approximately equal numbers of vessels north and south of the Forth-Clyde line.

There is much to suggest that there was a clear hierarchy between different sites, and it is notable that the sites closest to Hadrian's Wall (i.e. in north Northumberland) have relatively small assemblages. Some of the wealthiest sites are found in central and southern Scotland, a number of which have comparatively (or very) large glass assemblages. This includes sites such as Leckie broch, Stirlingshire; Traprain Law, East Lothian (fig. 4.4); Hyndford, Lanarkshire; and Torwoodlee, Selkirkshire. These are situated at some distance from each other, but are surrounded by sites with fewer imports.

The spatial distribution and quantities of the finds strongly suggests a system of redistribution within native societies,[39] which has been seen as a fundamental feature of stratified societies.[40] In the case of Traprain Law, Fraser Hunter has put forward convincing arguments for the site being a centre for distribution of Roman goods – primarily tablewares and personal ornaments – to subsidiary sites in the surrounding area.[41]

4.3 The categories of finds

It is possible to present an overall picture of the categories of glass found in native contexts, even if the original function of certain vessel types in their Roman context cannot be established with certainty,[42] and not all the fragmented material can be categorised. This

Figure 4.4: Traprain Law. F. Hunter

picture is markedly different in character, both in terms of the quantities of the various categories of vessels and the general level of quality, from what is normally found on Roman sites, both in Britain and on the Continent. However, partly as a consequence of the poor understanding of the chronology of native sites, and partly as a result of the vast differences in scale between Roman and native assemblages, such comparisons can be problematic to make. In the following the native assemblage will be treated in its entirety.

Ultimately the range of Roman glass vessels and objects available for Roman–native exchange would have been determined by trends in the use and manufacture of glass in Roman contexts. A brief overview of what characterised these assemblages is therefore given below. The categories of finds, and more importantly the proportions of these, normally found on a Roman site depended on a series of different factors: for instance, whether it was military or civilian, its function, size and status, the gender/s of its inhabitants, and its geographical setting.[43]

The single most important factor, however – as demonstrated in two influential papers written by Sophia van Lith and Klavs Randsborg, and Hilary Cool and Michael Baxter – was the periods during which the site was occupied.[44] Since there is an abundance of

sources available for dating the different periods and phases of individual Roman sites – numismatic, epigraphic, historical and archaeological evidence – it is possible to discuss changes in patterns of glass use over time in the Roman world.

If we study the assemblages from Roman contexts, one of the most evident trends which shifted over time is the employment of glass for the storage and transport of liquids, semi-liquids and solid foodstuffs. Bottles, and to some extent jars, formed a significant part of assemblages between the mid/late first century AD and the late second/early third century AD, after which there was a sharp decline in this category of finds.[45] Similarly vessels for serving food (bowls and plates) comprised a substantial part of the assemblages until the mid-second century AD, after which there was a marked decrease in the use of glass for this purpose.[46] In contrast, drinking vessels – cups, beakers and small bowls – which constituted a considerable component of the assemblages in the first and second centuries, became the dominant form of glass vessel in the late Roman period.[47]

The research of both van Lith and Randsborg and Cool and Baxter, has demonstrated how assemblages from military sites differ from those of major civilian settlements. Van Lith and Randsborg were able to show on the basis of Continental material that bowls, dishes,

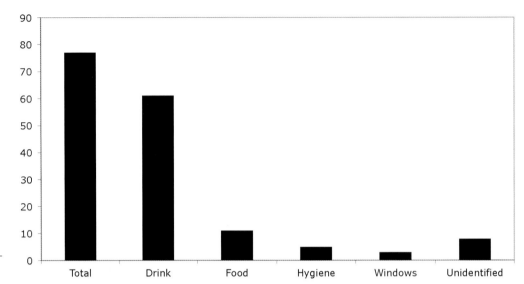

Figure 4.5

Functional categories represented in the glass.

cups, beakers, flasks/jugs, and bottles are found in roughly the same quantities as on the civilian sites, whereas perfume bottles are less frequent finds on the forts.[48] This is probably a reflection of the fact that the use of perfume was regarded as unmanly.[49] In Suetonius' (c. AD 70–130) work *De vita Caesarum (The Twelve Caesars),* an anecdote tells how the Emperor Vespasian (AD 69–79) told off a young soldier for wearing perfume with the words, 'I'd rather that you smelt of garlic'.[50]

Cool and Baxter could demonstrate that the glass assemblages from military sites were characterised by bowls and bottles, whereas the civilian sites had more varied assemblages.[51] Another trend noticeable in military assemblages of glass is the importance of bath flasks, a reflection of the importance of bathing in Roman culture.[52]

If we turn to the native assemblages of Roman glass, there is a very strong emphasis on categories linked to drink: cups, beakers, small bowls, jugs and flagons. With this I have chosen to include a category which in all probability is also linked to the serving and drinking of alcoholic beverages, namely bottles.[53] Figure 4.5 shows the number of sites which have yielded categories of vessels which in their Roman context were linked to drinking, the serving of food, hygiene, windows and unidentified material. The total number of sites is 77, and no fewer than 61 of these (79%) have assemblages which include vessels linked to drinking. As several sites have yielded material which was not identified, it is likely that the original percentage was still higher.

The most frequent type of Roman glass on native sites, both in terms of quantity and number of sites, is bottle glass: cylindrical and prismatic bottles, which had a wide distribution, from Orkney in the north to North-umberland in the south. There are regional differences in access to or interest in bottles. Fourteen sites which have yielded blue-green bottle glass are known from north of the Forth-Clyde line, and 24 south of this line (including recent finds which are not in the catalogue).[54] Whether or not these bottles reached native hands with their contents, and what this may have been, is a matter for debate. However, as bottle glass has been found on a number of sites that have produced a relatively wide range of Roman goods,[55] this implies it was valued; its intrinsically prosaic nature compared to other imports suggests it was the content rather than the actual bottle which was of primary interest.

There is abundant evidence to demonstrate the importance of cups and beakers as symbols of power in Iron Age society,[56] and not surprisingly this forms the second largest group of imported Roman glass; it has been found on at least 22 sites. In contrast to the bottles, finds of drinking vessels – cups, beakers and small bowls – appear to have been more numerous in the north than in the south. Sixteen sites lie north of the Forth-Clyde line, six to the south (fig. 4.6). It could be argued that this imbalance may be more apparent than real for two reasons. First, cups, beakers and small bowls are often in relatively thin glass, and a strongly fragmented assemblage cannot always be identified to type or even form/function. No fewer than four of the finds of cups in the northern area are from funerary contexts, and differences in practices of deposition may have created a bias in the material. Second, one of the largest categories of Roman imports is samian. It is quite possible that many of the cups and bowls in this material performed the same function as cups, beakers and small bowls in glass. Both glass and samian were markedly

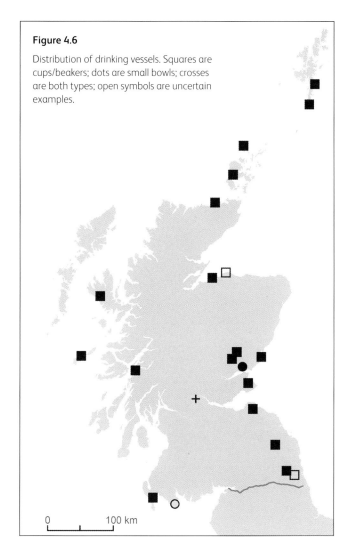

Figure 4.6

Distribution of drinking vessels. Squares are cups/beakers; dots are small bowls; crosses are both types; open symbols are uncertain examples.

0   100 km

A mere five sites (*c.*6%) had finds used for hygienic/cosmetic/medical purposes, i.e. oil-flasks or unguent bottles. Bath flasks (*aryballoi*), which were clearly linked to Roman bathing culture, have only been found on two sites, and in both cases had been reused. This suggests that Roman bathing culture had a very limited impact on the native cultures. Unguent bottles form an important category of finds in Roman contexts, and may have contained perfumes, cosmetics and medicines, but are very rare indeed in native contexts. Such finds have been found on a total of only four native/non-Roman sites, one of which also yielded a fragment of a bath flask: Traprain Law.

Window glass is another category which is common on Roman site but very rare on native ones. It is also important to note that two out of three sites which yielded window glass are early Medieval: Mote of Mark and Whithorn. Only a single site of Roman Iron Age date – Traprain Law – has any finds belonging to this category.

The clear contrast between the native and Roman assemblages of vessel (and window) glass demonstrates that the former had a narrower range of types and categories than that typically found on the latter. This has profound implications for interpretations of the mechanisms of Roman–native exchange. Moreover, there is much to suggest that it represents a selection of objects of particular value and meaning in the native societies.[58]

different from the pottery of indigenous manufacture, and it is clear that these materials were sought after.

Eleven sites have vessels which were probably linked to the serving or storage of foodstuffs in their original Roman context – that is bowls, plates and jars – which makes up 14% of the total number of sites. These constitute a notably less common category of Roman finds in a native context. This becomes even more accentuated if the possibility that larger bowls such as pillar-moulded bowls could also function as drinking vessels is taken into account. To some extent this may reflect the limited manufacture of bowls after the mid-second century AD; however, one has to bear in mind that before this time they formed an important category on Roman sites.[57] Nevertheless, the most likely cause for this scarcity is either that this category of vessels did not carry any particular significance in native societies, or that other imports, such as samian (which includes plates and large bowls), fulfilled this function.

4.4 The quality of the material

Any attempt to evaluate the quality and value of objects always contains a certain element of subjectivity: aspects of quality do not easily lend themselves to quantification. Ultimately any judgement of quality must depend on the object of comparison. None of the most exclusive types of glass manufactured in the Roman world such as cameo glass or *vasa diatreta,* found in very limited numbers on the wealthiest sites in the Empire, have been discovered on native sites in the area. Although there are single examples of these types found beyond the borders of the Empire, such as a find of *vasa diatreta* in Afghanistan[59] or cameo glass in Norway,[60] any comparison of native sites in Scotland and north Northumberland has to be made with the material from military and civilian sites in Roman Britain.

As argued above, the material found on native sites evidently constitutes a selection of goods that were of particular importance in native society, namely, vessels associated with the serving of drink. Furthermore, when it is possible to judge it appears to be a choice of objects mostly of high quality, as will be demonstrated below. Some categories of glass, however, such as bottles, defy any attempt to evaluate their value and quality, as their value ultimately depended on their contents, and whether they reached the native sites filled or empty.

As we have seen, the quality of all categories of Roman imports has long been a matter of scholarly debate, yet with few in-depth studies that could confirm or reject claims of low or high quality. To reiterate, Fulford and Macinnes contend that the imported goods on native sites were of indifferent quality,[61] whereas Robertson and Keppie argue that excavations have yielded relatively little mundane, everyday Roman goods: what is found tends to be of high quality.[62] As I hope to demonstrate, the present study strongly supports the latter view.

In the following discussion I consider the entire assemblage of Roman vessel glass found on non-Roman/native sites north of Hadrian's Wall. In doing so one must keep in mind all the inherent problems in comparing single Roman sites with the native assemblage as a whole, especially as the native sites with Roman vessel glass number 77 but still have a smaller number of sherds than that yielded on many a Roman site. However, the quality of the finds from the native sites is generally high.

Pillar-moulded bowls form a case in point. Of the 7 specimens found in native contexts, admittedly a small assemblage, three (43%) were in polychrome glass, one (14%) in strongly coloured glass, and three (43%) in blue-green glass.[63] This stands in inverse proportion to what is normally found on Roman sites; at Colchester, Essex (a site founded in AD 43), out of an estimated 82 glass specimens, 9% were polychrome, 19% in strong colours, and 72% in common blue-green glass.[64]

Likewise, around half of the cylindrical cups with fire-rounded rims found in native contexts were decorated (seven of 13–15 vessels identified to specific type), five of which were painted, one with an applied thread (a so-called Baldock cup), and one case so-called snake-thread technique.[65] The total number of decorated cups discovered in Roman Britain as a whole merely adds up to a few dozen, which can be compared with the literally thousands of undecorated cups yielded on innumerable sites.[66]

Yet another example that demonstrates an indigenous interest in relatively rare colours and/or variants are the collared jars of Isings Form 67. In Romano-British contexts blue-green is by far the most frequent colour for this type of vessel. In contrast, two of five finds from native contexts north of Hadrian's Wall were in strong colours: yellow-brown and deep blue glass.[67]

In some cases the types found in native contexts are exceedingly rare variants: for example, two vessels with polychrome marvered blobs. With the exception of a handful of objects, all vessels with marvered blobs found on Roman sites in Britain are bichrome.[68] Similarly, arcaded beakers, wheel-cut decorated cups, or jugs with chain-handles are very rare on Roman sites in Britain.[69] Further types, such as snake-thread glass, found on four or possibly five native sites, are found on a number of Roman sites, but in very small numbers.[70]

Although little or none of the glass found on the native sites can be said to be of exceptionally high quality, the indigenous peoples' preference for decorated glass and rare variants is clearly manifest. While all categories and types of Roman glass found on native sites can also be found on Roman sites, neither the range of objects nor the quality of the glass mirror what is typically found on the latter. This leaves little doubt that the material from native sites reflects the deliberate selection of objects of particular meaning and value to the indigenous societies.

4.5 The date of the material

Due to the lack of independent dating evidence for the native sites, their dating has often come to rely on the Roman material. In the following I hope to demonstrate that – at least for Roman glass – this is circumscribed by a series of source-critical problems. As a consequence of this, dating must be treated with much greater caution than has hitherto been the case. In discussing the results of this study, it is important to draw attention to the overarching problems.

First, it must be stressed that glass of early imperial date is easier to identify than late Roman glass. Much of the late glass is thin, fragile, and less variable in terms of colours and shapes, hence not always easy to identify to precise type. In contrast the early glass can sometimes be in strong colours, or have characteristic shapes and/or types of decoration. The result in a strongly fragmented assemblage is that the early glass can be given a date which is more or less exact, whereas the late material is often given a vague date such as 'late Roman'. Quite possibly the late material is under-represented in the total assemblage.

Second, as shown in figure 4.7 some glass types have extended periods of production and use. Pillar-moulded bowls, for instance, were produced for around a century and in use for decades after production ceased. Nevertheless, the colour of these can provide a

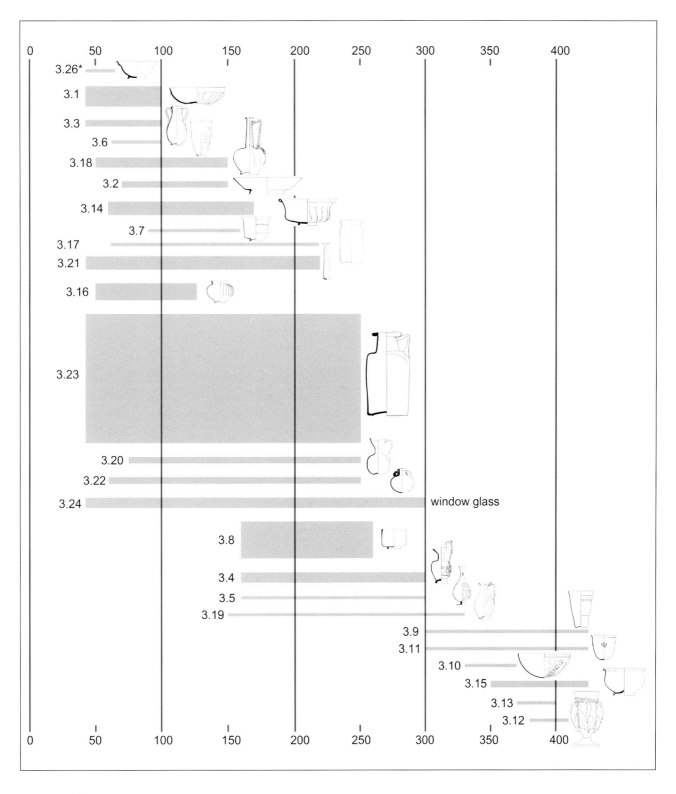

Figure 4.7

Summary of the date and occurrence of Roman vessels on Iron Age sites north of Hadrian's Wall. The bar length gives the likely chronological range; the height of each bar is proportional to the number of sites with this type of vessel. 3.26* is the cast vessel from Leckie which is a late addition to the catalogue (see ch. 3.26, additions).

more precise date for manufacture. Turning from the high-quality vessels to more mundane containers such as prismatic bottles, the dating is much less exact. Prismatic bottles were in production and use for around two centuries. This, of course, creates a source-critical problem.

From a purely hypothetical perspective, all bottle glass – both prismatic and cylindrical bottles – could have reached the native sites before the Agricolan invasion of northern Britain in the late 70s–early 80s. Or, in theory, all of the prismatic bottles might belong to the early third century. Most probably, however, prismatic bottles reached native hands from the late first century to the early third century. In contrast cylindrical bottles in all probability reached native sites from the late first to early second century AD and hence provide us with comparatively exact dating evidence.[71]

Third, the question of when the Roman imports reached native hands and when they were finally deposited is a complex one. There is a very small body of finds of Roman glass from early Medieval sites. Some of these may have had a Roman Iron Age phase, while other finds may represent long-term survival as heirlooms which were finally deposited on early Medieval sites. Part of this material, however, in all probability represents loot from long-abandoned Roman sites, and thus it does not provide us with any useful dating evidence. The overwhelming majority of sites belong to the Roman Iron Age, however; and, as pointed out above, these native assemblages do not reflect the source Roman assemblages. Rather they represent a choice of goods, and this suggests that the glass was in all probability obtained through some form of peaceful exchange between Roman and native, rather than representing loot, pilfer or plunder. If the glass can be regarded as an instance of Roman–native exchange, this suggests that the bulk of this glass reached native hands roughly in the period of its manufacture and use within the Roman world.

As regards the time of deposition of the material, the chances of long-term survival of intact objects in a fragile material such as glass must have been relatively slim. Despite the general lack of independent dating evidence, it seems reasonable to suggest that the major part of the material was deposited within a relatively limited span of time after it had reached native hands. This work has not attempted a detailed contextual study of the material's deposition, as so little is known of many of the key sites. However, clear examples of structured or deliberate deposits of fragments on settlement sites are very rare.

Due to these difficulties in dating the glass, it is difficult to give an accurate picture of the flows of goods between Roman and native hands. Most glass appears to have reached native hands in the first three centuries AD, both in terms of quantity of vessels and number of sites (fig. 4.7). In contrast, the number of sites with securely identified glass from the fourth century is limited: nine out of 77 (*c.* 12%) (fig. 4.8).[72] On a number of other sites there are sherds in natural-coloured greens belonging to the third and fourth centuries AD, and as argued above the late Roman glass may be under-represented. Yet the bulk of the glass must have reached native hands before this date; for example, large categories such as cylindrical and prismatic bottles and cylindrical cups ceased to be produced or used in the mid-third century. It is possible to point to four different factors in explaining why late Roman glass has been identified on so few native sites:

(1) The first factor is that the late Roman glass may be underrepresented due to the fact that much late material is very thin and fragile.

(2) The second and in my view, most important, factor must have been availability. In Romano-British contexts the range of vessel types had declined by the fourth century AD, and it appears that glass was not produced in the same quantities as earlier.[73] In a recent study by Jennifer Price of the Roman vessel glass from the northern Roman frontier, she demonstrated that only a small percentage of the total assemblages were of late Roman date, whereas the bulk of the material predated this period.[74]

(3) A possible third factor is that the decline could have had its cause in Roman–native conflicts.[75] We know that a period of conflict and unrest began in the concluding years of the third century, and these continued with interruptions throughout the fourth century.[76] It has been argued that this was partly a result of the political instability within the Empire.[77]

(4) A potential fourth factor could be that the Roman–native conflicts led to the repudiation of things Roman. This last possible factor is, in my view, a less probable cause of the decline. Conflicts between cultures and countries rarely result in the complete rejection of foreign goods.

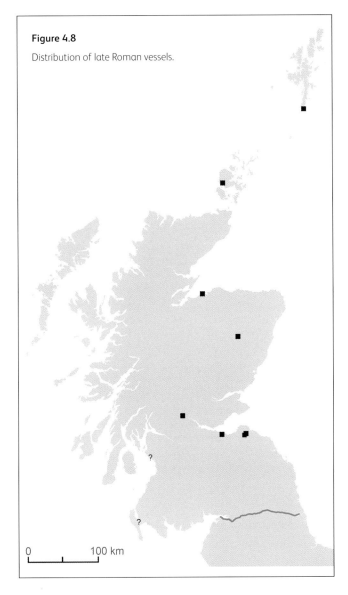

Figure 4.8

Distribution of late Roman vessels.

0   100 km

It has to be emphasized that it is not only the exchange of glass that appears to have decreased; a recent study by Fraser Hunter demonstrates a decline in Roman–native exchange as a whole in the last phase of the Roman Iron Age. A mere 40 native sites have yielded late Roman imports (defined as AD 250–400), in comparison to 170 sites with finds dating to AD 75–250. This decline is visible not only in the number of sites, but also in the quantities of material.[78]

It is important to stress that the decline in import starts in the mid-third century. Therefore there is little to uphold Michael Erdrich, Kristina Giannotta and William Hanson's claim that Roman material reached the Lowland sites only during the periods of Roman occupation,[79] for judging by both the glass and other imports, Roman–native exchange – whatever its nature – may

well have continued a century after the withdrawal from the Antonine Wall around AD 160. Their assertion, based on Erdrich's study of a single category of Roman import (samian), from a single, albeit rich and important site (Traprain Law), does not consider the inherent variations involved in access to the material,[80] nor does it take into consideration the possibility that other categories of Roman imports could yield other results.

It is also important to stress that the Roman imports can rarely be employed to provide exact dates. It is impossible to pin-point the exact time when the material reached native hands (see fig. 4.7). Even if we assume that the material was broken and deposited roughly within the same time-spans that it was in production and use in Roman contexts, the dating given is not precise enough to link it to specific historic events or periods such as the Agricolan invasion or the occupation of the Antonine Wall.

4.6 The glass – loot or exchange?

Although exchange in itself is often clearly visible in the archaeological record,[81] it is rarely, if ever, possible to discern the precise mechanisms which lie behind this exchange.[82] As pointed out by Stuart Needham, 'the life cycles of objects are effectively hidden from our view'. Although the place of manufacture is sometimes reasonably well known, we have no way of establishing how, when, how many times and where the objects changed hands before they were deposited finally.[83] What is possible, however, at least in the specific case of Roman glass found on non-Roman/native sites, is to differentiate between loot and exchange; in this discussion it is important to differentiate between the Roman Iron Age and the early Medieval sites.

If we commence with the sites of Roman Iron Age date, the distinction between loot and exchange is absolutely fundamental for our perception of Roman–native relations. If the glass found on native sites of Roman Iron Age date derived from the looting of abandoned Roman forts,[84] it would invariably have reached these sites in a fragmented state, taken either as raw material or as curios. Hence, it would not represent Roman–native exchange in any sense, and the discussion of the objects' original function would be largely irrelevant. Moreover, the dating would merely be a *terminus post quem* of limited use.

Several arguments can be presented to support the view that the finds of Roman glass represent exchange rather than loot, however. Most importantly, the assemblages of Roman glass from these sites are distinctly different from the Roman assemblages, both in terms of the categories of vessels found and the overall quality, suggesting that they represent a conscious and deliberate choice based on the qualities of the intact vessel.

Some of the types found on the native sites are in fact so scarce on Roman sites that it is only after several seasons of extensive excavation that single sherds have been unearthed. The notion that these could have been recovered by native looting thus appears less than likely. Although many of the vessels found on native sites are represented by a single sherd, there are a number of cases in which several sherds belonging to the same vessel have been found. Moreover, had the intent been to collect curios or souvenirs one would have expected more decorative pieces than the ones actually found. While a sherd of polychrome pillar-moulded bowl may be of decorative value, sherds of thin-walled cups seem inherently less attractive.

We know that glass was reused to make gaming pieces, and possibly also remelted in the manufacturing of glass bangles, on the native sites.[85] If the glass was looted with the primary intention to make gaming pieces or smoothers, the flat window glass which was relatively abundant on Roman forts would have constituted an eminently suitable raw material. However, window glass is *extremely* rare on native sites.[86] If the intention had been to remelt the glass, the quality and colour would have been of primary interest.[87] Thus it would have been of little use to gather rare types of decorated glass, or indeed to use only glass from particular types of vessels, whilst largely ignoring others. For the same reasons, it is also difficult to argue that the Roman glass found on the native sites represents Roman–native exchange in glass cullet. Moreover, if the material represented loot one would expect very little material post-dating the Antonine period; however, the glass assemblage cannot support such a view.

In fact, there is much to suggest that when the Roman army withdrew and had to abandon their forts, they tried to limit or hinder native looting. Many Roman forts appear to have been deliberately dismantled – for instance, Inchtuthil, Perthshire and Cardean, Angus – and objects that they had to leave behind were concealed in pits so as not to fall into enemy hands.[88] Thus there is little to support the view that the Roman vessel glass found on Roman Iron Age sites represents loot; regarding it as some form of peaceful exchange seems more plausible.

Turning to the early Medieval sites, their limited number (four or five in total, representing *c.* 5 to 6% of

the total number of the sites[89]) has yielded a mere 5% of the assemblage of the Roman glass found on non-Roman/native sites. In the debate concerning finds of Roman material on early Medieval sites, different hypotheses have been put forward, namely that they represent: (a) curios or raw material, picked off the ground or dug up at abandoned Roman sites; (b) heirlooms; (c) hitherto unrecognised earlier (i.e. Roman Iron Age) phases.

In an oft-quoted study of the glass from Dinas Powys, Glamorgan, Wales, Leslie Alcock argued that all the glass – both the small assemblage of Roman glass, and the considerably larger body of post-Roman/early Medieval glass – represent imported cullet intended for remelting,[90] and in other studies of early Medieval sites in Scotland he has pointed to Roman glass being collected as curios or 'reliquaries' from long-abandoned Roman sites.[91] In a reappraisal of the early Medieval (but not the Roman) glass from Dinas Powys, Ewan Campbell put forward convincing arguments that it represented the import of intact objects rather than cullet, although recycling of accidentally broken vessels did take place.[92]

In my view, however, there is much to suggest that Alcock was correct concerning at least some of the Roman glass on early Medieval sites. Two sites – Mote of Mark, Kirkcudbrightshire, and Whithorn, Wigtownshire – have yielded glass of types which are exceedingly rare on native sites of Roman Iron Age date, but which are frequent finds on Roman sites, namely window glass. This strongly implies that the material derived from a deserted Roman site, many of which were to be found in northern Britain.

In the case of other sites, however, alternative explanations must be given. In my opinion there is much to commend Fraser Hunter's notion that some sites traditionally considered to belong to the early Medieval period may have had a hitherto unrecognised Roman Iron Age phase.[93] Taking into account that some of these, often complex, sites were excavated long ago, this would hardly be surprising. In one case, a painted cylindrical cup found at Dunollie, Argyll, the excavator put forward plausible arguments for the find being an heirloom.[94]

4.7 Material culture and exchange as a means to achieve power

As demonstrated above, the Roman glass discovered on native sites represents a relatively narrow range of vessel types in comparison to what is normally found on Roman sites, and there is much to suggest that it primarily consisted of objects of particular meaning and importance within the indigenous culture. Moreover, a detailed analysis of this material shows that, contrary to some scholars' claims, it was of above-average quality and included types which are very rare in Roman contexts. Nonetheless all evidence implies that glass vessels were mass-produced and hence relatively inexpensive in the Roman world.[95] Are the assertions of Macinnes,[96] that the material represents mere 'trinkets' and 'baubles, beads and bangles' valid after all?

In the colonisation of Africa, America, Polynesia and other areas in early modern times, Europeans soon came to exploit the fact that relatively inexpensive goods could be used to obtain raw materials of great value in their homelands, marvelling at native naivety – even foolishness – in accepting what evidently constituted exceedingly unfavourable conditions of trade. For instance, in the early Native American–white trade in North America, the European merchants described the goods they offered as 'trash, trinkets, baubles, beads and bangles'.[97]

However, several scholars have pointed to the fact that objects do not have an absolute and universal value,[98] and what is perceived as of low value in one culture may be in high regard in another. The anthropological, archaeological and the historical scholarly literature contains abundant accounts of this phenomenon.[99] An example of this is how Native Americans in the sixteenth and seventeenth centuries viewed imported glass beads and glass vessels. Rather than regarding the glass as a novel and hitherto unknown material, it was conceived of as crystal – a material of great ritual significance – and hence aquired a substantial value.[100] And, as argued by Christopher Miller and George Hamell, 'far from being gullible, Indians were demanding and sophisticated consumers'.[101]

If we turn to the Roman glass in native contexts, the view on the value of these imported exotica ultimately depends on which perspective – Roman or native – is chosen. Undoubtedly much of the glass manufactured in the Roman world was considered cheap, even vulgar, by the Roman elites.[102] There is no indication that the native elites shared this view.

In most cases of cross-cultural trade of this kind, there was relatively limited interest in the practical and functional aspects of the imported goods. Instead it was the symbolic, ideological, and political value that was of importance.[103] As demonstrated by anthropological, sociological and archaeological research, material culture,[104] and in particular objects and materials of foreign derivation,[105] worked not only as symbols of status, but constituted the very tools or weapons with which

the elites could exert power. For material culture influences not only how others perceive an individual or group, but equally has a tremendous impact on the individual's self-image.[106]

To maintain or gain influence and political power the elite made use of material culture, either as a means of excluding all but themselves – what Mary Douglas and Baron Isherwood have called *weapons of exclusion* – or by controlling objects or resources which were indispensable to maintain the society's social relations. Several anthropologists have demonstrated how the sole access that leading members of society or the elders had to prestige objects used, for instance, in puberty rites or for bride price put people in social debt and a subordinate position: the so-called prestige goods systems model.[107] Originally many of these prestige goods would have been of indigenous manufacture, but in the case of Africa these were later replaced by European goods. Through their control over external trade the elites gained influence and political power.[108] However, a system dependent on foreign exotica is inherently unstable, for if the privileged classes' monopoly over the foreign trade is broken, or if the trade for some reason is disrupted, the basis of their power is threatened.[109]

It can be argued that certain aspects of the prestige goods systems model can be applied to the current study, namely that the underlying incentive for this import was essentially political rather than commercial. There is, however, nothing to suggest that any monopoly of Roman–native trade existed, for all the evidence seems to imply, as demonstrated by Fraser Hunter, that Roman artefacts were widely distributed in native societies.[110] The absence of such a monopoly points to the existence of other means of limiting social mobility. One of the most apparent means was the greater economic resources of the leading classes. Choosing goods of particularly high quality, and presumably great cost, which would have been far beyond the economic means of most, was a way of restricting the availability of prestige goods.

Far from an arbitrary choice of foreign exotica, this strongly suggests that these objects were of great symbolic significance. Some of the objects imported – namely the cups – were highly charged symbols of lordly power, and constituted a link between the leader and his war-band. As we have seen, cups and beakers in glass had a limited distribution, and it may be surmised that there were other means than strictly economic ones – probably moral or legal – restricting their spread. Cups and their symbolic significance will be discussed in greater depth in chapter 5.

Edward Luttwak and David Braund have both put

forward the idea that the Romans were acutely aware of how the leading classes in areas beyond the borders of the Empire could utilise prestige goods of Roman origin as political tools, and that they used this as a means to keep their allies in power.[111] As Luttwak has convincingly asserted, these client kingdoms or client tribes constituted one of the most economical means to protect the Empire, as they formed a buffer between Rome and her enemies.

It has often been argued, on the basis of various types of evidence, that the Votadini who lived in the Tyne-Forth province were philo-Roman, and that they may have been Roman allies.[112] On the basis of the glass from Traprain Law it can be argued that the Votadini must have had close and continuous contacts with the Romans from the first to early fifth century AD. In the light of the discussion above, this exchange between the Votadini and the Romans could reflect this aspect of the political use of these prestige goods. Whatever the nature of this exchange, access to Roman goods may have helped the Votadinian elite to remain in power.

Summing up the arguments above, the imported Roman glass was not merely a status marker employed by the Roman Iron Age elites in Scotland and north Northumberland, but also had a socio-political function in that it could be utilised as an instrument in the quest for influence and political power within indigenous societies. In this quest symbolically laden objects, often of foreign derivation, such as the imported glass cups and beakers, appear to have been of particular importance. Thus, far from being a random collection of foreign exotica, the Roman glass represents a deliberate choice of goods of particular meaning and value in native society.

Notes

1 Alcock 1963, 22–25; Alcock & Alcock 1988, 131; Alcock & Alcock 1990, 115–16.
2 MacKie 1965, 138.
3 MacKie 1982, 68.
4 Allason-Jones 1989a, 13.
5 Curle 1932a, 278.
6 Robertson 1970b, 201.
7 Welfare 1984, 315; Macinnes 1989, 114.
8 Robertson 1970, 200.
9 Robertson 1975, 418.
10 Keppie 1989, 68.
11 Fulford 1985, 102; Eggers 1951; Hedeager 1979.
12 Macinnes 1989, 114.
13 Robertson 1970, 200; Hunter 2007a, 10–15.
14 Hunter 2001a, 291; Hunter 2007a, 12.
15 Erdrich et al. 2000, 452–53.
16 Hunter 2001a, 291.
17 Curle 1913.
18 Curle 1932a, 347; contra Gillam 1958, 87.
19 Robertson 1970, 201–02; Macinnes 1989, 111; Wilson 1996–97, 22.
20 Allason-Jones 1989a, 13.
21 Tacitus, De Vita Iulii Agricolae, 31.
22 Fulford 1985, 103.
23 Breeze 1990, 93; Wilson 1996–97, 14.
24 Robertson 1990, 33.
25 Whittaker 1989, 67.
26 Dobson & Mann 1973; Gillam 1984; however, see also Scott 1976, 34–36.
27 Dio Cassius 75.5.4.
28 Robertson 1975b, 418–19; 1978, 187–92; 1983, 427.
29 Todd 1985.
30 Hunter 2007c, 217–18.
31 e.g. Hill 2006.
32 Hunter 2001a, 290, fig. 1; Hunter 2007a, 12, fig 4.
33 Westray, Orkney: a cylindrical cup originally found intact, now broken (Appendix A, B:3); Loch Kinnord, Aberdeenshire: an intact unguent bottle (Appendix A, G:1); Brackenbraes, Turriff, Aberdeenshire: an intact conical jug (Appendix A, G:3); Airlie, Angus: an intact cylindrical cup (Appendix A, I:1); Kingoldrum, Angus: an intact cylindrical cup, now lost (Appendix A, I:2); Hallowhill, St Andrews, Fife: one or two originally intact cylindrical cups, now lost (Appendix A, L:2); Torfoot, Lanarkshire: a prismatic bottle originally found intact, now lost (Appendix A, 0:2).
34 See p. 22.
35 Murray 2007, 25.
36 Dr Fraser Hunter, pers. comm.
37 See the discussion in ch. 2.3.
38 Piggott 1966, fig. 1.
39 Ingemark 1995, 15–16; Hunter 2001a, 295.
40 Earle 1977; Earle & d'Altroy 1982, 266; Johnson & Earle 1987, 208.
41 Hunter 2009b, 151.
42 See 'Catalogue', ch. 3.
43 Cool & Baxter 1999, 72.
44 van Lith & Randsborg 1985; Cool & Price 1995, 235–36; Cool & Price 1998, 179–80.
45 See Cool & Baxter 1999, Table 1, for an overview of patterns visible in Romano-British glass assemblages.
46 van Lith & Randsborg 1985, 417; Cool & Price 1995, 236.
47 Cool & Price 1998, 180; Cool & Baxter 1999, Table 4; see also Cool 1995b, 13–14.
48 van Lith & Randsborg 1985, 436.
49 See, for instance, Martial, Epigrammaton, 2.12.
50 Vespasianus, 8.
51 Cool & Baxter 1999, 83.

52 See 'Small globular flasks with looped handles – *aryballoi*', ch. 3.22.

53 Although both cylindrical and prismatic bottles were multi-purpose vessels, there is much to suggest that one of the most important functions was as a wine bottle; see ch. 3.23.

54 See 'Cylindrical and prismatic bottles', ch. 3.23.

55 Through the kind help of Dr Fraser Hunter, I have had access to the data which formed the basis for his study of Roman–native relations (Hunter 2001a).

56 See ch. 5.

57 van Lith & Randsborg 1985, 417; Cool & Price 1995, 236.

58 See chs 5. and 6.

58 Hackin 1939, fig. 37.

60 Lund Hansen 1987, fig. 61.

61 Fulford 1985, 102; Macinnes 1989, 110.

62 Robertson 1970, 200; Keppie 1989, 68.

63 See 'Pillar-moulded bowls', ch. 3.1.

64 Cool & Price 1995, 16.

65 See 'Cylindrical cups with fire-rounded rims and base rings', ch. 3.8.

66 Cool & Price 1995, 82.

67 See 'Jars with square, ovoid or globular bodies and collared rims', ch. 3.16.

68 See 'Vessels with marvered blobs' ch. 3.3.

69 See 'Arcaded beaker', ch. 3.6; 'Hemispherical cups with wheel-cut figured decoration', ch. 3.10; 'Globular or ovoid jug with chain-handle', ch. 3.19.

70 See 'Snake-thread glass', ch. 3.4; 'Beaker or flask with a beaded stem', ch. 3.5; 'Cylindrical cups with fire-rounded rims and base rings', ch. 3.8.

71 See ch. 3.23.

72 These are: Old Scatness, Shetland (Appendix A, A:2); Howe of Howe, Mainland Orkney (Appendix A, B:1); Culbin Sands, Morayshire (Appendix A, F:2); Waulkmill, Tarland, Aberdeenshire (Appendix A, G:2); East Coldoch, Stirlingshire (Appendix A, K:6); Edinburgh Castle, Edinburgh (Appendix A, M:3); Traprain Law, East Lothian (Appendix A, N:2) and ?Ardeer, Ayrshire or ?Luce Sands, Wigtownshire (Appendix A, P:1).

73 Price 2010, 37.

74 Price 2010, 40, tab. 5.1.

75 For a brief, but interesting, discussion on the impact of war on trade, see: Smith 2009, 52–53.

76 Breeze 1982, 125, 144.

77 Maxwell 1989, 36–37.

78 Hunter 2010, 96, fig. 11.1.

78 Erdrich et al. 2000, 452–53.

80 See Hunter 2001a, 291 referring to Going 1992.

81 Renfrew 1975, 3.

82 Renfrew 1993, 6.

83 Needham 1993, 166.

84 I use the word 'loot' as it is normally employed in Scottish archaeology, i.e. it does not designate war booty. When the latter is meant, the words pilfer or plunder are used.

85 See ch. 2.3.

86 See 'Matt/glossy cast window glass', ch. 3.24.

87 For a discussion concerning the recycling of post-Roman glass, see Campbell 1991, 80–81; Campbell 2000, 33; Campbell 2007, 92–93.

88 Wilson 1969, 202; Robertson 1970, 201.

89 Dunadd, Argyll (Appendix A, J:1) – note that this site may have a Roman Iron Age phase; Dunollie, Argyll (Appendix A, J:2); Dalmeny Park, South Queensferry, Midlothian – which is viewed as an Anglo-Saxon burial (Appendix A, M:2); Whithorn, Wigtownshire (Appendix A, Q:2); Mote of Mark, Kirkcudbrightshire (Appendix A, R:2). I have not included Hallowhill, St Andrews, Fife as there is very little to uphold the view that this find post-dates the Roman Iron Age (Appendix A, L:2).

90 Alcock 1963.

91 Alcock & Alcock 1988, 131; Alcock & Alcock 1990, 115–16.

92 Campbell 2007, 92–96; see also Campbell 1991, 75–83; Campbell 2000, 37–38.

93 Hunter 2001a, 292; Hunter 2007a, 11.

94 Alcock & Alcock 1988, 131.

95 See ch. 6.3.

96 Macinnes 1989.

97 Miller & Hamell 1986, 311.

98 See, for instance Appadurai 1986, 4; Thomas 1991, 4.

99 Miller & Hamell 1986; Appadurai 1986, 57; Kopytoff 1986, 74.

100 Miller & Hamell 1986, 314–15.

101 Miller & Hamell 1986, 313.

102 See ch. 6.3.

103 Hodder 1982a, 199; Hodder 1982b, 152; Appadurai 1986, 38; Helms 1988, 115.

104 Bourdieu 1977; Bourdieu 1984, 232; Douglas & Isherwood 1980, 85; Csikszentmihalyi & Rochberg-Halton 1981, 231; McCracken 1987, 121.

105 Meillassoux 1960; Dupré & Rey 1969; Ekholm 1972; Ekholm 1978; Frankenstein & Rowlands 1978.

106 Csikszentmihalyi & Rochberg-Halton 1981, 15; McCracken 1990, 118; Dittmar 1992, 143.

107 Meillassoux 1960, 63; Ekholm 1978, 131.

108 Meillassoux 1960, 63; Dupré & Rey 1969, 160.

109 Ekholm 1978, 131.

110 Hunter 2001a.

111 Luttwak 1976, 36; Braund 1984, 182; Braund 1989, 17.

112 Jobey 1976, 198–201; Macinnes 1984a, 195

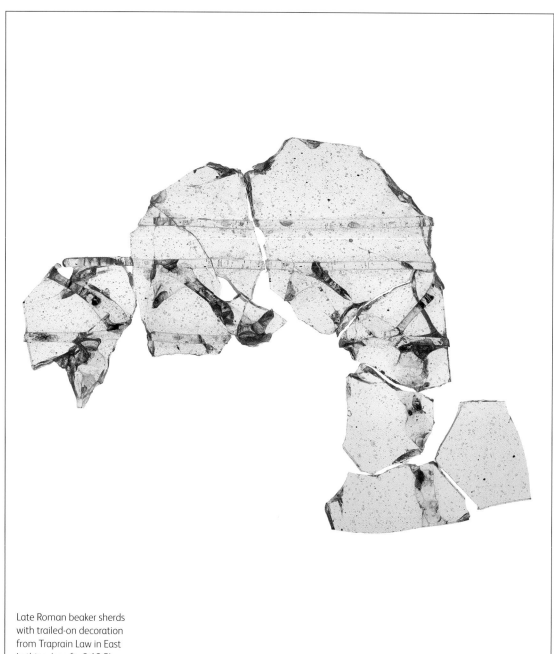

Late Roman beaker sherds
with trailed-on decoration
from Traprain Law in East
Lothian (see fig 3.12.5).

5

Alcohol, 'generosity'
and the exercise of power

IN comparison with the wide spectrum of objects found at Roman military and civilian sites in Roman Britain, including those in the militarised zone in the north, the Roman imports found on native sites beyond the border represent a relatively narrow range of objects.[1] This is also the case in Roman Iron Age Free Germany, where graves and settlements display a limited number of find categories.[2] In my view this reflects a deliberate choice by the native elites, as there would be no apparent reason for the Romans to limit or prohibit the export of non-military goods.[3]

As shown by anthropological and sociological research, demand is never a simple response to availability. Within societies the identity and self-identity of each group are made manifest in material culture; in other words, the objects functioned as social markers.[4] Consequently the choice of goods was far from insignificant to those who imported them – they chose things of particular value, meaning and status. Accordingly the study of material remains can reveal the power relations between different groups within a society.[5]

The aim of this chapter is to try to understand why one important category of imports, namely drinking vessels such as cups, beakers and small bowls, appear to have been so crucial to the Roman Iron Age elites living beyond the Roman border in Scotland and north Northumberland, and in contemporary Free Germany. In order to do that, an attempt will be made to demonstrate the symbolic significance of alcoholic drink and drinking vessels in Celtic[6] and Germanic societies by examining first the archaeological evidence, and second, pertinent literary sources describing the social implications of their use. This shows that the underlying reason why this category of imports was of such importance is that the drinking vessels and what was drunk out of them, mead or wine, were symbols of power and authority. Anthropological and archaeological research has clearly demonstrated that the fundamental role alcohol and feasting played as a political tool is a feature found in stratified societies worldwide.

In the last section of this chapter, I will take the ideas of the sociologist Pierre Bourdieu concerning 'symbolic capital' and 'symbolic violence' as a point of departure, and briefly explore the strategies employed by elites in the task of legitimating the established political order without the use of force, violence or even persuasion. In doing so, phenomena such as the transformation of low-value goods to high-value goods and social debt, are dealt with again, albeit from a somewhat different angle, in an attempt to elucidate the concealed mechanisms of domination. An example of this is the giving of feasts in traditional societies, where the elites control the large-scale brewing of beer for feasts: in other words, transforming relatively low-value agricultural surplus to high-value alcohol.

There have been very few, if any, societies whose peoples knew the use of alcohol and yet paid little attention to it. Alcohol may be tabooed; it is not ignored. In many societies, drinking behavior is considered important for the whole social order, and so drinking is defined and limited in accordance with fundamental motifs of the culture. *Hence it is useful to ask what the form and meanings of drink in a particular group tell us about their entire culture and society.*

D. G. Mandelbaum 1979, 14; my emphasis

Before we proceed to discuss the archaeological material, it is appropriate to present a brief overview of previous research concerning alcohol within anthropology and archaeology. For the last few decades there has been a focused beam of attention on the role of feasts as arenas for political action within anthropological research. Leaving earlier ideas of alcohol as something chiefly problematic,[7] much attention has been paid to the positive role of alcohol as a substance that works as a social lubricant at feasts. These feasts – which almost always involve alcohol, often also food – function as one of the elite's more important means of maintaining and achieving power.[8] As a result of its psychoactive, behaviour-altering effects,[9] alcohol is at the heart of the feast, and feasting has been widely used by the leading classes in societies around the world, creating and manifesting bonds within the elite itself, or between the elite and the rest of the population.[10]

Anthropological studies of traditional, stratified societies have shown that leadership is often dependent on the chieftain's ability to be generous: in particular, the provision of drink and food, the holding of feasts and gift giving. This 'generosity' can be regarded as a means of creating loyalty by placing someone in social debt (so-called indebtedness engineering).[11] Not surprisingly, great ritual and symbolic significance is attached to alcohol, and drinking parties are held during religious and profane festivals, and on major rites of passage, such as births, weddings and funerals.[12]

An equally important role of alcohol and feasting, however, is as a means of excluding parts of the population, and generating and manifesting the boundaries between the leading members in society and the rest of the population.[13] Depriving certain members of the society of alcohol – that is participating in parties and communal feasts – functions as a means of temporarily excluding them from a fundamental part of society. The underlying reasons for this exclusion can be a refusal to partake in work parties or as a punishment for theft.[14]

A similar scholarly interest has developed within archaeological research, taking as its starting point an influential paper published over three decades ago by Susan Frankenstein and Michael Rowlands.[15] Numerous papers have been published on this topic since, among which those of Michael Dietler have been particularly influential. For obvious reasons much of this research concerns the material culture that is related to feasts, and how this material could have been linked to the elite's struggle for power in the societies studied.[16] The evidence appears to demonstrate that feasting has formed a fundamental part of traditional societies both past and present.

5.1 The fundamental importance of vessels associated with drinking – the archaeological record

As we saw above, the native assemblages of Roman glass from the area north of Hadrian's Wall are manifestly different in character from ones found on Roman sites; at the former, a strong emphasis on vessels employed in the drinking and serving of wine in their original, Roman context can be discerned (fig. 4.1).[17] The fact that cups and beakers were symbols of lordly power is attested by various types of sources; thus it is not surprising that drinking vessels form the second largest category of Roman glass found in native contexts (fig. 4.5).

With the exception of some finds in funerary contexts and a relatively limited number of sites of other types, Roman glass vessels used for drinking have been discovered chiefly on settlement sites. Many of the settlement sites on which cups or beakers have been discovered must be termed as wealthy, as they have also yielded a wide range of other Roman imports.[18]

This category of vessels appears to have been more prevalent in the north than in the south of Scotland. This imbalance between north and south may in part be explained by the bias created by differences in depositional practices, as a significant part of the northern material derives from funerary contexts. It is also possible that there may have been a preference for cups made from other prestigious materials in the south, either having a lower degree of survival than glass, such as imported Roman bronze or silver vessels, or having largely remained unstudied by scholars. In other words, the seeming imbalance may not mirror the real state of affairs.

However, considering the role of the cup as a symbol of lordly power in Iron Age societies, the differences in distribution may reflect a more decentralized political situation north of the Forth-Clyde line. It seems from literary evidence that the tribes south of it were few in number at the time of the Roman invasion and remained so throughout the period, whereas the tribes in the north were more numerous until they merged into larger groups in the later Roman Iron Age.[19]

The contemporary archaeological material from Free Germany constitutes an interesting point of comparison. Needless to say there were many differences between the two areas. Focussing on the imports of Roman objects, there are also apparent similarities, although these should not be exaggerated. The Scottish and the Northumbrian assemblages of vessel glass consist solely of objects of Roman and provincial Roman origin,[20] whereas the Free German assemblages also include glass from the Chernjachov culture (Goths who inhabited the area north of the Black Sea).[21] The Roman and provincial Roman glass vessels found in rich funerary contexts in Free Germany were often parts of Roman drinking sets, possibly reflecting a basic understanding of Roman drinking customs. This may also have been the case in north Northumberland and Scotland, and is debated in chapter 6.7.

One of the most obvious similarities between the glass assemblages from these two areas is the importance of cups and beakers. This seems to have been even greater in Free Germany than in the area north of Hadrian's Wall; in Denmark, no less than 92% of the glass vessels found in graves dating to AD 175–400 were cups or beakers.[22] Remarkably little of the settlement material in Free Germany has been the object of in-depth study, but analyses of the glass from the Roman Iron Age and Migration-period settlement Eketorp, Öland, Sweden, appear to confirm this picture.[23]

The symbolic significance of the cup endured well after the end of the Roman Iron Age, for cups, beakers and small bowls in glass constituted a prominent class of vessels until the end of the Viking Age (AD 1050) in both Britain[24] and Scandinavia.[25] A typical example of this is the material from the Viking Age site of Kaupang in south-east Norway, where individual drinking vessels – funnel beakers and small squat jars – form the major part of the glass assemblage.[26]

5.2 Alcohol, feasting and generosity as symbols of authority and lordship

Through the use of historical sources, we can gain a deeper understanding of why cups and beakers appear to have been of such importance. As touched upon already, there seems to have been a very clear link between authority and generosity within the Iron Age and early Medieval societies in western, north-western and north-

ern Europe. Studying the Classical,[27] and more importantly the early Medieval insular sources (i.e. Welsh, Old Irish and Old English), it is evident that this generosity was made manifest by the holding of feasts. On these occasions ample quantities of alcohol and liberal amounts of food were served,[28] and sometimes gifts were distributed to participants. I make no claims of presenting a complete study of the symbolic meaning of alcohol and the role of feasting here, as this lies well beyond the scope of this work. Rather I will attempt to give a brief overview to enable understanding of the social use of the glass vessels.

The validity of these Medieval insular sources in throwing light on the Iron Age has been questioned by some scholars, most importantly by J. P. Mallory, who criticized Kenneth Jackson's idea of the Ulster cycle of tales representing a *window on the Iron Age*.[29] Mallory has convincingly demonstrated that the material culture described in the *Táin* (part of the Ulster cycle) is of Dark Age rather than of Iron Age date. Taking this as a point of departure, he argues that the Ulster cycle is a *window on the Dark Age*.[30] Mallory is doubtless correct in his identification and dating of the material culture in the epic, but whether this actually dates the core of the epic can be debated. Arguably, what is described in the Medieval sources was to no small extent pre-Christian in character, and was built upon long oral traditions, updated with contemporary colour.[31] In my view the ancient and Medieval insular sources can be regarded as an analogy which can be employed to shed light on the Iron Age societies.

The Greek author Athenaeus' *Deipnosophistae* (*The Learned Banquet*) – written in *c.* AD 200 – constitutes one of the best sources on Celtic ethnography, quoting at length several of the most important works on the Celts, some no longer preserved.[32] The following quotation, which originally derives from a lost work of Phylarchus – a Greek historian living in the third century BC – illustrates the importance of feasting:

> Ariamnes, who was a very rich Celt, publicly promised to entertain all Celts for a year, and he fulfilled this promise by the following method. At various points in their country he set stations along the most convenient highways, where he erected booths of vine-props and poles of reed and osiers, each booth holding four hundred men and even more, according to the space demanded in each station for the reception of the crowds which were expected to stream in from towns and villages. Here he set up large cauldrons, containing all kinds of meat, which he

had caused to be forged the year before he intended to give the entertainment, sending for metal-workers from other cities. Many victims were slaughtered daily – bulls, hogs, sheep, and other cattle – casks of wine were made ready, and a large quantity of barley-meal ready mixed.

> Phylarchus, frag. 2, *FGH* 2A (1926), 163
> [= Athenaeus *Deipnosophistae*, 4.150e–f,]

In the 90s BC, Poseidonius (*c.*135–*c.*51 BC), a Syrian Greek philosopher and historian, embarked on a tour which included both Spain and southern Gaul. His work gives valuable information on the traditions and customs of the Celts there, and it is most unfortunate that only fragments have been preserved. The following passage, quoted by Athenaeus, elucidates the importance of generosity and feasting among the Celtic elite:

> Lovernius, father of Bituis, who was deposed by the Romans, says that to win the favour of the mob he rode in a chariot through the fields scattering gold and silver among the myriads of Celts who followed him; he also made an enclosure twelve stades square, in which he set up vats filled with expensive wine, and prepared a quantity of food so great.

> Poseidonius, frag. 18, *FGH* 2A (1926), 231
> [= Athenaeus *Deipnosophistae*, 4.152e,][33]

The Medieval texts confirm what can be gathered from the Classical sources, namely the fundamental role of generosity of the elite, manifested in particular by the giving of feasts.[34] An illustrative example of this is the *Gododdin* and the three related *gorchanau*.[35] This work, found in Wales and written in Welsh, is preserved in a thirteenth-century manuscript. Its core, however, is attributed to the poet Aneirin who lived in Din Eidyn (Edinburgh)[36] in the second half of the sixth century AD, and originally it was probably composed in a dialect of Brittonic called 'Cumbric'. *Gododdin* is Welsh for the tribe called Votadini, who probably inhabited the area that is now Lothian and Borders in the south-east of Scotland.[37] Parts of this tribe are said to have moved to Wales in the mid-fifth century AD.

Throughout the *Gododdin* there are numerous references to mead – less often to wine – and feasting at the great halls of chiefs or kings. The vessels mentioned in connection with this are in most cases drinking horns; however, sometimes glass vessels and vessels in other materials[38] are referred to as well: 'he drank off wine from brimming glass vessels';[39] 'he would take up his spear just as if it were sparkling wine from glass ves-

sels'.[40] As apparent from the account below, the relation between the warlord and the members of the war-band was one of reciprocity. *Earning one's mead* was a metaphor for the drink and food, the feasts, lodging, gifts and protection that the chief bestowed on his fellow companions in the war-band:

> The men hastened forth, they were bounding forwards together, short-lived they were, drunk over the clarified mead, the retinue of Mynyddog famous in [battle-] straits; *their lives were payment for their feast of mead*.

> *Gododdin* A.31 = CA. xxxi, 1969, 129,
> my emphasis

The holding of feasts was a way to create bonds between the leader and his followers, as is stated in the following passage from an Irish text, *Mesca Ulad* (the intoxication of the Ultonians):

> When they were merry, Senchas clapped his hands. They all listened to him. 'Give ye, now, your blessing on the Prince who has protected you, who has been generous to you. It is not a hand in a poor garnered field. Plentiful are food and ale for you with the Prince who has protected you.'

> *Mesca Ulad*,
> quoted from B. Arnold 1999, 79

The connection between fighting for a king and his provision of sumptuous liquor is also evident in other insular sources, for example in an Irish text of ninth-century date, *Aided Oenfir Aife* (The tragic death of Aife's only son) where the hero Cú Chulainn exclaims: 'The good spear drinks good liquor'.[41] Equally, having deserved one's mead/wine is a stock metaphor used in the *Gododdin* for those who fell in battle, having fought bravely in the service of the king. Here the poet evokes the bitterness felt by those lured into tasting the *ensnaring* mead:[42]

> The exalted men went from us, they were fed on wine and mead. Because of the feast of Mynyddog I have become sorrowful, for the loss of the harsh warrior. Shields resounded like the thunder of heaven before the onslaught of Eithinyn.

> *Gododdin* B.31 = CA. xli, 1969, 109–10

The men hastened forth, they were feasted together for a year over the mead; great were their boasts. How sad to tell of them, what insatiable longing! Cruel was their resting-place; no mother's son succoured them. How long was the grief for them and the yearning, after the fiery men from the lands of wine-feasting! For the spirited men, Gwlyged of Gododdin contrived the famous feast of Mynyddog – and the costly, when paid for by the battle (?) at Catraeth.

Gododdin A.32 = CA. xxxii, 1969, 130

So fundamental was the link between feasting and lordship that those who were in opposition to a chief or a king 'fasted against him', i.e. did not attend the feast, and hence threatened and questioned his lordly power.[43] Lordship was, in other words, tantamount to generosity, which is apparent in many of the insular Medieval texts, for instance the *Gododdin*:

… since he was the son of a rightful king, lord of the men of Gwynedd, of the blood of Cilydd the gentle, before the cheek of the generous, thoughtful, sage man was buried in the earth his gifts and his fame brought visiting throngs; …

Gododdin B.3. = CA lxxxvii, 1969, 100

In *Timna Chathaír Máir* (the Testament of Cathaír Már), an Irish text of eighth-century date,[44] the obligations of a king are clearly stated:

For he has the gift of generosity
may he not hoard wealth
who apportions good grants to everyone,
flower of the kindreds of the Gáiliain.

Timna Chathaír Máir 1962, 151

In Germanic society, the same phenomenon existed: lordly generosity and munificence in the form of convivial communal feasting and lavish gift giving was a means to sustain or create bonds between the king or chieftain and the war-band, reflected, for instance, in *Beowulf*. There is much debate concerning the date and provenance of *Beowulf*; however, most scholars argue that it was composed in Northumbria or Mercia between the mid-seventh and the late ninth century AD.[45] Although the story takes place in pre-Christian times, it was written in a Christian attire.[46] Nevertheless it sheds light on various Germanic social customs and values, and is an invaluable source when it comes to understanding these phenomena.

In Germanic literature, the cup functioned as a metaphor for lordly power and as a vivid symbol of the glorious and joyful life in the royal mead-hall.[47] A recurrent theme, or rather *leit-motif*, is 'the lady with the mead cup', serving the warriors at the feast according to their rank and status. At Heorot – the splendid mead-hall built by Hrothgar, ruler over all of Denmark – Queen Wealththeow's proffering of the cup to Hrothgar formally marks the beginning of the feast:

There men's laughter / made merry sound;
the words were fair. / Wealththeow appeared,
Hrothgar's consort, / mindful of kinsmen,
gave her greeting / to the gold-adorned men.
The gentle lady / gave the cup first
to Denmark's lord / his land's protector,
bidding the prince, / beloved by his people,
joy at the revels; / the victorious ruler
gladly partook / of feast and goblet.
Wealththeow the Helming / then went about
among courtiers and warriors, / gave costly cups
to each in turn, / until the time came
for the bejeweled queen, / versed in courtesy,
to bear the beaker / for Beowulf to drink;

Beowulf, 611–24

As shown by Michael Enright in his important and thorough study of the Germanic war-band, this motif reflects the reality to a great extent among Germanic aristocrats.[48] For not only is 'the lady with the mead cup' represented in iconographic material from the Iron Age – such as depictions on gold foils (*guldgubbar*) found in Denmark and Sweden and picture stones (*bildstenar*) from Gotland, Sweden – it also sheds light on the rich women's graves of the Roman Iron Age, especially those in Denmark and Germany.[49]

The relation between the warlord or king and the members of the war-band was one of asymmetrical reciprocity (see below). The latter were furnished with armour and weapons, received costly gifts, were provided with food and given shelter, but most importantly they were held in honour and partook of the communal feast. This created strong bonds of loyalty by placing them in social debt to the generous king, as can be inferred from the passage in *Beowulf* quoted below. In this particular case – where Beowulf takes up battle with a fierce dragon – the warriors desert him at the time of need. And Wiglaf, who is the only one who is truly brave at heart, is ashamed of his fellow companions' unfaithful, unworthy and unmanly behaviour:

Wiglaf appealed   to his companions
with truth greatly   from his grieving heart:
'I remember the day   when we drank the ale
on the mead bench   when we made our boast
that when he had need as now he does
we would repay   our generous prince
for rewarding us   with war armour,
helmets and swords;   holding us honourable
and trusting us   he gave us treasure;
...   ...
I think it shameful   to carry our shields
back to our homes   without having
protected the life   of the nation's lord
and killed the enemy; I know clearly
that the debt we owe would still be due
if we abandon him   to do battle
and to die alone;   he and I will at least
stand together   with sword and armour.'

Beowulf, 2631–39, 2653–60

Normally, however, absolute loyalty was expected of those partaking in the feast, as the following declaration by Queen Wealththeow suggests:

'Here every peer   is peaceful in spirit
trusts his fellow,   protects his king;
the men who drink here obey my commands.'

Beowulf, 1228–30

Summing up the above, the fundamental importance of the feast as a means for the leading classes to establish and maintain their prestige and power is a theme which recurs in both the ancient and insular Medieval historical sources. Not only the historical sources, but also the archaeological and iconographic evidence attest to the cup as a symbol of lordly power, a symbol with continuity over time and space, from the pre-Roman Iron Age to the late Iron Age/early Medieval period.

5.3 Feasting and gift giving in an anthropological perspective – a means to achieve power

Anthropological analogy is an important and often indispensable tool in the understanding of societies in the past.[50] The study of feasts can provide a window of entry into the economic flows, social relations and power struggles within these societies.[51] The notion of generosity – in particular the giving of feasts – as a sign of leadership and authority is not culture-specific. On the basis of cross-cultural anthropological studies, it is evident that the elites of many traditional stratified societies used feasting and gift giving and other expressions of 'generosity' as means to gain prestige and create bonds of loyalty, which in turn was used to augment or achieve political power and influence. The fundamental importance of feasting in traditional societies has long been acknowledged, but it is only in recent years that archaeologists have really come to focus on this aspect of society.[52]

One of the earliest studies that emphasised the central role of feasting was Susan Frankenstein and Michael Rowlands' interesting – and influential – study of the power relations of the Early Iron Age in south-western Germany, which was published in 1978. This points towards much of what is the focus of interest in the scholarly work of today. In their view, which they based on anthropological research, groups were linked to each other through competitive feasting and gift giving to create or repay social debts.[53]

I should underline that I neither consider feasting to be merely an arena for those struggling for power, nor do I view the holding of feasts, gift giving and other aspects of 'generosity' as the sole means to achieve political influence in traditional societies. On the contrary, there is abundant evidence, anthropological as well as historical, to suggest that this was just one of several ways for the elite to achieve their goals. On the basis of these sources, however, it is apparent that it was one of the most important. Moreover, it is evident that it is strongly linked to other means – economic, military, legal, religious, and kinship – of obtaining political influence or accomplishing political dominance.

Feasts can be viewed as a specialised form of gift giving where the gifts, in the form of drink and food, are consumed and consequently cannot be reinvested in counter-gifts.[54] (Often other types of gift giving also take place at the feasts.) In stratified societies, feasts are often used as a form of what Raymond Firth has termed 'indebtedness engineering'[55] which inculcates social inequalities and gives prestige and power to the one holding the feast. Michael Dietler has called this 'commensal politics'[56] or 'commensal hospitality'.[57] Feasting, however, was also a way of strengthening the ties between people who, in other spheres of life, could be hostile towards each other, and thus a way of keeping the community together.[58]

Since feasting can be considered a form of gift giving, let us study the phenomenon in a wider perspective. One of the most important works is Marcel Mauss' *The Gift* (*Essai sur le don*), published in 1925.

Through the use of the ethnographic record and historical sources, Mauss was able to recognise some of the most fundamental aspects of gift giving, namely that the pretence that the giving and receiving was a voluntary and disinterested act was in fact a guise for the absolute opposite.[59] Not to accept a gift, or the failure to return one of equal or higher value, was considered a violation of etiquette which could lead to hostilities, and in extreme cases to socio-economic disruption and even warfare.[60]

In stratified societies a gift does not always presuppose a material counter-gift, or the return of services/labour (although this is often the case); however, this places the recipient in social debt, and hence in a subordinate position to the donor, as noted by Mauss:

> Between vassals and chiefs, between vassals and their henchmen, the hierarchy is established by means of these gifts. To give is to show one's superiority, to show that one is something more and higher, that one is magister. To accept without returning or repaying more is to face subordination, to become a client and subservient, to become minister.
>
> Mauss 1969 (1925), 72

The economic relation between donor and receiver, and the subsequent political relation of leader and follower, can be said to be dialectical, for in order to remain in a paramount position it was obligatory to be generous.[61] Leaders who no longer appear to be generous lose prestige, and at worst they lose their political influence and power. The most successful leaders are those who seem to be the most beneficial for the self-interest of the individual or group by providing for their physical, social and spiritual needs.[62]

Those who succeed are not those who have managed to accumulate large amounts of material goods. On the contrary, it is those who by lavish gift giving and by the holding of feasts have placed a large number of people in social debt. It often takes years, or a whole lifetime, for those indebted to repay their debt. Therefore they remain in a subordinate position until they can reciprocate the gift.[63] This phenomenon has been studied by a number of scholars;[64] it is known as 'asymmetrical reciprocity',[65] or more commonly indebtedness engineering.

How is it then that the chiefs appear to be generous? From an outside perspective the situation seems to be the opposite: they not only gain prestige and political influence by giving high-status gifts, but also make an economic profit in the form of agricultural produce

and raw materials when people try to buy their way out of the state of indebtedness. Alternatively, as in the case of the war-bands discussed above, people had to put their lives at stake in return for the right to partake in the lordly feasts.

The reason lies in the way that pre-monetary economies functioned. Different categories of goods were traded in different spheres; for example, cattle – which in many societies, past and present, were considered a sign of status and wealth – could not be exchanged for what was seen as low-value produce. This phenomenon has been observed, for example, on Tonga and Samoa where the chiefs gave durable prestige goods (toga) to the common people, who in return gave the chiefs perishable produce (oloa) such as food.[66] What was viewed as low value was generally what most households were able to produce themselves. Consequently it was difficult, if not impossible, for most individuals of low rank to return high-status objects, and hence gain prestige and political influence.[67]

The prerogative of the leading members of society to hold large feasts was another means of turning low-value agricultural surplus into labour, or status and prestige, by asymmetrical reciprocity. The labour could then, for instance, be used for producing metals, which could be turned into high-status objects by specialised craftsmen (who were also supported by the agricultural surplus).[68]

5.4 The transformation of 'economic capital' to 'symbolic capital' – a means to achieve power

The privileged classes, as we have seen, used 'generosity' through the hosting of feasts or presentation of gifts as a means to create bonds of loyalty, to obtain respect and renown, gain prestige, and consequently political influence and power from their followers or the populace in general by placing them in social debt. This 'generosity' was in turn based on the elite's ability to transform low-value goods, most importantly agricultural surplus, into either high-value goods – in this particular case imported Roman glass – or food and drink served at feasts. There is much to suggest that the elite gained not only in terms of prestige and power, but also in economic ones.[69]

Chris Gosden has termed this 'the trick of false generosity',[70] but I would argue that this is seen through the cold gaze of the scholar. For although it is apparent that the members of the elite were very much aware of their struggle for power, they may well have considered themselves generous. Moreover, as pointed out by Pierre Bourdieu, leadership in traditional societies is associated with responsibility, and it demands a great deal of time, effort and resources.[71]

Bourdieu's models are often viewed as *good to think with*,[72] or as *a set of thinking tools*[73] to use his own words. One of his key insights is that material wealth – so-called 'economic capital' – is just one of several resources available to individuals, families or 'classes', in their struggle to gain or maintain influence and power. He has designated these resources 'capital':

(a) Symbolic capital, an individual's or a group's honour, esteem, prestige, status, and objects of great symbolic value.[74]

(b) Social capital, a network of kin, friends and other personal contacts.

(c) Cultural capital, 'cultural competence', knowledge, education.[75]

In pre-modern societies (i.e. pre-capitalist) in particular, the economic realities which lie behind political dominance have to be euphemised, disguised, or otherwise obscured – lest they should lose in efficiency – by converting economic capital to other forms of capital; a form of collective denial of the 'objective economic truth'.[76] Bourdieu uses the all-embracing concept of 'symbolic violence' – a term I find misleading – to describe the *peaceful* modes of domination used by the elite, by employing different kinds of capital.[77] Despite the fact that efforts and a great deal of resources are involved, symbolic violence is an efficient and economical way to achieve or maintain political dominance, more so than the use of coercion, violence or even slavery.[78]

In my view, the Roman glass associated with drinking, primarily the cups and beakers, but also other forms of vessels, can be regarded as economic capital converted into symbolic capital, as they represent great wealth, and are the result of some form of peaceful exchange, probably trade.[79] The cup, in this case, is not only a symbol of lordship: it can in itself be used to exercise power. The notion of symbolic capital may thus appear paradoxical, for at the same time as it is disguised economic capital, its function is to convey a message – that of influence and power. As pointed out by Bourdieu: 'Symbolic capital is capital with a cognitive base, which rests on cognition and recognition' – and as a weapon to exclude all but the elite.

One aspect of society that Pierre Bourdieu pays remarkably little attention to is the leading classes' use of coercion and physical violence as means to maintain the established political order, or to achieve political domination. In his texts the exertion of force is only mentioned in passing,[80] thus down-playing the role of warriors and war-bands in pre-modern societies (and the function of the police force and the military in modern societies) considerably.[81] Although the employment of military force may be directed primarily against other societies, rather than turned against those of subordinate position in the same society, it can be argued that it was of indisputable importance as a basis of power for the elite.

In his studies of the Kabyle in Algeria, Bourdieu was able to show how symbolic capital – in particular the honour and prestige of those in a paramount position in society – was used to obtain a disguised form of corvée labour.[82] What is described in poetic works such as *Beowulf* or the *Gododdin* is but a martial variant of the same phenomenon, with one exception: those who were tempted to taste the *bitter mead*, lured by the glory and honour of drinking the queen's cup, had often to pay a costly price – their lives.

Notes

1   Curle 1932a; Robertson 1970; Hunter 2001a; Hunter 2007a.
2   Eggers 1951; Lund Hansen 1987.
3   There are of course exceptions to this rule: in the fourth century AD the Romans put restrictions on the export of food to the Visigoths (Thompson 1966, 14–20; Todd 1975, 41). See also Kunow 1986, for a discussion concerning military equipment.
4   Douglas & Isherwood 1978; Appadurai 1986; Bourdieu 1994.
5   Dietler 1996, 111.
6   Since Malcolm Chapman published *The Celts: The construction of a myth* in 1992, the validity of viewing the Iron Age peoples in Britain as 'Celtic' has been doubted (see, for instance Fitzpatrick 1996; James 1999), a criticism spurred by the fact that the peoples living in Britain were never called 'Celts' by the ancient authors – although similarities between them and the neighbouring Gauls were pointed out (Sims-Williams 1998, 26). This has implications for the application of 'Celtic analogy' – the use of 'Celtic' textual evidence in the interpretation of the archaeological material, which has been used to broaden understandings of Iron Age society. It can be argued, however, that we need not reject the textual evidence, merely utilise it with greater caution. In fact the ancient and Medieval sources can be better seen as analogies which are relatively close in terms time and space. There are a number of clear similarities over time and space,

analogies which are relatively close in terms time and space. There are a number of clear similarities over time and space, such as the fundamental role of feasting and warfare for the elites in these stratified societies. Moreover, there are indications that values and customs of the upper echelons of society in western, north-western and northern Europe in the pre-Roman and Roman Iron Ages, and to some extent also in the early Medieval period, were similar.

7   For an overview of earlier research see Heath 1976; Heath 1987.

8   Jennings et al. 2005, 275; Dietler 2006, 230.

9   Dietler 2006, 232; see also Heath 1976, 41; Marshall 1979, 2; Heath 1987, 99–100; Sherratt 1995.

10 Rehfisch 1987 (1962); Netting 1964; Carlson 1990; March 1998; Arthur 2003; see also Dietler 1990, 352.

11 Firth 1983, 101.

12 Dietler & Hayden 2001, 9; Wiessner 2001, 115.

13 Douglas 1987, 8.

14 Arthur 2003, 517.

15 Frankenstein & Rowlands 1978.

16 Jennings et al. 2005, 275; Dietler 2006, 237.

17 See ch. 4.3.

18 Hunter 2001a.

19 Mann 1974, 40; Mann & Breeze 1987. See also Hunter 2007a, 4–9 for a discussion of source-critical problems in naming the Iron Age tribes and confederations.

20 See 'Catalogue', ch. 3.

21 Näsman 1984; Straume 1987.

22 van Lith & Randsborg 1985, 454.

23 Näsman 1984.

24 Evison 2000; see also Campbell 1995; Campbell 2000; Campbell 2007, ch. 4.

25 Hunter 1975.

26 Gaut 2007, 32.

27 Tierney 1960; Champion 1985.

28 In the last two decades there have been several scholarly works which have dealt with the symbolic meaning of alcohol and feasting in 'Celtic' and Germanic societies: see Magennis 1985b; Dietler 1990; Enright 1996; Arnold 1999.

29 Jackson 1964.

30 Mallory 1992, 111.

31 Arnold & Gibson 1995; Arnold 1999, 72.

32 Tierney 1960, 201–3; see also Nash 1976.

33 This passage from Poseidonius is also quoted by Strabo (*Geographia* 4.2.3).

34 Jackson 1964, 20–22.

35 A number of translations of the *Gododdin* have been published over the years, most recently by Koch (1997). The quotes used here come from one of the most widely used versions, namely that of Kenneth Jackson (1969).

36 It has often been argued that Din Eidyn – or Eidïn Vre, i.e. the Hillfort of Eidïn – refers to the Iron Age settlement on the site which today is occupied by Edinburgh Castle (Koch 1997, xiii–xiv).

37 Jackson 1969, ix, 3, 69.

38 It is important to stress that the types of vessels described probably reflect what was used in the sixth and seventh centuries AD. For the use of glass in the Dark Age, see Harden 1956; Evison 2000; Campbell 2007, ch. 4. Glass has been found on several Scottish sites from this period (Campbell 2000, fig. 1b; Campbell 2007, fig. 39), for example Whithorn,

Wigtownshire (Campbell 1997), and Mote of Mark, Kirkcud-brightshire (Harden 1956, 149–50).

39 *Gododdin* B.10 = CA. xcii; Jackson 1969, 102.

40 *Gododdin* A.64 = CA. lxv; Jackson 1969, 141–42.

41 Quoted from Dillon 1948, 17. This text, which forms part of the Ulster Cycle, is preserved in a late fourteenth- or early fifteenth-century manuscript, the Yellow Book of Lecan (Dillon 1948, xviii, 16).

42 *Gododdin* A.11 = CA. xi; Jackson 1969, 119–20.

43 Dillon 1948, xv; Binchy 1958, 127; Arnold 1999, 79.

44 The Testament of Cathaír Már was written around the eighth century, but is probably based on an older oral tradition. It is preserved in several manuscripts, the oldest dating to *c*.1400. The text deals with the bequests made to the sons of Cathaír, king of the Lagin, who is supposed to have lived in the second or fourth century AD (Dillon 1962, 148–49).

45 Bjork & Obermeier 1997.

46 Irving 1997.

47 Bauschatz 1978, 290; Enright 1996. The cup as a symbol in Old English literature can also have Biblical and Christian connotations, however (Magennis 1985a; 1985b; 1986).

48 Enright 1996.

49 Enright 1996, ch. 4.

50 For a discussion of this topic, see Wylie 1985.

51 Frankenstein & Rowlands 1978, 76; Dietler 1990, 360; Dietler & Hayden 2001, 1; Hayden 2001, 30.

52 In particular the works of Michael Dietler and Brian Hayden are important; see Dietler 1990; Dietler 1996; Dietler 2001; Hayden 1995; Hayden 1996; Hayden 2001.

53 Frankenstein & Rowlands 1978. See also Gero 1992.

54 Dietler 2001, 73–74.

55 Firth 1983, 101.

56 Dietler 1990, 371–72; Dietler 1996, 88.

57 Dietler 2001, 73.

58 Anigbo 1996.

59 Mauss 1969 (1925), 1.

60 Mauss 1969 (1925), 37–38.

61 Orenstein 1980, 70; Gosden 1989, 359.

62 Clark & Blake 1994, 21.

63 Voss 1987, 131; Hayden 2001, 35.

64 See Mauss 1969 (1925); Orenstein 1980; Firth 1983; Voss 1987; Gosden 1989; Clark & Blake 1994.

65 Orenstein 1980.

66 Gosden 1989, 366.

67 Dietler & Herbich 2001, 251–53, fig. 9.4.

68 Hayden 1995, 40.

69 Bourdieu 1977, 180, 195.

70 Gosden 1989, 369.

71 Bourdieu 1977, 193–94; Bourdieu 1990, 128–29.

72 Jenkins 1992, 12.

73 Bourdieu in Wacquant 1989, 50.

74 Bourdieu 1977, 183.

75 Bourdieu 1980, 226–27; Bourdieu 1984; Bourdieu 1986b; Bourdieu 1988; see also Broady 1989.

76 Bourdieu 1977, 196; 1990, 118; 1998, 102.

77 Bourdieu 1977, 191.

78 Bourdieu 1977, 192.

79 For a discussion see ch. 4.6.

80 Bourdieu 1977, 190–91; 1990, 126; 1998, 41, 43.

81 Lash 1993, 200.

82 Bourdieu 1977, 178–80.

Bottle glass from Torwoodlee in Selkirkshire (see fig 8.15a).

6

Glass, wine and knowledge – intellectual imports as a weapon of exclusion

THE vast majority of imported Roman glass vessels found on non-Roman/native sites north of Hadrian's Wall are of types which were associated with serving, drinking, storing and (most probably) transporting wine in their original Roman setting (fig. 4.1). The aim of this chapter is to explore whether this material could have retained its original function; in other words, whether Roman drinking customs – albeit in their most basic form – were imitated by the native elites living in this area. Any venture to explain this highly fragmentary material is a difficult task, as there are a number of obstacles and source-critical problems involved. However, by using material from funerary contexts from Roman Iron Age Scandinavia and other parts of Free Germany as an analogy, it is possible to gain new insights into an otherwise almost unintelligible collection of sherds.

This choice of analogy has several reasons. First, the rich grave-material from Free Germany, with its intact vessels and closed contexts, can give us a greater understanding of how these imported objects might once have been used in their new setting (fig. 6.1). Second, while the cultural, economic and other differences between the two areas should not be underestimated, neither should the similarities, one crucial aspect being that both areas were situated beyond Rome's heavily militarised northern boundary. Third, though the archaeological assemblages of imported Roman goods were by no means identical in character, they show a great deal of resemblance, in particular in the focus on objects associated with drinking.[1]

Earlier scholarly works have considered whether Roman drinking customs were introduced in Free Germany (this has scarcely been discussed for Scotland and north Northumberland). However, the Roman and Germanic drinking customs have rarely been defined except in a very cursory and fleeting manner, often simply repeating the stereotypical views of the ancient authors. Yet it can be strongly argued that without a deeper understanding of these customs, it would be difficult, if not impossible, to address this query. Therefore I will examine Roman drinking customs in some detail, paying attention to their wider social context as well as to the practicalities of serving and drinking wine, with special focus on the glass. Thereafter the transport of wine in amphorae and, more importantly, in barrels, will be discussed. The drinking customs prevalent in the native societies are then described from the same perspectives, and I will go on to consider the case for an export of wine beyond the Roman frontier and, correspondingly, for the existence of Roman drinking sets in these areas. This part of the chapter culminates in a review of the evidence for the adoption of Roman drinking customs in Free Germany and Scotland.

The argument to be developed in this chapter is that the Roman glass found on native sites north of Hadrian's Wall may have been not merely exotic, exclusive and fragile articles which could not be produced by local craftsmen, but 'intellectual imports'. This term – first conceived by Kent Andersson[2] – denotes imported objects which had retained much of their original function and meaning, and hence required knowledge derived from this foreign culture to be used in an appropriate way. The inability to understand the meaning of these objects, or the lack of knowledge in how to use them, would have been intimidating, and would thus have functioned as a social barrier against those of lower social standing. Using anthropological and sociological theories as a point of departure for this discourse, an attempt will be made to show how these 'intellectual imports' functioned as a means for the leading members of society to maintain or gain status, influence and power.

6.1 A brief history of earlier research

The idea that the imported Roman vessels found in Free Germany could reflect an understanding of Roman drinking customs among the elites of Iron Age societies, and the possible import of wine along with these objects, is by no means new.[3] Several scholars from the 1930s onwards have tried to link the ancient historical sources speaking of a limited export of wine to the Germanic tribes with the finds of drinking sets in graves. In the first decades of the twentieth century, however, analyses of the organic remains in vessels of the Iron Age period revealed that they had once contained fruit beer and mead.[4] This was supported by historical sources of both ancient and Medieval date, in which mead and beer are mentioned as the traditional alcoholic beverages of the Germanic tribes. Hence, few have argued for a large-scale import of wine.

In 1934 Gunnar Ekholm published a paper in which he tried to link bronze ladle and sieve sets and bronze vessels of Hemmoor type with an import of wine to Free Germany. In this, however, it was suggested that those tribes further from the Roman frontier (i.e. parts of Scandinavia) had to be content with substitutes for wine, such as fruit beer.[5] A paper printed in 1949, written by Ole Klindt-Jensen, stresses the difficulties in trying to establish whether imported Roman objects found in Iron Age contexts could have retained their original function. Klindt-Jensen argues that there was an import of wine on the basis of the historical sources, but points out that this wine need not have been imbibed in a Roman manner.[6]

Other scholars have turned to the linguistic evidence in an attempt to elucidate the problem. In 1934, and again in 1942, Tönnes Kleberg commented on a loan-word in the Germanic languages, the Old High German *koufôn* which derives from Latin *caupo* – innkeeper, wine merchant. He argued that the German-speaking peoples came to view Roman *caupones* as merchants in general, owing to the fact that they first came into contact with these.[7]

In a paper printed in 1936, Olwen Brogan argued for an import of wine to Free Germany, using etymological evidence and drawing upon ancient historical sources. In her view, the loan-word 'wine' in the Germanic languages, which originates from Latin *vinum*, strongly suggests an acquaintance with that beverage. The scarcity of archaeological finds in Free Germany proving this (i.e. Roman wine amphorae) was explained by the use of wooden barrels for transporting wine which had long since disintegrated, leaving no trace.[8]

Figure 6.1

Rich burial with drinking set, Himlingøje 1894.

National Museum, Copenhagen
Photo L. Larsen

In a paper published by Joachim Werner in 1950, on the Roman drinking vessels found in graves of the Roman Iron Age period, a somewhat different – or rather, odd – hypothesis was put forward. In these graves drinking vessels often appear in pairs, for example two glass or silver beakers of the same type. On the basis that silver drinking cups found in Pompeii sometimes appear in pairs, that Pompeian wall-paintings often depict drinking vessels in pairs, and that Classical literary sources mention drinking vessels in pairs, Werner suggested that the finds beyond the Empire reflect the occurrence of Roman dinner parties – *convivia* among the Germanic elites.[9]

The idea that wine was imported, and that aspects of Roman drinking customs may have been introduced to Free Germany, did not remain unchallenged. In 1954 Rolf Nierhaus published a paper fiercely criticising earlier views, in particular those of Brogan and Werner. Nierhaus disputed the idea that wine was imported to the area, pointing to the virtual absence of Roman amphorae sherds further from the Roman border. The notion that barrels, rather than amphorae, were utilised was dismissed on the grounds that many of the Roman imports date from a period when wine was produced in Spain, southern Gaul and Italy, where it was drawn off into amphorae.[10]

Although Nierhaus' cutting criticism of earlier scholarship seems to have silenced almost all debate for nearly a generation, this was not the end of it. Jürgen Kunow's work on the imports of Roman bronze and glass vessels in Free Germany, published in 1983, attempted, amongst other things, to elucidate how these vessels functioned in their new context.[11] Using Werner Hilgers' detailed study of the names, forms and functions of Roman vessels within the Roman Empire,[12] Kunow tried to establish whether, and in that case to what extent, the original Roman use was retained within the Germanic setting.

Kunow argued that the drinking sets with large bronze vessels (so-called mixing vessels), ladles and sieves, and drinking vessels, reveal an understanding of the original function, in spite of the fact that the bronze wine-mixing vessels sometimes were replaced by Roman cooking vessels. According to Kunow this was not due to a misunderstanding, but rather a question of what was available. However, Kunow emphasised the difference between, on the one hand, maintaining the same function – in this case use as drinking and serving vessels – and on the other hand, representing actual Roman drinking customs.[13]

6.2 Roman drinking customs

In any discussion of Roman culture, it is important to bear in mind that this was far from homogeneous. As a result of military expansion, the Roman Empire came to cover vast expanses of land with a great number of different peoples and ethnic groups. And although the 'Roman' culture, with its roots in the Mediterranean area, came to influence these peoples, their old customs were maintained to a greater or lesser extent. In the case of Roman drinking customs, we know that the tradition of drinking wine in a manner that originated from the Graeco-Roman cultural sphere, spread to all the areas which came under Roman suzerainty. However, alongside the customs introduced from the Mediterranean area, the traditional alcoholic beverages retained much of their earlier popularity.[14]

To give a complete overview of the role of wine in Roman society lies well beyond the scope of this work. Instead an attempt will be made to give a rough picture of what I consider the most central aspects of Roman drinking customs; how these were manifested in the core of the Empire; and, albeit more briefly, to what extent these were conformed to in the north-western provinces. Wine was an essential part of Roman life, and to the Romans wine came to symbolise civilisation itself. Together with olives and cereals it constituted the most important staple foods in the Mediterranean world, the so-called 'eternal trinity'.[15]

Wine is life.   Petronius, *Satyrica*, 34

There are two liquids that are specially agreeable to the human body, wine inside and oil outside ...
        Pliny the Elder, *Naturalis historia*, 14. 29.149

... they [i.e. the Romans] require kneaded bread and wine and oil, ...
        Dio Cassius, *Roman History*, 62.5.5

Innumerable passages in ancient literature concern wine and drinking;[16] there are countless mentions in the epigraphic material[17] – not least in the graffiti. Frescoes, terracotta plaques and other types of iconographic material depict, for example, dinner parties (fig. 6.2), and the transportation of wine in amphorae and barrels.[18] Archaeological excavations have yielded millions of finds of wine amphorae, many from shipwrecks in the depths of the Mediterranean.[19] Other excavations have unearthed the remains of vineries, and even the actual vineyards.[20] In cities like Pompeii, Herculaneum

Figure 6.2

Roman fresco with banquet scene inside the House of Chaste Lovers, Pompeii.

and Ostia, a fair number of bars and inns have been preserved.[21] All this bears witness to the tremendous importance of wine in Roman society and life.

In the core of the Empire, the Mediterranean area, wine accompanied all meals: breakfast (*ientaculum*), lunch (*prandium*) and dinner (*cena*); but most importantly it was at the heart of the dinner party (*convivium*) and the drinking party (*comissatio*). In earlier scholarly works the Roman *convivium* was equated with the Greek s*ymposion*;[22] however, it has been convincingly argued by Katherine Dunbabin that there were important differences between the two.[23] The dinner – *convivium* or *cena* – was a social gathering[24] in which men and women partook,[25] on rare occasions also children.[26] The number of participants varied, and the Roman author Varro (116–27 BC) suggested that:

> ... the number of guests ought to begin with that of the Graces and end with that of the Muses; that is, it should begin with three and stop at nine ...
>
> Varro, cit. Aulus Gellius, *Noctes Atticae*, 13.11.2–3

The number of attending guests had to do with the tradition of reclining on couches (*clinae*) in the dining room (*triclinium*). As suggested by its name there were three couches in the triclinium, and each couch was normally shared by three people, rarely more.[27] Instead of three couches there could also be one larger couch of semicircular shape (*sigma* or *stibadium*) on which six to eight people could fit.[28] To dine and drink seated was viewed as vulgar by wealthy Romans,[29] and was considered fit only for children[30] or slaves.[31] Not all parties were held in the triclinium, however; wealthy and influential people often hosted parties with very large

numbers of guests, which sometimes could be counted by the hundred.[32] Alongside the guests were servants – usually slaves – who took care of the serving.[33]

During the actual dinner relatively little wine was drunk:[34] it was more an occasion for eating, talking and merry-making.[35] The dinner was sometimes followed by a *comissatio* – a drinking party, where the wine flowed in abundance.[36] A fundamental feature, perhaps even the most important aspect, of the *convivium* and the *comissatio*, was to maintain and strengthen the bonds with one's friends (*amici*) and clients (*clientes*).[37] The way different individuals were treated depended on their social rank and status. Clients and 'lesser friends' – *amici minores* – were habitually served cheaper wine and food, and on occasions when larger parties were held they were 'seated' further from the host.[38] Those of lesser rank could be treated rudely, a cause of great anger and frustration.[39] However, not all approved of this; the Roman author Pliny the Younger (*c.* AD 61–*c.*112), for example, strove for equality at his own dinner parties.[40]

Notwithstanding that the hierarchical order of society was clearly perceptible to all those partaking, these parties were generally considered to be most pleasurable occasions. *Hilaritas* – cheerfulness and merriment – was expected at *convivia*.[41] Good company, interesting discussions on various topics, the cracking of jokes, the reading of poetry, entertainment of different kinds, food, and most importantly the lavish quantities of wine being served, ensured this.[42]

Roman drinking customs involved a great deal of paraphernalia in the various procedures of serving and drinking of the wine. The wine first had to be transferred, either directly from the vessel in which it had been fermented (a *dolium*) or from the vessel in which it had been transported (an *amphora*) to a serving vessel. There were several kinds of serving vessels, one of which was the *crater*.[43] In a Greek context this type of vessel functioned as a mixing bowl, where wine was mixed with water. Dunbabin has, however, put forward convincing arguments for the wine being mixed directly in the cup in Roman times, rather than in a communal mixing vessel.[44]

Each participant had his or her own individual drinking vessel[45] – a cup, beaker or small bowl. These were manufactured in a wide variety of shapes and different materials.[46] Although there was a great deal of diversity in terms of shape, the majority of vessel types had some basic features in common: they were relatively small in size, and had a flattened base or foot which allowed them to be placed on the table.[47] Despite countless mentions of different types and categories of vessels in the ancient literature, it is often difficult to link these with the actual archaeological finds. If they are described at all in the literary sources, it is often in general terms. Nevertheless, the thorough scholarly work by Werner Hilgers in particular[48] has enhanced our knowledge within this field of research.

Before the wine could be drunk, however, it had to be sieved through cloth[49] or a metal colander or sieve[50] (*colum*),[51] removing wine dregs and giving it a smoother and milder taste (fig. 6.3).[52] Whether this sieving was done before it was poured into a serving vessel, or as it was poured into the drinking vessel, is not clear. Despite earlier claims for an extensive use of metal sieves in a Roman context, finds of these are relatively rare within the Roman Empire. This stands in contrast to a significant number of finds in Free Germany, where sieves formed parts of the so-called 'Roman wine-sets'.[53] Hilary Cool has argued that metal sieves were employed to remove not wine dregs but spices of various kinds:[54] for wine was not only served plain, but also mulled, i.e. sweetened with honey (*mulsum*) or infused with spices and sweetened (*conditum*).[55] Wine was almost always diluted with water, either hot[56] or cold[57] – sometimes in the form of snow or ice.[58] The hot water was probably heated in ordinary saucepans, directly in the metal jug used for serving,[59] or in exclusive and expensive 'samovar-like' hot-water heaters.[60] Both hot and cold water was served from flagons or jugs,[61] or the wine was measured up and served with a ladle (*cyathus*).[62]

What the proportions between wine and water were in Roman times is not entirely evident; according to Martial, wine was mixed 'half and half' during the festivities at Saturnalia (17–23 December).[63] This, however, was a holiday when excessive drinking was not only socially accepted but encouraged.[64] Most days of the year the proportion of water would have been much higher.[65] To drink undiluted wine, *merum*, was regarded

as truly uncivilized behaviour,[66] something which might be expected of barbarians[67] or drunkards.[68] Moreover, to drink wine neat was viewed as being potentially dangerous,[69] possibly even lethal.[70]

Among the upper classes, negative views were held against excessive eating and drinking. But whereas gluttons were held in utmost contempt,[71] the views on heavy drinking were less condemning.[72] Nevertheless temperance was a highly valued characteristic,[73] something to be expected of the members of the elite:

> At times we ought to reach the point even of intoxication, not drowning ourselves in drink, yet succumbing to it; …
> But, as in freedom, so in wine there is a wholesome moderation.
>
> Seneca the Younger, *De Tranquillitate Animi*, 17.8–9

Far from all were temperate: in the literature there are numerous mentions of drinking bouts,[74] and alcoholism was a well-known problem in Antiquity.[75] From the ancient sources we can gather that heavy drinkers and alcoholics could be found amidst the rich as well as the poor, among men as well as women. In this respect there was a marked difference between ideals and morals, and reality.

While we know a great deal about drinking and drinking customs in the core of the Empire, and in particular those of the elite, we do not have the same understanding of these customs in the provincial areas, neither for the Roman army nor for the civilian population. There is a great deal of archaeological evidence from Roman forts along the *Limes* and in northern Britain which suggests that traditional Roman drinking customs were observed at least to some extent. First, there are finds of amphorae and barrels,[76] which show that there was an import of wine.[77] Second, finds which had once constituted parts of drinking sets are common on military sites.[78] Finds from other parts of Britain show a wide range of imported wines, including the exclusive Falernian.[79]

A number of historical sources mention what was drunk in the army; however, they are primarily concerned with field rations and the military *annona*. All evidence suggests that water, or sour wine (*acetum*),[80]

Figure 6.3

Dipper and strainer set from Gainerhall, Lanarkshire.

NMS: FT 5-6

diluted with water, a beverage called *posca*,[81] was drunk when on the march.[82] There are, however, indications that although it was not viewed as appropriate, wine was drunk not only when in camp but also on the march. For instance, it is said that Emperor Pescennius Niger (AD 193–194) forbade his soldiers to drink wine while on campaign:

> He gave orders, likewise, that in the time of campaign the soldiers should not drink wine but should all content themselves with vinegar.
>
> SHA, *Pescennius Niger*, 10

One of the laws in Justinian's *Codex* deals with field rations at the time of Constantius II (d. AD 361), which shows that the soldiers were given wine and sour wine on alternating days.[83] Another late source, Vegetius' *Epitoma rei militaris* (written sometime between AD 383 and 450), also says that wine was drunk within the army. In this it is argued that military supplies under no circumstances must fall into enemy hands, and among the foodstuffs listed as part of these supplies are wine as well as sour wine.[84]

However, there is epigraphical evidence in the form of wooden leaf tablets from Vindolanda (Chesterholm), Northumberland, showing that the army units stationed on the frontier (auxiliaries, so-called ethnic units recruited on the fringes of the Empire), alongside wine, retained some of their old drinking customs, and even brewed their own beer.[85]

The situation in the civilian settlements in the north-western provinces mirrors that of the military. In these areas wine originally came to represent the elite lifestyle, a tradition which stretches back a long time, centuries before these areas became part of the Roman Empire.[86] The popularity of wine led to the introduction of viticulture, for instance in the Moselle valley in the first century AD[87]; and there are even indications that vines were grown in Britain in the second and third centuries AD, possibly earlier, although the scale of this production remains unknown.[88]

There is much to suggest that many drank wine in a Roman fashion, i.e. diluted with water. For example, there are vessels from the province Gallia Belgica which bear inscriptions such as *misce*[89] or *misce copo*,[90] i.e. a request for the innkeeper to mix the wine with water; while from Dorchester, Dorset, is a Rhenish beaker bearing an inscription that has been interpreted as [*Parc*]*e a*[*quam*], i.e. 'spare the water!' – however, only a small part of the inscription survives.[91] Yet other Rhenish vessels from Britain seem to suggest that the

wine was sometimes drunk neat, for they bear inscriptions such as *da merum*, 'serve unmixed wine!'[92] Similarily there are pottery vessels from Gallia Belgica simply stating *merum*, undiluted wine.[93] Possibly this indicates a continuation of the earlier habit of drinking wine neat mentioned by a number of ancient authors.[94]

Alongside the drinking customs introduced from the Mediterranean world, the traditional alcoholic beverages such as beer and mead retained much of their earlier popularity in the north-western provinces throughout the Roman period.[95] And it is clear that the negative sentiments against the drinking of beer voiced by many ancient authors[96] were not shared by the majority of inhabitants in the north-western provinces, or for that matter in other areas such as Egypt,[97] particularly since beer was considerably cheaper than wine.[98] Indeed beer appears to have remained a popular beverage in Roman Britain.[99]

Due to a general dearth of evidence in the case of Roman Britain, it remains unclear to what extent Roman dining and drinking customs were conformed to. A number of reclining terracotta figures found in Colchester, Essex, appear to imply that the habit of lying on couches whilst dining was known at least in that city. Iconographic evidence on tombstones from various parts of Britain showing the deceased lying on a couch seems to confirm that this was a relatively widespread phenomenon.[100]

In summary, it is clear Roman drinking customs, such as mixing the wine, and dining on couches, were observed by some – presumably predominantly the elites – in the north-western provinces, whereas others maintained the old customs of drinking beer and mead, or were behaving as barbarians, imbibing their wine neat.

6.3 Glass associated with wine drinking in a Roman context

In the serving of wine a number of different vessels and objects were utilised in a wide array of materials ranging from simple household pottery and glass,[101] through bronze and silver, to gold and semi-precious stones. The aim of this section is to show how one of these materials, glass, was used.[102] Relatively little scholarly work has been devoted to the study of how glass was used in the Roman world, however. This is not due to a lack of interest, but reflects the difficulties involved in interpreting a limited, geographically dispersed and diverse body of evidence, consisting of:

(a) Written sources in Latin and Greek.
(b) Iconographic evidence.
(c) Epigraphic evidence.
(d) Archaeological material from graves and settlements.

The views on glass expressed by the ancient authors are contradictory; many praised glass for its qualities, whereas others voiced their opinions on glass being cheap and vulgar. One of the primary reasons why glass was so appreciated was because it was considered to be hygienic, and most importantly had no taste. This is clearly mirrored in a passage in Petronius' (d. AD 66) *Satyricon*:

You will forgive me if I say that personally I prefer glass; glass at least does not smell. If it were not so breakable I should prefer it to gold; as it is, it is so cheap.

Petronius, *Satyrica*, 50–51

The words quoted above were spoken at a dinner party by the literary character Trimalchio, a freedman whom Petronius depicts as a depraved and ignorant member of the nouveau riche. In early Imperial times, glass had become cheap,[103] partly as an effect of the invention of glass blowing in the mid-first century BC, and partly as the result of an expansion of the traditional methods of manufacturing glass at that time; however, by the second century AD the latter method was almost entirely replaced by blowing.[104] The cost of glass fell so sharply that broken glass – *vitrea fracta* – was used proverbially to mean 'rubbish'.[105] This led many among the elite to regard glass as vulgar. This is clearly attested in a late fourth century AD source, the *Historia Augusta*, where the Roman Emperor Gallienus (AD 253–268) is claimed to have disdained the use of glass for drinking wine:

He always drank out of golden cups, for he scorned glass, declaring that there was nothing more common.

SHA, *Gallieni Duo* (*The Two Gallieni*), 17.5–7

Not all glass was cheap, however; the intact material from funerary contexts and fragmentary material from settlements show that glass was manufactured in all qualities, ranging from crudely made, everyday household goods to highly elaborate vessels which sometimes far surpass what can be achieved by glass workshops today.[106] This verifies what is known from the written

sources regarding the prices of glass, which spanned from one *as* to thousands of *denarii*. In Apuleius' *Metamorphoses* the vessels used at an exclusive dinner party are described as:

… generous cups of varied appeal but alike in costliness – here skilfully moulded glass, there flawless crystal, elsewhere shining silver and glistening gold …

Apuleius, *Metamorphoses*, 2.19

The cost of glass is also stipulated in a fragment of Diocletian's *Edict of maximum prices* (AD 301) discovered in Aphrodisias, Caria, Turkey.[107] However, even mundane household glass was considerably more expensive than equivalent objects in pottery.[108]

In the ancient sources there are numerous mentions of the various uses of glass in connection with wine: drinking vessels,[109] even entire services made of glass,[110] and glass bottles for storing wine of the finest quality.[111] Martial mentions that wine of low quality was drunk out of glass vessels.[112] But although the literary sources can provide much insight into how glass was used in this period, it is very difficult to link written sources to the specific types, or even categories, of glass vessels found during archaeological excavations. Despite the meticulous and painstaking work of distinguished scholars such as Mary Luella Trowbridge and Werner Hilgers, it has not been possible to make unambiguous identifications. This stems from the fact that both Latin and Greek have a number of general terms which can denote a relatively wide variety of vessels with different uses and functions.[113]

But where the literary sources are of little help, much is to be gained from studying the iconographic material, particularly wall paintings, but also mosaics and depictions on grave stelae and sarcophagi. Notwithstanding that these are never exact representations, they can be used to identify individual types of glass, as well as to give insights into the use of different categories of vessels.[114] For instance, mosaics and frescoes depict wine in a cup,[115] a beaker filled with wine standing next to a bottle,[116] or a jug half-filled with wine.[117] Other depictions clearly show that certain vessels were intended for wine drinking: for example a bottle and a ladle,[118] or a jug and a glass.[119] A number of frescos, most importantly from Pompeii and Herculaneum, portray scenes from inns and bars.[120] In some cases these frescoes are furnished with painted inscriptions that mention it was wine that was served.[121]

On grave stelae and sarcophagi there are representations of funerary meals.[122] From Simpelveld, Limburg, the Netherlands, there is a unique sarcophagus which has carvings on the inside (fig. 6.4). This depicts the deceased – a well-dressed lady reclining on a dining room couch – surrounded by her furniture, household goods and the actual house in which she lived: a Roman-style villa.[123] On the left side of a three-legged table is a low shelf with three glass bottles, two prismatic and one cylindrical. On the right side of the table is a wine service placed on a shelf, which suggests that the three bottles were wine containers.[124] On the top row of this shelf three cups are depicted. On the basis of their shape, Hilary Cool has argued that these are likely to have been glass vessels.[125] On the middle row are two buckets: vessels employed in mixing the wine. On the

floor below are two beaked wine jugs in metal. Archaeological finds of jugs of this type have traces of limescale which demonstrate that they were employed to heat water in.[126]

In an illuminating study of grave material of first and second century AD date from the necropolis at Emona, Slovenia, Mary DeMaine discusses the finds of tableware and their function.[127] By using both iconographic and archaeological evidence, she has been able to demonstrate clearly how the tableware found in a number of these burials represents funerary banquets, and included both drinking vessels and food vessels. The banquet sets consisted of drinking vessels of different kinds – one-handled jugs, ladles, and occasionally also funnels – manufactured in a range of different

Figure 6.4

Sarcophagus from Simpelveld (NL).
Above left: general view; above right: detail of deceased woman reclining on couch; below: the wine service.
National Museum of Antiquities, Leiden

Figure 6.5

Gravestone with a dining scene,
from Bonn (Adenauerallee).

Hans Weingartz

materials such as glass, pottery and bronze. The food was served on plates and bowls, sometimes accompanied by knives. In addition to these, ash urns, unguent flasks, fibulae, and other types of objects, were included as grave gifts.[128]

Vessels of the same kinds as in Emona are depicted in scenes showing banquet settings on grave stelae, monuments, and frescoes from other parts of the Empire (fig. 6.5), and similar types of drinking sets have been discovered *in situ* in dining rooms at Pompeii.[129] DeMaine was also able to show, again by analysing the iconographic material, that each banqueter had an individual cup or beaker. As many graves contained more than one drinking vessel, this would suggest that it was a drinking set, intended for a group of people. Another interesting observation made by her is that two different categories of objects were employed for pouring the wine into the drinking vessels: on the one hand flagons, flasks and jugs; on the other hand ladles. Ladles and jugs were mutually exclusive; when a ladle was utilised there would be no need for a jug, and vice versa.

6.4 Visible and invisible wine – amphorae and barrels as transport vessels in a Roman context

This section provides a brief overview of the vessels used in the transport of wine *within* the Roman Empire, placing particular emphasis on the use of barrels. The point of departure, however, lies beyond the Roman border. In the case of Free Germany, it has been argued that the absence of amphora finds is a reflection of wine having been imported in barrels[130] – organic objects that have left no trace in the archaeological record – rather than the Germanic-speaking peoples abstaining from drinking wine,[131] or being hindered from bringing it across the border.

Finds of amphorae have been made on more than 20 indigenous sites in Scotland and north Northumberland, but the majority were of a common type of oil-carrier: Dressel 20. Only two or three sites have yielded finds of amphorae which could have carried wine.[132] Given that wine was imported in both amphorae[133] and barrels[134] to Roman sites in northern Britain, it is possible that there was an import of wine to native Iron Age sites that has left no trace in the archaeological record. But before we return to this topic – in chapter 6.6 – the use of amphorae and barrels in a Roman context will be discussed.

Before we commence discussion of wine transport, it is important to stress that neither amphorae nor barrels were exclusively used as wine-carriers. In the case of amphorae, these were not only used for the transport of wine, but also olive oil and fish sauces such as *garum*, *liquamen* and *muria*, and to some extent also a wide variety of other food stuffs like preserved olives, dried fruits and nuts.[135] Barrels were in all probability used for the storage, not transport, of beer,[136] as this is a beverage less well suited for long-distance transport.[137] But there is nothing to contradict the possibility that empty wine-barrels could be reused for the storage of locally produced beer. Besides beer we know that barrels served as containers of other liquids, such as the transport of holy water from sacred springs in barrels; there were even transport wagons with fitted barrels.[138]

Analysis of the timber used for the majority of British and Continental finds of barrels showed that this wood originates in the Alpine area. As we know that other types of locally grown timber were readily available on many of these sites, this supports the suggestion that most barrels found were transport vessels carrying wine.[139] This claim is also confirmed by an (albeit limited) number of finds of barrels with microscopic traces of wine.[140] Bung-holes, vent-peg holes and tapping cocks clearly indicate that they had once contained some fermented beverage,[141] and following the arguments above this is more likely to have been wine than beer. In summary, this seems to indicate that barrels were primarily intended for the transport of wine.

As we have seen, wine played a really important

Figure 6.6

Oak barrel from Arbon, Thurgau, Switzerland.

AATG, Rolg Kesselring

role in Roman culture and vast quantities of wine were transported across the Empire. There is ample evidence for this transport, but it is very biased in nature and consists predominantly of amphorae finds. Amphorae – large, sturdy vessels manufactured in a material, pottery, which is virtually indestructible – are highly visible and easily recognisable in the archaeological record. Other types of vessels were also employed in the transport of wine, but in sharp contrast to the amphorae these were manufactured in materials that are normally poorly preserved: wood or leather. So although archaeological evidence for the use of barrels is relatively limited,[142] the historical sources, epigraphic and iconographic material suggest an extensive use of these.

The iconographic evidence for the use of barrels shows how they were used for the transport of liquids in military as well as civilian contexts from the first to the fourth centuries AD.[143] Representations of barrels have been found on graves and other monuments, and miniature 'barrels' were manufactured in pottery and glass.[144] Representations on funerary and other types of monuments show how wine was transported in barrels on barges along rivers.[145] In some cases they show how the liquid was poured from an amphora into the barrel,[146] and on others that both amphorae and barrels

were transported on the same boats.[147] In one case, an amphora found in the river Saône near Lyon had a stopper made from a wooden barrel. This confirms the idea that amphorae and barrels were transported together.[148]

To my knowledge there are no archaeological finds of wine-skins, and yet both historical and iconographic evidence testify that wine-skins were widely used in short-distance transport.[149] In addition to this, there is some iconographic evidence for wine being transported from the vineyards to nearby cities and harbours using wagons with mounted-on leather tanks.[150]

The conditions of preservation are of profound importance: barrels were manufactured in a material subject to decay, and in a material which must have constituted an excellent fuel for frozen soldiers. Barrels are particularly prolific on the military areas along the Roman *Limes*, and seem to have survived through secondary use as ready-made well lining (fig. 6.6).[151] To some extent this distribution reflects the use of barrels in army supply, but it can also be argued that it mirrors a manner of making wells within the military. It has to be stressed that there are, as is the case in Britain, a number of finds from civilian contexts.[152] There are also single finds salvaged from the sea.[153] The date of the barrels falls within a time span from the Augustan period to the third century AD, with a majority of finds dating to the first and second centuries AD.[154] Although there is much to support the argument that barrels were important transport vessels, the actual number of finds is fewer than 200.

All this clearly demonstrates that amphorae were far from being the only type of transport vessels employed. Having said this, I do not want to devalue their role in the transport of wine, since millions of amphorae sherds bear clear testimony to their tremendous importance. In fact, amphorae form one of the most common kinds of archaeological artefacts in the Mediterranean area.[155] What I do want to emphasise is the biased nature of the material and the consequences of this, namely rather biased research. Amphorae have attracted a great deal of scholarly interest, resulting in innumerable reports. This focus is due in large measure to the – unintentional – fact of their survival.[156] In contrast, the relatively limited number of publications concerning other types of transport vessels for wine belie their actual importance in antiquity.

Wine was a commodity transported in quantity in antiquity. Most of it went on ships across the Mediterranean and along the major rivers in Roman Europe. This was due to the high costs of land transport in comparison to water transport.[157] The sturdy amphora was highly practical for long-distance sea transport on ships;[158] however, the vessel itself weighed almost as much as its contents (see below). This rendered it less practical for land transport, and there is much to suggest that the wine from vineyards at some distance from the coast was transported in wine-skins by donkeys,[159] on wagons loaded with wine-skins,[160] or on wagons with mounted barrels,[161] to the nearest port where it was drawn off into amphorae.[162] Though there is iconographic evidence for the transport of wine in barrels on wagons,[163] they were better suited for transport in barges and small ships.[164] This is reflected both in the riverine distribution of finds[165] and the many depictions on funerary monuments and other works of art.[166]

Günter Ulbert and George Boon have suggested that in the early Imperial period, before viticulture was established in the north-western provinces, wine was transported in amphorae across the Mediterranean, or in wine-skins from production areas in the northern Adriatic region, and then transferred to barrels in Aquileia or some other port for further shipping along the great rivers – the Danube, the Rhine and its tributaries – in particular to the Roman army, but also to civilian customers.[167] Historical sources confirm the importance of barrels for transport and storage in Aquileia[168] and areas near the Alps[169] from the first century AD and later.[170] Archaeological finds and art also demonstrate that amphorae and barrels were transported together to and within the north-western provinces of the Roman Empire.[171]

It can thus be argued that barrels had certain advantages to amphorae as transport vessels when it came to riverine rather than sea transport. Apart from the fact that both barrels and amphorae were sturdy vessels that could withstand shipment and rough handling, the most obvious one is the barrel's capacity to carry large quantities. Although there is reason to believe that large barrels were more likely to survive in the archaeological record than small ones, as they were used as ready-made lining for wells, sizes between 800 and 1000 litres were by no means uncommon,[172] and there are rare finds of barrels with a carrying capacity of up to 1350 litres.[173] This equals between 30 and 50 amphorae.[174]

Another advantage is that a filled barrel in some aspects is easier to handle than a full amphora, for though it is a burdensome task to roll a barrel, its bulging bilge shape makes it possible for a single person to handle rather large vessels.[175] In fact, one scholar has tellingly described the barrel as 'a container with a built-in wheel'.[176] An empty amphora weighs around 20 kilograms and as it can carry around 25–30 litres of wine; a full amphora must have weighed around 45–50 kilos.[177] A single person can carry an amphora on the shoulder, as evidenced in the iconographical record,[178] but it must have been very heavy indeed. Although it can never be said that the amphora was replaced by the barrel, the advantages of the latter led to its widespread use also in the Mediterranean area in the late Roman period.[179]

To sum up: much of the transport of wine in the Roman era is highly visible in the archaeological record, due to the innumerable finds of amphorae, and consequently this category of material has attracted a great deal of scholarly attention. In contrast, the transport of wine in barrels has left relatively little trace in the archaeological record. Had it not been for the many representations in the iconographic material, and a number of references in ancient literary sources, it would have remained almost invisible.

6.5. Traditional drinking customs in the later prehistoric period

I have suggested that the elites in western, north-western and northern Europe in the later prehistoric period (the pre-Roman and Roman Iron Age) appear to have shared some common values, and to some extent also common customs.[180] The different categories of evidence can also shed light on the customs and ways of different areas in different periods. In the following text I attempt to define the traditional drinking customs of the Iron Age elites, discussing the same phenomena as with Roman drinking customs. What was drunk, and in what fashion? Who were allowed to partake in the feast, and how were they seated? What were the traditional drinking vessels?

There are several difficulties involved in any such enterprise. In comparison to the profound insights into Roman drinking customs, our understanding of those of the Iron Age is more rudimentary. For although there can be little doubt as to what was drunk – beer and mead – our knowledge of other aspects is limited. These difficulties stem from the evidence available for study, in particular the lack of contemporary indigenous literary sources. Roughly speaking, there are three categories of evidence of particular importance in elucidating traditional drinking customs:

(a) Ancient literary sources in Greek and Latin.
(b) Medieval literary sources from the British Isles and the Continent.
(c) Archaeological evidence of Iron Age date from Britain and the Continent.

If we begin with the Early Iron Age elites on the Continent, there are a number of source-critical problems linked to the various categories of evidence. A fundamental aspect of the accounts given in the ancient literature is that these are seen through the eyes of someone living in the Classical world. Recurring genre motifs (*topoi*) in the descriptions of barbarians reflect a strong tendency to either idealise or demonise the peoples beyond the frontiers of the 'civilised world'.[181] The idealisation of other peoples, so-called *Randvölkeridealisierung*,[182] can primarily be viewed as a criticism of contemporary society, involving a sentimental longing for the imagined simplicity of the past: a Golden Age supposedly free of the vices, baseness and corruption which imbued the present.

More often than not, however, the descriptions are of a profoundly negative nature. This may have several reasons: cultural prejudices, conflicting sets of values, and

not least military conflicts. Some of these views stretch far back in time, and indeed many of these descriptions were based to a greater or lesser extent on earlier literary sources rather than eyewitness accounts.[183] An example of how prejudices emanate from different sets of values is the attitude towards drinking. For whereas temperance was a highly valued characteristic, something which was to be expected of the elite in the Graeco-Roman culture (see chapter 6.3), the ability to imbibe vast quantities of mead or beer was viewed as a sign of manliness among the Iron Age elites in north-western and northern Europe.[184]

This stands in stark contrast to the views held on beer and beer-drinking in the Classical cultures, in which it was considered to make men effeminate and weak.[185] These ideas stem from the medical thoughts of the time – namely the idea of the four humours – according to which men were dry and hot. In this notion wine was seen as hot, whereas beer was considered cold and hence an unmanly beverage.[186] (It is worth noting, however, that the negative notions on beer in Roman culture were not shared by the soldiers in the Roman army serving in Britain.)[187] Moreover, the negative sentiments voiced by the ancient authors on the Celts and Germans as being prone to drunkenness[188] – as opposed to the ideal of temperance in the Classical cultures[189] – clearly mirrors this cultural conflict.

Notwithstanding the cautions mentioned above, the written sources are of help in our attempt to understand the traditional drinking customs of the Celts.[190] Several ancient authors mention that the Celts traditionally drank beer and mead;[191] for example Diodorus of Sicily, in his work the *Library of History* (completed in 30 BC):

> Furthermore, since temperateness of climate is destroyed by the excessive cold, the land produces neither wine nor oil, and as a consequence those Gauls who are deprived of these fruits make a drink out of barley which they call zythos or beer, and they also drink the water with which they cleanse their honey-combs.
>
> Diodorus of Sicily, *Bibliotheke Historikes*, 5.26.2

Ancient authors' claim that mead and beer were widely drunk in a Celtic context is confirmed by archaeological material from the early Iron Age. Excavations at the late Hallstatt/early La Tène site of Hochdorf in south-west Germany – a site which was clearly in contact with Classical World, and where they had copied some Mediterranean manners – have yielded a 'brewery',[192] while the princely burial from the same site contained a very large bronze vessel that had once contained some 500 litres of mead.[193]

One problem in trying to establish what characterised the traditional Celtic drinking customs, however, is that there is much to suggest that the elites living in parts of present-day France and Germany were influenced by Etruscan and Greek drinking customs in the early Iron Age. A number of the ancient authors mention an export of wine to these areas,[194] and there is ample archaeological evidence from the late seventh century BC onwards (late Hallstatt period and La Tène period) in the form of imported drinking sets and wine amphorae found in princely graves[195] to support this claim.

Both men and women partook in the feasts, as shown by archaeological and literary evidence. This appears to be a tradition that stretches back at least to the La Tène period and the latest phase of the preceding Hallstatt period.[196] It was argued that this was a result of an Etruscan influence, for unlike the Greek tradition where only courtesans (*heterai*) and not 'honest' women were engaged in the parties, the Etruscan symposia were mixed.[197] I find this reasoning less convincing, however, as it could equally have been an indigenous tradition.

There is also some evidence to imply that the elites in the areas closest to the Mediterranean World had adopted the Greek/Etruscan habit of reclining on couches already in the early Iron Age.[198] What the 'original', uninfluenced customs were like, however, is not entirely clear. A passage from a lost work of the Syrian Greek philosopher and historian Poseidonius (*c.* 151–*c.* 51 BC), quoted by the Greek author Athenaeus (*fl. c.* AD 200), may reflect some traditional customs:

> The Celts place hay on the ground when they
> serve their meals, which they take on wooden
> tables raised only slightly from the ground.
>
> Poseidonius, frag. 15, *FGH* 2A (1926), 229–30
> (= Athenaeus, *Deipnosophistae*, 4.151e)

Several ancient authors give accounts which are similar to that of Poseidonus. The Roman geographer Strabo (64 BC – after AD 21) states that Celts sat on straw on the floor, and Diodorus of Sicily (*fl. c.* 30 BC) mentions the use of wolf or dog skins placed on the ground.[199] Vast amounts of food, predominantly meat, in particular pork, and lavish quantities of drink, were served at the feasts. Not to bring bad luck to the participants, the servants always moved sun-wise, and hence served the drink to the guest's left,[200] and the communal vessel was passed around by a slave:

> They sip a little, not more than a small cupful, from
> the same cup, but they do it rather frequently. The
> slave carries the drink round from left to right and
> from right to left; ...
>
> Poseidonius, frag. 15, *FGH* 2A (1926),
> 230 (= Athenaeus, *Deipnosophistae*, 4.152c–d)

Such communal vessels included drinking horns. A number have been found in rich graves, and in the case of Hochdorf these were of gargantuan size.[201] This has led many to believe that drinking from horns was an indigenous tradition. The reality, however, seems to have been far more complex. For although drinking from horns manufactured in various materials is a tradition that stretches back at least to the Bronze Age in northern Europe,[202] there is much to suggest that the particular role this type of vessel was given in later periods was a result of influences from the Mediterranean world. It has been convincingly demonstrated how the Celtic elites took up this tradition – which ultimately originates from Scythia – from the Etruscans and Greeks in the early Iron Age.[203] Archaeological finds indicate that this tradition was transferred from the Celts to the Germans in the last century BC.[204]

Although the Medieval written sources are not tainted by the prejudices, idealisations and other problems typical of many of the ancient texts, it is important to remember that these are often imbued with Christian, and occasionally also Classical, thoughts, ideas and motifs instead.[205] There is much, however, to suggest that the early Medieval Irish texts reflect earlier customs in that area, and in my view may shed light to some extent on other areas too.

The literary sources, *e.g.* the *Táin Bó Cúailnge*, mention both the traditional beverages – *cuirm*, ale, and *mid*, mead – as well as *fín*, wine.[206] The feasts were held in the chieftain's or the king's hall – a large wooden edifice.[207] The roof was held up by large wooden pillars, a large hearth was placed in the centre, and there were compartments along the walls. In each of the latter a hero and his closest followers would be seated,[208] placed according to their rank and status:

> His drinking house was afterwards arranged by
> Conor according to deeds, and parts, and families;
> according to grades, and arts, and customs, with a
> fair view to the fair holding of the banquet.
>
> *Mesca Ulad*, 1889, 13;
> quoted from Arnold 1999, 79

Figure 6.7 (above)

Small bronze cup, Lamberton, Berwickshire.
Diameter 117 mm.

NMS: FT 51

Figure 6.8 (below)

Wooden cup, Dervaird Moss, Wigtownshire.
Length 135 mm.

NMS: ME 70

There is nothing to indicate that the traditional Iron Age drinking customs involved such a wide array of different objects and vessels as the Roman drinking customs; on the contrary, focus was placed on the communal drinking vessel, the cup or drinking horn: both were symbols of kingship and power.[209]

If we turn to Scotland, our knowledge is much more limited than in the case of Ireland. The literary sources which specifically concern this area are very limited in number, and the body of archaeological evidence is small. In the *Gododdin* there are countless mentions of mead, whereas beer is referred to less often;[210] archaeological evidence intimates that the tradition of brewing both mead and beer stretches back at least to the Bronze Age.[211] Whether or not others than the warband and its warlord partook in the feasts is not stated in the *Gododdin*.

Drinking horns may have been used in the pre-Roman Iron Age. There are two examples of what are often viewed as drinking horn terminals mounted as horns on the well-known Torrs pony cap (Kirkcudbright-shire) that dates to the third to second century BC.[212] Single finds of bronze cups have also been made, such as the four cups found in Lamberton Moor, Berwickshire (fig. 6.7). These cups, it is worth noting, are relatively small in size.[213]

While there were high-status and high-value drinking vessels, the majority must have been made in other materials. In south-east England a category of Late Iron Age pottery vessels has been identified as 'beer bowls';[214] in contrast, there is no evidence to suggest that pottery fulfilled that function in Iron Age Scotland. Pottery vessels of indigenous make were predominantly large bucket-shaped vessels, which appear to have been used for the storage and cooking of food.[215]

Wood, on the other hand, was in all probability widely used, as shown by a number of finds of wooden vessels, ranging from large kegs to small cups, that have been made in bogs and other waterlogged contexts in Scotland.[216] Wooden cups or bowls of Roman Iron Age date have, for example, been discovered at Dervaird Moss, Wigtownshire (fig 6.8) and Ardgour, Argyll.[217] In the case of the latter, the size ranges from around 15 to 26 cm in diameter.[218] It is possible that these could have served as communal drinking vessels.

In the case of the Germanic peoples, feasting was of tremendous significance for the elites,[219] and in particular for the chieftains or kings, as a mechanism for enforcing and preserving the social order.[220] The feast – *symbel* (Old English) or *sumbl* (Norse),[221] meaning the gathering of ale – was, as the name suggests, primar-ily a drinking party.[222] The ancient authors refer to beer or mead as the native alcoholic beverages,[223] which is attested to by later literary sources such as *Beowulf*.[224] Archaeological evidence verifies that the tradition of brewing beer, fruit beer and mead stretches far back in time – at least to the Bronze Age, possibly earlier – and continues throughout the Iron Age,[225] the Middle Ages, and to early modern times.[226]

Although these feasts were predominantly for males, high-ranking women also participated.[227] Participants were placed according to their status in the mead hall,[228] something which could be a cause of hostility and quarrel.[229] The mead halls where the feast took place resounded with merry laughter, boisterous talk,[230] song and music.[231] The queen was at the centre of everyone's attention as she served the men in their order of rank.[232]

There is ample evidence to show that, at least in the later Iron Age, the Germanic tradition was to be seated. The king sat in the seat of honour, *heahsetl* (Old English) or *hásæti* (Norse), at the centre of the longer wall of the mead-hall, with the hearth in front,[233] surrounded by his followers, who sat on mead-benches. In fact, to 'sit on the mead-bench' was an expression for still dwelling among the living.[234]

Among the Germans, the communal vessel was passed from hand to hand by the followers themselves,[235] served by the queen[236] or by a servant.[237] The drinking horn occupied a place apart among the different types of drinking vessels used by the Germans.[238] Both Julius Caesar and Pliny the Elder refer to how the Germans used the horns of aurochs to drink from,[239] but this was not an indigenous tradition in the true sense of the word, as discussed above. According to an Anglo-Saxon law, it was strictly forbidden to put down the vessel during certain feasts;[240] this may explain the preference for vessels such as conical beakers, drinking horns, and other vessels that were difficult to put down.

To summarise, the congruence between certain aspects described in the ancient and Medieval sources seems to hint at a certain degree of continuity over time and space. There was a clear hierarchical order in how the participants were seated and served, and communal drinking vessels were either brought round or sent round. During these feasts, vast quantities of beverage would be consumed, as the ability to imbibe large amounts of alcohol was viewed as a sign of manliness. Although these social gatherings were predominantly male, the evidence implies that women partook at least to some degree.

6.6 The evidence for export of wine beyond the borders of the Roman Empire

Several scholars – most importantly Olwen Brogan – have argued that the import of Roman drinking sets to Free Germany in all probability was accompanied by an import of wine. Yet there is a total absence of archaeological finds from Scandinavia to support this claim, and the archaeological evidence from the rest of Free Germany is very slim indeed. It has been suggested that this lack of archaeological evidence is a reflection of wine having been imported in barrels, thus leaving no archaeological remains but some linguistic traces. These views, it is argued, are also supported by historical evidence.[241] In what follows, the different categories of evidence – archaeological, historical and etymological – which can shed light on whether wine was exported to Free Germany and the native sites north of Hadrian's Wall, will be explored.

Amphorae are not common, but have been found on a significant number of Iron Age non-Roman/native sites north of Hadrian's Wall – 21 to date.[242] Although not all have received the attention of amphora experts, the vast majority are Dressel 20 olive oil amphorae, and there are only two attested finds of wine amphorae: a Gauloise 12 from Carlungie I, Angus[243] (fig. 6.9) and a Pélichet 47/Gauloise 4 from East Brunton, Newcastle Great Park, Northumberland.[244] Additionally, from Broch of Gurness, Orkney, there is a single find of a Camulodunum 185A/Haltern 70 which is likely to have carried ripe olives in *defrutum*, *defrutum* on its own, or *sapa*. Andrew Fitzpatrick argues that *defrutum* and *sapa* were sweet wines,[245] whereas other scholars consider these to be concentrated grape must.[246] Discussing sweet wines, Pliny the Elder defines *defrutum* and *sapa* as grape must that had been reduced by boiling.[247] This non-alcoholic syrup functioned as both a sweetener of wine and a preservative.[248] The dominance of Dressel 20 amphorae – olive oil carriers – can be explained by a number of factors:

- In contrast to wine amphorae which could, and often were, reused, oil amphorae could not be refilled with oil but were normally discarded after use as remains of the oil turned rancid. (It has been argued on the basis of *post cocturam* graffiti on the vessels that there was some reuse of oil amphorae in Roman contexts for dry storage, for instance grain.)[249] Hence it cannot be ruled out that the amphorae could have carried other types of food stuff, but most probably the finds of oil amphorae reflect a native interest in importing olive oil, albeit in what appears to be small quantities.

- In the Roman world the amphora was the sole type of carrier used for the long-distance transport of olive oil. In contrast, wine was transported in both barrels and amphorae. This may explain the dominance of oil amphorae on military sites in northern Britain; study of the archaeological assemblages from a significant number

Figure 6.9

Gauloise 12 amphora, Carlungie, Angus.
Height 350 mm.

NMS: HD 1742

of military sites in Scotland has demonstrated that these assemblages have an average of around 80 percent Dressel 20.[250]

Thus the dominance of olive oil amphorae in native contexts is an indicator of some interest in importing oil – possibly for culinary use – but not necessarily an indication of a disinterest in importing wine, as this could have reached the area in barrels,[251] and as we shall see, bottles. Bottles constitute yet another category of archaeological finds which may reflect an import of wine, albeit on a small scale, as seen in the many finds of cylindrical and prismatic bottles on non-Roman/native sites in Scotland and north Northumberland. These have been found on 38 sites, making it the largest category of Roman glass.[252] (In contrast to the area north of Hadrian's Wall, only one single bottle has been found in Scandinavia, and there are very few finds in Free Germany as a whole.[253])

There are, however, a number of difficulties interpreting this material. First, there is no way of telling whether or not these vessels carried any contents when they reached native hands. Like amphorae and barrels, these bottles were transport vessels for beverages and foodstuffs, including wine and olive oil.[254] As with amphorae, there is little to suggest that bottles were traded in their own right, so unless they were emptied of their contents before being traded on to native hands – a scenario which in my view is improbable – their value must thus have lain in their contents rather than that of the container. It is also evident that these vessels had secondary use, as shown by the heavy wear on many finds.

Second, we do not know what the original contents of these vessels were. The diameter of the neck can give an indication of whether they carried a liquid or not, and most preserved necks are relatively narrow. We know that in its original Roman context these types of bottles were carriers for both wine and olive oil. Analysis of residues found in bottles have been made in a very limited number of cases, demonstrating that they had once contained oil.[255] A number of Roman literary sources show that high-quality wine was stored in glass bottles.[256] Similarly, the iconographic evidence, most importantly the sarcophagus from Simpelveld, Limburg, the Netherlands, shows that wine was stored in and served from cylindrical and prismatic bottles (fig 6.4).[257]

Brogan's idea of the wine having been imported in barrels was vehemently rejected by Rolf Nierhaus, who argued that amphorae rather than barrels were used at

the time when the drinking sets reached Free Germany, and that barrels were a relatively late phenomenon.[258] There is little to uphold Nierhaus' objections though, as there is abundant evidence for the use of barrels in the Roman provinces north of the Mediterranean area – particularly along the *Limes* – from early Imperial times onwards (see above). This cannot be taken as proof for an export beyond the frontiers actually having taken place, for there is not a single find of a barrel beyond the border of the Roman Empire, neither in Free Germany nor in native contexts north of Hadrian's Wall. Hence, this problem remains unresolved.

If we turn to the written sources, the evidence is scanty, ambiguous and chronologically diverse, with a minimum of four centuries between the earliest and latest source. In Julius Caesar's *Gallic War* (written around 50 BC),[259] it is claimed that the Germanic peoples did not import wine:

They suffer no importation of wine whatever, believing that men are thereby rendered soft and womanish for the endurance of hardship.

Caesar, *De Bello Gallico* 4.2

This can either be interpreted in its literal sense, or be understood to mean that they had acquired a taste for wine, and that attempts were made to prohibit the import, as it was believed to make them weak.[260] In a work written a century and a half later, Tacitus (*c.* AD 56–*c.* 120)[261] mentions the import of wine to parts of Free Germany in his *Germania* (written in AD 98):

The Germans who live nearest to the Rhine can actually get wine in the market.

Tacitus, *Germania*, 23

Third and finally, there is a passage in Justinian's *Codex*,[262] a law prohibiting the export of wine, olive oil and *liquamen*, i.e. fish sauce, to the barbarians.[263] This law was constituted in the time of the Roman Emperors Valens (AD 364–378) and Valentinian I (AD 364–375), i.e. in the turbulent late Roman period.[264] This passage clearly shows that there had been an export of wine to the areas beyond the Empire before this law was ratified, but it does not say to which areas.

The long-term contacts between the Roman and Germanic cultures also left linguistic traces, and there was an exchange of loanwords for new phenomena and new types of objects borrowed or exchanged.[265] In other words, those loanwords of Latin origin found in the Germanic languages in all probability reflect not only the borrowing of the word itself, but also the actual phenomenon or object.

The English word *wine*, the Gothic *wein*, Old Saxon *win*, and Old High German *win*, stem from Latin *vinum*[266] and constitute an early example of a loanword in the Germanic languages. Not surprisingly, the same loanword was incorporated into the Celtic languages too, in Old Irish *fin*.[267] However, as pointed out by Kleberg[268] and others, this is not the only loanword found in the Germanic languages indicating a first-hand acquaintance with this alcoholic beverage. The word for purchasing, the Gothic *kaupôn*, Old Saxon *côpôn*, and Old High German *kuofôn*, stem from Latin *caupo* – wine merchant. The Germanic **kaupon*, **kaupian* thus originally meant to pursue trade with a *caupo*, i.e. an innkeeper, wine merchant.[269] It is important to stress that the linguistic evidence yields no information on which Germanic groups would have imported wine from the Roman Empire. The historical evidence, supported by the archaeological evidence, proves that there was an import of wine to the areas adjacent to the *Limes*. If and to what extent wine reached areas distant from the Roman frontier thus remains unknown.

6.7 The Roman glass – parts of drinking sets?

As we have seen, the overwhelming majority of Roman vessel glass found on non-Roman/native sites in Scotland and north Northumberland are of types which were associated with the serving, drinking and storing of wine in their original, Roman setting.[270] In the following, I will explore whether the glass found on the native settlement sites, and other related categories of finds, such as ladles and sieves in bronze found in ritual deposits in moors and lochs, may in some cases originally have formed parts of imported Roman drinking sets. The fragmented state of the glass, however, makes any venture to explain the function of these vessels a difficult task; the obstacles, difficulties and source-critical problems that arise from this will be discussed in greater detail below.

Before doing so it is essential to have an idea of what constituted a Roman drinking set – in other words the material culture used in connection with the Roman drinking customs. Therefore, this section brings together the discussions from chapters 6.2 and 6.3. Our knowledge is based in part on intact material from funerary contexts within, as well as beyond, the borders of the Roman Empire. In addition to this archaeological evi-

dence, the iconographic record forms an important source of information.[271] To make in-depth studies of these materials lies beyond the scope of this work, and hence I have used published analyses as a point of departure for this discussion.

Scholarly studies concerning the question of whether Roman drinking customs were introduced beyond Rome's borders sometimes give the impression that there was a standard Roman drinking set. The evidence from within the Roman Empire does not support this; rather it suggests some variation in which objects would make up such a set. Moreover, objects that we tend to see as typical of Roman drinking sets on the basis of finds from funerary contexts in Free Germany are not always as frequent within the Roman Empire. This is the case with sieves – ladle and sieve sets are frequently part of the Scandinavian finds of imported Roman drinking sets, but in contrast are much less common in Roman contexts.[272] Sieves seem to have had several functions in a Roman context. Some scholars consider them to be parts of drinking sets – primarily to sieve spiced wine[273] – whereas others consider them as typical kitchen utensils.[274] In all probability both views are correct.

Another difficulty we face is that our way of classifying the material may not conform at all to how it was once perceived. Take the category 'jug' as an example: these were manufactured in different materials, such as metal, pottery or glass. Whereas the glass or pottery jugs often functioned as serving vessels for the actual wine,[275] evidence seems to suggest that at least some metal jugs were employed for the heating and serving of warm water.[276] The latter is of course a part of the Roman tradition of mixing wine with cold or warm water. In the central parts of the Empire other means of heating the water were employed, namely hot-water heaters.[277]

As we have seen in chapter 6.2, there is much to suggest that wine was drunk in a similar manner in large parts of the Roman Empire. The Roman drinking customs included a number of different steps in the serving of wine, and to perform these a relatively wide range of paraphernalia was used. But whereas these vessels and objects can be said to be typical parts of drinking sets, there was some variation as to what constituted such a drinking set. Wine was always stored – and transported – in larger vessels, be it amphorae, barrels or bottles. Hence it had to be poured into a smaller serving vessel such as a jug, or a ladle was used to scoop the wine either from these larger vessels or from a *crater*. The latter appears to have been a serving vessel rather than a mixing-bowl in Roman context.[278]

Before this was done the wine was sieved, as it was thought to have a smoother, rounder taste if sieved. But to what extent metal sieves rather than cloth were used is not clear. The next step involved the mixing of wine and water, and there is much to suggest that the wine was mixed straight in the glass.

In a Roman context drinking vessels were never shared; each participant had his or her individual cup or beaker. These were made in a wide array of materials ranging from the simple, such as pottery or glass, to the exclusive, such as silver or semi-precious stones. As we have seen in chapter 6.2, these drinking vessels had two features in common: they were comparatively small in size, and they had a flattened base or foot, making it possible to place them on the table regardless of whether they were full or empty.

Let us look closer at one example that has been discussed already and which demonstrates the variability of what could constitute a drinking set in Roman context, namely the Roman necropolis at Emona, Slovenia. The banquet sets found in the burials of this necropolis included both drinking and food vessels. Although a variety of materials were made use of, glass was employed relatively extensively, not only for cups and beakers, but also for jugs and occasionally also ladles. Mary DeMaine's analysis of this material demonstrated that jugs and ladles were mutually exclusive in the drinking sets. The archaeological finds, as well as iconographic representations of banquets, established that the wine was either served with a ladle from a larger vessel, or poured from a jug. In other words, these objects were mutually exclusive in the drinking sets found.[279]

This emphasises the point made previously; a standard drinking set does not seem to have existed in the Roman world. Instead a number of vessels and objects could be combined to form a wine-drinking set:

(a) Drinking vessels of various kinds: cups, beakers and small bowls in pottery, glass, metals such as silver, or semi-precious stone.
(b) Metal *craterae* (used in a Roman context as serving vessels).
(c) Ladles to serve the wine with, or jugs or flagons used for the same purpose, or
(d) Bottles, which were used both as storage and serving vessels.
(e) Jugs that were used to heat water in, or hot-water heaters of a 'samovar-type'.

Turning to Free Germany, imported Roman drinking sets have attracted a great deal of scholarly interest since the 1930s,[280] and although there has been some debate concerning their function, the generally accepted view is that they were utilised for drinking. A drinking set in this area could consist of:

(a) Drinking vessels of various kinds: cups, beakers and small bowls in glass of Roman manufacture; or, on rare occasions, imported Roman beakers in silver; or drinking horns with bronze mountings of indigenous make; or pottery vessels, mostly of local manufacture, in rare cases samian/*terra sigillata* vessels; or locally made wooden vessels.[281]
(b) A ladle, or a ladle and sieve set.
(c) A large bronze vessel – cauldron/bucket.
(d) Jugs in bronze or silver, which have been found in a limited number of burials.[282]

With few exceptions, all glass vessels in the sets were drinking vessels such as cups, beakers and small bowls,[283] all other vessels in the drinking set being in bronze, silver, pottery or wood. In a knowledgeable study of the drinking sets from this area, Jürgen Kunow discussed the variations in what these sets were made up of. In this he differentiated between drinking sets of 'Roman character' and 'Barbarian character'. The former consist entirely of objects of Roman manufacture, whereas the latter also include vessels of indigenous make. In the sets of 'Roman character', however, the so-called mixing vessels sometimes were replaced by cooking vessels. Kunow argues that this was not a result of misunderstanding, but rather a practical solution, using what vessels were available.[284]

If we compare this material with that from an area in Scandinavia where relatively few graves have been discovered[285] – the island of Öland, in the Baltic Sea – a different picture emerges. In an exemplary study of the glass from the fortified settlement Eketorp II, Ulf Näsman was able to show that a wealth of imported glass – both provincial Roman and from the Cernjachov culture (i.e. Goths living north-west of the Black Sea) – reached the site in the last phase of the Roman Iron Age and the Migration period (AD 250/300–550).[286] Although this site dates to a time when drinking sets were no longer imported, it nevertheless sheds light on the difference between material from funerary contexts and settlements. There is not a single piece of imported bronze, a fact which Näsman attributes to the extensive recycling of metal.[287] Contrary to this, there is very little evidence to show that glass was remelted. The fact that most glass vessels are merely represented by a single sherd is a result of most sherds having been swept up, Näsman argues. Taking only material from funerary contexts into consideration, Öland appears to be rather poor, with relatively few foreign goods. In contrast, the material from settlements and fortifications implies a fairly large import.[288]

The analogies referred to above give an idea of what constituted a drinking set. On the basis of this, it is clear that a number of categories of imported Roman vessels and objects found in non-Roman/native contexts in Scotland and north Northumberland were of types that may be linked to drinking sets:

(a) Drinking vessels in glass: cups, beakers and small bowls.
(b) Drinking vessels in pottery: cups, beakers and small bowls.
(c) Serving vessels in glass: jugs, flagons and flasks.
(d) Serving vessels in pottery: jugs and flagons.
(e) Ladles, strainers and *paterae* in metal.
(f) Jugs in metal.
(g) Vessels for the storage, transport and serving of liquids, possibly wine: bottles.
(h) Vessels for transport of liquids and semi-liquids, occasionally wine: amphorae.

Appendix B is an attempt to bring together the evidence in the form of a simple table. The study of the glass (i.e. the categories a, c and g) rests on the result of my own research, whereas the information on categories b, d, e, f and h is based on the published results of other scholars.[289] *Paterae* are taken into account in the present study, although the function of these is far from obvious. Werner Hilgers has shown how these were used both as libation vessels in rituals and as drinking vessels for wine in everyday life.[290] The other related types of finds, ladles and strainers, are considered primarily to have had a profane use.[291] In Appendix B not all finds of these types of objects are included: I have chosen to omit all finds from hoards due to the difficulty of linking these to the use of glass and other related vessels on the settlement sites.[292]

I have chosen to include the imported pottery in this table, despite the fact that this category of Roman imports in a number of cases is poorly documented in the original publications. The identification of function/category rests solely on other scholars and the traditions within this field of research. Thus types which are classified as cups, for instance Dragendorff 27, are included, whereas types classified as bowls are not.

Some overall patterns are visible. First, as noted in chapter 4.3, a significant proportion of the assemblage of Roman glass found on non-Roman/native sites north of Hadrian's Wall principally consists of vessels linked to the serving, drinking and storing of wine in their original, Roman context: namely cups, beakers, small bowls, jugs, flagons and bottles (fig. 4.5). I argue that it is likely the bottles were linked to wine, although they could be used to store and transport other liquids. The non-Roman/native assemblage of glass resembles the assemblage of glass from Emona, Slovenia, where a relatively wide range of objects was manufactured in glass.

Second, if one includes the Roman pottery, the importance of the cup becomes even more apparent. Twenty-two sites with cups, beakers or small bowls in glass or pottery (including five sites with uncertain identifications) are known from north of Forth-Clyde line. Fourteen sites with cups, beakers or small bowls in glass or pottery (including two sites with an uncertain identification) have been found south of this line. (Three of these sites – one of which is north of the Forth-Clyde line – are of early Medieval date, however.) Some of the types of cups or beakers found in Scotland and north Northumberland are of the same types as those found as parts of drinking sets in Free Germany.[293]

This brings us to the central question of this chapter: did drinking-sets exist that were similar to those found in funerary contexts in parts of Free Germany? If we look at the funerary gifts from the few indigenous graves containing Roman glass north of Hadrian's Wall, there are no such sets, but rather single vessels: a cup, a beaker or flask, a jug. On the whole this part of the assemblage is very limited indeed, and we need to study the material from other types of contexts. The task of linking different categories of finds to each other in an attempt to establish if such sets existed is, however, surrounded by a series of source-critical problems:

- What was the function of the different categories of material? Can we be certain these categories were used in the serving of wine?
- Are the different objects contemporary?
- If the material can be/is contemporary, can the different objects be linked to each other, i.e. were they parts of drinking sets?
- Can the finds from hoards – metal ladles, strainers, *paterae* and jugs – be used as an argument that these were accessible at settlement sites? In other words, did this type of material reach the settlement sites without leaving much trace, perhaps due to extensive recycling?

The function of the glass has already been discussed, and there is much to suggest that this material was linked to wine-drinking in its original Roman context. The amphorae are much more difficult to link to wine, as discussed in chapter 6.6, since they are dominated by olive oil containers. The presence or absence of this category of find thus yields little information on whether or not wine was drunk. As argued in chapters 6.3 and 6.6, wine may have reached northern Britain in barrels, a material rarely visible in the archaeological record.

Glass, pottery and other types of imported Roman material which form part of this study can have relatively extended periods of production and use. In a number of cases we know for certain that they cannot be linked. For instance, at East Coldoch fragments of a fourth-century beaker as well as fragments of prismatic bottles (which date from the mid-first to the mid-third century) were found on the site. It seems highly unlikely that these finds can be linked to each other. In many other cases, the date of the material remains uncertain, for although different categories in theory can be contemporary, this may not have been the case.

Ladles, strainers, *paterae* and jugs in metal are rare on settlements, and have predominantly been discovered in hoards. It is noteworthy that several of the types found in non-Roman/native contexts in the area beyond Hadrian's Wall are of exactly the same vessel types retrieved as parts of drinking sets in Free Germany, and are also found on Roman forts along Hadrian's Wall and on the Antonine Wall.[294] Some copper alloy vessel types used in wine-drinking sets were made from multiple component parts, so although copper alloy was mostly recycled, individual parts can occasionally be found on settlement sites.[295] For example, parts of a *patera* handle and the remains of what may have been a sieve were discovered in the broch at Hurly Hawkin, Angus.[296] On the whole, however, there are few remains of the original metal vessels, although scientific analysis – in particular the presence of zinc – shows the extent of recycling Roman copper alloys in objects of indigenous manufacture.[297]

Given these problems, is it at all possible to show that these finds may have formed parts of drinking sets? On the majority of settlement sites where finds associated with wine drinking have been made, these are only represented by one or two categories of finds. There may be several explanations for this:

(a) That there was an extensive recycling of Roman metal in native contexts, with the result that we do not find such a wide range of objects as would originally have been in use on the site; hoarding evidence suggests that copper alloy vessels did reach native hands.[298] As noted previously, analysis of indigenous copper alloys shows that Roman metal was remelted, and this may be true also of Roman glass.

(b) That the inhabitants could not access a wider range of imported Roman goods. Access to Roman goods was limited in some areas, as appears to be the case in northern Scotland.[299]

(c) That the inhabitants of many sites could not afford a wider range of imported Roman goods. Many of the richer sites are situated in relatively rich agricultural lands, and if we believe that the Roman imports were the result of peaceful exchange they must have had goods to trade with.

(d) That they only had interest in one category of vessel. This is probably the case with some of the drinking vessels, for on a number of sites in northern Scotland only cups or beakers were found. The cup or beaker was a highly charged symbol of lordly power, which explains its fundamental importance in a native context. In some regions which were in conflict with the Romans, the import of only a limited range of objects – like cups and beakers – may disclose a disinterestedness in Roman culture, or a negative view thereof.

(e) That objects such as *paterae*, possibly also ladles and sieves, were only used in religious rituals which were performed at liminal locations such as moors and lochs, and not in profane contexts such as the holding of feasts on the settlements.

Put together, the evidence indicates that drinking sets did occur on a number of sites, despite the fact that we very rarely find the whole range of categories used on one and the same site. In my view the near total absence of metal vessels such as cauldrons/buckets,[300] and the very few finds of ladles and sieves, may not be a reflection of these never having reached the native settlement sites, but rather is a result of the extensive recycling of Roman metal. There is also variation between sites. The majority of sites on which only one category of find was made are less likely to have had access to the whole range of vessels that constituted a drinking set. It may reflect that the inhabitants were less wealthy, less influential or lived at a great distance from the Roman border, and thus had less access to Roman goods. There is also a chronological aspect to take into consideration: much of the material which is dated – both glass and the samian – dates to the first three centuries AD. With one possible exception, this is the time-period when wine-drinking sets could have reached native sites.

6.8 Bringing the threads together – can Roman drinking customs be traced in Roman Iron Age Free Germany and Scotland respectively?

Anthropological research has clearly demonstrated the fundamental importance of feasting in stratified societies. The holding of feasts and the giving of gifts functioned as one of the fundamental mechanisms for elites to gain influence and exercise political power over the population, thus enforcing and preserving the existing social order. Although this feature was shared by the Iron Age cultures in western, north-western, northern and central Europe, these differ in a number of other ways, differences which were made manifest in the material culture.

Roman drinking customs involved a great deal of paraphernalia employed in the various steps in the serving of wine. Each participant in the party had an individual vessel to drink from, in a wide variety of shapes and materials, but typically small and with a foot or flat base for placing on the table. In contrast, the traditional Iron Age drinking customs evolved around the communal vessel – the cup, bowl or drinking horn – which normally would have been large, and in the case of the drinking horn impossible to put down unless it was empty. The only other vessels mentioned in the literary sources as part of the drinking customs are large cauldrons in which the traditional alcoholic beverages – mead, beer, or fruit beer – were fermented.

In Free Germany, elite burials of Roman Iron Age date – i.e. graves containing a wealth of goods of indigenous manufacture and Roman imports – often include drinking sets. These sets consist either exclusively of objects of Roman production or of both Roman and local craftsmanship. Though it cannot be proven beyond doubt, the strongly fragmented glass from non-Roman/native sites in Scotland and north Northumberland may once have formed parts of drinking sets resembling those in Free Germany. How widespread this phenomenon may have been is impossible to establish.

In my view, the imported drinking sets found in funerary contexts in Free Germany reflect an under-standing of Roman drinking customs. Had the Germanic elites' objective been to maintain the traditional drinking customs but nevertheless make use of highly valued, imported objects, one would have expected a narrower range of objects, and moreover different types of arte-facts which would have been more suited to their needs. The Roman drinking vessels in glass – cups, beakers and small bowls – could only hold small amounts of liquids, which would have rendered them impractical as communal vessels. The discovery of two, occasionally even three and four, drinking vessels in the same burial also seems to confirm the suggestion that these were individual rather than communal vessels.

Whether the adoption of Roman drinking sets was accompanied by an import of wine is difficult to ascertain, as touched upon already. The rarity of amphora sherds and the absence of finds of barrels beyond the borders of the Roman Empire frustrates any attempt to reach a definitive conclusion in this matter on the basis of the archaeological material alone, but other categories of evidence can be of some assistance. Historical sources imply that there was a limited export of wine to the Germanic tribes living closest to the border, and there is etymological evidence in the Germanic languages which indicates a first-hand acquaintance with wine. To sum up: there is proof for a small-scale export of wine to the areas bordering the Empire, but if, and to what extent, wine was exported to the areas further from the boundaries of Rome is difficult to ascertain; indeed, residue analysis of finds from waterlogged contexts so far has shown that alternatives to wine were used.

Is it then possible to envisage Roman drinking customs even though wine was rarely, if ever, drunk? I believe this may well be the case, given that there would be little use for imported drinking sets in the indigenous drinking customs. What were then the underlying reasons for this limited use of wine? The most probable explanation is that the cost of wine was too high, and hence substituted by some other beverage. Fruit beer strongly resembles wine in colour, has a high alcoholic content, and the substitution for wine would not be perceptible to an outside viewer. Rather than 'investing' their resources in something which had to be consumed within a limited period of time – lest it should go sour – they opted for imports of a more durable nature.[301] Thus they may well have copied Roman wine-drinking customs and employed wine-drinking sets. This agrees with Hilary Cool's argument concerning one category of finds: 'it seems more likely that the strainers are reflecting a taste for infused beer'.[302]

The attempt to copy Roman drinking customs attested by the occurrence of drinking sets was not mere mimicry, an imitation lacking a true understanding. Had this been the case, the drinking sets known from Free German graves would have been much more varied, and there would have been a great deal of misunderstanding of what ought to constitute one of these sets. Anthropological research has shown that for cultural as well as practical reasons, the adoption of foreign customs always involves a certain degree of reinterpretation and alteration of the phenomena in question. This would account for the displacement of so-called mixing vessels for cooking-vessels in some Germanic graves, and the replacement of wine with local beverages.

Although it can be argued on the basis on the various categories of evidence that some Iron Age elites in Free Germany and Scotland had a knowledge of – and insights into – certain aspects of Roman culture,[303] it cannot be assumed that all elites possessed it. Some may have had a personal experience of Roman culture, as a result of serving in the Roman army, for instance, and thus had a real understanding of the proper use of these objects. Other possible ways for the transfer of knowledge are through peaceful exchange, either gifts or more importantly trade. Whichever was the case, direct contact must have been a necessary prerequisite for the transmission of customs and knowledge. And in those cases where the Roman imports passed through several hands, the understanding of the original meaning and function must have been, if not lost, at least distorted on the way.

In my view there is nothing to suggest that the introduction of Roman drinking customs among some of the Iron Age elites came to replace the older traditions; rather it is likely that it functioned as a complement, as argued by Fraser Hunter in the case of Roman Iron Age Scotland.[304] One the one hand there would have been large feasts involving a large number of people sharing a communal vessel in a traditional manner, on other occasions only a small elite would partake in parties or ceremonial gatherings drinking in a Roman manner. It is important to underline, however, that Roman imports could also have functioned as communal vessels. Jeffrey Davies has argued that in Welsh indigenous contexts samian bowls of Dragendorff Type 37 functioned as communal drinking vessels.[305]

6.9 Knowledge as an instrument of power

Using the archaeological evidence – and in particular burials of the elites from Roman Iron Age Free Germany – as a point of departure, it is clear that there was a marked interest not only in Roman objects, but also in Roman ideas and customs. In the following, I attempt to explain why knowledge derived from Roman culture appears to have been of such fundamental importance.

Despite a long-term interest in the transmission of ideas, knowledge and technology within archaeological research, these studies have often remained in the shadow of the study of material goods and the mechanisms of exchange. The last two decades, however, have seen a focussed beam of light on the study of how knowledge was transferred between cultures, stemming especially from the anthropologist Mary Helms' work *Ulysses' sail: An ethnographic odyssey of power, knowledge and geographical distance* (1988). Addressing only the tangible remains – in this specific case, merely regarding the Roman imports as highly visible exotica, objects of trade and exchange – gives a one-sided view of the broader interaction between Romans and natives, and obscures a more complex reality.

Helms has convincingly shown how the elites in stratified societies exhibited not only an active interest in obtaining status objects of foreign origin, but more importantly in procuring knowledge from alien cultures and of distant areas as a means to achieve influence or maintain political power.[306] For the basis of influence and power in stratified societies – i.e. the very essence of inequality – does not lie only in the asymmetrical distribution of wealth in terms of access to food, material goods and shelter, and the possibility to redistribute these resources in order to place people in social debt, and hence in a subservient position,[307] but also in what Helms called the 'asymmetry of knowledge'.[308]

In 1978 Mary Douglas and Baron Isherwood argued along similar lines to Helms a decade later, namely that the elite's greater access to information and knowledge could be used to exclude the rest of society, or to use their own words, functioned as a 'weapon of exclusion'.[309] The inability to understand the significance and meaning of objects owned by the elite, the lack of knowledge or the failure to recognise these, are all highly intimidating and hence function as a social barrier against those of lower social standing.[310]

In the archaeological record at least three closely interrelated forms of transferred ideas/knowledge can be detected:

(a) Technology, crafts and skills.

(b) The transmission of ideas.

(c) 'Intellectual imports', a term designating the import of foreign objects as well as the knowledge of how to use them in a correct manner, derived from the same culture.[311]

If we leave the introduction of new technologies aside, as this does not concern the questions addressed in this chapter, and focus on the transmission of 'pure' ideas as well as 'intellectual imports', it is important to stress that these do not represent an arbitrary choice. Rather, they appear to be the result of an active selection, representing ideas/goods of practical value, and more importantly of great politico-ideological value in the recipient culture.

Moreover, the adoption of alien ideas, customs and the import of foreign objects does not mean that these phenomena remained identical with those in the originating culture. For cultural as well as practical reasons, these were always redefined and reinterpreted to a greater or lesser degree.[312] Anthropological research has shown that the extent of reinterpretation covers a wide spectrum, from only slightly altered to totally recontextualised (i.e. the objects were given an entirely new function and meaning).[313] The greater the spatial, temporal, cultural, and institutional distance from their origins, the less of their original function and meaning will be known and understood.[314]

Igor Kopytoff and Arjun Appadurai have pointed to yet another fundamental aspect which has to be taken into consideration in any attempt to discuss whether an imported object should qualify as an 'intellectual import' or not, namely the 'life history' or 'biography' of the object.[315] Stuart Needham has argued that these life histories or life cycles are often obscured from the archaeologist's view: we know where, when and how an object was deposited, and often where and when it was produced or extracted; whereas we know little of what happened between these two 'nodes' in space and time.[316]

I would argue that in most cases we must assume that a direct contact was a necessary prerequisite for the transmission of knowledge to qualify an object as an 'intellectual import', and that goods that have passed through a number of hands through exchange may retain little of their original meaning. It has been claimed that it is only through gift giving and gift-exchange that objects could maintain their original meaning, and that commodities were stripped of any kind of ideas and knowledge attached.[317] Nevertheless, there is much to

suggest that any form of peaceful exchange which has involved direct contact, such as gifts, gift exchange or trade, could be a medium of a transference of ideas and knowledge.

Although elites have often made use of alien ideas and knowledge of distant areas as instruments of political influence and power, they could also be viewed in negative terms as being potentially dangerous.[318] At the risk of pointing out the blatantly obvious, hostilities, conflicts and wars sometimes – though far from always – lead to a strong reluctance to introduce the ways, customs and material culture of the enemy. This may well have been the case in parts of Roman Iron Age Scotland, whereas there is much to indicate that other parts, in particular those inhabited by the Votadini, were Roman allies.

The value of the imported Roman objects was not just because they constituted emblems of the elite, i.e. functioned as status symbols. To use the imported drinking sets in a 'correct' manner required knowledge both of and from the powerful Roman Empire. These objects functioned as weapons of exclusion,[319] not only in economic terms but also in cultural ones, and thus served as a means to consolidate the elites' dominating position in society through the asymmetry of knowledge.[320]

The fundamental importance of knowledge as a political instrument has been stressed in several of the sociologist Pierre Bourdieu's works.[321] Bourdieu's models can function as powerful analytical instruments in the study of societies, past or present, and in particular, the notion of 'capital'.[322] Not just material wealth is distributed asymmetrically in a society, but also access to other forms of resources. Not surprisingly, knowledge, what Bourdieu has termed cultural capital, is essential as a means to gain influence and power.

Bourdieu differentiates between three types of cultural capital:

(a) The embodied state, i.e. knowledge gained through a great deal of labour.[323]

(b) The objectified state, i.e. material objects which presuppose knowledge to be appropriated, such as works of art.[324]

(c) The institutionalised state, i.e. knowledge in the form of formal education.[325] An important aspect of cultural capital is that the kind of knowledge which is valued is linked to the lifestyle of the elite – what Bourdieu has termed legitimate taste.[326]

The objects which are endowed with the greatest power, that function as 'weapons of exclusion'[327] or 'paraphernalia which separate',[328] are those which not only represent great material wealth, but which require 'cultural capital' as well.[329] Cultural capital of different forms not only functions as a means for the elite to distinguish itself from the rest of society; often it serves as a vehicle for strengthening the position of individuals or families within society by differentiating them from others in the leading classes.[330]

The glass and other objects which constituted Roman drinking sets can thus be said to represent objectified cultural capital, which in turn was strongly linked to cultural capital in the embodied state, i.e. they required knowledge to be used in an appropriate way. Thus the glass was a potent weapon in the struggle for political influence.

Notes

1. An obvious difference between the areas is that Scandinavia is situated at some distance from the actual border, whereas Scotland and Northumberland were not. Yet there are – in my view – striking similarities in the archaeological assemblages of Roman Iron Age date which justify further exploration.
2. Andersson 1983–85.
3. Little attention has been paid to this matter in Scotland and north Northumberland. See, however, Curle 1932a, 313, 346.
4. Gram 1911; Grüß 1931; Broholm 1960, 289 (analysed by B. Gram in 1919).
5. Ekholm 1934, 28–29.
6. Klindt-Jensen 1949, 27–29.
7. Kleberg 1934, 7–8; Kleberg 1942, 23–24.
8. Brogan 1936, 218.
9. Werner 1950.
10. Nierhaus 1954, 253–55.
11. Kunow 1983.
12. Hilgers 1969.
13. Kunow 1983, 69–80.
14. Nelson 2005, ch. 6.
15. Garnsey 1999, ch. 1.
16. Weeber 1993.
17. Examples of this are funerary inscriptions and signs for bars and inns; see Armini 1929.
18. See Ingemark, Gerding & Castoriano 2000, 32, 119, 124.
19. Paterson 1982.
20. Vines were even grown in the cities; see Jashemsky 1967.
21. Kleberg 1934; Kleberg 1942; Packer 1978; Ellis 2004.
22. A. Mau, s.v. 'Convivium', *RE* IV (1901), cols 1201–8; A. Mau, s.v. 'Comissatio', *RE* IV (1901), cols. 610–19. This view is explained by the fact that several ancient authors, most importantly Cicero, were of this opinion (Cicero, *Epistulae ad familiares*, 9.24.3.)
23. Dunbabin 1993; Dunbabin 2003a. For example in the Greek *symposia*, 'honest' women did not partake (Cicero, *In Verrem*, 2.1.66).
24. G. Binder, s.v. 'Gastmahl, III Rom', *Der Neue Pauly* 4 (1998), cols. 803–6.
25. See, for example Seneca, *Epistulae*, 95.20; Juvenal, *Saturae*, 6.425; Petronius, *Satyrica*, 67.
26. Suetonius, *Divus Claudius*, 5.32; Tacitus, *Annales*, 13.16; Plutarch, *Quaestiones convivales*, 7.8.4 (*Moralia* 712, e–f).

27. Horace, *Sermones*, 1.4.86.
28. Martial, *Epigrammaton*, 10.48.5–6; 14.87; See also Balsdon 1969, 35; Dunbabin 1991; Dunbabin 1995, 252, fig. 9.
29. When the Roman poet Martial (c. AD 40–104) mentioned a tavern with only chairs, it was with utter contempt (*Epigrammaton*, 5.70).
30. Suetonius, *Divus Claudius*, 5.32; Tacitus, *Annales*, 13.16; see also Booth 1991.
31. Columella, *De re rustica*, 11.1.19.
32. Suetonius, *Divus Claudius*, 5.32.
33. D'Arms 1991; Dunbabin 2003b.
34. Balsdon 1969, 44.
35. Balsdon 1969, 35–52; d'Arms 1990, 312.
36. Petronius, *Satyrica*, 72–73.
37. Seneca, *Epistulae*, 19.11; Plutarch, *Quaestiones convivales*, 1. (*Moralia* 612d); d'Arms 1990, 312–14; Peachin 2001, 136.
38. Martial, *Epigrammaton*, 3.60; Suetonius, *Divus Augustus*, 2.74; d'Arms 1990.
39. Macrobius, *Saturnalia*, 7.3.3; Peachin 2001.
40. Pliny the Younger, *Epistulae*, 2.6.3.
41. d'Arms 1990, 314; d'Arms 1995, 305–7.
42. Balsdon 1969, 35–52.
43. Hilgers 1969, 52–53, 156–59.
44. Dunbabin 1993, 127.
45. DeMaine 1990.
46. Glass (Petronius, *Satyrica*, 51; Martial, *Epigrammaton*, 4.85; 12.74; 14.94; 14.115); pottery (Martial, *Epigrammaton*, 14.102); and silver, gold, and semi-precious stones (Pliny the Elder, *Historia naturalis*, 33.2.5; Martial, *Epigrammaton*, 14.113). See also Loewenthal & Harden 1949; Bromehead 1952; Vickers 1996; Stern 1997.
47. In the case of glass vessels of the late Roman period, this was no longer the case. Conical beakers of Isings Forms 106 and 109 had to be emptied before they were placed on the table.
48. Hilgers 1969.
49. Pliny the Elder, *Historia Naturalis*, 14.28.138.
50. Lucretius, *De rerum natura*, 2. 391–92; Martial, *Epigrammaton*, 14.103; see also White 1975, 92–93, 99–102.
51. Hilgers 1969, 150–51.
52. Pliny the Elder, *Historia Naturalis*, 9.53; see also Plutarch, *Quaestiones convivales*, 6.7 (*Moralia*, 692b–693e).
53. Koster 1997, 46.
54. Cool 2006, 143–44.
55. Apicius, *De re coquinaria*, 1.1.2; Pliny the Elder, *Historia*

Naturalis, 14.15, 92–93; Symphosius, *Aenigmata*, 82; Dioscorides, *De Materia Medica*, 5.54; Diocletian, *Edictum de Maximis Pretiis*, 2.17–19.

56 Plautus, *Miles gloriosus*, 832; Plautus, *Trinummus*, 1015; Plautus, *Curculio*, 293; Juvenal, *Saturae*, 5.63.

57 Martial, *Epigrammaton*, 14.116; 14.118. It has been argued that this was a Roman custom, and that the Greeks did not use hot water at their banquets (Athenaeus, *Deipnosophistae*, 3.123; Dunbabin 1993, 127–28; Dunbabin 1995, 258–59).

58 Pliny the Younger, *Epistulae*, 1.15.1–2; Martial, *Epigrammaton*, 6.86; 9.22; 14.103.

59 Cool 2006, 137.

60 Dunbabin 1993, 120–27.

61 Martial, *Epigrammaton*, 14.105; see also DeMaine 1990, 136–40.

62 Dunbabin 1995, 253.

63 Martial, *Epigrammaton*, 11.6.9.

64 Lucian, *Saturnalia*, 2; see also Ingemark 2001.

65 At bars and inns, however, landlords and innkeepers were sometimes accused of cheating, by mixing the wine with too much water (Petronius, *Satyrica*, 39; Martial, *Epigrammaton*, 1.56; *CIL* IV, 3948; see also Kleberg 1940).

66 Seneca, *Epistulae*, 122.6; see also Petronius, *Satyrica*, 41. There were, of course, exceptions to the rule against drinking undiluted wine: in cases of insomnia (Horace, *Sermones*, 2.1.9) or stomach complaints (Celsus, *De Medicina*, 2.30.3) doctors could prescribe neat wine as a form of medicine (Athenaeus, *Deipnosophistae*, 10.429a).

67 Horace, *Carmina*, 2.7.26; Athenaeus, *Deipnosophistae*, 10.427.

68 Plautus, *Curculio*, 77; Ausonius *Epigrammata*, 19.41.9–12. The Emperor Tiberius (AD 14–37), is an example of an alcoholic who was accused of drinking his wine straight. This gave him the nickname *Biberius Caldius Mero* – a wine-imbiber who drank hot, undiluted wine – based on his true name: Tiberius Claudius Nero (Suetonius, *Tiberius*, 42). See also Pliny the Elder, *Historia naturalis*, 14.28, 143.

69 Horace, *Carmina*, 3.19.13–15

70 Pausanias, *Descriptio Graeciae*, 10.23.12–13.

71 See for example Suetonius, *Vitellius*, 13.

72 See Seneca, *De tranquillitate animi*, 17.9; Seneca, *Epistulae*, 83.10–26; d'Arms 1995, 305–7.

73 Plutarch, *Gaius Gracchus*, 1.2; Suetonius, *Divus Julius*, 1.53; Suetonius, *Divus Augustus*, 2.77. See also McKinlay 1948.

74 See for example Petronius, *Satyrica*, 72, 78; Seneca, *Epistulae*, 18.1; 95.21, 122.4–7; McKinlay 1950; d'Arms 1995.

75 Plautus, *Curculio*, 75–90; Terence, *Andria*, 228–32; Cicero, *Orationes Philippicae*, 2.42.107; Pliny the Elder, *Historia Naturalis*, 14.28.139; 14.28.142–48; Pliny the Younger, *Epistulae*, 3.12; Horace, *Epistulae*, 1.1.38; Martial, *Epigrammaton*, 1.28; 1.87; 2.89; Ovid, *Amores*, 1.8.1–18; Plutarch, *Cato Minor*, 6; Plutarch, *Quaestiones convivales*, 3.5 (*Moralia*, 652 f); Suetonius, *Tiberius*, 42; Seneca, *Epistulae*, 77.16; 83.10–26; 95.16; 122.4–6; Clemens of Alexandria, *Stromata*, 2.2; *Philogelos*, 227–30; Ausonius, *Epigrammata*, 19. 41; St Augustine, *Confessiones*, 9.8. See also Rolleston 1927; McKinlay 1945; McKinlay 1946–47; McKinlay 1950; Leibowitz 1967; Jellinek 1976; d'Arms 1995.

76 See ch. 6.4.

77 See Cool 2006, 130–36.

78 Eggers 1966.

79 Sealey & Davies 1984; *RIB* II.6, 2493.12

80 For a discussion on the difference between sour wine and vinegar, see Tchernia 1986, 12.

81 Plutarch, *Cato Maior*, 1.7; SHA, *Avidius Cassius*, 5.3; SHA, *Gordiani tres*, 28.2; Vegetius, *Epitoma rei Militaris*, 3.3. See also F. Wotke, s.v. 'Posca', *RE* XXIV (1953), cols 420–21; Tchernia 1986, 12–14. *Posca* was also drunk by civilians in central parts of the Empire, by those who were so impoverished that they could not even afford cheap wine (Plautus, *Miles Gloriosus*, 837; Plautus, *Truculentus*, 609; Suetonius, *Vitellius*, 12), or too mean to do so (Horace, *Sermones*, 2.115–17; Martial, *Epigrammaton*, 10.45).

82 Davies 1971, 124.

83 *Codex Iustinianus*, 12.37.1.

84 Vegetius, *Epitoma rei militaris*, 4.7.

85 *Tab. Vind.* 182, 14 (Bowman & Thomas 1994, 131–33).

86 There is a vast number of publications written on this topic: see, for instance, Peacock 1971; Frankenstein & Rowlands 1978; Tchernia 1983; Fitzpatrick 1985; Williams 1989; Dietler 1989; Dietler 1990; Fischer 1990; Krauße 1993; Arafat & Morgan 1994; Arnold 1995; Dietler 1995; Carver 2001; Fitzpatrick 2003b; see also Pitts 2005, 143–44; Cool 2006, 131.

87 Cüppers (1970) suggests that viticulture was introduced as early as the first century AD in the Moselle area, i.e., around a century after it was incorporated into the Empire. However, most evidence seems to show that it was in the second and third centuries that production was firmly established.

88 The archaeological evidence for the growing of vines and the production of wine in Roman Britain has traditionally been considered as limited in extent, and on the basis of this and the literary sources, it has been suggested that viticulture never took place on a grand scale in this area. The Emperor Domitian (AD 81–96) prohibited growing of vines in Britain (Suetonius, *Domitianus*, 7.2); and it is argued that it was only after the Emperor Probus (AD 276–282) had lifted previous restrictions on this industry in AD 277 that vineyards could be established again (SHA, *Probus*, 18.8; Collingwood 1937, 78; Frere 1967, 293; Webster & Petch 1967; Williams 1977). Recent research has, however, suggested that there was production of wine in Britain in the second century, too, possibly on a somewhat larger scale than hitherto believed (Brown & Meadows 2000; Brown et al. 2001).

89 *CIL* XIII. 10018, no. 119.

90 *CIL* XIII. 10018, no. 120.

91 *RIB* II. 2498, no. 19.

92 *RIB* II. 2498, nos. 4–5.

93 *CIL* XIII. 10018, no. 116; see also *CIL* XIII. 10018, no. 61 *Merum dal Escipe vita*.

94 Diodorus of Sicily, 5.26.3; Athenaeus, *Deipnosophistae*, 4.152c.

95 Not surprisingly there is ample historical, archaeological and epigraphic evidence for the importance of beer in the areas where this beverage was traditionally drunk. One of many examples are the architectural remains of breweries, which have been discovered in the north-western provinces (Rieckhoff 1992), and brewers are mentioned on funerary inscriptions (*CIL* XIII. 11319; see also Ruprechtsberger 1992).

96 Strabo, *Geographia*, 4.5.5; 17.2.2; Columella, *De Re Rustica*,

10.115–16; Pliny the Elder, *Historia Naturalis*, 14.29.149; 22.82.164; Athenaeus, *Deipnosophistae*, 10.447; Ammianus Marcellinus, *Res Gestae*, 26.8; Julian, *Epigrammaton*, 1.

97   Nelson 2005, ch. 6. For a further discussion, see ch. 6.5.

98   Diocletian, *Edictum de Maximis Pretiis*, 2.10–12.

99   Nelson 2005, 65–66; Cool 2006, 140–43.

100 Alcock 2001, ch. 11.

101 Roman law-texts mention the wide array of materials used for household goods: *Digesta* 33.10.3; 33.10.7.

102 For a discussion of the original function of the individual types/forms found in non-Roman/native sites in Scotland and north Northumberland, see 'Catalogue', ch. 3.

103 Strabo, *Geographia*, 16.2.25: 'one can buy a glass beaker for a copper'. (trans. H. L. Jones 1930). Cicero mentions cheap glass which was shipped from Alexandria in quantity (*Pro Rabiro Postumo*, 40).

104 See for instance Grose 1984b; Grose 1989, ch. 5; Stern 1999; Stern 2008.

105 Petronius, *Satyrica*, 10. See also Martial, *Epigrammaton*, 1.41; Statius, *Silvae*, 1.4.74.

106 For instance, the Lycurgus cup (Harden et al. 1968, 77–79, pl. 2; Harden et al. 1988, 245–49; Freestone 1991, 52–54).

107 Erim et al. 1973; Barag 1987, 113–16; Stern 1999, 460–67; Stern 2007, 374–75.

108 Stern 1999, 462.

109 Martial, *Epigrammaton*, 2.40; 4.85; Pseudo-Vergil, *Copa*, 29; Juvenal, *Saturae*, 5.48; Apuleius, *Metamorphoses*, 2.19; Lucian, *Verae Historiae*, 2.14; SHA, *Gallieni Duo*, 17.5–7.

110 Propertius, *Elegiarum*, 4.37; SHA, *Tacitus*, 11.3; *Digesta*, 33.10.3; 33.10.7.

111 Petronius, *Satyrica*, 34.

112 Martial, *Epigrammaton*, 4.85.

113 Trowbridge 1930 (1922), chs 2–3, 5; Hilgers 1969; van Lith & Randsborg 1985, 415.

114 DeMaine 1990; Naumann-Steckner 1991.

115 Naumann-Steckner 1991, 94, pl. 22; Ceselin 1998, fig. 6 (a fresco from Herculaneum, Casa dei Cervi, Reg. IV, 21, which depicts a skyphos – possibly of a late Hellenistic type).

116 Masseroli 1998, fig. 7 (a mosaic from Tunisia, which depicts a cylindrical bottle of Isings Form 50).

117 Kleberg 1942, 56 (a fresco from Pompeii, Reg. IX 5, 1).

118 Masseroli 1998, fig. 6 (a mosaic; its origin not mentioned. This depicts a jug of Isings Form 13).

119 Ling 1991, fig. 162; Naumann-Steckner 1991, fig. 23a (a fresco from Herculaneum; Archaeological Museum, Naples no. 8644. This depicts a cup of Isings Form 12 (i.e. a Hofheim cup)).

120 Kleberg 1942, 50–52; Ceselin 1998, fig. 10 (a fresco from Hadrumentum, Sousse, Tunisia).

121 Naumann-Steckner 1991, 97.

122 DeMaine 1990, figs. 2b, 3a–c; Ceselin 1998, fig. 11 (a grave stele from Cologne, Germany).

123 Holwerda 1931, Afb. 18a & 18b.

124 In contrast to the iconographic evidence which seems to support the view that these bottles were used for the storage of wine (see ch. 3.23), analyses of residues suggest that they were also used for storing olive oil. It has to be noted, however, that this is based on a very limited number of finds (Cool 2006, 63–64). Given that other types of transport and storage vessels, most notably amphorae, could carry a wide range of liquids, semi-liquids and even solid foodstuffs, it is

hardly surprising that glass bottles could carry different contents.

125 Cool 2006, 137; fig. 15.1

126 Cool 2006, 136–38.

127 DeMaine's analysis was based on a detailed study of the contents of 1,617 graves – most of which included table wares of various types.

128 DeMaine 1990, 130, fig. 1a.

129 DeMaine 1990; see also Petru 1974; DeMaine 1983.

130 Brogan 1936, 218.

131 'They suffer no importation of wine whatever, believing that men are thereby rendered soft and womanish for the endurance of hardship.' (Caesar, *De Bello Gallico* [*The Gallic War*], 4.2).

132 See ch. 6.6.

133 Davies 1971, 131; Fitzpatrick 1992; Fitzpatrick 2003b; Cool 2006, 134–35 (with references).

134 In northern Britain finds of barrels have been made at Bar Hill, on the Antonine Wall (North Lanarkshire) (*RIB* II:4, 2442.9); Inveresk, East Lothian (Crone 2004, 163–67); Newstead, Roxburghshire (Ulbert 1959, 17; *RIB* II:4, 2442.10); Kirkby Thore, Cumbria (Boon 1975, 54, footnote 9); Carlisle, Cumbria; Vindolanda (Chesterholm), Northumberland (*RIB* II:4, 2442.4, 11 & 16) and York (Alcock 2001, 88).

135 Will 1977, 264, see also Davies 1971, 131. Determining the original contents of an amphora can be done in a number of ways. The shape of the vessel can often reveal whether it once held wine, olive oil or some other commodity (Will 1977, 264). Occasionally there are preserved written/painted inscriptions – *tituli picti* – on the amphorae which can also yield information on the contents (Peacock & Williams 1986, 13–16; Manacorda & Panella 1993). Intact vessels have on rare occasions been found in shipwrecks, and some contained residues of fish-bones, oyster-shells, olive-kernels or nuts, thus revealing what the vessel once carried (Peacock & Williams 1986, 17). Chemical analysis can provide an insight into the original contents of an amphora (Formenti & Duthel 1996). Finally, DNA analysis seems to surpass all previous methods. For a discussion of DNA analysis of residues inside amphorae, see Hansson & Foley 2008.

136 Greene 1986, 76. Max Nelson has pointed out the fact that the Celtic god Sucellus, who is often associated with barrels and the tools that coopers employ in the making of barrels, is a beer god. (Nelson 2005, 50). This could suggest the use of barrels as containers for beer in some of the Roman provinces.

137 Beers of most types have a very short shelf life; consequently in most societies – past and present – the production of beer took place not far from where it was consumed (Jennings et al. 2005, 286–87, Table 1; Dietler 2006, 238).

138 A silver patera dated to the Flavian period from Salus Umeritana (Castro Urdiales), Santander, Spain, depicts a 'tank-wagon' being filled with holy water (Molin 1984, 99, 102, fig. 6; Tchernia 1986, 290).

139 Viérin & Léva 1961, 781.

140 Viérin & Léva 1961, 779–80; Boon 1975, 55; Galsterer 1992, 213; Kühlborn 1992, 104.

141 Viérin & Léva 1961, 779–81.

142 Ulbert 1959; Viérin & Léva 1961; Boon 1975; Ellmers 1978; Molin 1984; Tchernia 1986, 285–90; Galsterer 1992; Crone

143 See, for instance, J. B. Keune, s.v. 'dolium', *RE* Suppl. III (1918), cols 342–46; Drexel 1920, Abb. 10–11; Lehmann-Hartleben 1926, Taf. 6, 30, 60; von Massow 1932, 285, Taf. 54–56, Abb. 15, 129–30; Boon 1975, 55; Ellmers 1978; Cüppers et al. 1983, nos. 38, 182–84; Molin 1984; Tchernia 1986, 285–91, figs 2, 4–5.

144 So-called Frontinus bottles, Isings Forms 89/128, are glass bottles in the shape of barrels. The earliest finds of this type date to around AD 100, possibly somewhat earlier (Isings 1957, 107); however, the majority of finds date to the fourth century AD (Cool & Price 1995, 204–6; Price 2005, 157). These vessels are typical of the north-western provinces, and are particularly common in north-west France (Price 2005, 156); this may reflect the widespread use of barrels in this area.

145 The most important example, Trajan's Column, was completed in AD 113. The relief covering the entire column depicts Trajan's Dacian Wars (AD 101–102 and 105–106), and not the situation in contemporary Italy. Several scenes show the use of barrels, and it is interesting to note that not a single amphora is represented on the monument (Lehmann-Hartleben 1926, Taf. 6, 30, 60). See also Drexel 1920, Abb. 10 (Cabrières d'Aigues, Vaucluse, France); von Massow 1932, Taf. 54–56, Abb. 125, 129–30 (Neumagen, Rhineland-Pfalz, Germany). In the case of the latter, Detlev Ellmers has argued that it was in a warship carrying wine barrels, and that this suggests it was army or navy supply (Ellmers 1978, 7).

146 Molin 1984, fig. 6.

147 See, for instance, von Massow 1932, 54–56, Abb. 125, 129–30.

148 Fitzpatrick 2003a, 22–23.

149 Varro, *De Re Rustica*, 2.6, 5; Dionysius Halicarnassus, *Antiquitates Romanae*, 13.10, 3; *Digesta*, 33.7.12, 1; Hug, s.v. 'Saccus', *RE* I (1920), cols 1622–24; Déchelette 1934: II, 601.

150 Real Museo di Napoli (1833), tav. A; for another possible example, see Molin 1984, fig. 11.

151 Ulbert 1959; Crone 2004, 165. Although barrels were primarily reused for lining wells, other forms of reuse are known in a Roman context: at Vindolanda staves were reused as flooring (Crone 2004, 165), and at Droitwich brine tanks were made from barrels cut in half lengthways (Crone 1992).

152 Such as London, Silchester, Wickford and Droitwich (Ulbert 1959, 17, 24; Boon 1975, 54; Crone 1992, 111; Collingwood & Wright 1992).

153 Cool 2006, 20 with references.

154 Ulbert 1959, 24.

155 Peacock & Williams 1986, xvi.

156 Greene 1986, 162.

157 Duncan-Jones 1974, 366–69; Greene 1986, ch. 2; Junkelmann 2006, 59–60.

158 Peacock & Williams 1986, 2.

159 Varro, *De Re Rustica*, 2.6.5; *Digesta*, 33.7.12.1; See also Hug, s.v. 'Saccus', *RE* I (Zweite Reihe; 1920), cols 1622–24; Purcell 1985, 12.

160 A passage in Dionysius of Halicarnassus, *Antiquitates Romanae* 13.10.3, suggests that wineskins could be transported relatively long distances: 'he loaded many skins of wine and many baskets of figs on the wagons and set out for Gaul'.

161 Molin 1984.

162 Purcell 1985, 12.

163 See for instance Molin 1984, figs. 3–5, 7–10.

164 George Boon has pointed to the fact that legal texts of fifth century AD date, postulate a limit of 500 kgs on the heaviest wagons of the Government postal service, presumably to prevent damage to the metalling of the road. This, argues Boon, suggests that heavily loaded wagons were rarely used for long distance transport (Boon 1975, 55). As pointed out above, land-transport was far more costly than transport along waterways (Duncan-Jones 1974, 366–69; Greene 1986, ch. 2).

165 Boon 1975, 54.

166 Ellmers 1978, 13; see also above.

167 Ulbert 1959, 27; Boon 1975, 54.

168 Strabo, *Geographia* (64/63 BC–c. AD 25), 5.1.8; Herodian, *Ab excessu Divi Marci Libri Octo* (3rd century AD), 8.4.4; SHA (probably 4th century AD), *Maximini Duo*, 22.4–5.

169 Pliny the Elder (AD 23/24–79), *Historia Naturalis*, 14.27.133.

170 Finds of coopers' axes and epigraphic material mentioning coopers have been found in present-day France and Germany (Boon 1975, fig. 3; *CIL* XII, 2669; XIII, 744; XIII, 3104).

171 Iconographic evidence: Ellmers 1978, 13.

172 Ulbert 1959, 26; Boon 1975, 55; Galsterer 1992, 213; Collingwood & Wright 1992, 1.

173 Galsterer 1992, 211.

174 This calculation is based on the size of large barrels (800 to 1,350 litres) in comparison to the standard Roman unit for measuring liquids such as wine – the amphora quadrantal – that is around 26 litres using modern units of measurement (H. Chantraine, *RE* XXIV, s.v. 'quadrantal' (1964)).

175 For a depiction of dockers rolling barrels aboard a ship, see Ellmers 1978, fig 16.

176 Twede 2005, 255.

177 Will 1977, 264.

178 A Roman mosaic from Piazzale delle Corporazioni at Ostia illustrates this; see Will 1977, 265.

179 Tchernia 1986, 288–91.

180 See ch. 5.2.

181 Arnold 1999, 72.

182 Tierney 1960, 214.

183 Champion 1985.

184 Grønbech 1931 II: 162; Magennis 1985b, 129.

185 Interestingly, Caesar claims that the Germanic peoples thought that wine-drinking made them 'soft and womanish' (Caesar, *De Bello Gallico*, 4.2).

186 For a discussion see Nelson 2005, 33–34.

187 For a discussion on beer in Roman Britain see Nelson 2005, 65–66; Cool 2006, 140–43. For example beer was drunk at the Roman fort of Vindolanda on the Stanegate (Bowman & Thomas 1994, 131–33) and in a number of areas under Roman supremacy, such as Egypt, the Iberian Peninsula and Gaul (Nelson 2005, 67–70).

188 Plato, *Leges*, 1.637d–e; Diodorus of Sicily, 5.26.3; Tacitus, *Annales*, 11.16; Tacitus, *Germania*, 22; Athenaeus, *Deipnosophistae* 10.432; Ammianus Marcellinus, *Res Gestae*, 15.12.4.

189 McKinlay 1948; McKinlay 1950.

190 The use and definition of the terms 'Celt' and 'Celtic' are

1992; Collingwood & Wright 1992; Cool 2006, 129–35.

far from unproblematic (see ch. 5).

191 Diodorus of Sicily, 5.26.2; Dionysius of Halicarnassus, *Antiquitates Romanae*, 13.11(16); Athenaeus, *Deipnosophistae*, 4.152c; Pliny the Elder, *Historia naturalis*, 14.29. 149; 22.82.164.

192 Stika 1996.

193 Biel 1985, 130.

194 Athenaeus, *Deipnosophistae*, 4.150d, 4.152c–e; Dionysios of Halicarnassus, *Antiquitates Romanae*, 13.11.1; Diodorus of Sicily, 5.26.2; Ammianus Marcellinus, *Res Gestae*, 15.12.4.

195 There is a vast number of publications written on this topic; see, for instance Christlein 1963–64; Tchernia 1983; Dietler 1989; Dietler 1990; Fischer 1990; Krauße 1993; Arafat & Morgan 1994; Arnold 1995; Dietler 1995.

196 The well-known female grave from Vix, Burgundy, France dated to *c.*480 BC (i.e., the latest phase of Hallstatt D) included – amongst other elite markers, such as a four-wheeled cart – an enormous bronze *crater* of Greek manufacture. There are also female graves from central and southern Germany of La Tène date which contained drinking sets (Arnold 1995, 154, 160).

197 Arnold 1995, 160.

198 The tradition was originally Iranian, and taken up by Assyrians, Medes and Lydians, perhaps under the influence of the Scythians. These customs were later introduced in the Greek world, from which it was transferred to the Etruscans, and eventually to the Celts (Krauße 1993; Krauße 1996). Objects like the Hochdorf 'kline' (a reclining couch) bear testimony of this (Biel 1985; Enright 1996, 134–37; see also Fischer 1990).

199 Strabo, *Geographia*, 4.4, 3; Diodorus of Sicily, *Bibliotheke Historikes*, 5.28.

200 Athenaeus, *Deipnosophistae*, 4.152d.

201 Biel 1985.

202 Krauße 1996, 392.

203 Krauße 1993.

204 Redlich 1977, 66–67; Stjernquist 1977–78b, 131.

205 Enright 1996, 166; see, also ch. 5.2.

206 Mallory 1992, 120.

207 The prehistoric architecture of Scotland is fundamentally different from that of the early Medieval period, and there are no halls of the type found in Scandinavia. However, other edifices could have fulfilled the same function.

208 Jackson 1964, 20.

209 Arnold 1999; see also ch. 5.

210 Jackson 1969.

211 The archaeological evidence for the making of mead- or beer-like beverages in prehistoric Scotland is rather scanty (see Nelson 2005, map 1). Neolithic pot sherds from Kinloch on the isle of Rum had a residue consisting of 'mashed cereal straw, cereal-type pollen, meadowsweet, types of heather (including ling), and royal fern' (Nelson 2005, 12). Analysis of plant pollen found in a Bronze Age cist burial at Ashgrove, Fife, suggested that a beaker filled with mead made from lime honey and flavoured with meadowsweet flowers had been deposited in the grave (Dickson 1978, 112). Another find of Bronze Age date – a 'Yorkshire Vase' from North Mains, Strathallan, Perthshire – may suggest that beer was drunk too: 'at least some food vessels may have contained a cereal-based liquid'

(Cowie 1983, 255–56). For further discussion on Neolithic and Bronze Age beverages from, and brewing in, Scotland, see Dineley & Dineley 2000; McGovern 2009, 137–39.

212 MacGregor 1976a, 146–47; MacGregor 1976b, nos. 285–86.

213 MacGregor 1976a, 149–50; MacGregor 1976b, nos. 292–96.

214 Pitts 2005, 155.

215 Hunter 2007a, 16; Dr Fraser Hunter pers. comm.

216 See Barber 1982; Crone 1993; Earwood 1993; Hunter 1997, 118–119.

217 Maxwell 1950–51, 163–65, fig. 4; Earwood 1993, 60–67, 265, fig. 38. Dervaird (Dalvaird): Canmore ID 78979, Ardgour: Canmore ID 78943; www.rcahms.gov.uk [retrieved 28.06.2010].

218 Maxwell 1950–51, 164.

219 Tacitus, *Germania*, 22.

220 Grønbech 1931 II, 90; see ch. 5.

221 Lönnroth 1997, 33.

222 Bauschatz 1978, 289–91; Magennis 1985b, 127.

223 Tacitus, *Germania*, 23. Strabo mentions what was drunk in Thule: however, whether or not it can be equated with Germanic areas can be questioned (Strabo, *Geographia*, 4.5.5).

224 *Beowulf* 1016.

225 A vessel in the well-known female grave dating to the Bronze Age, found at Egtved, Jutland, Denmark, contained the remains of mead (Thomsen 1923, 184 [analysed by B. Gram]). Analysis of the remains in two drinking horns of the Roman Iron Age found in Skudstrup Mose, a bog in southern Jutland, Denmark, showed that these once had contained fruit beer/wheat beer and mead respectively (Grüß 1931). The remains of a fruit beer – containing barley, bilberry, cranberry, possibly lingonberry and bog myrtle – were found in a bronze vessel in a female grave in Juellinge, Lolland, Denmark (Gram 1911). Analysis of the remains in a cauldron of Östland type found in a grave in Vogn, Mosbjerg, Jutland, Denmark, showed that it originally had been filled with a beer brewed of millet and flavoured with bog myrtle (Broholm 1960; analysis by B. Gram in 1919). Finally, there is a find – a hoard from Havor, Hablingbo socken, Gotland, Sweden – on which scholarly views differ significantly. This consists of a *situla*, a sieve and ladle set, three *paterae*, two Roman bells and a massive golden neck-ring (Nylén 2005). Patrick McGovern has argued that the *situla* once contained a beverage in which 'grape wine was the principle fruit ingredient' (McGovern 2009, 156). Whether this was made of wild grapes or imported wine remains unclear (Professor Patrick McGovern, pers. comm.). Sven Isaksson's interpretation is more cautious; he is of the opinion that there is no positive evidence to show that it was wine (Isaksson 2005, 156). The residues consist of carbohydrates and organic salts according to his analysis. Whether these can be interpreted as the remains of fruit or berry juices – let alone fermented juices – is in Isaksson's view, a question that remains unresolved (Dr Sven Isaksson pers. comm.).

226 The tradition of brewing fruit beer has continued in several areas. In Blekinge (south-east Sweden), for instance, the tradition of making *dros* – a beverage consisting of sloe and crab apples, spiced with juniper berries, wormwood and hops – survived until the mid-20th century AD (Ingrid Ingemark

pers. comm.). Similarly, the tradition of using bog myrtle rather than hops in beer continued in parts of rural Norway until early modern times (Nordland 1969, 216).

227 Lönnroth 1997, 33.
228 *Beowulf*, 1164, For a discussion, see also Enright 1996, 11.
229 *Beowulf*, 1085–96.
230 Bauschatz 1978, 290.
231 *Beowulf*, 89–90, 496.
232 *Beowulf*, 615–24; see ch 5.2.
233 Lönnroth 1997, 33–34.
234 Grønbech 1931 II, 99.
235 Grønbech 1931 II, 91.
236 *Beowulf*, 615–29.
237 *Beowulf*, 494.
238 Grønbech 1931 II, 150.
239 Caesar, *De Bello Gallico*, 6.28; Pliny the Elder, *Historia Naturalis*, 11.45.126.
240 Grønbech 1931 II, 152.
241 Brogan 1936, 218; see also Broholm 1960, 286.
242 1: Broch of Gurness, Orkney – Haltern 70 (Robertson 1970, 208; Hedges 1987 III, 82; Fitzpatrick 1989a, 24).
 – 2: Ardestie, Angus – Dressel 20 (Wainwright 1963, 132).
 – 3: Carlungie I, Angus – Gauloise 12 (wine) (Wainwright 1953, 228; Wainright 1963, 147; Fitzpatrick 2003a, 63; Hunter 2007a, Appendix 1).
 – 4: West Grange of Conan, Angus – Dressel 20 (Jervise 1860–62, 496; Curle 1932a, 287; 388, no. 71; Robertson 1970, Table 4).
 – 5: Constantine's Cave, Fife – Dressel 20 (Wace & Jehu 1914–15, 241; Curle 1932a, 288, 383–84, no. 55; Robertson 1970, 208).
 – 6: Fairy Knowe Broch, Stirlingshire – Dressel 20 (Willis 1998, 330).
 – 7: Bow Castle/Broch of Bow, Gala Water, Midlothian – Dressel 20 (Curle 1892, 68–70; Curle 1932a, 288; 351, no. 1; Robertson 1970, 208).
 – 8: Ghegan Rock, Seacliff, East Lothian – Dressel 20 (Curle 1932a, 288; 354 no. 11; see also Hunter 2009a, 155).
 – 9: Traprain Law, East Lothian – Dressel 20 (Robertson 1970, Table 10).
 – 10: Fast Castle, Berwick – possible Dressel 20 (Hunter 2001a, Table 1).
 – 11: Lilliesleaf, Roxburghshire (Hunter 2001a, Table 1).
 – 12: Bankhead, Darvel, Ayrshire (Robertson 1970, Table 1).
 – 13: Torwoodlee, Selkirkshire – one carrot amphora (Camulodunum 189), one Dressel 20 (Curle 1932a, 368; Piggott 1950–51, 102–3: Steer 1950–51; 110–11; Robertson 1970, 204).
 – 14: Whithorn, Wigtownshire 'probably from Dressel 20' (Millet 1997, 294).
 – 15: Huckhoe, Northumberland – 'south Spanish globular' (Dressel 20?) (Gillam 1959, 257; Jobey 1959).
 – 16: Burradon, Northumberland – 'Spanish amphorae' (Dressel 20?) (Jobey 1970, 78).
 – 17: Belling Law, Northumberland – 'fragments of a large globular-shaped vessel' (Dressel 20?) (Gillam 1979; Jobey 1979).
 – 18: Murton High Crags, Northumberland – 'south Spanish globular amphora' (Dressel 20?) (Jobey & Jobey 1987, 182).
 – 19: Middle Gunnar Peak, Northumberland – 'pinkish-buff amphora' (Jobey 1981, 70).
 – 20: East Brunton, Northumberland – Pélichet 47 (wine) (Burnham et al. 2004, 272–73).
 – 21: In addition to the above mentioned finds, there is a possible find of an amphora from Milking Gap, High Shield, Northumberland, a native site situated in the military zone between the Wall and the Vallum of Hadrian's Wall (Birley 1938, 348).
243 Fitzpatrick 2003a, 63.
244 Burnham et al. 2004, 272–73.
245 Fitzpatrick 1989a, 24–26.
246 Junkelmann 2006, 149.
247 Pliny the Elder, *Historia naturalis*, 14.11. See also Palladius, *Opus agriculturae*, 11.18.
248 Cato the Elder, *De agricultura*, 7.
249 Mattingly & Aldrete 2000, 147–48. Secondary use of oil amphorae, see: van der Werff 1987; van der Werff 1989; *RIB* 2494 (*RIB* II: 6, 33).
250 Fitzpatrick 2003a, 61.
251 Barrels have been found on a number of Roman sites in northern Britain; see ch. 6.4.
252 See 'Cylindrical and prismatic bottles', ch. 3.23.
253 Lund Hansen 1987, 103; ch. 3.23.
254 Alcock 2001, 89; Cool 2006, 62–64.
255 Cool 2006, 62–64 with references.
256 See Petronius, *Satyrica*, 34.
257 See the discussion in ch. 6.3.
258 Nierhaus 1954, 253–55. See also discussion in ch. 6.4.
259 The Gallic wars (58–51 BC), i.e., the Roman conquest of Gaul, were led by Julius Caesar in person. As a result of this, he was uniquely well informed on Gaul and the adjacent areas; however, his accounts cannot be unquestioningly accepted in their entirety. Roman cultural prejudices, and ethnographic ideas which may have their origins in older written accounts have influenced some of his descriptions. In my opinion, however, there is little to suggest that the passage quoted is a literary *topos*, i.e. a genre-motif.
260 Bruun & Lund 1974 II, 39.
261 Tacitus' accounts were based partly on earlier literary works, and partly on information he had gathered from his contacts with a number of people who had come into direct contact with the Germanic areas (Bruun & Lund 1974 I, 24–27).
262 The *Codex Iustinianus*, a compilation of Imperial laws, was finished in AD 529.
263 *Codex Iustinianus*, 4.41.1; see also Ammianus Marcellinus, *Res Gestae*, 27.5.7.
264 Thompson 1966, 14–20; Todd 1975, 41.
265 For a discussion on how such linguistic evidence can be used to shed light on archaeological problems, see Wild 1970, 125–26; Wild 1976, 57–58.
266 Lehmann 1986, 399.
267 Lehmann 1986, 399.
268 Kleberg 1934, 7–8; Kleberg 1942, 23–24.
269 Lehmann 1986, 216.
270 Vessels such as large bowls, plates and jars were associated with the serving of food in a Roman context; see chs 3.1, 3.2, 3.14, 3.16. Some of these probably retained their original function in a native context. It is, however, possible that some vessel types not associated with drinking in a Roman context – primarily large bowls – could have functioned as communal drinking vessels in the native societies, for example large pillar-moulded bowls (ch. 3.1).

271 See, for instance Dunbabin 1993; Dunbabin 1995; Dunbabin 2003a.

272 Koster 1997, 46; Cool 2006, 143–44.

273 Cool 2006, 144. It should also be noted that sieves of a somewhat similar shape to those of early Imperial date were used to sieve the wine employed in the Christian liturgy in the late Roman and early Medieval period (Martin 1984, 111; Cessford 1994). One such *colatorium* has been found in the Traprain Treasure (Curle 1920, 106, fig. 30).

274 Nuber 1973.

275 DeMaine 1990, 136.

276 Cool 2006, 136–37.

277 Dunbabin 1993, 120–27; Dunbabin 1995, 258–59.

278 Dunbabin 1993, 127.

279 DeMaine 1990, 136.

280 There is a vast number of studies published on the finds of Roman imports in Free Germany, as indeed from other areas beyond the border of the Roman Empire. Most important are the corpora of finds by H.-J. Eggers, which deals with material from Free Germany as a whole (1951), and that of U. Lund Hansen, which concern the finds from the Nordic countries (1987). For the area beyond the north-eastern border of the Empire, see V. V. Kropotkin (1970). For discussion of the function of the finds of drinking sets, see, *e.g.*, Ekholm 1934, 28–29; Klindt-Jensen 1949, 27–29; Werner 1950; Nierhaus 1954, 253–55; Lindeberg 1973, 39 ff; Gebühr 1974, 120; Stjernquist 1977–78a, 65–69; Kunow 1983, 69–80. For a discussion on similar finds in the area beyond the north-eastern border of the Empire, see Wielowiejski 1973. Besides the drinking sets, which are found in the entire Free Germany, there is a small group of washing-sets found in an area with very close connections with the Roman culture: Bohemia and Slovakia (Nuber 1973; Kunow 1983, 80–81).

281 Eggers 1951; Lindeberg 1973, 5; Stjernquist 1977–78a, 67–68; Stjernquist 1977–78b; Redlich 1980; Kunow 1983, ch. 5; Lund Hansen 1987.

282 Eggers 1951.

283 Eggers 1951; Hunter 1975; van Lith & Randsborg 1985, 454; Lund Hansen 1987; Lund Hansen 1989.

284 Kunow 1983, ch. 5.

285 Lund Hansen 1987, 444–45.

286 Näsman 1984.

287 Näsman 1984, 7.

288 Näsman 1984, 37.

289 Most importantly on the following works: Curle 1932a; Eggers 1966; Robertson 1970; Hunter 1997; Hunter 2001a. For references concerning the individual sites see Appendix A and/or the CANMORE database.

290 Hilgers 1969, 242–43.

291 Hilgers 1969, 150–51, 166–67.

292 For an overview of these finds, see Hunter 1997.

293 See 'Catalogue', ch. 3.

294 Eggers 1966.

295 Cool 2006, 138.

296 Taylor 1982, 226 no. 8, 228 no 24.

297 Hunter 1996; Dungworth 1997.

298 It has been convincingly argued by Fraser Hunter that many of these deposits were made by the native inhabitants of the area (1997, 117), and not, as advocated by Lindsay

Allason-Jones, by soldiers in the Roman army (1989a, 14).

299 Hunter 2001a, 297.

300 There is a 'camp-kettle' (a bucket) from a crannog at Barean, Kirkcudbrightshire (Curle 1932a, 372).

301 It is interesting to note that as late as in eighteenth-century England, so-called British wine (i.e. fruit beer) was drunk as a substitute for wine – even among the wealthiest – except on particular festivities (McNiell 1956, 238–39).

302 Cool 2006, 143–44.

303 Numerous scholarly works have dealt with what have been considered as borrowings from the Roman culture in Free Germany – the adoption of customs, the transmission of ideas, knowledge and skills. Examples are: Charon's fee, i.e. a Graeco-Roman burial custom which involved the placing of a coin in the mouth of the deceased (Gräslund 1965–66) or, as in some Scandinavian graves of the Roman Iron Age, a glass sherd replacing the coin (Boye 2002); the use of golden finger-rings as a sign of high rank (Andersson 1983–85); the introduction of writing – there is much to suggest that the runes were a Germanic adaption of the Latin alphabet (Rausing 1992); the introduction of Roman board games (Krüger 1982; Kjer Michaelsen 1992; Fonnesbech-Sandberg 2002). For an overview, see Klindt-Jensen 1949; Broholm 1960; Axboe & Kromann 1992.

304 Hunter 2007a, 16.

305 Arnold & Davies 2000, 112.

306 Helms 1988; Helms 1992, 161; Helms 1993, 4.

307 See, for instance, Orenstein 1980; Gosden 1989; Clarke & Blake 1994.

308 Helms 1988, 14–15.

309 Douglas & Isherwood 1978, 89, 113; see also Appadurai 1986, 38.

310 Bourdieu 1980, 245; see also Bourdieu 1984, 2, 173, 228–29.

311 Andersson 1983–85.

312 Kopytoff 1986, 67; Helms 1993, 4; see also Shils 1981, 13, 78, 89.

313 Helms 1988, 207; Thomas 1991, 187; Vandkilde 2000, 28–33.

314 Appadurai 1986, 56.

315 Kopytoff 1986; Appadurai 1986, 41.

316 Needham 1993, 166.

317 Vandkilde 2000, 32–33.

318 Helms 1988, 50.

319 Douglas & Isherwood 1978, 85.

320 Helms 1988, 14–15.

321 See, for example Bourdieu 1980; Bourdieu 1984; Bourdieu 1986a, ch. 3; Bourdieu 1986b; Bourdieu 1988; Bourdieu 1990; Bourdieu 1998.

322 For a discussion, see Calhoun 1993.

323 Bourdieu 1986b, 243–44.

324 Bourdieu 1986b, 243, 246–47.

325 Bourdieu 1986b, 243, 247.

326 Bourdieu 1980, 229; Bourdieu 1984, 173.

327 Douglas & Isherwood 1978, 89, 113.

328 Bourdieu 1980, 238.

329 Bourdieu 1984, 2, 173, 226, 228–29, 232, 281.

330 Bourdieu 1984.

Conclusions
and summary

A reworked sherd from Traprain Law in East Lothian.

7

Glass and the triad of status and power: wealth, 'generosity' and knowledge

7.1 Some reflections on the methodological problems

WE shall start with a consideration of the methodological implications of working with fragmented material. The basis of this study is Roman glass found on non-Roman/ native sites beyond Rome's primary border in Britain – Hadrian's Wall – that is, present-day Scotland and north Northumberland. In contrast to contemporary Scandinavia with its wealth of intact material deriving from funerary contexts, the lion's share of the Scottish and Northumbrian finds stems from settlement sites, with the consequence that almost all of the material is fragmented to a greater or lesser degree. The fragmented state of the material not only has a number of methodological implications, but also consequences for how we perceive it.

The impression of an intact glass vessel displayed in all its splendour in a museum such as the National Museum in Copenhagen, is utterly different from that of a minute sherd of an *identical vessel* from a Scottish or Northumbrian Iron Age settlement kept in a dusty matchbox that was tucked away in storage for decades after its discovery. The fragmented state of the objects gives the false impression that the import of Roman goods to the Iron Age societies beyond Hadrian's Wall was minor and unimportant, when it actually is a reflection of differing archaeological contexts. Indeed, the glass from Scandinavian settlements is equally fragmented and at first sight not particularly impressive; nevertheless, these also were once intact objects.

Moving beyond the visual and psychological impressions and onto the methodological problems involved in dealing with fragmented material, it is clear that detailed analysis also gives very low estimates of how large the import once was. A significant number of vessels are merely represented by a single sherd or very few sherds. It seems clear that when a vessel was broken, the sherds in most cases were carefully collected to prevent people from cutting their feet and not to waste valuable material. Evidence indicates that at least part of the material was either knapped into gaming pieces and polishers or remelted to form beads and bangles. In my view, much evidence suggests that estimates of the original number of imported vessels are very low, and it seems probable that many of the vessels once imported have become 'invisible' as not a single sherd has survived.

Another methodological problem derived from the fragmented condition is the obstacles involved in identifying it to type and form. To be able to establish whether a fragment derived from a cup or some other type of vessel is fundamentally important in studying a culture where the cup – or rather its alcoholic contents, mead – was of a highly symbolic significance. Yet in many cases the fragmented state of the material prevents close identification. It is possible that part of the assemblage, notably the late Roman glass which is generally thin and hence very fragile, is under-represented.

Despite all methodological difficulties, however, I would argue that the overall picture is clear. In the Roman world a wide range of different types of glass vessels was available, whereas the finds of Roman glass found beyond Rome's northern border in Britain represents a selection of vessel types. Moreover, many of the imported vessels are of variants and subtypes that were relatively rare in a Roman context, and thus are likely to represent a great value in a native context. This is far from the idea of the Iron Age societies as receivers of a random selection of cheap 'beads, bangles and baubles'.

7.2. Revisiting the prestige goods systems model: wealth, 'generosity' and knowledge

The ultimate aim of this work has been to steer away from the lures of reflectionist views – seeing the Roman imports simply as status symbols – and to present a more complex picture of the reception of foreign goods, a picture in which the native societies are depicted not as passive receivers of an essentially random selection of foreign exotica, but rather the opposite, viewing the native elites as a dynamic and discerning clientele, choosing objects of particular political usefulness. This follows anthropological and sociological research, where demand is never a simple response to availability.

Thus it can be argued that certain aspects of the prestige goods systems model can be applied in the study of Roman imports from non-Roman/native sites north of Hadrian's Wall, and that the underlying incentive for this import was essentially political rather than commercial. There is, however, nothing to suggest that any monopoly of Roman/native trade existed in northern Britain, for all the evidence seems to imply that Roman artefacts were widely distributed to the native societies. The absence of such a monopoly points to the existence of other means of limiting social mobility, and legitimating the established political order, through the use of material culture of a foreign derivation. I propose a tripartite model comprising the following elements:

(a) Wealth. Material culture functioned as an instrument of power, and the elites' greater economic resources enabled them to pursue exchange in order to obtain objects of particular symbolic significance or representing great wealth in the indigenous culture.

(b) 'Generosity'. The elites made use of symbolically charged objects to manifest their power. One particularly important symbol of power was the cup and its alcoholic contents; this symbol embodied the chieftain's ability to be generous, and represented the bonds of loyalty between him and his war-band.

(c) Knowledge. The elites strove to obtain not only objects of foreign origin, but also to procure knowledge from alien cultures and of distant areas in how to use these imports in an appropriate way. The inability to understand the meaning of these objects, or the lack of knowledge of how to use them in a correct manner, would have been intimidating, and hence functioned as a social barrier between them and those of lower standing.

One of the most apparent means of limiting social mobility and maintaining influence and power was through the elite's greater economic resources, in other words their wealth. Choosing goods of particularly high quality and presumably great cost – which would have been far beyond the economic means of most inhabitants of indigenous societies – was a way of restricting the availability of prestige goods.

Contrary to some scholars' claims that the Roman imports were low grade, a detailed analysis of the Roman vessel glass demonstrated that in comparison to Roman sites the material was of above-average quality, and includes types which are rare in a Roman context. Moreover, the native assemblage constitutes a relatively narrow range of vessel types in comparison to what is generally found on Roman sites. In native contexts there was a very strong emphasis on objects related to drink: cups, beakers, small bowls, jugs, flagons and bottles.

The fact that the native assemblage of Roman glass does not mirror that typically found on Roman sites, and it includes scarce types, implies it was acquired through peaceful exchange between Roman and native rather than representing loot from abandoned Roman forts, as suggested by some scholars. All evidence seems to indicate that the selection of goods was made by the native elites, and far from being an arbitrary choice of foreign exotica, the present study strongly suggests that these objects were of great symbolic significance within the indigenous culture.

Anthropological and sociological research has showed how material goods can be utilised not merely to denote status, but also to function as the very instrument through which the leading classes could exert power. This worked in two ways. First, resources and objects that were indispensable in maintaining the society's social relations, for instance prestige goods used in important *rites-de-passage* such as puberty rites or marriage, were controlled by the leading members of society, and could be used as an instrument of power. When people needed access to the objects or resources, they were put in social debt and consequently into a subordinate position. Second, material goods had a profound influence on how others perceived a group or an individual, and equally on that individual's self-image, and could thus be employed as weapons of exclusion, i.e. as a means to exclude all but the elite.

There are notable regional differences between different areas in Scotland and north Northumberland. The native sites nearest to the frontier – north Northumberland – have yielded comparatively few finds of Roman glass. Moving beyond this area to southern and central Scotland we find a number of wealthy sites: Torwoodlee, Selkirkshire; Hyndford, Lanarkshire; Traprain Law, East Lothian, and Leckie broch, Stirlingshire. Excavations of sites in northern Scotland have yielded small numbers of imported glass vessels, but in a number of cases objects of high quality and presumably also high value. The reasons for this may be several, but one underlying factor could be the existence of one or more political alliances.

It has been argued that the Romans were acutely aware of the political usefulness of prestige goods within the indigenous societies, and that it was in their interest to help their allies remain in power, by giving access to these goods through trade or diplomatic gifts. These client kingdoms or client tribes constituted a relatively inexpensive means of creating a buffer between Rome and her enemies. One example of this may have been the Votadini tribe who lived in south-east Scotland, a tribe who are commonly viewed as philo-Roman. Traprain Law, East Lothian, constitutes the single most important site within this tribe's area, and on the basis of the glass from this site it can be argued that the tribe had very close contact with the Romans.

Elites in traditional societies make use of symbolically charged objects as a means to manifest and maintain their political power. The importance of these objects can in some cases be reflected in the archaeological record. Drinking vessels in glass – cups, beakers and small bowls – form an important category of Roman imports in the area beyond Hadrian's Wall. The underlying reason for

this importance is that the cup or its alcoholic contents – mead or wine – was a symbol of power in Iron Age societies in western, north-western and northern Europe, as convincingly argued by several scholars on the basis of historical and archaeological evidence. In Germanic literature of Medieval date, for instance, the cup functioned as a metaphor for lordly power, the strong bond between the war-leader and his followers, and the joyful life in the mead hall. The archaeological and historical evidence suggests that the use of these charged symbols was restricted.

In the *Gododdin* – the core of which is attributed to the poet Aneirin living in Din Eidyn (Edinburgh) in the second half of the sixth century AD – having 'deserved one's mead/wine' is a stock metaphor used for those who fell in battle, having fought bravely in the service of the king. Here the poet evokes the bitterness felt by those enticed into tasting the 'ensnaring mead':

> His gifts to the enemy were frequent after the feast;
> he was venomous … ; and before he was buried
> under the sods of earth Edar deserved to drink his
> mead.
>
> *Gododdin* B.34 = CA. ci;, 110–11

Anthropological research of traditional stratified societies has demonstrated that the chieftain's ability to be generous, in particular by providing drink and food, by hosting feasts and giving gifts, is essential for his enjoyment of prestige and power. This 'generosity' can be regarded as a means of creating loyalty by placing someone in social debt. As a result of its psychoactive, behaviour-altering effects, alcohol is at the heart of the feast, working as a social lubricant and creating bonds between the host and his guests. An equally important role of feasting, however, is as a means of shutting out parts of the population, and generating and manifesting the boundaries between the elite and the rest of the population. In other words, the interest in importing Roman glass vessels was a result of their symbolic meaning and their political value as instruments of power.

The imports of Roman vessels, however, are not restricted to cups and beakers alone. As mentioned above, the finds of Roman glass in native contexts north of Hadrian's Wall cover a range of vessels which in their original Roman context were used in the serving and drinking of wine. In addition to these finds, there is a related category of finds – copper alloy ladles, *paterae*, sieves and jugs – found in what have been interpreted as ritual deposits in moors and lochs, and more rarely on settlement sites. Roman drinking sets in glass and metal have also been discovered in substantial numbers of inhumation graves in Free Germany, and this material can be used as an archaeological analogy to shed light on the fragmented and poorly understood settlement material from north of Hadrian's Wall.

In my view the imported drinking sets found in funerary contexts in Free Germany reflect an understanding of Roman drinking customs. This may also have been the case in Scotland and north Northumberland, but due to the dearth of graves this cannot be proved beyond doubt. However, a similar range of material is represented in settlements and hoards, rendering it very plausible. Archaeological and historical evidence clearly shows that traditional Iron Age drinking customs revolved around the communal vessel – the cup, tankard or drinking horn – which would normally have been large and, with horns, impossible to put down unless empty. Had the objective of the elites in the respective areas been to maintain traditional drinking customs while using highly valued imported objects, one would have expected a narrower range of objects and different types of artefacts to have been more suited to their needs.

In contrast, Roman drinking customs involved a great deal of paraphernalia – such as jugs, flagons, flasks, bottles, ladles, sieves, and so-called mixing-bowls – employed in the various steps in the preparation and serving of wine. Each participant in the party had an individual drinking vessel, manufactured in a variety of different shapes and materials, but mostly of relatively small size and able to be placed on a table.

Several scholars have argued that these drinking sets found in Free Germany were accompanied by the import of wine, despite the fact that few archaeological finds appear to substantiate this claim. Not a single amphora sherd has been published from Scandinavia, and the number of finds in the areas in Free Germany adjacent to the Roman frontier is very limited. The scarcity of archaeological corroboration, it is argued, is a reflection of wine having been imported in barrels — a material long since decayed, leaving no trace. Although there is ample evidence for a relatively extensive use of barrels in the forts along the *Limes* and in Britain from early Imperial times onwards, the question of whether these were actually exported beyond the borders remains open to debate. Historical sources imply that there was a limited export of wine to the Germanic tribes living

closest to the border, and etymological features in the Germanic languages indicate a first-hand acquaintance with wine. Equally, the archaeological evidence to demonstrate an export of wine beyond Hadrian's Wall is very limited: amphorae are attested, but it is clear that most carried olive oil, at least in their original incarnation. Bottles form the single largest group of Roman glass on native sites, and although it is quite possible that these originally contained wine, it cannot be proved.

Is it then possible to envisage the employment of Roman drinking customs, even though wine was rarely – if ever – drunk? In my opinion this may well be the case, as there would be little use for imported drinking sets within the context of indigenous drinking customs. What were then the underlying reasons for this limited use of wine? The most probable explanation is that the cost of wine was too high, or supply in quantity was difficult, and hence some other alcoholic beverage substituted it. Fruit beer resembles wine in colour, has a high alcoholic content, and its substitution for wine would not be perceptible to an outside viewer. However, this attempt to copy Roman drinking customs should not be dismissed as mere mimicry or imitation lacking a true understanding of the Roman practice. Anthropological research has demonstrated that the adoption of foreign customs always involves a certain degree of reinterpretation and alteration of the phenomena in question. The reasons for these changes may be of a practical nature, and/or a question of adapting them to fit into the receiving culture.

The evidence suggests that there was a marked interest not only in Roman objects, but also in Roman customs. Thus these imports have not merely been exotic and exclusive articles – objects that could not be produced by local craftsmen – but 'intellectual imports'. This term – coined by Kent Andersson – designates imported objects that had retained much of their original function and meaning, and hence required *knowledge* derived from this foreign culture to use in an appropriate way. The inability to understand the meaning of these objects, or the lack of knowledge of how to use them correctly, would have been daunting for the uninitiated, and thus functioned as a social barrier between the elites and those of lower standing.

I hope this work demonstrates that it is possible to breath new life into an old theory – the prestige goods systems model – by treating not only the material goods, but also bringing in the possible immaterial aspects of foreign contacts in an attempt to understand how indigenous elites maintained and gained political power and influence. For in my view there is much to suggest the idea that the native elites maintained and gained influence and power not merely through possessions in the material objects, but also through immaterial resources in the form of a knowledge of certain aspects of foreign customs and culture.

In some cases, but by no means always, the three different aspects – wealth, 'generosity' and knowledge – could be embodied in a single glass object – an object which was a weapon in the struggle for political power. Addressing only the tangible remains – in this case merely regarding the Roman glass imports as highly visible exotica denoting status – gives a one-sided view of the function of these imports, and obscures a considerably more complex reality.

Appendices

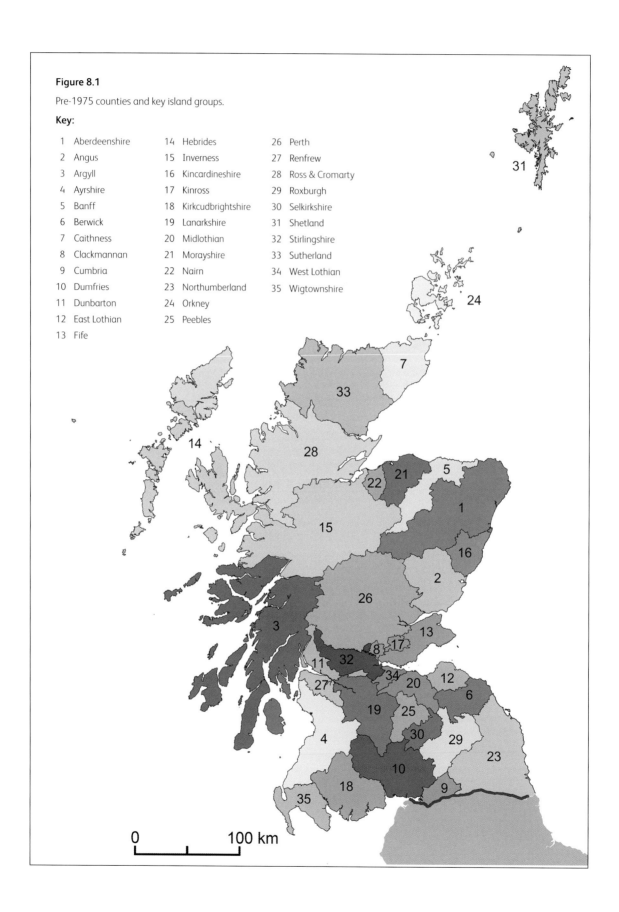

Figure 8.1

Pre-1975 counties and key island groups.

Key:

1	Aberdeenshire	14	Hebrides	26	Perth
2	Angus	15	Inverness	27	Renfrew
3	Argyll	16	Kincardineshire	28	Ross & Cromarty
4	Ayrshire	17	Kinross	29	Roxburgh
5	Banff	18	Kirkcudbrightshire	30	Selkirkshire
6	Berwick	19	Lanarkshire	31	Shetland
7	Caithness	20	Midlothian	32	Stirlingshire
8	Clackmannan	21	Morayshire	33	Sutherland
9	Cumbria	22	Nairn	34	West Lothian
10	Dumfries	23	Northumberland	35	Wigtownshire
11	Dunbarton	24	Orkney		
12	East Lothian	25	Peebles		
13	Fife				

A

A brief description of the sites

THE information presented here is based on the publications I have had access to, which includes printed reports in various journals, as well as unpublished preliminary reports. I have also had enormous help from the CANMORE database,[1] the computerised version of the National Monuments Record of Scotland provided by the Royal Commission on the Ancient and Historical Monuments of Scotland. Equally PASTMAP, which is linked to CANMORE, has proved to be very valuable for my work.

For the identification of materials other than the Roman glass, I have used published accounts. With the identification and dating of Roman pottery, Anne Robertson's work (1970) has been of particular use. Similarly, many of the identifications of beads derive from Margaret Guido's study (1978). Identifications of glass bangles are mostly based on the studies of H. E. Kilbride-Jones (1938a) and Robert Stevenson (1954–56, 1976). The sites are roughly arranged from north to south, following the old (i.e. pre-1975) county divisions for consistency with previous works (fig. 8.1), although the Inner and Outer Hebrides are grouped together in a single category. The following particulars are given for each entry:

- Area code: site number. Site name.
- Map reference (Ordnance Survey).
- Site location.
- Excavation dates.
- Brief summary of archaeological remains.
- Roman vessel glass: each category on a new line, with a unique catalogue number as a subdivision of the site number.
- Other finds of glass.
- Other Roman artefacts.
- Key publications.

The reader should consult chapter 3.26 for discoveries after the catalogue closed in 2007, as these do not feature in the appendix.

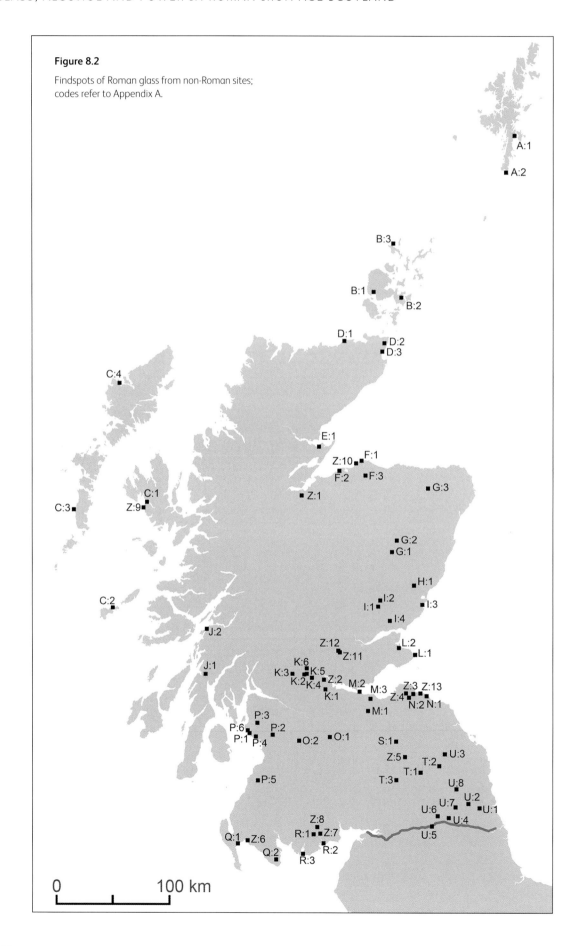

Figure 8.2

Findspots of Roman glass from non-Roman sites;
codes refer to Appendix A.

0   100 km

Shetland

A:1 Clickhimin

- Map reference: HU 464 408.
- Clickhimin is situated in the western outskirts of Lerwick on Mainland Shetland. The site lies on a low isthmus – originally an islet – in a small loch, Clickhimin Loch, very close to the sea.
- Excavated in 1953–57; however, the site was partially cleared and excavated in 1861.
- Archaeological remains: Clickhimin is a multi-period site occupied from the late Bronze Age to the later Iron Age. The Roman material comes from a phase when the site had a wheelhouse. This was created by partially dismantling the broch tower, and lowering it. A stone wall enclosed the settlement.
- Roman vessel glass:
  A:1:1 One fragment of a cast and lathe-turned vessel (Flavian to Antonine). Ch. 3.2.
  A:1:2 One fragment of a painted cylindrical cup (AD 160–260). Ch. 3.8.
- Other finds of glass: six plain yellow beads (Guido class 8); a dumb-bell-shaped bead; and a glass bangle with coloured stripes in blue, white and yellow, Kilbride-Jones type 1.
- Publications: Hamilton 1968; Fojut 1998.

A:2 Old Scatness

- Map reference: HU 3898 1065.
- Old Scatness is situated about 1.5 km from Jarlshof on the southern part of Mainland Shetland.
- Excavated in 1995–2004; the site was first discovered during road construction near Sumburgh Airport.
- Archaeological remains: this well-preserved multi-period site focuses on a broch, later reused for a major wheelhouse, which was surrounded by other wheelhouses. The central structure was rebuilt once again in a later phase to form a cellular house. There were also Norse and post-Medieval structures found on the site.
- Roman vessel glass:
  A:2:1 Fragments from a minimum of one painted cylindrical cup (AD 160–260). Ch. 3.8 & ch. 3.26.
  A:2:2 One fragment of a fourth-century vessel.[2] Ch. 3.26.
- Other finds of glass: a fragmented glass bangle.
- Other Roman artefacts: late Roman pottery.[3]
- Publications: Fojut 1998; Dockrill et al. 2002.

Orkney

B:1 Howe of Howe

- Map reference: HY 275 109.
- Howe (of Howe) is situated 1.5 km north-east of Stromness, Mainland Orkney. The site lies near the shore; the Bay of Ireland is 500 m to the south-east and the Loch of Stenness is 500 m to the north.
- Excavated in 1978–83; however, some excavations took place in 1888.
- Archaeological remains: this multi-period site has remains from the Neolithic to the late Iron Age/early Medieval period. There is no clear Bronze Age phase, indicating a hiatus from the Neolithic to the early Iron Age. During the Roman Iron Age, a broch tower on the site was partly dismantled. In the fourth century AD, six buildings surrounding the broch were pulled down and replaced by a single farmstead.
- Roman vessel glass:
  B:1:1 Two fragments of a beaker of late Roman type with trailed-on decoration (late fourth century AD). Ch. 3.13.
- Other finds of glass: two globular beads of Guido class 14 (one translucent with purple, white and yellow bands, and one colourless with white and yellow bands); two annular beads of Guido's class 8 in opaque yellow; a dumb-bell-shaped bead.
- Other Roman artefacts:
  Samian: a small piece.
  Metalwork: a bronze pin of possible Roman origin; an insect-shaped brooch.
  Other Roman finds: a Roman intaglio in carnelian with agate banding, with an engraved eagle.
- Publications: Ballin Smith 1994; MacKie 1998.

B:2 Mine Howe, Tankerness

- Map reference: HY 5105 0603.
- Mine Howe is situated about 100 m south-east of the cemetery on Churchyard Road, Tankerness, Mainland Orkney.
- This site was originally discovered in 1946 and partly cleared out, but was later resealed and forgotten. Rediscovery in 1999 led to an achaeological survey of the site in that year, and excavations from 2000–05.
- Archaeological remains: in the centre of a mound, a staircase in drystone masonry led down to a corbelled chamber. This site is extremely unusual,

and some role as a ritual gathering place seems assured. Survey and excavations revealed a major ditch surrounding the mound, outside which lay a workshop and other structures.

- Roman vessel glass (fig. 8.3):
  B:2:1 Three fragments from a minimum of one prismatic bottle (AD 43–250). Ch. 3.23, 3.26.
  B:2:2 One fragment of a snake-thread vessel (late second to third century AD). Ch. 3.4.
  B:2:3 Sixteen sherds of unidentified Roman vessel glass, most in pale green. Ch. 3.25.
- Other finds of glass: one cast gaming piece of triangular shape in blue-green (possibly recycled Roman) glass, one cast object of triangular shape in blue-green glass, one fragmented glass bangle, one fragmented spherical bead, and a splinter of opaque blue glass; sherd of decorated Saxon glass.
- Other Roman artefacts:
  Samian: fragments, reused.
  Other Roman pottery: fragments of late Roman coarse-ware.
  Metalwork: brooches.
- Publications: Card et al. 2000.

B:3 Links of Trenabie, Westray

- Map reference: HY 44 50.
- The site lies in sand dunes on the north coast of Westray.
- It is unclear when and by whom the site was excavated, but the finds had been found by 1778. They were donated to NMS in 1827 by Reverend Dr Brunton.
- Archaeological remains: the find is reported to have come from a stone cist, possibly in a tumulus, in an area which also produced Viking Age burials. In a manuscript by Reverend George Low written in 1778, a description of the finds is given: 'In one [burial] was found a metal spoon, and a neat Glass Cup which may contain two Gills Scottish measure.'
- Roman vessel glass (fig. 8.4):
  B:3:1 An undecorated cylindrical cup, intact when found but later broken (AD 160–260). Ch. 3.8.
- Publications: Low 1778 (quoted in Graham-Campbell 2004, 213); Pennant 1794; *Archaeologia Scotica* 3, 1831, appendix II; Davidson 1886; Cuthbert 1995.

Figure 8.3

Glass from Mine Howe.

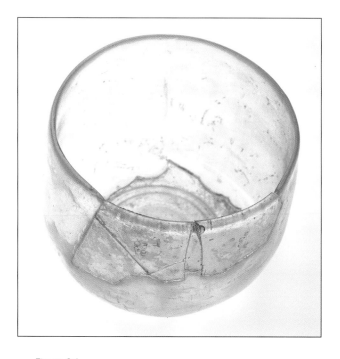

Figure 8.4

Cup from Links of Trenabie, Westray.

Hebrides

C:1 Dun Ardtreck, Skye

- Map reference: NG 335 358.
- Dun Ardtreck is situated on the cliff-edge of a rocky knoll near Ardtreck Point on the west coast of Skye.
- Excavated in 1964–65.
- Archaeological remains: Dun Ardtreck is a D-shaped galleried dun or partly-collapsed broch, protected by a wall on the landside and a cliff on the seaside. Excavations revealed three phases, the latest a rebuilding after a fire had destroyed the structures.
- Roman vessel glass:
  C:1:1 An unidentified fragment of a cup/beaker. Ch. 3.25.
- Other finds of glass: a fragmented melon bead; 29 small glass ring-beads in a wide range of colours (Guido group 6 ivb; 7 iv; Guido class 8 and 14; Guido Roman period II).
- Other Roman artefacts
  Samian: one fragment of a cup of Dragendorff 33 or a platter of Dragendorff 18/31 (Antonine); one fragment of Central Gaulish samian, reworked to a counter; one fragment of a bowl of Dragendorff 30 or 37 (Antonine).
  Other Roman pottery: eight sherds of a single jug in Severn Valley ware (post-Antonine).
- Publications: MacKie 2000.

C:2 Dun Mor Vaul, Tiree, Argyll

- Map reference: NM 042 492.
- Dun Mor broch is situated about 300 m north-west of Vaul, on the island of Tiree in the Inner Hebrides.
- Excavated in c. 1880 and 1962–64.
- Archaeological remains: the site was inhabited from the late sixth or fifth century BC to the second or third century AD, and there are also remains from the Norse period. Of interest here is the Roman Iron Age phase – a broch was built at the site in the early first century AD or somewhat earlier (a point of extended debate), and this was later partly demolished and turned into a round farmstead (fig. 8.5).
- Roman vessel glass:
  C:2:1 One prismatic bottle (c. AD 43–250). Ch. 3.23.
  C:2:2 Six fragments not identified to type, possibly belonging to the same vessel as above (c. AD 43–250). Ch. 3.23.
  C:2:3 Two fragments from a minimum of one painted cylindrical cup (AD 160–260). Ch. 3.8.
- Other finds of glass: a fragment of a glass bangle in opaque blue with yellow inlays; twelve glass beads in various colours, including Guido class 14; a Roman gaming counter in opaque white glass.

Figure 8.5

Dun Mor Vaul, Tiree.

Euan MacKie

- Other Roman artefacts:
  Samian: four fragments of samian and imitation samian were found: a platter of Dragendorff 18/31 (or 37); a cup of Dragendorff 33; a bowl of Dragendorff 38 (imitation); and a bowl of Dragendorff 37.
  Other Roman pottery: a spindle whorl made of a Roman coarse-ware jar.
- Publications: MacKie 1974; MacKie 1997.

C:3 Dun Vulan, South Uist

- Map reference: NF 714 298.
- Dun Vulan, also known as Rudha Ardvule, is situated on the west coast of South Uist, the Outer Hebrides (the Western Isles).
- Excavated in 1991–96.
- Archaeological remains: the site has been occupied since the Late Bronze Age till modern times. A broch was built in the late pre-Roman Iron Age, which was followed by a late Iron Age cellular house.
- Roman vessel glass:
  C:3:1 A fragment of what may have been Roman clear, colourless glass was found. Ch. 3.26.
- Other finds of glass: 15 small beads in blue and grey glass were unearthed, but subsequently lost.
- Publications: Parker Pearson & Sharples 1999.

C:4 Loch na Berie, Lewis

- Map reference: NB 103 351.
- Loch na Berie (sometimes Loch na Beirgh) is situated on what originally was a small island in a loch around 400 m from the coast on the Bhaltos (Valtos) peninsula in the western part of the island of Lewis.
- Excavated in 1985–88; 1993–95.
- Archaeological remains: a broch, rebuilt into a cellular building in the late Iron Age, has been partly excavated on the site, and on the same site – but outside the broch – a wheelhouse, and what is called a 'souterrain'.
- Roman vessel glass:
  C:4:1 Roman glass is said to have been discovered on the site. It has, however, not been possible to obtain any information on this material as it has subsequently been lost. Ch. 3.26.
- Other finds of glass: a blue bead (information is lacking on any other finds).

- Other Roman artefacts: a fragment of samian platter was discovered in the so-called 'souterrain'.
- Publications: Harding & Armit 1990; Harding & Gilmour 2000

Caithness

D:1 Crosskirk

- Map reference: ND 025 701.
- Crosskirk is named after the ruins of St Mary's Chapel, and is situated 8 km west of Thurso. The site lies on the cliff on the northern coast of Caithness. To the north it faces the Pentland Firth, and east of the site is the river Forss.
- Excavated in 1966–72.
- Archaeological remains: excavations revealed a multi-period site with a promontory fort succeeded by a broch surrounded by a settlement. The exact phasing is uncertain, but the broch was eventually abandoned, and only the settlement lived on. Not all of the site could be excavated; parts of it had eroded away and fallen into the sea.
- Roman vessel glass:
  D:1:1 One fragment from a minimum of one cylindrical bottle (c. AD 43–110). Ch. 3.23.
  D:1:2 One fragment of an unidentified beaker. Ch. 3.25.
- Other Roman artefacts:
  Samian: one fragment of a samian bowl, Dragendorff 37 (second century); six sherds of unidentified samian.
  Other Roman pottery: one fragment of a Castor Ware beaker (early fourth century).
- Publications: Fairhurst 1984; Heald & Jackson 2001.

D:2 Everley

- Map reference: ND 369 682.
- Everley Broch (Tofts of Freswick) is situated 5 km south of John O'Groats in the north-eastern part of Caithness.
- Excavated 1897; 2001–02.
- Archaeological remains: this site was originally excavated by Sir Frances Tress Barry, an amateur archaeologist. However, apart from a very brief summary by Joseph Anderson in 1901, relatively little was known about the site until re-examined by Andrew Heald. The latter demonstrated that

there still are *in situ* Iron Age deposits in the broch, and that there is late Norse/Medieval occupation on the same site.

- Roman vessel glass:
  D:2:1 One yellow-brown fragment of a globular jar (Isings Form 67b or 67c) (Neronian to early Flavian). Ch. 3.16.
- Other Roman artefacts: one fragment of a samian jar of Déchelette 72 (of Antonine date); fragments of samian bowls of Dragendorff 29 and 37 forms.
- Publications: Anderson 1901; Ross 1909; Hartley 1972; Heald & Jackson 2001; Heald & Jackson 2002.

D:3 Keiss Harbour

- Map reference ND 35 61.
- Keiss Harbour is situated on the coast at Sinclair's Bay, in the immediate vicinity of the village of Keiss, Caithness.
- Excavated 1893 and 2006.
- Archaeological remains: as with Everley Broch, this site was excavated by the amateur archaeologist Sir Frances Tress Barry. The excavations focused on the remains of a broch; later re-examination showed that it was occupied from the mid-first millenium BC to the late first millenium AD.
- Roman vessel glass:
  D:3:1 A rim fragment of blue-green glass, possibly reused cylindrical or prismatic bottle (*c.* AD 43–250). Ch. 3.23.
- Other finds of glass: a cylindrical glass bead; a glass ring.
- Other Roman artefacts:
  Samian: three fragments of samian (two fragments of Dragendorff 37 [first century date], possibly reused; a fragment of a plain samian vessel [second century date]).
  Other Roman pottery: three fragments of Lower Nene valley colour-coat pottery (3rd-century date).
- Publications: Anderson 1901; Ross 1909; Hartley 1972; Heald & Jackson 2001.

Figure 8.6

Sherd from Fendom Sands.

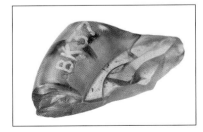

Ross & Cromarty

E:1 Fendom Sands

- Map reference NH 82 82.
- Fendom Sands are extensive sand dunes along the south coast of Dornoch Firth, near Tain, Easter Ross.
- Stray finds.
- Archaeological remains: sand dunes with traces of activity from several prehistoric periods.
- Roman vessel glass (fig. 8.6):
  E:1:1 One fragment of a cup, beaker, bowl or jug with a pushed-in tubular base-ring. Ch. 3.25.
- Other finds of glass: one bead.
- Publications: Guido 1978.

Morayshire

F:1 Covesea

- Map reference NJ 175 707.
- The Sculptor's Cave, Covesea, Morayshire, is a sea cave on the south coast of the Moray Firth, 7 km north of Elgin. Its name derives from the Pictish carvings on the walls.
- Excavated in 1928–30 and 1979.
- Archaeological remains: this site is protected by the sea and was only readily accessible during low tide. The 1970s excavations and a recent campaign of radiocarbon dating have clarified the sequence. This appears to be a long-lived ritual site, with two major foci of deposition in the late Bronze Age (linked to remains of a wooden platform) and Roman Iron Age. Radiocarbon dates show that deposits continued at a lower intensity throughout the Iron Age, while Pictish and Early Christian carvings around the cave entrance indicate a continuing sanctity. Many human bones were unearthed, and it is clear that during the late Bronze Age the site functioned as an ossuary. A second phase of deposition of human remains dates to the third to fourth centuries AD.
- Roman vessel glass:
  F:1:1 One fragment of a vessel with a pushed-in tubular base, possibly a cup or beaker. Ch. 3.25.
  F:1:2 One fragment of a cup, beaker or flask with snake-thread decoration (late second to third century AD). Ch. 3.4.
- Other finds of glass: several glass beads in various shapes: translucent blue with waves (Guido group 5a); annular yellow-green (Guido group 6 iib);

annular light yellow-green (Guido group 6 iiib); annular blue (Guido group 6 iva); a globular blue bead (Guido group 7 iv); long bead; pentagonal bead (Guido Roman period); a chip of opaque red glass.

- Other Roman artefacts:
Samian: five reused and polished fragments of samian from four vessels (four fragments of bowls of Dragendorff form 37, one cup of Dragendorff form 33).
Other Roman pottery: fragments of an *olla*.
Metalwork: the bolt and key of a barrel-lock; a bronze object of unknown function with the letters 'TRES'; toilet instruments (tweezers and nail-cleaners).
- Other Roman finds: a coin hoard of around 230 coins (nine genuine, the remainder imitation), dated between AD 337 and 354 was found. Three of the coins were pierced and must have been used as ornaments.
- Publications: Armit et al 2011; Benton 1931; Shepherd & Shepherd 1979; Shepherd 1993; Robertson 2000, 330, no. 1359.

F:2 Culbin Sands

- Map reference NJ 0 6.
- The Culbin Sands occupies a substantial area of coast immediately west of Findhorn Bay, 20 km west of Elgin.
- A number of excavations have taken place in this area over the years, but the bulk of the material is from casual finds.
- Archaeological remains: Culbin Sands is an area with sand dunes, now largely wooded, with re-mains from Mesolithic to post-Medieval period.
- Roman vessel glass:
F:2:1 One fragment of a convex-bodied vessel with marvered blobs (Claudian to Neronian or somewhat earlier). Ch. 3.3.
F:2:2 One fragment of a cup, beaker or flask with snake-thread decoration (late second to third century AD). Ch. 3.4.
F:2:3 One fragment of a cup/beaker unidentified to type. Ch. 3.25.
F:2:4 One fragment of a late Roman tubular-rimmed bowl in greenish colourless glass (later fourth century). Ch. 3.15.
- Other finds of glass: beads of several types have been found in this area, and it has been argued that production of certain types took place here. Eighteen annular blue beads (Guido group 6 ivb);

an amber-coloured annular bead (Guido group 6 v); a black annular bead (Guido group 6 ix); 85 small opaque yellow beads (Guido class 8); Meare 'spiral' bead (Guido class 10); spiral brown and blue beads (Guido class 13); Guido class 14 in various colours; Guido Roman period beads class a. Three finds of yellow-green glass bangles of Kilbride-Jones type 1; two finds of glass bangles of Kilbride-Jones type 2.
- Other Roman artefacts: a furniture mount in bronze; a trumpet brooch; a silver signet-ring with a cornelian intaglio.
- Publications: Black 1891; Henig 1971; Henderson 1989.

F:3 Birnie

- Map reference NJ 210 585.
- Birnie is located on a sand terrace above the River Lossie, 4 km south of Elgin (fig. 8.7).
- In 1996 a metal detectorist found a scatter of Roman *denarii* in a field with an open settlement known from cropmarks. The site was excavated from 1998 to 2011.
- Archaeological remains: this is a multi-period site with remains ranging from the Neolithic to the Medieval period. Of primary concern in this context is a very rich Iron Age site. Remains of a minimum of at least 25 – some very large – roundhouses have been discovered at the site.
- Roman vessel glass (fig. 8.8):
F:3:1 One fragment of a blue-green pillar-moulded bowl (*c.* AD 43–100; earlier production and use on the Continent). Ch. 3.1.
- Other finds of glass: several Guido class 13 beads; a number of yellow beads; blue biconical bead; Type 1 glass bangle fragment; ball with inlaid spirals.
- Other Roman artefacts: Samian: one sherd. Other Roman pottery: a sherd of Roman coarse-ware pottery. Metalwork: five Roman brooches, including an enamelled plate brooch and an enamelled taper-ing-bow brooch; a small enamelled Romano-British bronze bird; a Flavian *as*.
Other Roman finds: Two coin hoards containing several hundred *denarii* ranging from Nero to Septimius Severus (AD 193 and 196).
- Publications: Hunter 1999; Hunter 2000; Hunter 2001b; Hunter 2002; Hunter 2003; Hunter 2004; Hunter 2005; Hunter 2007b.

Figure 8.7

Above: aerial photograph of the Birnie settlement.

© Barri Jones

Figure 8.8

Right: pillar-moulded bowl sherd from Birnie.

Aberdeenshire

G:1 Loch Kinnord

- Map reference NO 43 95.
- Loch Kinnord is situated 7 km north-east of Ballater.
- Archaeological remains: very little is known about this find, except that it was found intact in the loch. However, in 1931 an account of the archaeology in the area was published by Sir Alexander Ogston. In the same loch there is a crannog; and in the area around the loch, roundhouses and souterrains have been found.
- Roman vessel glass:
  G:1:1 An intact unguent flask of Isings Form 8 in blue-green glass (first century AD, probably a Claudian to Flavian date). Ch. 3.21.
  No other finds are linked to this.
- Publications: Ogston 1931; Curtis & Hunter 2006; Ingemark 2006a.

G:2 Waulkmill, Tarland (fig. 8.9)

- Map reference: NJ 475 049.
- Tarland Waulkmill lies approximately 42 km west of Aberdeen.
- Found 1898.
- Archaeological remains: a gamekeeper was digging in a sand-pit when he discovered a stone cist consisting of four undressed stones. Finds of teeth

and fragmented bones suggests that this was an inhumation burial. Later digs in the same sand-pit yielded several more finds, possibly from the same grave. Apart from the objects mentioned below, the following finds were made: a studded bronze cup (probably a miniature cauldron), and what may have been a knife (identification by F. Hunter).

- Roman vessel glass:
  G:2:1 A beaded stem in greenish colourless glass from a beaker or flask – possibly with snake-thread decoration. This find is either a *pars pro toto* deposit, i.e. a fragment representing the intact vessel, or – less likely – it was a crude gaming piece. Dated from the mid-second to the early fourth century AD; the colour suggests it is more likely to be of a late date. Ch. 3.5.
- Other finds of glass: a minimum of four intact and one fragment of gaming pieces in glass, three in blue transparent glass, two in polychrome glass.

- Other Roman artefacts:
  Metalwork: a silver pennanular brooch may be of Roman origin.
  Other Roman finds: a minimum of seven gaming pieces in quartzite of possible Roman manufacture, belonging to the same set as the gaming pieces in glass.
- Publications: Callander 1915.

G:3 Brackenbraes, Turriff

- Map reference: NJ 737 480.
- The site is situated between the railway and a sandy hillock in Brackenbraes, Turriff.
- Found in 1857.
- Archaeological remains: the site was accidentally discovered after the railway between Turriff and Banff had been constructed in 1855–57. A glass jug and a number of beads were unearthed. No bones or ashes were discovered, but it may nevertheless have been a grave.

Figure 8.9

Waulkmill grave group.

- Roman vessel glass:
  G:3:1 An intact conical jug (Isings Form 55) (late first to early/mid second century AD). Ch. 3.18.
- Other finds of glass: 'a large number of dark-brownish, wine-coloured glass beads' were found, but were later given away, and their whereabouts remains unknown.
- Publications: Dunbar 1930; Thorpe 1934.

Kincardineshire

H:1 Dalladies

- Map reference NO 626 673.
- Dalladies is situated less than 2 km south-east of Edzell in the parish of Fettercairn, close to the North Esk river. To distinguish it from a long barrow nearby it was named Dalladies 2.
- Excavated in 1971–73.
- Archaeological remains: the site was discovered during rescue excavation of a nearby long barrow, which was threatened by gravel-extraction. An adjacent site was partly destroyed, and the haste in which the excavations had to be done means that it is not fully understood. However, it is clear that there was a series of roundhouses, pits, and a number of timber-lined souterrains. Remains of iron working were also found. Radiocarbon dates showed that the site had been in use at least intermittently from the third century BC to the sixth century AD.
- Roman vessel glass:
  H:1:1 One fragment of a square bottle (c. AD 43–250). Ch. 3.23.
- Other Roman artefacts:
  Samian: one piece of samian, Curle form 11 (late first to early second century date).
  Other Roman pottery: nine sherds of Romano-British coarse-ware, from a single-handled flagon.
- Publications: Watkins 1980.

Angus

I:1 Airlie

- Map reference NO 314 501.
- The burial was situated near the school in Airlie, Angus.
- Found in 1885.
- Archaeological remains: a workman digging a drain discovered a stone cist, not far from where

two stone cists were found 20 years previously.
- Roman vessel glass:
  I:1:1 An undecorated cylindrical cup (AD 160–260). Ch. 3.8.
- Publications: Davidson 1886.

I:2 Kingoldrum

- Map reference NO 334 550.
- The finds come from a stone cist discovered at the old parish churchyard of Kingoldrum Kirkton, Angus, which is situated approximately 20 km north of Dundee.
- Found c. 1843.
- Archaeological remains: excavations revealed a stone cist with three remaining slabs (the fourth had been removed), in which were the remains of an inhumation burial. The skeleton is described as 'doubled up, with the head and knees together, and placed in a sitting posture.'[4] On the wrist of the deceased was a chain armlet, and a small bronze cross was also unearthed. In the original report by Patrick Chalmers, a number of other finds – including a glass cup, a bronze vessel (now lost), and a bell – are mentioned as 'found at the same time'. Whether all the above finds actually belong to a single find is open to questioned on the basis of the wide range of dates.[5]
- Roman vessel glass:
  I:2:1 Lost, probably an undecorated cylindrical cup (AD 160–260). Ch. 3.8.
- Publications: Chalmers 1854; Stuart 1867; Davidson 1886.

I:3 Redcastle, Lunan Bay

- Map reference NO 687 508.
- The site is situated close to Red Castle, which lies where Lunan Water reaches the sea at Lunan Bay.
- Excavated in 1997–98.
- Archaeological remains: archaeological features from several periods were discovered during excavation: isolated flint artefacts of Neolithic date; a souterrain; and a series of square and round barrows of early Medieval date. A souterrain, originally with wattle and daub walls, was the only structure belonging to the Roman Iron Age on the site. It was later backfilled, and the finds came from this event.

Figure 8.10 Redcastle glass.

- Roman vessel glass (fig. 8.10):
  I:3:1 Seven fragments from one tubular-rimmed bowl of Isings Form 44b (AD 60/65–160/170). Ch. 3.14.
  I:3:2 Twenty-five or more fragments of a minimum of one cylindrical cup (AD 160–260). Ch. 3.8.
- Other Roman artefacts:
  Samian: one fragment of a black samian bowl of Dragendorff type 18/31; this may be an imitation of London Ware manufacture.
  Other Roman pottery: one fragment of a globular or round gray-ware jar of second-century date.
- Publications: Alexander & Rees 1997; Alexander 1998; Alexander 2005; Ingemark 2005.

I:4 Tealing

- Map reference: NO 412 381.
- Tealing is situated approximately 5 km north of Dundee.
- The site was accidentally discovered during agricultural work in the summer of 1871, and was dug the same year under the supervision of Mr Walter M'Nicoll. It was not until 1939 that parts of what was found were handed in to National Museums Scotland.
- Archaeological remains: Tealing III is a typical Angus souterrain with a curved plan, and was found in an area with three other souterrains.
- Roman vessel glass:
  I:4:1 One fragment of a small polychrome pillar-moulded bowl (c. AD 43–50, in use in Romano-British contexts throughout the first century AD; earlier production and use on the Continent). This find was not reported in the original publication

in 1873, but belongs to the group of finds donated to National Museums Scotland in 1939. Ch. 3.1.
- Other Roman artefacts
  Samian: one piece (possibly second-century date).
- Publications: Jervise 1873; Thorpe 1940; Wainwright 1963.

Argyll (mainland)

J:1 Dunadd

- Map reference NR 8365 9356.
- Dunadd is a prominent and isolated rocky massif in mid-Argyll surrounded by the flat and marshy Crinan Moss, through which the river Add meanders to the coast at Loch Crinan c. 4 km away.
- Excavated in 1904–05; 1929; 1980–81.
- Archaeological remains: due to the perfunctory excavations in the beginning of the twentieth century, this site is relatively poorly understood. Since the nineteenth century it has been considered the capital of the early Medieval kingdom of Dál Riata, and most structural remains and artefacts are of this date, along with a body of rock carvings. The evidence suggests that there was an earlier Roman Iron Age hillfort phase, while artefactual evidence ranges from the Mesolithic to the Medieval period.
- Roman vessel glass:
  J:1:1 One fragment of an oil flask (*aryballos*) of Isings Form 61 (mid-late first to mid-third century AD). Ch. 3.22.
  J:1:2 One fragment of unidentified blue-green bottle glass (c. AD 43–250). Ch. 3.23.
- Other finds of glass: small blue annular bead (Guido group 6 ivb); long drum-shaped bead (Guido exotic beads of the Roman period); finds of early Medieval glass vessels and beads.
- Other Roman artefacts: fragments of samian plates (Dragendorff 18/31); indeterminate fragments of samian.
- Publications: Christison & Anderson 1905; Hewat Craw 1930; Guido 1978; Lane & Campbell 2000; Campbell 2007.

J:2 Dunollie

- Map reference NM 852 314.
- Dunollie is situated on a rock promontory at the north end of Oban Bay.
- Excavated in 1978.

- Archaeological remains: the excavations were very limited in extent, covering a mere two percent of the rock promontory. These revealed a series of occupation phases from the seventh century onwards, and its importance as an early Medieval stronghold in the kingdom of Dál Riata is attested in historical sources. On the site there are also the ruins of a Medieval castle.
- Roman vessel glass:
  J:2:1 One fragment from a minimum of one painted cylindrical cup (AD 160–260). Ch. 3.8.
- Publications: Alcock & Alcock 1988; see also Campbell 2007.

Stirlingshire

K:1 Camelon

- Map reference NS 863 812.
- Camelon native site is situated on a promontory overlooking the River Carron, in eastern Falkirk.
- Excavated in 1961.
- Archaeological remains: the site was partly destroyed by quarrying and bulldozing, and excavations had to be done hastily. There were three phases of occupation, and although it is not clear how long these lasted, finds suggest that it belongs to the earlier part of the Roman Iron Age (first to second century AD). A circular hut (rather oval) was replaced by a similar structure on the same spot. Parts of a rectilinear structure, possibly Roman, may represent a phase between the first and the second hut. Multiple temporary Roman camps as well as forts of the Flavian and Antonine periods lie very close to the site. The native site was strongly defended: a multivallate system with four deep ditches and palisades (all of which may not have been contemporary) surrounded the south side.
- Roman vessel glass:
  K:1:1 A fragmentary unguent flask in colourless glass (first to second century). Ch. 3.21.
- Other finds of glass: two Roman glass gaming pieces, one dark blue and one white.
- Other Roman artefacts:
  Samian: one fragment of unidentified samian. Other Roman pottery: fragments of a carinated bowl, and a jar; fragments of a jug, Gillam 105 (AD 140–180); fragment of a flagon, Gillam 14 (AD 130–170); fragments of coarse-ware.

Metalwork: 20 iron nails; two iron studs; a thong tag in bronze.
- Publications: Proudfoot 1978.

K:2 Castlehill Wood

- Map reference NS 750 909.
- Castlehill Wood dun is situated on the east slopes of the Touch Hills, 5 km south-west of Stirling.
- Excavated in 1955.
- Archaeological remains: excavations revealed a thick stone wall roughly oval in shape with a narrow entrance on the eastern side. Near the entrance passage were the remains of a staircase leading up to the top of the wall. Remains of fireplaces were discovered in the interior, as well as daub with wattle impressions. Outcropping rock covers much of the interior, and as a result no postholes were discovered. However, it is likely that the area was covered by huts, or (more likely) roofed over. In addition to the Iron Age structure and artefacts, some Medieval pottery was found. However, there are no Medieval structures.
- Roman vessel glass:
  K:2:1 One fragment of a polychrome pillar-moulded bowl (c. AD 43–50, in use in Romano-British contexts throughout the first century AD; earlier production and use on the Continent). Ch. 3.1.
  K:2:2 Two fragments from a minimum of one cylindrical bottle (c. AD 43–110). Ch. 3.23.
- Other Roman artefacts: a small sherd of what is described as probably Roman pottery.
- Publications: Feachem 1956–57.

K:3 Fairy Knowe, Buchlyvie

- Map reference NS 585 942.
- Fairy Knowe is situated in the flat carse-lands of the Forth valley, 1 km east of the village of Buchlyvie and 21 km west of Stirling.
- Excavated in 1975–78.
- Archaeological remains: a timber roundhouse of Iron Age date was replaced by a broch in the Roman Iron Age. The site was destroyed by fire and the deliberate dismantling of the broch walls. All Roman imports came from the broch phase. During an earlier – unpublished – excavation a stone cist was found on the site; however, little is known about this.
- Roman vessel glass:
  K:3:1 Sixteen fragments from a minimum of one,

Figure 8.11

Leckie glass assemblage.

probably more cylindrical bottles (*c.* AD 43–110). Ch. 3.23.

- Other finds of glass: two glass beads (Guido class 7 and 8); a Roman gaming counter in opaque white.
- Other Roman artefacts:
  Samian: 31 fragments of Dragendorff forms 15/17, 18, 22/23, 27, 29 and 37, from an estimated 19 vessels, were found.
  Other Roman pottery: 125 sherds from four or more amphorae of Dressel 20, i.e. south Spanish vessels which normally contained olive oil. Three sherds from two *mortaria*. Eight fragments of several – possibly five – flagons. An imitation 'Pompeian Red Ware' bowl. Many of the pottery sherds were reused as rubbers/polishers.
  Metalwork: two penannular brooches. Objects of lead, and melted lead.
- Other Roman finds: two Roman bronze coins – *as* – of Vespasian, one minted in AD 71 and one minted in Lyon in AD 71–78.
- Publications: Main 1998; Ingemark 1998.

K:4 Leckie

- Map reference NS 692 939.
- Leckie Broch is situated on a rock promontory formed by two streams, in the southern foothills of the Forth Valley, some 11 km west of Stirling. The site was originally surrounded by flat, marshy ground.
- Excavated in 1970–78.
- Archaeological remains: excavations revealed that a wooden roundhouse built in the first century was replaced by a broch in the late first century AD (the excavator suggests soon after AD 79–80). This broch was occupied for 50 or 60 years, after which there was considerable destruction. The remaining ruins were converted into a round-house.
- Roman vessel glass (fig. 8.11):
  K:4:1 One fragment of a convex-bodied vessel with marvered blobs (Claudian to Neronian or somewhat earlier). Ch. 3.3.
  K:4:2 Two joining fragments of an arcaded beaker (Neronian to Flavian). Ch. 3.6.
  K:4:3 One fragment of a vessel with optic-blown decoration, either a jar of Isings Form 67c or a jug of Isings Form 52b or 55 (Neronian to early Flavian). Ch. 3.16.
  K:4:4 Six fragments from a minimum of one cylindrical bottle (*c.* AD 43–110). Ch. 3.23.
  K:4:5 Fourteen fragments from a minimum of one, probably more prismatic bottles (*c.* AD 43–250). Ch. 3.23.
  K:4:6 Seventeen fragments in blue-green bottle glass, including rims, necks, and handles, which could not be determined to type (*c.* AD 43–250). Ch. 3.23.
  K:4:7 One fragment from a cylindrical cup with snake-thread decoration (AD 160–260). Ch. 3.8; see also ch. 3.4.
  K:4:8 One fragment from a cast and lathe-turned opaque red constricted convex cup (*c.* AD 43–65). Ch. 3.26.
- Other finds of glass: ten fragments of glass ban-gles, many of which were reworked, of Kilbride-Jones types 1, 2 and 3. Melon beads; yellow beads, Guido class 8; beads in clear glass with yellow spirals, Guido class 10.
- Other Roman artefacts:
  Samian: fragments of south Gaulish make including one with a potter's stamp (Flavian date); fragments of Antonine date.

Metalwork: a mirror (first-century date); an enamelled bow brooch; a pair of enamelled disc brooches.
- Other Roman finds: one intaglio; two silver *denarii* (Caesar, minted 45 BC; Trajan, minted *c*.AD 105).
- Publications: MacKie 1982; MacKie 1987.

K:5 Keir Hill, Gargunnock

- Map reference NS 706 942.
- Keir Hill is a prominent grassy knoll in the east end of Gargunnock village, 8 km west of Stirling.
- Excavated in the 1950s; the report does not give the exact year of excavation.
- Archaeological remains: underneath a layer of later debris was a flat area on top of the knoll, and excavations revealed a series of post holes belonging to a circular hut. The interior had a stone-paved floor with a rectangular hearth in the centre. A layer of ash and burnt material showed that the building had burned to the ground, and the excavator suggests that the hut had only been occupied for a relatively short period of time.
- Roman vessel glass:
  K:5:1 Fragments from a unguent bottle in blue-green glass (first to second century AD). Ch. 3.21.
  K:5:2 Fragments possibly from a cup/beaker. Ch. 3.25.
- Other finds of glass: one melon bead in blue translucent glass.
- Other Roman artefacts: a decorated fragment of Roman pottery, light brown in colour with red decoration.
- Publications: MacLaren 1958.

K:6 East Coldoch

- Map reference NS 703 986.
- East Coldoch is *c*.9 km north-west of Stirling, and 3 km south-west of the Roman fort at Doune.
- Excavations began on a small scale in 1996 with subsequent excavations in 2000 and 2002–04.
- Archaeological remains: multi-period site stretching from the late Bronze Age or early Iron Age onwards, including a Roman Iron Age phase. Belonging to the latter period was one large defended roundhouse, in addition to which are at least five small roundhouses and a four-post structure.
- Roman vessel glass:
  K:6:1 Fragments of prismatic bottles (AD 43–250). Ch. 3.23.

K:6:2 Fragments of a fourth-century glass vessel. Ch. 3.26.
- Other finds of glass: beads of third or fourth century date.
- Other Roman artefacts: Antonine samian.
- Publications: Woolliscroft & Lockett 1996; Davies 2000; Annual Reports for the years 2002, 2003 and 2004.[6]

Fife

L:1 Constantine's Cave

- Map reference: NO 632 100.
- Constantine's Cave – named after Constantine II, King of Alba (AD 903–943) – lies on the north face of a rocky crag on the shore of Fife Ness, Fife.
- Excavated in 1914.
- Archaeological remains: at least three periods are represented. The oldest remains belong to the first part of the Roman Iron Age; the second from the period *c*.AD 800–1000, and the third recent times. It is the first period which is of interest here. On the floor were the remains of iron smelting: iron slag, metal debris and burnt clay. Across the mouth of the cave are the remains of a mortar-built wall of unknown date.
- Roman vessel glass:
  L:1:1 One fragment of a cylindrical bottle (*c*.AD 43–110). Lost. Ch. 3.23.
- Other Roman artefacts: three fragments of red-surfaced Romano-British ware; many fragments of amphorae, representing a minimum of three vessels of Dressel 20.
- Publications: Wace & Jehu 1915.

L:2 Hallowhill, St Andrews

- Map reference NO 494 156.
- Hallowhill is situated on the rising ground at the side of Kinness Burn, St Andrews.
- Excavated in 1861 and 1975–77.
- Archaeological remains: in 1861, 20 stone cists were excavated in the area, most of which were long-cists of seventh century and later date. In 1975–77 an additional 140 long-cists were dug. On the same site, however, a small and extremely deeply cut grave was found in 1861 [cist 51B]. This contained the remains of a child and a number of Roman artefacts. In the 1975–77 excavations this grave was rediscovered and excavated

once again, and a small fragment of bronze and a pig incisor were found in it.

On the same site another grave of similar type was unearthed [cist 54], which held the remains of a child and some rare objects of Roman manufacture: a bronze millefiore seal box; a stylised snake-head silver bracelet fragment; a bronze finger-ring; and an enamelled brooch. In the grave fill, a piece of figured samian was found. The date of these graves is discussed by the excavator, who considers them post-Roman. The wide range of Roman objects, however, seems to suggest a Roman Iron Age date for the shorter cists.

- Roman vessel glass:
  L:2:1 One or two undecorated cylindrical cups (AD 160–260). Now lost. Ch. 3.8.
- Other finds of glass: a glass bangle of Kilbride Jones type 1; a small blue-green glass bead.
- Publications: Stuart 1867; Proudfoot 1976; Proudfoot 1996.

Midlothian

M:1 Castlelaw

- Map reference: NT 229 638.
- Castlelaw fort is situated on the north-eastern slopes of the Pentland Hills, less than 2 km north-west of Penicuik.
- Excavated in 1931–32 and 1948.
- Archaeological remains: the low knoll is surrounded by a series of ditches and banks forming a standard multivallate fort. A palisade belonging to the first millennium BC was later replaced by a rampart in the late pre-Roman or early Roman Iron Age. In a later phase – when the defences were no longer functioning – a souterrain was constructed in the ditch of the inner rampart. The souterrain has a 'beehive' annexe, in which two hearths were found. A bloom of iron and other remains suggest that iron-working had taken place in the souterrain.
- Roman vessel glass:
  M:1:1 One fragment of blue-green glass, probably a cylindrical bottle (c. AD 43–110). Ch. 3.23.
- Other Roman artefacts:
  Samian: four sherds: a cup, Dragendorff 27 (second century); a platter, Dragendorff 18/31, bowls of Dragendorff 37 (second century).
  Metalwork: a *Trompetenmuster* openwork mount; an enamelled eagle brooch.

- Publications: Childe 1933a; Childe 1933b; Piggott & Piggott 1952.

M:2 Dalmeny Park, South Queensferry

- Map reference: NT 158 793.
- Dalmeny Park is situated in the eastern parts of South Queensferry, on the south coast of the Firth of Forth. The grave was discovered on the highest point of a projecting promontory.
- Excavated in 1915.
- Archaeological remains: this site was discovered by accident by the British army while building fortifications along the coast during World War I. The excavations revealed a grave formed of rough sandstone slabs, which lay in an east-westerly direction. The finds – a bead necklace and teeth – showed that the head lay in the west. This grave is generally considered to be of Anglo-Saxon date, on the basis of the beads, although Margaret Guido considers them to be Roman beads found in a later context.
- Roman vessel glass:
  M:2:1 One base fragment of a vessel with a tubular pushed-in base-ring, reused as a bead. Ch. 3.25.
- Other finds of glass: 11 beads in opaque green, yellow, orange, white, light blue, etc. (small segmented beads of Guido class a – Roman period?).
- Publications: Brown 1915; Guido 1978.

M:3 Edinburgh Castle

- Map reference NT 251 735.
- Edinburgh Castle, or Castle Rock, is situated in the centre of Edinburgh.
- Excavated in 1988–91.
- Archaeological remains: the earliest remains date to the Late Bronze Age and there is apparent continuity to modern times. In the Iron Age there was probably a hillfort on the site. The phase which is of interest here – the Roman Iron Age – is represented by a midden, or refuse-heap. As yet no structures belonging to this phase have been excavated.
- Roman vessel glass:
  M:3:1 One fragment of a prismatic bottle of Isings Form 50 (c. AD 43–250). Ch. 3.23.
  M:3:2 A jug or flask with an applied thread in blue glass (fourth century). Ch. 3.25.
- Other Roman artefacts:
  Samian: one or two sherds from La Graufe-

senque, Dragendorff 29 (late Neronian or early Flavian date); two Lezoux pots (first century AD); a number of Central Gaulish fragments of Antonine date – bowls of Dragendorff 37, a dish of Dragendorff 18, etc.

Other Roman pottery: a Nene Valley jar (mid-third to early fourth-century date AD); Black-burnished ware (Antonine); a jar, Gillam 30 (Flavian to Trajanic), an unidentified flagon, etc. One hundred and twenty fragments representing 37 vessels of Roman coarse-ware (dated to AD 90–160).

Metalwork: a trumpet brooch; a dragonesque brooch; a pennanular brooch; a bar brooch; a bronze hair pin.

- Other Roman finds: a coin of Hadrian (AD 117–138).
- Publications: Driscoll & Yeoman 1997.

East Lothian

N:1 Dryburn Bridge

- Map reference NT 724 755.
- Dryburn Bridge lies 5.5 km south-east of Dunbar, and approximately 1 km from the North Sea coast.
- Excavated in 1978–79.
- Archaeological remains: activity at the site starts in the Mesolithic, and there is also an Early Bronze Age phase with two burial cists. In the Early Iron Age there was large palisaded enclosure with a number of roundhouses and burials. This was succeeded by an open settlement. Roman Iron Age activity on the site is demonstrated by radio-carbon dating and the find of Roman glass, the latter from a ring-ditch house.
- Roman vessel glass:
  N:1:1 One fragment of blue-green bottle glass, of Isings Form 50 or 51 (c. AD 43–250). Ch. 3.23.
- Other Roman artefacts: a possible penannular brooch
- Publications: Triscott 1982; Dunwell 2007; Ingemark 2007.

N:2 Traprain Law

- Map reference NT 580 747.
- Traprain Law is approximately 30 km east of Edinburgh.
- Excavated in 1914–15, 1919–23, 1939, 1947, 1986, 1996–97, 1999–2000, 2003–06.

- Archaeological remains: Traprain Law is an isolated hill (a volcanic intrusion) which dominates the East Lothian plain (see fig. 4.4). The site is very complex indeed, and due to the early excavators' inability to cope with this it is poorly understood. Despite all difficulties, however, it is clear that Traprain Law stands out as an exceptionally rich site.

  Many periods are represented from the Mesolithic to Medieval times, with major occupations in the later Bronze Age and the Roman Iron Age. There may have been a hiatus in the pre-Roman Iron Age. A series of ramparts on different levels surround the hillfort, and the remains of buildings – circular houses and sub-rectangular buildings with several rooms – have been found. Ample evidence shows that the site was not merely used as a settlement, but also as a production centre for craftsmen working with bronze, enamelling, and possibly the manufacture of beads and bangles in glass.
- Roman vessel glass:
  N:2:1 Two fragments from a polychrome pillar-moulded bowl (c. AD 43–50, in use in Romano-British contexts throughout the first century AD; earlier production and use on the Continent). Ch. 3.1.
  N:2:2 Two fragments from one blue-green pillar-moulded bowl (c. AD 43–100; earlier production and use on the Continent). Ch. 3.1.
  N:2:3 Two fragments from a minimum of two colourless wheel-cut beakers (late first to mid-late second century AD). Ch. 3.7.
  N:2:4 Three fragments from a minimum of three tubular-rimmed bowls of Isings Form 44b or 45 (AD 60/65–160/170; see catalogue for discussion). Ch. 3.14.
  N:2:5 Twenty-four fragments from a minimum of seven cylindrical bottles (c. AD 43–110). Ch. 3.23.
  N:2:6 Sixty-six fragments from a minimum of 16, probably more, prismatic bottles (c. AD 43–250). Ch. 3.23.
  N:2:7 Sixty-seven fragments of blue-green bottle glass, probably of Isings Forms 50 or 51 (c. AD 43–250). Ch. 3.23.
  N:2:8 Seven fragments from a minimum of seven jugs – globular or conical – of Isings Form 52 and/or 55 (one is in a strong colour, and of Neronian or early Flavian date; the rest dates to last third of first to third quarter of second century AD). Ch. 3.18.

N:2:9 One fragment of an oil-flask (*aryballos*) (mid-late first to mid-third century AD). Ch. 3.22.

N:2:10 One unguent flask in pale purple (first to second century AD). Ch. 3.21.

N:2:11 One fragment, possibly a square jar of Isings Form 62 (first to second century AD). Ch. 3.17.

N:2:12 One fragment of a jar possibly of Isings Form 67b or 67c (early-mid second century AD?). Ch. 3.16.

N:2:13 One fragment representing an undecorated cylindrical cup; one fragment representing a painted cylindrical cup; one fragment representing a so-called Baldock cup and one fragment from a cylindrical cup of indeterminate type (AD 160–260). Ch. 3.8.

N:2:14 Ten fragments from a minimum of nine hemispherical cups of Isings Form 96, with abraded bands (late third to fourth century AD). Ch. 3.9.

N:2:15 Three fragments from one hemispherical cup of Isings Form 96, with wheel-cut figured decoration (AD 330–370). Ch. 3.10.

N:2:16 Three fragments from a minimum of two, possibly three conical beakers with cracked-off rims of Isings Form 106 (late third to early fifth century AD). Ch. 3.9.

N:2:17 Two fragments from a minimum of two cups or beakers of either of Isings Form 96 or 106, with marvered applied blobs (fourth century AD). Ch. 3.11.

N:2:18 Six fragments from a minimum of five conical cups with fire-rounded rims of Isings Form 106 (mid-fourth to early fifth century AD). Ch. 3.9.

N:2:19 One fragment of a jug with a chain-handle, possibly of Isings Form 120c? (third or fourth century AD). Ch. 3.19.

N:2:20 Two fragments representing a minimum of two vessels with out-splayed base-rings and high concave bases; these could not be positively identified to type, but may have come from deep tubular-rimmed bowls of late date (fourth century AD). Ch. 3.25.

N:2:21 Twenty-six fragments of a beaker with zigzag decoration, possibly a claw-beaker of Evison Type 1 (c. AD 370–400), and one fragment from a second vessel of similar type and date. Ch. 3.12.

N:2:22 One fragment of a late Roman bottle – possibly a tall cylindrical bottle of late third to fourth century AD. Ch. 3.25.

N:2:23 Fifteen fragments representing a minimum of eight cups or beakers with abraded or wheel-cut decoration. Five vessels were in colourless, two in blue-green and one in late Roman yellow-brown glass. Ch. 3.25.

N:2:24 Seven fragments representing a minimum of five cups or beakers with applied threads. One in colourless, one in greenish colourless, one in blue-green, one in natural green and one in yellow-green glass. Ch. 3.25.

N:2:25 Forty-nine fragments representing a minimum of ten undecorated cups or beakers in colourless, blue-green, Late Roman yellow-green, brown-green and green glass. Ch. 3.25.

N:2:26: One fragment representing a minimum of one jug of uncertain type, possibly an ovoid jug with a funnel mouth. Ch. 3.25.

N:2:27 One fragment of a jug or flask of uncertain type. Ch. 3.25.

N:2:28: Ten fragments of bases representing a minimum of five vessels in blue-green and green glass. Ch. 3.25.

N:2:29 Forty-five unidentified sherds in colourless, blue-green, green and pale yellow glass. Ch. 3.25.

- Other finds of glass:
Four or possibly five fragments from a minimum of two cast matt/glossy window glass panes (c. AD 43–300). Ch 3.24.

Around 200 fragments of glass bangles, including all of Kilbride-Jones' types (see Kilbride-Jones 1938).

A large number of beads of different colours and varieties, including melon beads (see Guido 1978). Three fragments representing two – or possibly three – vessels of Roman Mediterranean glass of fifth or sixth century date. Ch. 3.25.

One fragment of a late Roman or post-Roman bowl. Ch. 3.25.

- Other Roman artefacts:
The sheer quantity of Roman material makes it impossible to mention but a fraction of all that has been found; however, Fraser Hunter has summarised these finds (Hunter 2009b).

Samian: around 150 sherds of south, central and east Gaulish samian.

Other Roman pottery: a wide array of pottery of Romano-British manufacture; imported amphorae (Dressel 20); *mortaria*.

Metalwork: the Traprain treasure, which includes an array of Roman silver objects, including a late Roman wine-sieve. Locks and keys; door hinges; furniture fittings; tweezers, nail-cleaners, an ear-scoop; brooches; finger-rings; ear-rings; lead weights, etc.

- Other Roman finds: sixty-five coins, dating from Mark Anthony to *c.*AD 400 (not including those in the treasure); a *stylus*; beads in jet, etc.
- Publications: Curle 1915; Curle & Cree 1916; Curle 1920; Curle 1921; Cree & Curle 1922; Cree 1923; Cree 1924; Curle 1932a; Cruden 1940; Burley 1956; Feachem 1956; Jobey 1976; Sekulla 1982; Close-Brooks 1983; Strong 1986; Hill 1987; Erdrich et al. 2000; Rees & Hunter 2000; Hunter 2009b.

Lanarkshire

O:1 Hyndford

- Map reference NS 906 418.
- Hyndford Crannog is situated in a small natural pond near the river Clyde, outside Lanark.
- Excavated in 1898.
- Archaeological remains: the site was excavated by amateurs, albeit under the supervision of the well-known archaeologist Robert Munro. No proper plans were made and not much can be said of the structure, except that it was circular and built of wood. The remains of hearths and clay flooring were found.
- Roman vessel glass (fig. 8.12):
  O:1:1 Two fragments of a blue-green pillar-moulded bowl of Isings Form 3 (*c.*AD 43–100; earlier production and use on the Continent). Ch. 3.1.
  O:1:2 Two fragments from one tubular-rimmed bowl of Isings Form 44b (AD 60/65–160/170). Ch. 3.14.
  O:1:3 Fourteen fragments from a minimum of one, possibly more, cylindrical bottles (*c.*AD 43–110). Ch. 3.23.
  O:1:4 Two fragments from a minimum of two prismatic bottles (*c.*AD 43–250). Ch. 3.23.
  O:1:5 Six fragments of blue-green bottle glass not closely identifiable, including rims and necks: probably of Isings Forms 50 or 51 (*c.*AD 43–250). Ch. 3.23.
  O:1:6 Two fragments of unidentified Roman glass. Ch. 3.25.

- Other finds of glass: three melon beads; fragments of three glass bangles.
- Other Roman artefacts:
  Samian: fragments of a cup, Dragendorff 27 (first century); fragments of platters, Dragendorff 18 and Curle 6 (first century); fragments of barbotined cup, Dragendorff 35 (first century); fragments of bowl, Dragendorff 29 (first century); fragments of bowl, Dragendorff 30 (first century); fragments of flask, Déchelette 67 (first century).
  Other Roman pottery: fragments of a small buff jar and lid (first century); fragment of a *mortarium* (first century); fragments of white jar (second century).
- Publications: Munro 1899; Robertson 1970.

O:2 Torfoot

- Map reference NS 640 385.
- Torfoot is situated in Avondale, approximately 10 km south-west of Strathaven.
- Found in 1803.
- Archaeological remains: a boy cleaning out a drain found a prismatic bottle containing a coin hoard with about 400 Roman silver coins.
- Roman vessel glass:
  O:2:1 Lost – probably a prismatic bottle (*c.*AD 43–250). Ch. 3.23.

Figure 8.12

Hyndford glass assemblage.

Figure 8.13

Tubular-rimmed bowl fragment from Ardeer or Luce Sands.

- Other Roman artefacts
  Denarii of Trajan, Antoninus Pius, Faustina; the latest coins are of Crispina, wife of Commodus.
- Publications: Robertson 1978; Robertson 2000, no 347.

Ayrshire

P:1 Ardeer/Stevenston Sands

- Map reference NS 28 41.
- Ardeer Sands or Stevenston Sands is an area of sand dunes situated 1 km south-east of Stevenston in north Ayrshire, and just inland from the present coast.
- Stray finds in the later nineteenth/early twentieth century; souterrain excavated in 1960 and 1973.
- Archaeological remains: a wide range of objects from many periods have been recovered as casual finds from the sand dunes; many were collected and published by John Smith (1895, 33–48), and subsequently donated to National Museums Scotland (Callander 1933). Among the collections of the Museum is a box of glass finds, including items P:1:1–4. These glass finds are not mentioned in these published accounts, and were not registered when they were acquired; labels in the box read 'Stevenston Sands Smith Collection 1931' and 'Glenluce Sands'; the box is also labelled 'Glenluce'. This uncertainty over provenance cannot be resolved, and they are referred to here as ?Ardeer/?Luce Sands. The lack of any mention in the relatively well-published Ardeer/Stevenston Sands material, and the absence of any other glass known from Luce Sands, makes it perhaps

more likely that they are from Luce Sands, but this cannot currently be demonstrated. See also Q:1.

Apart from these casual finds, there has been one excavation in the area, at Ardeer House (NS 271 419). The site was partly dug in 1960, but rediscovered and excavated in 1973. A natural cave had been turned into a souterrain. The walls were built with large boulders and sandstone slabs. The remains of a hearth used for cooking as well as iron smelting were found. With the exception of a fragment of glass and a piece of worked antler, no artefacts are mentioned in the report. The current location of these finds is not known.

- Roman vessel glass (fig. 8.13) (numbers 1–4 from the sand dunes at Ardeer or Luce Sands, 5 from the Ardeer souterrain):
  P:1:1 One fragment of a cylindrical bottle (*c.*AD 43–110). Ch. 3.23.
  P:1:2 Two fragments of undiagnostic blue-green bottle glass, probably of Isings Forms 50 or 51 (*c.*AD 43–250). Ch. 3.23.
  P:1:3 One fragment of a tubular-rimmed bowl of Burgh Castle type (later fourth to early fifth century AD). Ch. 3.15.
  P:1:4 Two fragments of unidentified Roman glass (the colours suggest a late Roman date). Ch. 3.25.
  P:1:5 'A fragment of glass showing considerable efflorescence … [details of stratification follow] …. There is thus no reason to believe that the glass is modern; since it is clear glass it is tentatively suggested that it may be Roman.'
- Other finds of glass (from either Ardeer or Luce Sands dunes): one possible fragment of eastern Mediterranean engraved glass; one fragment of post-Roman window glass; two sherds which could not be closely identified.
- Other Roman artefacts: two Roman brooches, a *denarius* of Faustina I.
- Publications: Callander 1933; Hunter 1974; Smith 1895, 33–48.

P:2 Buston

- Map reference NS 415 435.
- Buston crannog, also known as Mid Buiston farm, is situated in a former loch between Kilmaurs and Stewarton in North Ayrshire.
- Excavated in 1880–81; 1989–90.
- Archaeological remains: the remains of a crannog

which was occupied in the Roman Iron Age and the early Medieval period were found. The site was extended at least once, and a circular hut was built on the extension in the late sixth century AD. Most artefacts come from a rubbish-heap or midden. In 1880 a logboat was discovered outside the crannog, but this was later destroyed in a fire. In 1990 another logboat was unearthed.

- Roman vessel glass:
P:2:1 Two fragments from a minimum of one prismatic bottle (*c.* AD 43–250). Ch. 3.23.
P:2:2 One fragment of unidentified blue-green bottle glass, probably the same vessel (*c.* AD 43–250). Ch. 3.23.
- Other finds of glass: two glass beads, a ball of glass. Finds of early Medieval glass have also been made.
- Other Roman artefacts: fragments of a samian platter of Dragendorff 18/31.
- Publications: Munro 1890; Crone 2000; see also Campbell 2007.

P:3 Castlehill, Dalry

- Map reference NS 285 536.
- Castlehill is situated on an isolated rock on the farm of South Howrat, Dalry.
- Excavated in 1901–02.
- Archaeological remains: the remains of an Iron Age fort were unearthed. The excavator believed that there were two periods of occupation, the early Roman Iron Age and the Viking period. The artefactual record, however, seems to suggest that it was occupied in the Roman Iron Age and the early Medieval period.
- Roman vessel glass:
P:3:1 One fragment of a cylindrical bottle of Isings Form 51 (*c.* AD 43–110). Ch. 3.23.
P:3:2 Two fragments from a minimum of one prismatic bottle of Isings Form 50 (*c.* AD 43–250). Ch. 3.23.
P:3:3 One fragment of undiagnostic blue-green bottle glass, probably of Isings Forms 50 or 51 (*c.* AD 43–250). Ch. 3.23.
- Other finds of glass: annular brownish-yellow bead (Guido group 6 iiia); blue melon bead; fragments of early Medieval glass vessels.
- Other Roman artefacts:
Samian: fragments of samian platters, Dragendorff 31 (later than AD 160).
Metalwork: dragonesque brooch.

- Publications: Smith 1919; Hartley 1972; see also: Campbell 2007.

P:4 Glenhead (Gourock Burn)

- Map reference NS 214 453.
- Glenhead double fort/Gourock Burn is situated 3 km south-east of West Kilbride.
- Excavated in 1962, 1968, 1969, 1972.
- Archaeological remains: this so-called 'fort' consisted of two flat-topped mounds surrounded by earthworks, and divided by a ditch. The remains of wooden roundhouses were found on the mounds. The site was destroyed by fire, and then reoccupied.
- Roman vessel glass:
P:4:1 Two fragments of a prismatic bottle (*c.* AD 43–250). Ch. 3.23.
P:4:2 One fragment of blue-green bottle glass, possibly the same vessel (*c.* AD 43–250). Ch. 3.23.
- Other finds of glass: a fragmented glass bangle, Kilbride-Jones type 3A.
- Other Roman artefacts:
Samian: fragments of a plate of Dragendorff 18, and a bowl of Dragendorff 29.
Other Roman finds: a *sestertius* of Sabina, wife of Hadrian (AD 128–138).
- Publications: Hendry 1962; Hendry 1968; Hendry 1969; Hendry 1972; publication from Hillfort Study Group 1983.

P:5 Lochspouts

- Map reference NS 288 058.
- Lochspouts is situated in a small loch approximately 4 km south-west of Maybole, south Ayrshire.
- Excavated in 1880.
- Archaeological remains: excavations showed that this was a crannog whose occupation included the Roman Iron Age.
- Roman vessel glass (fig. 8.14):
P:5:1 A fragment of blue-green bottle glass reused as a gaming piece. Probably of Isings Form 50 or 51. (*c.* AD 43–250). Ch. 3.23.
- Other finds of glass: three melon beads; a polychrome bead; opaque yellow annular bead (Guido class 8).
- Other Roman artefacts
Samian: fragments of a platter of Dragendorff 18/31 and a bowl of Dragendorff 37.
Other Roman pottery: fragments of a white jar.
- Publications: Munro 1890.

Figure 8.14

Reworked sherd from Lochspouts.

P:6 Seamill, West Kilbride

- Map reference NS 203 471.
- Seamill, West Kilbride is situated on a tongue of land on the coast of north Ayrshire.
- Excavated around 1840, and in 1880.
- Archaeological remains: a small stone-walled fort.
- Roman vessel glass:
  P:6:1 Two fragments from a minimum of one, possibly two, cylindrical bottles (*c.* AD 43–110). Ch. 3.23.
- Other Roman artefacts: Roman coarse-ware.
- Publications: Munro 1882.

Wigtownshire

Q:1 Luce Sands

- Map reference NX 1 5.
- Luce Sands occupies an area of coast at the head of Luce Bay, approximately 20 km east of Stranraer.
- When the finds were made is unclear.
- Archaeological remains: numerous casual finds from the Mesolithic to the post-Medieval period have been made in the area; and at High Torrs a cremation grave, which may have been Roman rather than native, was excavated.
- Roman vessel glass:
  Q:1:1 A fragment of what may be a prismatic bottle (*c.* AD 43–250). Ch. 3.23.

  Q:1:2 An unidentified fragment of a cup or beaker of Roman date. Ch. 3.25.

  See also P:1 for material which may come from Luce Sands

- Other finds of glass: two melon beads and various other beads.
- Other Roman artefacts:
  Metalwork: trumpet brooches, a handle of a key.
  Other Roman finds: two fourth-century coins.
- Publications: Breeze & Ritchie 1980.

Q:2 Whithorn

- Map reference NX 4447 4031.
- Excavated in 1984–91.
- Archaeological remains: Whithorn is an early monastic site. There has been some debate, however, on the basis of the Roman finds, as to whether there was a Roman Iron Age phase on the site.
- Roman vessel glass:
  Q:2:1 Two fragments from a minimum of one cylindrical bottle (*c.* AD 43–110). Ch. 3.23.
  Q:2:2 Two fragments of prismatic bottles (*c.* AD 43–250). Ch. 3.23.
  Q:2:3 Four fragments of blue-green glass, identified as prismatic bottles of Isings Form 50 or late Roman double-glossy window panes. Ch. 3.23.
  Q:2:4 Two fragments of unidentified cups or small bowls of first or second century date.[7]
- Other finds of glass: one fragment of a matt/glossy window pane (*c.* AD 43–300). Ch. 3.24.
  Thirteen Roman glass tesserae. A biconical bead. Post-Roman glass, including claw-beakers.
- Other Roman artefacts:
  Samian: seven sherds, including bowls of Dragendorff 30 and/or 37 and platters of Dragendorff 18/31.
  Other Roman pottery: five fragments of coarse-ware, including one fragment of a south Spanish amphora (probably Dressel 20), and one sherd of Nene valley pottery.
  Other Roman finds: a fourth-century *nummus*: Constantius II or Constans (AD 347–48).
- Publications: P. Hill 1997; Wilson 1996–97; see also Campbell 2007.

Kirkcudbrightshire

R:1 Carlingwark Loch

- Map reference NX 763 609.
- Carlingwark Loch lies on the outskirts of Castle Douglas; the find is reported to have been found on the bottom of the shallow loch, near Fir Island.

- Archaeological remains: around 1866 two local fishermen dredged up a hoard in a cauldron from the loch; it was later donated to the National Museum of Antiquities, Edinburgh.
- Archaeological remains: the large bronze cauldron (*c.* 66 cm in diameter) contained about 100 objects of metal and three pieces of glass. The nature of such hoards has been debated, and they are today commonly interpreted as ritual deposits.
- Roman vessel glass:
  R:1:1 Three fragments of a prismatic bottle, with parts of the maker's mark preserved (*c.* AD 43–250). Lost. Ch. 3.23.
- Other Roman artefacts: among those finds which beyond doubt are of Roman origin are: a gridiron and a tripod, both objects associated with cooking; a padlock-spring and fragments of the bronze mounting of a wooden box. Although studied and discussed by Piggott in 1953, and Manning in 1972 and 1981, it is still not clear what proportion of the objects can be considered as Roman imports. The majority of objects – whatever their origin – are tools; however, sword-tips and chain-mail were also found. (A find of a tankard-handle in so-called Celtic style is also worth mentioning.)
- Publications: Skene 1866; Piggott 1952–53; Manning 1972; Manning 1981.

R:2 Mote of Mark

- Map reference NX 845 540.
- Mote of Mark is situated on a rocky knoll west of the village of Rockcliffe.
- Excavated in 1913; 1973; 1979.
- Archaeological remains: The remains of a vitrified fort of early Medieval date were found, whereas no earlier phase has been documented on the site.
- Roman vessel glass: None.
- Other finds of glass: one fragment of matt/glossy cast window glass (*c.* AD 43–300), Ch. 3.24; a possible find of a glass tessera. Sixty-nine sherds of glass vessels from the early Medieval period. A glass disc with enamel; Ewan Campbell has suggested that this was a plaque inset in a piece of decorative metalwork.
- Other Roman artefacts: a piece of unidentified samian, and a piece of a *mortarium*.
- Publications: Curle 1914; Laing 1973; Laing 1975; Longley 1979; Longley 1980; Laing & Longley 2006; see also Campbell 2007.

R:3 Torrs Cave

- Map reference NX 676 445.
- Torrs Cave – also known as Dirk Hatteraik's Cove – is situated on the eastern shore of Kirkcudbright Bay, approximately 5 km south of the town of Kirkcudbright.
- The report does not mention when the excavation took place, only that it lasted for three seasons. Considering the publication date, it must have taken place in the mid-1930s.
- Archaeological remains: excavations in a natural cave revealed a multi-period site. The date of the earliest phase is unclear, but the later – datable – phases range from the Roman Iron Age to the eighteenth century.
- Roman vessel glass (from the Iron Age phase):
  R:3:1 One fragment from a prismatic bottle (*c.* AD 43–250). Ch. 3.23.
- Other finds of glass (from the Iron Age phase): one melon bead in blue glass.
- Other Roman artefacts (from the Iron Age phase) fragments of two samian vessels (second century).
- Publications: Morris 1936–37.

Selkirkshire

S:1 Torwoodlee

- Map reference NT 465 384.
- Torwoodlee is situated just below the summit of a hill overlooking the valley of Gala Water, north-west Galashiels, Selkirkshire.
- Excavated in 1891 and 1950–51.
- Archaeological remains: there are two main phases on the site: an earlier hillfort, and the later broch. A stone cist burial was found in the hillfort ditch, and dates to the period when the broch was dismantled. A wealth of Roman material was found in the broch.
- Roman vessel glass (fig. 8.15):
  S:1:1 Forty-three fragments from a minimum of three, probably more cylindrical bottles (*c.* AD 43–110). Ch. 3.23.
  S:1:2 Fourteen fragments of blue-green bottle glass of Isings Form 50 or 51 (*c.* AD 43–250). Ch. 3.23.
  S:1:3 Nine fragments from a minimum of one tubular-rimmed bowl of Isings Form 44b (AD 60/65–160/170). Ch. 3.14.
  S:1:4 Four fragments from one globular jar of

Isings Form 67c (early to mid second century?). Ch. 3.16.

S:1:5 Three fragments of unidentified Roman glass. Ch. 3.25.

- Other finds of glass: a yellowish-green and opaque yellow glass bangle, Kilbride-Jones type 3H.
- Other Roman artefacts:
  Samian: fragments of a platter, Dragendorff 18 or

15/17 (first century); fragments of platter, Dragendorff 18 (first century).

Other Roman pottery: a carrot-shaped amphora, Camulodunum 189 (first century); a Dressel 20 amphora (first century); fragments of flagons (first century); jars of bluish-grey ware, dark grey ware (first century); fragments of *mortarium* (first century).

Other Roman finds: a *denarius* of Titus.

- Publications: Curle 1892; Harden 1951; Piggott 1951.

Roxburghshire

T:1 Edgerston

- Map reference NT 679 124.
- Edgerston is situated on a high spur between the Jed Water and the Kaim Burn, 1 km south of Camptown.
- Excavated in 1928–39.
- Archaeological remains: a multivallate fort was constructed some time before the mid-first century AD. This was replaced by an enclosed settlement with stone-walled huts around the late first century AD. There were also traces of a Medieval military occupation. This site is relatively poorly understood – the result of it being excavated by an amateur – and has never been published properly.
- Roman vessel glass:
  T:1:1 One fragment of blue-green bottle glass, probably of Isings Forms 50 or 51 (*c.* AD 43–250). Ch. 3.23.
- Other finds of glass: a melon bead; three bangles of Kilbride-Jones type 2, four of type 3A, and three of type 3I.

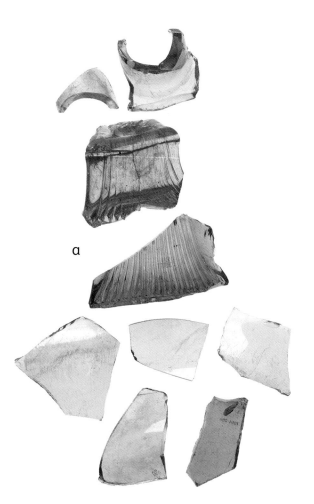

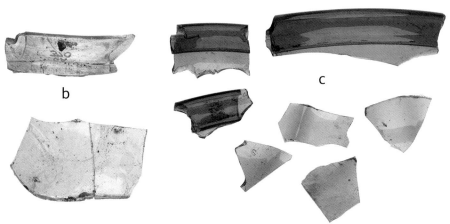

Figure 8.15

The glass from Torwoodlee: (a) bottle; (b) globular jar; (c) tubular-rimmed bowl. (Reproduced at different scales)

- Other Roman artefacts:
  Samian: fragment of a repaired cup, Pudding Pan Rock type 3 (second century); a samian cup, Dragendorff 35/36 (second century); fragment of a platter, Dragendorff 31 (second century).
  Other Roman pottery: a fragment of coarse-ware (second century).
  Metalwork: rim fragment of bronze *patera*; dragonesque brooch (second century).
- Other Roman finds: a *denarius* of Trajan (AD 114), and other Roman coins.
- Publications: *RCAHMS*, Roxburghshire no. 457.

T:2 Crock Cleuch

- Map reference NT 833 176.
- Crock Cleuch – in earlier research also referred to as Sourhope – is situated in the Cheviots, just north of the Northumbrian/Roxburghshire border at Windy Gyle. The two sites lie near a small burn in the Crock Cleuch valley.
- Excavated in 1939.
- Archaeological remains: two adjacent settlements, in all likelihood of contemporary date, were excavated. Each site had a drystone walled enclosure of oval shape, in the centre of which was a circular house/hut. In the eastern site, excavations revealed the remains of one or possibly two additional huts. The western site only had one house. North-west of the latter site there was an ancient field-system.
- Roman vessel glass (fig. 8.16):
  T:2:1 One fragment of a conical jug of Isings Form 55 (Neronian to early Flavian). Ch. 3.18.
- Publications: Steer & Keeney 1948.

T:3 The Dod

- Map reference NT 4726 0600.
- The Dod is situated in a western extension of the Cheviots, 11 km southwest of Hawick, at the head of a valley stream: Dod Burn.
- Excavated in 1979–81.
- Archaeological remains: a small number of round-houses – one of which had a souterrain integrated into the structure – were surrounded by a complex system of earthworks.
- Roman vessel glass:
  T:3:1 Three fragments representing a minimum of one prismatic bottle (*c.* AD 43–250). Ch. 3.23.
- Other finds of glass: fragments: two bangles of Kilbride Jones type 3A, one of type 3C, one of

Figure 8.16

Crock Cleuch jug fragment.

type 3J, and one that was difficult to classify, but which resembles type 3I and 3J. Two annular beads (one blue-green and one yellow-green).
- Other Roman artefacts:
  Metalwork: a bronze button or stud (possibly Roman?).
  Other Roman finds: a stone lamp was interpreted by Hilary Cool as a native copy of a Roman type.
- Publications: Smith 2000 & Worrell 2000.

Northumberland

U:1 Gubeon Cottage

- Map reference NZ 17 83.
- Gubeon Cottage lies in the Wansbeck area, approximately 5 km west of Morpeth.
- Excavated in 1956.
- Archaeological remains: the settlement was situated in a circular enclosure. The remains of a circular house and several pits, possibly rubbish pits, were excavated.
- Roman vessel glass:
  U:1:1 Fragments of two glass vessels, one of which may have come from a cup. Lost. Ch. 3.26.
- Other Roman artefacts:
  Samian: one piece.
  Other Roman pottery: a rim of Romano-British coarse-ware; complete *mortarium* bowl.
- Publications: Jobey 1957.

U:2 Hartburn

- Map reference NZ 081 867.
- Hartburn is situated *c.* 500 m from the Roman road known as the 'Devil's Causeway', approximmately 15 km north of Hadrian's Wall.
- Excavated in 1971.
- Archaeological remains: the settlement has an enclosure of two surrounding ditches. The outer ditch follows the natural contours, whereas the inner one is of roughly square form. Excavations inside the enclosure revealed traces of over 30 circular houses. Many of these overlap each other, revealing a long period of occupation rather than a large number of houses. Radiocarbon dating showed that the settlement was in use during the Roman Iron Age.
- Roman vessel glass:
  U:2:1 Fragment of a cup or beaker with engraved lines. Lost. Ch. 3.26.
- Other finds of glass: one fragment of an opaque green glass bangle, Kilbride-Jones type 3H; an intaglio in yellow-orange glass, showing a scene from Homer's *Illiad*.
- Other Roman artefacts: the excavation yielded 15 sherds of Roman coarse-ware: fragment of a cooking pot (Antonine); fragment of a bowl, Gillam type 306 (AD 125–160); fragment of jar (third century?); fragments of flagons (first–second century AD); jar (pre-Hadrianic to Hadrianic); cooking pot (Antonine or later); jar or pot, possibly Gillam type 96 (first to second century AD).
- Publications: Jobey 1973.

U:3 Hetha Burn, Hethpool

- Map reference NT 881 275.
- Hetha Burn is situated in the Cheviots, approximately 10 km west of Wooler.
- Excavated in 1969.
- Archaeological remains: at Hetha Burn the visible remains were found of 9–10 circular houses set on terraces cut into a steep hillside. Two of the houses were partially excavated, as well as the entrance of the settlement. Both houses had stone walls.
- Roman vessel glass:
  U:3:1 Two fragments from an engraved cup. First century AD? Ch. 3.25.
- Other finds of glass: a fragment of a blue glass bangle with white trailing. Two melon beads in blue glass.
- Publications: Burgess 1970.

U:4 Middle Gunnar Peak, Barrasford

- Map reference NY 915 749.
- Middle Gunnar Peak is situated approximately 5 km north of Hadrian's Wall at Chester, near the Barrasford Quarry.
- Excavated in 1978.
- Archaeological remains: within a stone-built enclosure of roughly rectangular shape there were five circular huts. East and south of the enclosure were an additional five circular huts, as well as a rectangular building (a 'longhouse').
- Roman vessel glass:
  U:4:1 Possible fragments of vessel glass. Lost; no identification could be made. Ch. 3.26.
- Other finds of glass: one fragment of a glass bangle in clear glass with blue and white inlays, Kilbride-Jones type 2; two fragments of opaque white glass bangles, type 3A; a pale green glass bangle with white inlays, type 3 F/G; lumps of blue-green and pale green glass.
- Other Roman artefacts:
  Samian: a rim fragment of Dragendorff 18/31. Other Roman pottery: sherds of Castor ware beakers and a Castor Ware cup; fragments of jars, Gillam type 105 (AD 80–120); fragments of Romano-British cooking pots, BB1 (early to mid-second century); several sherds of amphorae; fragments of a *mortarium*.
- Publications: Jobey 1981.

U:5 Milking Gap, High Shield

- Map reference NY 773 678.
- Milking Gap is situated between Hadrian's Wall and the Vallum, east of Milecastle 38.
- Excavated in 1937.
- Archaeological remains: the site consists of five circular houses. Three of these are situated within a rectangular enclosure, two outside. In addition to the houses there was a small cairn of uncertain date, possibly Iron Age. All features were excavated.
- Roman vessel glass:
  U:5:1 The reported Roman vessel glass was missing from its case in the Museum of Antiquities, Newcastle, and thus could not be examined. H. E. Kilbride-Jones describes it as 'a few pieces of green bottle glass'. This may have been cylindrical or square bottle glass of Isings Forms 50 or 51, but as this cannot be ascertained, no date can be given. Ch. 3.23.

- Other finds of glass: several fragments of blue glass bangles with white trailing, Kilbride-Jones type 3I; fragments of opaque white bangles, type 3A; fragment of a translucent yellowish-green glass bangle, type 3H. One bead in deep blue and opaque white (Guido group 5). Two melon beads in blue glass. One glass bead of cylindrical shape.
- Other Roman artefacts:
  Samian: several fragments of Dragendorff forms 18, 18/31, 33, 37. Both plain and decorated fragments were found.
  Other Roman pottery: Roman coarse-ware of several types, including Castor ware; a possible amphora sherd.
  Metalwork: Roman plumb-bob; a dragonesque bridge.
- Publications: Kilbride-Jones 1938b.

U:6 West Longlee

- Map reference NY 823 766.
- West Longlee is situated in the Wark Forest.
- It is unclear when it was excavated, possibly 1958 or 1959.
- Archaeological remains: this site is discussed in a publication by G. Jobey, albeit very fleetingly, and very little can be said except that a stone-paved roundhouse with a central hearth was found in a roughly rectangular enclosure.
- Roman vessel glass:
  U:6:1 Blue-green bottle-glass (c. AD 43–250). Lost. Ch. 3.23.
- Other finds of glass: fragment of a glass bangle, opaque white with green tinge, Kilbride-Jones type 3A.
- Other Roman artefacts: fragment of flagon in pink fabric (late first to late second century); fragment of cooking pot in grey fabric.
- Publications: Jobey 1960.

U:7 West Whelpington

- Map reference NY 974 837.
- West Whelpington is situated approximately 15 km north of Hadrian's Wall and 2 km west of Kirkwhelpington.
- Excavated in 1958–60 and 1970–76.
- Archaeological remains: during the excavations of the deserted Medieval and later village an earlier Iron Age phase was found. These excavations revealed two enclosures of different dates, as well as roundhouses of different dates. The earlier Iron Age phase had a minimum of two timber-built houses, which were later replaced by stone-built ones.
- Roman vessel glass:
  U:7:1 A possible find of a blue pillar-moulded bowl (c. AD 43–50); in use in Romano-British contexts throughout the first century AD; earlier production and use on the Continent). Lost. Ch. 3.1.
- Other finds of glass: one fragment of an opaque yellow glass bangle, Kilbride-Jones type 3B.
- Other Roman artefacts: one sherd of a colour-coated vessel.
- Publications: Jarrett & Evans 1989 (Iron Age phase); Jarrett 1962 (Medieval and later periods).

U:8 Witchy Neuk, Hepple

- Map reference NY 98 99.
- Witchy Neuk is situated near Hepple Whitefield in Upper Coquetdale.
- Excavated in 1936.
- Archaeological remains: within a fortified enclosure, two circular houses, an area covered with stones and a cooking pit were found. Several cairns and barrows were discovered in the vicinity of the site.
- Roman vessel glass:
  U:8:1 This find is believed to be lost and could not be studied. However, it was examined by W. A. Thorpe of the Victoria & Albert Museum, London. He identified it as a globular jug with a spouted rim. (Second or third century). Ch. 3.20.
- Publications: Wake 1939.

Notes

1 www.rcahms.gov.uk
2 I would like to thank Dr Hilary Cool for bringing my attention to this find.
3 Colin Wallace and Dr Fraser Hunter, pers. comm.
4 Chalmers 1851–54.
5 Dr Fraser Hunter, pers. comm.
6 Retrieved from The Roman Gask Project's homepage www.theromangaskproject.org.uk [accessed 2 March 2014].
7 Identifications made by Prof. Jennifer Price.

B

Vessels associated with wine in a Roman context found on non-Roman/native sites

Site	Type of site	a Cup Glass	b Cup Pottery	c Jug Glass	d Jug Pottery	e Ladle Strainer Paterae Metal	f Jug Metal	g Bottle Glass	h Amphora (wine)
Shetland									
Clickhimin	broch/ wheelhouse	x							
Old Scatness	broch/ wheelhouse	x							
Orkney									
Howe of Howe	broch	x							
Mine Howe	ritual & craft centre	?						x	
Midhowe	broch					x ladle			
Links of Trenabie	burial	x							
Hebrides									
Dun Ardtreck	dun	x	?		x				
Dun Mor, Vaul	broch	x	x					x	
Dun Vulan	broch/ cellular house	unidentified glass							
Loch na Berie	broch/ cellular house	unidentified glass							
Caithness									
Crosskirk	broch	x	x					x	
Keiss Harbour	broch							x	

Site	Type of site	a Cup Glass	b Cup Pottery	c Jug Glass	d Jug Pottery	e Ladle Strainer Paterae Metal	f Jug Metal	g Bottle Glass	h Amphora (wine)
Ross-shire									
Fendom Sands	sand-dunes	?							
Morayshire									
Covesea	cave	?	x						
Culbin Sands	sand dunes	x		?					
Aberdeenshire									
Tarland Waulkmill	burial	?							
Turriff	burial?			x					
Kincardineshire									
Dalladies	roundhouses souterrains				x			x	
Angus									
Airlie	burial	x							
Kingoldrum	burial	x							
Redcastle	souterrain	x							
Tealing	souterrain	x small bowl							
Carlungie I	souterrain								x
Hurly Hawkin	broch					x patera			
Argyll									
Dunadd	fort (post-Roman)							x	
Dunollie	fort (post-Roman)	x							
Stirlingshire									
Camelon	huts				x				
Castlehill Wood	dun							x	
Fairy Knowe	broch							x	
Leckie	broch	x		?	x			x	

Site	Type of site	a Cup Glass	b Cup Pottery	c Jug Glass	d Jug Pottery	e Ladle Strainer Paterae Metal	f Jug Metal	g Bottle Glass	h Amphora (wine)
Stirlingshire (cont.)									
Keir Hill	settlement	?							
East Coldoch	roundhouse	?						x	
Fife									
Kinkell Cave	cave						x		
Constantine's Cave	cave							x	
Hallow Hill	burial	x							
Midlothian									
Castlelaw	fort		x					x	
Dalmeny Park	burial	?							
Dryburn Bridge	roundhouse							x	
Traprain Law	fort	x	x	x				x	
Edinburgh Castle	fort			x	x			x	
Lanarkshire									
Hyndford	crannog		x					x	
Ayrshire									
?Ardeer/ ?Luce Sands	sand dunes	x						x	
Buston	crannog							x	
Castlehill, Dalry	fort							x	
Glenhead	fort							x	
Lochspouts	crannog		x					x	
Seamill	fort							x	
Wigtownshire									
Luce Sands	sand dunes	x						x	
Whithorn	monastic site (post-Roman)	x	?					x	

Site	Type of site	a Cup Glass	b Cup Pottery	c Jug Glass	d Jug Pottery	e Ladle Strainer Paterae Metal	f Jug Metal	g Bottle Glass	h Amphora (wine)
Kirkcudbright-shire									
Torrs Cave	cave							x	
Selkirkshire									
Torwoodlee	broch				x			x	?
Roxburghshire									
The Dod	roundhouses & souterrain							x	
Crock Cleuch	huts			x					
Northumberland									
East Brunton	roundhouses							x	
Hartburn	roundhouses	x			x				
Hetha Burn	roundhouses	x							
Middle Gunnar Peak	roundhouses/ 'longhouse'	unidentified glass	x						
Milking Gap	roundhouses		x					x	
West Longlee	roundhouse				x			x	
Witchy Neuk	fortified enclosure			x					

Decorated cylidrical cup fragment from
Traprain Law (see fig. 3.8.6a and plate 12).

C

Stratigraphic and spatial analysis of the Traprain Law glass

FRASER HUNTER

DOMINIC Ingemark's detailed analysis of the Traprain Law glass provides an excellent opportunity for study of what it can tell us about this key site. Since the major excavations by Alexander Curle and James Cree from 1914–23, various authors have commented on the reliability of the results, especially in terms of their grasp of stratification. While this was undoubtedly far from perfect, comment has tended to be anecdotal rather than analytical; study of a complete material category allows more detailed appraisal of this, for comparison with the results which Erdrich obtained from close study of samian ware from the site.[1]

Three hundred and seventy-five sherds of glass are recorded from the site, all vessel glass apart from five sherds of window glass. Of these, 112 cannot be closely identified to type (although they can be split into bottle and non-bottle); the remaining 263 sherds represent a minimum of 107 vessels. Within this, there is both chronological and typological variation.

It is not certain how rigorous Curle and Cree were in the recovery and retention of material; although they record that they riddled all soil, it is clear that many artefact categories show a strong bias to the larger and more distinctive items. Much of the later pre-historic pottery was discarded, for instance, and recent work has recovered markedly smaller Roman potsherds than those which now survive in the earlier assemblage. A plot of glass sherd recovery by excavation season, divided by broad date category, is interesting; the 1914 and (especially) 1921 seasons had notably low recovery of glass (fig. 9.1). Quantities of other Roman finds are known from the 1921 season, suggesting that the lack of glass might be of significance rather than a systematic bias.

For chronological analysis, Ingemark has provided a detailed discussion of each type. Here, they are simplified into the broad categories proposed by the author elsewhere[2]: early Roman Iron Age, c. AD 75–160; mid-Roman Iron Age, c. AD 160–250; late Roman Iron Age, c. AD 250–400. Much of the glass ware can only be broadly dated to first/second century, here referred to as early-middle.

The question of the 'levels' used by Curle and Cree has been much discussed. Fig. 9.2 splits the finds from each level by the production date assigned to the glass. There is a concentration of late and post-Roman glass in the upper levels (1 and 2), although it is found throughout the sequence, and early-middle Roman-period glass is found from the lowest levels (most likely to be late Bronze Age) to the highest. This confirms earlier scepticism over the value of Curle and Cree's layers. However, the areas (identified by letter) seem to be more robust; sherds from the same vessel noted by Ingemark tend to be in the same or adjacent squares. Thus the excavation squares provide a useful level of analysis.

Roman artefacts were found in every square, with variations in recorded numbers most likely due to factors of recovery. The glass is likewise widely spread across the western plateau, with no convincing difference between early/middle and later distributions.[3] However, there are some interesting concentrations: all the early Medieval glass concentrates in area T, in the northwest of the plateau. There is also a notable sparsity in areas L–O, along the eastern edge of the plateau (as there is with the samian). Beyond this, the glass is too coarse a tool to be confident about extracting spatial meaning.

Analysis of Ingemark's data by type and by date confirms the broader patterns he noted in the overall assemblage; the early-middle assemblage has a broader functional range, although with a focus on the consumption of food and drink; the late assemblage is entirely dominated by cups and beakers. Interestingly, the minimum numbers of vessels remain reasonably constant in the different periods; only the middle Roman Iron Age is sparse, but this is largely because only one type, the Airlie cups, can be confidently assigned to this period; others fall into the early-middle category. It is hard to spot any significant gaps in the data, and it is notable that there is a good amount of first-century material; while the samian showed a strong focus on second-century material, the glass serves to rebalance this view, and indicates extensive contact during the Flavian period.

Notes

1   Erdrich et al. 2000.
2   Hunter 2007a, 20, table 1.
3   This contrasts with the samian distribution; Erdrich et al. 2000. The current analysis uses a fuller range of material than was available to those authors in discussing the glass distribution.

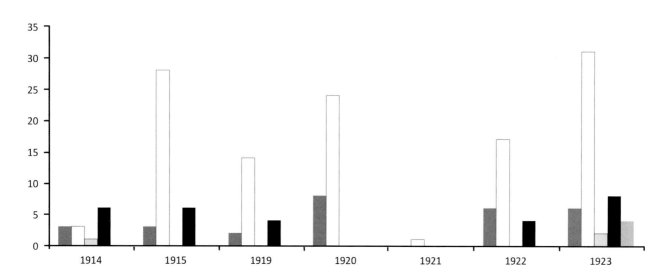

Figure 9.1

Quantity of glass sherds recovered in each season at Traprain Law, subdivided by date.

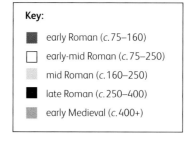

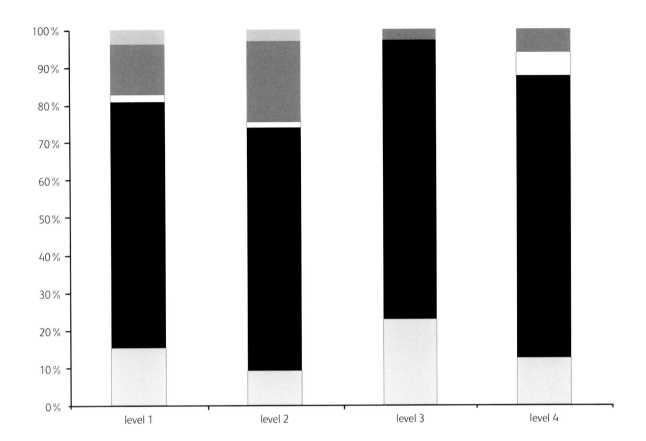

Figure 9.2

Distribution of dated glass sherds across the different excavation levels (with level 1 the highest).

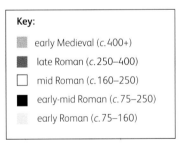

Key:

early Medieval (*c.*400+)

late Roman (*c.*250–400)

mid Roman (*c.*160–250)

early-mid Roman (*c.*75–250)

early Roman (*c.*75–160)

Figure 9.3 (overleaf)

Plan of Traprain Law, showing the subdivisions of the main excavated area.

Drawn by Marion O'Neil, with additions

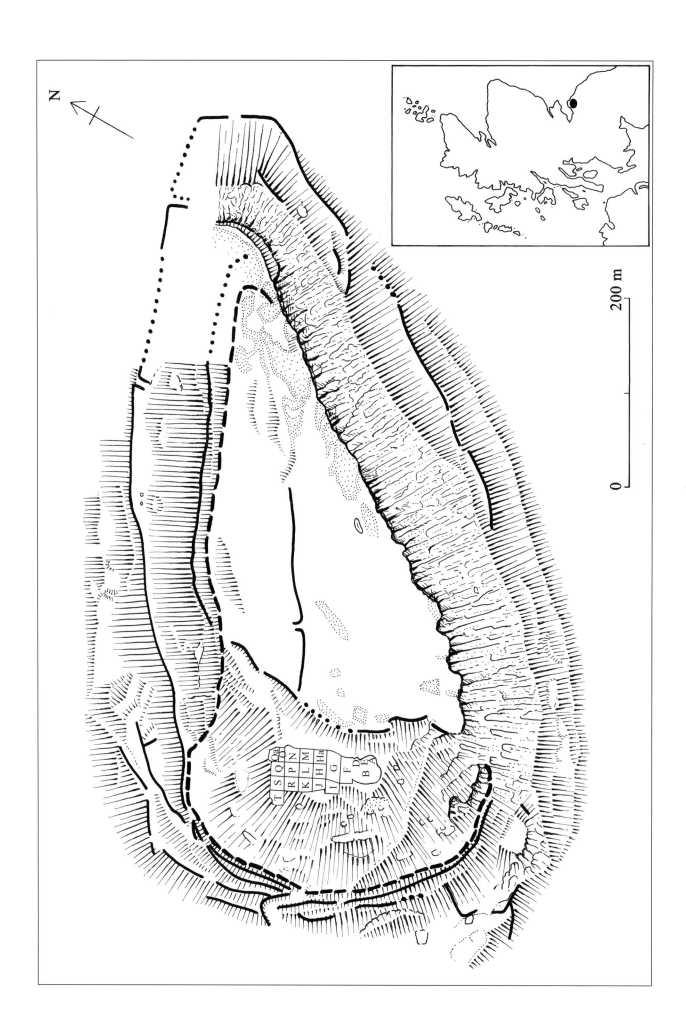

N

200 m

0

Bibliography
and index

Part of the Leckie glass assemblage (see fig 8.11).

Bibliography

Abbreviations

AA	Archäologischer Anzeiger (Beiblatt zum Jahrbuch des Deutschen Archäologisches Instituts)	CBA	Research Report = Council for British Archaeology Research Report	KölnJb	Kölner Jahrbuch für Vor- und Frühgeschichte
AIHV	Association Internationale pour l'Histoire du Verre	CIL	Corpus Inscriptionum Latinarum, Berlin 1863–	PSAS	Proceedings of the Society of Antiquaries of Scotland
AntJ	Antiquaries Journal	CRFB	Corpus der römischen Funde im europäischen Barbaricum	RE	Paulys Real-encyclopädie der Classischen Altertumswissenschaft, Stuttgart 1893–1972
ArchAel	Archaeologia Aeliana	D & E	Discovery and Excavation in Scotland	RIB	The Roman Inscriptions of Britain, Collingwood, R. G. & Wright, R. P., Oxford 1965–95
ArchJ	Archaeological Journal				
BAR	British Archaeological Reports. Brit.Ser. = British Series Int.Ser. = International Series	Der Neue Pauly	Der Neue Pauly: Enzyclopädie der Antike, Stuttgart 1996–	RRCSAL	Reports of the Research Committee of the Society of Antiquaries of London
BonnJbb	Bonner Jahrbücher des Rheinischen Landesmuseums in Bonn und des Vereins von Altertumsfreunden im Rheinlande	GlasAJ	Glasgow Archaeological Journal		
		JGS	Journal of Glass Studies		
		JRA	Journal of Roman Archaeology		
		JRS	Journal of Roman Studies		

Ancient and Medieval sources

Anthimus, *De Obseruatione Ciborum* [*On the Observance of Foods*], trans. and ed. Grant, M. (1996), Totnes.

Apuleius, *Metamorphoses* [*The Golden Ass*], trans. Hanson, J. A. (1989) (Loeb Classical Library), Cambridge, MA.

Athenaeus, *Deipnosophistae* [*The Deipnosophists*], trans. Gulick, C. B. (1937) (Loeb Classical Library), Cambridge, MA.

Beowulf = Huppé, B. F. (1984): *The Hero in the Earthly City: A Reading of Beowulf*, New York, NY.

Caesar, *De Bello Gallico* [*The Gallic War*], trans. Edwards, H. J. (1958) (Loeb Classical Library), Cambridge, MA.

Columella, *De Re Rustica* [*On Agriculture*], trans. Forster, E. S. & Heffner, E. H. (1954) (Loeb Classical Library), Cambridge MA.

Dillon 1962 = *Timna Chathaír Máir* (the *Testament of Cathaír Már*) in Dillon, M. (1962): *Lebor na Cert: the Book of Rights* (Irish Texts Society Publication 46), Dublin.

Dio Cassius, *Historia Romana* [*Roman history*], trans. Cary, E. (1955) (Loeb Classical Library), Cambridge, MA.

Diocletian, *Edictum de Maximis Pretiis* [*Edict on Maximum Prices*], trans. Barag, D. (see Barag 1987; Lauffer 1971).

Diocletian, *Diokletians Preisedikt*, trans. Lauffer, S. (1971) Berlin.

Diodorus of Sicily, *Bibliotheke Historike* [*The Library of History*], trans. Oldfather, C. H., Sherman, C. L. & Geer, R. M. (1946–56) (Loeb Classical Library), Cambridge, MA.

Dionysius of Halicarnassus, *Antiquitates Romanae* [*Roman Antiquities*], trans. Cary, E. (1948–50) (Loeb Classical Library), Cambridge, MA.

FGH = Jacoby, F. (1926): *Die Fragmente der Griechischen Historiker* (2A), Berlin.

Gellius, Aulus, *Noctes Atticae* [*Attic Nights*], trans. Rolfe, J. C. (1948) (Loeb Classical Library), Cambridge, MA.

Gododdin = Jackson, K. H. (1969): *The Gododdin: the oldest Scottish poem*, Edinburgh.

Koch, J. T. (1997): *The Gododdin of Aneirin: text and context from Dark-Age north Britain*, Cardiff.

Mesca Ulad = Hennesey, W. M. (1889): *Mesca Ulad, or the intoxication of the Ultonians* (Royal Irish Academy Todd Lecture Series 1), Dublin.

Periplus Maris Erythraei [*The Periplus of the Erythean Sea*], trans. Huntingford, G. W. B. (1980) London.

Petronius, *Satyrica* [*Satyricon*], trans. Heseltine, M. (1956) (Loeb Classical Library), Cambridge, MA.

Pliny the Elder, *Historia Naturalis* [*Natural History*], trans. Rackham. H., Jones, W. H. S. & Eichholz, D. E. (1944–52) (Loeb Classical Library), Cambridge, MA.

Pliny the Younger, *Epistulae* [*Letters*], trans. Radice, B. (1969) (Loeb Classical Library), Cambridge, MA.

Seneca the Younger, *De Tranquillitate Animi* [*On Tranquility of Mind*], trans.

Basore, J. W. (1958) (Loeb Classical Library), Cambridge, MA.

SHA = *The Scriptores Historiae Augustae* [*Historia Augusta*], trans. Magie, D. (1953) (Loeb Classical Library), Cambridge, MA.

Strabo, *Geographia* [*The Geography of Strabo*], trans. Jones, H. L. (1908–32) (Loeb Classical Library), Cambridge, MA.

Suetonius, *De Vita Caesarum* [*The Lives of the Caesars*] trans. Rolfe, J. C. (1951) (Loeb Classical Library), Cambridge, MA.

Symphosius, *Aenigmata* [*Enigmas*], trans. Ohl, T. (1928), Philadelphia, PA.

Tacitus, *Germania* [*Germania*], trans. Mattingly, H. (1948) (The Penguin Classics), Bungay.

Tacitus, *Germania* [*Germaniens historie, geografi og befolkning*], trans. Bruun, N. W. & Lund, A. A. (1974), Århus.

Voyage of Mael Duin, The = Stokes, W. (1888) *Revue Celtique* 9, 447–95.

Modern Literature

Abramić, M. & Colnago, A. (1909): 'Untersuchungen in Norddalmatien', *Jahreshefte des Österreichischen Archäologischen Institutes in Wien* 12, 13–112.

Agoston, G. A. (1987): *Colour theory and its application in art and design* (2nd ed.), Berlin & New York, NY.

Aguilar-Tablada Marcos, B. & Sanchez de Prado, D. (2006): 'Evidencias de un taller de vidrio en la cuidad romana de *Augustobriga* (Talavera la Vieja, Cáceres)', *Lucentum* 25, 177–93.

Alarcão, J. & Alarcão, E. (1965): *Vidros Romanos de Conimbriga*, Lisbon.

Albrechtsen, E. (1968): *Fynske jernalders-grave III: Yngre romersk jernalder*, Odense.

Albrechtsen, E. (1971): *Fynske jernalders-grave IV: Gravpladsen på Møllegårds-marken ved Broholm*, Odense.

Alcock, J. (1996): *Life in Roman Britain*, London.

Alcock, J. (2001): *Food in Roman Britain*, Stroud.

Alcock, L. (1963): *Dinas Powys*, Cardiff.

Alcock, L. & Alcock, E. A. (1988): 'Reconnaissance excavations on Early Historic fortifications and other royal sites in Scotland, 1974–84: 2, Excava-tions at Dunollie Castle, Oban, Argyll, 1978', *PSAS* 117, 119–48.

Alcock, L. & Alcock, E. A. (1990): 'Reconnaissance excavations on Early Historical fortifications and other royal sites in Scotland, 1974–84: 4 Excava-tion at Alt Clut, Clyde Rock, Strathclyde, 1974–75', *PSAS* 120, 95–149.

Alexander, D. (1998): *Redcastle, Lunan Bay, Angus: archaeological excavations* (University of Edinburgh Department of Archaeology Angus and South Aberdeenshire Field School – Data structure report 445), Edinburgh.

Alexander, D. (2004): 'Early Historic and Medieval Activity at Chapleton, Haugh of Urr, Dumfries and Galloway', *Transactions of the Dumfriesshire & Galloway Natural History & Antiquarian Society* 78, 59–77.

Alexander, D. (2005): 'Redcastle, Lunan Bay, Angus: the excavation of an Iron Age timber-lined souterrain and a Pictish barrow cemetery', *PSAS* 135, 41–118.

Alexander, D. & Rees, A. (1997): *Redcastle, Lunan Bay, Angus: archaeological excavations* (University of Edinburgh Department of Archaeology Angus and South Aberdeenshire Field School: Data structure report 364), Edinburgh.

Allason-Jones, L. (1989a): 'Introductory remarks on native and Roman trade in the north of Britain', in van Driel-Murray, C. (ed.), *Roman military equip-ment: the sources of evidence* (BAR Int.Ser. 476), Oxford, 13–24.

Allason-Jones, L. (1989b): *Women in Roman Britain*, London.

Allen, D. A. (1986a): 'Roman glass', in Buckland, P. C. & Magilton, J. R. (eds), *The archaeology of Doncaster 1. The Roman civil settlement* (BAR Brit. Ser. 148), Oxford, 103–8.

Allen, D. A. (1986b): 'The glass vessels', in Zienkiewicz J. D. (ed.), *The legionary fortress baths at Caerleon. Vol. II The finds*, Cardiff, 98–116.

Allen, D. A. (1986c): 'The Roman glass', in Dool, J. et al. (eds), *Roman Derby: Excavations 1968–83* (The Derbyshire Archaeological Journal 105), 133–35.

Allen, D. A. (1986d): 'Glass', in Dool, J. et al. (eds), *Roman Derby: Excavations 1968–83* (The Derbyshire Archaeo-logical Journal 105), 268.

Allen, D. A. (1989): 'The Roman glass', in Blockley, K. (ed.), *Prestatyn 1984–85: An Iron Age farmstead and Romano-British industrial settlement in north Wales* (BAR Brit.Ser. 210), Oxford, 117–24.

Allen, D. A. (1996): 'Roman glass', in Park-house, J. & Evans E. (eds), *Excavations in Cowbridge, South Glamorgan, 1977–88* (BAR Brit.Ser. 245), Oxford, 211–14.

Allen, D. A. (1997): 'The Roman glass', in Driscoll, S. T. & Yeoman, P. A. (eds), 131–33.

Allen, D. A. (1998a): 'The Roman glass', in Clarke, J. P. (ed.), *Excavations to the south of Chignall Roman villa, Essex 1977–81* (East Anglian Archaeology Report 83), Chelmsford, 94–96.

Allen, D. A. (1998b): *Roman Glass in Britain* (Shire Archaeology 76), Princes Risborough.

Allen, D. (2002): 'Roman Window Glass', in Aldhouse-Green, M. & Webster, P. (eds), *Artefacts and Archaeology: Aspects of the Celtic and Roman World*, Cardiff, 102–11.

Allen, D. (2006): 'The Late Roman Glass' & 'Catalogue of the Glass', in Fulford, M. et al. (eds), 116–19, 314–27.

Almgren, O. (1916): 'Ett uppländskt grav-fält med romerska kärl', *Fornvännen* 11, 76–103.

Anderson, J. (1901): 'Notices of nine brochs along the Caithness coast from Keiss Bay to Skirza Head, excavated by Sir Francis Tress Barry, Bart., M.P., of Keiss Castle, Caithness', *PSAS* 35, 112–48.

Andersson, K. (1983–85): 'Intellektuell import eller romersk *dona*?', *Tor* 20, 107–54.

Andersson, K. (2001): 'Romerska kärl i Upp-land och Västmanland', *Fornvännen* 96, 217–34.

Andersson, K. (2002): 'Sällsyntare än vad man tror: den romerska importen från Gödåker-gravfältet, Uppland', in Pind, J. et al., 239–44.

Anigbo, O. A.C. (1996): 'Commensality as cultural performance: the struggle for leadership in an Igbo village', in Parkin, D., Caplan, L. & Fisher, H. (eds), *The politics of cultural performance*, Providence, RI & Oxford, 101–14.

Anonymous (1939): 'Roman Britain in 1938', *JRS* 29, 199–230.

Anonymous (1953): 'Roman Britain in 1952', *JRS* 43, 104–32.

Anonymous (*sine anno*): *Führer für einen Besuch des Staatlichen Archäologi-schen Museums von Adria*.

Apakidze, A. & Nikolaishvili, V. (1994): 'An aristocratic tomb of the Roman period from Mtskheta, Georgia', *AntJ* 74, 16–54.

Appadurai, A. (1986): 'Introduction: Commodities and the politics of value', in Appadurai, A. (ed.), *The social life of things: commodities in cultural perspective*, Cambridge, 3–63.

Arafat, K. & Morgan, C. (1994): 'Athens, Etruria and the Heuneburg: Mutual misconceptions in the study of Greek-barbarian relations', in Morris, I. (ed.), *Classical Greece: ancient histories and modern archaeologies*, Cambridge, 108–34.

Arbman, H. (1937): *Schweden und das Karolingische Reich*, Stockholm.

Archaeologia Scotica 3 (1831): Appendix II.

Armini, H. (1929): 'Värdshusskyltar och gravinskrifter hos romarna', *Eranos* 27, 205–28.

Armit, I & McKenzie, J. (2013): *An Inherited Place: Broxmouth and the southern Scottish Iron Age*, Edinburgh.

Armit, I., Schulting, R., Knüsel, C. J. & Shepherd, I. A. G. (2011): 'Death, decapitation and display? The Bronze and Iron Age human remains from the Sculptor's Cave, Covesea, north-east Scotland', *Proceedings of the Prehistoric Society* 77, 251–78.

d'Arms, J. H. (1990): 'The Roman *convivium* and the idea of equality', in Murray, O. (ed.), *Sympotica: a symposium on the symposion*, Oxford, 308–20.

d'Arms, J. H. (1991): 'Slaves at Roman *Convivia*', in Slater, W. J. (ed.), *Dining in a Classical Context*, Ann Arbor, MI, 171–83.

d'Arms, J. H. (1995): 'Heavy drinking and drunkenness in the Roman world: Four questions for historians', in Murray, O. & Tecusan, M. (eds), 304–17.

Arnold, B. (1995): '"Honorary males" or women of substance? Gender, status, and power in Iron Age Europe', *Journal of European Archaeology* 3:2, 153–68.

Arnold, B. (1999): '"Drinking the feast": alcohol and the legitimation of power in Celtic Europe', *Cambridge Archaeological Journal* 9:1, 71–93.

Arnold, B. & Gibson, D. B. (1995): 'Introduction. Beyond the mists: forging an ethnological approach to Celtic studies', in Arnold, B. & Gibson, D. B. (eds), *Celtic chiefdom, Celtic states: the evolution of complex social systems in prehistoric Europe*, Cambridge, 1–10.

Arnold, C. J. & Davies, J. L. (2000): *Roman & Early Medieval Wales*, Stroud.

Arrhenius, B. (2006): 'Gullhögen i Husby-Långhundra', in Arrhenius, B. & Eriksson, G. (eds), *Gulldens hög i Husby-Långhundra* (Rapporter från Arkeologiska forskningslaboratoriet 6), Stockholm, 3–58.

Arthur, J. W. (2003): 'Brewing beer: status, wealth and ceramic use among the Gamo of south-western Ethiopia', *World Archaeology* 34:3, 516–28.

Arveillier-Dulong, V. et al. (2003): 'Verriers du Nord-Ouest de la Gaul: productions et importations', in Foy, D. & Nenna, M.-D. (eds), 147–60.

Åström, P. (1964): 'Collections of Cypriote glass', *Opuscula Atheniensia* 5, 123–58.

Avent, R. & Howlett, T. (1980): 'Excavations in Roman Long Melford, 1970–1972', *Proceedings of the Suffolk Institute of Archaeology and History* 34:4, 229–50.

Axboe, M. & Kromann, A. (1992): 'DN ODINN PF AUC ? Germanic "Imperial portraits" on Scandinavian gold brac-teates', *Acta Hyperborea* 4, 271–305.

Baatz, D. (1991): 'Fensterglastypen, Glasfenster und Architektur', in Hoffmann, A. et al. (eds), *Bautechnik der Antike* (Disussionen zur Archäologischen Bauforschung 5, Deutsches Archäologische Institut – Arkitekturreferat), Mainz, 4–13.

Ballin Smith, B. (ed.) (1994): *Howe: four millennia of Orkney prehistory* (Society of Antiquaries of Scotland Monograph 9), Edinburgh.

Balsdon, J. P. V. D. (1969): *Life and leisure in ancient Rome*, London.

Baluta, C. L. (1981): 'Fond de moule romaine pour la fabrication de bouteilles carrées trouvé a Apulum (Dacie)', *Annales du 8e Congrès du AIHV*, Liège, 111–13.

Barag, D. (1963): 'The glassware', in Yadin, Y., *The finds from the Bar Kokhba period in the Cave of Letters*, Jerusalem, 101–10.

Barag, D. (1967): 'The glass vessels', in Dothan, M. & Freedman, D. N., (eds), *Ashdod I: the first season of excavations 1962 (Atiquot 7)*, 36–37, 72–73.

Barag, D. (1969): '"Flower and bird" and snake-thread glass vessels', *Annales du 4e Congrès du AIHV*, Liège, 55–66.

Barag, D. (1972): 'Two Roman glass bottles

with remnants of oil', *Israel Exploration Journal* 22, 24–26.

Barag, D. (1987): 'Recent important epigraphic discoveries related to the history of glassmaking in the Roman period', *Annales du 10e Congrès du AIHV*, Amsterdam 1987, 109–16.

Barber, J. (1982): 'A wooden bowl from Talisker Moor, Skye', *PSAS* 112, 578–79.

Barkóczi, L. (1988): *Pannonische Glasfunde in Ungarn* (Studia Archaeologica 9), Budapest.

Barrett, J. C., Fitzpatrick, A. P. & Macinnes, L. (eds) (1989): *Barbarians and Romans in north-west Europe from the later Republic to late Antiquity* (BAR Int.Ser. 471), Oxford.

Basch, A. (1972): 'Analyses of oil from two Roman glass bottles', *Israel Exploration Journal* 22, 27–32.

Bateson, J. D. (1973): 'Roman material from Ireland: a re-consideration', *Proceedings of the Royal Irish Academy* 73C, 21–97.

Bauschatz, P. C. (1978): 'The Germanic ritual feast', in Weinstock, J. (ed.), *The Nordic languages and modern linguistics* 3, Austin, TX, 289–95.

Baxter, M. J. et al. (1995): 'Compositional variability in colourless Roman vessel glass', *Archaeometry* 37:1, 129–41.

Baxter, M. J. et al. (2005): 'Further Studies in the compositional variability in colourless Romano-British vessel glass', *Archaeometry* 47:1, 47–68.

Behrens, G. (1925): *Römische Gläser aus Deutschland* (Kulturgeschichtliche Wegweiser durch das Römisch-Germanische Central-Museum 8), Mainz.

Behrens, G. (1925–26): 'Römische Gläser aus Rheinhessen', *Mainzer Zeitschrift* 20–21, 62–77.

Bel, V. (1990): 'Le verre de la nécropole de Saint-Paul-Trois-Châteaux', *Annales de 11e Congrès du AIHV*, Basel, 145–51.

Benea, D. (2000): 'Les verres d'époque romaine du vicus militaire de Tibiscum', *Annales du 14e Congrès du AIHV*, Lochem, 178–81.

Benton, S. (1930–31): 'The excavation of the Sculptor's Cave, Covesea, Morayshire', *PSAS* 65 (1930–31), 177–216.

Béraud, I. & Gébara, C. (1990): 'La datation du verre des necropoles gallo-romaines de Fréjus', *Annales du 11e Congrès du AIHV*, Basel, 153–65.

Berger, L. (1960): *Römische gläser aus*

Vindonissa (Veröffentlichungen der Gesellschaft pro Vindonissa IV), Basel.

Bernhard, H. (1982): 'Germanische Funde der Spätantike zwischen Strassburg und Mainz', *Saalburg Jahrbuch* 38, 72–107.

Biaggio Simona, S. (1990): 'Buntgefleckte Gläser aus dem Kanton Tessin (Süd-schweiz)', *Annales du 11e Congrès du AIHV*, Basel, 95–104.

Biaggio Simona, S. (1991): *I vetri Romani* I–II, Locarno.

Biddle, M. (1967): 'Two Flavian burials from Grange Road, Winchester', *AntJ* 47, 234–50.

Biel, J. (1985): *Der Keltenfürst von Hoch-dorf*, Stuttgart 1985.

Binchy, D. A. (1958): 'The fair of Tailtiu and the feast of Tara', *Ériu* 18, 113–38.

Birley, E. (1938): 'Pottery', in Kilbride-Jones, H. E. (1938b), 347–48.

Bjork, R. E. & Obermeier, A. (1997): 'Date, provenance, author, audiences', in Bjork, R. E. & Niles, J. D. (eds), *A Beowulf handbook*, Exeter, 13–34.

Björklund, E. & Hejjl, L. (1996): *Roman reflections in Scandinavia*, Roma.

Bjørn, A. (1929): *Bronsekar og glasbegre fra Folkevandringstiden i Norge* (Det kgl norske videnskabers selskabs skrifter 1929:6), Trondhjem.

Black, G. (1891): 'Report on the archaeo-logical examination of the Culbin Sands, Elginshire, obtained under the Victoria Jubilee gift of his excellency Dr R. H. Gunning, F.S.A. Scot', *PSAS* 25, 484–511.

Blake, M. E. (1947): *Ancient Roman con-struction in Italy from the prehistoric period to Augustus*, Washington.

von Boeselager, D. (1989): 'Zur Datierung der Gläser aus zwei Gräbern an der Luxemburger Strasse, Köln', *KölnJb* 22, 29–36.

Boon, G. C. (1959): 'The latest objects from Silchester, Hants.', *Medieval Archaeology* 3, 79–88.

Boon, G. C. (1966): 'Roman window glass from Wales', *JGS* 8, 41–45.

Boon, G. C. (1969): 'Roman glass in Wales', *Annales du 4e Congrès des Journées Internationales du Verre, Ravenne-Venise 13–20 Mai 1967*, Liège, 93–102.

Boon, G. C. (1974): *Silchester: the Roman town of Calleva*, London.

Boon, G. C. (1975): 'A Roman stave of larch-wood and other unpublished finds mainly of organic materials,

together with a note on late barracks', *Archaeologia Cambrensis* 124, 52–67.

Booth, A. (1991): 'The age for reclining and its attendant perils', in Slater, W. J. (ed.), *Dining in a Classical context*, Ann Arbor, MI, 105–20.

Booth, P. (1982): 'A Romano-British burial from Mancetter', *Transactions of the Birmingham and Warwickshire Archaeological Society* 92, 134–36.

Bourdieu, P. (1977): *Outline of a theory of practice*, Cambridge.

Bourdieu, P. (1980): 'The aristocracy of culture', *Media, Culture and Society* 2, 225–54.

Bourdieu, P. (1984): *Distinction: a social critique of the judgement of taste*, London.

Bourdieu, P. (1986a): *Kultursociologiska texter; i urval av Broady, D. & Palme, M.*, Lidingö.

Bourdieu, P. (1986b): 'The forms of capital', in Richardson, J. G. (ed.), *Handbook of theory and research of the sociology of education*, New York, NY, 241–58.

Bourdieu, P. (1988): *Homo Academicus*, Stanford, CA.

Bourdieu, P. (1990): *The logic of practice*, Cambridge.

Bourdieu, P. (1994): 'Distinction: a social critique of the judgement of taste', in Grusky, D. B. (ed.), *Social stratification: class, race, and gender in sociological perspective*, Boulder, CO, 404–29.

Bourdieu, P. (1998): *Practical reason*, Stanford, CA.

Bourke, E. (1994): 'Glass vessels of the first nine centuries AD in Ireland', *Journal of the Royal Society of Anti-quaries of Ireland* 124, 163–209.

Bowman, A. K. & Thomas, J. D. (1994): *The Vindolanda writing-tablets* (Tabulae Vindolandenses II), London.

Boye, L. (2002): 'Glasskår i munden – en upåagtet gravskik i yngre romersk jernalder', in Pind, J. et al., 203–9.

Braund, D. (1984): *Rome and the friendly king: the character of the client king-ship*, London.

Braund, D. (1989): 'Ideology, subsidies and trade: the king on the northern frontier revisited', in Barrett, J. C., Fitzpatrick, A. P. & Macinnes, L. (eds), 14–26.

Breeze, D. (1982): *The northern frontiers of Roman Britain*, London.

Breeze, D. (1990): 'The impact of the Roman army on the native peoples of north Britain', *Akten des 14.*

Internationalen Limeskongress 1986 in Carnuntum I, Wien, 85–97.

Breeze, D. J. & Ritchie, J. N. G. (1980): 'A Roman burial at High Torrs, Luce Sands, Wigtownshire', *Transactions of the Dumfriesshire and Galloway Natural History and Antiquarian Society* 55, 77–85.

Broady, D. (1989): *Kapital, habitus, fält. Några nyckelbegrepp i Pierre Bourdieus sociologi* (UHÄ arbetsrapport 1989:2), Stockholm.

Brogan, O. (1936): 'Trade between the Roman Empire and the Free Germans', *JRS* 26, 195–222.

Broholm, H. C. (1954): 'Fra yngre Romertid i Sydsjælland', *Fra Nationalmuseets Arbejdsmark*, 95–107.

Broholm, H. C. (1960): *Kulturforbindelser mellem Danmark og syden i ældre Jærnalder*, København.

Bromehead, C. N. (1952): 'What was Murrhine?', *Antiquity* 26, 65–70.

Brown, A. G. & Meadows, I. (2000): 'Roman vineyards in Britain: finds from the Nene Valley and new research', *Anti-quity* 74, 491–92.

Brown, A. G. et al. (2001): 'Roman vine-yards in Britain: stratigraphic and palynological data from Wollaston in the Nene Valley, England', *Antiquity* 75, 745–57.

Brown, G. B. (1915): 'Notes on a neck-lace of glass beads found in a cist in Dalmeny Park, South Queensferry', *PSAS* 49, 332–38.

Brun, J.-P. (2000): 'The production of perfumes in Antiquity: the cases of Delos and Paestum', *AJA* 104, 277–308.

Brun, J.-P. (2003): 'Le verre dans le Désert Oriental d'Égypte: contexts datés', in Foy, D. & Nenna, M.-D. (eds), 377–87.

Bruun & Lund (1974): see Tacitus, Ancient and Medieval sources.

Bucovală, M. (1984): 'Roman glass vessels discovered in Dobrudja', *JGS* 26, 59–63.

Buechner, T. S. (1960): 'The glass from Tarrha', *Hesperia* 29:1, 109–17.

Bulat, M. (1974): 'Verrerie antique au Musée de la Slavonie', *Arheološki Vestnik* 25, 88–101.

Buora, M. (1998): 'La circolazione vetraria nell'Italia Nordorientale nel periodo Tardoantico e la produzione di un maestro vetrario a Sevegliano', in La Guardia, R. & Tibiletti, T. (eds), 165–72.

Burgess, C. B. (1970): 'Excavations at the

scooped settlement Hetha Burn 1, Hethpool, Northumberland, 1969', *Transactions of the Architectural and Archaeological Society of Durham and Northumberland* 2, 1–25.

Burley, E. (1956): 'A catalogue and survey of the metalwork from Traprain Law', *PSAS* 89, 118–226.

Burnham, B. et al. (2004): 'Roman Britain in 2003', *Britannia* 35, 253–349.

Bushe-Fox, J. P. (1949): *Fourth report on the excavations of the Roman fort at Richborough, Kent* (RRCSAL 16), Oxford.

Calhoun, C. (1993): 'Habitus, field, and capital: the question of historical specificity', in Calhoun, C., LiPuma, E. & Postone, M. (eds), *Bourdieu: critical perspectives*, Cambridge, MA & Oxford, 61–88.

Callander, J. G. (1914–15): 'Notice of a bronze cup and other objects found apparently in a sepulchral deposit near Tarland, Aberdeenshire', *PSAS* 49, 203–6.

Callander, J. G. (1932–33): 'A collection of prehistoric relics from the Stevenston Sands, Ayrshire, and other objects in the National Museum', *PSAS* 67, 26–34.

Callender, M. H. (1965): *Roman amphorae*, London.

Calvi, M. C. (1968): *I vetri romani del Museo di Aquileia* (Pubblicazioni dell' Associazione Nationale per Aquileia 7), Aquileia.

Calvi, M. C. (1969): *I vetri romani* (Pubblicazioni dell'Associazione Nationale per Aquileia 8), Aquileia.

Campbell, E. (1991): *Imported goods in the Early Medieval Celtic West: with special reference to Dinas Powys* (unpublished PhD thesis, University of Wales, College of Cardiff), Cardiff.

Campbell, E. (1995): 'New evidence for glass vessels in western Britain and Ireland in the 6th/7th centuries AD', in Foy, D. (ed.), 35–40.

Campbell, E. (1997): 'The Early Medieval vessel glass', in Hill, P. (ed.), 297–314.

Campbell, E. (2000): 'A review of glass vessels in western Britain and Ireland AD 400–800', in Price, J. (ed.), (2000b), 33–46.

Campbell, E. (2007): *Continental and Mediterranean imports to Atlantic Britain and Ireland, AD 400–800* (CBA Research Report 157), York.

Campbell, L. (2012): 'Modifying material: social biographies of Roman material culture', in Kyle, A. & Jervis, B. (eds) *Made do and mend: the archaeologies of compromise* (BAR Int. Ser. 2408), Oxford, 11–25.

Campbell, R. (2008): 'Manufacturing evidence of Romano-British glass bangles from Thearne, near Beverley East Yorkshire', *Yorkshire Archaeological Society: Roman Antiquities Section Bulletin* 24, 12–17.

Capo, G. (1972–76): 'Vetro', in Carandini, A. & Panella, C. (eds), *Ostia IV* (Seminario di Archeologia e Storia dell'Arte Greca e Romana dell'Università di Roma, Studi Miscellanei 23), Roma, 336–43.

Caputo, G (1951): 'Parte seconda', in Pace, B., Sergi, S. & Caputo, G., 'Scavi Sahariani. Ricerche nell'Uadi el-Agial e nell'Oasi di Gat', *Monumenti Antichi: pubblicati dall'Accademia dei Lincei* 41, 201–442.

Card, N. et al. (2000): 'Minehowe', *D & E*, 65–66.

Cardonell, A. M. C. (1790): *Relicta Antiqua* (unpublished manuscript at National Museums Scotland, Edinburgh).

Carington-Smith, J. (1982): 'A Roman chamber tomb from the south-east slope of Monasteraki Kephala, Knossos', *The Annual of the British School at Athens* 77, 255–93.

Carlson, R. G. (1990): 'Banana beer, reciprocity, and ancestor propriation among the Haya of Bukoba, Tanzania', *Ethnology* 29:4, 297–311.

Caron, B. (1997): 'Roman figure-engraved glass in the Metropolitan Museum of Art', *Metropolitan Museum Journal* 32, 19–50.

Carter, J. (1796): 'Account of sepulcral monuments discovered in Lincoln', *Archaeologia* 12, 107–13.

Carver, E. (2001): *The visibility of imported wine and its associated accoutrements in Later Iron Age Britain* (BAR Brit. Ser. 325), Oxford.

Cavers, G., Crone, A., Engl, R., Fouracre, L., Hunter, F., Robertson, J. & Thoms, J. (2011): 'Refining chronological resolution in Iron Age Scotland: excavations at Dorman's Island crannog, Dumfries and Galloway', *Journal of Wetland Archaeology* 10, 71–108.

Cermanovic-Kuzmanovic, A. (1974): 'Entwicklungsübersicht des römischen Glases in Montenegro', *Arheološki Vestnik* 25, 175–90.

Ceselin, F. (1998): 'Il vetro in epoca Romana: un bene suntuario? Risultato di un'analisi delle fonti iconografiche', in La Guardia, R. & Tibiletti, T. (eds), 131–38.

Cessford, C. (1994): 'Wine in Early Historic Scotland', *Journal of Wine Research* 5:1, 5–17.

Chalmers, P. (1851–54): 'Notice of the discovery of a curious bronze cross and chain in a stone cist, at Kingoldrum, Forfarshire', *PSAS* 1, 191.

Champion, T. C. (1985): 'Written sources and the study of the European Iron Age', in Champion, T. C. & Megaw, J. V. S. (eds), *Settlement and society: aspects of West European prehistory in the first millennium BC*, Leicester, 9–22.

Chapman, M. (1992): *The Celts: construction of a myth*, New York, NY & London.

Charleston, R. J., Evans, W. & Werner, A. E. (eds) (1968): *Studies in glass history and design* (Papers read to committee B. Sessions of the VIIIth international congress on glass, held in London 1–6 July 1968), London.

Charlesworth, D. (1959a): 'Roman glass in northern Britain', *ArchAel* (Series 4) 37, 33–58.

Charlesworth, D. (1959b): 'The glass', in Daniels, C. M. et al., 'The Roman bath-house at Red House, Corbridge', *ArchAel* (Series 4) 37, 164–66.

Charlesworth, D. (1966): 'Roman square bottles', *JGS* 8, 26–40.

Charlesworth, D. (1968): 'The dating and distribution of Roman cylindrical bottles', in Charleston, R. J., Evans, W. & Werner, A. E. (eds), 6–8.

Charlesworth, D. (1971): 'A group of vessels from the Commendant's house, Housesteads', *JGS* 13, 34–37.

Charlesworth, D. (1972): 'The glass', in Frere, S. S. (ed.), *Verulamium excavations I* (RRCSAL 28), Oxford, 196–212.

Charlesworth, D. (1973): 'Glass', in Hobley, B., 'Excavations at "the Lunt" Roman military site, second interim report', *Birmingham and Warwickshire Archaeological Society: Transactions for 1971–1973*, vol. 85, 78–79.

Charlesworth, D. (1974–76a): 'The glass', in Neal, D. S., 31–33, 92, 101–3.

Charlesworth, D. (1974–76b): 'The glass bowl', in Neal, D. S., 117.

Charlesworth, D. (1975a): 'A Roman cut glass plate from Wroxeter', *AntJ* 55, 404–6.

Charlesworth, D. (1975b): 'The Commendant's house, Housesteads', *ArchAel* (Series 5) 3, 17–42.

Charlesworth, D. (1976a): 'Glass', in Stead, I. M. (ed.), *Excavations at Winterton Roman villa and other Roman sites in north Lincolnshire* (Department of the Environment Archaeological Reports 9), London, 244–50.

Charlesworth, D. (1976b): 'Glass vessels', in MacGregor, A. (ed.), *Finds from a Roman sewer system and an adjacent building in Church Street* (The archaeology of York: the small finds), York, 15–18.

Charlesworth, D.(1978): 'The Roman glass', in Down, A. (ed.), *Chichester excavations* 3, Chichester, 267–72.

Charlesworth, D. (1979a): 'Glass', in Daniels, C. M., Dore, J. N. & Gillam, J. P., 'The Agricolan supply base at Red House, Corbridge', *ArchAel* (Series 5) 7, 58–61.

Charlesworth, D. (1979b): 'Glass (including material from other Exeter sites excavated between 1971 and 1976)', in Bidwell, P. T. (ed.), *The legionary bath-house and basilica and forum at Exeter*, Exeter, 222–31.

Charlesworth, D. (1979c): 'Glass from the excavations of 1966, 1967 and 1973', in Dore, J. N. & Gillam, J. P. (eds), *The Roman fort at South Shields*, Newcastle, 166–67

Charlesworth, D. (1979d): 'Glass, beads, armlets', in Potter, T. W., *Romans in north-west England. Excavations at the Roman forts of Ravenglass, Watercrook and Bowness on Solway* (Cumberland and Westmoreland Antiquarian and Archaeological Society Research Series 1), Kendal, 230–34.

Charlesworth, D. (1981): 'The glass', in Partridge, C. (ed.), *Skeleton Green: a late Iron Age and Romano-British site* (Britannia Monograph Series 2), London, 119, 268–71.

Charlesworth, D. (1984): 'The Xanten glass', *Beiträge zur Archäologie des römischen Rheinlands* 4, Köln, 283–300.

Charlesworth, D. (1985a): 'The glass', in Niblett, R. (ed.), *Sheepen: an early Roman industrial site at Camulodunum* (CBA Research Reports 57), London, Microfiche 1:A6–9, 3:F1–11.

Charlesworth, D. (1985b): 'Glass', in Draper, J. (ed.), *Excavations by Mr H. P. Cooper on the Roman site at Hill Farm, Gestingthorpe, Essex* (East Anglian Archaeology Report 25), Chelmsford, 64–66.

Cherian, P. J. (ed.) (2013): *Interim report of the Pattanam excavations/explorations – 2013*, Trivandrum.

Chiaramonte Trerè, C. (1973a): 'Vetri', in Frova, A. (ed.), 724–26.

Chiaramonte Trerè, C. (1973b): 'Vetri', in Frova, A. (ed.), 772–85.

Childe, V. G. (1933a): 'Excavations at Castlelaw, Midlothian, and the small forts of north Britain', *AntJ* 13, 1–12.

Childe, V. G. (1933b): 'Excavations at Castlelaw fort, Midlothian', *PSAS* 67, 362–88.

Christison, D. & Anderson, J. (1905): 'Report on the Society's excavations of forts on the Poltalloch estate, Argyll, 1904–05', *PSAS* 39, 259–322.

Christison, D. et al. (1902–03): 'Excavations of Castlecary fort on the Antonine *vallum*', *PSAS* 37, 271–346.

Christlein, R. (1963–64): 'Ein Bronzesiebfragment der Spätlatènezeit vom Zugmantel', *Saalburg Jahrbuch* 21, 16–19.

Clairmont, C. W. (1963): *The glass vessels* (Excavations at Dura Europos: Final report IV, part 5), New Haven.

Clark, J. E. & Blake, M. (1994): 'The power of prestige: competitive generosity and the emergence of rank societies in lowland Mesoamerica', in Brumfiel, E. M. & Fox, J. W. (eds), *Factional competition and political development in the New World*, Cambridge, 17–30.

Close-Brooks, J. (1983): 'Dr Bersu's excavations at Traprain Law, 1947', in O'Connor, A. & Clarke, D. V. (eds), *From the Stone Age to the 'Forty-five: studies presented to R. B. K. Stevenson*, Edinburgh, 206–23.

Collingwood, R. G. (1937): 'Roman Britain', in Frank, T. (ed.), *An economic survey of ancient Rome* III, Baltimore.

Collingwood, R. G. & Wright, R. P. (1992): *The Roman Inscriptions of Britain II:4: Instrumentum Domesticum*, London.

Colls, D. et al. (1977): *L'épave Port-Vendres II et le commerce de la Bétique a l'époque de Claude* (Archaeonautica 1), Paris.

Comfort, H. (1958): 'Imported pottery and glass from Timna', in LeBaron Bowen, R. & Albright, F. P. (eds), *Archaeological discoveries in South Arabia*, Baltimore, 199–212.

Cool, H. E. M. (1992): 'The vessel glass', in Caruana, I., 'Carlisle: excavation of a section of the annexe ditch of the first Flavian fort, 1990', *Britannia* 23, 63–68.

Cool, H. E. M. (1995a): 'Glass vessels', in Cool, H. E. M., Lloyd-Morgan, G. & Hooley, A. D. (eds), *Finds from the fortress* (The archaeology of York: the small finds 17/10), York, 1559–88.

Cool, H. E. M., (1995b): 'Glass vessels of the fourth and early fifth century in Roman Britain', in Foy, D. (ed.), 11–23.

Cool, H. E. M. (1996): 'Sedeinga and the glass vessels of the Kingdom of Meroe', *Annales du 13e Congrès du AIHV*, Lochem, 201–12.

Cool, H. E. M. (2000): 'Quernstones and other items of worked stone', in Smith, I. M. [Taylor, J. (ed.)], 304–11.

Cool, H.E.M. (2003): 'Local production and trade in glass vessels in the British Isles in the first to seventh centuries AD', in Foy, D. & Nenna, M.-D. (eds), 139–45.

Cool, H. E. M. (2004): 'The glass vessels', in Cool, H. E. M. (ed.), *The Roman cemetery at Brougham, Cumbria: excavations 1966–67* (Britannia Monograph Series 21), London, 364–73.

Cool, H. E. M. (2006): *Eating and drinking in Roman Britain*, Cambridge.

Cool, H. E. M. & Baxter, M. J. (1999): 'Peeling the onion: an approach to comparing vessel glass assemblages', *JRA* 12, 72–100.

Cool, H. E. M. & Price, J. (1987): 'The glass', in Meates, G. W. (ed.), *The Roman villa at Lullingstone, Kent II: the wall paintings and finds* (Monograph Series of the Kent Archaeological Society 3), Maidstone, 110–41.

Cool, H. E. M. & Price, J. (1989): 'The glass vessels', in Britnell, J. (ed.), *Caersws Vicus, Powys: excavations at the Old Primary School, 1985–86* (BAR Brit. Ser. 205), Oxford, 31–43.

Cool, H. E. M. & Price, J. (1991): 'The Roman vessel and window glass', in Padley, T.G. (ed.), *The metalwork, glass and stone objects from Castle Street, Carlisle: excavations 1981–2* (Cumberland and Westmorland Antiquarian and Archaeological Society Res. Ser. 5), Carlisle,165–76.

Cool, H. E. M. & Price, J. (1993–94): 'The glass vessels', in Booth, P., 'A Roman burial near Welford-on-Avon', *Transactions of the Birmingham and Warwickshire Archaeological Society* 98, 45–47.

Cool, H. E. M. & Price, J. (1995): *Roman*

vessel glass from excavations in Colchester, 1971–85 (Colchester Archaeological Report 8), Colchester.

Cool, H. E. M. & Price, J. (1998): 'The vessels and objects of glass', in Cool, H. E. M. & Philo, C. (eds), *Roman Castleford: excavations 1974–85 vol I: the small finds* (Yorkshire Archaeology 4), York, 141–81.

Cool, H. E .M. & Price, J. (2008): 'The glass vessels', in Cool, H. E. M. & Mason, D. J. P. (eds), *Roman Piercebridge: excavations by D. W. Harding and Peter Scott 1969–1981* (The Architectual and Archaeological Society of Durham and Northumberland. Research Report 7), Durham, 235–40.

Cowie, T. G. (1983): 'The pottery from North Mains: general discussion', in Barclay, G. J. (ed), 'Sites of the third millennium BC to the first millennium at North Mains, Strathallan, Perthshire', *PSAS* 113, 248–57.

Cramp, R. (1968): 'Glass finds from the Anglo-Saxon monastery of Monkwearmouth and Jarrow', in Charleston, R. J., Evans, W. & Werner, A. E. (eds),16–19.

Cree, J. E. (1923): 'Account of the excavations on Traprain Law during the summer of 1922', *PSAS* 57, 180–225.

Cree, J. E. (1924): 'Account of the excavation on Traprain Law during the summer of 1923', *PSAS* 58, 241–85.

Cree, J. E. & Curle, A. O. (1922): 'Account of the excavations on Traprain Law during the summer of 1921', *PSAS* 66, 189–260.

CRFB D1 (1994): *Corpus der römischen Funde im europäischen Barbaricum, Deutschland Band 1: Bundesländer Brandenburg und Berlin*, Laser, R. & Voß, H.-U. (eds), Bonn.

CRFB D2 (1995): *Corpus der römischen Funde im europäischen Barbaricum, Deutschland Band 2: Freistaat Sachsen*, Laser, R. & Schultze, E. (eds), Bonn.

CRFB D3 (1998): *Corpus der römischen Funde im europäischen Barbaricum, Deutschland Band 3: Bundesland Mecklenburg-Vorpommern*, Voß, H.-U. (ed.), Bonn.

CRFB D4 (2002): *Corpus der römischen Funde im europäischen Barbaricum, Deutschland Band 4: Hansestadt Bremen und Bundesland Niedersachsen*, Erdrich, M. (ed.), Bonn.

CRFB D5 (2004): *Corpus der römischen Funde im europäischen Barbaricum, Deutschland Band 5: Freie und Hansestadt Hamburg und Land Schleswig-Holstein*, Erdrich, M. & von Carnap-Bornheim, C., Bonn.

CRFB D6 (2006): *Corpus der römischen Funde im europäischen Barbaricum, Deutschland Band 6: Land Sachsen-Anhalt*, Becker, M., Bemmann, J., Laser, R., Leineweber, R., Schmidt, B., Schmidt-Thielbeer, E. & Wetzel, I. (eds), Bonn.

CRFB D7 (2009): *Corpus der römischen Funde im europäischen Barbaricum, Deutschland Band 7: Land Nordrhein-Westfalen, Landesteile Westfalen und Lippe*, Berke, S. (ed.), Bonn.

CRFB L (2001): *Corpus der römischen Funde im europäischen Barbaricum, Litauen*, Michelbertas, M. (ed.), Vilnius.

CRFB P1 (1998): *Korpus znalezisk rzymskich z europejskiego Barbaricum. Polska, Suplement 1: Corpus der Römischen Funde im Europäischen Barbaricum, Polen Band* 1, Kolendo, J. (ed.), Warszawa.

CRFB P2 (2001): *Korpus znalezisk rzymskich z europejskiego Barbaricum. Polska, Suplement 2: Corpus der Römischen Funde im Europäischen Barbaricum, Polen Band* 2, Kolendo, J. & Bursche, A. (eds), Warszawa.

CRFB P3 (2006): *Korpus znalezisk rzymskich z europejskiego Barbaricum. Polska, Suplement 3: Corpus der Römischen Funde im Europäischen Barbaricum, Polen Band* 3, Bursche, A. & Ciolek, R. (eds), Warszawa.

Crone, A. (1992): 'Wood' in Woodiwiss, S. (ed.), *Iron Age and Roman salt production and the medieval town of Droitwich: excavations at the old Bowling Green and Friar Street*, London, 106–13.

Crone, A. (1993): 'A wooden bowl from Loch a'Ghlinne Bhig, Bracadale, Skye', *PSAS* 123, 269–75.

Crone, A. (2000): *The history of a Scottish Lowland crannog: excavations at Buiston, Ayrshire 1989–90*, Edinburgh.

Crone, A. (2004): 'The barrel and its wooden contents', in Bishop, M. C., *Inveresk gate: excavations in the Roman civil settlement at Inveresk, East Lothian, 1996–2000*, Edinburgh, 163–67.

Crowfoot, G. M. & Harden, D. B. (1931): 'Early Byzantine and later glass lamps', *Journal of Egyptian Archaeology* 17, 196–206.

Cruden, S. H. (1939–40): 'The ramparts of Traprain Law: excavations in 1939', *PSAS* 74, 48–59.

Csikszentmihalyi, M. & Rochberg-Halton, E. (1981): *The meaning of things: domestic symbols and the self*, Cambridge.

Cummings, K. (1980): *The technique of glass forming*, London.

Cüppers, H. (1970): 'Wein und Weinbau zur Römerzeit im Rheinland', in Bömer, F. & Voit, L. (eds), *Germania Romana III: Römisches Leben aus Germanischen Boden* (Gymnasium Beihefte 7), Heidelberg, 138–45.

Cüppers, H. et al.(1983): *Die Römer an Mosel und Saar*, Mainz.

Curle, A. O. (1914): 'Report on the excavation, in September 1913 of a vitrified fort at Rockcliffe, Dalbeattie, known as the Mote of Mark', *PSAS* 48, 125–68.

Curle, A. O. (1915): 'Account of excavations on Traprain Law in the parish of Prestonkirk, county of Haddington, in 1914', *PSAS* 49, 139–202.

Curle, A. O. (1920) 'Report of the excavation on Traprain Law in the summer of 1919', *PSAS* 54, 54–123.

Curle, A. O. (1921): 'Account of excavations on Traprain Law during the summer of 1920', *PSAS* 55, 153–206.

Curle, A. O. & Cree, J. E. (1915–16): 'Account of excavations on Traprain Law in the parish of Prestonkirk, county of Haddington, in 1915', *PSAS* 50, 64–144.

Curle, J. (1892): 'Notes on two brochs recently discovered at Bow, Midlothian, and Torwoodlee, Selkirkshire', *PSAS* 26, 68–84.

Curle, J. (1913): 'Roman and native remains in Caledonia', *JRS* 3, 99–115.

Curle, J. (1932a): 'An inventory of objects of Roman and provincial Roman origin found on sites in Scotland not definitely associated with Roman construction', *PSAS* 65, 277–397.

Curle, J. (1932b): 'Roman drift in Caledonia', *JRS* 10, 73–77.

Curtis, N. G. W. & Hunter, F. (2006): 'An unusual pair of Roman bronze vessels from Stoneywood, Aberdeen, and other Roman finds from north-east Scotland', *PSAS* 136, 199–214.

Cuthbert, O. D. (1995): *The life and letters of an Orkney naturalist. Reverend George Low, 1747–95*, Kirkwall.

Czurda-Ruth, B. (1979): *Die römischer Gläser vom Magdalensberg* (Kärntner Museumsschriften 65), Klagenfurt.

Czurda-Ruth, B. (1989): 'Zu den römischen Gläsern aus den Hanghäusern von Ephesus', *KölnJb* 22, 129–40.

Damevski, V. (1974) 'A survey of the types of glass vessels from Italic, Gallic, Mediterranean, and Rhenish workshops on the territory of Croatia during the Roman Empire', *Arheološki Vestnik* 25, 62–87.

Dasnoy, A. (1966): 'Quelques ensembles archéologiques du bas empire provenant de la région namuroise (Spontin, Flavion, Tongrinne, Jamiolle, Jambes, Treigne)', *Annales de la Société Archéologique de Namur* 53, 169–232.

Dasnoy, A. (1968): 'La nécropole de Samson (IVe–VIe siècles)', *Annales de la Société Archéologique de Namur* 54, 277–334.

Dasnoy, A. (1969): 'La nécropole de Furfooz', *Annales de la Société Archéologique de Namur* 55, 121–94.

Davidson, J. (1886):'Notice of a small cup-shaped glass vessel found in a stone cist at the public school, Airlie, and now presented to the museum by the school board of Airlie', *PSAS* 20, 136–41.

Davidson Weinberg, G. (ed.) (1998): *Excavations at Jalame: site of a glass factory in late Roman Palestine*, Columbia, MO.

Davies, M. H. (2000): 'East Coldoch (Kincardine parish): palisaded enclosures; barrow; cists; homestead', *D & E*, 90.

Davies, R. W. (1971): 'The Roman military diet', *Britannia* 2, 122–42.

Déchelette, J. (1934): *Manuel d'archéologie préhistorique, celtique et gallo-romaine* 6, Paris.

Dell'Acqua, F. (2004): 'Le finestre inveriate nell'antichità romana', in Beretta, M. & Di Pasquale, G. (eds), *Vitrum: Il vetro fra arte e scienza nel mondo romano*, Firenze, 109–19.

DeMaine, M. R. (1983): 'Ancient glass distribution in Illyricum', *JGS* 25, 79–86.

DeMaine, M. R. (1990): 'The northern necropolis at Emona: banquet burials with ladles', *Annales du 11e Congrès du AIHV*, Basel, 129–44.

De Tommaso, G. (1985): 'Vetro', in Ricci, A. (ed.), *Settefinestre: una villa schiavistica nell'Etruria romana*, Modena.

De Tommaso, G. (1989): 'Vetri incisi dalle collezioni del Museo Nazionale Romano di Roma', *KölnJb* 22, 99–104.

De Tommaso, G. (1994): 'Vetri incisi dalla Tuscia annonaria. Note sulla produzione di vetri incisi tra III e IV secolo', *Archeologia Classica* 46, 261–78.

De Tommaso, G. (2000): 'Alcuni vetri incisi dalle collezioni del Museo Nazionale Romano', *Annales du 14e Congrès du AIHV*, Lochem, 113–16.

Dickson, J. H. (1978): 'Bronze Age mead', *Antiquity* 52, 108–13.

Dietler, M. (1989): 'Greeks, Etruscans, and thirsty barbarians: Early Iron Age interaction in the Rhône Basin of France', in Champion, T. C. (ed.), *Centre and periphery: comparative studies in archaeology*, London, 127–41.

Dietler, M. (1990): 'Driven by drink: the role of drinking in the political economy and the case of Early Iron Age France', *Journal of Anthropological Archaeology* 9, 352–406.

Dietler, M. (1995): 'The cup of Gyptis: rethinking the colonial encounter in Early Iron Age Western Europe and the relevance of world-system models', *Journal of European Archaeology* 3:2, 89–111.

Dietler, M. (1996): 'Feasts and commensal politics in the political economy: food, power, and status in prehistoric Europe', in Wiessner, P. & Schiefenhövel, W. (eds), 87–125.

Dietler, M. (2001): 'Theorizing the feast: rituals of consumption, commensal politics, and power in African contexts', in Dietler, M. & Hayden, B. (eds), 65–114.

Dietler, M. (2006): 'Alcohol: anthropological/archaeological perspectives', *Annual Review of of Anthropology* 35, 229–49.

Dietler, M. & Hayden, B. (2001): 'Digesting the feast: good to eat, good to drink, good to think. An introduction', in Dietler, M. & Hayden, B. (eds), 1–22.

Dietler, M. & Hayden, B. (eds) (2001): *Feasts: archaeological and ethnographic perspectives on food, politics and power*, Washington & London.

Dietler, M. & Herbich, I. (2001): 'Feasts and labor mobilization: dissecting a fundamental economic practice', in Dietler, M. & Hayden, B. (eds), 240–66.

Dillon, M. (1948): *Early Irish literature*, Chicago, IL.

Dillon 1962: see Ancient and Medieval sources.

Dineley, M. & Dineley, G. (2000): 'Neolithic ale: barley as a source of sugars for fermentation', in Fairbairn, A. (ed.), *Plants in the Neolithic and beyond* (Neolithic Studies Group Seminar Papers 5), Oxford, 137–53.

Dittmar, H. (1992): *The social psychology of material possessions: to have is to be*, New York, NY.

Dobson, B. & Mann, J. C. (1973): 'The Roman army in Britain and Britons in the Roman army', *Britannia* 4, 191–205.

Dockrill, S. J. et al. (2002):'Old Scatness and the broch lairds of the Northern Isles', *Current Archaeology* 177 (2002), 382–90.

Doppelfeld, O. (1966): *Römisches und fränkisches Glas in Köln*, Köln.

Doppelfeld, O. (1970): 'Ein farbiger Muschelpokal aus Köln', in Keller, H. et al. (eds), *Festschrift für Gert von der Osten*, Köln, 17–23.

Douglas, M. (ed.) (1987): *Constructive drinking: perspectives on drink from anthropology*, Cambridge.

Douglas, M. & Isherwood, B. (1980): *The world of goods: towards an anthropology of consumption*, Harmondsworth. First published in 1978.

Drexel, F. (1920): 'Die Bilder der Igeler Säule', *Mitteilungen des Deutchen Archaeologischen Instituts: Roemische Abteilung* 35, 83–142.

Driscoll, S. T. & Yeoman, P. A. (eds) (1997): *Excavations within Edinburgh Castle in 1988–91* (Society of Antiquaries of Scotland Monograph 12), Edinburgh.

Dunbabin, K. M. D. (1991): 'Triclinium and stibadium', in Slater, W. J. (ed.), *Dining in a Classical context*, Ann Arbor, MI, 120–48.

Dunbabin, K. M. D. (1993): 'Wine and water at the Roman *convivium*', *JRA* 6, 116–41.

Dunbabin, K. M. D. (1995): 'Scenes from the Roman *convivium: frigida non derit, non derit calda petenti* (Martial xiv. 105)', in Murray, O. & Tecusan, M. (eds), 252–65.

Dunbabin, K. M. D. (2003a): *The Roman banquet: images of convivality*, Cambridge.

Dunbabin, K. M. D. (2003b): 'The waiting servant in later Roman art', *American Journal of Philology* 124, 443–68.

Dunbar, D. (1930): 'Note on a Roman glass bottle from the parish of Turriff, found about 1857', *PSAS* 64, 147–48.

Duncan-Jones, R. (1974): *The economy of the Roman empire: quantitative studies*, Cambridge (revised 1982).

Dungworth, D. (1997): 'Copper metallurgy in Iron Age Britain: some recent research', in Gwilt, A. & Haselgrove, C. (eds), 46–50.

Dunwell, A. (2007): *Cist burials and an Iron Age settlement at Dryburn Bridge,*

Innerwick, East Lothian (Scottish Archaeological Internet Report 24), Edinburgh. (www.sair.org.uk)

Dupré, G. & Rey, P.-P. (1969): 'Réflexions sur la pertinence d'une théorie de l'histoire des échanges', *Cahiers Internationaux de Sociologie* 46, 133–62.

During Caspers, E. C. L. (1980): *The Bahrain tumuli: an illustrated catalogue of two important collections*, Leiden.

Dusenbery, E. B. (1967): 'Ancient glass from the cemeteries of Samothrace', *JGS* 9, 34–49.

Earle, T. K. (1977): 'A reappraisal of redistribution: complex Hawaiian chiefdoms', in Earle, T. K. & Ericson, J. E. (eds), *Exchange systems in prehistory*, New York, NY, 213–32.

Earle, T. K. & d'Altroy, T. N. (1982): 'Storage facilities and state finance in the Upper Mantaro Valley, Peru', in Ericson, J. E. & Earle, T. K. (eds), *Contexts for prehistoric exchange*, New York, NY, 265–90.

Earwood, C. (1993): *Domestic wooden artefacts in Britain and Ireland from Neolithic to Viking times*, Exeter.

Eckardt, H. (2006): 'The character, chronology and use of the late Roman pits: the Silchester finds assemblage', in Fulford, M. et al. (eds), 221–45.

Ecroyd Smith, H. (1852): *Reliquiae Isurianae: the remains of the Roman Isurium (now Aldborough, near Boroughbridge, Yorkshire)*, London.

Edgren, B. et al. (1976): 'Bygd och borg i Hässelby: rapport från ett bebyggelsehistoriskt forskningsprojekt på mellersta Öland', *Öländsk Bygd* (Åkerbo Hembygdsförening Årsbok), 4–50.

Eggers, H.-J. (1940): *Das römische Einfuhrgut in Pommern* (Beiheft zum Erwerbungs- und Forschungsbericht Pommerisches Landesmuseum Stettin), Stettin.

Eggers, H.-J. (1948–49): 'Das Körpergrab von Woldegk, Mecklenburg-Strelitz', *Hammaburg* I, 230–37.

Eggers, H.-J. (1949–50): 'Lübsow, ein Germanische Fürstensitz der älteren Kaiserzeit', *Praehistorische Zeitschrift* 34/35, 58–111.

Eggers, H.-J. (1951): *Der römische Import im freien Germanien* (Atlas der Urgeschichte I), Glückstadt 1951.

Eggers, H.-J. (1964): 'Das Kaiserzeitliche Gräberfeld von Pollwitten, Kreis Mohrungen', *Jahrbuch des Römisch-Germanischen Zentralmuseums Mainz* 11, 154–75.

Eggers, H.-J. (1966): 'Römische Bronzegefässe in Britannien', *Jahrbuch des Römisch-Germanischen Zentralmuseum Mainz* 13, 67–164.

Eggers, H.-J. & Stary, P. F. (2001): *Funde der Vorrömischen Eisenzeit, der Römischen Kaiserzeit und der Völkerwanderungszeit in Pommern* (Beiträge zur Ur- und Frühgeschichte Mecklenburg-Vorpommerns 38), Lübstorf.

Ekholm, G. (1934): *Romerska vinskopor och kärl av Hemmoortyp i skandinaviska fynd*, Uppsala.

Ekholm, G. (1937a): 'Romerska glasvaror i Skandinavien', *Fornvännen* 32, 65–83.

Ekholm, G. (1937b): 'Bornholms fynd av romerska importvaror', *Bornholmske Samlinger* 25, 333–43.

Ekholm, G. (1956): 'De orientaliska glasens vägar mot Norden', *Fornvännen* 51, 246–66.

Ekholm, G. (1958a): 'De ribbade skålarnas ursprung', *Fornvännen* 53, 17–25.

Ekholm, G. (1985b): 'Westeuropäische Gläser in Skandinavien während der späten Kaiser- und der früher Merowingerzeit', *Acta Archaeologica* 29, 21–50.

Ekholm, K. (1972): *Power and prestige: the rise and fall of the Kongo kingdom*, Uppsala.

Ekholm, K. (1978): 'External exchange and the transformation of Central African social systems', in Friedman, J. & Rowlands, M. J. (eds), *The evolution of social systems*, Liverpool, 115–36.

Ellis, S. J .R. (2004): 'The distribution of bars at Pompeii: archaeological, spatial and viewshed analyses', *JRA* 17:1, 371–84.

Ellmers, D. (1978): 'Shipping on the Rhine during the Roman period: the pictorial evidence', in du Plat Taylor, J. & Cleere, H. (eds), 1–14.

Engelhardt, C. (1865): *Nydam mosefund 1859–1863*, Kjøbenhavn.

Engelhardt, C. (1866–71): 'Trouvailles danoises du commencement de l'Age de Fer', *Mémoires de la Société Royale des Antiquaires du Nord*, 262–72.

Engelhardt, C. (1871): 'Romerske statuetter og andre kunstgjenstande fra den tidlige nordiske jernalder', *Aarbøger for Nordisk oldkyndighed og historie*, 432–54.

Engelhardt, C. (1873): 'Valløby fundet', *Aarbøger for Nordisk oldkyndighed og historie*, 285–320.

Engelhardt, C. (1875): 'Klassisk industri og kulturs betydning for Norden i oldtiden', *Aarbøger for Nordisk oldkyndighed og historie*, 1–94.

Enright, M. J. (1996): *Lady with a mead cup: ritual, prophecy and lordship in the European warband from La Tène to the Viking Age*, Dublin.

Erdrich, M., Hanson, W. S. & Giannota, K. (2000): 'Traprain Law: native and Roman on the northern frontier', *PSAS* 130, 441–56.

Erim, K. T. et al. (1973): 'The Aphrodisias copy of Diocletian's edict on maximum prices', *JRS* 63, 108–9.

Espérandieu, É. (1911): *Recueil general des bas-reliefs de la Gaule romaine* E4, Paris.

Ethelberg, P. (1995): 'Skovgårde-gravpladsen: sydsjællandsk "fyrstegrave" fra 3. årh. e.Kr.', *Kulturhistoriske studier: Sydsjællands Museum*, 46–64.

Ethelberg, P. (2000): *Skovgårde: ein Bestattungsplatz mit reichen Frauengräbern des 3. Jhs. n.Chr. auf Seeland*, København.

Evison, V. I. (1974): 'An Anglo-Saxon glass claw-beaker from Mucking, Essex', *AntJ* 54:2, 277–78.

Evison, V. I. (1982): 'Anglo-Saxon glass claw-beakers', *Archaeologia* 107, 43–76.

Evison, V. I. (1983): 'Some distinctive glass vessels of the post-Roman period', *JGS* 25, 87–93.

Evison, V. I. (2000): 'Glass vessels in England AD 400–1100', in Price, J. (ed.), *Glass in Britain and Ireland AD 350–1100* (British Museum Occasional Paper 127), 47–98.

Facchini, G. M. (1990): 'Roman glass in an excavational context: Angera (VA)', *Annales du 11e Congrès du AIHV*, Basel, 105–15.

Fagan, G. G. (1999): *Bathing in public in the Roman world*, Ann Arbor, MI.

Faider-Feytmans, G. (1940): 'Les verreries des époques romaine et mérovingienne au Musée de Mariemont', *Revue belge d'archéologie et d'historie de l'art* 10:4, 211–29.

Fairhurst, H. (1984): *Excavations at Crosskirk broch, Caithness* (Society of Antiquaries of Scotland Monograph 3), Edinburgh.

Feachem, R. W. (1955–56): 'The fortifications on Traprain Law', *PSAS* 89, 284–89.

Feachem, R. W. (1956–57): 'Castlehill Wood dun', *PSAS* 90, 24–51.

Firth, R. (1983): 'Magnitudes and values in Kula exchange', in Leach, J. W. &

Leach, E. (eds), *The Kula: new perspectives on Massim exchange*, Cambridge, 89–102.

Fischer, C. (1981): 'En romersk glasskål med jaktmotiv fra en yngre romersk jernaldersgrav', *Kuml*, 165–81.

Fischer, J. (1990): 'Zu einer griechischen Kline und weiteren Südimporten aus dem Fürstengrabhügel Grafenbühl, Asperg, Kr. Ludwigsburg', *Germania* 68, 115–27.

Fitzpatrick, A. P. (1985): 'The distribution of Dressel 1 amphorae in north-west Europe', *Oxford Journal of Archaeology* 4:3, 305–21.

Fitzpatrick, A. P. (1989a): 'The submission of the Orkney Islands to Claudius: new evidence?', *Scottish Archaeological Review* 6, 24–33.

Fitzpatrick, A. P. (1989b): 'The uses of Roman imperialism by the Celtic barbarians in the later Republic', in Barrett, J. C., Fitzpatrick, A. P. & Macinnes, L. (eds), 27–54.

Fitzpatrick, A. P. (1992): 'La place des amphores dans l'approvisionnement militaire de l'Écosse romaine', *Journal of Roman Pottery Studies* 5, 179–83.

Fitzpatrick, A. P. (1996): '"Celtic" Iron Age Europe: the theoretical basis', in Graves-Brown, P., Jones, S. & Gamble, C. (eds), *Cultural identity and archaeology: the construction of European communities*, London & New York, NY, 238–55.

Fitzpatrick, A. P. (2003a): 'The place of Gaulish wine in the military supply of amphorae-born commodities to Roman Scotland', in Plouviez, J. (ed.), 60–63.

Fitzpatrick, A. P. (2003b): 'Roman amphorae in Iron Age Britain', in Plouviez, J. (ed.), 10–24.

Fleming, S. J. (1996): 'Early Imperial Roman glass at the University of Pennsylvania Museum', *Expedition* 38:2, 13–37.

Fleming, S. J. (1999): *Roman glass: reflections on cultural change*, Philadelphia, PA.

Fojut, N. (1998): 'How did we end up here? Shetland Iron Age studies to 1995', in Nicholson, R. A. & Dockrill, S. J. (eds), *Old Scatness broch, Shetland: Retro-spect and prospect*, Bradford, 1–15.

Follmann, A.-B. & Piepers, W. (1963): 'Laurenzberg, Kr. Jülich', in von Petrikovitz, H., 'Bericht über die Tätigkeit des Rheinischen Landesmuseums Bonn in Jahre 1961', *BonnJbb* 163, 539–45.

Follmann-Schulz, A.-B. (1990): 'Die römischen Gläser aus Bonn im Rheinischen Landesmuseum Bonn', *Annales du 11e Congrès du AIHV*, Basel, 117–27.

Follmann-Schulz, A.-B. (1992): *Die römischen Gläser im Rheinischen Landesmuseum Bonn*, Köln.

Follmann-Schulz, A.-B. (1995): 'À propos des precurseurs romains du Rüsselbecher', in Foy, D. (ed.), 85–87.

Fonnesbech-Sandberg, E. (2002): 'Romerske spillebrikker og anden import i en sjaellendsk fyrstegrav', in Pind, J. et al. (eds), 211–15.

Formenti, F. & Duthel, J. M. (1996): 'The analysis of wine and other organics inside amphoras of the Roman period', in McGovern, P. E., Fleming, S. J. & Katz, S. H. (eds), *The origins and ancient history of wine*, Amsterdam [3rd ed. 2000], 79–88.

Fortuna Canivet, M. T. (1969): 'I vetri Romani di Cornus conservati al Museo di Cagliari', *JGS* 11, 19–26.

Foy, D. (ed.) (1995): *Le verre de l'Antiquité Tardive et du Haut Moyen Age: typologie-chronologie-diffusion* (Association Française pour l'Archéologie du Verre, Musée Archéologique Departmentale du Val d'Oise), Val d'Oise.

Foy, D. (2003): 'Le verre en Tunisie: l'apport des fouilles récentes tuniso-françaises', *JGS* 45, 59–89.

Foy, D. et al. (2005): 'La circulation du verre en Méditerranée au début du IIIe siècle: le témoignage de *L'Épave Ouest Embiez 1* dans le sud de la France (fouilles 2001–03)', *Annales du 16e Congrès du AIHV*, Nottingham, 122–26.

Foy, D. & Hochuli-Gysel, A. (1995): 'Le verre Aquitane du IVe au IXe siecle: un état de la question', in Foy, D. (ed.), 151–75.

Foy, D. & Nenna, M.-D. (2001): *Tout feu: tout sable. Mille ans de verre antique dans le Midi de la France*, Aix-en-Provence.

Foy, D. & Nenna, M.-D. (eds), (2003): *Échanges et commerce du verre dans le monde antique*, Montagnac.

Frankenstein, S. & Rowlands, M. J. (1978): 'The internal structure and regional context of Early Iron Age society in south-western Germany', *Bulletin of the Institute of Archaeology of the University of London* 15, 73–112.

Frazer, A. (1964): 'The Cologne circus bowl: Basileus Helios and the cosmic hippodrome', in Freeman Sandler, L. (ed.), *Essays in memory of Karl Lehmann*, New York, NY, 105–13.

Freestone, I. (1991): 'Looking into glass', in Bowman, S. (ed.), *Science and the past*, London, 37–56.

Fremersdorf, F. (1926): 'Weitere Ausgrabungen unter dem Kreuzgang von St Severin in Köln', *BonnJbb* 131, 290–324.

Fremersdorf, F. (1933–34): 'Zur Geschichte des fränkischen Rüsselbechers', *Wallraf Richartz Jahrbuch* 2/3, 7–30.

Fremersdorf, F. (1938): 'Römische Gläser mit bunt-gefleckter Oberfläche', in von Petrikovitz, H. & Steeger, A. (eds), *Festschrift für August Oxé*, Darmstadt, 116–21.

Fremersdorf, F. (1939a): 'Erzeugnisse Kölner Manufacturen in den Funden von Kastell Saalburg und Zugmantel', *Saalburg Jahrbuch* 9, 6–22.

Fremersdorf, F. (1939b): 'Zur Zeitstellung und der herkunft der Millifiori-Gläser aus den vandalischen Fürstengräben von Sacrau bei Breslau', *Altschlesien* 8, 85–90.

Fremersdorf, F. (1955a): 'Aus der Tätigkeit des Römisch-Germanischen Museums Köln' *KölnJb* 1, 117–23.

Fremersdorf, F. (1955b): 'Zu dem blauen Glasbecher aus dem Reihengräberfeld von Pfahlheim (Kr. Ellwangen) im Germanischen Nationalmuseum, Nürnberg', *KölnJb* 1, 33–35.

Fremersdorf, F. (1958a): *Römisches Buntglas in Köln* (Die Denkmäler des Römischen Köln 3), Köln.

Fremersdorf, F. (1958b): *Das Naturfarbene, sogennante Blaugrüne Glas in Köln* (Die Denkmäler des Römischen Köln 4), Köln.

Fremersdorf, F. (1959): *Römische Gläser mit fadenauflage in Köln* (Die Denkmäler des römischen Köln 5), Köln.

Fremersdorf, F. (1961): *Römisches Geformtes Glas in Köln* (Die Denkmäler des Römischen Köln 6), Köln.

Fremersdorf, F. (1962): *Die Römischen Gläser mit Aufgelegten Nuppen* (Die Denkmäler des Römischen Köln 7), Köln.

Fremersdorf, F. (1965–66): 'Die anfänge der Römischen Glashütten Kölns I', *KölnJb* 8, 24–43.

Fremersdorf, F. (1967): *Die Römischen Gläser mit Schliff, Bemalung und Goldauflagen aus Köln* (Die Denkmäler des Römischen Köln 8), Köln.

Fremersdorf, F. (1970a): 'Seltene Varianten steilwandiger römischer Glasbecher des 3. Jh. aus Köln', *KölnJb* 11, 59–72.

Fremersdorf, F. (1970b): 'Die antiken Glasfunde', in Beck, H., 'Funde aus der germanischen Siedlung Westick bei Kamen, Kreis Unna', *Spätkaiserzeitliche Funde in Westfalen* (Bodenaltertümer Westfalens XII), Münster, 50–64.

Fremersdorf, F. (1970c): 'Die antiken Glasfunde', in Beck, H., 'Die germanische Siedlung auf dem Gelände der Zeche Erin in Castrop-Rauxel', *Spätkaiserzeitliche Funde in Westfalen* (Bodenaltertümer Westfalens XII), Münster, 83–106.

Fremersdorf, F. (1975): *Antikes, Islamisches und Mittelalterliches Glas* (Catalogo del Museo Sacro 5), Città del Vaticano.

Fremersdorf, F. & Fremersdorf-Polónyi, E. (1984): *Die Farblosen Gläser der Frühzeit in Köln: 2. und 3. Jahrhundert* (Die Denkmäler des Römischen Köln 9), Köln.

Frere, S. S. (1967): *Britannia: a history of Roman Britain*, London.

Friedhoff, U. (1989): 'Beigaben aus Glas in Körpergräben des späten 3. und des 4. Jahrhunderts: ein Indiz für den sozialen Status des Bestatteten', *KölnJb* 22, 37–48.

Frova, A. (ed.) (1973): *Scavi di Luni: relazione preliminare delle campagne di scavo 1970–1971*, Roma.

Fulford, M. G. (1985): 'Roman material in barbarian society c. 200 BC–c. AD 400', in Champion, T. C. & Megaw, J. V. S. (eds), *Settlement and society: aspects of West European prehistory in the first millenium BC*, Leicester, 91–108.

Fulford, M. G. (1989): 'Roman and barbarian: the economy of Roman frontier systems', in Barrett, J. C., Fitzpatrick, A. P. & Macinnes, L. (eds), 81–96.

Fulford, M. et al. (eds) (2006): *Life and labour in late Roman Silchester: excavations in Insula IX since 1997* (Britannia Monograph Series 22), London.

Funck, E. (1912): 'Römische Brandgräber in Remagen', *BonnJbb* 122, 256–70.

Fünfschilling, S. (1987): 'Beobachtungen zu Rippenschalen von Schweizer Fundorten', *Annales du 10e Congrès du AIHV*, Amsterdam, 81–103.

Fünfschilling, S. (2000): 'Form und funktion spätrömischen Glases im Castrum Rauracense (Kaiseraugst/AG)', *Annales du 14e Congrès du AIHV*, Lochem, 163–67.

Gage, J. (1834): 'A plan of barrows called the Bartlow Hills, in the parish of Ashdon, in Essex, with an account of Roman sepulchral relics recently discovered in the lesser barrows', *Archaeologia* 25, 1–23.

Galsterer, B. (1992): 'Stempel und Graffiti auf Holzfässern aus Oberaden', in Kühlborn, S. (ed.), *Das Römerlager in Oberaden* III, Münster, 203–14.

Garbacz, K. (2001): 'Importy rzymskie ze wschodniej czesci Niecki Nidzianskiej' (with a German summary), in *CRFB* P2, 177–237.

Garbsch, J. (1978): 'Glasgefässe und Fensterglas', in Schönberger, H. (ed.), *Kastell Oberstimm – Die Grabungen von 1968 bis 1971* (Limesforschungen 18), Berlin, 279–85.

Garnsey, P. (1999): *Food and society in Classical Antiquity*, Cambridge.

Gaut, B. (2007): 'Vessel glass from Kaupang: a contextual and social analysis', *Norwegian Archaeological Review* 40:1, 26–41.

Gebühr, M. (1974): 'Zur Definition älterkaiserzeitlicher Fürstengräber vom Lübsow-Typ', *Praehistorische Zeitschrift* 49, 82–127.

Gerharz, R. R. et al (1986): 'Munsell-Farbtafeln: Eine Notwendigkeit für Archäeo-logen?', *Acta praehistorica et archaeologica* 18, 177–87.

Gero, J. M. (1992): 'Feasts and females: gender ideology and political meals in the Andes', *Norwegian Archaeological Review* 25, 15–30.

Gillam, J. P. (1958): 'Roman and native, AD 122–197', in Richmond, I. A. (ed.), *Roman and native in north Britain*, Edinburgh, 60–89.

Gillam, J. P. (1959): 'The Roman coarse pottery', in Jobey, G., 255–58.

Gillam, J. P. (1979): 'Roman pottery', in Jobey, G., 22.

Gillam, J. P. (1984): 'A note on the Numeri Brittonum', in Miket, R. & Burgess, C. (eds), 287–94.

Goethert-Polaschek, K. (1977): *Katalog der römischen Gläser des Rheinischen Landesmuseums Trier* (Trierer Grabungen und Forschungen 9), Mainz.

Going, C. J. (1992): 'Economic "long waves" in the Roman period? A reconnaissance of the Romano-British ceramic evidence', *Oxford Journal of Archaeology* 11, 93–117.

Gosden, C. (1989): 'Debt, production, and prehistory', *Journal of Anthropological Archaeology* 8, 355–87.

Graham-Campbell, J. (2004): '"Danes … in this Country": discovering the Vikings in Scotland', *PSAS* 134, 210–39.

Gram, B. (1911), 'Mikroskopiske undersøgelser', in Müller, S., 'Juellinge-fundet og den romerske periode', *Nordiske Fortidsminder* 2, Kjøbenhavn 1911–1935, 40–46.

Gräslund, A.-S. (1965–66): 'Charonsmynt i vikingatida gravar?', *Tor* 11, 168–97.

Grazia Diani, M. (2000): 'Nuove attestazioni di vetro a mosaico e di bottiglie con bolli in Lombardia', *Annales du 14e congrès du AIHV*, Lochem, 76–81.

Green, M. J. (1998): 'Vessels of death: sacred cauldrons in archaeology and myth', *AntJ* 78, 63–84.

Greene, K. (1986): *The archaeology of the Roman economy*, London.

Greiff, S. & Schuster, J. (2008): 'Technological study of enamelling on Roman glass: the nature of opacifying, decolourizing and fining agents used with the glass beakers from Lübsow (Lubieszewo, Poland)', *Journal of Cultural Heritage* 9, e27–e32.

Grønbech, W. (1931): *The culture of the Teutons* I–III, Copenhagen.

Grose, D. F. (1974): 'Roman glass of the first century AD: a dated deposit of glassware from Cosa, Italy', *Annales du 6e Congrès du AIHV*, Liège, 31–52.

Grose, D. F. (1973–76): 'The glass from the Roman "colonia" of Cosa', *Bulletin du AIHV* 7, 175–82.

Grose, D. F. (1977): 'Early blown glass: the Western evidence', *JGS* 19, 9–29.

Grose, D. F. (1982): 'The Hellenistic and early Roman glass from Morgantina (Serra Orlando), Sicily', *JGS* 24, 20–29.

Grose, D. F. (1984a): 'The origins and early history of glass', in Klein, D. & Lloyd, W. (eds), *The history of glass*, Verona, 9–38.

Grose, D. F. (1984b): 'Glass forming methods in Classical Antiquity: some considerations', *JGS* 26, 25–34.

Grose, D. F. (1989): *Early ancient glass, core-formed, rod-formed, and cast vessels and objects from the late Bronze Age to the early Roman Empire, 1600 BC to AD 50*, New York, NY.

Grose, D. F. (1991): 'Early Imperial Roman cast glass: the translucent coloured and colourless fine wares', in Newby, M. & Painter, K. (eds), 1–18.

Grüß, J. (1931): 'Zwei altgermanischen

Trinkhörner mit Bier- und Metresten',
Praehistorische Zeitschrift 22, 180–91.

Gudenrath, W. (1991): 'Techniques of
glassmaking and decoration', in Tait,
H. (ed.), *Five thousand years of glass*,
London, 213–41.

Gudiol Ricart, J. (1936): *Eis vidres catalans*
(Monumenta Cataloniae III),
Barcelona.

Gueury, M.-C. & Vanderhoeven, M. (1989):
'La tombe gallo-romaine de Vervoz aux
Musées Royaux d'Art et d'Histoire',
*Bulletin des Musées Royaux d'Art et
d'Histoire* 60, 107–24.

Guido, M. (1978): *The glass beads of the
prehistoric and Roman periods in
Britain and Ireland* (RRCSAL 35),
London.

Gwilt, A. & Haselgrove, C. (eds) (1997):
*Reconstructing Iron Age societies:
new approaches to the British Iron
Age* (Oxbow Monograph 71), Oxford.

Haberey, W. (1942): 'Spätantike Gläser aus
Gräbern von Mayen', *BonnJbb* 147,
249–84.

Hackin, J. (1939): *Recherches archéologiques à Bégram* 2 (Memoires de la
Délégation Archéologique Francaise
en Afganistan IX), Paris.

Hackin, J. (1954): *Nouvelles recherches
archéologiques à Bégram* (Memoires
de la Délégation Archéologique
Francaise en Afganistan XI), Paris.

Haevernick, T. E. (1981a): 'Antike
Glasarmringe und ihre Herstellung';
originally published in *Glastechnische
Berichte* 25 (1952), 212–15, republished in Haevernick, T. E. (1981c), 8–11.

Haevernick, T. E. (1981b): 'Römische
Fensterscheiben', *Glastechnische
Berichte* 27 (1954), 464–66; republished in Haevernick, T. E. (1981c),
24–27.

Haevernick, T. E. (1981c): *Beiträge zur
Glasforschung*, Mainz.

Haevernick, T. E. & Hahn-Weinheimer, P.
(1981): 'Untersuchungen römischer
Fenstergläser'; originally published in
Saalburg Jahrbuch 14 (1955), 65–73,
republished in Haevernick, T. E.
(1981c), 33–38.

Hagberg, U. E. (1965): 'Hotade gravfält i
Gärdslösa', *Fornvännen* 60, 42–49.

Hamilton, J. R. C. (1968): *Excavations at
Clickhimin, Shetland* (Ministry of
Public Building and Works. Archaeo-
logical reports 6), Edinburgh.

Hansson, M. C. & Foley, B. P. (2008):
'Ancient DNA fragments inside Classical Greek amphoras reveal cargo of

2400-year-old shipwreck', *Journal of
Archaeologiccal Science* 35:5, 1169–
76.

Harden, D. B. (1934): 'Snake-thread glasses found in the East', *JRS* 25, 50–55.

Harden, D. B. (1936a): 'The glass', in
Ralegh Radford, C. A., 'The Roman
villa at Ditchley, Oxon', *Oxoniensia* 1,
62–64.

Harden, D. B. (1936b): *Roman glass from
Karanis*, Ann Arbor, MI.

Harden, D. B. (1945): 'Glass', in O'Neil, H.
E., 'The Roman villa at Park Street, near
St Albans, Hertfordshire: report of the
excavations of 1943–45', *ArchJ* 102,
68–72.

Harden, D. B. (1947): 'Camulodunum, the
glass', in Hawkes, C. F. C. & Hull, M. R.,
Camulodunum (RRCSAL 14), Oxford,
287–307.

Harden, D. B. (1950–51): 'The Roman
glass from Torwoodlee', in Piggott, S.,
112–13.

Harden, D. B. (1956): 'Glass vessels in
Britain and Ireland AD 400–1000', in
Harden, D. B. (ed.), *Dark-Age Britain:
studies presented to E. T. Leeds*,
London, 132–67.

Harden, D. B. (1958): 'The glass objects',
in Aywin Cotton, M. A. & Gathercole,
P. W., *Excavations at Clausentum,
Southampton 1951–1954* (Ministry
of Works Archaeological Reports 2),
London, 47–50.

Harden, D. B. (1959): 'The Highdown Hill
glass goblet with Greek inscription',
Sussex Archaeological Collections 97,
3–20.

Harden, D. B. (1961): 'Domestic window-
glass: Roman, Saxon and Medieval',
in Jope, E. M. (ed.), *Studies in building
history: essays in recognition of the
work of B. H. St J. O'Neil*, London,
39–63.

Harden, D. B. (1962): 'Glass in Roman
York', in *An inventory of the historical
monuments in the City of York I:
Eburacum, Roman York*, London,
136–41.

Harden, D. B. (1967): 'The glass jug', in
Biddle, M., 238–40.

Harden, D. B. (1968a): 'The glass', in Han-
worth, R., 'The Roman villa at Rapsley,
Ewhurst', *Surrey Archaeological Collections* 65, 65–69.

Harden, D. B. (1968b): 'The glass', in
Brodribb, A. C. C., Hands, A. R. & Walker,
D. R. (eds), *Excavations at Shakenoak
Farm, near Wilcote, Oxfordshire 1: Sites
A & D*, Oxford, 74–81.

Harden, D. B. (1968c): 'A Roman glass
from a cremation group at Braughing,
Hertfordshire', *AntJ* 48, 309–10.

Harden, D. B. (1968d): 'Roman glass from
Huntingdon and Rapsley, Surrey', *AntJ*
48, 308.

Harden, D. B. (1971–73): 'Glass', in Hobley,
B., 'Excavations at "the Lunt" Roman
military site, second interim report',
*Birmingham and Warwickshire
Archaeological Society: transactions
for 1971–1973*. vol. 85, 77–78.

Harden, D. B. (1974): 'Window-glass from
the Romano-British bath-house at
Garden Hill, Hartfield, Sussex', *AntJ* 54,
280–81.

Harden, D. B. (1975): 'The glass', in
Cunliffe, B. (ed.), *Excavations at Portchester Castle* I (RRCSAL 32), London,
368–74.

Harden, D. B. (1979): 'Glass vessels', in
Clark, G. (ed.), *The Roman cemetery
at Lankhills* (Winchester studies III),
Oxford, 210–20.

Harden, D. B. (1983): 'The glass hoard', in
Johnson, S (ed.), *Burgh Castle: excava-
tions by Charles Green, 1958–61* (East
Anglian Archaeology Report 20),
London, 78–89.

Harden, D. B. & Price, J. (1971): 'The glass',
in Cunliffe, B. (ed.), *Excavations at
Fishbourne 1961–1969*. Vol II *The
finds* (RRCSAL 27), London, 317–68.

Harden, D. B. et al. (1968): *Masterpieces
of glass*, London.

Harden, D. B. et al. (1988): *Glas der
Caesaren*, Milano.

Harding, D. W. & Armit, I. (1990): 'Survey
and excavation in West Lewis', in
Armit, I. (ed.), *Beyond the brochs:
changing perspectives on the later
Iron Age in Atlantic Scotland*, Edinburgh, 71–107.

Harding, D. W. & Gilmour, S. M. D. (2000):
*The Iron Age settlement at Beirgh,
Riof, Isle of Lewis: excavations 1985–
95. I: structures and stratigraphy*,
Edinburgh.

Harter, G. (1999): '"Eier im Glas" –
Gläserne Gefäße in der römischen
Kochkunst und Tischkultur', Klein, M. J.
(ed.), *Römische Glaskunst und Wandmalerei*, Mainz am Rhein, 34–40.

Hartley, B. R. (1972): 'The Roman occupation of Scotland: the evidence of
Samian ware', *Britannia* 3, 1–54.

Haselgrove C. (ed.) (2009): *The Traprain
Law Environs Project: excavations
and fieldwork 2000–2004* (Society of
Antiquaries of Scotland), Edinburgh.

Haverfield, F. & Taylor, M. V. (1908): 'Romano-British Shropshire', in *Shropshire I, the Victoria History of the Counties of England*, London, 205–78.

Hayden, B. (1995): 'Pathways to power: principles for creating socio-economic inequalities', in Price, T. D. & Feinman, G. M. (eds), *Foundations of social inequality*, New York, NY & London, 15–86.

Hayden, B. (1996): 'Feasting in prehistoric and traditional societies', in Wiessner, P. & Schiefenhövel, W. (eds), 127–46.

Hayden, B. (2001): 'Fabulous feasts: a prolegomenon to the importance of feasting', in Dietler, M. & Hayden, B. (eds), 23–64.

Hayes, W. C. (1928): 'An engraved glass bowl in the Museo Cristiano of the Vatican Library', *American Journal of Archaeology* 32, 23–32.

Hazzledine Warren, S. (1915): 'The opening of the Romano-British barrow on Mersea Island', *Transactions of the Essex Archaeological Society* 13, 116–32.

Heald, A. & Jackson, A. (2001): 'Towards a new understanding of Iron Age Caithness', *PSAS* 131, 129–47.

Heald, A. & Jackson, A. (2002): 'Caithness archaeological project: excavations at Everley broch, Freswick', *Antiquity* 76, 31–32.

Heath, D. B. (1976): 'Anthropological perspectives on alcohol: an historical review', in Everett, M. W., Waddell, J. O. & Heath, D. B. (eds), *Cross-cultural approaches to the study of alcohol: an interdisciplinary perspective*, The Hague & Paris, 41–101.

Heath, D. B. (1987): 'Anthropology and alcohol studies: current issues', *Annual Review of Anthropology*, 99–120.

Hedeager, L. (1979), 'A quantitative analysis of Roman imports in Europe north of the Limes (0–400 AD), and the question of Roman-Germanic exchange', in Kristiansen, K. & Paludan-Müller, C. (eds), *New directions in Scandinavian archaeology*, København, 191–216.

Hedges, J. W. (1987): *Bu, Gurness and the brochs of Orkney*, Part III: *the brochs of Orkney* (BAR Brit.Ser. 165), Oxford.

Helms, M. W. (1988): *Ulysses' sail: an ethnographic odyssey of power, knowledge, and geographical distance*, Princeton, NJ.

Helms, M. W. (1992): 'Long-distance contacts, elite aspirations, and the age of discovery in cosmological context', in Schortman, E. M. & Urban, P. A. (eds), *Resources, power, and interregional interaction*, New York, NY & London, 157–74.

Helms, M. W. (1993): *Craft and the kingly ideal: art, trade and power*, Austin, TX.

Henderson, J. (1989): 'The evidence for regional production of Iron Age glass in Britain', in Feugère, M. (ed.), *Le verre préromain en Europe occidentale*, Montagnac, 64–72.

Henderson, J. (1994): 'The glass', in Ballin Smith, B. (ed.), 234–36.

Henderson, J. & Kemp, M. M. B. (1992): 'Glass', in Rideout, J. S., Owen, O. A. & Halpin, E. (eds), *Hillforts of southern Scotland*, Edinburgh, 42–45.

Hendry, T. A. (1962): 'Gourock Burn', *D & E*, 22–23.

Hendry, T. A. (1968): 'Gourock Burn (Glenhead)', *D & E*, 13.

Hendry, T. A. (1969): 'Gourock Burn', *D & E*, 12.

Hendry, T. A. (1972): 'Gourock Burn', *D & E*, 14–15.

Henig, M. (1970–71): 'Three Roman objects from the Culbin Sands, Morayshire', *PSAS* 103, 231–33.

Henricson, L. G. (2006): 'En circusbägare samt ytterligare två glas möjligen härrörande från gruppen Schlangenfädenglas från Vackersberga, Husby-Långhundra sn, Uppland', in Arrhenius, B. & Eriksson, G. (eds), *Gulldens hög i Husby-Långhundra* (Rapporter från Arkeologiska forskningslaboratoriet 6), Stockholm, 81–82.

Herbig, R. (1929): 'Fensterstudien an antiken Wohnbauten in Italien', *Mitteilungen des Deutschen Archaeologischen Instituts: Roemische Abteilung* 44, 260–321.

Herbst, C. F. (1861): 'Varpelev fundet', *Aarbøger for Nordisk oldkyndighed og historie*, 305–22.

Herschend, F. (1972–73): 'Bobler i snabelbaegre', *Tor* 15, 110–21.

Hewat Craw, J. (1930): 'Excavations at Dunadd and at other sites on the Poltalloch estates, Argyll', *PSAS* 64, 111–46.

Hilgers, W. (1969): *Lateinische Gefässnamen* (Beihäfte der Bonner Jahrbücher 31), Düsseldorf.

Hill, J. D. (1997): '"The end of one kind of body and the beginning of another kind of body"? Toilet instruments and "Romanization" in southern England during the first century AD', in Gwilt, A. & Haselgrove, C. (eds), 96–107.

Hill, J. D. (2006): 'Are we any closer to understanding how later Iron Age societies worked (or did not work)?' in Haselgrove, C. (ed.) *Les mutations de la fin de l'Âge du Fer*, Glux-en Glenne, 169–79.

Hill, P. (1987): 'Traprain Law: the Votadini and the Romans', *Scottish Archaeological Review* 4:2, 85–97.

Hill, P. (ed.) (1997): *Whithorn and St Ninian: the excavation of a monastic town 1984–91*, Phoenix Mill.

Hillfort Study Group (1983): *Hillfort Study Group, Ayr, 22–24 April 1983*.

Hochuli-Gysel, A. (1993): 'Römisches Glas aus dem Südwesten von Frankreich', *Annales du 12e Congrès du AIHV*, Wien, 79–88.

Hochuli-Gysel, A. (2003): 'L'Aquitaine: importations et productions au Ier siècle av. J.-C. et au Ier siècle ap. J.-C.', in Foy, D. & Nenna, M.-D. (eds), 177–93.

Hodder, I. (1982a): 'Toward a contextual approach to prehistoric exchange', in Ericson, J. E. & Earle, T. K. (eds), *Contexts for prehistoric exchange*, New York, NY, 199–212.

Hodder, I. (1982b): *The present past: an introduction to anthropology for archaeologists*, London.

Hogg, A. H. A. (1944–45): 'Roman fragments from Castle Dykes near Cockburnspath and from St Abb's Head', *PSAS* 79, 172–73.

Holwerda, J. H. (1931): *Een vondst uit den Rijn bij Doorwert en romeinische sarcophaag uit Simpelveld* (Oudheidkundige Mededeelingen uit's Rijksmuseum van Oudheiden te Leiden Supp. 12), Leiden.

Hope, St John W. H. (1902): 'Excavations on the site of the Roman city at Silchester, Hants., in 1901', *Archaeologia* 58, 17–36.

Hunter, F. (1996): 'Recent Roman Iron Age metalwork finds from Fife and Tayside', *Tayside and Fife Archaeological Journal 2*, 113–25.

Hunter, F. (1997): 'Iron Age hoarding in Scotland and northern England', in Gwilt, A. & Haselgrove, C. (eds), 108–33.

Hunter, F. (1999): 'Birnie (Birnie parish), Roman coin hoard; Iron Age settlement; medieval settlement', *D & E*, 63.

Hunter, F. (2000): 'Birnie, Moray (Birnie parish), Roman coin hoard; Iron Age

settlement; medieval settlement',
D & E 2000, 58–59.

Hunter, F. (2001a): 'Roman and native in
Scotland: new approaches', JRA 14,
289–309.

Hunter, F. (2001b): 'Birnie, Moray (Birnie
parish), Iron Age settlement', D & E,
67–68.

Hunter, F. (2002): 'Roman Britain in 2001
1. Sites explored 2. Scotland', Britannia 33, 284–90.

Hunter, F. (2003): 'Birnie (Birnie parish),
Iron Age and medieval settlement',
D & E, 96.

Hunter, F. (2004): 'Birnie (Birnie parish),
Iron Age and medieval settlement',
D & E, 84–85.

Hunter, F. (2005): 'Birnie, Moray (Birnie
parish), Late Bronze Age metalworking
area; later prehistoric and medieval
settlement', D & E, 93–94.

Hunter, F. (2007a): Beyond the edge of
the empire: Caledonians, Picts and
Romans, Rosemarkie.

Hunter, F. (2007b): 'Birnie, Moray (Birnie
parish), excavation', D & E, 131.

Hunter, F. (2007c): 'Silver for the barbarians: interpreting denarii hoards in
north Britain and beyond', in Hingley,
R. & Willis, S. (eds), Roman finds:
context and theory. Proceedings of a
conference held at the University of
Durham, Oxford, 214–24.

Hunter, F. (2009a): 'The finds assemblages in their regional context', in
Hunter, F., Lowther, P. & MacSween,
A., 'The material remains', in Haselgrove, C. (ed.), 140–56.

Hunter, F. (2009b): 'Traparin Law and the
Roman world', in Hanson, W. S. (ed.),
The army and frontiers of Rome:
papers offered to David J. Breeze on
the occasion of his sixty-fifth birthday
and his retirement from Historic
Scotland, Portsmouth, RI, 225–40.

Hunter, F. (2010): 'Beyond the frontier:
interpreting late Roman Iron Age
indigenous and imported material
culture', in Collins, R. & Allason-Jones,
L. (eds), Finds from the frontier:
material culture in the 4th–5th
centuries (CBA Research Report 162),
York, 96–109.

Hunter, F., Lowther, P. & MacSween, A.
(2009): 'The material remains', in
Haselgrove, C. (ed.), 117–56.

Hunter, J. (1972–74): 'Excavations at
Ardeer, Ayrshire', PSAS 105, 296–301.

Hunter, J. R. (1975): 'Glasses from Scandinavian burials in the first millennium',
World Archaeology 7:1, 79–86.

Hunter, J. R. & Jackson, C. M. (1993):
'Glass', in Rodgers, N. S. H. (ed.),
Anglian and other finds from Fishergate (The archaeology of York. The
small finds) 17 (9), York, 1331–44.

van den Hurk, L. J. A. M. (1977): 'The
tumuli from the Roman period of
Esch, province of north Brabant, III',
Berichten van de Rijksdienst voor het
Ouidkundig Bodemonderzoek 27, 91–
138.

Ingemark, D. (1995): En teoretisk studie
av varuutbytet mellan romare och
barbarer i Skottland under romersk
järnålder (0–400 e Kr), (unpublished
MA thesis, Dept of Archaeology, Lund
University, Sweden).

Ingemark, D. (1998): 'Roman glass', in
Main, L. (ed.), 335–37.

Ingemark, D. (2000): 'Roman glass from
non-Roman contexts in Scotland &
north Northumberland: some preliminary thoughts', Annales du 14e
Congrès de l'AIHV Italia i Venezia –
Milano, Lochem, 175–77.

Ingemark, D. (2001): 'Saturnalierna: en
folklig fest under romersk tid', in Swahn,
J.-Ö. (ed.), Tidernas fester, Lund, 36–
49.

Ingemark, D. (2005): 'Roman glass', in
Alexander, D., 80–82.

Ingemark, D. (2006a): 'Perfume bottle
from Loch Kinnord', in Curtis, N. G. W.
& Hunter, F., 211.

Ingemark, D. (2006b): 'Glass', in Anderson, S. & Rees, A. R., 'The excavation
of a large double-chambered souterrain at Ardownie Farm Cottages,
Monifieth, Angus', Tayside and Fife
Archaeological Journal 12, 33.

Ingemark, D. (2007): 'Roman glass', in
Dunwell, A., 79–81.

Ingemark, D. (2012): 'The glass from San
Lorenzo in Lucina' in Brandt, O (ed.),
San Lorenzo in Lucina: the transfor-
mation of a Roman quarter. Skrifter
utgivna av Svenska Institutet i Rom/
Acta Instituti Atheniensis Regni
Sueciae, 4/61, Stockholm, 321–30.

Ingemark, D., Gerding, H. & Castoriano,
M. (2000): Liv och död i antikens Rom,
Lund.

Inskip, T. (1846): The Journal of the British
Archaeological Association 1, 52.

Irving, Jr, E. B. (1997): 'Christian and pagan
elements', in Bjork, R. E. & Niles, J. D.
(eds), A Beowulf handbook, Exeter,
175–92.

Isaksson, S. (2005): 'Food for the gods', in
Nylén, E., Lund Hansen, U. & Mannecke,
P. (eds), The Havor hoard: the gold,
the bronzes, the fort (Kungl. Vitterhets-
historie och Antikvitets Akademiens
Handlingar, Antikvariska serien 46),
Stockholm, 145–57.

Isings, C. (1957): Roman glass from dated
finds, Groningen & Djakarta.

Isings, C. (1965): 'The glass', in Vermas-
eren, M. J. & van Essen, C. C. (eds), The
excavations in the mithraeum of the
church of Santa Prisca in Rome, Leiden,
508–29.

Isings, C. (1968): 'Some of the 10th
Legion's glass at Nijmegen', in Charleston, R. J., Evans, W. & Werner, A. E.
(eds), 9–11.

Isings, C. (1971): Roman glass in Limburg
(Archaeologica Traiectina 9),
Groningen.

Isings, C. (1980): 'Glass from the Canabae
Legionis at Nijmegen', Berichten van
de Rijksdienst voor het Ouidkundig
Bodemonderzoek 30, 281–346.

Itten, J. (1971): Färg och färgupplevelse,
Stockholm.

Iversen, R. (2008): Rapport om den
arkæologiske udgravning ved Ellekilde
Heldagsskole, Thorslunde, Ishøj Kom-
mune, TAK 1355 (Bygherrerapport nr.
29 Januar 2008).

Iversen, R. (2011): 'Ellekilde – en grav-
plads fra yngre romersk jernalder med
fyrstegrav og cirkusbægre', Aarbøger
for nordisk Oldkyndighed og Historie
2009, 69–120.

Jackson, K. H. (1964): The oldest Irish
tradition: a window on the Iron Age,
London.

Jackson 1969: see Goddoddin, Ancient
and Medieval sources.

James, S. (1999): The Atlantic Celts:
ancient people or modern invention?,
London.

Jarrett, M. G. (1962): 'The deserted village
of West Whelpington, Northumber-
land', ArchAel (Series 4) 40, 189–225.

Jarrett, M. G. & Evans, D. H. (1989):
'Excavation of two palisaded enclosures at West Whelpington, Northumberland', ArchAel (Series 5) 17, 117–39.

Jashemsky, W. F. (1967): 'The caupona of
Euxinos at Pompeii', Archaeology 20:
1, 36–44.

Jasim, S. A. (1999): 'The excavation of a
camel cemetery at Mleiha, Sharja,
U. A. E.', Arabian archaeology and
epigraphy 10, 69–101.

Jasim, S. A. (2006): 'Trade centres and
commercial routes in the Arabian Gulf:

post-Hellenic discoveries at Dibba, Sharja, United Arab Emirates', *Arabian archaeology and epigraphy* 17, 214–37.

Jellinek, E. M. (1976): 'Drinkers and alcoholics in ancient Rome', *Journal of Studies on Alcohol* 37, 1721–41.

Jenkins, R. (1992): *Pierre Bourdieu*, London & New York, NY.

Jennings, J. et al. (2005): '"Drinking beer in a blissfull mood": alcohol production, operational chains, and feasting in the ancient world', *Current Anthropology* 46:2, 275–303.

Jennings, S. (2000): 'Late Hellenistic and early Roman cast glass from the Souks excavation (BEY 006), Beirut, Lebanon', *JGS* 42, 41–59.

Jennings, S. (2002): 'Late Hellenistic and early Roman glass from the Souks excavation, Beirut, Lebanon', in Kordas, G. (ed.), 127–32.

Jervise, A. (1860–62): 'An account of the round or "bee-hive" shaped house, and other underground chambers, at West Grange of Conan, Forfarshire', *PSAS* 4, 492–99.

Jervise, A. (1873): 'Notice regarding a "Pict's house" and some other antiquities in the parish of Tealing, Forfarshire', *PSAS* 10, 287–92.

Jobey, G. (1957): 'Excavation at the native settlement, Gubeon Cottage, Northumberland', *ArchAel* (Series 4) 35, 163–79.

Jobey, G. (1959): 'Excavations at the native settlement at Huckhoe, Northumberland, 1955–57', *ArchAel* (Series 4) 37, 217–78.

Jobey, G. (1960): 'Some rectilinear settlements of the Roman period in Northumberland', *ArchAel* (Series 4) 38, 1–38.

Jobey, G. (1970): 'An Iron Age settlement and homestead at Burradon, Northumberland', *ArchAel* (Series 4) 48, 51–95.

Jobey, G. (1973): 'A native settlement at Hartburn and the Devil's Causeway, Northumberland', *ArchAel* (Series 5) 1, 11–53.

Jobey, G. (1976): 'Traprain Law: a summary', in Harding, D. W. (ed.), *Hillforts: later prehistoric earthworks in Britain and Ireland*, London, 192–204.

Jobey, G. (1979): 'Iron Age and later farmsteads on Belling Law, Northumberland', *ArchAel* (Series 5) 5, 1–38.

Jobey, I. (1981): 'Excavations on the Romano-British settlement at Middle

Gunnar Peak, Barrasford, Northumberland', *ArchAel* (Series 5) 9, 51–74.

Jobey, I. & Jobey, G. (1987): 'Prehistoric, Romano-British and later remains on Murton High Crags, Northumberland', *ArchAel* (Series 5) 15, 151–98.

Johnson, A. W. & Earle, T. K. (1987): *The evolution of human societies: from foraging group to agrarian state*, Stanford, CA.

Jones, J. (1987): 'The glass', in Parker, S. T. (ed.), *The Roman frontier in Central Jordan: interim report on the Limes Arabicus project, 1980–1985* vol II (BAR Int.Ser. 340), Oxford, 621–53.

Junkelmann, M. (2006): *Panis Militaris: Die Ernährung des römischen Soldaten oder der Grundstoff der Macht* (3rd rev. ed.), Mainz [originally pub. 1997].

Keppie, L. (1989): 'Beyond the northern frontier: Roman and native in Scotland', in Todd, M. (ed.), *Research on Roman Britain 1960–89* (Britannia Monograph Series 11), London, 61–73.

Kessler, P. T. (1927): 'Ein frührömisches Brandgrab aus Weisenau bei Mainz', *Mainzer Zeitschrift* 22, 47–51.

Kilbride-Jones, H. E. (1938a): 'Glass armlets in Britain', *PSAS* 72, 366–95.

Kilbride-Jones, H. E. (1938b): 'The excavation of a native settlement at Milking Gap, High Shield, Northumberland', *ArchAel* (Series 4) 15, 303–50.

Kisa, A. (1908): *Das Glas im Altertume* I–III, Leipzig.

Kivikoski, E. (1954): 'Skandinavisches in der Römischen Eisenzeit Finnlands', *Acta Archaeologica* 25, 151–70.

Kivikoski, E. (1973): *Die Eisenzeit Finnlands*, Helsinki.

Kjer Michaelsen, K. (1992): *Braet og brik: spil i Jernaldern*, Højberg.

Kleberg, T. (1934): *Värdshus och värdshusliv i den romerska antiken*, Göteborg.

Kleberg, T. (1940): 'Weinfälschung: ein stilistisches Klischee bei den Kirchenvätern', *Eranos* 38, 47–54.

Kleberg, T. (1942): *På värdshus och vinstugor i antikens Rom*, Stockholm.

Klein, M. J. (ed.) (1999): *Römische Glaskunst und Wandmalerei*, Mainz am Rhein.

Klindt-Jensen, O. (1949): 'Foreign influences in Denmark's Early Iron Age', *Acta Archaeologica* 20, 1–198.

Koch 1997: see Ancient and Medieval sources.

Koltes, J. (1982): *Catalogue des collections archéologiques de Besançon VII: la verrerie Gallo-Romaine* (Annales

Littéraires de l'Université de Besançon 270), Paris.

Kopytoff, I. (1986): 'The cultural biography of things: commoditization as process', in Appadurai, A. (ed.), *The social life of things: commodities in cultural perspective*, Cambridge, 64–94.

Kordas, G. (ed.) (2002): *Hyalos vitrum glass: history, technology and conservation of glass and vitreous materials in the Hellenistic world*, Athens.

Kordmahini, H. A. (1994): *Glass from the Bazargan collection*, Teheran [1st edition 1988].

Koster, A. (1997): *Description of the collections in the Provinciaal Museum G. M. Kam at Nijmegen XIII: the bronze vessels* 2, Nijmegen.

Krauße, D. (1993): 'Trinkhorn und Kline. Zur griechischen Vermittlung orientalischer Trinksitten an die frühen Kelten', *Germania* 71, 188–97.

Krauße, D. (1996): *Hochdorf III: Das Trink- und Speiseservice aus dem späthallstattzeitlichen Fürstengrab von Eberdingen-Hochdorf (Kr. Ludwigsburg)*, Stuttgart.

Kropotkin, V. V. (1970): *Rimskie importnye izdeljia v Vostcnoj Evrope*, Moskva.

Krüger, E. (1909): 'Ein gravierter Glasbecher mit Darstellung eines Wagenkämpfers aus Trier', *BonnJbb* 118, 353–69.

Krüger, T. (1982): 'Das Brett- und Würfelspiel der Spätlatènezeit und römischen Kaiserzeit im freien Germanien', *Neue Ausgrabungen und Forschungen in Niedersachsen* 15, 135–324.

Kühlborn, S. (1992): *Das Römerlager in Oberraden* III, Münster.

Kunisch, N. (1967): 'Neuerworberne antike Gläser der Antikenabteilung der Staatlichen Museen Berlin', *AA* 82, 179–96.

Kunow, J. (1983): *Der römische Import der Germania libera bis zu den Markomannenkriegen: Studien zu Bronze- und Glasgefässen*, Neumünster.

Kunow, J. (1986): 'Bemerkungen zum Export römischer Waffen in das Barbarikum', in Unz, C. (ed.), *Studien zu den Militärgrenzen Roms III: 13. Internationaler Limeskongreß Aalen 1983* (Forschungen und Berichte zur Vor- und Frühgeschichte in Baden-Württemberg 20), Stuttgart, 740–46.

La Baume, P. (1976): 'Außergewöhnliche Stücke römischer Kleinkunst aus einer Privatsammlung', in Haevernick, T. E. & von Saldern, A. (eds), *Festschrift für Waldemar Haberey*, Mainz, 79–83.

Lagler, K. (1989): *Sörup II und Südensee:*

Zwei eisenzeitliche Urnenfriedhöfe in Angeln (Offa-Bücher 68), Neumünster.

La Guardia, R. & Tibiletti, T. (eds), (1998): *Il vetro dall'Antichità all'Età contemporanea: aspetti tecnologici, funzionali e commerciali*, Milano.

Laing, L. (1973): 'Mote of Mark', *D & E*, 32–34.

Laing, L. (1975): 'Mote of Mark and the origins of Celtic interlace', *Antiquity* 49, 98–108.

Laing, L. & Longley, D. (2006): *The Mote of Mark: a Dark Age hillfort in southwest Scotland*, Oxford.

Lamberg-Karlovsky, C. C. & Fitz, W. (1987): 'Cairn burials in the Soghun Valley, southeastern Iran', in Gnoli, G. & Lanciotti, L. (eds), *Orientalia Iosephi Tucci memoriae dicata*, Roma, 747–70.

Lancel, S. (1967): *Verrerie antique de Tipasa*, Paris.

Lane, A. & Campbell, E. (2000): *Dunadd: an early Dalriadic capital*, Oxford.

Lantier, R. (1929): *La verrerie: Musée des Antiquités Nationales Chateau de Saint-Germain-en-Laye*, Paris.

Lapp, N. L. (1983): 'Ancient glass', in Lapp, N. L., *The excavations at Araq El-Amir*, vol. 1 (The Annual of the American Schools of Oriental Research 47–48), Ann Arbor, MI, 43–62.

Lash, S. (1993): 'Pierre Bourdieu: cultural economy and social change' in Calhoun, C., LiPuma, E. & Postone, M. (eds), *Bourdieu: critical perspectives*, Cambridge & Oxford, 193–211.

Lazar, I. (2000): 'Ribbed glass bowls from the territory of modern Slovenia', *Annales du 14e congrès du AIHV*, Lochem, 63–67.

Le Maho, S. & Sennequier, G. (1996): 'A propos d'un verre à peint trouvé à Roen (fin 2e–milieu 3e siècle)', *Annales du 13e Congrès du AIHV*, Lochem, 175–84.

Leciejwicz, L. (1960): 'Tombe "princiére" a inhumation no. 3 Mus. Archeol., Poznan – Łęg Piekarski', in Abramowicz, A. et al. (eds), *Inventaria Archaeologica, Pologne, Periode Romaine*, Lodz, pl. 26.

Lehmann, W. P. (1986): *A Gothic etymological dictionary* [based on 3rd ed. of Feist, S., *Vergleichendes Wörterbuch der Gotischen Sprache*], Leiden.

Lehmann-Hartleben, K. (1926): *Die Trajanssäule: ein römisches Kunstwerk zu beginn der Spätantike*, Berlin & Leipzig.

Lehrer Jacobson, G. (1987): 'Greek names on prismatic jugs', *Annales du 10e Congrès du AIHV*, Amsterdam, 35–43.

Leibowitz, J. O. (1967): 'Studies in the history of alcoholism II: acute alcoholism in ancient Greek and Roman medicine', *British Journal of Addiction* 62, 83–86.

Lewis, C. T. & Short, C. (1962): *A Latin dictionary*, Oxford (1st edition 1879).

Lierke, R. (1993): *'Aliud torno teritur'*, *Antike Welt* 24:3, 218–34.

Lierke, R. (1996): 'Glass vessels made on a turning wheel in Roman times (survey)', *Annales du 13e Congrès du AIHV*, Lochem, 55–62.

Lightfoot, C. S. (1990): 'Some types of Roman cut-glass vessels found in Turkey', in [editor not mentioned], *1st international Anatolian glass symposium*, Istanbul, 7–15.

Lindeberg, I. (1973): 'Die Einfuhr römischer Bronzegefässe nach Gotland', *Saalburg Jahrbuch* 30, 5–65.

Ling, R. (1991): *Roman painting*, Cambridge.

van Lith, S. (1977): 'Römisches Glas aus Velsen', *Berichten van de Rijksdienst voor het Ouidkundig Bodemonderzoek* 58, 1–62.

van Lith, S. (1978–79): 'Römisches Glas aus Valkenburg Z. H.', *Berichten van de Rijksdienst voor het Ouidkundig Bodemonderzoek* 59–60, 1–150.

van Lith, S. (1984): 'Glas aus Asciburgium', *Beiträge zur Archäologie des römischen Rheinlands* 4, Köln, 211–81.

van Lith, S. (1987): 'Late Roman and early Merovingian glass from a settlement site at Maastricht (Dutch South Limburg) I', *JGS* 29, 47–59.

van Lith, S. (1988): 'Late Roman and early Merovingian glass from a settlement site at Maastricht (Dutch South Limburg) II', *JGS* 30, 62–76.

van Lith, S. & Isings, C. (1981): 'Recent finds from the Netherlands', *Annales du 8e Congrès du AIHV*, Liège, 97–105.

van Lith, S. M. E. & Randsborg, K. (1985): 'Roman glass in the West: a social study', *Berichten van de Rijksdienst voor het Ouidkundig Bodemonderzoek* 35, 413–532.

Liversidge, J. (1977): 'Roman burials in the Cambridge area', *Proceedings of the Cambridge Antiquarian Society* 67, 11–38.

Loewenthal, A. I. & Harden, D. B. (1949): 'Vasa murrina', *JRS* 39, 31–37.

Longley, D. (1979): 'Mote of Mark, Dalbeattie', *D & E*, 5–6.

Longley, D. (1980): 'Mote of Mark, Dalbeattie', *D & E*, 3–4.

Lönnroth, L. (1997): 'Hövdingahallen i fornnordisk myt och saga: ett mentalitetshistoriskt bidrag till förståelsen av Slöingefyndet', in Callmer, J. & Rosengren, E. (eds), *… gick Grendel att söka det höga huset … Arkeologiska källor till aristokratiska miljöer i Skandinavien under yngre järnålder* (Slöingeprojektet 1/Hallands Länsmuseers Skriftserie 9/GOTARC C. Arkeologiska Skrifter 17), Halmstad, 31–37.

Low, G. (1778): *Tour through the Northern Isles and part of the Mainland of Orkney in the year 1778*. Manuscript account, published in Cuthbert 1995, 111–22.

Lund Hansen, U. (1980): 'Herlufmagle: et splittet gravfund med glas fra yngre romertid', *Aarböger for nordisk oldkyndighed og historie 1979*, København, 88–101.

Lund Hansen, U. (1987): *Römischer Import in Norden. Warenaustausch zwischen dem Römischen Reich und dem freien Germanien während der Kaiserzeit unter besonderer Berücksichtigung Nordeuropas* (Nordiske Fortidsminder Ser. B 10), København.

Lund Hansen, U. (1989): 'Römischer Glasexport in das Freie Germanien', *KölnJb* 22, 177–85.

Lund Hansen, U. (2000): 'Die Glasbecher' in Ethelberg, P., 320–47.

Luttwak, E. N. (1976): *The grand strategy of the Roman Empire*, Baltimore.

Lux, G. V. & Roosens, H. (1971): 'Een Gallo-Romeins grafveld te Gors-Opleeuw', *Archaeologica Belgica* 128, 5–43.

Lysons, S. (1792): 'Account of Roman antiquities discovered in the county of Gloucester', *Archaeologia* 10, 131–36.

Magennis, H. (1985a): 'The cup as symbol and metaphor in Old English literature', *Speculum* 60:3, 517–36.

Magennis, H. (1985b): 'The treatment of feasting in the Heliand', *Neophilologus* 69, 126–33.

Magennis, H. (1986): 'The exegesis of inebriation: treading carefully in Old English', *English Languages Notes* 23, 36.

Main, L. 1998: 'Excavation of a timber roundhouse and broch at the Fairy Knowe, Buchlyvie, Stirlingshire, 1975–78', *PSAS* 128, 293–417.

Maioli, M. G. (1974): 'I vetri della necropoli Romana de «Le Palazzette» nel territorio di Classe', *Felix Ravenna* 7–8 (107–08), 15–36.

Mallory, J. P. (1992): 'The world of Cú

Chulainn: the archaeology of the Táin Bó Cuailnge', in Mallory, J. P. (ed.), *Aspects of the Táin*, Belfast, 103–59.

Manacorda, D. & Panella, C. (1993): 'Anfore', in Harris, W. V. (ed.), *The inscribed economy: production and distribution in the Roman empire in the light of instrumentum domesticum*, Ann Arbor, MI, 55–64

Mandelbaum, D. G. (1979): 'Alcohol and culture', in Marshall, M. (ed.), *Beliefs, behaviors & alcoholic beverages: a cross-cultural study*, Ann Arbor, MI, 14–30.

Mann, J. C. (1974): 'The northern frontier after AD 369', *GlasAJ* 3, 34–42.

Mann, J. C. & Breeze, D. J. (1987): 'Ptolemy, Tacitus and the tribes of north Britain', *PSAS* 117, 85–91.

Manning, W. H. (1972): 'Ironwork hoards in Iron Age and Roman Britain', *Britannia* 3, 224–50.

Manning, W. H. (1981): 'Native and Roman metalwork in northern Britain: a question of origins and influences', *Scottish Archaeological Forum* 11, 52–61.

March, K. S. (1998): 'Hospitality, women, and the efficacy of beer', in Counihan, C. M. & Kaplan, S. L. (eds), *Food and gender: identity and power*, Amsterdam, 45–80.

Mariën, M. E. (1984): 'Romeins glaswerk met krokelende glasdraden uit België', *Bulletin des Musées Royaux d'Art et d'Histoire* 55:2, 63–74.

Marshall, J. (1951): *Taxila: an illustrated account of archaeological excavations carried out at Taxila under the orders of the Government of India between the years 1913 and 1934*, Cambridge.

Marshall, M. (1979): 'Introduction', in Marshall, M. (ed.), *Beliefs, behaviors & alcoholic beverages: a cross-cultural study*, Ann Arbor, MI, 1–11.

Marstrander, S. (1947): 'Et provinsial-romersk glass fra Telemark', *Stavanger Museum årbok 1946*, Stavanger, 73–85.

Martin, C. (1995): 'Le verre de l'Antiquité Tardive en Valais: notes preliminaries', in Foy, D. (ed.), 93–107.

Martin, M. (1984): *Der spätrömische Silberschatz von Kaiseraugst*, Basel.

Masseroli, S. (1998): 'Analisi di una forma vitrea: la bottiglia Isings 50 nella Cisalpina Romana', in La Guardia, R. & Tibiletti, T. (eds), 41–49.

von Massow, W. (1932): *Die Grabmäler von Neumagen* (Römische Grabmäler des Mosellandes und der angrenzenden Gebiete II), Berlin & Leipzig.

Mattingly, D. J. (1990): 'Paintings, presses and perfume production at Pompeii', *Oxford Journal of Archaeology* 9:1, 71–90.

Mattingly, D. S. & Aldrete, G. S. (2000): 'The feeding of imperial Rome: the mechanics of the food supply system', in Coulston, J. & Dodge, H. (eds), *Ancient Rome: the archaeology of the Eternal City* (Oxford University School of Archaeology Monograph 54), Oxford, 142–65.

Mauss, M. (1969): *The gift: Forms and functions of exchange in archaic societies*, London [1st edition 1925].

Maxwell, G. S. (1974): 'Objects of glass', in Rae, A. & Rae, V., 'The Roman fort at Cramond, Edinburgh: excavations 1954–66', *Britannia* 5, 197–99.

Maxwell, G. S. (1989): *The Romans in Scotland*, Edinburgh.

Maxwell, S. (1950–51): 'Discoveries made in 1934 on King Fergus' Isle and elsewhere in Loch Laggan, Inverness-shire', *PSAS* 85, 160–65.

McCracken, G. (1987): 'Clothing as language: an object lesson in the study of the expressive properties of material culture', in Reynolds, B. & Stott, M. A. (eds), *Material anthropology: contemporary approaches to material culture*, Lanham, 103–28.

McCracken, G. (1990): *Culture and consumption: new approaches to the symbolic character of consumer goods and activities*, Bloomington & Indianapolis, IN. First edition 1988.

McGovern, P. E. (2009): *Uncorking the past: the quest for wine, beer, and other alcoholic beverages*, Berkeley, CA. & London.

MacGregor, A. (1972–74): 'The broch of Burrian, North Ronaldsay, Orkney', *PSAS* 105, 63–118.

MacGregor, M. (1976a): *Early Celtic art in north Britain*: vol. 1 (text), Leicester.

MacGregor, M. (1976b): *Early Celtic art in north Britain*: vol. 2 (catalogue), Leicester.

Macinnes, L. (1984a): 'Settlement and economy: East Lothian and the Tyne-Forth province', in Miket, R. & Burgess, C. (eds), 176–98.

Macinnes, L. (1984b): 'Brochs and the Roman occupation of lowland Scotland', *PSAS* 114, 235–49.

Macinnes, L. (1989): 'Baubles, bangles and beads: trade and exchange in Roman Scotland', in Barrett, J. C., Fitzpatrick, A. P. & Macinnes, L. (eds), 108–16.

MacKie, E. W. (1965): 'The origin and development of the broch and wheel-house building cultures of the Scottish Iron Age', *Proceedings of the Prehistoric Society* 31, 93–146.

MacKie, E. W. (1974): *Dun Mor Vaul: An Iron Age broch on Tiree*, Glasgow.

MacKie, E. W. (1982): 'The Leckie broch, Stirlingshire: an interim report', *GlasAJ* 9, 60–72.

MacKie, E. W. (1987): 'Impact on the Scottish Iron Age of the discoveries at Leckie broch', *GlasAJ* 14, 1–18.

MacKie, E. W. (1997): 'Dun Mor Vaul revisited: fact and theory in the reappraisal of the Scottish Atlantic Iron Age', in Ritchie, G. (ed.), *The archaeology of Argyll*, Edinburgh, 141–80.

MacKie, E. W. (1998): 'Continuity over three thousand years of northern prehistory: the "tel" at Howe, Orkney', *AntJ* 78, 1–42.

MacKie, E. W. (2000): 'Excavations at Dun Ardtreck, Skye, in 1964 and 1965', *PSAS* 130, 301–411.

McKinlay, A. P. (1945): 'The Roman attitude towards women's drinking', *Classical Bulletin* 22, 14–15.

McKinlay, A. P. (1946–47): 'The wine element in Horace', *Classical Journal* 42, 160–68, 229–35.

McKinlay, A. P. (1948): 'Temperate Romans', *Classical Weekly* 41:10, 146–49.

McKinlay, A. P. (1950): 'Roman sobriety in the early Empire', *Classical Bulletin* 26, 31–36.

MacLaren, A. (1958): 'Excavations at Keir Hill, Gargunnock', *PSAS* 91, 78–83.

McNeill, F. M. (1956): *The Scots cellar: its traditions and lore*, Edinburgh.

Meconcelli Notarianni, G. (1979): *Vetri antichi nelle collezione del Museo Civico Archeologico di Bologna*, Bologna.

Meconcelli Notarianni, G. (1987): 'Römische Gläser aus Claterna: Alte und neue Erwerbungen des Städtischen Archäologischen Museums Bologna', *Annales du 10e Congrès du AIHV*, Amsterdam, 37–60.

Meillassoux, C. (1960): 'Essai d'interprétation du phénomène économique dans les sociétés traditionelles d'auto-subsistance', *Cahiers d'Études Africaines* 1, 38–67.

Meyer, C. (1992): *Glass from Quseir al-Qadim and the Indian Ocean trade* (Studies in Ancient Oriental Civilization 53), Chicago, IL.

Middleton, B. C. (1950): 'Glass', in Meates, G. W., Greenfield, E. & Birchenough, E., 'The Lullingstone Roman villa', *Archaeologia Cantiana* 63, 22–28.

Miket, R. & Burgess, C. (eds) (1984): *Between and beyond the walls: essays on the prehistory and history of north Britain in honour of George Jobey*, Edinburgh.

Miller, C. L. & Hamell, G. R. (1986): 'A new perspective on Indian-White contact: cultural symbols and colonial trade', *Journal of American History* 73:2, 311–28.

Millet, M. (1997): 'The Roman coarse wares', in Hill, P. (ed.), 293–94.

Molin, M. (1984): 'Quelques considérations sur le charoit des vendanges de Langres (Haute-Marne)', *Gallia* 42, 97–114.

Montague Benton, G. (1926): 'Roman burial group discovered at West Mersea', *Transactions of the Essex Archaeological Society* 17, 128–30.

Moriconi, M. P. (1969–72): 'Vetro', in Carandini, A. & Panella, C. (eds), *Ostia III, parte seconda* (Seminario di Archeologia e Storia dell'Arte Greca e Romana dell'Università di Roma, Studi Miscellanei 21), Roma, 363–95.

Morin-Jean [pseud.] (1913): *La verrerie en Gaule sous l'empire Romaine*, Paris.

Morris, S. V. (1936–37): 'Excavation of Torrs Cave, Kirkcudbright', *PSAS* 71, 415–30.

Morrison, H. (1983): 'Glass and trade of the ancient Aksumite kingdom', *Annales du 9e Congrès du AIHV*, Nancy, 113–26.

Morrison, H. (1989): 'The glass', in Munro-Hay, S. C. (ed.), *Excavations at Aksum* (Memoirs of the British Institute in Eastern Africa 10), London, 188–209.

Motte, S. & Martin, S. (2003): 'L'atelier de verrier antique de la Montée de la Butte à Lyon et ses productions', in Foy, D. & Nenna, M.-D. (eds), 303–19.

Munro, R. (1882): 'Notice of excavations made on an ancient "fort" at Seamill, Ayrshire', *Archaeological & Historical Collections of Ayr & Wigtown* 3, 59–65.

Munro, R. (1890): *The lake-dwellings of Europe: being the Rhind lectures in archaeology for 1888*, London, Paris & Melbourne.

Munro, R. (1899): 'Notes on a crannog at Hyndford, near Lanark, recently excavated by Andrew Smith', *PSAS* 33, 373–87.

Murray, O. & Tecusan, M. (eds) (1995): *In vino veritas*, London.

Murray, R. (2007): 'Iron-masters of the Caledonians', *Current Archaeology* 212, 20–25.

Mutz, A. (1972): *Die Kunst des Metalldrehens bei den Römern*, Basel.

Nash, D. (1976): 'Reconstructing Poseidonios' Celtic ethnography: some considerations', *Britannia* 7, 111–26.

Nash-Williams, V. E. (1953): 'The Roman villa at Llantwit Major, Glamorgan', *Archaeologia Cambrensis* 192, 89–151.

Näsman, U. (1984): *Glas och handel i senromersk tid och folkvandringstid: en studie kring glas från Eketorp-II, Öland, Sverige*, Uppsala.

Naumann-Steckner, F. (1991): 'Depictions of glass in Roman wall paintings', in Newby, M. & Painter, K. (eds), 86–98.

Neal, D. S. (1976): 'Northchurch, Boxmoor and Hemel Hempstead station: The excavation of three Roman buildings in the Bulborne valley', *Hertfordshire Archaeology* 4.

Neal, D. S. et al. (1990): *Excavations of the Iron Age, Roman and Medieval Settlement at Gorhambury, St Albans* (English Heritage Monograph 14), London.

Needham, S. (1993): 'Displacement and exchange in archaeological methodology', in Scarre, C. & Healy, F. (eds), *Trade and exchange in prehistoric Europe* (Oxbow Monograph 33), Oxford, 161–69.

Nelson, M. (2005): *The barbarian's beverage: a history of beer in ancient Europe*, London & New York, NY.

Netting, McC. R. (1964): 'Beer as a locus of value among the West African Kofyar', *American Anthropologist* 66, 375–84.

Neumann, H. (1953): 'Et Løveglas fra Rinlandet', *Kuml*, 137–54.

Newby, M. & Painter, K. (eds) (1991): *Two centuries of art and invention* (Occasional papers from the Society of Antiquaries of London 13), London.

Newton, R. G. (1971): 'A preliminary examination of a suggestion that pieces of strongly coloured glass were articles of trade in the Iron Age in Britain', *Archaeometry* 13:1, 11–16.

Newton, R. G. & Davidson, S. (1996): *Conservation of glass*, Cambridge. First edition 1989.

Nierhaus, R. (1954): 'Kaiserzeitlicher Südweinexport nach dem Freien Germanien?', *Acta Archaeologica* 25, 252–60.

Nordland, O. (1969): *Brewing and beer traditions in Norway: the social anthropological background of the brewing industry*, Oslo.

Norling-Christensen, H. (1940): 'Der Stenlille-fund: ein Grabfund aus der römischen Kaiserzeit mit römischen Bronze- und Glasgefässen', *Acta Archaeologica* 11, 212–25.

Norling-Christensen, H. (1951): 'Jernaldersgravpladsen ved Himlingøje', *Fra Nationalmuseets Arbejdsmark*, 39–46.

Norling-Christensen, H. (1952): 'Gravfund fra Borritshoved med romerske glas og bronzekar', *Kuml*, 84–92.

Norling-Christensen, H. (1953a): 'Vestlandskedler og malede glas', *Kuml*, 47–60.

Norling-Christensen, H. (1953b): 'Romerske glaskar i Danmark', *Fra Nationalmuseets Arbejdsmark*, 81–91.

Nuber, H. U. (1973): *Kanne und Griffschale: ihr Gebrauch im täglichen Leben und die Beigabe in Gräbern der römischen Kaiserzeit* (53. Bericht der Römisch-Germanischen Kommission), Berlin.

Nylén, E. (2005): 'The Havor hoard and the gold neckring', in Nylén, E., Lund Hansen, U. & Mannecke, P. (eds), *The Havor hoard: the gold, the bronzes, the fort* (Kungl. Vitterhetshistorie och Antikvitets Akademiens Handlingar, Antikvariska serien 46), Stockholm, 11–52.

Nylén, N. & Schönbäck, B. (1994): *Tuna i Badelunda: guld kvinnor båtar* 1 (Västerås kulturnämnds skriftserie 27), Västerås.

Oelmann, F. (1938–39): 'Bericht über die Tätigkeit des Landesmuseums in Bonn in der Zeit vom 1. April 1937 bis 31. März 1938', *BonnJbb* 143/144, 329–404.

Ogston, A. (1931): *The prehistoric antiquities of the Howe of Cromar*, Aberdeen.

Orenstein, H. (1980): 'Asymmetrical reciprocity: a contribution to the theory of political legitimacy', *Current Anthropology* 21:1, 69–91.

Orton, C. (1990): 'An introduction to the quantification of assemblages of pottery', *Journal of Roman pottery studies* 3, 94–97.

Osborne, R. (1980): *Lights and pigments. Colour principles for artists*, London.

Packer, J. (1978): 'Inns at Pompeii: a short survey', *Cronache Pompeiane* 4, 5–51.

Päffgen, B. (1989): 'Glasbeigaben in Römischen Gräbern bei St Severin in Köln', *KölnJb* 22, 17–23.

Painter, K. S. (1971): 'Six Roman glasses with cut decoration from Amiens', *British Museum Quarterly* 36:1–2, 41–50.

Paolucci, F. (2002): *L'Arte del vetro inciso a Roma nel IV secolo d. C.*, Firenze.

Parker Pearson, M. & Sharples, N. (eds), with Mulville, J. & Smith, H. (1999): *Between land and sea: Excavations at Dun Vulan, South Uist* (Sheffield environmental & archaeological research campaign in the Hebrides 3), Sheffield.

Paskavalin, V. (1974): 'Ancient glass from the territory of Bosnia and Herzegovina', *Arheološki Vestnik* 25, 109–38.

Pastorino, A. M. (2000): 'Vetri romani degli scavi urbani di Albenga', *Annales du 14e congrès du AIHV*, Lochem 2000, 108–12.

Paternoster, A. M. (2000): 'Contenitori vitrei bollati dalla necropoli dell'Università Cattolica di Milano', *Annales du 14e congrès du AIHV*, Lochem, 104–7.

Paterson, J. (1982): '"Salvation from the sea": amphorae and trade in the Roman West', *JRS* 72, 146–57.

Payne, G. (1874): 'Roman coffins, of lead, from Bex Hill, Milton-next-Sittingbourne', *Archaeologia Cantiana* 9, 164–73.

Peachin, M. (2001): 'Friendship and abuse at the dinner table'; in Peachin, M. (ed.), *Aspects of friendship in the Graeco-Roman World*, Portsmouth, RI, 135–44.

Peacock, D. P. S. (1971): 'Roman amphorae in pre-Roman Britain', in Hill, D. & Jesson, M. (eds), *The Iron Age and its hillforts, Southampton*, 161–88.

Peacock, D. P. S. & Williams, D. F. (1986): *Amphorae and the Roman economy: an introductory guide*, London & New York, NY.

Pellatt, A. (1849): *Curiosities of glass making*, London.

Penman, A. (1995): *Botel Bailey excavation: interim report 1995*, Castle Douglas.

Penman, A. (1997): *Botel Bailey excavation: interim report 1997*, Castle Douglas.

Pennant, T. (1794): *Arctic zoology Vol. 1. Introduction. Class 1. Quadrupeds*, London.

Pernice, E. (1912): 'Der Grabfund von Lübsow bei Greifenberg i. P.', *Praehistorische Zeitschrift* 4, 126–48.

Petch, J. A. (1927): 'Excavations at Benwell (*Condercum*): first interim report', *ArchAel* (Series 4) 4, 135–92.

Petersen, H. (1890–1903): 'Gravpladsen fra den ældre jernalder paa Nordrup Mark ved Ringsted', *Nordiske Fortidsminder* I, Kjøbenhavn.

Petersen, J. (1916): *Gravplassen fra Store-Dal i Skjeberg* (Norske Oldfund I), Kristiania.

Petru, S. (1974): 'Römisches Glas in Slowenien', *Arheološki Vestnik* 25, 21–34.

von Pfeffer, W. (1976): 'Ein Konchylienbecher in Schlangenfaden-technik aus Worms', in Haevernick, T. E. & von Saldern, A. (eds), *Festschrift für Waldemar Haberey*, Mainz, 95–99.

Piggott, S. (1950–51): 'Excavations in the broch and hillfort of Torwoodlee, Selkirkshire, 1950', *PSAS* 85, 92–117.

Piggott, S. (1952–53): 'Three metal-hoards of the Roman period from southern Scotland', *PSAS* 87, 1–50.

Piggott, S. (1966): 'A scheme for the Scottish Iron Age', in Rivet A. L. F. (ed.), *The Iron Age in northern Britain*, Edinburgh, 1–15.

Piggott, S. & Piggott, C. M. (1951–52); 'Excavations at Castlelaw, Glencorse, and at Craig's Quarry, Dirleton, 1948–49', *PSAS* 86, 191–96.

Pind, J. et al. (eds) (2002): *Drik: og du vil leve skønt. Festskrift til Ulla Lund Hansen på 60-årsdagen 18 August 2002* (Publications from the National Museum Studies in Archaeology & History vol. 7), Copenhagen.

Pitts, M. (2005): 'Pots and pits: drinking and deposition in late Iron Age southeast Britain', *Oxford Journal of Archaeology* 24:2, 143–61.

du Plat Taylor, J. & Cleere, H. (eds) (1978): *Roman shipping and trade: Britain and the Rhine provinces* (CBA Research Report 24), London.

Plouviez, J. (ed.) (2003): 'Amphorae in Britain and the Western Europe', *Journal of Roman Pottery Studies*, 10.

Price, J. (1976a): 'Glass', in Jarrett, M. G., *Maryport, Cumbria: a Roman fort and its garrison* (Cumberland and Westmoreland Antiquarian and Archaeo-

logical Society Extra Series 22), Kendal, 49–54.

Price, J. (1976b): 'Glass', in Strong, D. & Brown, D. (eds), *Roman crafts*, London, 110–25.

Price, J. (1977): 'The Roman glass', in Gentry A., Ivens, J. & McLean, H., 'Excavations at Lincoln Road, London Borough of Enfield, November 1974 – March 1976', *Transactions of the London & Middlesex Archaeological Society* 28, 154–61.

Price, J. (1978a): 'Trade in glass', in du Plat Taylor, J. & Cleere, H. (eds), 70–78.

Price, J. (1978b): 'The glass flask', in Collis, J. (ed.), *Winchester excavations volume II: 1949–1960*, Winchester, 102.

Price, J. (1980): 'The glass', in Gracie, H. S. & Price, E. G., 'Frocester Court Roman villa: second report', *Transactions of the Bristol and Gloucestershire Archaeological Society* 97, 37–46.

Price, J. (1981): 'The glass', in Jarrett, M. C. & Wrathmell, J. (eds), *Whitton. An Iron Age and Roman farmstead in South Glamorgan*, Cardiff, 149–62.

Price, J. (1982a): 'The glass', in Webster, G. & Smith, L., 'The excavation of a Romano-British rural settlement at Barnsley Park: Part II', *Transactions of the Bristol and Gloucestershire Archaeological Society* 99, 174–85.

Price, J. (1982b): 'The Roman glass', in Leach, P. (ed.), *Ilchester, vol. 1, excavations 1974–1975* (Western Archaeological Trust Excavation Monograph 3), Ilchester, 227–32.

Price, J. (1985a): 'The Roman glass', in Pitts, L. F. & St Joseph, J. K. (eds), *Inchtuthil* (Britannia Monograph, Series 6), Gloucester, 303–12.

Price, J. (1985b): 'The glass', in Bidwell, P. T. (ed.), *The Roman fort of Vindolanda* (Historic Buildings and monuments Commission for England Archaeological Report 1), London, 206–13.

Price, J. (1985c): 'Early Roman vessel glass from burials in Tripolitania: a study of finds from Forte della Vite and other sites now in the collections of the National Museum of Antiquity in Tripoli', in Buck, D. J. & Mattingly, D. J. (eds), *Town and country in Roman Tripolitania: papers in honour of Olwen Hackett* (BAR Int.Ser. 274), Oxford, 67–106.

Price, J. (1985d): 'Late Hellenistic and early Imperial vessel glass at Berenice: a survey of import tableware found during excavations at Sidi Khrebish,

Benghazi', in Barker, G., Lloyd, J. & Reynolds, J. (eds), *Cyrenaica in Antiquity* (BAR Int.Ser. 236), Oxford, 287–96.

Price, J. (1987a): 'Glass from Felmongers, Harlow in Essex. A dated deposit of vessel glass found in an Antonine pit', *Annales du 10e Congrès du AIHV*, Amsterdam, 185–206.

Price, J. (1987b): 'The Roman glass', in Frere, S. S., 'Brandon Camp, Hertfordshire', *Britannia* 18, 71–76.

Price, J. (1987c): 'Late Hellenistic and early Imperial cast vessel glass in Spain', *Annales du 10e Congrès du AIHV*, Amsterdam, 61–80.

Price, J. (1988): 'Romano-British glass bangles from East Yorkshire', in Price, J. et al. (eds), *Recent research in Roman Yorkshire* (BAR Brit.Ser. 193), Oxford, 339–66.

Price, J. (1989a): 'The Roman glass', in Frere, S. S. & Wilkes, J. J. (eds), *Strangeath. Excavations within the Roman fort 1973–86* (Britannia Monograph Series 9), London, 192–203.

Price, J. (1989b): 'Glass', in Stead, I. M. & Rigby, V. (eds), *Verulamium: the King Harry Lane site* (English Heritage Archaeological Report 12), London, 40–50.

Price, J. (1990a): 'Roman vessel and window glass', in McCarthy, M. R. (ed.), *A Roman, Anglian and Medieval site at Blackfriars Street, Carlisle: excavations 1977–79* (Cumberland and Westmoreland Antiquarian and Archaeological Society. Res. Ser. 4), 163–79.

Price, J. (1990b) 'The glass', in Wrathmell, S. & Nicholson, A. (eds), *Dalton Parlours: Iron Age settlement and Roman villa* (Yorkshire Archaeology 3), 99–105.

Price, J. (1991): 'Decorated mould-blown glass tablewares in the first century AD', in Newby, M. & Painter, K. (eds), 56–75.

Price, J. (1992a): 'Report on the vessel and window glass', in Rahtz, P. et al. (eds), *Cadbury Congresbury 1968–73. A late/post-Roman hilltop settlement in Somerset* (BAR Brit.Ser. 223), Oxford, 132–43.

Price, J. (1992b): 'Hellenistic and Roman Glass', in *Knossos: from Greek city to Roman colony: excavations at the Unexplored Mansion 2*, Oxford, 414–90.

Price, J. (1993a): 'Window glass' & 'Vessel glass', in Woodward A. & Leach, P.

(eds), *The Uley shrines. Excavation of a ritual complex on West Hill, Uley, Gloucestershire 1977–79* (English Heritage Archaeological Report 17), London, 189–92, 210–15.

Price, J. (1993b): 'The Romano-British glass', in Blockley, K. et al. (eds), 'Excavations on the Roman fort at Abergavenny, Orchard site, 1972–73', *ArchJ* 150, 215–20.

Price, J. (1995a): 'Glass vessels', in Manning, W. H., Price, J. & Webster, J. (eds), *Report on the excavation at Usk 1965–1976: the small finds*, Cardiff, 139–91.

Price, J. (1995b): 'The Roman glass', in Casey, P. J. & Hoffmann, B., 'Excavations at Alstone Cottage, Caerleon, 1970', *Britannia* 26, 80–89.

Price, J. (1995c): 'Glass tablewares with wheel-cut, engraved and abraded decoration in Britain in the fourth century AD', in Foy, D. (ed.), 25–33.

Price, J. (1995d): 'Roman glass', in Phillips, D. & Heywood, B. (eds), *Excavations at York Minster I: from Roman fortress to Norman cathedral*, London, 346–71.

Price, J. (1996): 'Glass', in Jackson, R. P. J. & Potter, T. W. (eds), *Excavations at Stonea, Cambridgeshire 1980–85*, London, 379–409.

Price, J. (1997a): 'The Roman glass', in Hill, P. (ed.), 294–95.

Price, J. (1997b): 'The glass', in Potter, T. W. & King, A. C. (eds), *Excavations at the Mola di Monte Gelato: a Roman and Medieval settlement in south Etruria* (Archaeological Monographs of the British School at Rome 11), London, 265–86.

Price, J. (1998): 'A glass drinking cup with incised decoration from Newton Kyme, North Yorkshire', in Bird, J. (ed.), *Form and fabric: studies in Rome's material past in honour of B. R. Hartley* (Oxbow Monograph 80), Oxford, 307–12.

Price, J. (2000a): 'Late Roman glass vessels in Britain and Ireland from AD 350 to 410 and beyond', in Price, J. (ed.), 1–31.

Price, J. (ed.) (2000b): *Glass in Britain AD 350–1100* (British Museum Occasional Paper 127), London.

Price, J. (2002): 'Two vessels from Llandovery, Carmarthenshire, and Piercebridge, County Durham: a note on Flavian and later polychrome mosaic glass in Britain', in Aldhouse-Green, M. & Webster, P. (eds), *Artefacts and*

Archaeology: aspects of the Celtic and Roman world, Cardiff, 112–31.

Price, J. (2004): 'Romano-British and early post-Roman glass vessels and objects', in Quinnell, H. (ed.), *Trethurgy: excavations at Trethurgy Round, St Austell. Community and status in Roman and post-Roman Cornwall*, Truro, 85–92.

Price, J. (2005): '"A glass vessel of peculiar form": a late Roman mould-blown bottle found with a burial at Milton-next-Sittingbourne in Kent', in Dannell, G. B. & Irving, P. V. (eds), *An archaeological miscellany: papers in honour of K. F. Hartley* (Journal of Roman Pottery Studies 12 (2005), 155–63.

Price, J. (2009): 'Glass', in Haselgrove, C. (ed.), *The Traprain Law environs project: fieldwork and excavations 2000–2004*, Edinburgh, 262.

Price, J. (2010): 'Late Roman glass vessels in the Hadrian's Wall frontier region', in Collins, R. & Allason-Jones, L. (eds), *Finds from the frontier: material culture in the 4th–5th Centuries* (CBA Research Report 162), York, 37–49.

Price, J. & Cool, H. E. M. (1983): 'Glass from the excavations of 1974–76', in Brown, A. E. & Woodfield, C., 'Excavations at Towcester, Northamptonshire: the Alchester Road suburb', *Northamptonshire Archaeology* 118, 115–24.

Price, J. & Cool. H. E. M. (1985): 'Glass (including glass from 72 Dean's Way),' in Hurst, H. R. (ed.), *Kingsholm* (Gloucester Archaeological Reports 1), Cambridge 41–45.

Price, J. & Cool. H. E. M. (1989): 'Report on the Roman glass found at the Cattle-market, County Hall and East Palant House sites, Chichester', in Down, A. (ed.), *Chichester excavations* 6, Chichester, 132–42.

Price, J. & Cool. H. E. M. (1991): 'The evidence for the production of glass in Roman Britain', in Foy, D. & Sennequier, G. (eds), *Ateliers de verriers, de l'Antiquité à la periode pre-industrielle* (Actes du 4ème Recontres de l'Association Française pour l'Archéologique du Verre), Rouen, 23–30.

Price, J. & Cool. H. E .M. (1993): 'The vessel glass', in Darling, M. J. & Gurney, D. (eds), *Caister-on-Sea excavations by Charles Green, 1951–55* (East Anglian Archaeology Report 60), London, 141–52.

Price, J. & Cottam, S. (1995a): 'The Roman glass', in Casey, J. & Hoffmann, B.,

'Excavations on the Corbridge bypass, 1974', *ArchAel* (series 5) 23, 25–28.

Price, J. & Cottam, S. (1995b): 'Late Roman glass bowls from Beadlam villa, North Yorkshire', in Vyner, B. (ed.), *Moorland monuments: studies in the archaeology of north-east Yorkshire in honour of Raymond Hayes and Don Spratt* (CBA Research Report 101), London, 235–42.

Price, J. & Cottam, S. (1996a): 'The Roman glass from Fishbourne 1983 and 1985–86', in Cunliffe, B. W., Down, A. G. & Rudkin, D. J. (eds), *Chichester excavations IX: excavations at Fishbourne 1969–1988*, Chichester, 161–88.

Price, J. & Cottam, S. (1996b): 'The glass', in Neal, D. S. (ed.), *Excavations on the Roman villa at Beadlam, Yorkshire* (Yorkshire Archaeological Report 2), York, 93–108.

Price, J. & Cottam, S. (1997a): 'Roman glass', in Wilmott, T. (ed.), *Birdoswald: excavations of a Roman fort on Hadrian's Wall and its successor settlements 1987–92* (English Heritage Archaeological Reports 14), London, 341–55.

Price, J. & Cottam, S. (1997b): 'The Roman glass', in Wenham, L. P. & Heywood, B. (eds), *The 1968 to 1970 excavations in the vicus at Malton, North Yorkshire* (Yorkshire Archaeological Report 3), York, 118–31.

Price, J. & Cottam, S. (1998a): *Romano-British glass vessels: a handbook*, (Practical Handbook in Archaeology 14), York.

Price, J. & Cottam, S. (1998b): 'Vessel glass', in Leach, P. (ed.), *Great Witcombe Roman villa, Gloucestershire* (BAR Brit.Ser. 266), Oxford, 73–81.

Price, J. & Cottam, S. (2000a): 'Glass tableware in use at Mytilene in Lesbos in the early-mid 1st century AD', *Annales du 14e congrès du AIHV*, Lochem, 58–62.

Price, J. & Cottam, S. (2000b): 'The vessel glass', in McCarthy, M. R. (ed.), *Roman and Medieval Carlisle: the Southern Lanes. Excavations 1981–82* (Department of Archaeological Sciences, University of Bradford Research Report 1), Bradford, 103–5.

Price, J. & Worrell, S. (2003): 'Roman, Sasanian, and Islamic glass from Kush, United Arab Emirates: a preliminary survey', *Annales du 15e Congrès du AIHV*, Nottingham 2003, 153–57.

Price, J. et al. (2005): '"All in a day's work?" The colourless cylindrical glass cups found at Stonea revisited', in Crummy, N. (ed.), *Image, craft and the Classical world: essays in honour of Donald Bailey and Catherine Johns*, Montagnac, 165–71.

Proudfoot, E. V. W. (1976): 'Hallowhill', *D & E*, 33–34.

Proudfoot, E. V. W. (1977–78): 'Camelon native site', *PSAS* 109 , 112–28.

Proudfoot, E. V. W. (1996): 'Excavations at the long cist cemetery on the Hallow Hill, St Andrews, Fife, 1975–77', *PSAS* 126, 387–454.

Purcell, N. (1985): 'Wine and wealth in ancient Italy', *JRS* 75, 1–19.

Raddatz, K. (1973): *Mulva I: die grabungen der Nekropole in den Jahren 1957 und 1958* (Madrider Beiträge 2), Mainz am Rhein.

Rademacher, F. (1942): 'Fränkische Gläser aus dem Rheinland', *BonnJbb* 147, 285–344.

Raftery, B. (1981): 'Iron Age burials in Ireland', in O'Corráin, D. O. (ed.), *Irish antiquity: essays and studies presented to professor M. J. O'Kelly*, Cork, 173–204.

Raftery, B. (1994): *Pagan Celtic Ireland: the enigma of the Irish Iron Age*, London.

Ralegh Radford, C. A. (1949–50): 'Castle Loch, Mochrum', *Transactions of the Dumfriesshire and Galloway Natural History & Antiquarian Society*, 3rd. ser. 28, 41–63.

Rashleigh, P. (1803): 'Account of a further discovery of antiquities at Southfleet', *Archaeologia* 14, 221–23.

Rausing, G. (1992): 'On the origin of the runes', *Fornvännen* 87, 200–5.

RCAHMS (1956): (The Royal Commisson on the Ancient and Historic Monuments of Scotland), *Roxburghshire* vol. I, Edinburgh.

Real Museo di Napoli (1833): *Real Museo di Napoli* 4

Redlich, C. (1977): 'Zur Trinkhornsitte bei den Germanen der älteren Kaiserzeit', *Praehistorische Zeitschrift* 52, 61–120.

Redlich, C. (1980): 'Politische und wirtschaftliche Bedeutung der Bronzegefäße an Unterelbe und Saale zur Zeit der Römerkriege', in Häßler, H.-J. (ed.), *Studien zur Sachsenforschung* 2, Hildesheim, 329–74.

Rees, T. & Hunter, F. (2000): 'Archaeological excavation of a medieval structure and an assemblage of prehistoric artefacts from the summit of Traprain Law, East Lothian, 1996–97', *PSAS* 130, 413–40.

Rehfisch F. (1987): 'Competitive beer drinking among the Mambila', in Douglas, M. (ed.), 135–45. Originally published in *Cahiers d'Etudes Africaines* III (1) (1962), 51–103.

Renfrew, C. (1975): 'Trade as action at a distance: questions of integration and communication', in Sabloff, J. A. & Lamberg-Karlovsky, C. C. (eds), *Ancient civilization and trade*, Albuquerque, NM, 3–59.

Renfrew, C. (1993): 'Trade beyond the material', in Scarre, C. & Healy, F. (eds), *Trade and exchange in prehistoric Europe* (Oxbow Monograph 33), Oxford, 5–16.

Ribechini, E. et al. (2008): 'Gas chromographic and mass spectrometric investigations of organic residues from Roman glass unguentaria', *Journal of Cromatography* A 1183, 158–69.

Richter, G. M. A. & Milne, M. J. (1935): *Shapes and names of Athenian vases*, New York, NY.

Rieckhoff, S. (1992): 'Eine römische "Brauerei" aus Regensburg', in Ruprechtsberger, E. M. (ed.), *Bier im Altertum: ein Überblick* (Linzer Archäologische Forschungen Sonderheft VII), Linz, 27–33.

Ritterling, E. (1913): *Das Frührömische Lager bei Hofheim I. T.* (Annalen des Vereins für Nassauische Altertumskunde und Geschichtsforschung 40), Wiesbaden.

Roach-Smith, C. (1842): 'Observations on Roman remains recently found in London', *Archaeologia* 29, 145–66.

Roach-Smith, C. (1859): *Illustrations of Roman London*, London.

Robertson, A. S. (1964): *The Roman fort at Castledykes*, Edinburgh.

Robertson, A. S. (1970): 'Roman finds from non-Roman sites in Scotland: more Roman "drift" in Caledonia', *Britannia* 1, 198–226.

Robertson, A. S. (1975a): *Birrens (Blatobulgium)*, Edinburgh.

Robertson, A. S. (1975b): 'The Romans in north Britain: The coin evidence', *Aufstieg und Niedergang der römischen Welt* II.3, 364–426.

Robertson, A. (1978): 'The circulation of Roman coins in north Britain: the evidence of hoards and site finds from Scotland', in Carson, R. A. G. & Kraay,

C. M. (eds), *Scripta nummaria Romana: essays presented to Humphrey Sutherland*, London, 186–216.

Robertson, A. S. (1983): 'Roman coins found in Scotland, 1971–82', *PSAS* 113, 405–48.

Robertson, A. S. (1990): *The Antonine Wall* (4th editon revised and edited by L. Keppie), Edinburgh.

Robertson, A. S. (2000): *An inventory of Romano-British coin hoards*, London.

Roffia, E. (1973): 'Vetri', in Frova, A. (ed.), 462–81.

Rolleston, J. D. (1927): 'Alcoholism in Classical Antiquity', *British Journal of Inebrity* 24:3, 101–20.

Ross, T. (1909): 'Donations to the museum and library', *PSAS* 43, 15.

Rotloff, A. (1999): 'Römische Vierkantkrüge', in Klein, M. J. (ed.), 41–49.

Ruprechtsberger, E. M. (1992): '"Wirtin, füll" die Flasche mit Bier! Bier in griechisch-römischer Zeit: ein Überblick', in Ruprechtsberger, E. M. (ed.), *Bier im Altertum: ein Überblick* (Linzer Archäologische Forschungen Sonderheft VII), Linz, 15–24.

Rütti, B. (1983): 'Das Schlangenfadenglas von Cham-Hagendorn', *Helvetia Archaeologica* 55/56, 217–24.

Rütti, B. (1991a): 'Early enamelled glass', in Newby, M. & Painter, K. (eds), 122–36.

Rütti, B. (1991b): *Die römischen Gläser aus Augst und Kaiseraugst*, Augst.

Rütti, B. (2003): 'Les verres peints du Haut Empire romain: centres de production et de diffusion', in Foy, D. & Nenna, M.-D. (eds), 349–56.

Rygh, K. (1880): *Trondheim Museum, tilveksten 1879*, Kristiania.

Sablerolles, Y. (1996): 'The glass finds from the auxiliary fort and civil settlements at Valkenburg (the Netherlands)', *Annales du 13e Congrès du AIHV*, Lochem, 139–50.

Saggau, H. E. (1981): *Bordesholm: der Urnenfriedhof am Brautberg bei Bordesholm in Holstein, Teil 2: Katalog, Tafeln und Plan des Gräberfeldes*, Neumünster.

Saggau, H. E. (1985): *Bordesholm: der Urnenfriedhof am Brautberg bei Bordesholm in Holstein, Teil 1: Text und Karten*, Neumünster.

Saguí, L. (1996): 'Un piatto di vetro inciso da Roma: contributo ad un inquardramento delle officine', in Picozzi, M.G. & Carinci, F. (eds), *Vicino oriente, Egeo, Grecia, Roma e mondo romano: tradizione dell'antico e collezionismo di antichità. Studi in memoria di Lucia Guerrini*, Roma, 337–58.

Sahlström, K. E. et al. (1931–32): *Gudhems härads fornminnen* (Skövdeortens Hembygds- och Fornminnes-förenings Skriftserie 3), Skövde.

von Saldern, A. (1980): *Ancient and Byzantine glass from Sardis* (Archaeological exploration of Sardis Monograph 6) Cambridge, MA & London.

von Saldern, A. (1980): *Glas von der Antike bis zum Jugendstil*, Mainz am Rhein.

Sanches de Prado, M. D. (1984): 'El vidrio romano en la Provincia de Alicante', *Lucentum* 3, 79–100.

Sanderson, D. C. W. & Hutchings, J. B. (1987): 'The origins and measurement of colour in archaeological glasses', *Glass Technology* 28:2, 99–105.

Sazanov, A. (1995): 'Verres à decor de pastilles bleus provenant des fouilles de la Mer Noire: typologie et chronologie', in Foy, D. (ed.), 331–41.

Scatozza Höricht, L. A. (1986): *I vetri Romani di Ercolano*, Roma (reprinted in 1995).

Scatozza Höricht, L. A. (1990): 'Die Verwendung der römischen Gläser im 1. Jh. n.Chr. und die Fundkomplexe der Vesuvstädte', *Annales du 11e Congrès du AIHV*, Basel, 43–48.

Schäfer, G. (1968): 'Bericht über die Auffindung und Untersuchung von Fürstengräbern der jüngeren Kaiserzeit bei Bornstein, Kr. Eckernförde', *Jahrbuch des Heimatsgemeinschaft Eckernförde*, 41–59.

Schirnig, H. (1969): *Die Keramik der Siedlung Böhme, Kreis Fallingbostel, aus der römischen Kaiserzeit* (Göttinger Schriften für Vor- und Frühges-chichte 11), Neumünster.

Schmidt, B. & Bemman, J. (2008): *Körperbestattungen der jüngeren Römischen Kaiserzeit unter Völkerwanderungszeit Mitteldeutschlands* (Veröffentlichungen des Landes-amtes für Denkmalpflege- und Archäologie Sachsen-Anhalt, Landesmuseum für Vorgeschichte 61), Halle 2008.

von Schnurbein, S. (1977): *Das Römische Gräberfeld von Regensburg* (Archäologische Forschungen in Regina Castra-Reganesburg 1), Kallmünz.

Schönberger, H. (1956): 'Ein weiterer bemalter Glasbecher von Zugmantel', *Saalburg Jahrbuch* 15, 41.

Schou Jørgensen, M. et al. (1978): 'Himlingøje-gravpladsens høje', *Antkvariske studier* 2, 47–80.

Schuldt, E. (1948–49): 'Das spätrömische Grab von Jesendorf, Kreis Wismar', *Hammaburg* 1, 225–30.

Schuler, F. (1959): 'Ancient glassmaking techniques. The molding process', *Archaeology* 12, 47–52.

Scott, J. G. (1976): 'The Roman occupation of south-west Scotland from the recall of Agricola to the withdrawal under Trajan', *GlasAJ* 4, 29–44.

Sealey, P. R. & Davies, G. M. R. (1984): 'Falernian wine at Roman Colchester', *Britannia* 15, 250–54.

Sekulla, M. F. (1982): 'Roman coins from Traprain Law', *PSAS* 112, 285–94.

Selinge, K.-G. (1977): 'Järnålderns bondekultur i Västernorrland', in Baudou, E. & Selinge, K.-G. (eds), *Västernorrlands förhistoria*, Motala, 153–418.

Sennequier, G. (1977): 'La verrerie', in Ratel, R., 'La nécropole gallo-romaine de "Gratte Dos" Commune de Meuilley, Côte d'Or', *Revue Archéologique de l'Est et du Centre-Est* 28:3–4, 255–62.

Sennequier, G. (1985): *Verrerie d'époque romaine*, Rouen.

Sennequier, G. (1994): 'Roman glass found in upper Normandy', *JGS* 36, 56–66.

Shepherd, I. A. G. (1993): 'The Picts in Moray', in Sellar, W. D. H. (ed.), *Moray: province and people*, Edinburgh, 75–90.

Shepherd, J. D. (1995): 'The glass vessels', in Elder, J. (ed.), *Excavations in the Marlowe car park and surrounding areas* (the Archaeology of Canterbury 5), Canterbury, 1227–59.

Shepherd, I. & Shepherd, J. (1979): 'Sculptor's Cave, Covesea', *D & E*, 14–15.

Sherratt, A. (1995): 'Alcohol and its alternatives: symbol and substance in pre-industrial cultures', in Goodman, J., Lovejoy, P. E. & Sherratt, A. (eds), *Consuming habits: drugs in history and anthropology*, London & New York, NY, 11–46.

Shils, E. (1981): *Tradition*, London & Boston, MA.

Simon-Hiernard, D. (2000): *Verres d'époque romaine: collection des Musées de Poitiers*, Poitiers 2000.

Simonett, C. (1941): *Tessiner Gräberfelder* (Monographien zur Ur- und Frühgeschichte der Schweiz III), Basel.

Simpson, P. (2004): 'Glass', in Alexander, D., 'Early Historic and Medieval activity at Chapleton, Haugh of Urr, Dumfries and Galloway', *Transactions of the*

Dumfriesshire & Galloway Natural History & Antiquarian Society 78, 70.

Simpson, StJ. (2005): 'Sasanian glass from Nineveh', *Annales du 16e Congrès du AIHV*, Nottingham, 146–51.

Sims-Williams, P. (1998): 'Celtomania and Celtoscepticism', *Cambrian Medieval Celtic Studies* 36, 1–35.

Skene, W. F. (1866): 'Donations to the museum', *PSAS* 7, 7–10.

Skilbeck, C. O. (1923): 'Notes on the discovery of a Roman burial at Radnage, Bucks.', *AntJ* 3, 334–37.

Smith, I. M. [edited by Taylor, J.] (2000): 'Excavations on Iron Age and Medieval earthworks at the Dod, Borders Region, 1979–81', *ArchJ* 157, 229–353.

Smith, J. (1895): *Prehistoric man in Ayrshire*, London.

Smith, J. (1919): 'Excavations of the forts of Castlehill, Aitnock, and Coalhill, Ayrshire', *PSAS* 53, 123–36.

Smith, R. L. (2009): *Premodern trade in world history*, New York, NY.

Sorokina, N. (1967): 'Das antike Glas des Nord-Schwarzmeerküste', *Annales du 4e congrès des journées internationales du verre, Ravenne-Venise*, Liège, 67–79.

Sorokina, N. (1972): 'Die Nuppengläser von der Nord-Küste des Schwarzen Meeres', *Annales du 5e Congrès International d'Etude Historique du Verre*, Liège, 71–79.

Sorokina, N. (1987): 'Glass aryballoi (first–third centuries AD) from the northern Black Sea region', *JGS* 29, 40–46.

Sorterup, J. B. (1844–45): 'Udsigt over urner, gravkar og jordfundne kar fra Nordens Hedenold', *Aarbøger for Nordisk oldkyndighed og historie*, 317–69.

Statens Historiska (1967): *Statens Historiska Muséer och Kungl. Myntkabinettet: Samlingarnas tillväxt 1965*, Stockholm.

Stawiarska, T. (2005): 'Roman period glass beakers with thread decoration (Eggers 188–92) from Poland: technical examination', *Annales du 16e Congrès du AIHV*, Nottingham, 75–79.

Steer, K. A. (1950–51): 'The Roman pottery from Torwoodlee', in Piggott, S., 110–112.

Steer, K. A. (1956–57): 'The Roman fort at Easter Happrew, Peeblesshire', *PSAS* 90, 93–101.

Steer, K. A. & Keeney, G. S. (1946–48): 'Excavations in two homesteads at

Crock Cleuch, Roxburghshire', *PSAS* 81, 138–57.

Stenberger, M. (1956): 'Tuna in Badelunda: a grave in central Sweden with Roman vessels', *Acta Archaeologica* 27, 1–21.

Stern, E. M. (1977): 'A glass bowl of Isings Form 2 from the tomb of an Ethiopian Candace', *Oudheidkundige Medelingen uit Rijksmuseum van Oudheden te Leiden* 58, 63–72.

Stern, E. M. (1981): 'Hellenistic glass from Kush (modern Sudan)', *Annales du 8e Congrès du AIHV*, Liège, 35–59.

Stern, E. M. (1987): 'Early Roman glass from Heïs on the north Somali coast', *Annales du 10e Congrès du AIHV*, Amsterdam, 23–36.

Stern, E. M. (1991): 'Early exports beyond the Empire: Roman glass', in Newby, M. & Painter, K. (eds), 141–55.

Stern, E. M. (1992): 'Early Roman export glass in India', in Begley, V. & De Puma, R. (eds), *Rome and India: the ancient sea trade*, Delhi, 113–24.

Stern, E. M. (1993): 'The glass from Heïs', in Desanges, J., Stern, E. M., & Ballet, P. (eds), *Sur les routes Antiques de l'Azanie et de l'Inde*, Paris, 21–61.

Stern, E. M. (1997): 'Glass and rock crystal: a multifaceted relationship', *JRA* 10, 192–206.

Stern, E. M. (1999): 'Roman glassblowing in a cultural context', *American Journal of Archaeology* 103:3, 441–84.

Stern, E. M. (2001): *Roman, Byzantine and Early Medieval Glass 10 BCE–700 CE. Ernesto Wolf Collection*, Ostfildern-Ruit.

Stern, E. M. (2007): 'Ancient glass in a philological context', *Mnemosyne* 60, 341–406.

Stern, E. M. (2008): 'Glass production', in Oleson, J. P. (ed.), *The Oxford handbook of engineering and technology in the Classical world*, Oxford, 520–47.

Sternini, M. (1995): 'Il vetro in Italia tra V e IX secoli', in Foy, D. (ed.), 243–76.

Sternini, M. (2001): 'Reperti in vetro da un deposito tardeantico sul Colle Palatino', *JGS* 43, 21–75.

Stevenson, R. B. K. (1954–56): 'Native bangles and Roman glass', *PSAS* 88, 208–21.

Stevenson, R. B. K. (1976): 'Romano-British glass bangles', *GlasAJ* 4, 45–54.

Stiaffini, D. & Borghetti, G. (1994): *I vetri romani del Museo Archeologico Nazionale di Cagliari*, Cagliari.

Stika, H.-P. (1996): 'Traces of a possible Celtic brewery in Eberdingen-Hochdorf, Kreis Ludwigsburg, southwest

Germany', *Vegetation History and Archaeobotany* 5, 81–88.

Stjernquist, B. (1977–78a): *Roman objects from the equipment of a Scandinavian warrior of the second century AD* (Scripta Minora 5), Lund.

Stjernquist, B. (1977–78b): 'Mountings for drinking horns from a grave found at Simris, Scania', *Meddelanden från Lunds historiska museum* 2, 129–50.

Stjernquist, B. (1986): 'Glass from the settlement of Gårdslösa, southern Sweden', *Meddelanden från Lunds historiska museum 1985–1986*. New Series vol. 6, 139–65.

Stolpe, H. (1896): 'Österhvarfsfyndet', *K. Vitterhets Historie och Antiqvitets Akademien och de under hennes inseende ställda Statssamlingarna: Riksantiqvariens årsberättelse för 1895*, Stockholm, 82–88.

Straume, E. (1987): *Gläser mit facettenschliff aus skandinavischen Gräbern des 4. und 5. Jahrhunderts n.Chr.*, Vojens.

Strong, P. (1986): 'Traprain Law', *D & E*, 20.

Stuart, J. (1867): *Sculptured stones of Scotland*, Edinburgh.

Subic, Z. (1974): 'Revue typologique et chronologique du verre romaine de Poetovio', *Arheološki Vestnik* 25, 39–61.

Tanichii, T. (1983): 'Pre-Roman and Roman glass recently excavated in China', *Bulletin of the Okayama Orient Museum* 3, 83–105.

Tarpini, R. (1998): 'Aspetti della circolazione del vetro in età romana nel territory modenese', in La Guardia, R. & Tibiletti, T. (eds), 55–60.

Taylor, D. B. (1982): 'Excavation of a promontory fort, broch and souterrain at Hurly Hawkin, Angus', *PSAS* 112, 215–53.

Tchernia, A. (1983): 'Italian wine in Gaul at the end of the Republic', in Garnsey, P., Hopkins, K., & Whittaker, C. R. (eds), *Trade in the ancient economy*, London, 87–104.

Tchernia, A. (1986): *Le vin de l'Italie romaine*, Roma 1986.

Thill, G. (1975): 'Frühkaiserzeitliche Grabbeigaben von Hellingen (G. H. Luxemburg)', *Archaeologisches Korrespondenzblatt* 5, 69–79.

Thomas, G. D. (1988): 'Excavations at the Roman civil settlement at Inveresk 1976–77', *PSAS* 118, 139–76.

Thomas, N. (1991): *Entangled objects: exchange, material culture, and* colonialism in the Pacific, Cambridge, MA.

Thompson, E. A. (1966): The Visigoths in the time of Ulfila, Oxford.

Thomsen, T. (1923): 'Egekistefundet fra Egtved, fra den ældre Bronzealder', Nordiske Fortidsminder 2, Kjøbenhavn 1911–35, 166–201.

Thorpe, W. A. (1933–34): 'A glass jug of Roman date from Turriff, Aberdeenshire', PSAS 68, 439–44.

Thorpe, W. A. (1938): 'Prelude to European cut glass', Transactions of the Society of Glass Technologists 22, 5–34.

Thorpe, W. A. (1940): 'A fragment of Roman glassware from Tealing, Angus', PSAS 74, 134–35.

Tierney, J. J. (1960): 'The Celtic ethnography of Poseidonius', Proceedings of the Royal Irish Academy 60, 189–275.

Timby, J. (2006): 'The pottery from the late Roman deposits', in Fulford, M. et al. (eds), 86–115.

Todd, M. (1975): The northern barbarians 100 BC–AD 300, London.

Todd, M. (1985): 'The Falkirk hoard of denarii: trade or subsidy', PSAS 115, 229–32.

Townend, P. & Hinton, P. (1978): 'Glass', in Bird, J. et al. (eds), Southwark excavations 1972–1974 (London & Middlesex Archaeological & Surrey Archaeological Society Joint Publication 1), London, 387–89.

Toynbee, J. M. C. (1967): 'The bronze jug', in Biddle, M., 240–45.

Trakosopoulou, E. (2002): 'Glass grave goods from Acanthus', in Kordas, G. (ed.), 79–89.

Triscott, J. (1982): 'Excavations at Dryburn Bridge, East Lothian, 1978–1979', in Harding, D. W. (ed.), Later prehistoric settlement in south-east Scotland (University of Edinburgh Department of Archaeology Occasional Paper 8), Edinburgh, 117–24.

Trowbridge, M. L. 1930: Philological studies in ancient glass, Urbana, IL [dissertation 1922].

Turno, A. (1989): 'Römische und Frühbyzantinische Gläser aus Novae in Bulgarien', KölnJb 22, 163–70.

Twede, D. (2005): 'The cask age: the technology and history of wooden barrels', Packaging Technology and Science 18, 253–64.

Ulbert, G. (1959): 'Römische Holzfässer aus Regensburg', Bayerische Vorgeschichtsblätter 24, 6–29.

Universitetets Oldsaksamling (1950): Universitetets Oldsaksamling Årbok 1945–48, Oslo.

Vandkilde, H. (2000): 'Material culture and Scandinavian archaeology: a review of the concepts of form, function, and context', in Olausson, D. & Vandkilde, H. (eds), Form, function, context: material cultural studies in Scandinavian archaeology, Lund, 3–49.

Vanpeene, N. (1993): Verrerie de la nécropole d'Èpiais-Rhus (Val-d'Oise), Guiry-en-Vexin.

Vedel, E. (1872): 'Den ældre Jernalders begravelser paa Bornholm', Aarbøger for Nordisk oldkyndighed og historie, 1–104.

Vessberg, O. & Westholm, A. (1956): The Swedish Cyprus expedition IV:3. The Hellenistic and Roman periods in Cyprus, Stockholm.

Vickers, M. (1996): 'Rock crystal: the key to cut glass and diatreta in Persia and Rome', JRA 9, 48–65.

Viérin, J. & Léva, C. (1961): 'Un puits à tonneau romain avec sigles et graffiti à Harelbeke', Latomus 20, 759–81.

Voss, J. (1987): 'The politics of pork and the rituals of rice: redistributive feasting and commodity circulation in northern Luzon, the Philippines', in Clammer, J. (ed.), Beyond the new economic anthropology, London, 121–41.

Wace, A. J. B. & Jehu, Prof. (1914–15): 'Cave excavations in East Fife', PSAS 49, 233–55.

Wacquant, L. D. (1989): 'Towards a reflexive sociology: a workshop with Pierre Bourdieu', Sociological Theory 7, 26–63.

Wainwright, F. T. (1953): 'Souterrains in Scotland', Antiquity 27, 219–32.

Wainwright, F. T. (1963): The souterrains of southern Pictland, London.

Wake, T. (1939): 'Excavations at Witchy Neuk, Hepple', ArchAel (Series 4) 16, 129–39.

Watkins, T. (1978–80): 'Excavation of an Iron Age open settlement at Dalladies, Kincardineshire', PSAS 110, 122–64.

Webster, H. & Petch, D. F. (1967): 'A possible vineyard of the Romano-British period at North Thoresby, Lincolnshire', Lincolnshire History and Archaeology 2, 55–62.

Weeber, K.-W. (1993): Die Weinkultur der Römer, Zürich.

Weigel, M. (1890): 'Der Grabfund von Bietkow, Kreis Prenzlau, Prov. Brandenburg', Nachrichten über deutsche Altertumsfunde, 39–41.

Weinberg, G. D. & Goldstein, S. M. (1988): 'The glass vessels', in Weinberg, G. D. (ed.), Excavations at Jalame. Site of a glass factory in late Roman Palestine, Columbia, MO, 38–102

Weinberg, G. D. & Stern, E. M. (2009): Vessel glass (The Athenian Agora vol. 34), Princeton, NJ.

Welfare, H. (1984): 'The southern souterrains', in Miket, R. & Burgess, C. (eds), 305–23.

Welker, E. (1974): Die römischen Gläser von Nida-Heddernheim (Schriften des Frankfurter Museums für Vor- und Frühgeschichte 3), Frankfurt am Main.

Welker, E. (1985): Die römischen Gläser von Nida-Heddernheim II (Schriften des Frankfurter Museums für Vor- und Frühgeschichte 8), Frankfurt am Main.

Welcomme, E. et al. (2006): 'Investigation of white pigments used as make-up during the Greco-Roman period', Applied Physics A 83, 551–56.

van der Werff, J. H. (1987): 'Roman Amphoras at "De Horder" (Wijk bij Duurstede)', Berichten van de Rijksdienst voor het Ouidkundig Bodemonderzoek 37, 153–72.

van der Werff, J. H. (1989): 'Sekundäre Graffiti auf römischen Amphoren', Archäelogisches Korrespondenzblatt 19, 361–76.

Werner, H. (1873): Antiqvariska berättelser afgivna till Vestergötlands Fornminnesförening II, Stockholm.

Werner, J. (1950): 'Römische Trinkgefässe in Germanischen Gräbern der Kaiserzeit', in Kirchner, H., Ur- und Frühgeschichte als historische Wissenschaft: Festschrift zum 60. Geburtstag von Ernst Wahle, Heidelberg, 168–76.

West, L. C. (1931): Roman Britain: the objects of trade, Oxford.

Westell, W. P. (1931): 'A Romano-British cemetery at Baldock, Herts.', ArchJ 88, 247–301.

Wheeler, R. E. M. (1946): 'Arikamedu: an Indo-Roman trading station on the east coast of India', Ancient India 2, 17–124.

Wheeler, R. E. M. (1956): Rom utanför imperiet, Stockholm.

Whimster, R. (1981): Burial practices in Iron Age Britain: a discussion and a gazetteer of the evidence c. 700 BC–AD 43, (BAR Brit. Ser. 90), Oxford.

White, K. D. (1975): *Farm equipment of the Roman world*, Cambridge.

White, R. H. (1988): *Roman and Celtic objects from Anglo-Saxon graves* (BAR Brit. Ser. 191), Oxford 1988.

Whitehouse, D. (1997): *Roman glass in the Corning Museum of Glass: Vol. 1*, New York, NY.

Whitehouse, D. (1998): *Excavations at ed-Dur (Umm al-Qaiwain, United Arab Emirates) I: the glass vessels*, Leuven.

Whitehouse, D. (2000): 'Ancient glass from ed-Dur (Umm al-Qaiwain, U.A.E.) 2. Glass excavated by the Danish expedition', *Arabian Archaeology and Epigraphy* 11, 87–128.

Whitehouse, D. (2003): *Roman glass in the Corning Museum of Glass: Vol. 3*, New York, NY.

Whittaker, C. R. (1989): 'Supplying the system: frontiers and beyond', in Barrett, J. C., Fitzpatrick, A. P. & Mac-innes, L. (eds), 64–80.

Wiedmann, K. (1965): 'Die Herstellung der römischen Schlangenfadengläser', *Technische Beiträge zur Archäologie* 2, 131–36.

Wielowiejski, J. (1973): 'Die Antiken trinkgelage-gebräuche bei den Völkern Osteuropas der römischen Kaiserzeit', *Archaeologia Polona* 14, 269–78.

Wiessner, P. & Schiefenhövel, W. (eds) (1996): *Food and the status quest: an interdisciplinary perspective*, Providence, RI & Oxford.

Wiessner, P. (2001): 'Of feasting and value: Enga feasts in a historical perspective (Papua New Guinea)', in Dietler, M. & Hayden, B. (eds), 115–43.

Wild, J. P. (1970): 'Borrowed names for borrowed things?', *Antiquity* 44, 125–30.

Wild, J. P. (1976): 'Loanwords and Roman expansion in north-west Europe', *World Archaeology* 8, 57–64.

Will, E. L. (1977): 'The ancient commercial amphora', *Archaeology* 30:4, 264–70.

Wilhelm, E. (1979): *Verrerie de l'Époque Romaine – Musée d'Histoire et d'Art Luxembourgh*, Luxembourg.

Williams, D. F. (1977): 'A consideration of the sub-fossil remains of Vitis vinifera L. as evidence for viticulture in Roman Britain', *Britannia* 8, 327–34.

Williams, D. F. (1989): 'The impact of the Roman amphora trade on pre-Roman Britain', in Champion, T. C. (ed.), *Centre and periphery: comparative studies in archaeology*, London, 142–150.

Willis, S. (1998): 'Iron Age and Roman pottery', in Main, L., 321–31.

Wilson, A. (1996–97): 'Roman penetration in Strathclyde south of the Antonine Wall', *GlasAJ* 20, 1–40.

Wilson, D. R. (1969): 'Roman Britain in 1968 I: sites explored', *JRS* 59 (198–234.

Wise, A. (1998): 'Hillhead, Lilliesleaf', *D & E*, 80.

Woolliscroft, D. J. & Lockett, N. J. (1996): 'East Coldoch (Kincardineshire parish): circular ditched enclosure', *D & E*, 102.

Worrell, S. (2000): 'The Roman glass', in Smith, I. M., 316–20.

Worsaae, J. J. A. (1850): 'Jernalderens begyndelse i Danmark, oplyst gjennem gravfund', *Aarbøger for Nordisk old-kyndighed og historie*, 358–62.

Wylie, A. (1985): 'The reaction against analogy', in Schiffer, M. B. (ed.), *Advances in archaeological method and theory* 8, London, 63–111.

Zimmer-Linnfeld, K. (1960): *Westerwanna I* (Beiheft zum Atlas der Urgeschichte 9), Hamburg.

Ziviello, C. (1998): 'Considerazioni su alcuni bolli in rilievo dalla collezione del Museo Archeologico Nazionale di Napoli', in La Guardia, R. & Tibiletti, T. (eds), 67–72.

Zobel-Klein, D. (1999): 'Glaskannen mit Kettenhenkel: eine Mainzer Spezialität', in Klein, M. J. (ed.), 91–105.

Non-Roman/native sites in Scotland and north Northumberland included in the catalogue

Airlie, Angus. I:1
Ardeer, Ayrshire. P:1
Birnie, Morayshire. F:3
Brackenbraes, Turriff, Aberdeenshire. G:3
Broxmouth East Lothian. Z:13
Buston crannog, Ayrshire. P:2
Buittle, Kirkcudbrightshire. Z:7
Camelon native site, Stirlingshire. K:1
Carlingwark Loch, Kirkcudbrightshire. R:1
Castle Craig, Perthshire. Z:11
Castlehill, Dalry, Ayrshire. P:3
Castlehill Wood, Stirlingshire. K:2
Castlelaw, Midlothian. M:1
Chapelton, Haugh of Urr, Kirkcudbrightshire. Z:8
Clarkly Hill, Morayshire. Z:10
Clickhimin, Shetland. A:1
Constantine's Cave, Fife. L:1
Covesea (the Sculptor's Cave), Morayshire. F:1
Crock Cleuch, Roxburghshire. T:2
Crosskirk, Caithness. D:1
Culbin Sands, Morayshire. F:2
Culduthel Mains Farm, Inverness, Inverness-shire. Z:1
Dalladies, Kincardineshire. H:1
Dalmeny Park, South Queensferry, Midlothian. M:2
Dod (the), Roxburghshire. T:3
Dryburn Bridge, East Lothian. N:1

Dun Ardtreck, Skye, Hebrides. C:1
Dun Mor Vaul, Tiree, Argyll. C:2
Dun Vulan, South Uist, Hebrides. C:3
Dunadd, Argyll. J:1
Dunollie, Argyll. J:2
East Coldoch, Stirlingshire. K:6
Easter Moss, Cowiehall/Cowiehall Quarry, Stirlingshire. Z:2
Edgerston, Roxburghshire. T:1
Edinburgh Castle, Midlothian. M:3
Everley, Caithness. D:2
Fairy Knowe, Buchlyvie, Stirlingshire. K:3
Fendom Sands, Ross & Cromarty. E:1
Fiskavaig, Skye, Hebrides. Z:9
Gilmerton House, Athelstaneford, East Lothian. Z:4
Glenhead (Gourock Burn), Ayrshire. P:4
Gubeon Cottage, Northumberland. U:1
Hallowhill, St Andrews, Fife. L:2
Hartburn, Northumberland. U:2
Hetha Burn, Hethpool, Northumberland. U:3
Hillhead, Lilliesleaf, Roxburghshire. Z:5
Howe of Howe, Orkney. B:1
Hyndford, Lanarkshire. O:1
Kay Craig, Perthshire. Z:12
Keir Hill, Gargunnock, Stirlingshire. K:5
Keiss Harbour, Caithness. D:3
Kingoldrum, Angus. I:2
Knowes, East Lothian. Z:3

Leckie, Stirlingshire. K:4
Links of Trenabie, Westray, Orkney. B:3
Loch Kinnord, Aberdeenshire. G:1
Loch na Berie, Lewis, Hebrides. C:4
Lochspouts, Ayrshire. P:5
Luce Sands, Wigtownshire. Q:1
Middle Gunnar Peak, Barrasford, Northumberland. U:4
Milking Gap, High Shield, Northumberland. U:5
Mine Howe, Tankerness, Orkney. B:2
Mote of Mark, Kirkcudbrightshire. R:2
Old Scatness, Shetland. A:2
Redcastle, Lunan Bay, Angus. I:3
Seamill, West Kilbride, Ayrshire. P:6
Stevenston Sands *see* Ardeer
Tealing, Angus. I:4
Torfoot, Lanarkshire. O:2
Torrs Cave, Kirkcudbrightshire. R:3
Torwoodlee, Selkirkshire. S:1
Traprain Law, East Lothian. N:2
Waulkmill, Tarland, Aberdeenshire. G:2
West Longlee, Northumberland. U:6
West Whelpington, Northumberland. U:7
Whitefield Loch, Wigtownshire. Z:6
Whithorn, Wigtownshire. Q:2
Witchy Neuk, Hepple, Northumberland. U:8

The sites listed above are detailed in Appendix A.
Those sites prefixed 'Z' are found in chapter 3.26 of the catalogue.

Places and sites in Britain
(Iron Age, Roman and early Medieval)